LESSONS ENCOUNTERED

LESSONS ENCOUNTERED

LEARNING FROM THE LONG WAR

Edited by Richard D. Hooker, Jr., and Joseph J. Collins

National Defense University Press
Washington, D.C.
September 2015

Library of Congress Cataloging-in-Publication Data

Lessons encountered : learning from the long war / edited by Richard D. Hooker, Jr., and Joseph J. Collins.
    pages cm
  Includes bibliographical references.
1. National security—United States—History—21st century. 2. United States—Military policy—History—21st century. 3. Afghan War, 2001- 4. Iraq War, 2003-2011. 5. United States—Armed Forces—Operations other than war—History—21st century. 6. United States—History, Military—21st century—Case studies. 7. Strategy. I. Hooker, Richard D., editor of compilation. II. Collins, Joseph J., editor of compilation.
  UA23.L484 2015
  355'.033073—dc23

                                                                    2015030056

National Defense University Press
260 Fifth Avenue (Building 64)
Suite 2500
Fort Lesley J. McNair
Washington, DC 20319

NDU Press publications are sold by the U.S. Government Printing Office. For ordering information, call (202) 512-1800 or write to the Superintendent of Documents, U.S. Government Printing Office, Washington, DC, 20402. For GPO publications online, access its Web site at: http://bookstore.gpo.gov.

Book design by Chris Dunham, U.S. Government Printing Office

Cover photo: U.S. Army Soldiers with Echo Company, 5th Cavalry Regiment, 172nd Infantry Brigade, prepare to clear building during combined training exercise with Iraqi soldiers near Bahbahani, Iraq, June 6, 2009 (DOD/Kim Smith)

Human nature will not change. In any future great national trial, compared with the men of this, we shall have as weak and as strong, as silly and as wise, as bad and as good. Let us therefore study the incidents in this [war] *as philosophy to learn wisdom from and none of them as wrongs to be avenged.*

—Abraham Lincoln, November 10, 1864

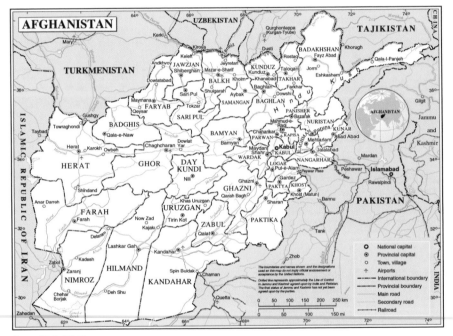

Source: United Nations

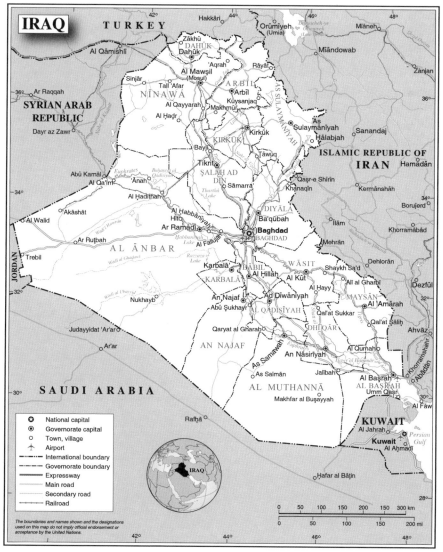

IRAQ

TURKEY

Hakkâri Orūmīyeh (Umia) Miāneh

Zākhū Biljvicheh-ye Ormiveh (Lake Urmia)

DAHŪK Dahūk Miāndowab

Al Qāmishlī 'Aqrah Rāyāt

Al Mawṣil (Mosul) Zanjan

Sinjār Tall 'Afar **ARBĪL** Arbīl Kūysanjaq

NĪNAWĀ Makhmūr

Al Qayyarah **AS SULAYMĀNĪYAH**

SYRIAN ARAB REPUBLIC Ar Raqqah Al Ḥaḍr As Sulaymānīyah Sanandaj

Dayr az Zawr **KIRKŪK** Kirkūk Ḥālabjah

Bayjī Ṭāwūq

ISLAMIC REPUBLIC OF

Tikrīt **IRAN** Hamādān

ṢALĀḤ AD DĪN

Abū Kamāl Euphrates Buhavrat al Qādisiyah Sāmarra' Qaṣr-e Shīrīn Kermānshāh

'Ānah Khānaqīn

Al Qā'im Thartha Lake Khānaqīn Borūjerd

Al Ḥadīthah

Akāshāt Al Ḥabbānīyah **DIYĀLĀ** Īlām Khorramābād

Al Walid Hīt Ba'qūbah

Ar Ramādī Al Fallūjah Mehrān

Wadi Hawran Habbaniyah Lake **Baghdad** BAGHDAD

Trebil **AL ĀNBAR** Razzaza Lake **WĀSIT** Dehlorān

Ar Ruṭbah Wadi al Ghadaf Karbalā' **BĀBIL** Shaykh Sa'd

KARBALĀ' Al Ḥillah Al Kūt 'Alī al Gharbī Dezfūl

Nukhayb Wadi al Ubayyid An Najaf Ad Dīwānīyah Al Hayy **MAYSĀN**

Abū Ṣukhayr **AL QĀDISĪYAH** Qal'at Sukkar Al 'Amārah

Judayyidat 'Ar'ar Qaryat al Gharab **DHĪ QĀR** Qal'at Ṣāliḥ Ahvāz

Ar'ar **AN NAJAF** Euphrates At Qurnaho Khorramshahr

As Samāwah An Nāṣirīyah Hawr al Hammar Abadan

As Salmān Jalībah Al Baṣrah

SAUDI ARABIA **AL MUTHANNĀ** **AL BAṢRAH** Umm Qaṣr

Makhfar al Buṣayyah Al Fāw

Rafḥā **KUWAIT**

Al Jahrah *Persian Gulf*

Kuwait

Al Ahmadī

Ḥafar al Bāṭin

JORDAN

⊛	National capital
⊚	Governorate capital
○	Town, village
✈	Airport
---·---	International boundary
---·---	Governorate boundary
━━━	Expressway
────	Main road
-----	Secondary road
+++++	Railroad

The boundaries and names shown and the designations
used on this map do not imply official endorsement or
acceptance by the United Nations.

IRAQ

0	50	100	150	200	150	300 km
0	50		100		150	200 mi

Source: United Nations

Contents

Chapter 5

Chapter 6

ANNEXES

ACKNOWLEDGMENTS

This volume was a great team effort that enabled us to accomplish a 2-year project in only 10 months. The first acknowledgment goes to the nearly one dozen people who wrote chapters and annexes. Next we thank Lieutenant General Thomas D. Waldhauser, USMC, Director for Joint Force Development, Joint Staff J7, and Major General Frederick Padilla, USMC, President of the National Defense University (NDU). They were a critical sounding board and gave great advice to the team.

Many others helped us and gave unselfishly of their time and effort. A number of senior officers and civilians gave hours of their time to provide interviews (or written responses) for this project. Among them were General Martin E. Dempsey, Chairman of the Joint Chiefs of Staff; the Honorable Stephen J. Hadley, former National Security Advisor; General Lloyd J. Austin III, USA, Commander, U.S. Central Command (USCENTCOM); General David Petraeus, USA (Ret.), former Commander, USCENTCOM, and commander in Iraq and Afghanistan; General James N. Mattis, USMC (Ret.), former Commander, USCENTCOM; Admiral James G. Stavridis, USN (Ret.), former Supreme Allied Commander, Europe; General Stanley A. McChrystal, USA (Ret.), former commander in Afghanistan; General John R. Allen, USMC (Ret.), former commander in Afghanistan; Lieutenant General Douglas E. Lute, USA (Ret.), former Deputy National Security Advisor and now U.S. Ambassador to the North Atlantic Treaty Organization; the Honorable Michèle Flournoy, former Under Secretary of Defense for Policy; Dr. Michael Mazaar of RAND, a former member of the Chairman of the Joint Chief of Staff's Commander's Action Group; and John Wood, a long-serving member of the National Security Council Staff.

The authors also had access to over 100 additional senior officer interviews conducted by organizations such as the Center for Military History (CMH),

Acknowledgments

Military History Institute (MHI), Combat Studies Institute (CSI) at Fort Leavenworth, and Chief of Staff of the Army's Operation *Iraqi Freedom* (OIF) Study Group. We would like to thank Dr. Donald Wright of CSI, Dr. Conrad Crane of MHI, Colonel E.J. Degen, USA, of CMH, the leader of the Army's operational study of Operation *Enduring Freedom*, and Colonel Joel Rayburn, USA, the leader of the Army's OIF study, for their assistance in facilitating access to these interviews, which allowed the authors to exploit previous research on Afghanistan and Iraq, thus saving months of work in the process.

As always, the Center for Complex Operations (CCO) staff earned our deepest appreciation. Some commented on chapters, while others transcribed, took notes, edited, scheduled, or pointed out errors. CCO Deputy Bernie Carreau provided management and expert commentary. Giorgio Rajao, Nathan White, Fulbright scholar Hiram Reynolds, Maxwell Kelly, Michael Davies, and Major Claude Lambert, USA, a graduate student at George Mason University, took notes, made expert comments, and worked on formal summaries or transcripts of multiple interviews. Captain Sam Rosenberg, USA, a graduate student in Georgetown's Security Studies Program, did excellent work on the timelines and fact-checking. The CCO staff who participated in this project also include Michael Miklaucic, Dale Erickson, Sara Thannhauser, Christoff Luehrs, Talley Latimore, Connor Christensen, Ryan Lester, and Jonathan Reich. Becky Harper worked tirelessly behind the scenes to direct support to the project, the project's workers, and two complex conferences.

In addition to the authors and the support staff, the team wants to extend its appreciation to the many people who read the manuscript and commented on the chapters. We owe our special gratitude to our senior reviewers, who not only commented on the manuscript as a whole but also sat with us for a long day discussing it in detail, the academic version of trench warfare. Our senior reviewers were Professor Richard Betts of Columbia University; Professor Dan Caldwell of Pepperdine University; Lieutenant General H.R. McMaster, USA, of the U.S. Army Training and Doctrine Command (TRADOC); Major General Rick Waddell, USAR, who is both director of the NDU renowned Capstone Course and Deputy Commander of U.S. Southern Command; and Lieutenant General David Deptula, USAF (Ret.), who is is the Dean of the Mitchell Institute of Aerospace Power Studies.

Our chapter reviewers, who also made great and detailed contributions, include John Wood of the Near East South Asia Center, Dr. Pete Mansoor of The Ohio State University, Ryan Henry and Linda Robinson of RAND, Robert Perito, Dr. Jack Kem of the Combined Arms Center, the Honorable James Baker of the Court of Military Appeals, and Amy Belasco of the Congressional Research Service.

A number of other invited reviewers went above and beyond and submitted detailed comments on the manuscript. The editors and authors want to thank in particular Professor Cynthia Watson of the National War College, who read the manuscript twice; Professor Steve Brent and Professor Sorin Lungu of the Dwight D. Eisenhower School for National Security and Resource Strategy; Colonel Tim Ryan, USA (Ret.), of the Joint and Coalition Operational Analysis Division, J7, Joint Staff; and Lieutenant Colonel John Gallagher, USA, Lieutenant Colonel Blair Sokol, USMC, and Colonel Charlie Miller, USA, of the Office of the Chairman of the Joint Chiefs of Staff. Others who weighed in at our review conference include Norine MacDonald, Queen's Counsel; Major Dave McNatt, USA, TRADOC Army Capabilities Integration Center; Major Erica Iverson, USA, TRADOC; and Colonel Joel Rayburn.

The *Small Wars Journal* (SWJ), for the last decade led by Dave Dilegge—Marine, journalist, and entrepreneur—published a review essay by one of our authors on lessons learned and invited reader responses. Among those who contributed their thoughts were Dr. John Fairlamb, Dr. Jeff McCausland, Jeff Goodson, Brian Petit (who sent along his own book), Keith Nightingale, David Ronfeldt, Dr. John Kuehn, and many others on the SWJ blog whose use of aliases prevent us from naming them. National War College faculty members and alumni added powerful and precise commentary. Thanks also to Colonels Dave Arnold, USAF; John Hall, USA; Ivan Shidlovsky, USA; Andrew Nielsen, USAF; and Mark Roberts of the Department of Homeland Security for their expert commentary. Professors Dan Dailey and Mark Clodfelter of the National War College mixed intelligence and strategic commentary in appropriate proportions. The Army War College's Steve Metz also lent us his considerable wisdom. Lastly, Jerry Lynes of J7 was supportive through every step of the process.

A final note of thanks goes to our friends and partners at NDU Press. The skillful work of Dr. William T. Eliason, Dr. Jeffrey D. Smotherman, Dr. John

Acknowledgments

J. Church, Joanna E. Seich, and Erin L. Sindle, along with Lisa M. Yambrick, made this a better book.

The editors and authors alone are responsible for any errors of fact or interpretation. This work is theirs alone and does not purport to represent the assessment, interpretation, or views of the Department of Defense, Joint Staff, or National Defense University.

INTRODUCTION

By Richard D. Hooker, Jr., and Joseph J. Collins

We shall not cease from exploration
And the end of all our exploring
Will be to arrive where we started
And know the place for the first time.

—T.S. Eliot, "Little Gidding"

Not learning from wars can be catastrophic. The next cohort of national security leaders may not achieve the sublime mental state envisioned by T.S. Eliot, but they must make every effort to learn the lessons of the Long War. For that reason, in his second term's *Strategic Direction to the Joint Force*, Chairman of the Joint Chiefs of Staff General Martin E. Dempsey charged senior officers "to apply wartime lessons learned to provide best military advice and inform U.S. policy objectives and strategic guidance."[1] Major General Gregg F. Martin, USA, then–President of National Defense University (NDU), wrote:

> In addition to continuing to analyze and teach the lessons of past conflicts, [NDU] *must research, disseminate, and teach the strategic and operational lessons of over 10 years of war. These efforts will play an important role in both improving the quality of strategic leadership and performance of our graduates and contributing to new national and military security strategies and innovative operational concepts to meet emerging needs.*[2]

1

This volume represents an early attempt at assessing the Long War, now in its 14th year. Forged in the fires of the 9/11 attacks, the war includes campaigns against al Qaeda, major conflicts in Iraq and Afghanistan, and operations in the Horn of Africa, the Republic of the Philippines, and globally, in the air and on the sea. The authors herein treat only the campaigns in Afghanistan and Iraq, the largest U.S. efforts. It is intended for future senior officers, their advisors, and other national security decisionmakers. By derivation, it is also a book for students in joint professional military education courses, which will qualify them to work in the field of strategy. While the book tends to focus on strategic decisions and developments of land wars among the people, it acknowledges that the status of the United States as a great power and the strength of its ground forces depend in large measure on the dominance of the U.S. Navy and U.S. Air Force in their respective domains.

This assessment proceeds from two guiding sets of questions about the wars in Iraq and Afghanistan. The core set of questions was suggested by the Chairman of the Joint Chiefs: What did we gain? What did we lose? What costs did the United States pay for its response to 9/11, particularly from operations in Afghanistan and Iraq? How should the answers to these questions inform senior military leaders' contributions to future national security and national military strategy? The second set of questions proceeds from the first: what are the strategic "lessons learned" (or "lessons encountered," as the British and the authors of this work prefer) of our experience in Operation *Enduring Freedom* (OEF) in Afghanistan, and Operations *Iraqi Freedom* (OIF) and *New Dawn* in Iraq.

This inquiry is constrained by a number of factors. First, the conflicts in Afghanistan and Iraq continue. Our combat forces withdrew from Iraq in 2011 and that campaign was formally brought to a close, but it was reopened because of the advances by the Islamic State of Iraq and the Levant (ISIL) since 2014. Thus, this book reviews two incomplete stories. Second, focusing on the primary operations in Iraq and Afghanistan leaves the lessons of secondary, but still important, operations for another day. For example, the advisory and assistance experience in the Republic of the Philippines may well provide important lessons for the future. Indeed, future U.S. operations in this war are much more likely to resemble what our trainers and advisors did in the Philippines than what their comrades did in Iraq or Afghanistan.

Third, in asking the questions posed above, the book may pay inadequate attention to the nearly 50 nations that have been involved with the United States as coalition partners in various theaters. Warfare today is coalition warfare. While this book focuses on the United States, nothing here should be seen as devaluing the contributions of host nations or coalition partners. Finally, our primary audience is future senior military officers who will work at the strategic level in peace and war: the Chairman, Service chiefs, combatant commanders, their senior staff officers, and all those—military and civilian—who interact with interagency partners, the National Security Council, and the President. Given its focus and audience, this study does not include an examination of the tactical and operational levels of these conflicts.[3]

This inquiry must also contend with the difficulties of learning from history, an arduous task under any circumstances. Great effort is no guarantee of learning the right lessons. There are numerous cases of great powers making significant efforts to learn—only to fail. The French had one of the greatest armies of the 19th and 20th centuries but twice learned the wrong lessons from wars against Germany, including a world war in which they were part of the victorious alliance. The causes of faulty learning are varied but include lack of imagination, poor information, misperception, stress, organizational preferences, bureaucratic politics, and inflexible military doctrine.[4] Ideology and personal experience may enlighten or blind the observer to lessons.[5] As noted by military historian Jay Luvaas:

> *We should understand the reasons why military men in the past have failed sometimes to heed the correct lessons. Often it has been the result of an inability to understand local conditions or to accept another army or society on its own terms. Sometimes the guidance to observers has been so specific that the major lessons of the war went unheeded simply because observers had not been instructed to look in different directions. . . . Sometimes, doctrine has narrowed the vision or directed the search, as in the case of the French army after World War I. Often, there has been a failure to appreciate that once removed from its context, a specific lesson loses much of its usefulness.[6]*

Henry Kissinger has reminded us that "the study of history offers no manual of instruction that can be applied automatically; history teaches by analogy, shedding light on the likely consequences of comparable situations. But each generation must determine for itself which circumstances are in fact comparable."[7] Strategic lessons from comparable cases can appear to present the student with conflicting advice. Adam Gopnick, comparing the onset of the two world wars, wrote:

> *The last century, through its great cataclysms, offers two clear, ringing, and, unfortunately, contradictory lessons. The First World War teaches that territorial compromise is better than full-scale war, that an "honor-bound" allegiance of the great powers to small nations is a recipe for mass killing, and that it is crazy to let the blind mechanism of armies and alliances trump common sense. The Second teaches that searching for an accommodation with tyranny by selling out small nations only encourages the tyrant, that refusing to fight now leads to a worse fight later on, and that only the steadfast rejection of compromise can prevent the natural tendency to rush to a bad peace with worse men. The First teaches us never to rush into a fight, the Second never to back down from a bully.*[8]

At the strategic level, there are no cookie-cutter lessons that can be pressed onto every batch of future situational dough. A lesson from one era or locale may not fit another. The only safe posture is to know many historical cases and to be constantly reexamining the strategic context, questioning assumptions, and testing the appropriateness of analogies. The lessons of OIF and OEF will join those of other wars, competing for the attention of future decisionmakers and, no doubt, at times confounding them. The difficulty of learning lessons from history, however, should not stop us from trying to learn. Indeed, the rewards of successful learning—think Franklin D. Roosevelt in the run-up to World War II or John F. Kennedy in the Cuban missile crisis—cannot be overestimated. A final caveat: one's enemies can learn faster and better. The defeated will often learn better than the victors.

For national security professionals, technical and tactical lessons are relatively easy to digest, but operational and strategic lessons are much more difficult, though not impossible, to capture. Lessons for military or national security strategy are the most important lessons of all, and the ones that military observers often ignore. In the Armed Forces, one often hears, even from senior officers, that certain strategic subjects are "above my pay grade." That is sometimes true, but at the highest levels of command, the larger strategic lessons must be the focal point of study and education. Carl von Clausewitz reminded his readers that policy, politics, statecraft, and military affairs come together at the highest levels:

> *To bring a war or one of its campaigns to a successful close requires a thorough grasp of national policy. On that level, strategy and policy coalesce:* [the general who] *is commander in chief, is simultaneously a statesman . . . but he must not cease to be a general. On the one hand, he is aware of the entire political situation; on the other, he knows exactly how much he can achieve with the means at his disposal.*[9]

President Kennedy covered similar themes in his 1961 instructions to the Joint Chiefs. Disappointed by senior officers who looked narrowly at issues during the Bay of Pigs crisis, he wrote, "While I look to the Chiefs to present the military factor without reserve or hesitation, I regard them to be more than military men and expect their help in fitting military requirements into the over-all context of any situation, recognizing that the most difficult problem in Government is to combine all assets in a unified, effective pattern."[10]

Finally, for senior officers and their civilian masters, learning from history is complicated by the nature of organizational life. It is one thing for an individual to experience a phenomenon, learn from it, and apply lessons to a subsequent experience. When generals and admirals talk about learning, however, they are talking about distilling experience, drawing complex conclusions, debating them, resolving differences, packaging lessons, and then inculcating them into the force through doctrine, training, exercises, and joint professional military education.[11] The Armed Forces can forget lessons that are not institutionalized, that lose bureaucratic sponsorship, or that are misapplied in the future. The retention, nurturing, and propagation of relevant lessons are difficult at the tactical and operational levels but even more so at the context-sensitive strategic level.

In a similar vein, the failure to inculcate lessons can cause the apparent repetition of national security disasters, commonly referred to as history repeating itself. For example, the decisionmaking pathologies associated with Athens' Sicilian expedition in the Peloponnesian Wars, the introduction of U.S. combat troops into Vietnam in 1965, and the invasion and occupation of Iraq in 2003 all demonstrate the difficulties of learning, institutionalizing, and consistently applying even well-known or obvious strategic lessons. Sadly, faulty learning and poor decisionmaking echo throughout the ages, but so do the cases of accurate learning, adaptation, and innovation.

Encountering lessons is relatively easy; understanding and institutionalizing them over time is more difficult, especially in the realm of national strategy. The ultimate value of this volume should be determined by the future senior officers and national security decisionmakers who refine and internalize its strategic lessons. Those leaders must then ensure that the lessons are passed down to succeeding generations and applied under appropriate circumstances. If this book assists future military and civilian decisionmakers, it will have achieved its goal.

This book is an edited volume but not a collage of independent efforts. The authors worked together for 10 months and twice met in conference along with expert commentators. At the same time, the authors do not necessarily agree on all the key assessments.

The book is divided in this manner: chapter one focuses on the early, pre-Surge years in both campaigns. Chapter two continues the chronological thread but focuses on assessment and adaptation in the Surges in Iraq and Afghanistan. Chapter three examines decisionmaking at the national level and implementation. Chapter four discusses security force assistance, the coalition's development of indigenous armies, and police forces. Chapter five analyzes the complex set of legal issues attendant to irregular conflict, including detention and interrogation policy. Chapter six develops the capstone conclusions of the study and isolates the most important lessons. Supporting these chapters are three annexes: one on the human and financial costs of war, and, for reference, two others on the key events in both campaigns.

To orient the reader, the lessons encountered in these chapters are divided into a few functional areas: national-level decisionmaking, unity of effort/unity of command, intelligence and understanding the operational environment, character of contemporary conflict, and security force assistance. Clearly, each observer of the Long War would characterize his lessons in a different manner, but the following observations are what the contributors of this volume thought to be most important.[12]

National-Level Decisionmaking

Strategic lessons begin with decisionmaking, which here entails efforts at shaping goals, developing strategies, crafting plans at the national and departmental levels, and developing ways to carry out those plans. Every chapter in this book raises observations and lessons on these complex processes. Here are the lessons encountered in this study:

- Military participation in national decisionmaking is both necessary and problematic. Part of this comes from normal civil-military tension, but many instances in the Long War also show unnecessary misunderstandings. Civilian national security decisionmakers need a better understanding of the complexity of military strategy and the military's need for planning guidance. Senior military officers for their part require a deep understanding of the interagency decisionmaking process, an appreciation for civilian points of view, and a willingness to appreciate the complexities and challenges inherent in our system of civilian control.[13] Both civilian and military planners should cultivate the art of backward planning, starting with the desired political endstate and working back toward the present.[14]
- In a similar vein, inside the Pentagon, future senior officers also need to study cases in wartime decisionmaking. The case of Iraq is particularly instructive. In the run-up to the Iraq War, the Secretary of Defense—as is his legal prerogative—interjected himself into the military-technical aspects of war planning to a high, perhaps unprecedented degree. History will judge the wisdom of this managerial technique, but it serves as a reminder to future senior officers that the civil-military relationship, in Eliot Cohen's term, is characterized by an unequal dialogue.[15] Secretaries of Defense in the future can leave war planning to the com-

batant commander and the Joint Chiefs or, like Secretary Donald Rumsfeld, dive into the details with a regular stream of questions and memoranda. Senior officers need to be ready for either method, or a hybrid of both.

▪ Vigorous discussion and clearly presented military perspectives are essential for successful strategy. The best military advice should be provided without fear or favor, but always nested within a larger appreciation of the strategic context and its political, economic, diplomatic, and informational dimensions. This conversation must be carried on in private, not in the public square.

▪ In most cases civilian leaders will look for a range of suitable, feasible, and acceptable military options, with clear cost and risk estimates. In cases where the objective is poorly defined, military leaders should press for clarity. In so doing, senior officers must remember that civilian policymakers generally lack a military planning background and that formulating policy goals is usually based on discussion and consensus. In this milieu, persuasive arguments matter and will often prevail.

▪ Four-star officers are presumed to be masters of joint warfare, but at the highest levels, knowledge of the interagency community, the press, and Congress, as well as defense budgeting and international affairs, are also critical. Not every successful flag officer will be well equipped in these fields. In some of the cases examined in this volume, lack of experience in these areas probably inhibited success.

▪ While the civilian leadership remains firmly in charge of the policy process, senior military figures also have an obligation to provide their military expertise and, if necessary, their respectful dissent to help prevent strategic disaster. In this regard, military officers like their civilian counterparts do not shed personal and professional values when they reach the top. Whenever the use of force is contemplated, the advice they bring to bear must come with a firm moral-ethical component.

▪ National security is a highly personalized process where trust is the coin of the realm. That trust may take years to evolve but can be lost in a day. Good working relationships between civilian and military partners, despite differences that may arise on specific issues, will go far toward resolving the natural tension inherent in the civil-military relationship.

■ Senior military planners must pay more attention to the linkage between political and military objectives. Civil and military planning for postconflict stability operations was inadequate. Poor postconflict planning set back operations in Afghanistan and Iraq. The worst failing in Iraq was, early on, an inadequate number of troops on the ground to establish order and initiate stability operations. This failure sped the onset of an insurgency that evolved into a sectarian civil war.

■ Policy and strategy are highly sensitive to budget, election, and news cycles. The health of the Nation's economy is also a key factor. Career military officers are not always attuned to these realities, but civilian decisionmakers are. Awareness of and flexibility with respect to this reality will improve the quality of military advice.

Unity of Effort/Unity of Command

The best strategic decisions exemplify unity of command on the military side and unity of effort in all areas. The campaigns in Afghanistan and Iraq suffered from significant problems in this regard, both in the military and in the interagency aspects of the operations.

■ Whole-of-government efforts are essential in irregular conflicts. The military must improve its efforts to reach across departmental divides. The Department of State and U.S. Agency for International Development (USAID) have improved over time but need to work harder on planning for expeditionary activities. Unfortunately, emphasis on working whole-of-government issues is fading across the U.S. Government, except in the field of joint concept and doctrine development.[16] For popular support and policy effectiveness, the national security system must routinely generate vertical and horizontal unity of effort at every level.

- The United States was often unable to knit its vast interagency capabilities together for best effect.[17] The implementation of national decisions by various agencies and departments was a continuing problem for senior officials. The inability to integrate, direct, prioritize, and apply capabilities in the optimal manner diminished success as much as any faulty strategy or campaign plan. The converse is also true: our greatest successes were those pockets of interagency collaboration stimulated by innovative leaders.

- Continuous monitoring of strategy implementation is part of the portfolio of the National Security Council, Office of the Secretary of Defense, Joint Staff, and field commanders. At national, theater, and high commands, U.S. departments and agencies must work closely early on to develop performance metrics and use them consistently over time to manage the conflict. Honest periodic reassessments should be meticulously planned and ruthlessly executed. This is important for combat, personnel, logistics, and replacement training and education. Short tours are likely to be a constant, and we need to ensure that new personnel and units know the physical territory and demographics of their areas of operations.

- Unity of command is a key tenet in the principles of joint operations and remains relevant to how the Armed Forces use combat power across a range of operations. Unity of command is a time-proven American tradition that has been applied to great effect in the Civil War, World War I, and World War II. This principle, however, seems to have been bypassed in the development of disjointed command and control structures in the wars in Iraq and Afghanistan.[18] Indeed, General David Petraeus noted that we did not get the strategy and command and control architecture right in Afghanistan until 2010.[19] Creating unity of command within large coalitions will remain a high point of military art.

Intelligence and Understanding the Operational Environment

Intelligence in war is always problematic. Not only are understanding, analysis, and prediction difficult, but the thinking enemy also attempts to deceive us at every twist and turn. In these two campaigns, the difficult mission of intelligence agencies has been compounded by the need for additional intelligence on the indigenous population.

■ Neither national nor military intelligence in Iraq and Afghanistan was a success in supporting decisionmakers. Intelligence on Afghanistan itself was initially scant and not actionable. In Iraq, prewar intelligence was wrong about weapons of mass destruction, the Iraqi police, and the state of Iraqi infrastructure. U.S. forces had little information on tribal dynamics and the potential role of Iran. In both wars, U.S. intelligence failed in telling battlespace owners about the people whom they were protecting. The effects of these shortcomings were grave.

■ The biggest advances in intelligence came in improved support for the warfighter at the tactical level, and the intimate relationship that developed between special operations forces and all-source intelligence. General Martin Dempsey stated that a captain at a remote site in Afghanistan in 2008 had more access to national technical means and high-level intelligence than he had as a division commander in 2003.[20]

■ Neither national-level figures nor field commanders fully understood the operational environment, including the human aspects of military operations.[21] To fight, in Rupert Smith's term, war among the people, one must first understand them. We were not intellectually prepared for the unique aspects of war in Iraq and Afghanistan. In both conflicts, ethnic, religious, and cultural differences drove much of the fighting. Efforts to solve this problem—Human Terrain Teams and the Afghanistan-Pakistan Hands Program, for example—came too little and too late. Our intelligence system was of little help here primarily because the Intelligence Community did not see this as its mission. The need for information aggregation stands as an equal to classical all-source intelligence. Our lack of understanding of the wars seriously retarded our efforts to fight them and to deal with our indigenous allies, who were often more interested in score-settling or political risk aversion than they were in winning the war.

■ Understanding the operational environment calls for a whole array of fixes, such as improving language training, predeployment training, area expertise, and reforming the intelligence/information apparatuses. The Army's regionally aligned forces concept appears a step in the right direction. The renewed emphasis on the human domain and human aspects of military operations should be reinforced and sustained over time. There can be no substitute for excellent joint professional military education, reinforced by dedicated self-study by career officers and noncommissioned officers. For senior officers and advisors, every dollar spent on civilian graduate education in policy sciences and history is returned many times over.

■ U.S. leaders must also know themselves and the social, political, and systemic constraints that will affect the ability to respond well to the threat. If we ask more than the public and its representatives in Congress can bear or the national security system can provide, our ability to counter the threat will be handicapped. For example, public support for war depends on the perception that we are defending vital or important U.S. interests. Even in those cases, political support for policy or strategy in war is short-lived and can be extended only by success.

■ In the same vein, future senior officers and policymakers must understand constitutional, domestic legal, and international legal norms. This is fundamental to honoring their oath to the Constitution. Moreover, if the United States is seen as violating these norms, it damages U.S. standing and undercuts the legitimacy of our policy.

■ To address legal norms and intelligence-gathering, planning for military operations must include detention planning. Policymakers and joint force commanders must sort out the complex legal and practical issues in advance of arrival in the country in question.

Character of Contemporary Conflict

The analysis of these two campaigns reinforced a number of lessons about the nature of war and the character of contemporary conflict. Again, few of these lessons are new.

- When conventional warfare or logistical skills were called for in Iraq and Afghanistan, the Armed Forces generally achieved excellent results. At the same time, the military was insensitive to needs of the postconflict environment and not prepared for insurgency in either country. Our lack of preparation for dealing with irregular conflicts was the result of a post-Vietnam organizational blindspot. Military performance improved over time. Indeed, field-level innovation on counterinsurgency showed an admirable capacity for learning and innovation. Furthermore, the development of Army and Marine Corps doctrine on counterinsurgency and the inculcation of the doctrine into the force was an excellent example of systemic adaptation. The doctrine for counterinsurgency and stability operations needs revision, and this work is well under way.
- In a similar manner, with great fits and starts and a great deal of managerial attention, the acquisition system of the Department of Defense was able to create, field, and deploy the equipment needed to turn the military we had into the military we needed. Long-term planning in the Services for future wars can retard warfighting adaptations in the near term. The speed of battlefield learning was admirable, and the speed of technological innovation in this war was satisfactory.[22]
- A prudent great power should avoid being a third party in a large-scale counterinsurgency effort. Foreign expeditionary forces in another country's insurgency have almost always failed. Exceptions to this rule came only where the foreign expeditionary

force controlled the government and did not have to contend with insurgents who possessed secure sanctuaries.[23] At the same time, it should be remembered that the wars in Iraq and Afghanistan did not begin as insurgencies, but evolved in that direction. The Armed Forces must be ready for combat across the spectrum of conflict, and irregular wars on the low end of the spectrum will remain the most frequent form of conflict that they encounter.

■ Another salient issue in irregular conflicts is the question of sanctuary. In Iraq and Afghanistan, our enemies exploited base areas in adjacent countries. This presents the United States with a dilemma. Does the Nation violate international understandings about the sanctity of borders, or does it allow an enemy to have secure bases from which to launch attacks?

■ Wars that involve regime change are likely to be protracted conflicts. They require a substantial, patient, and prudent international effort to bring stability and foster reconstruction, especially in the wake of weak, corrupt, or failed states. These exercises in armed nation-building are complex, uncertain, and, with the passing of time, increasingly unpopular in the United States. In the often used words of General Petraeus, progress in such conflicts will be "fragile and reversible." Nevertheless, regime change and long-duration stability operations will at times be necessary. The alternatives are inaction or kinetic "success" followed by political chaos. In the view of the editors, there was an option not to invade Afghanistan or Iraq, but there was never a politically acceptable option to leave Afghanistan or Iraq shortly after the conclusion of the initial phase of major combat operations.

■ Long and complex conflicts are likely to be coalition efforts, which lend legitimacy and ease manpower and material requirements. Coalitions also confound unity of command and may hurt unity of effort. On balance, sound coalitions of the willing contribute more to success than they detract from it. In the modern world, they are also a foolproof guide to public support and acceptance. Robust coalitions endure and show international support, which is somewhat self-replicating. Lesser coalitions are a reminder of perceived illegitimacy and an indicator of serious problems.

■ In a counterinsurgency, success will depend in part on the political development of the host government, whose weakness, corruption, and ineffectiveness are ironically an important factor in the development of the insurgency. There are few assets in the State Department or USAID inventory to mentor and assist a host government in political development. In collateral areas, such as humanitarian assistance, development, rule of law, and reconstruction, State and USAID have more assets, but far fewer than large-scale contingencies require. Ideally, the United States should have a civilian response corps, but the urge to develop whole-of-government capabilities is waning. As former National Security Advisor Stephen J. Hadley notes, there needs to be a national discussion on these critical issues.[24]

■ Strategic communications was a weak point in our performance in Washington, DC, and in the field. Making friends, allies, and locals understand our intent has proved difficult. At times, the situation on the ground will block good messaging. However, our disabilities in this area—partly caused by too much bureaucracy and too little empathy—stand in contradistinction to the ability of clever enemies to package their message and beat us at a game that was perfected in Hollywood and on Madison Avenue. War crimes and clear evidence of abuse of locals or detainees have further hobbled our efforts, especially when every person with a cellular phone is a photojournalist. This is not a psychological operation or public affairs issue. Strategic communications is a vital task for commanders and senior policymakers at every level.

Security Force Assistance

Security force assistance—especially the building of indigenous police and military forces—is a key strategic activity, which in Iraq and Afghanistan was the centerpiece of the coalition exit strategy. It was also an area where successes followed a painful process of trial and error, and coalition approaches were often mismatched with the local population and circumstances.

- In Iraq and Afghanistan, the United States developed host-nation ministries and military forces modeled on Western institutions and structures. In Iraq, initial efforts focused on creating an army to defend the country from external enemies. In Afghanistan, the decision to focus on a national army and police force, albeit at the insistence of the government of Afghanistan, increased tensions with local tribes and ethnic groups. The political, economic, social, and cultural conditions of these countries made U.S. approaches problematic and perhaps unsustainable without a significant long-term presence.

- Whenever possible, U.S. forces should be placed in a supporting role to the host nation. U.S. assistance should usually be framed as "transactional" and "conditional," based on shared objectives and situational variables.[25] Where possible, the host nation must take ownership of the training effort and associated architecture. It must be held accountable for its progress and shortcomings.

- Improving our ability to teach others to defeat an insurgency or terrorists is likely the key to future U.S. participation in irregular conflicts. U.S. advisors can only train what they know. Before they deploy, advisors must be educated culturally and politically to organize ministries and/or train forces that fit the operational environment and local needs. Except for the special operations forces, the United States is not well organized to accomplish this mission. The Services generally do not reward individuals for this kind of service. Two possibilities commend themselves: the United States can form military assistance groups, or it can develop and refine ways to prepare conventional units for this mission in a rapid and effective manner. The ad hoc approach to preparing advisory and assistance forces should not be our primary methodology.

In conclusion, this book is an assessment of two unfinished campaigns, written for future senior officers, their key advisors, and other national security professionals. The lessons identified here emerged from a study rich in strategic context and immediate circumstances. Any application of these lessons must be done with an understanding of situational context, particular circumstances, and mission at hand. The lessons identified here will be theirs to debate, accept or reject, refine, and institutionalize. They will have to mix them generously with the lessons of other wars and apply them appropriately, guided by their mission and the situation at hand. Learning strategic lessons will be difficult but not impossible. In the future, the national interest and the lives of our men and women in uniform will be hostage to how well we have learned and institutionalized these strategic lessons.

Notes

[1]   Martin J. Dempsey, *18th Chairman's 2nd Term Strategic Direction to the Joint Force* (Washington, DC: The Joint Staff, n.d.), 4, available at <www.jcs.mil/portals/36/Documents/CJCS_2nd_Term_Strategic_Direction.pdf>.

[2]   National Defense University 2020 Design Paper, unpublished, December 2012.

[3]   For operational lessons, see Joint and Coalition Operational Analysis (JCOA), *Decade of War, Volume 1: Enduring Lessons from the Past Decade of Operations* (Suffolk, VA: JCOA, June 15, 2012), available at <http://blogs.defensenews.com/saxotech-access/pdfs/decade-of-war-lessons-learned.pdf>. As this book was being prepared, two teams of Army officers were working on operational histories of the U.S. Army in Iraq and Afghanistan.

[4]   For an earlier discussion on the problems of learning, see Joseph J. Collins, "Desert Storm and the Lessons of Learning," *Parameters* (Autumn 1992), 83–92.

[5]   David Petraeus, "Lessons of History and Lessons of Vietnam," *Parameters* (Autumn 1986; reprinted Winter 2010–2011), 48–50.

[6]   Jay Luvaas, "Lessons and Lessons Learned: A Historical Perspective," in *The Lessons of Recent Wars in the Third World: Approaches and Case Studies*, volume 1, ed. Robert Harkavy and Stephanie Neuman (Lexington, MA: Lexington Books, 1985), 68.

[7]   Henry Kissinger, *Diplomacy* (New York: Simon & Schuster, 1994), 27.

[8]   Adam Gopnick, "The Big One: Historians Rethink the War to End All Wars," *The New Yorker*, August 23, 2004, 78–79.

⁹ Carl von Clausewitz, *On War*, ed. and trans. Michael Howard and Peter Paret (Princeton: Princeton University Press, 1984), 111–112.

¹⁰ National Security Action Memorandum no. 55, Subject: Relations of the Joint Chiefs of Staff to the President in Cold War Operations, June 28, 1961. In General Petraeus's and General Lloyd Austin's conception, general and statesman is the correct formulation, but in their interviews for this volume, they stressed the importance of the general first getting the military advice right, based on the facts on the ground and other considerations. David Petraeus, interview by Joseph J. Collins and Nathan White, March 27, 2015; and Lloyd Austin, interview by Richard D. Hooker, Jr., April 7, 2015.

¹¹ For a precis on the learning organization, see John Nagl, *Learning to Eat Soup with a Knife: Counterinsurgency Lessons from Malaya and Vietnam* (Chicago: University of Chicago Press, 2005), 6, 10–11, 215–223. Nagl attributes much of his discussion on learning theory to Richard Downie, *Learning from Conflict: The U.S. Military in Vietnam, El Salvador, and the Drug War* (Westport, CT: Praeger, 1998).

¹² For an example of how an evaluator would have shifted emphasis, Lieutenant General David Deptula, USAF (Ret.), noted in correspondence with the editors, "I offer that perhaps more attention could have been given to the issue of the importance of greater encouragement and consideration of options at the strategic level. Also, greater attention could have been given to the important topic of the application—or lack thereof—of the tenets of joint doctrine/operations in the context of organization and employment. The complete failure of strategic communications/perception management and an anachronistic structure for the optimal application of a whole-of-government approach are also areas that I believe deserve greater attention and elaboration."

¹³ Chairman of the Joint Chiefs of Staff General Martin E. Dempsey in his interview for this study offered the following guidelines (in shortened paraphrasing) for participants in the national decisionmaking system: Learn the civilian national security decisionmaking system. The military starts with objectives and works toward options. The civilian leadership begins with options and works backward toward objectives. Military leaders must accommodate this system and offer options that are suitable, feasible, and acceptable. Civil-military or interdepartmental friction is not necessarily bad. Accept it and embrace it. Develop relationships and then build trust with civilian contemporaries. Be prepared to engage in national discussions and speak on grand strategy issues. The most persuasive arguments normally win. Most big decisions are made in conjunction with budget cycles. Adapt to the leadership style of the President and Secretary of Defense, but above all, in every decision, maintain your moral compass. Martin E. Dempsey, interview by Richard D. Hooker, Jr., and Joseph J. Collins, January 7, 2015. For a collateral discussion of civilian and military decisionmakers talking past each other, see Janine Davidson, "Civil-Military Friction and Presidential Decision-Making," *Presidential Studies Quarterly* 43, no. 1 (March 2013).

¹⁴ John Allen, interview by Richard D. Hooker, Jr. and Joseph J. Collins, January 27, 2015.

¹⁵ Eliot Cohen, *Supreme Command: Soldiers, Statesmen, and Leadership in Wartime* (New York: Free Press, 2002), 208–224.

[16] For a table showing the decline of unity of effort organizations and initiatives, see Linda Robinson et al., *Improving Strategic Competence: Lessons from 13 Years of War* (Santa Monica, CA: RAND), 117–119.

[17] Some close observers believe that in any conflict or postconflict situation, the United States should have one person, military or civilian, who is in charge of all American policy and people in the theater in question. See, for example, Stanley A. McChrystal, interview by Joseph J. Collins and Frank G. Hoffman, April 2, 2015. General David Petraeus recommended that in complex contingencies, we should make better use of existing headquarters, even if they have to be repurposed. See David Petraeus, interview by Joseph J. Collins and Nathan White, March 27, 2015.

[18] For example, in Afghanistan in 2006, Combined Forces Command–Afghanistan passed control of the ground fight to the International Security Assistance Force, and operations became fragmented among the U.S. Central Command commander; Supreme Allied Commander, Europe; and U.S. Special Operations Command (USSOCOM) commander. As former Secretary of Defense Robert Gates notes in his memoir, "efforts in Afghanistan during 2007 were being hampered not only by muddled and overambitious objectives but also by confusion in the military command structure" (page 205). Furthermore, Gates adds that command relationships in Afghanistan were a "jerry-rigged arrangement [that] violated every principle of the unity of command" (page 206). The problem persisted even after Secretary Gates ordered it rectified in the summer of 2010, nearly 9 years after the war started. In both Iraq and Afghanistan, the often raw relationships between conventional forces, who were battlespace owners, and various types of special operations forces (SOF, such as theater SOF, USSOCOM-subordinated SOF, non-U.S. SOF, and so forth) were common complaints. This problem improved over time but is still an issue. Efforts to bridge the gap between conventional and SOF must continue. The editors thank Major Claude Lambert, USA—a strategist and intern in the Center for Complex Operations at the National Defense University—for this observation.

[19] Petraeus, interview.

[20] Dempsey, interview. In his interview for this volume, General Lloyd J. Austin III, U.S. Central Command commander, noted that intelligence support to the warfighter was "light years ahead of where it was in 2003." Austin, interview by Richard D. Hooker, Jr., April 7, 2015.

[21] This was a major point first made in JCOA, *Decade of War, Volume I: Enduring Lessons from the Past Decade of War* (Suffolk, VA: JCOA, June 15, 2012), 2–5. It was also a major finding in Robinson et al., 59–71.

[22] The problems in developing and fielding the equipment that matched current warfighting requirements are discussed in Robert M. Gates, *Duty: Memoirs of a Secretary at War* (New York: Knopf, 2014), 115–148. General Austin lauded in particular rapid equipment fielding efforts, the Joint Improvised Explosive Device Defeat Organization, and advances in intelligence, surveillance, and reconnaissance. Austin, interview.

[23] In the past, among the great failures in third-party expeditionary force participation in

insurgencies are the French in Indochina and Algeria and the United States in Vietnam. One can find many successes against insurgents that used unconscionable tactics. The two great successes among great power efforts were the United States in the Philippines (1899–1902) and United Kingdom in Malaya. There have been many cases in which the United States achieved positive outcomes when it did not have to use a major expeditionary force.

[24] Stephen J. Hadley, interview by Joseph J. Collins and Nicholas Rostow, October 7, 2014.

[25] Dempsey, interview.

1

Initial Planning and Execution in Afghanistan and Iraq

By Joseph J. Collins

Al Qaeda's 9/11 attacks on the United States had devastating effects. Not only were nearly 3,000 people killed at the World Trade Center, the Pentagon, and in Shanksville, Pennsylvania, but also the physical and emotional security of the United States was shattered by a major foreign attack on the homeland for the first time since the Japanese attack on Pearl Harbor. Fear of the next attack, the desire to punish the enemy, the pressure of military preparations, the urgent need to improve homeland security, and a "never again" attitude animated the policy of the United States. The North Atlantic Treaty Organization (NATO), for the first time, invoked Article 5 of its charter, which proclaims that "an attack on one is considered an attack on all." France's *Le Monde*, not always an American partisan, proclaimed in an editorial, "*Nous sommes tous Américains.*"[1] The United States crossed the threshold from the post–Cold War era to an era of global conflict that came to be known as the Long War or the war on terror. Afghanistan and Iraq were the two largest campaigns in this war. While the military was the dominant tool, these campaigns involved all of the Nation's intelligence, defense, diplomatic, developmental, informational, and financial instruments of statecraft.

This chapter analyzes the U.S. decision to go to war in Afghanistan in 2001, operations in Afghanistan through 2008, the coercive diplomacy with Iraq, the planning for the Iraq War, and U.S. operations there through 2006. The aim of the chapter is to develop observations or perspectives to help future senior officers and other national security professionals contribute to national security and military strategies.[2] Subsequent chapters complete the analysis, and the volume is capped off by a discussion of the strategic lessons of the two campaigns.

War in Afghanistan: The First Few Years

Once the Taliban refused to surrender Osama bin Laden and close the terrorist training camps in Afghanistan, there was never a question of whether the United States would use force against al Qaeda and the Taliban; it was only a question of when it would go to war. Congress acted quickly and granted wide authority to use force. In part, the Authorization for Use of Military Force gave President George W. Bush the power "to use all necessary and appropriate force against those nations, organizations, or persons he determines planned, authorized, committed, or aided the terrorist attacks that occurred on September 11, 2001, or harbored such organizations or persons, in order to prevent any future acts of international terrorism against the United States by such nations, organizations or persons."[3]

Afghanistan is a forbidding place to make war. The so-called graveyard of empires is landlocked, mountainous, and fractious. By 2001, it was the victim of two decades of nationwide fighting, followed by 5 years (1996–2001) of disastrous Taliban rule.[4] The Taliban were strongly backed by Pakistan. They were religious zealots who fought well against other Afghan groups but were ineffective and ruthless governors. Aside from being serial violators of human rights, the Taliban adopted bin Laden and his al Qaeda henchmen, allowing their country to play host to the world's most dangerous terrorist organization. Their 5-year rule further impoverished and damaged Afghanistan in many areas, especially health care and education. Only three countries—Pakistan, Saudi Arabia, and the United Arab Emirates—recognized this highly authoritarian and ineffective government.

A small group of American officials—including Director of the Central Intelligence Agency (CIA) George Tenet—understood the al Qaeda threat based in Afghanistan. These officials advocated a strong national policy toward al Qaeda but were unsuccessful in moving the White House to effective action during either the Presidency of William Clinton or President George W. Bush's first 7 months in office. In August 2001, the CIA warned Bush in a general way about an imminent al Qaeda attack on the United States involving aviation. The United States had never effectively retaliated against previous al

Qaeda attacks, and it did not take concrete steps to prepare for an attack after the Agency's August warning. The attacks on 9/11 were in part an intelligence and a homeland security failure, but they were also a failure of the national security bureaucracy to adapt to a new and growing threat.[5] For its part, prior to 9/11, the U.S. Armed Forces were primarily focused on high-tech, conventional warfare. Their long-range vision papers, *Joint Vision 2010* (1996) and *Joint Vision 2020* (2000), barely mentioned counterterrorism or counterinsurgency as major defense requirements. Combating al Qaeda was not a major focus of the 2001 Quadrennial Defense Review, which was in the final draft stage in the days prior to the attack.[6] On September 11, 2001, America's national security leadership was simply on the wrong page.

It is not clear what Taliban leader Mullah Mohammed Omar or al Qaeda's leaders thought would happen in Afghanistan after the 9/11 attacks. Perhaps bin Laden thought that the Bush administration would conduct a lengthy investigation, treat this act of terrorism as a law enforcement issue, and be slow to respond. The United States had failed to take significant retaliatory action after other terrorist attacks: the 1983 bombing of the Marine barracks in Lebanon, the 1993 bombing of the World Trade Center, the 1996 Khobar Towers attack in Saudi Arabia, the 1998 Embassy bombings in East Africa, and the 2000 bombing of the USS *Cole* off the coast of Yemen. The Taliban and al Qaeda may have believed the United States would only strike with its airpower and cruise missiles, as it had done frequently in Iraq and once in Afghanistan after the 1998 Embassy bombings. Osama bin Laden and Mullah Omar may have believed that the United States might attack on the ground but that it would get bogged down just as the Soviet Union had. After the fact, bin Laden suggested that drawing the United States into Middle Eastern and Southwest Asian wars and thus draining its power was an integral part of the al Qaeda strategy.[7]

With the Pentagon and World Trade Center sites still smoldering, the President met with his advisors at Camp David on September 15. Chairman of the Joint Chiefs of Staff General Hugh Shelton presented three generic options to the President and his advisors: a cruise missile strike, a cruise missile attack with airstrikes, and "boots on the ground" with cruise missile and air attacks. Neither President Bush nor Secretary of Defense Donald Rumsfeld was comfortable with the presentation and found the idea of a deliberate buildup of U.S. ground forces to be too slow even to contemplate. Rumsfeld characterized the presentation as unimaginative and unoriginal.[8] The President wanted a plan that featured the rapid use of military force and the insertion of troops on the ground as soon as possible.

It should be noted here that some Defense officials believed that the terrorists likely had the help of a state sponsor and that Saddam Hussein's Iraq was the most likely suspect.[9] The issue of simultaneously attacking Iraq was brought up at Camp David by Deputy Secretary of Defense Paul Wolfowitz, but the suggestion had little support among the National Security Council (NSC) principals and was sidelined by the President. The timing was not fortuitous. However, on September 26, President Bush asked Rumsfeld in private to "look at the shape of our plans on Iraq" and asked for "creative" options.[10] In any event, U.S. Central Command (USCENTCOM) planning for a potential war in Iraq would begin in earnest in November 2001 before the conclusion of the initial fighting in Afghanistan.[11]

On September 21, USCENTCOM Commander General Tommy Franks, USA, briefed the President on a plan to destroy al Qaeda in Afghanistan and remove the Taliban government.[12] Despite recent air and missile attacks against al Qaeda in Afghanistan, USCENTCOM had no preexisting plans for conducting ground operations there. The September 21 plan emerged after extensive dialogue, but Secretary Rumsfeld also asked for broader plans that looked beyond Afghanistan.[13] In all of his planning commentary, the Secretary's stated goal was not to seek revenge but to prevent another attack on the U.S. homeland. However, all the participants in the briefing agreed that real-time intelligence about Afghanistan was in short supply.[14] The plan also depended heavily on access to facilities in nearby countries and support by U.S. airlift and sealift.

The basic concept was to put U.S. Army Special Forces and CIA operators with Northern Alliance forces and anti-Taliban forces in the south, exploiting the combination of U.S. airpower, tactical advice, communications, and experienced Afghan resistance forces.[15] The plan also featured making humanitarian food drops and, later, having U.S. and coalition conventional forces mop up and go after the remaining Taliban and al Qaeda elements.[16] In President Bush's hopeful words, "We would [then begin to] stabilize the country and help the Afghan people to build a free society."[17]

The air war and humanitarian food drops, coordinated from the Combined Air Operations Center in Saudi Arabia, began on October 7, but Special

Forces personnel, delayed by helicopter issues and weather, did not arrive in the north until October 19. When they arrived, they joined a small number of CIA paramilitary officers already on the ground. With Special Forces advising Afghan ground commanders and calling in airstrikes, the Taliban defenses unraveled, and Afghanistan's major cities fell quickly. A combined force of Special Forces, Joint Terminal Attack Controllers, Navy and Air Force attack aircraft, and Northern Alliance infantry and horse cavalry under General Abdul Rashid Dostum captured Mazar-e-Sharif on November 9. At the same time, Deputy Secretary of State Richard Armitage gave an ultimatum to Pakistani authorities; as a result, he secured their full cooperation in fighting al Qaeda, access to their critical ground lines of communication, and promises (albeit short-lived ones) to restrain the Afghan Taliban. In short order, Herat in the west, Kabul in the center, and Kandahar in the south fell to the resistance. Army Rangers conducted raids and a Marine brigade seized a base south of Kandahar. Later, in the December battle at Tora Bora, a CIA-advised Afghan ground element eliminated an al Qaeda stronghold where bin Laden may have been present. A CIA officer there requested help from U.S. ground forces, but his request was disapproved by General Franks. Secretary Rumsfeld did not learn of this request until after the battle, but it is far from clear that the insertion of a U.S. battalion or brigade, even if it were available, would have made a difference in that mountainous terrain.[18]

In less than 10 weeks, the United States and its partners were able to accomplish significant military objectives without a large-scale ground invasion and without alienating the Afghan people. While the operation was successful, it was not decisive. The Taliban had been defeated and ousted and al Qaeda's bases and organizational structure in Afghanistan had been destroyed, but the Taliban and al Qaeda leadership, along with many of their senior cadre, escaped, mostly into Pakistan. For its part, Pakistan would be helpful in rounding up foreign radicals and members of al Qaeda, but it generally accommodated the Afghan Taliban, with major pockets of Taliban settling near Quetta in Baluchistan, in Waziristan, in other areas in northwest Pakistan, and, later, in Karachi.

With the help of the Germans and the United Nations (UN), an international conference in Bonn, Germany, established an Afghan Interim Administration with Hamid Karzai as its leader, backed by a multi-ethnic cabinet.[19]

The interim government quickly began to work on organizing a *Loya Jirga*, a nationwide assembly of tribal leaders, and preparing a draft constitution. While the formation of the government looked impressive, the truth was that the Afghan government was invisible in the countryside and had few police officers or army forces under its control. The country had been devastated by 24 years of war. The warlords and narcotics traffickers, who did have thousands of men under arms, often called the shots in the 34 provinces. The legal, health, and educational systems were in shambles, as were many aspects of civil society. (More than a decade later, revisionists argue that the United States could have avoided much pain in Afghanistan by leaving immediately upon forming the new government. That argument ignores the fact that the country was destitute. Taliban and al Qaeda forces would have returned in short order.[20])

The United States and its coalition partners, who formed the International Security Assistance Force (ISAF) in the Kabul region, became a stabilizing presence and a hedge against terrorist attacks and Taliban operatives, but the international community's "light footprint"—5,000 coalition and 10,000 U.S. troops focused on counterterrorism—was inadequate to secure nearly 30 million Afghans in a state as large as Texas. Years later, in his memoirs, President Bush wrote that although he had changed his mind and embraced "nation building" in Afghanistan, "We were all wary of repeating the experience of the Soviets and the British, who ended up looking like occupiers. This [light footprint] strategy worked well at first. But in retrospect, our rapid success with low troop levels created false comfort, and our desire to maintain a light footprint left us short of the resources we needed. It would take several years for these shortcomings to become clear."[21]

Stability Operations

Allied commanders and diplomats who arrived in Afghanistan in January 2002 were astounded by the devastation that nearly two and a half decades of war had wrought. The country also had suffered mightily from 5 years of Taliban mismanagement and authoritarian rule, further complicated by a few years of drought. The country they found was only 30 percent literate, and 80 percent of its schools had been destroyed. The Taliban severely restricted female education and did little for that of males. Twenty-five percent of all

Afghan children died before the age of 5. Only 9 percent of the population had access to health care. The professional and blue collar work forces had virtually disappeared.[22] The former Afghan finance minister, noted scholar, and later president, Ashraf Ghani noted that:

> *Between 1978, when the Communist coup took place, and November 2001, when the Taliban were overthrown, Afghanistan (according to a World Bank Estimate) lost $240 billion in ruined infrastructure and vanished opportunities. While the rest of the world was shrinking in terms of spatial and temporal coordination, the travel time between Kabul and every single province in the country significantly increased. . . . Millions of Afghan children grew up illiterate in refugee camps, where they learned that the gun rather than the ballot was the key instrument for the acquisition of power and influence.*[23]

The government of Afghanistan and its coalition partners had a relatively easy time of it from 2002 to 2004. Although starting from rock bottom in nearly every category, progress was made in security, stabilization activities, and economic reconstruction. Pushed by foreign aid, post-Taliban Afghanistan had nearly a decade of double-digit economic growth per year. From 2003 to 2005, the U.S. leadership team, led by Ambassador Zalmay Khalilzad and Lieutenant General Dave Barno, USA, focused on teamwork and elementary organization for counterinsurgency operations, albeit with very small forces. General Barno—who moved his office next door to the Ambassador's office in the Embassy—unified the field commands and divided the country into regional areas of responsibility, where one colonel or general officer would command all maneuver units and Provincial Reconstruction Teams.[24] Secretary Rumsfeld described the Khalilzad-Barno field relationship as a "model of how civilian-military relations should work."[25]

Barno was a self-taught expert in counterinsurgency. Although he initially had only a small force of 14,000 soldiers to work with, he concentrated on the Afghan people, not the Taliban, and worked along five lines of effort: defeating terrorism and denying sanctuary, enabling the Afghan security structure, sustaining area ownership, enabling reconstruction and good governance, and engaging regional states, especially Pakistan. Underpinning these efforts was an emphasis on information operations, which Barno saw as a Taliban strength and a coalition weakness.[26]

Pursuant to U.S. initiative and a series of NATO decisions, the ISAF mandate was increasingly enlarged until it took over all the regions of Afghanistan. The drive behind NATO expansion was designed to energize the alliance and relieve the United States of the two-war burden.[27] Initially in control of only the 200 square miles around Kabul, in the fall of 2004, ISAF took charge of the regional command in the north. In the spring of 2006, it took over in the west. In the summer of 2006, ISAF control moved into the south, parts of which, especially in Helmand Province, were Taliban strongholds with little government presence and influence. In the fall of that year, ISAF took over fighting and stability operations in the east, marking its command over coalition forces in the entire country. By 2006, most U.S. combat forces were put under the enlarged and empowered ISAF. In November 2009, the coalition stood up ISAF Joint Command to supervise combat operations, a task that had become too much for ISAF, which spent most of its time on policy, planning, and politico-military affairs.

While NATO action brought the Alliance on line in Afghanistan, it also magnified the caveats issued by countries to limit the activities of their forces. Many NATO nations did not allow their forces to engage in offensive combat operations. The United States, Canada, the United Kingdom, France, Denmark, the Netherlands, and a few others did most of the fighting and combat advising.[28] Still, the international coalition in Afghanistan was a powerful force in both operations and training. When Barack Obama was elected in 2008, NATO nations and other coalition partners provided 30,000 of the 68,000 conventional forces in country.

The advent of ISAF and NATO in Afghanistan created a complex relationship between the Supreme Allied Commander, Europe, and the USCENTCOM commander. While the latter remained in command of U.S. forces there, the former became responsible for supervising the strategic guidance, which came through NATO's Joint Forces Command in Brunsuum, the Netherlands. At the same time, after 2007, the ISAF commander was an American general responsible both to his NATO superiors and to USCENTCOM. Complicating matters, it took ISAF and NATO a few years to take over the training of the Afghan army and police from the United States. The NATO-ISAF regime also did not see Pakistan as part of its area of influence, magnifying the all too powerful tendency to look at Afghanistan and Pakistan as separate issues.[29]

General John P. Abizaid, USA, who commanded USCENTCOM for nearly 4 years, admired the strength of the coalition, but he noted in an interview in 2007 that the command arrangements in Afghanistan violated the principle of unity of command; he would have preferred that "unity of regional efforts stay within CENTCOM's purview."[30] In a similar vein, the seams between conventional and special operations forces (SOF) were a problem, but one that improved over time.

From 2003 to 2005, the relationship between Ambassador Khalilzad, born in northern Afghanistan to Pashtun parents, and President Karzai was close and productive. The government of Afghanistan, with much help from the international community, conducted nationwide Loya Jirgas in 2002 and 2003, passed a modern constitution modeled on the 1964 Afghanistan constitution, and held fair presidential and parliamentary elections in 2004 and 2005, respectively.[31] The new constitution was highly centralized and gave the president much of the power that the king held in the constitutional monarchy from 1964 to 1973. While the Kabul government was weak in capability and nationwide coverage, it was responsible for national and local policy, as well as all significant personnel appointments, to include provincial and district governors. Warlords still played major roles in Afghanistan, but with Japanese funding and UN leadership, the central government confiscated and cantoned all heavy weapons. This process was called disarmament, demobilization, and reintegration. By 2004, major fighting between contending warlords that featured the use of heavy weapons ceased to be an important issue. The UN mission, with the support of the government of Japan, performed yeoman's service on this major project.

Afghanistan attracted a fair amount of international aid, but far less than the Balkan nations did after their conflicts in the 1990s. U.S. security and economic assistance from 2002 to 2004 was a modest $4.4 billion, but nearly two-thirds of that sum went to economic assistance, with only slightly more than one-third to security assistance. Afghanistan ranked poorly when compared to other nation-building efforts. RAND Corporation experts noted that in the first two postconflict years, the international community provided

$1,400 per capita for Bosnia and over $800 for Kosovo but less than $100 for Afghanistan.[32]

The Bush administration had hoped that the UN and international financial institutions such as the World Bank would lead reconstruction and stabilization. It learned that the international actors would follow only in areas where the United States led. Initiatives by so-called lead nations—Germany for the police, Great Britain for counternarcotics, and Italy for law and justice—were often disappointing. Similarly, the U.S. buildup of the Afghan National Army lagged, and police development in the first few years was slow and unproductive. By 2008, 70 percent of U.S. assistance funds was assigned to security or counternarcotics.[33] In the first 2 years after the expulsion of the Taliban, fighting was infrequent and at a low level. In 2004, nationwide, the worst weeks had about 100 security incidents. By 2009, after 4 years of Taliban offensives, the worst weeks topped 900 incidents.[34]

From 2002 to 2003, under the guidance of finance minister Ashraf Ghani, the Afghan government swapped out the several currencies in use across the country, established a single stable currency, negotiated international contracts for a nationwide cellular phone service, and began to work on economic reconstruction. With the help of the international community, there was rapid reconstruction in health care and education. The United States and international financial institutions rebuilt most of the ring road around the country, improving travel and commerce. Access to medical care was extended from 9 percent of the population under the Taliban to more than 60 percent of the population by 2010.[35] Spurred by foreign aid, rapid licit economic growth began and has continued, but it exists alongside a booming illegal economy marked by bribery, smuggling, and narcotics trafficking.

To make up for inherent weakness in the Afghan government, various countries followed the U.S. lead and set up Provincial Reconstruction Teams (PRTs), which had varying names when led by coalition partners. The generic purposes of the PRTs were to further security, promote reconstruction, facilitate cooperation with nongovernmental organizations (NGOs) and international organizations in the field, and help the local authorities in governance and other issues. These small interagency elements were initially established in a third of the provinces but rapidly went nationwide. At their height, these

26 teams—half led by U.S. allies—played a key role in reconstruction and development.

PRTs consisted of a headquarters, a security element, civil affairs teams, diplomats, aid and assistance experts, and, where possible, agricultural teams. Many U.S. PRTs were commanded by Navy and Air Force officers. Without a nationwide peacekeeping force, these teams were often the only way that diplomats and government aid professionals could get out to the countryside. From 2002 to 2009, the U.S.-hosted PRTs were instrumental in helping to disburse nearly $2.7 billion of Commander's Emergency Response Program (CERP) money and other PRT-designated funds.[36]

The PRTs were, on balance, a positive development. They did, however, exacerbate interagency tensions within the U.S. Government. In 2002, providing diplomats and development experts to each of the eight initial PRTs consumed many hours of meetings at the deputies' committee level.[37] The PRTs remained a recurring problem with NGOs, which were reluctant to have military forces in the "humanitarian space." Some donors found the PRTs a convenient excuse for ignoring the need to build Afghan government capacity. As the years passed, the Afghan government tried to grow in budgetary capacity, a key to improving management. It complained that the money going directly to NGOs and PRTs kept aid funds outside of the Afghan budget and prevented the government from managing business through its own budgetary control mechanisms. It became a vicious cycle: the government of Afghanistan's corruption and lack of management capacity became an excuse for bypassing it, which in turn ensured that it would not develop capacity. Toward the end of his presidency, Karzai, initially a fan, had become a critic of PRTs in general.

While many observers objected to the military flavor of these teams, the need for large-scale security elements dictated that condition. Regional commanders after 2004 controlled maneuver forces and PRTs in their region.[38] By 2009, "the U.S. Ambassador put civilian leadership at the brigade and Regional Command levels, creating a civilian hierarchical structure that mirrored the military [chain of command]."[39] Later, the U.S. Government in Afghanistan also used District Support Teams, with representatives from the Department of State, U.S. Agency for International Development (USAID), and Department of Agriculture, to go with deployed military units or other security to hotspots to work directly with Afghan government representatives. There were 19 of these teams in Regional Command–East alone. In a similar vein, the U.S. National Guard fielded nine Agribusiness Development Teams with military and state university agronomists to help Afghan agriculture and animal husbandry enter the 21st century.

In terms of reconstruction and development, the coalition, reinforced by the UN and international financial institutions, did outstanding work and markedly improved Afghanistan's lot. Through the end of fiscal year 2009, nearly $40 billion of U.S. foreign and security assistance was pledged or delivered to Afghanistan. Other nations or international financial institutions delivered at least $14 billion of economic assistance through fiscal year 2008.[40] Although there are no reliable figures for its allies' expenditures, the United States devoted more than half its total aid to security assistance.

Progress in education, health care, road-building, and some areas of agriculture was good. A RAND study, citing NATO statistics, noted the military and development wings of allied nations had built or repaired thousands of kilometers of roads.[41] While it is fair to note that the areas under the most Taliban pressure received the least amount of aid, there were significant accomplishments. Five million refugees returned, and school enrollment increased six-fold from Taliban days, with 35 percent of the student body being female. (For its part, the Taliban burned or bombed over 1,000 schools from 2007 to 2009.) USAID alone, through the end of 2008, spent over $7 billion helping the Afghan people.[42] Among its accomplishments were 715 kilometers of major highways built, 670 health clinics built or refurbished, 10,600 health workers trained, over 600 schools constructed, more than 60 million school textbooks purchased, and 65,000 teachers trained in various courses. From time to time, these projects caused local frictions, but in significant ways they also transformed life for many Afghans.

In all, from 2001 to 2005, the coalition did well, but it did not do enough. Despite significant economic progress, poverty remained widespread, and the insurgents did their best to interfere with aid workers and disrupt their efforts at progress. Neither Afghan government capacity nor anticorruption efforts improved to an appreciable level. Some areas, especially in southern Afghanistan, had little coalition or Afghan government presence. Poppy cultivation and drug production increased despite coalition efforts. Warlords, even those co-opted by President Karzai, remained independent and often toxic power brokers. The level of international aid was not enough to stem the tide of an insurgency designed in part to render such aid ineffective. In many areas, but particularly in the southern and eastern parts of the country, the Taliban, from its sanctuaries in Pakistan, covertly began to restore its infrastructure, unimpeded by absentee or ineffective government structures.

The Situation Deteriorates, 2005–2009

From 2002 to 2005, the Taliban rebuilt its cadres with drug money, donations from the Gulf states, extortion, and help from al Qaeda.[43] Their sanctuaries in Pakistan enabled them to rearm and retrain. By 2005, the Quetta Shura Taliban (led by Mullah Omar), the Hezb-i-Islami Gulbuddin (under Gulbuddin Hekmatyar), and the Haqqani Network (led initially by Jalaluddin Haqqani and his son, Sirajuddin) were all working together to subvert the Karzai regime and wear down the coalition. All three of these groups continue to swear at least nominal allegiance to Mullah Omar and to coordinate major plans, but they are distinct operational entities with their own territories of interest in Afghanistan and independent fundraising mechanisms. Mullah Omar is also revered by the Pakistani Taliban, who have opposed Pakistan's government since 2006.[44] In 2005, the Afghan government's lack of capacity and the allies' light footprint scheme allowed many districts and a few provinces to fall under the "shadow" control of the Taliban. Some provinces, such as poppy-rich Helmand, had little government or coalition presence before 2006.

In 2005, encouraged by the U.S. attention to its troubled war in Iraq, the Taliban began a nationwide offensive to regain its influence. From 2004 to 2009, there was a nine-fold increase in security incidents nationwide and a forty-fold increase in suicide bombing, a technique imported from Iraq. Conflict spread to most of the 34 provinces, but 71 percent of the security incidents in 2010 still took place in only 10 percent of the more than 400 districts nationwide.[45] The war in Afghanistan remains primarily a war over control of Pashtun areas in the eastern and southern portion of the country, but Taliban subversion and terrorism also became important factors in many other provinces. Efforts to combat narcotics growth and production generally failed or met with only temporary success. As corruption inside Afghanistan increased, Taliban revenue increased accordingly.

With lessons learned from al Qaeda in Iraq, the flow of components from Pakistan, and some later support from Iran, the use of improvised explosive devices (IEDs) became the Taliban tactic of choice.[46] IED strikes rose from 300 in 2004 to more than 4,000 in 2009. In later years, more than half of all U.S. fatalities in Afghanistan resulted from IEDs.[47] Suicide bombers, almost unknown before 2004, became commonplace. By 2009, there were Taliban shadow governments of varied strength in nearly all provinces. Even in areas dominated by the government or government-friendly tribes, Taliban subversion or terror tactics became potent facts of life.

Beginning in 2005, the Taliban added more sophisticated information operations and local subversion to their standard terrorist tactics. "Night letters," a Soviet–Afghan war–era method of warning or intimidating the population, made a comeback, in some places as early as 2003. Letters were aimed at students, teachers, those who worked for Americans, and even children who fraternized with Americans.[48] In addition to subversion, terror tactics remained standard for the Taliban. In October 2008, for example, "the Taliban stopped a bus in the town of Maiwand in the western part of Kandahar Province, forcibly removed 50 passengers, and beheaded 30 of them."[49]

A UN study noted that in 2010, civilian casualties had increased by 10 percent from the previous year. The UN also noted that three-quarters of the civilian casualties were caused by "anti-government enemies," a marked increase of 53 percent from 2009.[50] While the population appreciated coalition restraint, the terror tactics of the Taliban kept many Afghans, especially in Pashtun areas, on the fence. Civilian casualties drove a wedge between the United States and the Karzai government, which began to harshly criticize the coalition while often ignoring the Taliban's reckless, inhumane behavior.

How did the war effort in Afghanistan deteriorate? First, in the early years, there was little progress in building Afghan capacity for governance, security, or economic development. There was little Afghan government and administrative capacity, and much economic and security assistance from the coalition bypassed the Afghan government. Nations and international organizations found it more convenient to work through NGOs and contractors. Over the years, these habits continued, and corruption among Afghan government officials increased. Key ministers, such as Ashraf Ghani (Finance), Abdullah Abdullah (Foreign Affairs), and Ali Jalali (Interior), resigned over time. After the departure of Ambassador Khalilzad in 2005, Karzai lost his closest confidant on the American side. Subsequent Ambassadors—Ronald Neumann, William Wood, and Karl Eikenberry—did fine work but did not have the close relationship with Karzai that Khalilzad had. At the same time, Karzai lost faith in his American allies, who were often driven to distraction by Karzai's unfair and one-sided tirades. The leaking of sensitive cables in the WikiLeaks scandal undoubtedly contributed to the breakdown in trust between Karzai and the U.S. Government and its representatives.

Second, there was also substantial government corruption in Afghanistan, often tied to police operations or the drug trade. Karzai took the lead in dealing with the so-called warlords, the regional strongmen. Many of them ended up in the government, which was both a blessing and a curse. Others continued their viral existence in the provinces, often using their local power and cunning to take money from reconstruction projects or even from U.S. security contracts. Money-laundering through Kabul International Airport became well developed. Later, as assistance increased, journalists discovered that pallets of convertible currencies were being moved to the United Arab Emirates by individuals, corporations, and even Afghan government officials.[51] President Karzai's brothers and some of his immediate subordinates also became the subject of corruption investigations, especially after the Kabul Bank fell apart in 2010.

The drug trade fueled corruption and funded part of the Taliban operation. The United Kingdom, the United States, and the United Nations focused on various strategies to block the narcotics traffic but to no avail. Various attempts at crop eradication were particularly dysfunctional. Brookings Institution analyst Vanda Felbab-Brown offered this bleak assessment: "The counternarcotics policies pressed on the post-Taliban government prior to 2009 had serious counterproductive effects not only on the Afghan economy but also on the counterinsurgency, stabilization, anticorruption, and rule of law efforts being pursued in Afghanistan by the United States and its allies."[52]

Third, U.S. intelligence was a problem in the beginning and throughout the war. Human intelligence in particular was difficult to gather. While national and local intelligence learned more about the enemy's forces, the military leadership had inadequate information about the population that U.S. forces were protecting, a central focus of the campaign. The necessary rotation of units compounded this situation. In 2010, Major General Michael T. Flynn, USA, the senior intelligence official in theater, wrote:

> *Eight years into the war in Afghanistan, the U.S. intelligence community is only marginally relevant to the overall strategy. Having focused the overwhelming majority of its collection efforts and analytical brainpower on insurgent groups, the vast intelligence apparatus is unable to answer fundamental questions about the environment in which U.S. and allied forces operate and the people they seek to persuade. Ignorant of local economics and landowners, hazy about who the powerbrokers are and how they might be influenced, incurious about the correlations between various development projects and the level of cooperation among villagers, and disengaged from people in the best position to find answers—whether aid workers or Afghan soldiers—U.S. intelligence officers and analysts can do little but shrug in response to high level decision-makers seeking the knowledge, analysis, and information they need to wage a successful counterinsurgency.*[53]

Combat units were slow to develop cultural awareness, and Human Terrain Teams and other specialists who tried to make up for this defect were often unable to bridge the information gap in their areas of concern. Units frequently knew the enemy situation, but not the people whom they were supposed to protect.[54] Compounding these factors, the senior-most U.S. commanders in Afghanistan had an average tenure of less than 13 months, nearly matching that of their combat soldiers.[55] In Afghanistan, neither generals nor sergeants had much time for on-the-job learning and even less for reflection.

The lack of information on local people and conditions hampered counterinsurgency efforts, which were further complicated by troop rotations. Years later, Lieutenant General H.R. McMaster, USA, a veteran of the fighting in Operation *Desert Storm* as well as in Iraq and Afghanistan, summed up the effects of not knowing the human terrain:

> *In Afghanistan, coalition forces struggled to understand local drivers of conflict and instability. Coalition forces sometimes unintentionally empowered predatory and criminal actors, fostered exclusionary*

political and economic orders, and alienated thereby key elements of the population. The Taliban, regenerating in safe houses in Pakistan, portrayed themselves as patrons and protectors of aggrieved parties in Afghanistan.[56]

Fourth, coalition arms, aid, trainers, and advisors ended up being insufficient in number, speed, and efficiency. The U.S. light footprint strategy, reinforced by a few years of low-level fighting, proved in retrospect to be inadequate to the task and the capacity of the threat. U.S. and allied combat troops fared well militarily, but the coalition was unsuccessful in building the capacity of the Afghan security forces, especially the police. Responsibility for police training bounced from Germany to the State Department to the Department of Defense (DOD) to a combined NATO-U.S. lead under Lieutenant General William Caldwell, USA, who finally stabilized police training.

The Afghan police remained an especially weak link in the security chain, and the Taliban made attacking them a priority. From 2007 to 2009, Afghan security forces killed in action (3,046) outnumbered U.S. and allied dead in those 3 years (nearly 800) by more than three to one. More than two out of every three Afghan servicemembers killed were policemen.

The coalition operations in Afghanistan also became an exemplar of "contractorization," with more Western-sponsored contractors, many of them armed, than soldiers in country. This in part reflected the limitations of a relatively small volunteer force and the ravages of protracted conflict. In the end, reliance on contractors proved both boon and burden. Contractors extended the force's capabilities but at great cost to the nation. The legal regime that controlled contractors was also problematic.

In all, from 2004 to 2008, there were insufficient coalition forces or Afghan national security forces to conduct what became known as a strategy to clear, hold, build, and then transfer responsibility to Afghan forces. The Taliban had a wide pool of unemployed tribesmen and former militia fighters to recruit from, as well as greater latitude in picking targets. Over time, the coalition also became increasingly unsuccessful in gaining Pakistani cooperation to control the Taliban and the permeable Pakistan-Afghanistan border. By 2009, the insurgency spread from its home base in the Pashtun areas in the south and east to the entire nation. Ironically, the war spread geographically in part because of the greater presence and more vigorous activities of coalition forces in the south and east after 2009.

Taliban penetration of many areas deepened over time. In areas with scant Pashtun population, the Taliban also used motorcycle squads and IEDs to make headway in controlling the population. In areas under their control, Taliban judges administered sharia-based (and ethnically and tribally compatible) judgments, trumping Karzai's broken and corrupt civil courts. The Afghan people had little love for the Taliban, but insecurity and government ineptitude made the general population hesitant to act against them.

It is not literally true that initial U.S. operations in Iraq in 2003 stripped Afghanistan of what it needed to fight the Taliban. Indeed, 2004 was the last "good" year for Afghan security. While some intelligence, surveillance, and reconnaissance assets and Special Forces units were removed from Afghanistan, most of the assets needed to continue what appeared to be a low-risk operation there in the short term were wisely "fenced" by Pentagon and US-CENTCOM planners before the invasion of Iraq.[57]

It is fair to say, however, as the situation in Afghanistan began to decline after 2005, the greater scope and intensity of problems in Iraq worked against sending reinforcements or adequate funds to Afghanistan. National decision-makers knew that there were problems in Afghanistan, but the problems in Iraq were so much greater and of a higher priority that they deferred the problems in Afghanistan until after the success in 2008 of the Surge in Iraq. Another policy fault plagued U.S. war efforts: while U.S. fortunes declined in two wars, DOD leadership refused until 2006 to expand the end strength of the Armed Forces. For a short time, hoping against experience, the Pentagon even slightly reduced U.S. troops in Afghanistan when NATO took over command and control of the mission there in 2006.

Funding for the war did grow, usually matching modest increases in troop strength. In the first 3 years of the U.S. commitment (2001–2003), expenditures averaged $12 billion per year; in the next 3 years, $18 billion per year; and for 2007–2009, $48 billion per year.[58] Even as the funding picture for development assistance improved, it was not always done effectively and efficiently. At times, the military, with its CERP funds and stability operations mindset, was out of sync with the longer term view of USAID officials in Kabul or in the PRTs. Years later, both civil and military elements were criticized by the Office of the Special Inspector General for Afghanistan, who criticized USAID in Afghanistan in particular for creating projects that were not Afghan-supportable.[59] In the end, the logic of stability operations and peacetime development assistance often will remain at odds. Both war and simultaneous reconstruction are inherently wasteful. *Armed nation-building*—a term popularized by the Center for Strategic and International Studies' Anthony Cordesman—is for neither the faint of heart nor the impatient.

Also complicating the war was the fact that the regional powers—Saudi Arabia, Pakistan, Iran, India, Russia, and China—did little to help the situation. Each had its own interests and timetables. Iran and Pakistan were actually part of the problem, and the other four were unable to further a solution.

Pakistan was wary of American staying power and hedged its bets, allowing the Afghan Taliban to operate from its territory with minimal interference. Its objectives were to restore some sort of strategic depth in Afghanistan and block the spread of Indian influence, which grew daily with billions of dollars in Indian aid and commercial contracts. India worked hard to earn contracts in Afghanistan and forged a logistical alliance with Iran to work around Pakistan's geographic advantages. In a vicious circle, Indian success fueled Pakistani insecurity and tended to increase its attachment to the Afghan Taliban. In turn, the more Pakistan did for the Afghan Taliban, the more Pakistan alienated the people and the government of Afghanistan. Ironically, the more Pakistan supported the Afghan Taliban, the easier it was for India to expand its influence in Afghanistan. Pakistan, in its defense, would remind its interlocutors (and correctly so) that Pakistan has lost more soldiers and civilians in the war on terror than any other nation on Earth.[60]

Iran was no friend of the Taliban, and it worked (often with bags of cash) with authorities in Kabul and Herat in the western part of Afghanistan both to spread its influence and to improve trade and border control. Iran cooperated well during the Bonn Process but was alienated early in 2002 when President Bush declared the country to be a part of the "axis of evil." Tehran has also erratically aided the Taliban to ensure serious American problems, if not outright defeat.

China, for its part, seemed interested only in exploiting Afghanistan's strategic minerals and played a minimal role before 2010. Now that China has major financial interests, Afghan officials hope that it will work harder for peace and stability, exerting a more positive influence on Pakistan, its close ally. China is poised today to help Afghanistan develop its mineral deposits but to date has little taste for security cooperation there.

Saudi Arabia tried hard to use its good offices to end the war but was frustrated by the Afghan Taliban's refusal to break relations with al Qaeda, a sworn enemy of the Kingdom of Saudi Arabia. Russia and China exploited commercial contracts, and Russia began slowly to improve counternarcotics cooperation with the coalition. In later years, Russia participated with other nations in the region in forming a northern logistics route.

In all, by 2009 the regional powers were not the primary cause of the war in Afghanistan, but their policies had not worked toward a solution. Pakistan is particularly noteworthy here. While the U.S. policy has been one of patient engagement to wean Islamabad from its dysfunctional ways, analysts from other countries could be openly bitter. One Canadian military historian who served in Afghanistan wrote that Pakistan was behind the external support to the insurgents in southern Afghanistan and that it was "a country with a 50-year history of exporting low-intensity warfare as a strategy."[61]

American officials tended to be more circumspect in public, but even Chairman of the Joint Chiefs of Staff Admiral Michael Mullen, who devoted tremendous effort to working with the Pakistani military leaders, unleashed a broadside right before he retired in 2011, "The Haqqani Network—which has long enjoyed the support and protection of the Pakistani government and is, in many ways, a strategic arm of Pakistan's Inter-Services Intelligence Agency—is responsible for the September 13th [2011] attacks against the U.S. Embassy in Kabul." He went on to detail Haqqani attacks on Afghan and American targets and concluded that it is difficult to defeat an insurgency with a secure sanctuary in a neighboring country.[62]

By the end of the Bush administration, security in Afghanistan was down, as was Afghan optimism about the future. From 2005, Karzai's popularity had declined at home by a third. His standing in the West also fell after widespread fraud occurred in the 2010 presidential elections. His habit of criticizing the coalition and the United States was galling. Bad feelings were multiplied by his reluctance to criticize the Taliban and his habit of referring to them as "our brothers." In 2008, polls showed Afghan confidence in the United States and its allies had been halved. Many Afghans believed that the Taliban had grown stronger every year since 2005, and incentives for fence-sitting increased, along with fear and disgust at government corruption.[63]

In the Bush years, the lack of progress came at a price: 630 U.S. Service-members died, and the United States spent $29 billion in Afghanistan on security assistance, counternarcotics, economic development, and humanitarian assistance. With the Iraq effort finally back on a more solid footing, President Bush's deputy national security advisor, Lieutenant General Douglas Lute, USA, conducted an assessment of the campaign in Afghanistan. He concluded that more troops and resources were needed, but in the final days of the administration, the President decided quietly to pass the Lute assessment on to the Obama administration. He decided that "the new strategy would have a better chance of success if we gave the new team an opportunity to revise it as they saw fit and then adopt it as their own."[64]

In early 2009, Ambassador Eikenberry returned to Kabul and noticed the changes in Afghanistan since his departure as the military commander there in 2007. He opined that the security situation deteriorated, especially in the south; training of the army and police lagged; the challenge of the Pakistani sanctuary had increased; and the level of mistrust between President Karzai and the United States was peaking, as was Afghan government corruption, complicated by a glut of foreign aid and assistance. Ambassador Eikenberry found the Taliban "enjoying increasing amounts of political support inside of Afghanistan."[65]

We now turn to the conflict in Iraq, beginning with a short comparison of the two campaigns.

Comparing the Two Campaigns

The conflicts in Afghanistan and Iraq had significant commonalities and differences.[66] Both began as conventional conflicts with the aim of regime change. Both turned into protracted insurgencies compounded by nation-building activities. In Afghanistan, U.S. Army Special Forces on horseback calling in close air support might seem highly unconventional, but when considering the whole picture—Afghan infantry and cavalry facing entrenched Taliban fighters along well-established frontlines, air support, coalition activity, and so forth—the initial campaign that culminated by December 2001 with the capture of Mazar-e-Sharif, Kabul, Kandahar, Herat, and Jalalabad was, on balance, a conventional force-on-force fight.[67] The Iraq invasion was clearly a modern, conventional assault. Both conflict zones featured powerful regional actors on their borders who were often more a part of the problem than the solution. Sectarian violence was a real threat in both countries but especially so in Shia-majority Iraq, which had long been under the boot of the largely Sunni Ba'athists.

There were also many differences between the two conflicts. The retaliatory war in Afghanistan was a come-as-you-are, hot-blooded affair, while the deliberate, preventive war in Iraq was the result of a decade-long crisis and was actively planned for more than a year. Although smaller and slightly less populous than Afghanistan, Iraq's location, oil wealth, and potential for weapons of mass destruction (WMD) proliferation made it a vastly more important nation than Afghanistan in the U.S. strategic calculus. Afghanistan was impoverished and had been at war for over two decades before the U.S. invasion. Iraq had the potential to be rich but was stifled by the regime of Saddam Hussein. It was more a damaged state than it was an underdeveloped one. It still possessed great oil wealth, an educated population, and relatively modern infrastructure in its urban areas. Afghanistan had none of that, and still does not. The embryonic Afghan civil elite, middle class, and governmental bureaucracy had ceased to exist after a decade of war with the Soviet Union, followed by a civil war that continued up to the U.S. invasion. In 2009, USCENTCOM Commander General David Petraeus, USA, stated, "Given the fact that you have police who can't read the law that they are enforcing, local government officials who can't read the directives that have been sent to them . . . that does create a few handicaps and challenges that certainly weren't present to the same extent in Iraq, to put it mildly."[68]

Iraq's conflictual relationship with the United States began in the first Gulf War and continued, albeit at a lower level, right up to the U.S. invasion in 2003, a 13-year struggle. The United States was not distracted from Afghanistan and lured into Iraq. Indeed, the quick march to war in Afghanistan took a few weeks, but the movement to war for a second time with Iraq was more than a decade in the making.

One final difference is the character of the two wars. The retaliatory war against the Taliban and al Qaeda in Afghanistan was a classical just war. It attracted a large and willing coalition of U.S. allies and partners. It had more enduring popularity with the American people than the conflict in Iraq. The war in Iraq was a preventive war, unpopular abroad, and, in short order, unpopular at home as well. It temporarily hurt U.S. standing around the world, and it drove a wedge between the United States and two of its closest allies, France and Germany. The issue of legitimacy retarded the development of the coalition force in Iraq, but over time, it grew to be a large and effective field force, with nearly three dozen partners and two-fifths of the division headquarters commanded and dominated by allied nations. To understand the 2003 invasion of Iraq, it is necessary to begin with the first Gulf War.

Context of the War in Iraq

After favoring Saddam in his war with Iran, the United States was shocked when the unpredictable dictator invaded Kuwait, a state that he owed billions of dollars to for its support in the Iraqi struggle with Iran. In August 1990, the United States organized a vast international coalition and in the following year forced Saddam from Kuwait. Down but not out, Saddam managed to put down subsequent rebellions in the south (among the Shia) and the north (among the Kurds) of Iraq. Today, the coalition's failure to "finish the job" in Iraq in 1991 is often seen as a huge mistake. Critics have argued that Saddam was on the ropes and that he was ripe for not just a knockdown, but for a knockout blow. In 1991, however, President George H.W. Bush and his National Security Advisor, Brent Scowcroft, saw it differently. Years later, they wrote:

> *While we hoped that a popular revolt or coup would topple Saddam, neither the United States nor the countries of the region wished to see the breakup of the Iraqi state. We were concerned about the long-term balance of power at the head of the Gulf. Breaking up the Iraqi state would pose its own destabilizing problems. . . . Trying to eliminate Saddam, extending the ground war into an occupation of Iraq, would have violated our guideline about not changing objectives in midstream, engaging in "mission creep," and would have incurred incalculable human and political costs. . . . We would have been forced to occupy Baghdad, and, in effect, rule Iraq. The coalition would instantly have collapsed. . . . Had we gone the invasion route [in 1991], the United States could conceivably still [in 1998] be an occupying power in a bitterly hostile land.*[69]

From 1991 to 2003, Saddam continued to rule Iraq, brutally putting down sporadic revolts and turning the Iraqi state into a money-making enterprise for himself and his cronies. Public and private infrastructure decayed. The regular Iraqi army and air force remained formidable by regional standards but much less potent than in 1990. Following a doctrine of dual containment for Iran and Iraq, the United States and coalition partners kept Saddam's regime constrained by using their air forces to enforce UN-supported (but not explicitly authorized) no-fly zones in the northern and southern thirds of the country. This required complex and continuous air operations run out of the Gulf states—especially Saudi Arabia—and Turkey. On a daily basis, enforcing the two no-fly zones required up to 200 aircraft and 7,500 airmen. In all, 300,000 sorties were flown. In 2002 alone, Iraq attacked coalition aircraft on 500 occasions, 90 of which resulted in coalition airstrikes, some of which were calculated to be helpful in a potential future conflict.[70] For the U.S. Air Force, there was precious little rest in the decade between the first and second gulf wars.

Saddam's regime was also subject to strict economic sanctions, and the UN later came to provide food and medicine for the Iraqi people in return for regulated oil exports in the oil-for-food program. Over the years, Saddam found a way to profit from the sanctions, stockpiling cash and building palaces as the Iraqi economy withered. After the 2003 invasion of Iraq, UN investigators exposed many people (including some foreign government and UN officials) who had taken bribes of one sort or another for cooperating with Saddam. As the 20th century came to an end, however, Saddam had convinced many in the West that the UN-approved sanctions were hurting the people and especially the children of Iraq.[71] The sanctions regime was on thin ice. Indeed, the steady unraveling (and outflanking) of international sanctions became a subsidiary factor in the litany of reasons to go to war with Saddam.

After Operation *Desert Storm* in 1991, UN inspectors hunting WMD played a long cat-and-mouse game with Saddam's military and intelligence bureaucracies. In 1998, Saddam unilaterally ended the inspections, raising suspicion in the West and at the UN that he was accelerating his WMD programs. President Clinton later conducted punitive strikes on Iraq with the tacit support of many nations in the UN Security Council. Prodded by Congress, he later declared regime change in Iraq to be U.S. policy.

The George W. Bush administration was composed of many veterans of the first Gulf War—including Vice President Richard Cheney and his chief of staff, Lewis "Scooter" Libby; National Security Advisor Condoleezza Rice and her deputy Stephen Hadley; Deputy Secretary of Defense Paul Wolfowitz; and NSC staff member Zalmay Khalilzad—all of whom saw Saddam as an ugly piece of unfinished business from their collective past.[72] In retrospect, the shock of 9/11 and anxiety about future strikes encouraged the U.S. Government to take counsel of its fears about Iraq, which had roots in terrorism, Saddam's reputation as a regional aggressor who had used chemical weapons, and, most importantly, his apparent WMD possession and research programs.

Despite the suspicions of some in the Pentagon, Saddam never had an operational relationship with al Qaeda. Iraq had neither supervised al Qaeda assets nor conducted joint terrorist operations. At the same time, his active relationship with terrorists of all stripes was a concern and was never in doubt.[73] He was among the most active supporters of Palestinian terrorism. The Mujahideen-e-Khalq, a leftist, anti-Iranian terrorist/military force, was resident in Iraq, conducted operations against Iran, and cooperated with Saddam's paramilitary and armed forces. Also, Abu Musab al-Zarqawi, who became al Qaeda's leader in Iraq, was resident for a time in a remote Kurdish-controlled section of northern Iraq with his small terrorist group before the U.S. invasion. He had visited Baghdad and received medical treatment there.[74]

Zarqawi did not have an operational relationship with Saddam's intelligence force, but they clearly had communications and a symbiotic coexistence. Initially, Zarqawi was independent and not yet a subordinate of Osama bin Laden. However, the similarities between Zarqawi's and bin Laden's organizations attracted the attention of U.S. friends in Kurdistan, who made U.S. planners aware of it. In the run-up to the war, the radical Zarqawi was cooperating with both the Ba'athist regime and al Qaeda. After establishing his reputation as the most energetic Salafist terrorist leader in Iraq, he later merged his group with al Qaeda and became its emir in Iraq.[75] (After the invasion, the CIA examined the files of Saddam's intelligence apparatus. Michael Morrell, former Deputy Director of the Agency, noted that "the United States never found anything in the files of the Iraqi intelligence service, or any other Iraqi ministry, indicating that there was ever any kind of relationship between the Iraqis and al Qa'ida."[76])

Despite the obvious decay in his regime, "what to do about Saddam" was an important issue for the new Bush administration. In all, it was not just WMD either. The Iraq threat also included Saddam's past regional violence, his multi-faceted relationships with terrorists, and his outlandish tyranny. The complete Iraq threat was, in the words of Under Secretary of Defense Douglas J. Feith, "WMD and the 3 Ts," which stood for terrorism, threats to neighbors, and tyranny. Saddam was a threat not only inside Iraq but also abroad due to the absence of all restraints on his aggressive tendencies.[77]

After the 9/11 attacks, Saddam's regime took on a more ominous appearance. Early on, some Bush administration officials believed it was likely that Saddam was involved with 9/11, and they saw new reason to be concerned about him and his WMD programs. When terrorists can strike the U.S. homeland and cause mass casualties, terrorism ceases to be only a law enforcement issue. In the introduction to the 2002 National Security Strategy, Bush stated, "The gravest danger our Nation faces lies at the crossroads of radicalism and technology. Our enemies have openly declared that they are seeking weapons of mass destruction, and evidence indicates that they are doing so with determination. The United States will not allow these efforts to succeed."[78]

Because of the new threat from al Qaeda and the dangers of WMD proliferation, the President embraced the so-called doctrine of preemption—which experts saw as a doctrine of preventive war—and declared Iraq (along with North Korea and Iran) a member of the "axis of evil."

Preparation for War

Planning for a potential war against Iraq was largely sidelined during the first 2 months of fighting in Afghanistan. In November 2001, however, on the edge of achieving initial military success in Afghanistan, President Bush again asked Secretary Rumsfeld to begin planning in secret for potential military operations against Iraq. That mission was passed quickly to USCENTCOM, now headed by General Franks.[79] Chairman of the Joint Chiefs of Staff General Richard B. Myers and Vice Chairman General Peter Pace played a supporting role, with the activist Secretary of Defense exercising his legal authority to be the direct supervisor of the combatant commanders. While most Defense secretaries in recent memory chose to work war-planning issues with the combatant commanders through the Chairman, Secretary Rumsfeld played a hands-on role in the development of the details of the battle plan and the flow of the invasion force.

Over the next 14 months, Franks and Rumsfeld remained in frequent contact. Not only were there dozens of briefings and face-to-face conversations, usually with the Chairman or Vice Chairman in attendance, there also was a steady stream of memos (known as "snowflakes") from the energetic Secretary who posed probing questions for the Pentagon and USCENTCOM staffs. Rumsfeld wanted to conduct a quick, lightning-like operation in Iraq, followed by a swift handover of power to the Iraqis, as was done in Afghanistan in 2001. He did not want a large-scale, ponderous operation such as *Desert Storm*, which he saw as wasteful and outmoded. In his memoir and frequently in conversations, the Secretary criticized the wastefulness of *Desert Storm* by pointing out that "more than 80 percent [of the ammunition shipped to theater] was returned to the United States untouched."[80]

Secretary Rumsfeld also did not want U.S. troops unnecessarily bogged down in a long, costly, manpower-intensive peace operation. He was vitally interested in force modernization and "transformation," which further predisposed him against prolonged military operations.[81] In some ways, the war in Afghanistan—with a small U.S. force on the ground ably assisted by CIA paramilitary forces, mated to superb communications, high-tech air assets, precision-guided munitions, and timely intelligence—was a conceptual model for what Rumsfeld wanted to see in the new Iraq war plan. In February 2003, a few weeks before the invasion, he stated in New York:

> *If the United States were to lead an international coalition in Iraq . . . it would be guided by two commitments. Stay as long as necessary, and to leave as soon as possible. . . . We would work with our partners as we are doing in Afghanistan to help the Iraqi people establish a new government that would govern a single country, that would not have weapons of mass destruction, that would not be a threat to its neighbors. . . . The goal would not be to impose an American style template on Iraq, but rather to create conditions where Iraqis can form a government in their own unique way just as the Afghans did with the Loya Jirga. . . . This is not to underestimate the challenge that the coalition would face. . . . General Franks in an interagency process has been working hard on this for many months.[82]*

Throughout their dialogue and into the deployment of the force, Rumsfeld urged a small force and a lightning-fast operation. Later, he shut down the military's automated deployment system, questioning, delaying, or deleting units on some of the numerous deployment orders that came across his desk.[83]

Franks may have briefed the President on his war plan as many as 10 times. He started using a modified version of the old 1003V war plan but then developed three new varieties: a generated start plan, a running start plan, and a hybrid plan. In the end, the last version, Cobra II, was strongly influenced by edits from the field.[84] It called for an initial combat force of about 140,000 troops—one-third the size of the force in the plan that was on the shelf when the administration came to power. In the end, General Franks insisted that the plan was a USCENTCOM plan and not the concoction of anyone in Washington:

> *The sessions in the White House, the sessions with Rumsfeld were initiated by me and my staff and then critiqued and questioned by the White House or by the Office of the Secretary of Defense (OSD). But there was not a leadership role wherein we would walk in and the President or Rumsfeld would say, "Now here is how I would like to do this and here is what I'm thinking." That never happened. That never occurred. . . . They were there to listen, and we would spend hour upon hour with me doing what I am doing right now, talking. . . . So it was asking questions, receiving answers, and . . . these sessions . . . went on repetitively over the course of 14 months.[85]*

The main strike elements of the plan were a few thousand special operators and three ground divisions (one U.S. Army mechanized division, one Marine division, and one British armored division), along with elements of three other Army divisions and an Army parachute infantry brigade that was later inserted into the fray. Given the effects of previous air operations and the need to be unpredictable, the notion of a long, preliminary air operation was discarded, aiding the element of surprise on the ground. A high level of allied hesitancy no doubt encouraged an already reluctant Turkish government—faced with strong public opinion against the war—to disallow the use of its territory to launch a northern front in Iraq with the U.S. 4th Infantry Division, which the Iraqis saw as a potent threat. Consequently, much of the division's assets loitered at sea, which had the salutary effect of forcing the Iraqis to hold a significant portion of their army in the north.

Unlike in Afghanistan, the CIA lacked an extensive set of relationships with movements in Iraq.[86] Much critical intelligence about Iraq was not verifiable against sources on the ground. The United States had excellent technical intelligence but apparently lacked a network of agents in the country. There were grave limits on the U.S. ability to confirm judgments that it believed were true. Faulty intelligence estimates on the status of WMD were compounded by numerous mis-estimates that complicated the postconflict phases of the operation.

For their part, the Joint Chiefs of Staff—statutory military advisors to the Secretary of Defense, President, and National Security Council—also met with the President twice on the war plan, the second time in January 2003. Army Chief of Staff General Eric Shinseki commented in the second meeting that the on-scene force was small and that "it would be important to keep reinforcements flowing," but all of the chiefs supported the basic plan.[87] None of them brought up specific misgivings about Phase IV, postcombat stability operations, but that issue would be raised by Senator Carl Levin (D-MI) a month later in a Senate Armed Services Committee hearing.

The administration's key congressional effort, however, had already taken place. In October 2002, President Bush sought congressional approval for a prospective military operation against Iraq. Propelled by a post-9/11 threat perception, the resolution passed both houses handily. More than half of the Senate Democrats and 81 House Democrats voted along with Republicans to authorize military force.[88] The Congressmen and Senators no doubt remembered the political penalty assigned to those legislators, mostly Democrats, who had voted against the first Gulf War, Operation *Desert Storm*, which passed the Senate by only five votes.[89]

International Support and WMD

On the international front, Secretary of State Colin Powell, with the strong backing of the United Kingdom and other U.S. allies, convinced the President in August 2002 to exhaust diplomatic efforts before going to war. Late in 2002, with strong U.S. support, weapons inspections restarted, and Saddam's regime again interfered with them. After 400 inspections, however, the UN personnel came to no firm conclusions. Their cautious on-scene report was drowned out by many other briefings about Iraqi WMD, including one by Secretary Powell. In all, the existence of a large stockpile of chemical weapons and missiles and, perhaps more importantly, active missile, biological, and nuclear research programs became the overriding reason for invading Iraq and the reason that brought together many different U.S factions and international partners in their desire to forcibly oust Saddam and his regime.

On the eve of the 2003 war, despite the many disputes on such details as the purpose of aluminum tubes in grainy imagery and reports of the potential transfer of uranium oxide ("yellowcake"), most international intelligence agencies believed, as did former President Clinton, that Saddam still possessed a major chemical weapons stockpile, a significant missile force, and active research and development programs for biological and nuclear weapons. There is nothing in credible sources to support the notion that the WMD threat was concocted by U.S. Government officials and then sold to a gullible public, nor is it clear that a small number of Iraqi sources tricked the U.S. Government into its beliefs.[90] No special offices within the Office of the Secretary of Defense or secret advisors created the dominant perception of the danger of Iraqi WMD. There were many holes in the knowledge base, but senior officials and analysts were almost universally united in their core beliefs. As the lead key judgment in the Intelligence Community's October 2002 National Intelligence Estimate on WMD in Iraq stated, "We judge that Iraq has continued its weapons of mass destruction (WMD) programs in defiance of UN resolutions and restrictions. Baghdad has chemical and biological weapons as well as missiles with ranges in excess of UN restrictions; if left unchecked, it probably will have a nuclear weapon during this decade."[91]

This perception was aided and abetted by Saddam himself, who wanted the great powers and his hostile neighbor, Iran, to believe that he had WMD programs and stockpiles. His use of chemical weapons against Iran and the Kurds, who were Iraqi citizens, also gave weight to the danger of Iraqi WMD programs. Saddam's destruction of his stockpiles and the suspension of much of his research and development work fooled the West, as well as his own generals.[92] In his eyes, this deception was critical to Iraqi security. According to the U.S. Joint Forces Command–Institute for Defense Analyses (USJFCOM-IDA) project on Iraqi perspectives, "Saddam walked a tightrope with WMD because, as he often reminded his close advisors, they lived in a very dangerous global neighborhood where even the perception of weakness drew wolves. For him, there were real dividends to be gained by letting his enemies believe he possessed WMD, whether it was true or not."[93]

Saddam also had many reasons to convince the great powers that he had destroyed these weapons and that the UN should end the sanctions. Inside his regime, a tangled web of lies and secrecy confused even his own generals. According to the USJFCOM-IDA study, "The idea that in a compartmentalized and secretive regime other military units or organizations might have WMD was plausible to . . . [the Iraqi generals]."[94] Saddam's record of deception was a key factor in why intelligence analysts continued to believe in Iraqi WMD. His own duplicity and the U.S. inability to penetrate it were factors in his undoing. Former National Security Advisor Stephen Hadley, years after the mistake, stated, "Thinking back, I now wonder if our mistakes may have been in not considering whether the reason that Saddam Hussein was so secretive about his weapons of mass destruction capabilities was not because he had the weapons and wanted to conceal them, but because he did not have them and wanted to hide that."[95]

While Secretary Powell was successful in restarting weapons inspections in Iraq, he was never able to build a consensus for decisive action in the UN Security Council. In mid-January 2003, with CIA Director Tenet at his side, Powell gave a highly publicized briefing on Iraqi WMD programs to the Security Council. He was later embarrassed to discover that some details that he highlighted were incorrect.

When in the following month UN inspections came to naught, the die was cast for war without the blessing of many key U.S. allies or the UN Security Council. Iraq was declared to be in material breach of UN Security Council Resolution (UNSCR) 1441, which demanded that Iraq give a detailed accounting of its WMD programs. With urging from its closest ally, Great Britain, the United States decided to try for yet another resolution, one that might explicitly authorize the use of force. The attempt broke down for lack of allied, Russian, and Chinese support. The failure of this risky diplomatic move cast doubt on the legitimacy of the preventive war that the United States and Great Britain were planning. Adding to the sting of rejection was the fact that France and Germany led the way in trying to block the resolution. Later, U.S. failure to find either WMD stockpiles or active research and development programs compounded the damage to U.S. credibility, further retarding efforts to gain international support.

Of the nations in the Middle East, only Israel, Kuwait, and Qatar were openly behind the coalition effort; many other regional states, such as Saudi Arabia and Bahrain, privately supported it. Of major U.S. allies, only the United Kingdom was ready to provide a significant military formation for combat operations.[96]

Military and Interagency Postwar Plans

In many of his war-plan briefings to the President, General Franks mentioned Phase IV, the transition period after the end of major combat operations. Indeed, he did not underestimate the work that might have to be done. On two occasions, Franks's memoir indicates that he told first the Secretary of Defense and then the President and National Security Council that Phase IV might require up to 250,000 troops, over 100,000 more combatants than were in the initial invasion force. He also noted that this phase might last for years, although he did believe that it might be done more quickly with a smaller force under the right circumstances.[97] Despite these estimates, USCENTCOM was not adequately prepared for the post–major combat difficulties that it faced in Iraq.

It was ironic that DOD civilian leadership severely criticized General Shinseki when he mentioned a similar level of effort ("several hundred thousand") in response to questions about postcombat troop requirements in a February 2003 Senate hearing. These estimates were consistent with the outside estimates of USCENTCOM's land component headquarters and its Phase IV planners. While it has never been confirmed, Secretary Rumsfeld and Deputy Secretary Wolfowitz may have been worried about not alarming Congress on the eve of the war. It is clear that they expected a relatively quick, easy, and inexpensive occupation. They were also conscious of inflated cost and casualty estimates in previous conflicts such as Operation *Desert Storm*.

Franks's many briefings to the President did not cover critical postwar issues that were not ordinarily in the military's sphere of competence: governance, constitutions, sectarian relations, and so forth. He emphasized tasks that the military had to do in the short run: security and humanitarian assistance.

Some analysts have criticized Franks for not being interested in postwar Iraq, an area where many in uniform believed that civilians should dominate decisionmaking. Most war planning was handled by Franks and his staff, but most military postwar planning efforts were left to USCENTCOM's land component. Franks announced his retirement soon after the fighting, and this act negatively affected perceptions concerning his enthusiasm for post–major conflict stability operations.[98] Years later, Franks explained his focus on the combat phase of the operation:

> *The key that unlocked the door in Iraq was the removal of the regime and so the force level initially was planned to remove the regime. So we said, depending on whether we see the left end of the continuum, peace breaking out, or the right end, tending toward chaos, we will continue to modify both the structure and the number of troops involved in Iraq until we "win," that is, that the Iraqis are able to take charge of their own destiny. That was the plan from the beginning to the end and that is the way that we looked at Phase IV in every iteration. . . . You don't know what you are actually going to find.*[99]

While USCENTCOM and its land component had Phase IV plans, some of the divisions making up the force—including the 3rd Infantry Division, the main attack division—did not have them. Division planners wrote in their after action review that the division had not been fully and completely briefed on the highly detailed postwar plan of its higher headquarters, the land component command.[100] The Marine headquarters, I Marine Expeditionary Force, and its divisional element under Major General James Mattis did formulate plans and standard operating procedures. After the seizure of Baghdad, however, they were redeployed to the south, a less contested area in the immediate postcombat phase.[101]

The Coalition Forces Land Component Command (CFLCC) plan did not generate supporting division plans, and this represented a shortcoming. In all, while the military did begin to plan for this issue before civilians did, the USCENTCOM and CFLCC Phase IV planning efforts were not an effective guide for immediate post–conventional combat military policy, were not shared fully with implementing units, and did not make adequate allowances for supporting civilian entities in the reconstruction and stabilization business. In CFLCC's defense, however, it is important to note that it was never able to supervise Phase IV operations. It was sent home early, an unusual decision (discussed below).[102]

While war planning was in high gear from November 2001 until March 2003, civilian planners in the interagency community were not included in the close-hold war-plan briefings. Civilian planners, for the most part, did not begin to make meaningful independent contributions until the summer of 2002. By then General Franks had briefed the President six times on the battle plan. Thus, instead of a military plan being built to line up with a national plan, the interagency work on Iraq generally followed in the wake of the war plan. Postwar issues were broken up and handled by different groups that sometimes worked in isolation from one another for security reasons or for bureaucratic advantage.

The NSC-led Executive Steering Group did valuable work to attempt to break down agency barriers and pull together the strands of a postwar plan, concentrating on humanitarian and economic issues. They began their work in the summer of 2002, following up on a Pentagon-run interagency effort. The planning efforts of the Pentagon were so powerful and the nature of war so uncertain that the President—with the concurrence of Secretary Powell, first in October and then in December 2002—put the Pentagon in charge of initial postwar operations, a fairly typical pattern in U.S. military history.

Although the outline of the postwar plan was approved in October 2002, the President did not formally approve the organization that would carry out initial stabilization and reconstruction activities, the Office of Reconstruction and Humanitarian Assistance (ORHA), until December 2002. It was not brought into existence until January 2003. This office was subordinated to the Secretary of Defense, who put it under USCENTCOM.

Policy queuing was a natural and unavoidable problem. Not all planning efforts can be seamlessly started or terminated with optimal timing. One reason for the slow start in postwar planning had to do with diplomacy. The tentative scheme to manage postwar Iraq was approved in October 2002, but little could be done as diplomats attempted in vain to solve the problem without recourse to arms. One can plan war in secret, but to do postwar planning and programming, diplomacy must be winding down and war must be nearly inevitable. In a recent interview, Stephen Hadley, who served President Bush first as deputy and then, in the second term, as National Security Advisor, lamented the fact that diplomatic efforts retarded postwar planning:

> *The dilemma was the following: the President wanted coercive diplomacy; he wanted to prepare a war plan, and to be seen preparing forces in order to give strength to the diplomacy. But he was hopeful that Iraq could be resolved diplomatically, and that Saddam could be convinced either to change his policies or to leave. There were a lot of people who, of course, didn't believe that. They thought that Bush came in with the settled intention to go to war, and that diplomacy was just a cover. . . . But the dilemma was, if we started, and it became known publicly that we were planning for a post-conflict, post-Saddam Iraq, everybody would say: "See, we told you, the diplomatic effort is not real, they're already preparing for war." And we would undermine our own diplomacy. So we had a dilemma, you had to delay the post-war planning as much as you could because you didn't want to jeopardize the diplomacy, but you still want enough time to develop the postwar plan.*[103]

According to Hadley, another problem with postwar planning was implementation. Summarizing a study that he had commissioned, he reflected on a basic problem with civil planning:

> *But what you didn't understand was that while military plans were being developed by CENTCOM, there was a system for translating those military plans into operational orders all the way down to the squadron level. There wasn't an established way of taking that postwar planning and putting it into the process, and implementing orders all the way down to the squadron level. So, you did all the planning, but it had no legs.*[104]

According to National Security Advisor Condoleezza Rice, the President's designation of the Pentagon as the lead on postwar issues appeared to streamline the chain of command, but it also dampened interagency cooperation.[105] It also caused intense friction between State and Defense over who would be assigned to ORHA. The disruptive tension between clear lines of command and interagency cooperation continued when ORHA was replaced by the Coalition Provisional Authority (CPA) led by Ambassador L. Paul Bremer. The head of the CPA emphasized his status as the Presidential envoy and did not report consistently to or through either the Secretary of Defense or National Security Advisor.[106]

The President received several major civilian briefings that were relevant to postwar issues, all of which were arranged by the NSC-driven Executive Steering Group. In January, based on interagency deliberations, Elliot Abrams of the NSC and Robin Cleveland of the Office of Management and Budget briefed the President on potential humanitarian issues during and right after the war. The work of this interagency group focused mainly on humanitarian assistance and the handling of refugees and internally displaced persons. The group's initial estimate of reconstruction costs was only a few billion dollars.[107] In early February, the NSC staff briefed the President on postwar relationships in Iraq, and on February 24, 2003, the President was briefed on the status of the Iraqi oil industry and the oil-for-food program.[108]

On February 28, 2003, Lieutenant General Jay Garner, USA (Ret.), briefed the President and his advisors on the initial estimates of his interagency ORHA team, which reported to Franks and the Secretary of Defense and was to be the lead office in postwar operations.[109] Because Garner had only been hired in January, his briefing was not detailed. Indeed, Garner's team was only partially formed when it deployed. In all, his staff officers did not have time to develop relationships with their peers in OSD Policy or on the Joint Staff.

Immediately before the war began, the NSC staff briefed the President in two sittings on the postwar reconstruction, governance, and security plans that had been cleared by the deputies and principals. The essence of the plan briefed to President Bush was essentially to turn over power quickly to an Iraqi entity, administer the country through the Iraqi ministries, use the existing police and military to help run the country, and pay for most reconstruction by using Iraqi funds, mainly from the sale of oil. This briefing was entirely in keeping with Garner's plans, as well as the DOD approach. In a few weeks, however, it would be completely overcome by events and scrapped without further interagency discussions.

One final briefing deserves highlighting. On March 4, 2003, the President and NSC reviewed for a final time the U.S. and coalition objectives in Iraq. This was one of the last major briefs before the war began, and in retrospect, it was an important symbol of how high U.S. hopes were for postwar Iraq.[110] The formal goals for the Iraq policy had been laid out in October 2002 and were frequently mentioned in planning guidance to USCENTCOM. The desired endstate was an Iraq that:

- does not threaten its neighbors
- renounces support for, and sponsorship of, international terrorism
- continues to be a single, unitary state
- is free of WMD, their means of delivery, and associated programs
- no longer oppresses or tyrannizes its people
- respects the basic rights of all Iraqis, including women and minorities
- adheres to the rule of law and respects fundamental human rights, including freedom of speech and worship
- encourages the building of democratic institutions.[111]

The major combat operations, which began on March 23, 2003, went well. The Iraqis never significantly challenged the invading force's vulnerable supply lines. The overwhelming power of U.S. and British forces quickly accomplished tactical objectives, and the major conventional fight was over by mid-April, months ahead of schedule. The only real surprise during the fighting—and a bad omen for the future—was the sporadic but vigorous resistance put up by paramilitary irregulars, such as the Fedayeen Saddam. The much-anticipated bloody battle for Baghdad and the use of WMD did not happen, and the predicted flood of refugees never took place due to the speed of the operation and the attacking forces' avoidance of many cities and towns.

On May 1, 2003, after landing on the aircraft carrier USS *Abraham Lincoln*, President Bush stood in front of a banner that proclaimed "Mission Accomplished" and stated, "Major combat operations in Iraq have ended. In the battle of Iraq, the United States and our allies have prevailed."[112] He then told the allies and the UN that their help was now needed and could be provided in safety. Although Franks had talked of the possible need for a long occupation, and many others warned of the complexity of postcombat events, some officials in OSD at the urging of the Secretary of Defense were soon speaking of a rapid turnover and withdrawal, with the invasion force possibly being reduced to 25,000 to 30,000 by August 2003.[113]

In May, war A was ending, but war B was about to begin. The United States had a complex, flexible plan for war A but no such plan for war B. War A was a rapid, high-tech, conventional battle—war, American style. War B would become a protracted conflict, an insurgency with high levels of criminality and sustained sectarian violence; it was just the sort of ambiguous, irregular conflict that the American public finds hard to understand and even harder to endure. The military was not initially prepared for insurgency and took more than a year to adjust well in the field. In 2006, the drastic increase in sectarian violence—in some eyes, a Sunni-Shia civil war—compounded the insurgency and cast a pall over coalition military efforts until the Surge began early in 2007. Political development and progress in reconstruction both continued to lag behind military efforts.

Pitfalls in Decisionmaking and Initial Execution

Underlying nearly all of these mistakes was a series of faulty assumptions.[114] These initial assumptions were a thread that ran through many missteps, and thus it is important to ask where assumptions come from. In every case, assumptions are affected by wishful thinking, stress, predispositions of the key actors, uncertainty, and the process used to arrive at decisions. In complex national security operations, intelligence estimates also play a vital role. In the case of Iraq, intelligence was faulty on WMD, the state of Iraqi infrastructure, and the usefulness of Iraqi police and military. Later, other shortfalls came in the provision of information about Iraqi tribal structures, as well as in the interests and intentions of neighboring states. Secretary Rumsfeld and Under Secretary Feith also complained that while intelligence did include the possibility of civil disturbances, it never predicted the possibility of an insurgency.[115] Incorrect, incomplete, or dated intelligence contributed in large measure to the assumptions that infected what became a "best case" war plan.

The core assumption held by many leaders in the national security establishment—and nearly all of the civilian leadership in the Pentagon—was that war in Iraq would be difficult, the peace relatively easy, and the occupation short and inexpensive.[116] This assumption—as implicit as it was powerful—was reflected in many leadership statements, actions, and planning priorities. Right up to the start of operations, the amount of time and effort spent on the major combat operation war plan was impressive; the amount of time and effort placed on postwar planning was relatively slight in comparison. Battle plans had branches and sequels, and combat troops were prepared for eventualities. The postwar plans had little such flexibility built into them.

The supporting assumptions were five in number. First, the war was expected to include tough fighting and end in a climactic battle. Most senior national security officials expected (and realistically so) that *Iraqi Freedom* would be a fight that could include the use of chemical or biological weapons. The battle for Baghdad in particular was seen as the logical bloody end to months of combat. Every DOD, State Department, and CIA expert expected battle-related refugees and internally displaced people or populations to be a major complicating factor in the war and its aftermath. These judgments were prudent, plausible, and consistent with previous conflicts. But none of them came to pass.

Second, leaders were repeatedly told by exiles that U.S. soldiers would be seen as liberators, welcomed with "sweets and flowers," as renowned scholar Kanan Makiya told President Bush.[117] General Abizaid called this the "Heroic Assumption." He criticized it because he believed that the liberation theme was connected in the minds of many decisionmakers with the liberation of Europe in World War II. Abizaid rightly believed that Iraq was not France.[118] In the minds of many, the fact of liberation would also facilitate early withdrawal. Our most senior leaders apparently believed this and frequently said so. General George W. Casey, Jr., USA, later stated, "CENTCOM bought into it. Franks bought into it. It was down to the tactical level. . . . Rumsfeld pushed that. . . . It was in everyone's mind that we were getting out of there."[119] No one was able to estimate the time that it would take for humiliation and impatience to turn appreciative welcomes into hatred for occupiers. It proved to be a painfully short interval.

While wiser heads had predicted a short honeymoon,[120] many officials such as Abizaid, Feith, Khalilzad, and Garner wanted a quick turnover of governmental authority to Iraqis. Indeed, this was the plan approved by President Bush just days before the invasion. It did not come to pass. There were significant situational difficulties. There was no Iraqi equivalent of a Hamid Karzai in Afghanistan. An international conference to legitimize an appointed government, as the UN-sponsored Bonn Conference did with Afghanistan, proved difficult to organize in the prevailing international climate. Many Iraqis were wary of a rapid turnover becoming Ba'athism without Saddam. Others worried about Shia domination. The Kurds worried about both of these scenarios and also kept one eye on Turkey.[121] Throughout it all, the rivalry between Iraqi "externals," such as Ahmed Chalabi, and "internals" was also a factor. In a similar vein, the few hundred Iraqi National Congress exiles led by Chalabi were not well or widely employed and accomplished little when they were brought into theater to help put an Iraqi face on coalition efforts. To complicate matters, there was another group of externals that had sought shelter in Iran during Saddam's regime. By mid-May 2003, any sense that Western-based Iraqi exiles or other externals—strongly distrusted in any event by the CIA and Department of State—might come to lead Iraq had evaporated in the spring heat.

The rapid turnover of power to Iraqis was key to the U.S. postwar plan, but it could not be arranged in advance or imposed by fiat. Khalilzad and Garner wanted to begin by holding a nationwide meeting of notables on May 15, 2003, a follow-up to three previous conferences in February and April 2003. Bremer, who had supplanted both of these officials, thought that such a meeting would be risky and canceled it; he also doubted the move to turn over elements of governmental authority rapidly to some sort of interim Iraqi body. In addition, he asked the President to end Khalilzad's status as a Presidential envoy under the premise that having two envoys would be confusing. However, removing Khalilzad took away the administration's de facto representative to all elements of Iraqi society. Khalilzad's popularity in Iraq and his status as an empathetic American of Muslim background were impossible to duplicate. Powell and Khalilzad were both surprised by this personnel shift, which was proposed by Bremer and approved by the President without benefit of interagency deliberation.[122]

Pursuant to UNSCR 1483, from May 2003 to June 2004 the United States and its coalition partners became the legal occupiers of Iraq, a fact that became more intolerable to many Iraqis as time passed and the dreams of reconstruction failed to come true. As Bremer settled into the headquarters—quickly canceling the nationwide meeting to prepare for an interim government, instituting de-Ba'athification, and disbanding the old Iraqi army—every major element of the plan briefed to President Bush right before the invasion had been abandoned because of changes on the ground without comprehensive reconsideration by the NSC principals.

In his back-brief to Rumsfeld (but not to President Bush), Garner—who had complained to Bremer in Baghdad about these three policy initiatives—referred to them as the "three tragic decisions."[123] In place of a quick turnover to Iraqis, a staple of prewar planning, the United States now had a full-scale occupation of Iraq without the requisite increase in resources to carry it off. Deprived of the assistance of over 100,000 Iraqi soldiers, the imbalance between aspirations and on-hand assets would continue up to the Surge.[124] The President approved these changes to postwar policy—the three tragic decisions—and he bears direct responsibility for not calling in all hands to create a new, well-balanced policy toward Iraq.

A third supporting assumption was that the Iraqi people hungered for democracy and human rights and that this hunger would suppress the urge to settle scores or to think in narrow tribal or sectarian terms. This presupposition undoubtedly was also enhanced by Iraqi exiles, many of whom had not been home in decades. This assumption had some validity, but it lived alongside the widely held perception that the United States and its partners were foreign occupiers and that democratic forms of government were a Western, Christian imposition on Islamic Iraq.

In the end, few Iraqis understood that democracy, in addition to majority rule, meant tolerance of and respect for minority rights. Ba'athists and al Qaeda–affiliated terrorists were able to create, magnify, and exploit sectarian tensions faster than the local government was able to imbue Iraqis with the spirit of democracy and unity. After the failure to find WMD, the White House—against Pentagon advice—pounded the democracy drum so loudly that in the minds of many, creating a democracy in Iraq, rather than bolstering national security, had become the centerpiece of U.S. policy.[125]

A fourth assumption was that Iraq without Saddam could manage and fund its own reconstruction. Unlike Afghanistan, Iraq had not been devastated by over 20 years of war, and its middle-class, educated population was mostly intact. If there were damages from the war, oil could pay for its modest reconstruction, a process that would be made easier by a small invading force and a highly successful effort to avoid collateral damage. In truth, unknown to policy planners and U.S. intelligence agencies, the country's prewar infrastructure was in disastrous shape. It was further devastated by the conventional battle that took place from March to May 2003 and by the looting and insurgency that followed the end of combat operations. Billions of dollars for reconstruction were required and later provided by the coalition or the international community, but any progress made was marred by a lack of security, inadequate capacity, and the ill effects of the insurgency. Compounding all of this, neither ORHA nor CPA had the right people or assets to make their presence felt throughout the country. Despite great personal sacrifices on the parts of hundreds of Americans and their allies, both organizations were often ineffective.[126] Few among them had any detailed knowledge of the Iraqi milieu.

Finally, based on the best available U.S. intelligence, as DOD and NSC officials had briefed the President, U.S. officials assumed that they would receive great help from the Iraqi police, the army, and the ministries, all of which were seen by many experts as salvageable, malleable, and professional. None of those things turned out to be true. The police were corrupt, ill trained (by Western standards), and not at all concerned with the rule of law. The virtual evaporation of the army during the war and its formal disbanding by Bremer (which surprised many outside the Pentagon), and even the de-Ba'athification that was ordered (and then expanded by Iraqis on the ground) did nothing to replace a system in which all national leadership had flowed from the Ba'ath party.[127] The Sunni minority—dominant in the army and the party—was alienated and became fodder for the insurgency. The ministries, deserted by cadres and looted repeatedly, did not continue to function effectively as had been hoped. It did nothing for their effectiveness when the coalition asked most ministries to report not to Iraqi authorities, but to the CPA. On top of all this, the urge for sectarian score-settling that was encouraged by al Qaeda in Iraq was strong. Later, the Shia-dominated Iraqi government did little to dampen sectarian violence and often encouraged it by Shiite militias, sometimes from within Iraqi security forces and ministries.

Sadly, much of the post-invasion state of affairs had been predicted. Many government and civilian experts had spoken well and loudly about the dangers of postwar Iraq, but their warnings were not heeded. For example, in September 2002, 33 of the most renowned U.S. international relations scholars, many of them normally considered right-wing realists, signed an open letter declaring the "war with Iraq is not in America's national interest."[128] Many analysts believed that the war and the subsequent peace would both be difficult. Planners and senior decisionmakers could have made better use of the report by the Department of State Future of Iraq Project, the 2002 National Defense University workshop "Iraq: Looking Beyond Saddam's Rule,"[129] or the Army War College's Strategic Studies Institute report titled *Reconstructing Iraq: Insights, Challenges, and Missions for Military Forces in a Post-Conflict Scenario,* all of which were U.S. Government–sponsored efforts.

The Army study, previewed at a conference in December 2002, concluded that "Iraq presents far from ideal conditions for achieving strategic goals. . . . Rebuilding Iraq will require a considerable commitment of American resources, but the longer U.S. presence is maintained, the more likely violent resistance will develop."[130] The study went on to recommend that the U.S. military prepare in detail for 135 postwar tasks. Senior NSC staff officials tried but failed to get the Army study briefed to interagency partners.[131]

Planners in OSD Policy, led by Deputy Assistant Secretary Christopher J. Lamb, also did a study on the significant potential for widespread lawlessness in postwar Iraq.[132] The OSD Policy leadership passed this study to the Pentagon's uniformed leadership and asked them to send it to USCENTCOM. The command did not respond to the analysis and likely did not have enough troops on hand to solve the security problems that arose after the completion of conventional operations.

The declassified January 2003 Intelligence Community Assessment—a document of lesser stature than a full National Intelligence Estimate—on postwar Iraq also concluded that building "an Iraqi democracy would be a long, difficult, and probably turbulent process, with potential for backsliding into Iraq's tradition of authoritarianism." It went on to highlight postwar Iraq as an environment offering opportunity to al Qaeda and to note the high probability of sectarian violence, "score settling," and Iranian meddling.[133] Warnings on various aspects of the plan were also made by Representative Ike Skelton (D-MO), former USCENTCOM Commander General Anthony Zinni, USMC (Ret.), as well as Secretary Powell, Senator Joseph Biden (D-DE), former National Security Advisor Brent Scowcroft, and others.

In addition to a complex set of sensitive, inaccurate assumptions, another problem—in part related to the sensitive assumptions, but at the same time a separate issue—was the inability of the coalition and the United States to put enough security forces—U.S., allied, or Iraqi—on the ground to control a country the size of California and create the security needed for governance and reconstruction. The small initial USCENTCOM combat force accepted significant risk in its rear area, but it accomplished its mission. The forces adequate to win the war, however, were not sufficient for providing local security, enabling reconstruction, defeating the insurgents, or protecting the population. General Abizaid, then USCENTCOM deputy commander, stated in a recent interview, "I went to Baghdad right after it had been captured, and I was shocked at how little control there was in Baghdad. I went to the [3rd] Division Commander, and then I went to Lieutenant General McKiernan [Land Component Commander Lieutenant General David McKiernan, USA] and I said, hey you have got to get control of what's going on in Baghdad. You may think the war is over, but the war isn't over yet."[134]

Sadly, while looters were demonstrating the inadequacy of the force on hand and implicitly encouraging insurgents, General Franks, responding to an inquiry by the Secretary of Defense, changed his mind and "off ramped" the nearly 20,000 Soldiers of the 1st Cavalry Division, ending its land, air, and sea movement toward Iraq and leaving the in-country troops without reinforcements.[135] The guidance from Washington to its forces was to "take as much risk getting out of the country as you took getting into the country."[136] General Abizaid concluded, "For all intents and purposes, we were still fighting in Iraq, and everyone else was saying how glad they were that [the war] was over with. We were going to turn it into Bosnia, except it wasn't Bosnia, it was Iraq."[137]

DOD civilian leadership did not want to admit—perhaps for public relations or legal reasons—that by mid-summer 2003, there was an insurgency going on. General Abizaid, the new USCENTCOM commander, publicly and clearly stated that there was an emerging guerrilla war there.[138] The August

2003 bombing by insurgents of the Jordanian embassy, the destruction of the UN headquarters, the attempted assassination of Deputy Secretary Wolfowitz in Baghdad, and the assassination of Shiite faction leader Ayatollah Mohammad Baqir al-Hakim left little doubt that a new type of war was beginning. Indeed, as one senior officer joked, the varieties of insurgents later became as numerous as the flavors of Baskin-Robbins ice cream.[139]

The Campaign, 2003–2006

The campaign for Iraq from the summer of 2003 to the beginning of the 2007 Surge is a well-told tale. From the summer of 2003 to the summer of 2004, the President appointed Ambassador Bremer and the CPA as the civil leadership. As already noted, on orders from or with the concurrence of Washington, Bremer launched a de-Ba'athification initiative, disestablished the Iraqi army (which had melted away during the fighting), and ended the movement by Garner and Khalilzad to quickly form an interim Iraqi government. The United States formally occupied Iraq, a fact legitimized in UN Security Council resolutions after May 2003.

On the military side, the large and general officer–filled CFLCC, built around 3rd Army headquarters, was the principal planner for Phase IV and was to take charge after the shooting stopped. It appears that this headquarters was too big for the desired strength of U.S. occupation forces. The USCENTCOM chief of staff told Army historians that "Franks and others were interested in lowering the size of the military footprint in Iraq in line with prewar planning for a very brief period of military operations after toppling Saddam Hussein."[140] General Franks ordered CFLCC replaced with a smaller combined joint task force, built around the arriving V Corps staff. This move confounded Army Vice Chief of Staff General Jack Keane, who had filled CFLCC with the best and brightest of the Army's senior officers to maximize their service in both Phase III and Phase IV of the operation.[141] A Baghdad division commander noted that V Corps was not suited to the mission and observed that the forces in the capital were "a bit adrift," engaged in what was "a bit of almost discovery learning" as they transitioned from maneuver elements in a grand fight to governing a fractious capital city.[142]

The U.S. force, commanded by Lieutenant General Ricardo Sanchez, USA, and his small headquarters, Combined Joint Task Force 7 (CJTF 7), tried to bring order to a complex insurgency in a large country beset by disgruntled Ba'athists, Shiite militias, restless Sunni tribes, and al Qaeda cadres, all vying for power and chafing under the coalition's presence. To become capable, Sanchez's organic corps headquarters built up from a strength of 280 to a strength of 1,000 over a year's time.[143] General officer strength went from 3 to nearly 20 on hand in roughly the same period. To compound command issues, Bremer and Sanchez did not work smoothly together.

There were a few positive developments on the ground during Sanchez's command. Saddam was captured in December 2003. Another highlight was the movement of a brigade of the 1st Armored Division to the south of Baghdad to secure the lines of communication. General Abizaid stated that "the best division fight of the war is the way that [then–Major General Martin] Dempsey handled his division in that period of combat. I don't think he has ever gotten enough credit for that. He sent a brigade down to Najaf and Karbala," and they severely damaged Muqtada al-Sadr's militia, thus securing "the lines of communication to the south."[144]

Despite such isolated bright spots, the insurgency spread and the ruthless pursuit of insurgents was often counterproductive. Years later, H.R. McMaster noted, "in Iraq, an inadequate understanding of tribal, ethnic, and religious drivers of conflict at the local level led to military operations (such as raids against suspected enemy networks) that exacerbated fears or offended the sense of honor of populations in ways that strengthened the insurgency."[145]

Thousands of Iraqis were incarcerated during this period, and the explosion in the prison population led indirectly to overcrowding and problems at Abu Ghraib prison. This overcrowding was a contributing factor in the national disgrace that emerged in the spring of 2004 with the publication of hundreds of pictures of a small group of U.S. Soldiers subjecting detainees to cruel and degrading abuse. Scooter Libby, the Vice President's chief of staff, summed up the devastating effect the photos would have on strategic communications: "This just goes against every message we are trying to send." The war grew increasingly unpopular at home and abroad.[146]

Around the same time, in response to the murders and mutilations of U.S. contractors, CJTF 7, with approval from higher authorities and over the initial objections of local Marines, began a comprehensive offensive in Fallujah, a Sunni insurgent stronghold not far from Baghdad. Partway through the bloody operation, with the concurrence of a reluctant USCENTCOM, Ambassador Bremer stopped the battle to prevent the carnage from destroying the cohesion of the Iraqi Governing Council.[147]

Some elements of the situation improved with time: the CPA gave way to an interim government in the summer of 2004, and then three sets of elections were held in 2005 for an elected Iraqi government. Bremer was replaced in the summer of 2004 by Ambassador John Negroponte, and the undermanned headquarters of Lieutenant General Sanchez was replaced by a four-star headquarters under General George Casey, ably mentored by General Abizaid, a former Middle East foreign area officer who had been USCENTCOM deputy commander or commander for over 18 months. Casey's headquarters now also had a subordinate, separate corps headquarters, Multi-National Corps–Iraq, to supervise the fight.

Casey commanded for 30 months through the tenures of 3 Ambassadors and 3 Iraqi governments. He had a succession of warfighting corps commanders under him—Lieutenant Generals Thomas Metz, John Vines, Peter Chiarelli, and Raymond Odierno—as well as two commanders for police and army training, Lieutenant Generals David Petraeus and Martin Dempsey. Sanchez and Casey were ably assisted by counterterrorist forces of the JSOC under Lieutenant General Stanley A. McChrystal, USA. Multi-National Force–Iraq (MNF-I) was established in the spring of 2004. Casey's description shows the complexity of the coalition force: "At the time [of his assumption of command] MNF-I consisted of around 162,000 coalition forces from 33 countries, organized into five Multi-National Division and one Multi-National Brigade area[s] of operation in northwest Iraq." Two of these five divisions were commanded by coalition members and contained most of the non-U.S. forces. The United States was responsible for three multinational division areas, the Marine sector in the west, and a brigade area of operations in the northwest.[148]

General Casey quickly published a full campaign plan, which was out in August 2004. His initial priorities were setting the conditions for the election and building Iraqi security forces and institutions, while respecting Iraqi sovereignty in all things.[149] The command also went to work on terrorist and militia strongholds in Samarra and Sadr City.

The problem of Fallujah did not go away. Working closely with the new interim government under Prime Minister Ayad Allawi, General Casey turned his attention to the destruction of the insurgent base there. In November 2004, with the support of the Allawi government, Marines and Army forces reattacked the reinforced stronghold. It was one of the costliest battles of the war. Between the two offensives in Fallujah, U.S. forces lost nearly 150 killed and 1,000 wounded. This time, the Iraqi government stood up under the strain of a major battle.[150]

In other areas, while still awaiting the new counterinsurgency doctrine, many units—for example, the 101st Airborne Division in Mosul in 2003, the Marines in Anbar, the 3rd Armored Cavalry Regiment in Tal Afar, and various battalions inside fractious Baghdad—began the practice of counterinsurgency operations, despite being short of supporting resources. From 2005 on, coalition forces improved their operations against the insurgents and laid the security groundwork for successful nationwide elections and the further development of Iraqi security forces. While repetitive tours stressed the ground forces, learning and experience counted when they returned to Iraq. Throughout this period, the command worked closely with the Embassy and the emerging Iraqi government. The training of police and army units improved, as did partnering between U.S. and Iraqi units.

Nationwide, however, violence continued to grow from around 500 violent incidents per month in July 2003 to 2,500 in January 2005, the month of the first successful Iraqi election. In February 2006, Iraq exploded in sectarian violence after the bombing of the Shiite al-Askari mosque (also called the Golden Mosque) in Samarra; total security incidents grew to over 1,400 per week in the worst periods.[151] Shiite militias went on the warpath after the bombing, and al Qaeda exploited the alienation of the Sunni from the Shia-dominated Iraqi government under Nouri al-Maliki. The government could not control the fighting. Iraqi soldiers and policemen were too few in number and inadequate in capacity to get the job done.[152] In June 2006, al Qaeda chief Abu Musab al-Zarqawi was killed in an airstrike. Unfortunately, his demise did not lessen al Qaeda–inspired violence. By the end of 2006, more than 50 Iraqi civilians were being killed in the fighting every day.[153]

It was increasingly clear that there were insufficient troops on the ground to clear, hold, and build, while simultaneously standing up the Iraqi security forces.[154] The coalition could no longer wait for the maturation or growth of Iraqi security forces to "fix" the growing violence. Any number of close observers, civilian and former military, opined that the coalition needed more troops. According to his memoir, Bremer also told President Bush or his key deputies on a few occasions, including during his predeployment orientation, that security was poor and more troops were needed. Bremer concluded that the United States had become the worst of all things: an ineffective occupier. Near the time of his departure in the spring of 2004, he asked Rumsfeld for one or two more divisions; he did not receive a reply, most likely because neither Sanchez nor Abizaid had asked the Secretary to add more troops.[155] In 2006, Chairman of the Joint Chiefs of Staff General Peter Pace, an inter-Service team of colonels, as well as an unusual combination of scholars, retired officers, Active-duty generals, and National Security Council staffers—with the encouragement of the President—began to look for the way out. Their story is in the next chapter.

The self-imposed cap on troops no doubt had much to do with the small size of U.S. ground forces. Neither the regional commander nor the theater commander, however, asked for more troops, favoring limiting the size of the U.S. forces in country. In any case, the United States did not have the ground troops in its base force to support the kind of troop rotations and in-country force levels necessary in both Afghanistan and Iraq to create the appropriate level of security and move toward success. Even when the President surged forces and civilians to Iraq, the question was not how many, but how many more the United States could afford to send. The protracted nature of the Iraq and Afghanistan commitments made Soldiers, Marines, and special operators endure an excessive number of rotations. For example, in the fall of 2007, 4 years before the war ended in Iraq, General Casey told the Senate:

> *Over 1.4 million American troops have served in Iraq or Afghanistan; more than 420,000 troops have deployed more than once. The* [Active] *Army has a total of 44 combat brigades and all of them except one . . .* [based in South Korea] *have served at least one tour of duty . . . and the majority of these 43 brigades have done multiple tours: 17 brigades have had two tours . . . 13 brigades have had three tours . . . and 5 brigades have had four tours in Iraq or Afghanistan.*[156]

By 2014, of the 72 Active and Army Reserve Component Brigade Combat Teams, 2 had deployed once, 24 had deployed twice, and 44 had deployed 3 or more times. Of that last category, 26 brigades had deployed 4 or 5 times.[157] The Army and Marine Corps later tried to ameliorate this multiple deployment problem after 2006 with a rapid buildup of the Active-duty personnel. Unfortunately, the enlistment of too many substandard recruits who required legal or moral waivers later became a source of its own set of problems for the Army.[158]

From 2003 to 2007, reconstruction and stabilization activities in Iraq, a partner to the military side of counterinsurgency, made slow progress. The condition of Iraq's infrastructure, including its oil industry, represented another prewar intelligence failure. Iraq needed much more reconstruction than anticipated, and in the early years there was precious little oil revenue to pay for it. Reconstruction was a struggle, compounded by the rapidly expanding demands of a liberated Iraqi population. Indeed, after the expenditure of many billions of dollars, electricity and oil production in 2007 still only matched prewar levels.[159] Toward the end of the U.S. presence, the bulk of reconstruction and construction financing came from the Iraqi government, which coalition advisors pushed to spend their growing surpluses on the needs of their own country.

In the early years, Iraqi capacity even to accept, operate, and maintain completed projects was wanting. According to a 2007 U.S. Government report, after the United States spent nearly $6 billion and completed nearly 3,000 reconstruction projects, the new government of Iraq had agreed to take possession of just 435 of them, worth only half a billion dollars. The rest remained idle or had been turned over to weak local governments.[160] In his final report, Stewart Bowen, the Special Inspector General for Iraq Reconstruction, highlighted the key role of security in enabling reconstruction and concluded that the lessons of the various periods of reconstruction from 2003 to 2009 "taken collectively . . . underscore the need for the U.S. Government to reform its approach to contingency relief and reconstruction operations and to develop greater capacity to execute them."[161]

In all, U.S. forces in Iraq in 2007 and in Afghanistan in 2008 were at an impasse. In both cases, there was a significant gap between the host country's objectives and preferences and those of the United States. In Iraq, after the destruction of the Golden Mosque in 2006, the addition of open sectarian warfare and the growing strength of al Qaeda made the slow buildup of

Iraqi forces inadequate by itself to bring stability to Iraq. The elections that were pursued with great diligence also created a highly sectarian government that expressed majority views but did nothing to protect minority rights. It served neither U.S. interests nor the long-term welfare of the Iraqi people. In Afghanistan, by the end of the Bush administration, years of insufficient funding and increasing Taliban momentum left the coalition unable to clear, hold, and build. More forces were needed quickly to provide a space to build up the Afghan police and army forces needed for the United States to begin to withdraw from the Hindu Kush. First in Iraq and later in Afghanistan, the addition of more coalition forces would be necessary before the endgame could be reached in either country.

Observations and Lessons

Lessons involving decisionmaking, intelligence and knowledge of the operational area, and the character and conduct of war itself were encountered in these conflicts.

Decisionmaking

Military participation in national decisionmaking is both necessary and problematic. Part of the difficulty comes from normal civil-military tension, but many instances in the war on terror also show unnecessary misunderstandings. Civilian national security decisionmakers need a better understanding of the complexity of military strategy and the military's need for planning guidance. Senior military officers for their part require a deep understanding of the interagency decisionmaking process, an appreciation for the perspectives and frames of reference of civilian counterparts, and a willingness to embrace and not resist the complexities and challenges inherent in the system of civilian control.[162]

In a similar vein, inside the Pentagon, future senior officers also need to study cases in wartime decisionmaking. The case of Iraq is particularly instructive. In the run-up to Iraq, the Secretary of Defense, as is his legal prerogative, inserted himself into the military-technical aspects of war planning to a high, perhaps unprecedented, degree. History will judge the wisdom of this managerial technique, but it serves as a reminder to future senior officers that the civil-military relationship, in Eliot Cohen's term, is characterized by an unequal dialogue.[163]

The U.S. Government also needs a better system for managing the implementation of interagency decisions and then exporting interagency efforts and unity of effort to the field. Good interagency policy decisions are often made, but execution is usually done by stovepiped departments and agencies.[164] Senior officers need to be able to participate in and assist with managing implementation of interagency systems.

Unity of command and effort in Iraq and Afghanistan were often lacking. Indeed, General Petraeus noted that we did not get the strategy and command and control architecture right until 2010.[165] In both Kabul and Baghdad, the arrangements have not always worked as well as they did with Lieutenant General Barno and Ambassador Khalilzad in Kabul or with General Petraeus and Ambassador Crocker in Baghdad and Kabul. Other, better arrangements may be possible. In a similar vein, the interagency community and command in Afghanistan were slow to see the importance of Pakistan to the solution of problems in Afghanistan. NATO nations (and headquarters) were sometimes reluctant to deal with Pakistan, which was outside of their mandate.[166]

Intelligence and the Operational Environment

Neither national nor military intelligence in Iraq and Afghanistan was a success in supporting decisionmakers. Intelligence on Afghanistan itself was scant and initially not actionable. In Iraq, prewar intelligence was wrong in a number of areas.

The biggest advances in intelligence came in improved support for the warfighter at the tactical level and the intimate relationship that developed between SOF and all-source intelligence. General Dempsey has stated that a captain at a remote site in Afghanistan in 2008 had more access to national technical means and high-level intelligence than he had as a division commander in 2003.[167]

Neither national-level figures nor operational commanders fully understood the operational environment, including the human aspects of military operations and the importance of Pakistan's milieu to the solution of Afghanistan's problems. To fight, in Rupert Smith's term, "war among the people," understanding them is a primary task.[168] The United States was not intellectually prepared for the unique aspects of war in Iraq and Afghanistan. Efforts to solve this problem—the Afghanistan-Pakistan Hands Program, for example—were insufficient and came too late to have a profound effect. Moreover, these efforts were inorganic adaptations, something apart from the normal unit activities. This devalued their potential contributions.[169] The intelligence system was of little help here. The need for information aggregation stands as an equal to classical all-source intelligence. This problem calls for a whole array of fixes, from improving language training, predeployment training, and area expertise to reforming the intelligence/information apparatuses.

Character and Conduct of War

When conventional warfare or logistical skills were called for, the U.S. Armed Forces usually achieved excellent results, but the military was insensitive to the needs of the postconflict environment and not well prepared for insurgency in either country. Military gains were not connected to political objectives. The lack of preparation for dealing with irregular conflicts was a result of failing to learn and internalize post-Vietnam lessons. Military performance improved over time. Indeed, field-level innovation on counterinsurgency showed an admirable capacity for learning and innovation. Later on, the development of Army and Marine Corps doctrine on counterinsurgency and its inculcation of the doctrine in the force were excellent examples of systemic adaptation under fire. In a similar manner, with great fits and starts and lots of managerial attention, the DOD acquisition system was able to create, field, and deploy the equipment needed to turn the military that existed into the military that was needed to fight these wars. The focus on preparation for future wars can retard warfighting adaptations in the near term. Even with bureaucratic resistance, however, the speed of battlefield learning and technological innovation in these wars was admirable.[170]

A prudent great power should avoid becoming a third-party expeditionary force in a large-scale counterinsurgency. Large-scale foreign expeditionary forces in another country's insurgency have almost always failed, except when the foreign power was the de facto government and the local insurgents had no sanctuaries.[171] At the same time, it should also be remembered that the U.S. participation in the wars in Iraq and Afghanistan did not begin as insurgencies but evolved in that direction. It is not possible for a superpower to disregard completely the possibility of future large-scale counterinsurgency or stability operations.

Another salient issue in irregular conflicts is the question of sanctuary. In Iraq and Afghanistan, U.S. enemies exploited base areas in adjacent countries. Some world-class experts believe that such sanctuaries make success nearly impossible for the counterinsurgents.[172] This situation presents the United States with a dilemma: Does it violate international understandings about the sanctity of borders, or should it respect borders and allow the enemy to rest, recover, and reattack at will?

Wars that involve regime change are likely to be protracted conflicts. They will require a substantial, patient, and prudent international effort to bring stability and foster reconstruction, especially in the wake of weak, corrupt, or failed states. These exercises in nation-building are complex, uncertain, and, with the passing of time, increasingly unpopular at home. In the words of General Petraeus, progress in such conflicts will always be "fragile and reversible." Nevertheless, regime changes and long-duration stability operations will sometimes be necessary. The alternative may be kinetic "victory" followed by political chaos. This author does not believe that coalition forces could have or should have left Afghanistan or Iraq right after the conclusion of major combat operations.

In a counterinsurgency, success will depend in part on the political development of the host government, whose weakness, corruption, and ineffectiveness are, ironically, an important factor in the development of an insurgency. There are few assets in the State Department or USAID inventory to mentor and assist a host government in political development. In collateral areas, such as humanitarian assistance, development, rule of law, and reconstruction, State and USAID have more assets, but still far fewer than these contingencies required. Ideally, the United States should have a civilian response corps, but the urge to develop whole-of-government capabilities is waning.

Getting better at teaching others how to handle an insurgency is likely to be one of the most important ways for the United States to participate in irregular conflict. Outside of SOF, the Armed Forces are not well organized to accomplish the training mission.

Notes

[1]   *Le Monde* editorial, September 13, 2001.

[2]   This chapter draws heavily on two of the author's previous works: *Choosing War: The Decision to Invade Iraq and Its Aftermath*, Institute for National Strategic Studies Occasional Paper 5 (Washington, DC: NDU Press, April 2008); and *Understanding War in Afghanistan* (Washington, DC: NDU Press, 2011).

[3]   For the full text of Public Law 107-40, "To authorize the use of United States Armed Forces against those responsible for the recent attacks launched against the United States," September 18, 2001, see <www.gpo.gov/fdsys/pkg/PLAW-107publ40/html/PLAW-107publ40.htm>.

[4]   On Afghanistan as the graveyard of empires, see Seth Jones, *In the Graveyard of Empires: America's War in Afghanistan* (New York: Current Affairs–Norton, 2009); and David Isby, *Afghanistan: Graveyard of Empires—A New History of the Borderland* (New York: Pegasus-Norton, 2010). The common expression is an exaggeration, but it is indicative of the fact that the Hindu Kush is a crossroads of history and that Afghanistan is a difficult place in which to fight.

[5]   For background on the U.S. Government and imminent al Qaeda threats, see *Final Report of the National Commission on Terrorist Attacks Upon the United States* (Washington, DC: U.S. Government Printing Office, 2004), 254–277. For her appreciation of the August warning, see Condoleezza Rice, *No Greater Honor: A Memoir of My Years in Washington* (New York: Crown, 2011), 63–70. For a mention of the difficulty of target-relevant intelligence in Afghanistan, see Chief of Staff of the Army's (CSA's) Operation *Iraqi Freedom* (OIF) Study Group, interview of General John Abizaid, September 19, 2014.

[6]   The two joint vision documents that outlined the long-range vision of the Joint Chiefs and the Quadrennial Defense Review 2001 document can be found at <www.dtic.mil/jv2010/jv2010.pdf>; <www.fs.fed.us/fire/doctrine/genesis_and_evolution/source_materials/joint_vision_2020.pdf>; and <www.defense.gov/pubs/qdr2001.pdf>.

[7]   A complete strategy of al Qaeda is laid out in Bruce Reidel, *The Search for Al Qaeda: Its Leadership, Ideology, and Future* (Washington, DC: The Brookings Institution Press, 2010), 121–133. Reidel believes that al Qaeda sought as a first strategic step to entice the United States to engage in "bleeding wars" in Afghanistan and Iraq.

[8]   Donald Rumsfeld, *Known and Unknown* (New York: Penguin, 2011), 358–359.

[9]   This perceptual bias toward Iraqi involvement in the 9/11 attack can be seen in the Camp David intervention by Deputy Secretary of Defense Paul Wolfowitz, but it was also mentioned by Under Secretary Douglas Feith to then–Lieutenant General John Abizaid, who were together overseas on September 11, 2001. Abizaid noted this in his interview with the OIF Study Group.

[10] Rumsfeld, 425; Rice, 86–87. President Bush does not mention the September 26 conversation in his memoir. He dates his request to Secretary Donald Rumsfeld to review Iraq war plans to "two months after 9/11." See George W. Bush, *Decision Points* (New York: Crown, 2010), 234.

[11] General Tommy Franks clearly thinks that his work on Iraq began in November. His first major meeting with the President came in December 2001. See Pete Connors, "Interview with General (Ret.) Tommy Franks," Fort Leavenworth, KS, June 23, 2006.

[12] Tommy Franks with Malcolm McConnell, *American Soldier* (New York: Regan Books–HarperCollins, 2004), 252.

[13] The best guide to the Pentagon planning can be found in Douglas J. Feith, *War and Decision: Inside the Pentagon at the Dawn of the War on Terrorism* (New York: HarperCollins, 2008), 63–78. Rumsfeld and Feith credit Wolfowitz with raising the profile of special operations forces working with Afghans in the initial plan.

[14] Franks, 211.

[15] Rumsfeld, 358–372.

[16] Franks, 268–272.

[17] Bush, 194.

[18] Gary Berntsen with Ralph Pezzulo, *Jawbreaker: The Attack on Bin Laden and al Qaeda* (New York: Three Rivers–Random House, 2005), 278–288; Rumsfeld, 403.

[19] For a full account of the Bonn process by the U.S. lead negotiator, see James F. Dobbins, *After the Taliban: Nation-Building in Afghanistan* (Washington, DC: Potomac Books, 2008), 1–116.

[20] The notion of the value of a quick exit from Afghanistan is developed in Daniel Bolger, *Why We Lost: A General's Inside Account of the Iraq and Afghanistan Wars* (New York: Houghton Mifflin Harcourt, 2014), especially xiii–xvii, 416–426. For a critique of his thesis, see Joseph J. Collins, "The Long War: Four Views," *Small Wars Journal*, January 5, 2015, available at <http://smallwarsjournal.com/jrnl/art/the-long-war-four-views>.

[21] Bush, 207.

[22] On comparative development, see the *UN Development Program's Human Development Index* and report, available at <http://hdr.undp.org/en/statistics/>. This report includes economics, education, health, security, and many other factors. Afghanistan has consistently been in the bottom 10 countries in the world. Along with the CIA's *World Factbook*, there are many statistics on Afghanistan on assistance and aid on the U.S. Agency for International Development's (USAID's) Web site at <http://afghanistan.usaid.gov/en/index.aspx>.

[23] Ashraf Ghani and Clare Lockhart, *Fixing Failed States* (New York: Oxford University Press, 2008), 75.

[24] On his strategy for counterinsurgency, see David W. Barno, "Fighting 'the Other War': Counterinsurgency Strategy in Afghanistan," *Military Review* (September–October 2007).

[25] Ibid. See also Rumsfeld, 684. The conventional wisdom that David Barno and Zalmay Khalilzad's successors did not get along well is disputed by the individuals in question. See, for example, Peter Connors, "Interview with Ambassador Ronald E. Neuman," Fort Leavenworth, KS, August 24, 2009.

[26] Donald Wright, *A Different Kind of War: The United States Army in Operation Enduring Freedom, October 2001–September 2005* (Fort Leavenworth, KS: Combat Studies Institute Press, May 2010), 245–247.

[27] For the Secretary of Defense perspective, see Rumsfeld, 689–690.

[28] For studies on the evolution of North Atlantic Treaty Organization (NATO) commit-ment to Afghanistan, see Andrew Hoehn and Sarah Harting, *Risking NATO: Testing the Limits of the Alliance in Afghanistan* (Santa Monica: RAND, 2010), 25–40. For an excellent analysis of NATO in Afghanistan, see David Auerswald and Stephen Saideman, *NATO in Afghanistan: Fighting Together, Fighting Alone* (Princeton: Princeton University Press, 2014).

[29] Despite the formal prohibition for the International Security Assistance Force (ISAF), General Stanley A. McChrystal as commander of U.S. Forces kept in close contact with the Pakistani military leadership. Stanley A. McChrystal, interview by Joseph J. Collins and Frank G. Hoffman, April 2, 2015.

[30] James Embrey and Thomas Riley, "Exit Interview with General John P. Abizaid," Carl-isle, PA: U.S. Army Military History Institute, 2007, 5.

[31] The current constitution of Afghanistan, Year 1382, can be found in English at <www.afghan-web.com/politics/current_constitution.html> and its 1964 predecessor at <www.afghan-web.com/history/const/const1964.html>.

[32] James Dobbins et al., *America's Role in Nation-Building: From Germany to Iraq* (Santa Monica, CA: RAND, 2003), 146, 157–158.

[33] U.S. Embassy–compiled statistics, 2009, provided by former Ambassador William Wood.

[34] ISAF briefing material, "Security Incidents," Afghanistan JOIIS NATO SIGACTS, 2004 to September 2009, unclassified.

[35] USAID statistics available at <http://afghanistan.usaid.gov/en/index.aspx>. Also see presentation by General David Petraeus, Royal United Services Institute, London, October 15, 2010, available at <www.rusi.org/events/past/ref:E4CB843C349F2E>.

[36] Kenneth Katzman, *Afghanistan: Post-Taliban Governance, Security, and U.S. Policy*, RL30588 (Washington, DC: Congressional Research Service, August 17, 2010), 88–90, available at <http://assets.opencrs.com/rpts/RL30588_20100817.pdf>.

[37] The author participated in at least five sessions of the deputies committee where the recruitment and provision of agreed-on State Department and USAID personnel was an issue akin to pulling teeth. The problem was few personnel and the inflexibility of the State and USAID personnel systems. The posting of State and USAID employees to

combat zones, especially for duty outside the Embassy, remained an issue throughout the war. By the end of the Afghan Surge, over 500 diplomats and U.S. Government specialists were in the field, and over 1,500 civilians were under Chief of Mission authority in Afghanistan.

[38] Prior to 2004, the Provincial Reconstruction Teams had a chain of command separate from troop units. This was ended by Lieutenant General Barno, in part to create more unity of command and in part to free up civil affairs assets.

[39] Written comments of an anonymous Supreme Headquarters Allied Powers Europe staff officer to the author, November 18, 2010.

[40] U.S. figures to 2009 come from Katzman, table 21, 91. Foreign data are adapted from Ian Livingston et al., *Afghanistan Index: Tracking Variables of Reconstruction and Security in Post-9/11 Afghanistan* (Washington, DC: The Brookings Institution Press, October 4, 2010), table 3.15, available at <www.fas.org/sgp/crs/row/RL30588.pdf>.

[41] Hoehn and Harting, 33.

[42] USAID Web site, available at <http://afghanistan.usaid.gov/en/index.aspx>.

[43] Most observers believe that narcotics and criminal activity are the Taliban's best source of financing—up to $500 billion per year by the highest estimates. Ambassador Richard Holbrooke, the first Special Representative to Afghanistan and Pakistan, often mentioned in public that he believed that donations from wealthy people in the Gulf were the Taliban's biggest source of revenue. One instance where Holbrooke mentioned this assessment was the Washington, DC, New Ideas Forum, October 1, 2010, author's notes.

[44] For a superb analysis of the Afghan and Pakistan Taliban, see Hassan Abbas, *The Taliban Revival: Violence and Extremism on the Pakistan-Afghanistan Frontier* (New Haven: Yale University Press, 2014).

[45] Data from U.S. Central Command (USCENTCOM), various briefings.

[46] On Iran, see Lara Setrakian, "Petraeus Accuses Iran of Aiding Afghan Taliban," ABC News, December 15, 2009, available at <http://abcnews.go.com/Politics/Afghanistan/gen-petraeus-iran-backing-iraq-militias-afghan-taliban/story?id=9346173>.

[47] For data on casualties and causes of death, see Livingston et al., tables 1.21, 1.22, available at <www.brookings.edu/~/media/Files/Programs/FP/afghanistan%20index/index.pdf>.

[48] Examples of night letters can be found in USCENTCOM release, available at <http://centcom.dodlive.mil/2010/08/29/taliban-aims-to-hinder-development-by-threatening-civilian/>.

[49] Testimony of former Under Secretary of State James K. Glassman before the Senate Foreign Relations Committee, March 10, 2010. The original report of the 2008 beheadings can be found in Carlotta Gall and Taimoor Shah, "Taliban Behead 30 Men from Bus," *New York Times*, October 19, 2008, available at <www.nytimes.com/2008/10/19/world/asia/19iht-19afghan.17083733.html>.

[50] United Nations Assistance Mission in Afghanistan (UNAMA), *Afghanistan: Mid Year Report on Protection of Civilians in Armed Conflict 2010* (Kabul: UNAMA, August 2010), 1, available at <http://unama.unmissions.org/Portals/UNAMA/Publication/August102010_MID-YEAR%20REPORT%202010_Protection%20of%20Civilians%20in%20Armed%20Conflict.pdf>; and Livingston et al., figure 1.29.

[51] Greg Miller and Josh Partlow, "U.S., Afghanistan Plan to Screen Cash at Kabul Airport to Prevent Corruption," *Washington Post*, August 20, 2010, available at <www.washington-post.com/wp-dyn/content/article/2010/08/20/AR2010082004049.html>.

[52] Vanda Felbab-Brown, *Aspiration and Ambivalence: Strategies and Realities of Counter-insurgency and State Building in Afghanistan* (Washington, DC: The Brookings Institution Press, 2013), 161. The standard work on the ways in which narcotics funded the Taliban and al Qaeda is Gretchen Peters, *Seeds of Terror: How Heroin is Bankrolling the Taliban and al Qaeda* (New York: St. Martin's Press, Thomas Dunne Books, 2009).

[53] Michael T. Flynn, Matt Pottinger, and Paul D. Batchelor, *Fixing Intel: A Blueprint for Making Intelligence Relevant in Afghanistan* (Washington, DC: Center for a New American Security, 2010), 7.

[54] For a thoughtful critique of human terrain teams, see Ben Connable, "All Our Eggs in a Broken Basket: How the Human Terrain System Is Undermining Sustainable Military Cultural Competence," *Military Review* (March–April 2009), 57–64.

[55] The author thanks Major Claude Lambert, USA, for this insight, April 2015.

[56] H.R. McMaster, "Continuity and Change: The Army Operating Concept and Clear Thinking about Future Warfare," *Military Review* (March–April 2015), 7–9.

[57] Conversations with various Active and retired senior officers from USCENTCOM and U.S. Forces–Afghanistan, 2008.

[58] Adapted from Amy Belasco, *The Cost of Iraq, Afghanistan, and Other Global War on Terror Operations Since 9/11*, RL33110 (Washington, DC: Congressional Research Service, March 2011), 1–6.

[59] Statement of John F. Sopko, "Lessons Learned from Oversight of the U.S. Agency for International Development's Efforts in Afghanistan," testimony before the Subcommittee on National Security, Committee on Oversight and Government Reform, U.S. House of Representatives, April 2014, available at <http://oversight.house.gov/wp-content/uploads/2014/04/Mr.-John-F.-Sopko-Testimony-Bio.pdf>.

[60] Pakistani officials—who tend to speak from the same talking points—are proud of their post-2006 operations against the Pakistani Taliban, but they are apparently blind to the connection between the Afghan and Pakistani Taliban, as well as the ill effects of their support of the Afghan Taliban or their standing in Kabul and their competition with India there. As the years passed, India's stock rose and Pakistan's fell in Kabul.

[61] Sean Maloney, "Afghanistan: Not the War It Was," *Policy Options* (November 2010), 44.

[62] Statement of Admiral Michael Mullen on Afghanistan and Iraq before the Senate

Armed Services Committee, September 20, 2011, available at <www.armed-services. senate.gov/imo/media/doc/Mullen%2009-22-11.pdf>.

[63] Various ABC-BBC and Asia Foundation Polls, 2005–2009. For January 2010 ABC-BBC polls, see <http://abcnews.go.com/images/PollingUnit/1099a1Afghanistan-WhereThings-Stand.pdf>; and for October 2009 Asia Foundation polls, see <http://asiafoundation.org/ resources/pdfs/Afghanistanin2009.pdf>.

[64] Bush, 228.

[65] Don Wright, "Interview with Karl Eikenberry," Fort Leavenworth, KS, April 30, 2012.

[66] Two books that treated both conflicts equally well were Dan Caldwell, *Vortex of Conflict: U.S. Policy Toward Afghanistan, Pakistan, and Iraq* (Stanford: Stanford University Press, 2011); and John Ballard, David Lamm, and John Wood, *From Kabul to Baghdad and Back: The U.S. at War in Afghanistan and Iraq* (Annapolis, MD: Naval Institute Press, 2012).

[67] For an interesting dissection of the initial Afghanistan campaign, see Stephen D. Biddle, "Afghanistan and the Future of Warfare," *Foreign Affairs* (March–April 2003), available at <www.foreignaffairs.com/articles/58811/stephen-biddle/afghanistan-and-the-future-of-warfare>.

[68] Pete Connors, "Interview with General David Petraeus," Fort Leavenworth, KS, May 2009.

[69] George H.W. Bush and Brent Scowcroft, *A World Transformed* (New York: Knopf, 1998), 489.

[70] Suzanne Chapman, "The War before the War," *Air Force Magazine* (February 2004), available at <www.afa.org/magazine/Feb2004/0204war.asp>.

[71] For one such report on how sanctions hurt children, see M. Ali and Iqbal Shah, "Sanctions and Childhood Mortality in Iraq," *The Lancet* 355, Issue 9218 (May 27, 2000), 1851–1857.

[72] A number of these officials were behind a movement for regime change as U.S. policy, and some had even publicly opined about military options against Iraq. For example, see the series of articles in the *Weekly Standard* of December 1, 1997, that were bannered on the cover page as "Saddam Must Go: A How-to Guide," with individual pieces by Wolfowitz, Peter Rodman, and Khalilzad, all of whom served as senior Bush administration officials in the run-up to the 2003 war.

[73] On the Saddam–al Qaeda connection, see Stephen Hayes, *The Connection: How al Qaeda's Collaboration with Saddam Hussein Has Endangered America* (New York: Harper Collins, 2004).

[74] In his memoir *At the Center of the Storm*, George Tenet confirms the activities of Zarqawi in Iraq and his relationship with Saddam's regime. See the extensive excerpts from the memoir in William Kristol, "Inadvertent Truths: George Tenet's Revealing Memoir," *Weekly Standard*, May 14, 2007, available at <www.weeklystandard.com/content/

public/articles/000/000/013/615cglnt.asp>. On terrorist affiliations with Saddam, see also Lawrence Wright, *The Looming Tower: Al-Qaeda and the Road to 9/11* (New York: Knopf, 2006), 295–296.

[75] An Arab expert's account of the inner workings of Zarqawi and al Qaeda can be found in Abdel Bari Atwan, *The Secret History of Al Qaeda* (Berkeley: University of California Press, 2006), 179–206.

[76] Michael Morell with Bill Harlow, *The Great War of Our Time: The CIA's Fight Against Terrorism from Al Qa'ida to ISIS* (New York: Twelve-Hachette Book Group, 2015), 88–89.

[77] Feith, 283.

[78] *The National Security Strategy of the United States of America* (Washington, DC: The White House, September 2002).

[79] For a complete examination of planning, see Michael Gordon and Bernard Trainor, *Cobra II: The Inside Story of the Invasion and Occupation of Iraq* (New York: Pantheon, 2006), 75–117.

[80] Rumsfeld, 428.

[81] One of the most developed arguments about how transformation ideas affected the war plan can be found in James Kitfield, *War and Destiny: How the Bush Revolution in Foreign and Military Affairs Redefined American Power* (Washington, DC: Potomac Books, 2005).

[82] Secretary Rumsfeld's clearest presentation on his postwar strategic concept—light footprint, quick occupation, a preference for a short-term presence—can be found in his "Beyond Nation Building" speech at the *Intrepid* Museum, New York City, February 14, 2003, less than a month before the war began. This speech is available at <www.defense.gov/speeches/speech.aspx?speechid=337>.

[83] For an example of Army shortages connected to interrupted or curtailed deployments, see Kitfield, 146.

[84] 1003V was the existing pre-9/11 war plan. The only book to cover the critical inputs to the plan made by Lieutenant General McKiernan and his staff at the land component command is Gordon and Trainor, 75–117.

[85] Pete Connors, "Interview with General (Ret.) Tommy Franks," Fort Leavenworth, KS, June 2006.

[86] Feith's memoir is highly critical of intelligence. See, in particular, 222–224, 517–518.

[87] Gordon and Trainor, 101.

[88] Vote count in Feith, 358–359.

[89] In a case of historical irony, many mainstream Democrats in the 2008 election were penalized politically for their vote to authorize and support the second Gulf War, just as their predecessors were penalized for not supporting the first Gulf War.

[90] *U.S. Commission on the Intelligence Capabilities of the United States Regarding Weapons*

of Mass Destruction (Washington, DC: U.S. Government Printing Office, March 2005). This group, the so-called Silberman-Robb Commission, concluded in its transmittal letter that there was "no indication that the Intelligence Community distorted the evidence regarding Iraq's weapons of mass destruction. What the intelligence professionals told you [President Bush] about Saddam Hussein's programs was what they believed. They were simply wrong." For a brief restatement, see Laurence H. Silberman, "The Dangerous Lie that Bush Lied," *Wall Street Journal*, February 8, 2015.

[91] The declassified key judgments of the 90-page National Intelligence Estimate can be found at <http://fas.org/irp/cia/product/iraq-wmd.html>. It should be noted that the Bureau of Intelligence and Research at the State Department objected to the timing and criticality of the Intelligence Community's judgment about Iraq's nuclear program. While this author maintains that we went to war on agreed-upon intelligence, some at the Central Intelligence Agency (CIA) believed that analysts there had been pressured or overlooked. See, for example, Paul Pillar, "Intelligence, Policy, and the War in Iraq," *Foreign Affairs* (March–April 2006).

[92] For a readily available summary of the U.S. Joint Forces Command–Institute for Defense Analyses study referred to in the text, see Kevin Woods, James Lacey, and Williamson Murray, "Saddam's Delusions: The View From the Inside," *Foreign Affairs* (May–June 2006), 2–26. Ironically, during the U.S. troop presence in Iraq, the CIA and Army technical experts collected thousands of abandoned yet lethal munitions from all around Iraq. See C.J. Chivers and Eric Schmitt, "CIA Is Said to Have Bought and Destroyed Iraqi Chemical Weapons," *New York Times*, February 15, 2015, available at <www.nytimes.com/2015/02/16/world/cia-is-said-to-have-bought-and-destroyed-iraqi-chemical-weapons.html?_r=0>.

[93] Woods, Lacey, and Murray, 91.

[94] Ibid., 92.

[95] David Rothkopf, "Can Obama's Foreign Policy Be Saved," *Foreign Policy* (September–October 2014), 50.

[96] A former senior National Security Council (NSC) official told the author in October 2007 that he believed the Pentagon was not eager initially to have combat forces from allies other than Australia and the United Kingdom but wanted maximum allied participation in Phase IV operations in Iraq.

[97] Franks, 366, 393.

[98] This was the opinion of senior generals in the Pentagon, as reported to the author in the fall of 2014 by a former White House official.

[99] Connors, interview with Franks, 8.

[100] The 3rd Infantry Division after action review is available at <www.globalsecurity.org/military/library/report/2003/3id-aar-jul03.pdf>.

[101] For a precis of the Marine Phase IV planning effort, see Nicholas Reynolds, *Basrah,*

Baghdad, and Beyond: The U.S. Marine Corps in the Second Iraq War (Annapolis, MD: Naval Institute Press, 2005), 42–46, 145–156.

[102] The most complete account of postwar planning is in Nora Bensahel et al., *After Saddam: Prewar Planning and the Occupation of Iraq* (Santa Monica, CA: RAND, 2008). The author was a reader and commentator on this study. A shorter version can be found in Nora Bensahel, "Mission Not Accomplished: What Went Wrong with Iraqi Reconstruction," *Journal of Strategic Studies* 29, no. 3 (June 2006), 453–473.

[103] Stephen J. Hadley, interview by Joseph J. Collins and Nicholas Rostow, October 7, 2014.

[104] Ibid.

[105] Rice, 192.

[106] Conversations and correspondence with a senior Joint Staff planner and a former senior NSC official, September 2007. Secretary Rumsfeld was frustrated by Bremer's reporting and finally told the President and all concerned that Bremer no longer reported to him. See Rumsfeld, 527.

[107] Bob Woodward, *Plan of Attack: The Definitive Account of the Decision to Invade Iraq* (New York: Simon & Schuster, 2004), 276–277. The author was the Defense Department representative on that group.

[108] Correspondence with a former senior NSC official in September 2007; on the oil briefing, Woodward, *Plan of Attack*, 322–323.

[109] Bob Woodward, *State of Denial: Bush at War, Part III* (New York: Simon & Schuster, 2006), 131–133.

[110] Woodward, *Plan of Attack*, 328–329.

[111] NSC Memorandum, signed by Condoleezza Rice, APNSA, SUBJECT: Principals Committee Review of Iraq Policy Paper, October 29, 2002, as reproduced in Feith, 541–543.

[112] For transcription of the speech, see "Bush makes historic speech aboard warship," *CNN.com*, May 1, 2003, available at <www.cnn.com/2003/US/05/01/bush.transcript/>.

[113] On plans for rapid drawdown, see Gordon and Trainor, 98, 103, 464; Woodward, *State of Denial*, 162. Many in the Office of the Secretary of Defense (OSD) continued to argue for a rapid turnover well into the Coalition Provisional Authroity period. See L. Paul Bremer with Malcolm McConnell, *My Year in Iraq* (New York: Simon & Schuster, 2006), 168–170, 188, 205–206.

[114] On assumptions, see also, Caldwell, 111–126; and chapter six in this volume. There are major interpretive differences between this chapter and the more granulated analysis in chapter three of this volume. The readers are invited to compare both approaches and make up their own minds.

[115] On the CIA's failure to predict insurgency, see Rumsfeld, 463–464, 520–521; and Feith, 517–518.

[116] These assumptions were reflected in numerous statements by Dick Cheney, Rumsfeld,

and Wolfowitz. They were also reflected by actions taken by various members of the national security team. For example, reaction by civilian leaders to the accurate judgments by General Shinseki (and USCENTCOM planners) as to the need for a large postwar force, the rush to begin postcombat withdrawal planning in the midst of looting, and the insistence that the Iraqis could pay for much of their own reconstruction all suggest that many leaders expected the peace to be easy relative to the war and that reconstruction would not be expensive. For many other officials, these assumptions remained unspoken but no less powerful. The sources of these assumptions included poor intelligence, the opinions of Iraqi exiles, and the policy predispositions of the members of the national security team. The dominant effect of assumptions was noted in David Petraeus, interview by Joseph J. Collins and Nathan White, March 27, 2015.

[117] Accounts of Kanan Makiya's meeting with the President and the Vice President's subsequent public declaration that we would be met as liberators can be found in George Packer, *The Assassins' Gate: America in Iraq* (New York: Farrar, Straus and Giroux), 97–98. An Iraqi émigré who lived in the United States for many years, Makiya wrote *Republic of Fear: The Politics of Modern Iraq* (Los Angeles: University of California Press, updated edition, 1998), a guide to the horrors of Saddam's regime.

[118] OIF Study Group interview with General Abizaid.

[119] Interview of General George W. Casey, Jr., May 19, 2014, filed in General Raymond T. Odierno, Chief of Staff of the Army Archives, 9.

[120] In the author's personal conversations with him in 2003 and thereafter, General Abizaid has been a continuing supporter of a rapid turnover to Iraqi control and broadening international participation. See also Gordon and Trainor, 163, 314. Khalilzad, Wolfowitz, Feith, and Garner were all dedicated proponents of rapid turnover. Many in the Department of State, as well as Ambassador Bremer, saw that up to 2 years of occupation would be a necessary phase in the operation. State had even floated a paper to that effect in the months before the war. However, a rapid turnover of power to some sort of Iraqi authority had been approved by the NSC and the President in the days before the war but was abandoned in the aftermath of the fighting and the difficulty in finding Iraqi partners.

[121] On the issue of why rapid turnover to an unelected Iraqi government was problematic, see Bremer, 162–167. There remained adherents of rapid turnover to Iraqis in the Pentagon and NSC well into the year of occupation.

[122] On this surprise decision, see Roger Cohen, "The MacArthur Lunch," *New York Times*, August 27, 2007, 17. This article recounts Khalilzad and Powell's surprise that the quick turnover concept had been abandoned and that Khalilzad had been ousted as a Presidential envoy to Iraq, not at an NSC meeting, but at a luncheon discussion between the President and Bremer. Bremer clearly envisioned a long occupation; see Feith, 496–497.

[123] Woodward, *State of Denial*, 219.

[124] In his interview for this volume, Hadley highlighted the problems of not having the

assistance of 100,000 or more Iraqi soldiers to assist the coalition in the postcombat environment.

[125] Feith, 475–477.

[126] For a precis on organizational and personnel problems, see Bensahel, "Mission Not Accomplished," 460–466; and Bensahel et al., *After Saddam*, 115–119.

[127] Ironically, some psychological operations and counter–command and control activities encouraged the Iraqi army to dissolve and for the soldiers to desert, while other plans were relying on Iraqi army units to remain intact to be used for reconstruction. See, for example, Gordon and Trainor, 145–146; and interview, former NSC official, August 15, 2007. The poor staffing and consequent bureaucratic surprise generated by the orders on de-Ba'athification and disbanding the Iraqi army were associated with a lull in NSC staff activism in managing day-to-day activities in Iraq. Sadly, Bremer was unfairly blamed for these decisions, which he had brought with him from Washington.

[128] Published as an advertisement on the op-ed page of the *New York Times*, September 26, 2002, emphasis in the original. The author thanks Christoff Luehrs for reminding him of this important statement.

[129] The National Defense University report of its November 2002 workshop "Iraq: Looking Beyond Saddam's Rule" highlighted the complexities of the postwar era and recommended a strong emphasis on postwar security. Copies of this report were provided directly to selected offices of OSD and Joint Staff leadership by memorandum on December 16, 2002. The author participated in the conference; his office funded it and helped to design it.

[130] Conrad C. Crane and W. Andrew Terrill, *Reconstructing Iraq: Insights, Challenges, and Missions for Military Forces in a Post-Conflict Scenario* (Carlisle, PA: Strategic Studies Institute, February 2003), v–vi.

[131] Discussions with a former senior NSC staff official in September and October, 2007.

[132] Feith, 362–364.

[133] *Intelligence Community Assessment: Principal Challenges in Post-Saddam Iraq*, January 2003, as summarized in an unpublished document of the Senate Select Committee on Intelligence and in the *Washington Post*, May 20, 2007, A6.

[134] In the OIF Study Group interview.

[135] Gordon and Trainor, 462. In a postwar interview with the Combat Studies Institute, General Franks admitted that he made a mistake in off-ramping the 1st Cavalry Division, an action that previously had been suggested by Rumsfeld. See Connors, interview with Franks, 9.

[136] OIF Study Group interview with General Abizaid.

[137] Ibid.

[138] See, for example, the transcript of Secretary Rumsfeld's July 13, 2003, appearance on

ABC's *This Week*, available at <www.defenselink.mil/transcripts/transcript.aspx?transcriptid=2842>. Compare that to the transcript of General Abizaid's remarks at the Pentagon on July 16, soon after he assumed command, on the nature of the guerrilla war, available at <www.defenselink.mil/transcripts/transcript.aspx?transcriptid=2845>. In his memoir, Rumsfeld salutes Abizaid's forthrightness on this subject and acknowledges post facto that the general's position made sense. Rumsfeld complained about faulty intelligence in regard to the prospect for insurgency in Iraq. See Rumsfeld, 521–522.

[139] A comment on an earlier draft by an anonymous major general with multiple tours in Iraq and Afghanistan, February 2015.

[140] Donald Wright and Timothy Reese, *On Point II: Transition to the New Campaign* (Fort Leavenworth, KS: Combat Studies Institute, 2008), 145.

[141] Ibid., 146.

[142] Martin E. Dempsey, interview by Richard D. Hooker, Jr., and Joseph J. Collins, January 7, 2015.

[143] Ibid.

[144] OIF Study Group interview with General Abizaid.

[145] McMaster, 8.

[146] On Abu Ghraib, see Tom Ricks, *Fiasco: The American Military Adventure in Iraq* (New York: Penguin Press, 2006), 197–200, 238–240, 258–261, 296–297. The Libby quotation is in Hadley, interview.

[147] The USCENTCOM perspective on the first battle in Fallujah can be found in Embrey and Reilly, "Exit Interview with General John P. Abizaid," 27–29.

[148] George W. Casey Jr., *Strategic Reflections: Operation* Iraqi Freedom, *July 2004–February 2007* (Washington, DC: NDU Press, October 2012), 20–24.

[149] Ibid.

[150] Among the best coverage of the battle in Fallujah was a series of articles by Dexter Filkins of the *New York Times*. A summary of some of his best coverage can be found in Dexter Filkins, "My Long War," *New York Times Magazine*, August 22, 2008. In it he surveys the material covered in his book *The Forever War* (New York: Knopf, 2008).

[151] See the command's statistics in Wright and Reese, *On Point II*, 101; and Ricks, photo collection.

[152] Joseph J. Collins, "The Surge Revisited," *Small Wars Journal*, November 4, 2013, 1, available at <http://smallwarsjournal.com/jrnl/art/the-surge-revisited>. One of the best books on the Surge, written from the command post perspective, was Pete Mansoor, *Surge: My Journey with General Petraeus and the Remaking of the Iraq War* (New Haven: Yale University Press, 2013).

[153] This figure was cited by Petraeus, interview. By the end of the Surge, levels of violence had been reduced by 90 percent.

[154] In a rare tiff between the theater commander and a Secretary of State, George Casey told the Secretary of State that she was out of line prescribing a strategy of clear, hold, and build, the first two of which were military tasks. The Secretary stood her ground. See Rice, 373.

[155] According to Bremer, his complaints to Cabinet officers or the President on poor security and/or the lack of troops started before he entered the theater and continued throughout his tenure. See Bremer, 12, 14, 71, 106, 170, 221, 228. The report of Bremer's 2004 memorandum requesting more troops can be found on 357–358.

[156] Army figures cited by Senator Ted Kennedy in the *Congressional Record–Senate*, vol. 153, pt. 18, September 19, 2007, 24,846. The effect on units was greater than the effect on individual soldiers who leave Active duty, and if they stay often do not remain in a unit beyond 2 to 3 years. By 2012, over half of the members of the Active Army and Reserve Components had more than one deployment. The effects of wounds, post-traumatic stress disorder, traumatic brain injuries, and deaths are discussed in *HQDA, Army 2020: Generating Health and Discipline in the Force Ahead of the Strategic Reset* (Washington, DC: U.S. Government Printing Office, 2012), annex B.

[157] Official U.S. Army statistics provided to the author by Dr. Robert Rush, an Army historian.

[158] *HQDA, Army 2020*, 148–156. These pages show the behavioral and criminal problems associated with low-quality recruits.

[159] The monthly U.S. Government statistics are promulgated in a comprehensive Power-Point briefing. See, for example, *The Iraq Weekly Status Report*, compiled from various sources by the Department of State, Bureau of Near East Affairs, October 17, 2007.

[160] For a mid-2007 report, see Dana Hedgpeth, "Report Says Iraq Lags on Rebuilding: Special Inspector Derides Iraqi Government's Lack of Responsibility," *Washington Post*, July 29, 2007, A19.

[161] Special Inspector General for Iraq Reconstruction (SIGIR), *Hard Lessons: The Iraq Reconstruction Experience* (Washington, DC: SIGIR, 2009), 324.

[162] On the problems of civil-military interaction in national security decisionmaking, see Martin E. Dempsey, interview by Richard D. Hooker, Jr., and Joseph J. Collins, January 7, 2015. For a collateral discussion of civilian and military decisionmakers talking past each other, see Janine Davidson, "Civil-Military Friction and Presidential Decision-Making," *Presidential Studies Quarterly* 43, no. 1 (March 2013).

[163] Eliot Cohen, *Supreme Command: Soldiers, Statesmen, and Leadership in Wartime* (New York: Free Press, 2002), 208–224.

[164] General McChrystal, for one, believes that in all cases, there should be one person, military or civilian, in charge. McChrystal, interview.

[165] Petraeus, interview.

[166] For example, in Afghanistan in 2006, Combined Forces Command–Afghanistan passed control of the ground fight to ISAF, and operations became fragmented between the commander, U.S. Central Command, Supreme Allied Commander, Europe, and commander,

U.S. Special Operations Command (USSOCOM). As former Secretary of Defense Robert Gates notes in his memoir, "efforts in Afghanistan during 2007 were being hampered not only by muddled and overambitious objectives but also by confusion in the military command structure." Furthermore, Gates adds that command relationships in Afghanistan were a "jerry-rigged arrangement [that] violated every principle of the unity of command." Robert M. Gates, *Duty: Memoirs of a Secretary at War* (New York: Knopf, 2014), 205–206, 478. The problem persisted even after Gates ordered it rectified in the summer of 2010, nearly 9 years after the war started. In both Iraq and Afghanistan, the often raw relationships between conventional forces, who were battlespace owners, and various types of special operations forces (theater, USSOCOM-subordinated, non-U.S., and so forth) were common complaints. This problem improved over time but is still an issue. Efforts to bridge the gap between conventional and special operations forces must continue. The authors would like to thank Major Claude Lambert, USA, for this observation.

[167] Dempsey, interview. General Lloyd Austin noted that intelligence support to the warfighter was "light years ahead of where it was in 2003." Lloyd Austin, interview by Richard D. Hooker, Jr., April 7, 2015.

[168] General Sir Rupert Smith, *The Utility of Force: The Art of War in the Modern World* (New York: Knopf, 2007).

[169] This salient observation was contributed by Nathan White of the Center for Complex Operations, based on his own field research.

[170] The problems in developing and fielding the equipment that matched current warfighting requirements are discussed in Gates, 115–148. General Austin, in his interview for this book, lauded in particular rapid equipment fielding efforts, the Joint IED Defeat Organization, and advances in intelligence, surveillance, and reconnaissance.

[171] In the past, among the great failures in third-party expeditionary force participation in insurgencies are the French in Indochina and Algeria and the United States in Vietnam. One can find many successes against insurgents that used unconscionable tactics. The two great successes among great power efforts were the United States in the Philippines (1899–1902) and the United Kingdom in the Malaya. There have been many cases in which the United States achieved positive outcomes when it did not have to use a major expeditionary force.

[172] Steve Metz of the U.S. Army War College Strategic Studies Institute made this observation in an email to the author, January 6, 2015.

2

Strategic Assessment and Adaptation: The Surges in Iraq and Afghanistan

By Frank G. Hoffman and G. Alexander Crowther

War is the greatest test of a bureaucratic organization.

—James Q. Wilson, *Bureaucracy, What Government Agencies Do and Why They Do It*

In December 2004, Donald Rumsfeld responded to a Soldier's question about the lack of adequate armored vehicles in Iraq by claiming that "you go to war with the Army you have, not the one you'd liked to have." While pilloried for his glib reply, the Secretary was essentially right: all nations go to war with the military forces they have developed to face a range of possible threats. Rarely are they optimized for the particular crisis or conflict in which they are engaged, and even when they are, adaptive adversaries can be counted on to present unanticipated challenges. Historian Victor Davis Hanson observed, "As a rule, military leaders usually begin wars confident in their existing weapons and technology. But if they are to finish them successfully, it is often only by radically changing designs or finding entirely new ones."[1]

While we go to war with the army we have, we do not necessarily win that war with the same army or initial strategy. Per Carl von Clausewitz, war is a duel whose outcome is the result of competing strategies in which both sides interact. Throughout recorded history, military leaders who have been successful have often had to recognize that their initial plans were necessarily not successful and thus altered their forces (organizationally, doctrinally, or weapons and equipment) to adapt as needed.[2] Victory often depends on which side can recognize problems or gaps in performance and implement changes faster by an altered strategy and adapting its forces. Despite this well-grounded observation, only recently has interest arisen on how strategies and military organizations adapt during war.

The two protracted conflicts examined in this volume have spawned a number of studies on the nature of operational adaptation by military organizations.[3] The Joint Chiefs of Staff have also identified adaptation as a key lesson learned from the last decade of conflict.[4] However, strategic adaptation, historically and during this era, remains largely unexplored.

This chapter begins with an overview of the literature on assessment and adaptation. After this brief examination of the current state of affairs, we establish an analytical framework for both strategic assessment and adaptation that serves as the basis for our subsequent analysis of the major strategic adaptations of Operation *Iraqi Freedom* (the Surge of 2007) and Operation *Enduring Freedom* (2009). The outcomes of these two adaptations are then summarized. The chapter concludes with insights relevant to the joint warfighting community.

Assessment

Strategic assessment represents a crucial element in a state's ability to adapt strategy to changing wartime conditions, which in turn plays a critical role in determining the outcome and cost of wars.[5] Yet it is an understudied area, one in which senior military officers must be prepared to make substantive contributions. A major shortfall in the conduct of our national security system has been the lack of appreciation for a continuous assessment of strategy implementation. Our national security mechanisms should not stop at the issuance of a Presidential decision. Instead, an "end to end" approach must be considered that encompasses policy formulation, strategy development, planning guidance, resource allocation and alignment, implementation oversight, and performance assessment based on feedback loops.[6]

Figure 1 offers a model of a continuous strategic performance cycle and identifies where the focus of this chapter resides in that process. Research underscores the reality that functional agencies resist rigorous evaluation, and the National Security Council (NSC) system must ensure effective mechanisms and metrics for oversight and performance assessment.[7]

Figure 1. Strategic Performance Cycle

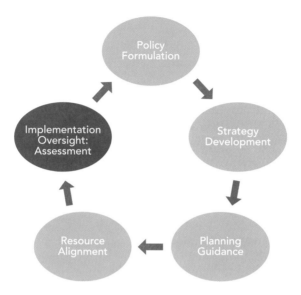

The importance of campaign and operational assessment is well known to the American military community. Critical issues involved in strategic assessment include evaluation of intelligence, likely international consequences of proposed actions, proposed operational plans to obtain defined political objectives, and a state's relative capabilities and how well they relate to the potential requirements in the proposed strategy.[8] The role of metrics in operational assessments and their complexity in accurately measuring progress in counterinsurgency (COIN) campaigns is also recognized. So too is the potential danger of politicization of metrics to satisfy bureaucratic or institutional politics.

During the Vietnam War, U.S. military operations were assessed using new techniques derived from systems analysis and the operations research community. Derived from the physical sciences, operations research proved its worth in World War II, but was less valuable in capturing the more political and socioeconomic aspects of the Vietnam War.[9] The assessment of progress in Vietnam was oversimplified in one sense by body counts and kill ratios but was also confused by an overabundance of sources and myriad metrics.[10] Military Assistance Command, Vietnam (MACV) used statistics as a substitute for understanding the war.[11] An extensive reporting system was eventually crafted to better capture vast amounts of data from the hamlet level and aggregated up to the provincial and corps levels. As the MACV strategy was increasingly challenged, there was strong pressure to generate favorable indicators to buttress the appearance of progress.[12]

American operations in Iraq and Afghanistan faced similarly daunting requirements for data collection.[13] The challenges involved in selecting, collecting, and analyzing metrics, both physical and from human sources, in combat theaters are significant. Holistic analyses of the myriad political, sociocultural, and economic factors relevant in combatting insurgencies and civil wars are rare. The volume of data is not the objective in assessments. The goal is to be able to monitor progress and adapt as necessary. As General James Mattis, USMC, observed of his experience in Iraq:

> *It's a very humanistic war, this war amongst the people. So it's hard to measure, but the indicators that I would consider most significant were when I walked down the street, did people look me in the eye and shake my hand? That was more significant than whatever. There was almost an over-quantification. We had a checklist of 77 questions to ask police in each station. We went out and asked those questions, and one of them that had the most yes's, when the fighting broke out badly against us, they joined the enemy.*[14]

American experience and official doctrine are limited, resulting in "inventive but ad hoc solutions."[15] The analytical community attempted to craft and promulgate regular indices to promote an understanding of strategic and operational effectiveness. Moreover, reflecting a lesson from Vietnam, the relationship between quantitative metrics and domestic political support for a protracted conflict was well recognized:

> *Only by tracking progress can we know whether a strategy is working. And only by examining a range of indicators can we determine how to adjust a strategy that may require improvement. Priorities must be set. Metrics can help in determining what they should be. Assessing progress*

is also important because the perception of progress has an effect on the sustainability of the war effort.[16]

Operational metrics and campaigns assessments are necessary but not sufficient. An operational assessment may provide valuable insights into the progress of a strategy or campaign plan, but it should not be confused with a national strategic-level assessment, which must incorporate a larger perspective involving international risks, coalition dynamics, and national resources. It must also account for domestic political constraints, resourcing, and opportunity costs. The policy community must be prepared to engage in strategic assessments, but the two cases studied here suggest that it is handicapped by a similar lack of grounded analytical structures and processes.

Adaptation

Historians identify the failure to adapt as a principal contributory cause of poor organizational effectiveness in conflict.[17] They fault institutions over individuals and focus on organizational elements in their analyses. Adapting to unexpected circumstances tests the organization, "revealing weaknesses that are partly structural and partly functional, whose full potential for disaster may not previously have been noticed."[18]

Scholarship in this field has been principally focused on operational and tactical, rather than strategic, adaptation. It is not enough to be tactically effective.[19] Historian Williamson Murray has stressed the importance of getting the strategy right, as any campaign's operations and tactics can always be fixed later. But good tactics cannot compensate for a poor strategy. As he puts it, "No amount of operational virtuosity [can] redeem fundamental flaws in political judgment. . . . it is more important to make correct decisions at the political and strategic level than it is at the operational and tactical level. Mistakes in operations and tactics can be corrected, but political and strategic mistakes live forever."[20] That said, strategic adaptation is also necessary.

This chapter is oriented at the strategic level to offer insights on the drivers and process of change at the strategic and national level of government.[21] There were numerous forms of operational and tactical adaptations made in both wars, including organizational changes (for example, Human Terrain Teams and Provincial Reconstruction Teams), enhanced integration of special operations forces with general purpose units, and materiel changes such as enhanced body armor and Mine-Resistant Ambush Protected vehicles.[22] There were also doctrinal adaptations including the rapid development of appropriate COIN doctrine. But this project and chapter are focused at the higher level of strategy.

This chapter's definition for adaptation is based on that of Theo Farrell, a leading scholar on military change. He defines *adaptation* as "change to strategy, force generation, and/or military plans and operation that is undertaken in response to operational challenges and campaign pressures."[23] The two Surge decision cycles examined herein certainly meet this definition for changes to strategy, the Services that generated forces, and military plans.

Analytical Framework

For an analytical framework, we modified Risa Brooks's four attributes of strategic assessment and adapted them to this study.[24] To extend her attributes to incorporate the strategic changes generated by the assessment, we added a fifth element. The five factors are defined as follows:

- Performance assessment mechanisms capture the quality of institutional structures and processes devoted to evaluations of our intelligence of enemy capabilities and capacities, as well the evaluation of our own political and military activities and progress. Due to the political-military character of irregular conflicts, such mechanisms must also include a capacity to assess the interdependent political, diplomatic, and developmental activities consistent with effective counterinsurgency.

- Collaborative information-sharing environment describes the routines and conventions of dialogue associated with exchanging information at the apex of decisionmaking. Key to information-sharing is the degree of openness and how forthcoming participants are about options and assessments not favorable to their preferred policy outcomes. Collaborative does not mean that all participants were comfortable. But the process should allow perspectives to be shared in a climate where parties are free to explore options, test assumptions, and debate merits of options.

- Strategic coordination captures the overall structure and mechanisms of the government used to develop and make policy decisions. These aspects influence how well policy is defined, how military strategies are tested, and how well they are coordinated with diplomatic activities and other aspects of the state. Without strong integrating mechanisms, senior leaders may not be aware of disconnects between the respective elements of a strategy, questionable assumptions, unintended consequences, or inconsistent objectives.[25]

- Decision authorization clarity captures how state leaders articulate and promulgate decisions and how they are unambiguously communicated. Within this dimension, the allocation of decisionmaking flexibility, prerogatives to subordinates, and accountability for constituent pieces of a larger strategy are allocated and defined.

- Strategic coherence evaluates the inherent logic of the proposed adaptation and its linkage of ends, ways, and means. Coherence integrates the use of all instruments of national power—diplomatic, informational, military, and economic tools. A coherent strategy matches the diagnosed problem to the selected approach and allocates commensurate responsibility and resources in relation to the mission and strategy.[26]

This set of factors is crucial to creating a foundation for understanding adaptation at the strategic level. Simply stated, one cannot understand strategic-level adaptation without considering the mechanisms and institutional capacity for strategic assessment and for implementing a change in strategy. The criteria employed in our evaluation of the strategic adaptations in this case study are presented in table 1.

Iraq Assessment and Adaptation

After the defeat of the Iraqi army in 2003, the United States and coalition partners occupied Iraq under the direction of the Coalition Provisional Authority (CPA)[27] led by Ambassador L. Paul Bremer,[28] while the Department of Defense (DOD) took the U.S. Government lead for matters relating to Iraq. Due to

Table 1. Assessment and Adaptation Analytical Framework

Assessment and adaptation factors	Criteria
Performance assessment mechanisms	Did the National Security Council have a process to gather and independently monitor relevant metrics and data on collected on progress and costs?
Collaborative information-sharing environment	Did the process allow perspectives and intelligence to be completely shared in a climate in which parties were open and free to explore options, assumptions, and debate merits of options?
Strategic coordination	Were all relevant parties present and engaged, positions defined, and shared in a timely way? Did the process produce both strategic options and Department positions to meet policy requirements? Were these integrated and coordinated?
Decision authorization clarity	Was a clear Presidential decision issued in writing with timely guidance regarding implementation and responsibilities?
Strategic coherence	Did selected strategy and adaptation resolve the diagnosed problem and logically balance or align end, ways, and means?

insufficient planning for the occupation of Iraq[29] and interpersonal frictions in Washington,[30] there were a number of interagency disagreements on how to proceed. Two major parts of the misunderstandings were the first two CPA orders, which called for de-Ba'athification and dissolution of Iraqi security forces. The upshot of these two orders was the political alienation and economic disenfranchisement of Sunni Arabs in Iraq, who had been the ruling elite since the early 1800s.[31] Because there were not enough forces to occupy the entirety of Iraqi population centers, these "Former Regime Elements" had time and space to recover and organize their forces for a campaign against the coalition.[32] Iraqi Kurds and Shiite Arabs had previously organized their own militias. The two different Kurdish political parties fielded the Peshmerga, while a variety of Shiite militias were active, including the Badr Corps of the Hakim family and the newly established Muqtada al-Sadr's Jaish al-Mahdi (JAM). By July 2003, General John Abizaid, USA, commander of U.S. Central

Command (USCENTCOM), stated that he thought that the coalition might face an insurgency.[33]

As the violence built between 2003 and 2006, the U.S. Government periodically sought to modify its approach to problems on the ground. In keeping with the "policy formulation," "strategy development," and "planning guidance" sections of the continuous strategic performance cycle described earlier, the Bush administration published a series of documents designed to delineate and achieve national goals in Iraq. As time passed without overall success, however, there was a widespread recognition that there was a lack of effective interagency collaboration,[34] and the focus changed across the U.S. Government. The Bush administration first published the *National Strategy for Victory in Iraq* on February 26, 2003. January 2004 saw the beginning of "a coordinated interagency process" involving both the State and Defense Departments to transfer authority from the CPA to an interim Iraqi government.[35] DOD stood up Multi-National Force–Iraq (MNF-I) in May 15, 2004,[36] while John Negroponte became the U.S. Ambassador to Iraq on June 23, 2004, taking charge of U.S. Embassy Baghdad on June 28 when CPA Chief Administrator L. Paul Bremer left Iraq.[37]

As it became apparent that current COIN doctrine (which had not been updated since Vietnam) was inadequate to guide operations in Iraq, the Army published Field Manual (FM) (Interim) 3-07.22, *Counterinsurgency Operations*, in October 2004. Reappraisal and modification of the military approach would continue through 2006. As U.S. Ambassador to Iraq Zalmay Khalilzad arrived in July 2005, he "initiated a full management review of the U.S. Mission in Iraq."[38] When the U.S. Government realized that a military-centric COIN campaign was insufficient, it expanded its scope and worked to improve interagency capability and stability operations and published:

- DOD Directive 3000.05, "Military Support for Stability, Security, Transition, and Reconstruction (SSTR) Operations," November 29, 2005
- an updated *National Strategy for Victory in Iraq*, November 30, 2005
- an interagency approach National Security Policy Decision 44, "Management of Interagency Efforts Concerning Reconstruction and Stabilization," December 7, 2005.

In addition to these national efforts back home, General George W. Casey, Jr., USA, who became the overall commander in Iraq on July 1, 2004, ordered the creation of a Counterinsurgency Center in Taji to teach coalition units to deal with the situation on the ground in Iraq.

The Iraqis had been making some political headway, promulgating a constitution, creating several interim governments, and holding a country-wide election at the end of 2005. Altogether these efforts codified an interagency approach that emphasized a combination of military and nonmilitary efforts toward stabilizing Iraq.

In spite of (and perhaps because of) these efforts to forge a solution to stabilize the situation in Iraq, these documents actually had little impact on the U.S. effort, and things were still not going well at the end of 2005. The Sunnis, for instance, bitterly contested the new constitution governing the country. The main issue continued to be the political alienation of the Sunni elite from the Iraqi government and their unwillingness to cooperate with U.S. and Iraqi leaders in charting a new way forward.

General Casey stood up a Red Cell to provide an external critique of options and plans, while he and Ambassador Khalilzad integrated DOD and State Department planning to better align their operations by forming an MNF-I/U.S. Embassy Iraq Joint Strategic Plans and Assessments cell in February 2006.[39] On February 22, 2006, al Qaeda in Iraq (AQI) bombed the al-Askari mosque in Samarra, north of Baghdad. This event triggered a civil war between Sunni and Shiite Arabs across Iraq. Violence continued to rise throughout the country after the attack. Sunni insurgents continued the fight against coalition forces, but al Qaeda–affiliated terrorists also added the Shiite population to their target list. The insurgent bombing of the golden dome in Samarra was designed to further ignite sectarian conflict—a goal that it accomplished. Shiite militias ramped up death squad activity and began the sectarian cleansing of Baghdad. By late 2006, Sunni Arabs realized that they were losing the war. They also chafed under the influence of AQI, which attacked, mutilated, and killed Iraqis who did not behave according to its strict rules. AQI proved incapable of protecting the Sunni Arab population from Shiite militias and the coalition. This situation led some Sunni Arabs, in particular several tribes in Anbar Province, to seek rapprochement with the coalition. Although the tribal rebellion was known as the Anbar Awakening, it was a movement that would later spread throughout the country with the full support of General David Petraeus, USA, and MNF-I. This development, combined with a new COIN approach manifested through the Surge, enabled the coalition to tamp down violence in an attempt to provide the conditions needed for Iraqi elites to develop a political solution to the conflict.

During 2006, the Iraqi government attempted to control the situation. On March 16, the Council of Representatives met for the first time. Ibrahim al-Jafari, the former prime minister in the Iraqi Transitional Government, was nominated as the candidate for prime minister under the permanent government of Iraq. He was a divisive figure who failed to obtain enough support and reacted to terrorist attacks with heavy-handed tactics employed by increasingly Shiite-dominated security forces. Evidence suggests that Jafari directed a campaign of sectarian cleansing that further inflamed the communal struggle and brought Iraq to the brink of civil war. On April 22, Nouri al-Maliki, a compromise candidate, was approved as the prime minister. Although Maliki had the support of the majority of the Council of Representatives, he was a Shiite, which limited Sunni Arab support and diminished Kurdish support for his government.

The year 2006 was a watershed year for the review of U.S. strategy in Iraq. Not only did the Army and Marine Corps rewrite their COIN doctrines, but the NSC, State Department, and DOD also reviewed the overall Iraq strategy. Then–Lieutenant General Petraeus, who had taken command of the Combined Arms Center at Fort Leavenworth after his second tour in Iraq, drove the rewrite of COIN doctrine.[40] He cooperated with then–Lieutenant General James N. Mattis, USMC, who had also returned from Iraq and was commanding the Marine Combat Development Command. This was a fortunate pairing. As Conrad Crane, one of the main authors of the new manual, stated, "The creation of the new Army/Marine Corps COIN manual resulted from the fortuitous linkage of two soldier-scholars with similar backgrounds and interests who had been forged in the crucible of Iraq to change their respective services, and were given simultaneous assignments where they could make that happen."[41]

The result was the December 2006 edition of FM 3-24, *Counterinsurgency*. Although this was a big step toward conceptualizing counterinsurgency, it had both supporters and critics. The COIN community welcomed serious thought about the issue, having been frustrated by Secretary Rumsfeld's continuing questioning that current operations had anything to do with insurgency.[42] The more conventional community, however, thought that too much emphasis on counterinsurgency was dangerous. They were personified by then–Lieutenant Colonel Gian Gentile, USA, who later stated, "This hyper emphasis on counterinsurgency puts the American Army in a perilous condition. Its ability to fight wars consisting of head-on battles using tanks and mechanized infantry is in danger of atrophy."[43] Some thought that the doctrine was "too soft" on insurgents, while others believed that the U.S. population and its military were incapable of mustering the patience required for victory. A critique more specific to Iraq was that the doctrine was not appropriate for a civil war where the United States had to act as an honest broker rather than taking sides with the government.[44] These various critics remarked on the new manual after its publication and, in a more limited form, continue to publish their commentaries to this day.

Because of continued controversy over Iraq, publications discussing the situation proliferated through the year. One good example was Stephen Biddle's "Seeing Baghdad, Thinking Saigon" in *Foreign Affairs*. In this article, Biddle argues that "turning over the responsibility for fighting the insurgents to local forces, in particular, is likely to make matters worse."[45]

As part of ongoing efforts to embrace and codify an approach to the situation in Iraq, the Bush administration continued to publish strategies, doctrines, and studies. On March 16, 2006, President George W. Bush published a new National Security Strategy. This policy document reflected the 2005 *National Strategy for Victory in Iraq* with three tracks (political, security, and economic) and three pillars to the security track (clear, hold, and build).[46] However, this was an update of the current strategy rather than a full strategic review.[47]

Also during that time, Congress officially announced the formation of the Iraq Study Group (ISG). The Center for Strategic and International Studies, Center for the Study of the Presidency, and James A. Baker III Institute for Public Policy at Rice University were asked to assist the bipartisan group. The ISG would work through 2006, observing spiraling violence and working to identify strategic options for the President. As the situation deteriorated, the studies and recommendations continued. President Bush would not suffer from a lack of advice. Although each analysis provided a different list and used varying phraseology, the options boiled down to five:

- pull out of Iraq
- do less to force the Iraqis to do more
- do the same
- do more of the same (that is, the same approach with more troops)
- go all in with a different strategy and a new operational concept.

Although President Bush did not favor one option over the others at this point, he did make it clear that he wanted to win the war.[48]

On July 11, 2006, the U.S. Government Accountability Office released *Rebuilding Iraq: More Comprehensive National Strategy Needed to Help Achieve U.S. Goals.* This report stated:

> *that there were three problems with the* National Strategy for Victory in Iraq: *First, it only partially identifies the current and future costs of U.S. involvement in Iraq, including the costs of maintaining U.S. military operations, building Iraqi government capacity at the provincial and national level, and rebuilding critical infrastructure. Second, it only partially identifies which U.S. agencies implement key aspects of the strategy or resolve conflicts among the many implementing agencies. Third, it neither fully addresses how U.S. goals and objectives will be integrated with those of the Iraqi government and the international community, nor does it detail the Iraqi government's anticipated contribution to its future security and reconstruction needs. In addition, the elements of the strategy are dispersed among the* [National Strategy for Victory in Iraq] *and seven supporting documents, further limiting its usefulness as a planning and oversight tool.*[49]

As the studies piled up, 2006 showed that there would be no end in sight for U.S. efforts in Iraq, and the U.S. Government was still looking for a way to prosecute the war successfully.

Biddle asserts that in the spring and summer of 2006, there was a "dawning realization at the White House" that a new approach was needed in Iraq.[50] Peter Feaver claims that during the late spring, the NSC staff started an internal review.[51] During the April/May timeframe, Megan O'Sullivan and Peter

Feaver realized that the failure they saw unfolding in Iraq was not the message or its implementation; the problem was the strategy. Although they did not envision an analysis at the level of Dwight Eisenhower's Project Solarium,[52] they saw a need to have a "no-kidding debate" at the principals' level. As preparation, they held an offsite at Camp David with "friendly critics" of the administration's policy in Iraq, including Michael Vickers from the Center for Strategic and Budgetary Assessments (who advocated accelerating the training and transition approach), Eliot Cohen from the School of Advanced International Studies at The Johns Hopkins University (who provided a historical perspective and argued for the need for accountability among senior military leadership), Robert Kaplan from the U.S. Naval Academy (who provided perspectives on past successful counterinsurgency campaigns), and Frederick Kagan from the American Enterprise Institute (who advocated a "double down" or Surge strategy). Kagan and Vickers were in opposition, with Vickers explaining how Iraq could be won with fewer troops and Kagan as a proponent for additional troops and a clear-hold-build approach.[53]

By the end of May and beginning of June, it became obvious the NSC would not get the bottom-up review it desired. Instead, the administration relaunched the *National Strategy for Victory in Iraq*. This highlighted a two-part approach: a Casey/Khalilzad strategy to gain control of Baghdad (a joint U.S.-Iraqi military operation featuring large unit operations) together with a 100-day political plan for Prime Minister Maliki (that is, legislative initiatives that met with U.S. approval). The result of this interim approach was that there was still no full review of U.S. strategy in Iraq.

At this point, General Casey and Ambassador Khalilzad were developing the 2006 Joint Campaign Plan while Casey was asking important questions about the effort in Iraq. As early as March 13, 2006, he had directed the MNF-I staff to look at the changing nature of violence[54] and was asking if something had changed to cause the coalition to alter what it was doing.[55] By April, he was asking if Iraq was in a civil war, but he decided that it was not.[56] Despite his questioning about the nature of change in Iraq, or more precisely because of his continuing belief that the nature of the war had not changed, General Casey was still dedicated to the original plan of transition, producing an updated campaign plan for Operation *Iraqi Freedom* transition to Iraqi self-reliance on April 28.[57]

As the military part of this plan, the government of Iraq and coalition attempted to gain control of Baghdad. Maliki announced the launch of Operation *Together Forward I* (OTF I), the newly formed government's plan to secure Baghdad, on June 13, 2006. An Iraqi-led operation, OTF I included "13 Iraqi Army battalions, 25 Iraqi National Police Battalions, and 10 Coalition Forces battalions. Altogether, nearly 50,000 Iraqi and Coalition troops were involved in the operation—21,000 Iraqi police, 13,000 Iraqi national police, 8,500 Iraqi army soldiers, and roughly 7,200 Coalition forces."[58] OTF I was a nascent attempt to provide protection to the population of Baghdad. At the same time, General Casey was reexamining his approach. One of his primary focuses in July 2006 was to rethink strategic priorities in Iraq.[59] By mid-July, he was considering the pros and cons of putting more coalition forces into Baghdad to support OTF I.[60] Even so, he continued to believe in the plan to transition security responsibilities to the Iraqis, meeting with the Joint Committee for Coalition Drawdown on July 16, and reporting to General Abizaid and Secretary Rumsfeld on July 18 on how the current situation was impacting drawdown plans. In spite of his desire to transition, by late July he recognized that he would need to keep more coalition troops in Iraq longer than originally intended.[61]

Even with OTF I efforts, over 3,400 Iraqi civilians died in Baghdad in July.[62] President Bush announced that he and Maliki would move more U.S. and Iraqi forces into Baghdad:

Our strategy is to remain on the offense, including in Baghdad. Under the Prime Minister's leadership, Coalition and Iraqi leaders are modifying their operational concept to bring greater security to the Iraqi capital. Coalition and Iraqi forces will secure individual neighborhoods, will ensure the existence of an Iraqi security presence in the neighborhoods, and gradually expand the security presence as Iraqi citizens help them root out those who instigate violence.[63]

This movement of more forces into Baghdad, called OTF II, started on August 7, 2006. An additional 6,000 Iraqi security forces and 5,500 coalition forces were sent to Baghdad. Although "protect the population" was not yet the strategy for the entirety of Iraq, OTF II called for forces "to move into neighborhoods, clearing the area of extremist elements, holding cleared areas securely, and building up essential services and infrastructure. Yet OTF II placed a far greater emphasis on the pace of clearing operations, rather than holding and rebuilding cleared neighborhoods."[64] As part of OTF II, the U.S. military extended tours for a Stryker Brigade from Alaska by 4 months at the request of Lieutenant General Peter Chiarelli, USA, the Multi-National Corps–Iraq (MNC-I) commander. This politically charged last-minute extension, which cut against the grain of General Casey's desire to draw down U.S. forces in Iraq, demonstrated the pace of the rapidly deteriorating security situation in Baghdad.

Even with the incapacity of the coalition to stem the violence, the U.S. military and diplomats in Iraq remained positive. On August 26, the Effects Assessment and Synchronization Board Composite Assessment was that "we are on track to achieve some but not all elements of Joint Campaign Plan Phase I by early 2007, that the campaign plan remains valid, even as conflict has grown more complex."[65]

In the end, however, insufficient forces were on hand to secure Baghdad, and many Iraqi security force units and leaders proved to be either undependable or excessively sectarian. The results were "disheartening," and violence "jumped more than 43 percent between the summer and October 2006."[66] On October 19, Major General William Caldwell, USA, the MNF-I spokesman, admitted that the campaign in Baghdad had "not met our overall expectations."[67] By the beginning of November 2006, OTF II was considered a failure and was abandoned.[68] Regardless, OTF II did demonstrate attributes that would contribute to the eventual success of the Surge the next year—concentration on security in Baghdad, flooding the zone with forces to protect the population, and using "clear" tactics as a prelude to holding and rebuilding neighborhoods.

By September 2006, old doubts in Washington were compounded by the failure of both the political and military plans for Iraq. The disquiet over the situation overcame bureaucratic inertia and personal agendas, so the "real strategic review" started at the end of the month. This review was quiet, reflecting the desire of the Bush administration to avoid a public discussion in the run-up to the midterm elections in November. Few even in the NSC knew about it. This process would discover that "distressingly few assumptions" remained plausible.[69] Three other strategic reviews were also conducted—by Lieutenant General Raymond Odierno, USA, before assuming command of MNC-I, by the "Council of Colonels" working for the Joint Chiefs of Staff, and within the State Department by Counselor Philip Zelikow and Coordinator for Iraq David Satterfield.[70]

Even as doubts grew, Secretary Rumsfeld continued to press ahead with the current strategy of transition, rejecting a recommendation by General John Keane, USA (Ret.), of a "Surge Plan" presented at the Defense Policy Review Board in September.[71]

General Peter Pace, USMC, Chairman of the Joint Chiefs of Staff, called for a Council of Colonels, which paralleled the NSC review, between September and December 2006. The council produced three major alternatives: "go big" by adding troops, "go long" by adding advisors, or "go home."[72] Unfortunately, by the time the council finished, "Layers of bureaucracy had sanded off the sharp edges of the analysis done by Pace's review team. Instead of presenting a clear alternative, the Joint Chiefs temporized."[73]

As part of the NSC review process, National Security Advisor Stephen Hadley traveled to Iraq in order to address the "Maliki question." Operation *Iraqi Freedom* was perceived as failing because of Maliki for three possible reasons:

- Maliki was the *Shiite prime minister* of Iraq as opposed to the prime minister of Iraq who was a Shia
- little institutional capability existed under Maliki
- Maliki was surrounded by bad advisors.

Although Hadley did not return with a specific answer, he did return with a classified memorandum for President Bush. This memo was reported to have addressed four major issues: what steps Maliki could take, what we could do to help Maliki, how to augment Maliki's political and security capabilities, and how to move ahead.[74]

On November 10, President Bush held an NSC meeting to launch "a formal deputy-level Iraq strategy review led by Deputy National Security Advisor [Jack Dyer] Crouch and involving senior participants from all the key departments and agencies, including the Departments of State and Defense, the [Joint Chiefs of Staff], the Office of the Director of National Intelligence, the Treasury, Vice President Dick Cheney's office, and the NSC staff."[75] The President had authorized the Joint Staff, DOD, Department of State, and NSC to work together for the formal review. The government needed to revisit the entire logic of the operations in Iraq and develop a series of options. The White House made it clear going into this process that there was no tolerance for defeat and withdrawal. Each one of the organizations produced papers for the review, which took place out of the public eye.

The NSC staff used its part of the review as an excuse to examine the assumptions that it had created for the *National Strategy for Victory in Iraq*. This turned out to be a sobering exercise. In the end, the NSC team lost faith in some assumptions and actually believed the opposite of others. The various efforts resulted in "a merged product which provided several options": tough it out (that is, more of the same), accelerate train and transition operations, hunker down (get out of cities and stay on forward operating bases), or ramp up.[76]

The NSC, Joint Staff, and State Department spent November discussing the options; Secretary of Defense Rumsfeld continued to hold the line. On November 6, the *New York Times* reported that Rumsfeld sent a classified memorandum to the President, reportedly articulating "above the line" options (that could and, in several cases, should be combined with others) and "below the line," or less attractive, options.[77] These less attractive options included continuing on the current path, moving a large faction of U.S forces into Baghdad in an attempt to control it, increasing Brigade Combat Teams and U.S. forces in Iraq substantially, and setting a firm withdrawal date. The above the line options reportedly included declaring that with Saddam Hussein gone and Iraq a sovereign nation, the Iraqi people could govern themselves, telling Iran and Syria to stay out, assisting in accelerating an aggressive federalism plan, moving toward three separate states—Sunni, Shia, and Kurd—or trying a Dayton-like peace process.[78] So Rumsfeld's reported above the line options were more of the same, while he did not support other newer options.

Although President Bush desired to keep the review out of the election, the election nevertheless had a large impact on the review. The day after the Republicans lost control of Congress in the 2006 mid-term, President Bush announced that he had accepted the resignation of Secretary Rumsfeld and was nominating Robert Gates as his successor.[79] Secretary Rumsfeld, now a lame duck, agreed to stay for the transition and eventually departed on December 18, 2006.

During the same period, President Bush started referring to "a new way forward" for Iraq. Although everyone now knew that a strategic review was under way and that there would be a new approach, the President had not yet made up his mind on which approach to take. There was no shortage of options covering the spectrum, from the full withdrawal that Congress wanted to doubling down and going for a win. As several commentators have mentioned about the Bush decisionmaking process, different staffs would work out an entire problem and then, having reached consensus, would brief the President. This review was different. During the Iraq relook, as appropriate, key actors took individual issues to the President rather than reaching overall consensus first. The President gave a key piece of guidance early in December when the NSC asked him, "'What is the U.S. role in population security?' The President stated that it was mission number one. All proposals logically flowed from this statement."[80]

On December 6, 2006, the Iraq Study Group released its official report to the President, Congress, and public. This report considered four options: precipitate withdrawal, stay the course, more troops for Iraq, and devolution to three regions. It also made 79 specific recommendations. It discussed the need for a new external approach titled "Building an International Consensus" and a new internal approach titled "Helping Iraqis Help Themselves." The diplomatic approach called for a "New Diplomatic Offensive" to put the problems into a regional context and to deal with issues in that region. The report also stipulated Iraqi milestones and new efforts for national reconciliation and governance. Additionally it addressed security, calling for a new "Military Strategy for Iraq" that required accelerated Iraqi control of security and embedding more advisors in the security forces.[81] It also called for changes in the police and criminal justice system, a new approach to U.S. economic and reconstruction assistance, the use of U.S. personnel, and U.S. intelligence.[82]

The report had supporters and detractors. On December 7, *Foreign Affairs* hosted a roundtable to discuss it.[83] Stephen Biddle, Larry Diamond, James Dobbins, and Leslie Gelb debated the issue. Biddle stated that the report "offers the political groundwork for a complete withdrawal more than it offers a sustainable solution to the conflict."[84] Diamond stated, "The seduction of a comprehensive approach . . . is that everything can seem equally urgent, and thus priorities may be difficult to discern." He also asked, "What matters most?"[85] Dobbins agreed with the report in that the "need to move toward a smaller U.S. presence and a more limited U.S. mission in Iraq is equally clear," and that "it is fairly obvious that one must try to move toward a level of engagement that could be sustained for the five to 10 years it may take to end the violence and stabilize Iraq."[86] Gelb lauded the "good bipartisan politics, a courageous analysis of the bleak situation in Iraq, and a compendium of useful policy steps," but argued that it "leaves the United States without an overall strategy—which will put the country in the position of having to confront the tough decisions all over again five months from now." He also criticized the middle-way approach adopted by the Iraq Study Group as sending two messages: that the "United States is leaving, and it's staying," which means that "neither Americans nor Iraqis would know which way the United States was really going."[87]

Different actors took different lessons from the report. People who wanted to withdraw used it to demand withdrawal. People who wanted a more Iraqi-centric political approach used it to demand that. Overall, the Iraq Study Group provided bipartisan top cover for the President to use should he choose to begin the withdrawal of U.S. forces from Iraq, but it did not provide a feasible strategy for him to adopt. It was dead on arrival in the Bush White House.

Another event generated more viewpoints for President Bush to consider. On December 11, 2006, the President met with retired General Wayne Downing, USA, of U.S. Special Operations Command, former Vice Chief of Staff of the Army General Jack Keane, and former commander of U.S. Southern Command General Barry McCaffrey, USA. Defense intellectuals Stephen Biddle and Eliot Cohen were also invited. Perhaps the most important input came from General Keane, who advocated changing the strategy from General Casey's clear and transition approach to protecting the population and putting more forces into Iraq to achieve that goal. President Bush considered the strategy review produced by the NSC, ISG, Joint Staff, and the meeting with defense specialists. As a background to his thoughts, on December 18, 2006—ironically, the day that Secretary Rumsfeld left office—the Pentagon reported that attacks were averaging 960 a week, the most since the reports began in 2005. With this in mind, on December 20, the President publicly articulated for the first time that the United States was not winning the war in Iraq.[88] On the same day, Secretary Gates visited Iraq and took a look at the situation on the ground. After his return, he delivered a proposal from General Casey for a two-brigade "mini-Surge" to President Bush, who disagreed with the idea as insufficient to alter the trajectory of the war.[89] The year ended with General Keane and Frederick Kagan publishing an op-ed in the *Washington Post* titled "The Right Type of 'Surge'—Any Troop Increase Must Be Large and Lasting." The op-ed discussed 30,000 soldiers for 18 months to bring security to Baghdad, "the essential precondition for political compromise, national reconciliation, amid economic development."[90]

This wide spread of input from disparate actors gave President Bush a variety of options: end the Iraq operation, do less and allow the Iraqis to assume more responsibility for the war effort, continue along the current path, do more of the same, undertake a different approach with the same force structure, and significantly increase activity while changing the overall approach. While the President was deep into examining strategic alternatives, his senior military advisors, particularly the Joint Chiefs of Staff and commanders in the region, were against larger U.S. forces on the ground. General Abizaid and General Casey were united against a significant troop increase because they shared a viewpoint that held U.S. forces were part of the problem, not the solution to Baghdad's woes, while some of the Joint Chiefs were concerned about the institutional state of the Army and Marine Corps after 4 years of conflict.

In the end, the President chose to go for the win. On January 10, 2007, President Bush announced a "New Way Forward" in Iraq.[91] "It is clear that we need to change our strategy in Iraq," the President stated in a nationally televised broadcast. He continued, "So my national security team, military commanders, and diplomats conducted a comprehensive review. We consulted Members of Congress from both parties, our allies abroad, and distinguished outside experts." He demonstrated that he clearly understood why:

> *Our past efforts to secure Baghdad failed for two principal reasons: There were not enough Iraqi and American troops to secure neighborhoods that had been cleared of terrorists and insurgents. And there were too many restrictions on the troops we did have. Our military commanders reviewed the new Iraqi plan to ensure that it addressed these mistakes. They report that it does. They also report that this plan can work.*

The President next talked about how the United States would change its strategic approach:

> *So America will change [its] strategy to help the Iraqis carry out their campaign to put down sectarian violence and bring security to the people of Baghdad. This will require increasing American force levels. . . . Our troops will have a well-defined mission: to help Iraqis clear and secure neighborhoods, to help them protect the local population, and to help ensure that the Iraqi forces left behind are capable of providing the security that Baghdad needs.*

President Bush then clarified that U.S. forces would now participate in the full clear-hold-build process:

> *In earlier operations, Iraqi and American forces cleared many neighborhoods of terrorists and insurgents, but when our forces moved on to other targets, the killers returned. This time, we'll have the force levels we need to hold the areas that have been cleared. In earlier operations, political and sectarian interference prevented Iraqi and American forces from going into neighborhoods that are home to those fueling the sectarian violence. This time, Iraqi and American forces will have a green light to enter those neighborhoods—and Prime Minister Maliki has pledged that political or sectarian interference will not be tolerated.*

President Bush then emphasized the interagency nature of the new approach:

> *We will give our commanders and civilians greater flexibility to spend funds for economic assistance. We will double the number of Provincial Reconstruction Teams. These teams bring together military and civilian experts to help local Iraqi communities pursue reconciliation, strengthen the moderates, and speed the transition to Iraqi self-reliance. And Secretary [of State Condoleezza] Rice will soon appoint a reconstruction coordinator in Baghdad to ensure better results for economic assistance being spent in Iraq.*

He also directly mentioned his analysis of the wide range of options that he had received:

We carefully considered these proposals. And we concluded that to step back now would force a collapse of the Iraqi government, tear the country apart, and result in mass killings on an unimaginable scale. Such a scenario would result in our troops being forced to stay in Iraq even longer, and confront an enemy that is even more lethal. If we increase our support at this crucial moment, and help the Iraqis break the current cycle of violence, we can hasten the day our troops begin coming home.

During late 2006, another change was occurring on the ground in Iraq. The Sunnis of Anbar Province had had enough of al Qaeda in Iraq and turned on them. At the same time, the Sunnis decided that the United States was the only actor in Iraq that was neutral enough for them to trust. The end result was that the Sunnis sided with the coalition, formed self-defense units called Concerned Local Citizens (which eventually became the Sons of Iraq) that cooperated with the coalition, and identified AQI actors on the ground so that the coalition could target them. This "Awakening" played a large part in bringing down violence in Iraq. The Awakening began before the decision on the Surge; however, the Awakening and Surge were mutually reinforcing.[92]

In the first half of 2007, the five Surge brigades deployed to Iraq. MNC-I and the Iraqi security forces cleared Baghdad neighborhood by neighborhood and then remained behind to secure the Iraqi people from insurgent and militia violence. Lieutenant General Odierno conceptualized fighting the "Battle of the Baghdad Belts," which would enable friendly forces to isolate Baghdad from neighboring regions of instability, where AQI and other groups had created safe havens. Violence reached a zenith in December 2006, remained at those high levels while the Surge forces arrived and began operations, and then began a precipitous drop in June 2006 after MNC-I launched Operation *Phantom Thunder*, the beginning of the "surge of offensive operations" that continued until the following summer. The Green Zone received 40 to 60 rocket and mortar rounds a day. Where coalition forces had previously cleared areas and then left the Iraqis to fend for themselves, U.S. forces now remained in cleared areas in more than 75 joint security stations and combat outposts, assisting the Iraqi security forces to hold and build. Although progress was slow and difficult to perceive, coalition and Iraqi security forces were taking back the city.

The next turning point occurred when Muqtada al-Sadr, the leader of the Jaish al-Mahdi militia, declared a ceasefire on August 29.[93] JAM fighters had instigated a gun battle at the holy shrines in Karbala that killed several hundred people, leading to wide condemnation from the Shiite community in Iraq. Since the Surge had already succeeded in lessening the threat to Shiite areas, JAM was no longer needed as the security force of last resort. Sadr bowed to public pressure and took his forces out of the fight. Violence dropped off immediately while indirect fire in the Green Zone ceased almost entirely.

The third major event during the first half of the Surge occurred during September 10–11, 2007, when Ambassador Ryan C. Crocker and General Petraeus testified before Congress. Many in Iraq, both coalition and Iraqi, thought that Congress might take advantage of the hearings to confront the President and force him to bring U.S. forces home. In the event, Crocker and Petraeus were able to convince Congress that enough progress had occurred and was continuing to warrant a continuation of the Surge. Many in Iraq were relieved when the two returned to Baghdad.

The Surge continued through late 2007 and into the new year. In early 2008, with violence ebbing, Iraqi politicians were finally able to make progress on a reform of the de-Ba'athification decree, amnesty legislation, delineation of provincial powers, a budget, and a redesigned Iraqi flag. These developments demonstrated that the assumption underpinning the Surge—that political progress was incumbent upon improved security—was accurate.

The next spring, Prime Minister Maliki finally had enough with the Jaish al-Mahdi's control of Basra, the oil capital of Iraq. He triggered Operation *Charge of the Knights* in Basra, which the coalition supported to the full extent of its capabilities. After a rough start, the operation successfully cleared the militia presence from Basra. JAM responded by launching rockets into the Green Zone from Sadr City, which triggered the battle of Phase Line Gold to bring Sadr City under control. After a month of hard fighting, the Jaish al-Mahdi was a spent force, and Iraqi security forces occupied Sadr City in May 2008 without firing a shot. By the end of the Surge in July 2008, violence had dropped to levels not seen since early 2004. The United States and

Iraq signed a pair of agreements that defined their bilateral relationship. This included a Status of Forces Agreement that stipulated the departure of U.S. forces from Iraq by the end of 2011.

In late 2009, the last of the coalition partners departed Iraq, and U.S. forces started to reorganize for a transition to a new security arrangement. On September 1, 2009, the United States declared the end of Operation *Iraqi Freedom* and the beginning of Operation *New Dawn*. On January 1, 2010, MNF-I, MNC-I, and Multi-National Security and Training Command–Iraq combined to form U.S. Forces–Iraq (USF-I). During 2011, when it became obvious that American forces would depart Iraq in their entirety by the end of the year, USF-I continued the drawdown. On December 18, 2011, the last U.S. forces in Iraq departed. The remaining forces were reorganized under the Office of Security Cooperation–Iraq under a lieutenant general and subordinate to U.S. Embassy Iraq. The mission was declared over.

Afghanistan Assessment and Adaptation

This section details the historical record of the Obama administration's assessment process and the resulting adaptation in strategy and force levels in Afghanistan in 2009.[94] It should be kept in mind that unlike the previous case study, this was a new administration, one in which routines, processes, and personalities had not yet gelled. The President campaigned, however, on an explicit platform that viewed the war in Afghanistan as a war of necessity, compared to the invasion and subsequent insurgency in Iraq. The Bush administration had conducted an exhaustive review in late 2008, recognizing that events in Afghanistan were not trending in a positive way.[95] The Afghan government did its own internal assessment and believed that nearly half of the country's 364 districts (166) were completely or substantially controlled by the Taliban.[96] The late 2008 American review, led by Lieutenant General Douglas Lute, USA, recommended a fully resourced COIN approach and additional force levels to implement it. President Bush did not commit to a decisive shift in strategy or force levels, given pending change in administration, and deferred to the incoming President.[97]

Within a few weeks of taking office, President Barack Obama requested that former Central Intelligence Agency analyst Bruce Riedel conduct a quick strategic assessment of the situation in Afghanistan.[98] Riedel had recently completed a manuscript on the ongoing conflict with al Qaeda including Operation *Enduring Freedom*. Riedel quickly assembled a small team, conducted a number of working group meetings with Office of the Secretary of Defense (OSD) and State Department representatives, and produced an overall scan of the current campaign strategy and its effectiveness. National Security Advisor General James L. Jones, USMC (Ret.), regional envoy Richard Holbrooke, and USCENTCOM Commander General Petraeus participated in group sessions over Riedel's report. Ultimately, Riedel briefed President Obama.[99] In short order and with no debate, the President approved force levels needed to help secure the upcoming Afghan election and dampen a Taliban resurgence.

The results of the review, however, were not debated. Moreover, the resourcing increase was not scrutinized by the NSC. The President did not engage any external insights or meet with his major military advisors. He approved the troop increase of 17,000 for Afghanistan and issued a hurried statement in late March 2009.[100] The President's speech clarified why the Nation was taking additional actions and with what priorities. He concluded, "If the Afghan government falls to the Taliban or allows al Qaeda to go unchallenged, that country will again be a base for terrorists who want to kill as many of our people as they possibly can."[101]

Both the principal policy aim and national security interest of the United States were articulated in this statement, but it was a compromise between fully resourced counterinsurgency and preventing an environment in which al Qaeda could return. It was based upon the recognized increased inroads that the surging Taliban was making and its long-term impact. The administration concluded that al Qaeda and Taliban leadership shared common bonds that could support terrorism from inside Afghanistan. Were the Taliban to succeed in toppling the government of Hamid Karzai and regain control of the major urban centers, it would embolden extremism in general and al Qaeda in particular. Thus, core U.S. interests were at risk.[102]

The initial assessment offered clarity on goals, in particular an emphasis on disrupting terrorist networks in both Afghanistan and Pakistan. Next, the review expanded the scope of the campaign to recognize the interdependent nature of both countries and the need to consider the strategy and operations from a regional perspective. Mr. Holbrooke's appointment as envoy with a portfolio over both countries reinforced this aspect of the strategy.[103] Finally, the new strategy defined the goals for enhanced governance in Afghanistan and greater partnership capacity in counterinsurgency in that country's growing security force.

Given the lack of progress in Afghanistan, Secretary Gates believed that the International Security Assistance Force (ISAF) commander, General David McKiernan, USA, was miscast in a role that required a different mindset. No one thought ill of McKiernan, but many thought a change in leadership was warranted. Subsequently, Mr. Gates announced General McKiernan's relief on May 9, 2009, and President Obama announced the selection of Lieutenant General Stanley A. McChrystal, USA, to replace him. McChrystal, then serving as Director of the Joint Staff, was quickly approved by the Senate and took up his post. He was directed to conduct a thorough evaluation of operations in Afghanistan and report back.

McChrystal formed a multidisciplinary team and oversaw a truly strategic assessment rather than merely a campaign or an operational evaluation. His strategic assessment was designed to be more than a purely military assessment.[104] The commander's personal involvement and the nontraditional perspectives from scholars and coalition members made this a notable effort. The civilian academics brought in diversity and served as a valuable resource in formulating and debating the contents of the assessment.[105] The end product was a better plan for conducting a comprehensive counterinsurgency inside Afghanistan, which the team perceived as its assigned task.[106]

In late August 2009, McChrystal delivered his initial assessment. His strategic review recognized the critical importance of the effectiveness of the Afghan National Security Forces and sought to elevate the importance of governance. The review made clear that additional resources were needed to blunt the Taliban's evident momentum but that those forces should focus on "those critical areas where vulnerable populations are most threatened."[107] This plan stressed the importance of governance to the success of the campaign, not just population security or other counterinsurgency related lines of effort.

McChrystal was told to wait until after the Afghanistan election and then submit his report via the chain of command.[108] When he did, the report soon found its way to the media, despite its classified and sensitive nature.[109] The report did not skirt with niceties or hedge on its conclusions: "Failure to provide adequate resources also risks a longer conflict, greater casualties, higher overall costs, and ultimately a critical loss of political support. Any of these risks in turn are likely to result in mission failure."[110] McChrystal made clear that his call for more forces was predicated on the adoption of a strategy in which troops emphasize protecting Afghans rather than killing insurgents or controlling territory. Most starkly, the report stated that what was needed most was an entirely reshaped strategy. "Inadequate resources will likely result in failure," he noted; however, "without a new strategy, the mission should not be resourced."[111] McChrystal explained that "success is achievable, but it will not be attained simply by trying harder or 'doubling down' on the previous strategy." He concluded that the key takeaway was the urgent need for a significant change to the U.S. strategy and "the way that we think and operate." He and Ambassador Karl W. Eikenberry translated their assessment into their own integrated campaign plan in August of that year even before Washington could assess the assessment.[112]

McChrystal's report kicked off a renewed White House strategy review that began with a far broader and blank canvas. It soon became apparent that there were different camps forming on the future of U.S. policy and strategy in Afghanistan, with civilian and military perspectives starting to emerge.[113] A scheduling opportunity existed in October for the President to meet with McChrystal in Denmark.[114] This marked the first opportunity for the President to have a one-on-one meeting with his field commander. This was followed by a video teleconference session in which McChrystal presented his findings to the NSC. The general requested additional force levels and outlined his ideas on how to implement a counterinsurgency approach.[115] This session initiated a second but more formal strategy review by the Obama administration.[116]

The President, with the assistance of his National Security Advisor, began a deliberate and extended review process that included nine meetings of the NSC principals and some 25 hours of discourse.[117] The President personally chaired these meetings and consistently demonstrated a willingness to challenge his assumptions as well as those of others in his Cabinet, immersed himself in detailed intelligence reports and policy details, and repeatedly asked probing questions.

Several different coalitions among the Cabinet members emerged. Secretary Gates, Chairman of the Joint Chiefs of Staff Admiral Michael Mullen, and both USCENTCOM and ISAF commanders consistently supported the comprehensive COIN approach and the concomitant requirement for 40,000 troops to execute that plan. The ISAF commander submitted three force levels for consideration, one for 85,000 troops, his preferred option of an increased end strength allocation of 40,000, and a smaller option of 8,500. The latter option would have added additional training and advisory capacity but would have had no additional combat power to offset Taliban inroads or increased population security in Afghanistan. This was derided by some in the NSC as a typical "Goldilocks" approach, two throwaway courses of action, and the preferred option for 40,000. The President desired true options, ones in which the ways of the strategy options were different, not only the means. On one occasion the President chided his Cabinet for not satisfying his expressed desire for real options.[118]

A second option was introduced by Vice President Joe Biden to rescope the U.S. objectives in Afghanistan—an option often turned into shorthand as counterterrorism (CT). He was supported by NSC staff members in developing this option, which focused on a narrower policy endstate, keeping pressure on al Qaeda, reducing force presence in Afghanistan, and relying more on special operations, drone strikes, and high-value targeting. This school was concerned about long-term national security issues and economic health risks driven by the U.S. economic situation. The CT option was efficient but may not have been effective. Even with a diminished objective, ISAF, the international community, and U.S. civilians from supporting agencies would have to consolidate their staffs and offices back to Kabul and a handful of consulates. Intelligence sources that enabled a precise CT campaign would be more exposed with fewer bases and troops to defend them, and less able to continue supporting U.S. special operations forces. Thus, the resources most needed to hold Afghanistan together would end up too far away from the areas that mattered to contribute to a positive outcome. This counterterrorism strategy would be unlikely to hold Afghanistan together, degrade the Taliban, or reduce al Qaeda's freedom of action.[119] However, this option would not have required a troop increase.

A third option emerged during debates, and a minority camp emerged that stated the real problem all along was Pakistan, the source of much of the Pashtun-dominated Taliban insurgency and a secure sanctuary for it. Eikenberry and Holbrooke held to this perspective. After a preliminary meeting

117

with NSC deputies in which the Ambassador expressed strong reservations about the proposed strategy, he was asked by General Jones to craft an official cable to Secretary of State Hillary Clinton. Ambassador Eikenberry sent his cable as requested. Like McChrystal's classified theater assessment, this highly sensitive cable was promptly leaked to major media outlets.[120] The Ambassador's candid evaluation of the critical U.S. ally, Hamid Karzai, as an improbable partner did not endear him to the Afghan leadership. Moreover, Eikenberry's strong reservations in the cable were not coordinated with his military partner in Kabul.[121] The cable argued that "the better answer to our difficulties could well be to further ratchet up our engagement in Pakistan."[122] The cable was at odds with the military's perspective of what counterinsurgency could achieve and directly contradicted the logic of both Petraeus and McChrystal on the efficacy of a comprehensive politico-military solution via counterinsurgency.[123]

Each of the options presented alternative goals, with requisite and distinct means to advance U.S. security interests. The full-scale counterinsurgency camp argued that the goal for U.S. policy should be to preserve Afghanistan's sovereignty and current constitutional government and defeat the Taliban insurgency in cooperation with building that country's institutions including its military and police force. For the CT school, large-scale operations and extensive nation-building were beyond U.S. national interests, which were defined narrowly as not allowing al Qaeda to have the freedom of action to plan future attacks against the U.S. homeland. The administration was more concerned with al Qaeda, not the Taliban. Eikenberry's preference was better defined in terms of what it would not do—it would not ensure the survival of the Afghan capital, and it would not ensure that al Qaeda shifted back into Afghanistan and reestablish its base infrastructure there. His emphasis was a shift toward resolving Pakistan's support to destabilizing networks in both Pakistan and Afghanistan.

While the three options produced a useful delineation of alternative ways and means, there was still a strong consensus among all the participants that the United States had a vital interest in degrading al Qaeda's capacity to threaten American citizens or allies. This ensured some common ground for the assessment. The only option that the President unilaterally removed from the table was an Afghan withdrawal.[124]

The Vice President continued to oppose increased force levels and the supporting strategy, retaining his position that reduced force levels, lower costs, and a renewed but narrow approach directed at al Qaeda were better. Key staffers including Lieutenant General Lute and Deputy National Security Advisor Thomas Donilon preferred the CT/al Qaeda connection and continued to pepper the Pentagon and ISAF with questions between major meetings. Their active role questioned the traditional "honest broker" role of the National Security Advisor and his team in the interagency process.[125]

During NSC debates, the Secretary of Defense and Secretary of State supported a substantive COIN campaign with a Surge. Their position aligned closely with the views of the Chairman of the Joint Chiefs of Staff, USCENTCOM, and ISAF. Secretary Gates was willing to adapt his views on U.S. goals and consider options less expansive than his military leaders. He was joined by Secretary Clinton, who saw the military's proposed troop increase, combined with a civilian surge and diplomatic efforts, as crucial to a transition process that would both strengthen the Afghan government and increase leverage for a diplomatic solution.[126]

In response to Presidential discomfort with the responsiveness of the Joint Staff, the Vice Chairman of the Joint Chiefs of Staff, General James Cartwright, USMC, produced a hybrid option that increased troop levels by 20,000–25,000 and employed them somewhat more narrowly in population protection rather than offensive clearing operations. This was an option that neither the Chairman nor field commanders wanted to have presented to the NSC, as it did not reflect their conception of counterinsurgency.[127] The development of this option and information exchanges between the OSD, Joint Chiefs of Staff, and NSC staff complicated interpersonal and institutional relations.

The internal debate on force levels spilled out again in the media. Lieutenant General McChrystal, speaking in London at the International Institute for Strategic Studies, talked about ongoing efforts in Afghanistan. During the question-and-answer period, however, he explicitly rejected counterterrorism as an option, despite the fact that it was an option under consideration in ongoing NSC discussions. The White House was not happy with a public critique of the internal council options.[128] Media sources continued to describe the contending camps and the President's desire for an exit strategy.[129] The military came off as if they were pressuring President Obama in the media to limit the range of options that he could consider.[130] The President (and his White House staff) complained to both Secretary Gates and Admiral Mullen about what appeared a concerted effort to box him in.[131] While not a deliberate campaign, the number of statements by senior military officers that made their way into the press influenced the candor of internal deliberations.

Given the strains of a decade at war, civil-military relations would naturally be tense. Both Secretary Gates and Admiral Mullen had to counsel subordinates about American traditions with regard to civil-military relations and how to be candid in counsel but far more discreet in public commentary.[132] The Chairman later made civil-military relations and professionalism an issue in his speeches and lectures.[133]

President Obama sought out the collective perspective of the Joint Chiefs early in the review. He held a full meeting with the Joint Chiefs on October 30 at the White House. The President received the chiefs' collective support for the shift in strategy, increased force levels, and resourcing ISAF, although some of them expressed a lack of support for protracted nation-building.[134]

During the course of the debates, the literature shows that President Obama became dissatisfied with the production of options that met his desired outcomes within the temporal and resource constraints he believed were politically feasible. He expressed his key objectives and the outline of his preferred strategy. This approach was discussed by officials and became the focal point for subsequent deliberations. Rather than select a discrete option from this menu, the President developed a hybrid option that sought to balance contending viewpoints. To restrain an expansive if not expensive solution, President Obama downgraded U.S. goals from the outright defeat of the insurgency in Afghanistan to the disruption of the Taliban and its effectiveness. To satisfy the Pentagon and ISAF request, he approved an additional 30,000 troops for ISAF and permitted Secretary Gates to generate another 3,000 at his own discretion. The President's final decision incorporated a faster deployment and peak of the increased force levels and incorporated a withdrawal timeline that surprised military officials. A phased withdrawal timetable, beginning in July 2011, was part of the strategy.

The specificity of the timeline presented a wrinkle. This issue was debated at an NSC meeting with the President, who held firm to the desire to both increase resources, but hold the theater commander to a fixed amount of time to demonstrate results, and terminate active U.S. fighting forces. The articulation of a fixed end date to U.S. participation in Afghanistan was not desired by military officials, who wanted subsequent assessment cycles and results on the ground to dictate the vector and pace of American force levels. The President asked for and received support for this final strategy, although subsequently some principals believed that its starker deadline was questionable.[135] Some reports suggest that military commanders believed they could generate demonstrable progress by the timeline and further extensions would be authorized to complete the mission.[136]

The timeline issue for the announced withdrawal issue raised concerns in some circles. Reportedly, NSC discussions on the issue suggest that the Service chiefs were consulted and supported it under the assumption that a deadline put the Afghan government on notice in terms of enhancing governance and building up the Afghan army.[137] This temporal element was briefed to USCENTCOM and ISAF in late November.[138] Senior administration officials were quick to suggest that any withdrawal starting in mid-2011 might be limited and would be conditions-based. In a brief public comment, Under Secretary of Defense for Policy Michèle Flournoy clarified, "The pace, the nature and the duration of that transition are to be determined down the road by the president based on the conditions on the ground."[139]

The President elected to roll out his decisions and garner public support by delivering a major speech at the U.S. Military Academy at West Point on December 1, 2009. He made it clear that he recognized "Afghanistan is not lost, but for several years it has moved backwards" and that the Taliban had gained momentum. He stated U.S. forces lacked the full support they needed to effectively train and partner with Afghan security forces and better secure the population.[140] He noted, too, that the commander in the field in Afghanistan had found the security situation more serious than he anticipated and that the President found the status quo unsustainable:

> *I make this decision because I am convinced that our security is at stake in Afghanistan and Pakistan. This is the epicenter of violent extremism practiced by al Qaeda. It is from here that we were attacked on 9/11, and it is from here that new attacks are being plotted as I speak. This*

is no idle danger; no hypothetical threat. In the last few months alone, we have apprehended extremists within our borders who were sent here from the border region of Afghanistan and Pakistan to commit new acts of terror. And this danger will only grow if the region slides backwards, and al Qaeda can operate with impunity.[141]

The President noted that the strategy would keep the pressure on al Qaeda, in not only the short term with U.S. forces but also the long term by increasing the stability and capacity of partners in the region. In the end, "Our overarching goal remains the same: to disrupt, dismantle and defeat al Qaeda in Afghanistan and Pakistan, and to prevent its capacity to threaten American and our allies in the future. . . . We must reverse the Taliban's momentum and deny it the ability to overthrow the government."[142] The bumper sticker for the strategy became "to disrupt, dismantle, and defeat al Qaeda," but notably the task was expanded by reference to safe havens in Pakistan. This became the central logic of the strategic communications plan. The strategy was articulated further in congressional testimony that week by Cabinet officials,[143] the Chairman,[144] and the political and military leaders seeking to execute it.[145]

General McChrystal did not survive in his post long enough to see his operational design applied. Indiscreet comments from his staff published in *Rolling Stone* forced the President to accept his resignation in June 2010.[146] General Petraeus, who was appointed to replace him, continued the campaign he had helped frame while commander of USCENTCOM.

All in all, the strategic adaptation developed for Afghanistan's Surge was a product of a protracted evaluation of U.S. interests, policy aims, and supporting strategies. Some found the sessions too extended and inconclusive, but they did include the kind of strategic discourse needed to produce a clear strategy.[147] President Obama's deliberate style strived to reassess U.S. policy and strategic requirements, including fundamental assumptions.[148] Some participants believed that the review was useful but too drawn out and reflected a lack of Presidential commitment.[149] The President observed that he was more engaged than was typical in deliberations and felt compelled to generate his own option. Ironically, the administration largely ended up where the Lute review of 2008 had finished a year earlier.

Iraq Outcomes

There is an ongoing discussion about whether the Surge in Iraq succeeded and whether it was worth the effort. As a holistic approach, there are a wide variety of both continuities and differences to examine. Peter Feaver identifies several:

> the surge of military forces, the surge of civilian forces, the prioritization of population protection, the emphasis on the bottom-up political accommodation that harnessed the so-called Tribal Awakening of Sunni tribes in al-Anbar Province that had begun to fight back against al-Qaida in Iraq's predations, the increased special operations attacks on al-Qaida in Iraq and on rogue Shiite militias, the greater decentralization and diversification of efforts beyond the Green Zone.[150]

Although each of these efforts has its proponents and its critics, it is impossible to disaggregate any one part of the Surge approach. In the long run, the Surge did not resolve Iraq's problems. No external military force can resolve another country's political issues in the modern world;[151] however, external forces in this case reduced violence dramatically, which provided an opportunity for the Iraqis to resolve their internal political issues. The fact that Nouri al-Maliki did not take the opportunity to unite Iraq does not diminish the military results of the Surge.[152]

The first question is to ask why President Bush took so long to make a decision. It appears that he was reluctant to impose himself on the decisionmaking of his senior subordinates. His own history and background as "a product of the Vietnam era" made him uncomfortable with getting into the details of decisions about the use of the military.[153] History suggested to him that there was a fine line between setting strategy and micromanaging combat. He consciously sought to avoid constraining his generals or impacting their abilities to win the war. Furthermore, the President valued loyalty and was accused of surrounding himself with people who placed a premium on conformity over debate or dissent.[154]

Feaver writes, "One study notes that President Bush mentioned delegating the decision on troop levels to his ground commanders in 2006 more than thirty times in that year alone."[155] It took the political disaster of losing control of Congress to get the President to override his subordinates in order to seek the ends he desired.[156]

As for the results of the Surge, the major result was a large-scale decline in violence. Figure 2 shows how much violence dropped over time. Another way to measure the decline is in U.S. casualties (see table 2). By either of those measures, the Surge was a success. Another way of examining success is to compare results to articulated goals. The Surge was clearly defined from the beginning. According to a fact sheet provided by the White House when President Bush announced the Surge:

> *The President's New Iraq Strategy is Rooted in Six Fundamental Elements:*
>
> *1. Let the Iraqis lead;*
> *2. Help Iraqis protect the population;*
> *3. Isolate extremists;*
> *4. Create space for political progress;*
> *5. Diversify political and economic efforts; and*
> *6. Situate the strategy in a regional approach.*[157]

By this definition, the Surge was a success; it did achieve all of these objectives.

If, however, we examine what President Bush defined as success in the body of the same fact sheet, we see he states:

> *Victory will not look like the ones our fathers and grandfathers achieved. There will be no surrender ceremony on the deck of a battleship. But victory in Iraq will bring something new in the Arab world—a functioning democracy that polices its territory, upholds the rule of law, respects fundamental human liberties, and answers to its people. A democratic Iraq will not be perfect. But it will be a country that fights terrorists instead of harboring them—and it will help bring a future of peace and security for our children and our grandchildren.*

Figure 2. Weekly Enemy-Initiated Attacks Against Coalition and Partners

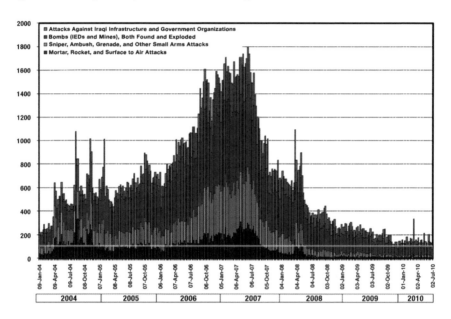

Source: Iraq Index: Tracking Variables of Reconstruction & Security in Post-Saddam Iraq (Washington, DC: The Brookings Institution, November 30, 2011), 4, available at <www.brookings.edu/~/media/Centers/saban/iraq%20index/index20111130.PDF>.

Table 2. Total U.S. Military Fatalities, by Year

2003	2004	2005	2006	2007	2008	2009	2010	2011
486	849	846	822	904	314	149	60	53

Source: Iraq Index: Tracking Variables of Reconstruction & Security in Post-Saddam Iraq (Washington, DC: The Brookings Institution, November 30, 2011), 7, available at <www.brookings.edu/~/media/Centers/saban/iraq%20index/index20111130.PDF>.

It would be difficult to define Iraq as being a functioning democracy that polices its territory, upholds the rule of law, respects fundamental human liberties, and answers to its people. By this measure, the Surge was not a success.

The final cost in lives in Iraq operations between 2003 and 2011 was 4,486 Americans, 218 coalition partners, and at least 103,775 Iraqis.[158] Some find it hard to assess whether this price was worth paying. Others tend to give credit to external forces such as the Sunni Awakening. But as Peter Mansoor has noted, "Without the surge, the Awakening would have been much more limited in its scope and impact."[159]

Afghanistan Outcomes

Naturally, after such an extended debate associated with the revised strategy in Afghanistan, we must ask, "Did the Surge Work?"[160] That is a more complex question than it seems since the number of variables are high, as are the number of actors. At this point, we can at least document the outcomes. Some context is necessary for a start. From 2004 to 2009, there was a 900 percent increase in security incidents across Afghanistan, and a 40-fold increase in suicide bombings. The conflict had spread throughout the country, but the violence was more concentrated with over 70 percent of all security incidents in 2010 taking place in only 10 percent of the country's 400 districts.[161]

This concentration of violence continued during the Surge period. Increased force levels and penetrations into Helmand Province generated resistance and higher casualty totals for friendly and coalition troops, as well as for the Taliban. The total U.S. military fatalities in Afghanistan were 317 in 2009 and spiked in 2010 to 500 killed in action (KIA) with the heavier operational tempo in the south. The 2010–2012 casualty totals reflect higher force levels directly engaging Taliban-held territory including both Helmand and Kandahar provinces.[162]

The campaign design supporting the ISAF Surge centered resources in key districts and subdistricts including Nawa, Marjah, Garmser, and Nad Ali. Before the Surge decision was reached, these districts were essentially Taliban bases with little Afghan or coalition presence. The Taliban imposed its will and judicial writ and built up its forces there and tried to rebuild. During early 2010, the deployment of coalition forces permitted the initiation of a serious and deliberate offensive to clear these districts of antigovernment elements and insurgents. The well-embedded Taliban resistance attempted to defend its strongholds and caches of supplies.

A dramatic turnaround like in Iraq may have been hoped for. Certainly, the significant impact obtained in Iraq back in 2007 raised expectations. Nothing of the sort occurred, but clear progress was made. The Taliban withdrew where it was directly confronted, and its momentum was checked. While the change in the level of violence is not as dramatic as in Iraq, the Taliban's influence waned, and ISAF efforts provided a breathing space for the Afghan government to build up institutional capacity.

The Taliban's coercive impact steadily declined in Helmand and Kandahar. After some tough battles in Helmand, some clear results could be discerned in the physical security domain. By May 2011, the Marines in Nawa had gone more than 12 months without a serious battle. The force in Nad Ali reported an 85 percent reduction in incidents by June 2010. Garmser, long a hot spot, had been tamed, with security attacks falling by 90 percent in the spring of 2011. Taliban attacks in Marja dropped by half, from almost 1,600 in 2011 to 782 in 2012. More than security improvements were noted. By early 2012, bazaars and shops had reopened with new wares to sell. Even in places where U.S. forces had withdrawn, violence levels decreased. To be sure, the Taliban had not been entirely defeated, but its efforts had been checked, and time for security force development and government reforms had been gained.

Violence ultimately fell dramatically in cleared areas. Of the coalition's nearly 3,500 KIA, almost half (1,505) occurred in just two provinces, Helmand and Kandahar.[163] In table 3, the human costs for the United States leading up to and subsequent to the Surge period are depicted. U.S. fatalities had doubled in 2009 while U.S. policy and strategy were being reassessed. The arrival of the Marines at the end of 2009 and the steady flow of other U.S. forces in 2010 eventually expanded ISAF capacity to thwart Taliban intrusions and to conduct clearing operations. In addition to American losses, coalition fatalities doubled from 2006 to the 3 years of escalated activity, from 54 KIA in 2006 to roughly 100 a year from 2009–2011.[164]

The same trend holds for indigenous security forces as well. As noted in table 4, the number of Afghan army/police fatality totals doubled from 2009 to 2011, and doubled again in 2012 as Afghan forces rapidly expanded capabilities and became more engaged.

While American and ISAF casualty totals are a common metric, we must also evaluate Afghanistan's losses. Here a different story emerges, which shows a steady total of Afghan civilians killed and wounded. This statistic appears to reflect the Taliban's deliberate shift to avoid well-prepared ISAF troops and to concentrate on attacking softer targets and the local population. Figure 3 depicts both killed/wounded civilian totals from 2009–2013.[165]

Table 3. U.S. Military Casualties by Year Through 2012

Year	U.S. Killed in Action	U.S. Wounded in Action
2001	11	22
2002	49	74
2003	45	99
2004	52	217
2005	98	268
2006	99	403
2007	117	748
2008	155	795
2009	311	2,144
2010	499	5,247
2011	414	5,204
2012	310	2,877

Source: Susan G. Chesser, *Afghanistan Casualties: Military Forces and Civilians,* R41084 (Washington, DC: Congressional Research Service, December 6, 2012); <http://icasualties.org/OEF/index.aspx>.

Table 4. Afghan National Army/Afghan National Police Fatalities, 2007–2012

	2007	2008	2009	2010	2011	2012
Army	209	226	282	519	550	1,200
Police	803	880	646	961	1,400	2,200
	1,012	1,106	928	1,480	1,950	3,400

Source: Ian S. Livingstone and Michael O'Hanlon, *Afghanistan Index: Also Including Selected Data on Pakistan* (Washington, DC: The Brookings Institution, October 2014), figure 1.20, available at <www.brookings.edu/~/media/Programs/foreign%20policy/afghanistan%20index/index20141029.pdf>.

Another commonly used metric in counterinsurgency is the raw number of incidents initiated by the insurgents.[166] This is a crude measure of the outputs of the insurgency and its ability to plan/conduct attacks. It counts the number of attacks, but not their scale or lethality. Data show that the pattern of attacks mirrors the annual campaign season in Afghanistan and that the number was not necessarily reduced by the surge adaptation. The increases in 2010 as Surge forces arrived and began operations reflect increased force size and activity levels by ISAF in clearing contested areas.

Figure 3. Afghan Civilian Casualties, 2009–2013

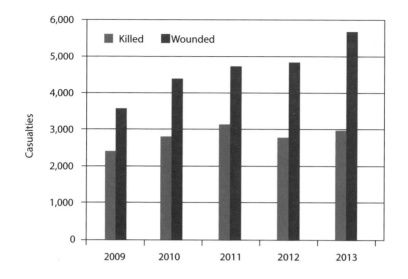

An element in the overall adaptation selected in 2009 was the increased emphasis on professionalizing the Afghanistan security forces and increasing their capabilities to deal with the Taliban.[167] Increased assistance levels and improved training resources were made available in the summer of 2010. By the fall of that year and over the past few years, there has been a measurable and clear progression in units able to be either independent of coalition assistance or effective with simply advisors.[168] Table 5 depicts these performance levels over time.[169]

Troop levels, incident rates, and casualties are only a crude measure of inputs and effort on the security front. As a limited counterinsurgency-based strategy, other lines of effort must also be assessed. There were dramatic results obtained in the developmental and economic portions of the strategy, too. The "other war" was not neglected.[170] A number of nonmilitary achievements include:

- Over 715 kilometers (km) of the Kabul to Kandahar to Herat Highway were reconstructed, and another nearly 3,000 km of paved and gravel roads were laid.
- Almost 700 clinics or health facilities were constructed or refurbished, and over 10,000 health workers were trained with over $6 million of pharmaceuticals distributed.

Table 5. Assessed Capability Levels of Afghan National Army, 2010–2013

Rating Levels	November 2010	April 2011	August 2011	December 2011	October 2012	March 2013
Independent with advisors	0	1	1	7	20	35
Effective with advisors	47	56	60	68	72	99
Effective with partners	35	55	56	63	22	16
Developing	46	32	22	16	7	10
Awaiting fielding	18	13	19	10	25	6

- 670 schools were constructed or refurbished and staffed with 65,000 teachers trained in modern teaching methods, and some 60 million textbooks were printed and distributed nationwide.
- School enrollment was 600 percent higher than before 2002, and between 33 and 40 percent of the students in Afghanistan are female. Some 11.5 million children are attending school across the country, more than 10 times the number in 2001. Of those 11.5 million students, 4.7 million are female.
- Almost 500,000 hectares of land received improved irrigation.
- Some 30 million head of livestock were vaccinated/treated.
- Over 28,000 loans were made to small businesses, 75 percent to women.
- Over 500 Provincial Reconstruction Team quick impact projects were completed.[171]

Not all of these improvements are tied to the additional resources the President authorized, but they do demonstrate the substantial achievements beyond security. In 2002, only 6 percent of Afghans had access to reliable electricity. Roughly 28 percent of the population has access to reliable electricity, including more than 2 million people in Kabul.[172] Less than 10 percent of the country had access to rudimentary health care when the war started, and by

2009, North Atlantic Treaty Organization (NATO) officials claimed this number had increased to 65 percent.[173] Afghanistan's infant mortality rate was cut by 25 percent. Schools are staffed by more than 180,000 teachers trained to Afghan standards, and more than 52,000 candidates enrolled in Afghan teacher training programs.[174] These education programs are limited, with many teachers unqualified by U.S. standards.[175]

Key performance parameters for other major objectives should also be factored in, including improving the quality of national and provincial governance, decreasing levels of corruption, and decreasing Pakistan's negative influence inside Afghanistan. Quantitative data for these objectives are not evident, but most interviewees believe progress has been made. Progress on the corruption front, however, has been limited. A September 2013 report from the U.S. Special Inspector General for Afghan Reconstruction claimed the United States has no discernable plan to fight corruption in Afghanistan, following more than a decade of American involvement.[176]

All in all, one could question whether the progress made to date is sustainable given Afghanistan's limited overall capacity of government, its limited economy, and the capacity of the Afghan National Security Forces. Reports today, years after the 2010 troop increase and resulting influx of attention, now depict greater violence or increased Taliban threats against civilians.[177] Yet the Afghan National Army (ANA) is still fighting and gaining competence despite high losses. There is little doubt of the Surge's impact on reversing the Taliban's momentum in 2010 or how the new strategy bolstered ANA competence and confidence.[178] Whether it can sustain this capability over time remains to be seen.

Overall, the campaign was similar to Iraq in that the military component delivered what it was designed to do. It bought space and time required for institutional development of a weak state and fragile leadership. It was not strategically effective in that the Karzai government struggled to enhance its capacity or minimize the perception of its corruption. The strategy was sound in design but was dependent on both U.S. civilian capacity that proved insufficient and changes from the Karzai leadership that were always problematic at best. In this respect, Ambassador Eikenberry may have been proved correct.

Evaluating Assessment and Adaptation

This analytical effort now turns to the evaluation phase. This is not a comparative analysis between two administrations.[179] The strategic context and personalities and timing of these two different cases varied in many ways. What we hope to identify here are common themes and issues attendant to strategic assessments and strategic adaptations. We again apply our analytical framework of the five assessment/adaptation decision factors to guide the evaluation.

Iraq

Performance Assessment Mechanisms. Assessments were widespread on Iraq long before the Surge decision was made in December 2006. Assessments began almost immediately after the bombing of the mosque in Samarra on February 22, when General Casey asked what civil war would look like and considered convening another Baghdad-based Red Cell to take a look at the question.[180] Khalilzad and Casey formed the Joint Strategic Planning and Assessments cell in February 2006.[181] Casey continued to ask the right questions throughout the summer of 2006.[182] By the fall of 2006, when it became obvious that efforts in Iraq were failing, the National Security Council, Congress, and the Chairman of the Joint Chiefs of Staff all developed their own analytic groups to assess the situation in Iraq.

Collaborative Information-sharing Environment. The main obstacle to a government-wide reassessment seems to have been Secretary Rumsfeld, who refused to approve a formal effort.[183] As such, groups such as the NSC performed private assessments. This slowed interagency communications but did not prevent them as Interagency Working Groups, deputies' committees, and principals' committee meetings all continued on their regular schedules. Communications between Washington and Iraq were constant. The MNF-I chronology refers to a constant series[184] of secure video teleconferences between MNF-I and the NSC, the Secretary of Defense, and the President. Casey also returned to Washington periodically to render reports to Congress and the Secretary of Defense. Communications within Iraq were also robust, with Casey meeting regularly with his senior officers as well as visiting all of his units deployed throughout Iraq.

Strategic Coordination. The NSC had already been deeply involved in Iraq decisionmaking before the events of 2006. In her role as National Security

Advisor, Condoleezza Rice produced the initial *National Strategy for Victory in Iraq* in 2003 and produced an updated version in 2005. The NSC knew that the wheels were coming off in Iraq in early 2006,[185] but felt bureaucratically blocked from performing a full-scale reassessment. The NSC eventually produced one of the several assessments of the situation in Iraq in late 2006. To participants on the NSC staff, the interagency coordination system performed well; they "argued their view [strongly], they interacted directly with the President, their needs were addressed, and at the end of the day they came on-board."[186] In terms of strategic coordination, the Bush Surge can be seen as a thoroughly structured decision process with intense Presidential engagement.[187]

The Surge decision in Iraq was no less controversial inside the Bush administration, and the President was personally engaged in the formulation of the policy and details behind the strategy. While the President had a strong instinct on where he wanted to go in terms of the Surge, his Cabinet was much more divided. The NSC had done estimates on troop requirements, and numerous staff members favored the Surge. The National Security Advisor worked to ensure the President's staff gave him all the options, not only what they thought he wanted or what the Defense Department would support.[188]

President Bush wanted his team to be on board, but key NSC members were reluctant. The Vice President, Secretary of Defense, and Secretary of State were not completely sure that they agreed with the President's decision. There were senior-level inputs from Defense and State that argued Iraq was essentially a civil war that was best to be avoided.[189] As noted earlier, the combatant and theater commanders were against the Surge, as were the Chairman and the Joint Chiefs.

Decision Authorization Clarity. In 2006, Iraq decisionmaking was understood, but more than one actor was making strategic decisions. Specifically, Secretary Rumsfeld ran the war while President Bush gave strategic guidance. His guidance was direct but did not necessarily shape the way the war was being prosecuted. As an example, on his June 14, 2006, visit to Iraq, President Bush, after receiving a briefing, stated, "[W]e have to win."[190] This was clear guidance but not detailed enough to shape how the war was being fought. Secretary Rumsfeld, on the other hand, was asking questions such as "How many [Iraqi security forces (ISF)] are there really? How many did the Iraqis really need? Did we have an effective methodology for tracking their development?

How was the ISF development effort integrated into the overall strategy?"[191] President Bush was not the sole decisionmaker until after the November 2006 elections, when he said of his nomination of Robert Gates as Defense Secretary, "He'll provide the department with a fresh perspective and new ideas on how America can achieve our goals in Iraq."[192] President Bush took charge of Iraq decisionmaking and was clearly the sole decider about the future of Iraq between mid-November 2006 and the Surge announcement on January 7, 2007.

Strategic Coherence. The various military adaptations in Iraq in 2006 clearly failed to dampen insurgent violence.[193] Political influence was even less successful. Although Ambassador Khalilzad sought to influence Iraqi decisionmaking in 2006, he failed, as seen by the length of time it took to form a new government, a lack of national reconciliation efforts by the new government, and a lack of cooperation on the part of Prime Minister Maliki, who did not allow targeting of Shiite groups until December 2006. The new approach announced in January 2007 was a logical and comprehensive whole-of-government approach, although the public face of the Surge was a larger U.S. military force required to reduce the high levels of violence, which would allow the political and economic efforts to succeed. Additionally, even though the emerging Awakening in Anbar Province was not widely understood at the time, it was consistent with the logic of the Surge decision, including increased engagement, focus on population protection, and corresponding levels of political and economic cooperation. The Surge was executed over the next year and a half and continued to adapt. It did succeed in buying time for a political solution in Iraq.

Afghanistan

Performance Assessment Mechanisms. State-of-the-art operational assessment leaves much to be desired, and there is little reason to believe that strategic assessment is any better. Multiple assessments by RAND, NATO Allies, and Service schools have concluded that complex collection systems used in Afghanistan did not meet the needs of policy or military decisionmakers. One group of scholars argues that "assessments often proceed from flawed assumptions with little real-world evidence. The varied cast of agencies performing assessments can at once be criticized for being too complex in their methodology and too simplistic in their analysis. This has resulted in understandable disenchantment with the assessments process."[194] As noted by another study on deficiencies in operational assessments:

> *The disconnect between counterinsurgency theory and the assessments process that had plagued operations assessment in Vietnam re-emerged and the result has been equally frustrating. The promise of technological advancement and the effects-based framework to help make sense of the vast amount of data coming from both theaters has fallen short. Once again, the pitfalls in trying to quantify complex dynamics has [sic] made the production of accurate and useful assessments a persistently elusive aim.*[195]

In particular, these analyses question the transparency and credibility of the operational assessments. One scholar concluded, "The flaws in the currently used approaches are sufficiently egregious that professional military judgment on assessments is, rightfully, distrusted."[196] The challenges in Afghanistan were the complexity of the counterinsurgency effort and complications of a large coalition. An extensive effort was put into data collection, but it was focused on operational and tactical data and was difficult to raise to strategic audiences. The ingrained optimism of the U.S. military may be an additional complicating factor.[197]

In Afghanistan, General McChrystal knew the critical important of assessment and indicators at both levels of war and for different audiences. He specifically understood that ISAF needed to identify and refine appropriate indicators to assess progress, clarifying the difference between operational measures of effectiveness critical to practitioners on the ground and strategic measures more appropriate to national capitals.[198] Both strategic and operational assessments in Afghanistan were clouded by uncertainty over the mission. In the presence of confusion over policy aims and strategy, the component agencies tended to define their contributions and metrics in terms of inputs or traditional tasks.[199]

McChrystal's strategic review, augmented by volunteer scholars, is an exception that warrants more study. That report proved to be a truly strategic assessment, even if its orientation focused narrowly on defining the requirements for a fully resourced counterinsurgency effort. It answered the presumed question about defeating the Taliban to succeed in Afghanistan as opposed to clear delineation of national interests, policy, and options. While the ISAF review proved quite impressive, it lacked a broad enough charter and representation to be the basis for subsequent NSC deliberations. Further study is warranted to determine if future theater commands should be tasked to undertake such strategic assessments given their priorities and largely military structure.

Collaborative Information-sharing Environment. In this portion of the Afghanistan case study, we found limitations stemming from Pentagon practices in framing options and a desire by DOD and the Joint Staff to unite behind the theater command's assessment and strategy rather than explore different missions and different strategies. The President's desire for disciplined debate, his request for options, and his explicit discomfort with early portions of the debate suggest that information-sharing was limited. The President's reaching out to his staff and to the Vice Chairman to gain additional insights and to push for more constrained options suggest that this component of the process was not fully satisfied.

Additionally, there is considerable agreement among participants that the candor and trust levels were corrupted early in the process and negatively impacted the decisionmaking process. On several occasions, speeches, leaks, and comments to the media or Congress inadvertently created the impression that the military was maneuvering the President into a box.[200] Civil-military relations are abetted by an open and professional tenor, which results in quality discourse and sound policy decisions and strategies.[201] This discourse is best achieved in a climate of trust and candor, but this decision process was colored by a lack of trust.

Strategic Coordination. In the case of Afghanistan initially, the NSC was not aware of confusion over the mission, resource gaps, or inconsistent objectives. However, with the personal involvement and pushing of the President, discrete policy options were developed and debated. Ultimately, again with the deliberate engagement of the President, a consensus between competing factions on both the aim and ways of a strategy were hashed out.

If there were weak spots in the Surge adaptation, the new approach did not create additional political leverage and conditionality for Karzai to reform his government and mitigate levels of corruption and incompetence. There is little doubt that security would be enhanced and that additional time could be gained by slowing and reversing Taliban momentum. This injection of additional forces could lead to a reconsideration by Taliban leaders that the United States was increasingly committed to securing its interests, which could lead to mutually beneficial negotiations within Afghanistan. Furthermore, the NSC decision did not assess and resolve the viability of the Afghan security forces to meet their recruiting goals and minimum effectiveness within the resources and timelines framed by the President. Creating sustainable Afghan National Security Forces would clearly be a longer term but relevant issue if U.S. security interests were to be served. Finally, the State Department's contributions were long on promise and short on delivery. Both the strategic assessment and oversight should have tested State's capacity to actually support the plan. Because of these nonmilitary elements, the strategic coordination phase was deliberate and robust but less than fully satisfactory.

Decision Authorization Clarity. There appears little doubt that the President was fully immersed and invested in the final strategic decisions in 2009. However, the six-page strategic memorandum President Obama purportedly authored contained contradictions. The President apparently intended that the lesson of unclear objectives from Vietnam would not be repeated, based on a reading of Gordon Goldstein's *Lessons in Disaster*.[202] While intended to reduce ambiguity and reflect his commitment to the decision, the President's strategic guidance evidences distinct tensions between the diagnosis of the problems in Afghanistan and a limited allocation of resources and time.

Clarity was augmented by the discourse of the principals and the President's direct question to each to expressly assent to the final strategy. The ISAF commander may have had some questions from the inauguration through late November as to what the new administration really wanted to achieve in Afghanistan. That doubt or ambiguity was clarified during the Surge debate. Our reading of the November 29 memo reinforces the clarity of the commander's intent. The U.S. goal in Afghanistan was "to deny safe haven to al Qaeda and to deny the Taliban the ability to overthrow the Afghan government." The military mission was defined in six operational objectives, which were to be "limited in scope and scale to only what is necessary to attain the U.S. goal."[203] In case there was any question, the President's memo noted, "*This approach is not fully resourced counterinsurgency or nation building.*"[204] But at the same time, the President articulated numerous military and civilian tasks at the operational level that are fully consistent with a broad counterinsurgency approach. The guidance instructs the military to reverse the Taliban's momentum, deny it access to and control of key population centers and lines of communication, disrupt the insurgency and its al Qaeda allies, and degrade their capability to the point where Afghan National Security Forces could manage the threat. There is little doubt that the President reshaped the mission's scale, authorized resources for specific purposes, and introduced a temporal dimension framing a faster introduction of U.S. forces—and a planned assessment and withdrawal. But while he narrowed the mission, he authorized a substantial force to accomplish many challenging tasks in a tighter timeframe. Moreover, the tighter timeframe was belatedly introduced into the debate. Overall, we judge this element of the framework as only partially satisfied.

Strategic Coherence. The adaptations proposed by the Obama administration in 2009 sought to better align U.S. strategy with policy aims, but ended up focusing almost entirely on the military means—the size and duration of the Surge—rather than the possible ways. Despite references to the centrality of Afghan politics and governance throughout the strategy review, there is little evidence that alternative political strategies were considered.

As Secretary Gates noted, the concept of an efficient, corruption free, effective Afghan central government was "a fantasy."[205] By 2009 there was growing recognition that the highly centralized power structure of the Afghan government created through the 2001 Bonn Agreement and 2004 constitution was resented and becoming untenable.[206] While McChrystal's staff was cognizant of the need for a bottom-up approach to complement efforts to build the capacity of the central government, neither the 2009 campaign plan nor the White House–led review process generated alternative political strategies to induce Kabul to devolve power, or bypass it by delivering U.S. assistance directly to subnational governments.[207] Despite a rhetorical nod to "working with the Karzai government when we can, working around him when we must," U.S. strategy remained dependent on the willingness of the Afghan government to implement reforms that involved reducing control and ceding power to rivals. As in most counterinsurgencies, the central government proved reluctant to do so, and the Obama administration did not integrate efforts to compel Kabul's cooperation or bypass it in pursuit of U.S. policy goals.[208]

The Surge decision better defined U.S. core interests, policy, and plans. Were that the total criteria, we would judge the strategy review a success. However, the decision was promulgated as both a Surge of military and nonmilitary resources and a defined time limit. This had some utility in that a sense of urgency was not only put in the deployment of troops, but it also generated the perception of limited U.S. commitment to success in Afghanistan. This signaled to both our allies and regional powers that American patience was waning and could be outlasted. This may have been necessary to satisfy domestic politics, but there is an argument that this did not contribute to success. Moreover, the civilian and political components of the Surge were not as integrated into the final strategy, leaving it less coherent in implementation.

Insights

Performance Assessment Mechanisms. Assessments in Afghanistan proved more problematic due to that campaign's dynamics, producing numerous recommendations for innovative solutions.[209] Assessment in both campaigns was complex and evolutionary in development. NATO produced a major evaluation of the transparency and credibility of assessment methods:

> *Like Vietnam, both Operation Iraqi Freedom and Operation Enduring Freedom . . . have been relatively ill-defined campaigns with shifting strategic end state objectives. In both of these campaigns, senior leaders across the various coalition nations demanded reams of quantitative data from their operational commanders which, in some cases, may have been an attempt to compensate for a lack of operational and strategic clarity and the inability to discern meaningful progress over time.[210]*

That study reports that at one time a regional command in Afghanistan demanded that subordinate units collect and report some 400 different metrics. A senior assessment officer in Kabul estimated that there were more than 2,000 mandatory reportable quantitative metrics leveraged on subordinate units across the theater in 2011.[211] In Iraq, General Casey understood the need to measure progress at the strategic level. He also faced the discrepancy between analysis and public opinion:

> *Going into Iraq, we made a conscious decision not to use enemy casual-*
> *ties—body count—to measure strategic progress. I believe that was the*
> *right decision, but the unintended consequence was that our casualties*
> *were reported and the enemy's were not. It appeared to some domestic*
> *audiences that the enemy had the upper hand—which was not at all*
> *true. Over time, I began selectively reporting enemy losses to give a more*
> *balanced picture of the situation to our home audiences.*[212]

Impatience in Washington influenced assessment mechanisms, accord-ing to a theater commander. General Casey has recounted that when looking at ways to measure progress at the strategic level, he sought to demonstrate steady progress toward an ultimate endstate. But "as these major events took months and even years to accomplish, I found that they did not compete with the daily reports of casualties and violence as a means of expressing our prog-ress." Over time and by virtue of the media's focus on visceral imagery and vi-olence levels, "casualties and violence became the de facto measure of strategic progress in Iraq, and *I should have forced a more in-depth discussion with my civilian leadership about their strategic expectations.*"[213]

Continuous monitoring of strategy implementation is part of the portfo-lio of the NSC, OSD, and Joint Staff (as well as any other agencies involved in the conflict). Periodic reassessment is important and necessary for the suc-cessful prosecution of an extended conflict and should include a total relook of everything that went into strategy development, including intelligence and assumptions. Optimistic progress reports should also be examined rigorously. Reassessments must be brutally objective and consider external and diverse viewpoints (including those of coalition partners).

New facts and a reassessment should have produced a strategy read-justment for Iraq by mid-2006 when everyone in Washington knew that the wheels were coming off in the country. A lack of mechanisms for routine mon-itoring, and a lack of cooperation by the Secretary of Defense, prevented the needed reassessment. The NSC and the deputy's committee should routinely develop those mechanisms rather than depend on ad hoc taskings. Oversight and continuous evaluation must become more routine but not tie up valuable executive time in tactical matters.

The Joint Staff evolved its structures to support operations and also provided resources to staff the NSC as needed. Unique assessment models (that is, the council of colonels or the ISAF review team) were also employed to stimulate strategic evaluation of ongoing wars. Further options for planning cells or boards should be considered to stimulate the sustained capacity to operationalize and continuously adapt ongoing U.S. strategies, and these structural options should examine representation beyond just military resources.[214] Given the importance of this element to initiating adaptation, a detailed study on assessments should be commissioned.[215]

Collaborative Information-Sharing Environment. Our understanding of Iraq and Afghanistan was profoundly thin and unbalanced. Strategy is driven by and serves politics, and military operations take place in the political environment of the state in which an intervention takes place. *Understanding the strategic context of an intervention* is the first fundamental requirement of policy formulation.[216] Based on numerous crisis management situations, the importance of a deeply grounded understanding of the sociopolitical complexities and cultural awareness in an operational area cannot be overlooked in policy and strategy development.[217]

Given the complex nature of contemporary conflict, integrated strategy development and assessment processes are necessary. This includes civilian-military integration within the U.S. Government as well as allies, partners, and nonmilitary and multinational partners. The tenor of deliberation, candor, and transparency should focus on maximizing the value of policy/strategic assessments in reviews. These processes should focus on providing decisionmakers with coherent options that consistently align ends, ways, and means and identify rather than obscure assumptions and risks.

It is important for senior military leaders to understand the decisionmaking process and to participate in that process fully. American history contains examples of problems in meshing civilian and military perspectives.[218] As General Casey noted, "Civil-military interaction around matters of policy and strategy is inherently challenging. The issues are complex, the stakes are high, and the backgrounds of the people involved can vary widely."[219]

Underlying the discourse in policymaking is a degree of mutual respect and understanding between civilian and military leaders, and the exchange of candid views and perspectives in the decisionmaking process. Senior joint leaders must strive to sustain a professional relationship with civilian policy-makers and avoid appearances of going around or trying to negate Presidential decisions. The absence of actual friction inside policy debates would be suspect, but it should never be publicly evident, at least from military professionals.[220]

The experience of the past 14 years suggests that effective civilian and military interaction is (and always has been) critical to the framing of real-istic policy objectives and effective strategy.[221] Senior military leaders should understand how decisions are made, and it is important for senior-most offi-cers to develop relationships with other agencies and officials. Military leaders should not expect this process to comport with military planning steps follow-ing a linear progress or flow diagram, and they should not expect the process to be without friction. The existing NSC system has inherent tensions built into it, which make it uncomfortable but productive. The diverse cultures of the NSC create friction and promote better decisions than a top-driven model that ignores different perspectives. Instead of fighting the process or trying to impose a military framework on civilian politicians, military leaders should understand the process and "embrace it."[222] DOD's education programs should be adapted to better prepare officers to accept that reality and work in a more iterative way rather than expect the current school model of progressive and deductive reasoning.[223] Colin Gray's metaphor of the "strategy bridge" may be an appropriate way of thinking about the "traffic" of options and assessments between policy and operational details.[224]

Senior military leaders should understand that influence and trust go to-gether and that just as networking and developing relationships with peers are important to professional success, the same relationship-building will pay dividends with civilian political leaders in terms of access, understanding, and trust.[225]

Strategic Coordination. Since the projected future operating environ-ment involves extensive interactions with interagency, coalition, and host-na-tion partners, coordinating the development of strategy and implementation among this disparate group of actors will have even greater salience. During reassessment, as during strategy development, senior military leaders should be prepared to challenge assumptions and vague policy aims, as well as offer creative options (ways) to satisfy desired ends.

A President and his policy team need options. These should include a full range of credible options, not just the preferred solution. Options not wholly acceptable or valid for military reasons may still be viable to policymakers and should be incorporated even when they are not preferred or not supported. If the President does not believe in the validity of options provided by the military, he will get them elsewhere. The military did not give President Bush a range of options for Iraq in 2006 until he insisted on their development, nor did they give President Obama a range of options for Afghanistan in 2009. The military must give the President views and options as well as pros and cons, but must also give him options because, at the end of the day, he is *the* accountable decisionmaker. As General Martin Dempsey observed, "That's what being Commander in Chief is all about."[226] A failure to provide more than a single solution will cede the initiative to the NSC staff or other outlets.

Since war should be approached holistically, strategic reassessments and adaptations require a whole-of-government and a whole-of-coalition approach. This is particularly true in periods in which the United States is engaged in longer term state-building projects where all instruments of national power are being employed at the operational and tactical levels. Effective strategy incorporates more than physical effects and application of military power. As such, senior military leaders need to be able to participate in and shape strategy discussions involving the use of all elements of national power, not just military strategy.[227]

Senior military leaders must be prepared to serve as the principal strategists in these assessments, ensuring a coherent linkage between desired policy objectives and the art of the possible. Policymakers are not generally school-trained in the military decisionmaking process or educated to follow linear planning processes. Instead, they are inclined to search iteratively for general options and reverse-engineer specific objectives. The military is trained to do exactly the opposite. This complicates the strategic conversation that must occur in two directions. Military leaders and their strategy cells must be able to clearly explain the tie between military actions and political objectives (explanation "up") while providing subordinate staffs with guidance to ensure that military actions support political objectives (guidance "down").

Military leaders should not expect clear, linear processing as taught in senior schools, according to General Mattis. An important insight for senior policy advisors is to understand how decisions are made and how information is processed and evaluated in the policy/strategy process. Policymakers are not hardwired for lockstep templates or well prepared to execute a military-style decisionmaking process out of joint doctrine. Most NSC staff officials will not be graduates of joint professional military education programs. Civilian political officials will often explore an array of options without defining a firm political endstate. They may be more comfortable exploring the art of the possible and examining political factors and risks differently. They may be more comfortable with ambiguity, political elements, and other intangibles. While embracing the fluid and iterative nature of policy and strategy formulation, some tense interaction should be expected in keeping a coherent strategy together, especially during the discourse tied to potential changes in strategy that is inherent to both assessment and adaptation.

It is important for senior military leaders to learn how to work within that culture/system and not fight it.[228] As former Chairman Mike Mullen noted:

> *Policy and strategy should constantly struggle with one another. Some in the military no doubt would prefer political leadership that lays out a specific strategy and then gets out of the way, leaving the balance of the implementation to commanders in the field. But the experience of the last nine years tells us two things: A clear strategy for military operations is essential; and that strategy will have to change as those operations evolve.*[229]

There is a role for actors outside the formal planning regime in the formulation and refinement of strategy. The Iraq Study Group and external inputs from think tanks and individuals such as General Keane, Eliot Cohen, and Stephen Biddle are examples. Senior joint leaders may want to prevent sources and options from reaching the President, but in doing so they may not serve the policy community well and could lose initiative and influence in the process.

Coalitions are notoriously difficult to manage but are superior to the alternative of fighting alone. Timely coalition inputs into any assessment process are better than selling a strategic shift after the decision to do so. This may be more important during strategic reassessments than in initial interventions due to the political impacts among international partners when we are considering changing course and speed. According to Admiral James G. Stavridis, USN (Ret.), former Supreme Allied Commander, Europe, and now the dean of the Fletcher School at Tufts University, the valuable experience that U.S. policy and military leaders acquired in coalition-building and coalition management should be captured and incorporated into leadership development programs.

Strategic Coherence. At the national level, policies and strategy are inseparable. National strategies must focus on achieving national (and therefore political) objectives. Because war is a political act, military strategies have to be embedded in and supportive of overall national strategies. The latter must address the use of all elements of national power, must be coherent, and must have a strategic logic that links the various parts of the U.S. Government into a whole-of-government approach. Americans expect their senior officers to be articulate in if not expert at these grand strategies, not only military strategy.[230] Civilian officials expect inputs from military leaders to be truly expert in their appropriate "lane" about the application of military force, but they also prize advice from senior officials who understand how the different components of U.S. power are best applied *coherently.*[231]

In the recent past, the development and conduct of U.S. strategy have lacked a common understanding and appreciation for strategy among the Nation's leaders. Policy guidance should be specific enough to drive theater/campaign plans and be clearly linked to larger national interests and regional concerns—and reflect an appreciation for logic, costs, and risks. Senior military leaders must often prepare to serve as the principal strategist in these assessments, ensuring a coherent linkage between policy "desires" (that is, objectives) and the art of the possible. Policymakers want options, but these need to be real options: they must be feasible and suitable, not merely expedient.[232]

There are claims that U.S. strategic adaptations ignored the political side of the Surge. We do not concur with that assertion but did find policy discussions too often focused on the familiar military component (force levels, deployment timelines, and so forth) and too little on the larger challenge of state-building and host-nation capacity. In 2006, MNF-I formed a Red Cell, while MNF-I and U.S. Embassy Baghdad formed the Joint Strategic Plans and Assessments Cell, which produced combined joint campaign plans. Civil-military interactions by U.S. leaders in Iraq with Maliki were intense, with both civilian and military leaders meeting Maliki together to send the message that the two sides sought the same results.[233] The political strategy to influence Karzai was less effective, but in both cases the political component of the overall strategic shift was recognized and incorporated into U.S. policy decisions. Execution and capacity shortfalls in nonmilitary aspects of both surges were evident. Politics and governance at the micro level appear to increasingly have an influence on policy and strategy from the bottom up.[234] If true, leadership development in military education should account for this.

Complex and wicked problems created by U.S. involvement in Iraq and Afghanistan require comprehensive and integrated solutions from the strategy toolkit. Both strategically and now operationally, we can expect to employ multiple tools in a synergistic manner. As Admiral Mullen observed, "Defense and diplomacy are simply no longer discrete choices, one to be applied when the other one fails, but must, in fact, complement one another throughout the messy process of international relations."[235] Because all the elements of national power must be brought to bear simultaneously to achieve national political objectives, "in the future struggles of the asymmetric counterinsurgent variety, we ought to make it a precondition of committing our troops, that we will do so only if and when the other instruments of national power are ready to engage as well."[236]

During the conduct of both these adaptation cycles, there was an overemphasis on military issues and insufficient focus on governance, economic, and information lines of efforts. The military got well ahead of the other instruments of power. Military leaders at all levels must be completely frank about the limits of what military power can achieve, with what degree of risk, and in what timeframe.[237] They should also ensure that required supporting components are in place to ensure that military resources are not being risked without commensurate support from other agencies.

Conclusion

As this chapter's epigraph notes, war is an audit of how well states have formulated policies and strategies, and how well prepared their armed forces and other tools are. Indeed, we go to war with the army we have and with an initial strategy. But we rarely win wars with the same force or the same strategy. Wars also require leaders to assess progress, recognize shortfalls, and resolve gaps in strategy or operational method as the conflict evolves. This assessment and adaptation function is often overlooked. As one historian concluded, "Over the course of the past century and a half, adaptation in one form or another has been a characteristic of successful military institutions and human societies under the pressures of war." Yet he notes, often "leaders attempt to impose prewar conceptions on the war they are fighting, rather than adapt their assumptions to reality."[238]

The same needs to be said for the highest level of government, and the nexus of policy and strategy. Prewar conceptions of the conflicts in Iraq and Afghanistan were eventually reassessed, and strategies and instruments were adapted to reflect reality on the ground and changed circumstances. The past 14 years suggest that the framing of policy and implementation of a coherent strategy remain challenges for the U.S. policymaking community. The conduct of two wars has been impressive in many respects, particularly the adaptations needed to conduct counterinsurgency and the contributions of the all-volunteer force in a protracted conflict. At the same time, the U.S. Government has revealed weaknesses in understanding the strategic context that it was operating in—and with initial policy and strategy development. The assessment and adaptation processes captured in this chapter reflect belated recognition that the United States was losing in both conflicts and that adapted responses were required.

The insights gleaned from these two cases suggest common themes for consideration. The development, implementation, and reshaping of policy and strategy remain worthy of detailed historical analyses and greater study. This chapter also concludes that we still have room for improvement in bridging the policy/strategy discourse that abets initial strategy development and its subsequent adaptation when unanticipated environmental conditions emerge. Ultimately, the Nation's best interests are served when strategy decisions are the product of a rigorous system in which civilian policymakers have options and are informed about risks.[239] Thorough examination of a full range of feasible options is required in such reviews. The interplay of political factors, including coalition and domestic politics, must also be incorporated. Moreover, civil-military relations are an important professional ethic and part of the educational process for both civilian and military leaders.[240] The capacity to oversee implementation, conduct assessments of progress, and alter strategy under fire during wartime is a clear contributor to strategic success. The case studies suggest also that institutionalizing these capacities at the strategic level would be valuable.

Future leaders should draw upon these cases to enhance their understanding of strategic decisionmaking and the assessment/adaptation processes inherent to national security. There is little reason to believe that strategic success in the future would not depend on the same qualities that generated successful strategy and adaptation in the past—proactive rather than reactive choices, flexibility over rigidity, and disciplined consistency instead of improvisation in applying force in the pursuit of political goals.[241]

Notes

[1] Victor Davis Hanson, *The Father of Us All: War and History* (New York: Bloomsbury, 2010), 123–124.

[2] Dan Caldwell, *Vortex of Conflict: U.S. Policy Toward Afghanistan, Pakistan, and Iraq* (Stanford: Stanford University Press, 2011), 262–263.

[3] On operational adaptations, see Richard H. Schultz, *The Marines Take Anbar: The Four-Year Fight Against Al Qaeda* (Annapolis, MD: Naval Institute Press, 2013); James Russell, *Innovation, Transformation, and War* (Stanford: Stanford University Press, 2009); Theo Farrell, Frans Osinga, and James Russell, eds., *Military Adaptation in Afghanistan* (Stanford: Stanford University Press, 2013).

[4] U.S. Joint Chiefs of Staff, *Decade at War: Enduring Lessons from a Decade of Operations, Vol. 1* (Suffolk, VA: Center for Joint and Coalition Operational Analysis, 2012); Elizabeth Young, "Decade of War: Enduring Lessons from a Decade of Operations," *PRISM* 4, no. 2 (March 2013), 123–141.

[5] Scott S. Gartner, *Strategic Assessment in War* (New Haven: Yale University Press, 1997), 163.

[6] Project on National Security Reform (PNSR), *Turning Ideas into Action* (Arlington, VA: PNSR, September 2009), 101–104.

[7] For a distillation of National Security Council (NSC) process challenges, see PNSR, *Forging a New Shield* (Arlington, VA: PNSR, November 2008), 221–256.

[8] Risa A. Brooks, *Shaping Strategy, The Civil-Military Politics of Strategic Assessment* (Princeton: Princeton University Press, 2008) 34–35.

[9] We thank Dr. T.X. Hammes for this insight.

[10] John E. Mueller, "The Search for the 'Breaking Point' in Vietnam," *International Studies Quarterly* 24, no. 4 (December 1980), 497–519; Gregory A. Daddis, "The Problem of Metrics: Assessing Progress and Effectiveness in the Vietnam War," *War in History* 19, no. 1 (January 2012), 73–98.

[11] Gregory A. Daddis, *No Sure Victory: Measuring U.S. Army Effectiveness and Progress in the Vietnam War* (New York: Oxford University Press, 2011), 234.

[12] Graham Cosmas, *MACV: The Joint Command in the Years of Escalation, 1962–1967* (Washington, DC: U.S. Army Center of Military History, 2006), 295.

[13] For challenges in assessment of counterinsurgencies, see Anthony Cordesman, *The Uncertain "Metrics" of Afghanistan (and Iraq)* (Washington, DC: Center for Strategic and International Studies, May 2007); James Clancy and Chuck Crossett, "Measuring Effectiveness in Irregular Warfare," *Parameters* 37, no. 2 (Summer 2007), 88–100; Jonathan Schroden, "Measures for Security in a Counterinsurgency," *Journal of Strategic Studies* 32, no. 5 (October 2009), 715–744; Jonathan Schroden, "Why Operations Assessments Fail: It's Not Just the Metrics," *Naval War College Review* 64, no. 4 (Autumn 2011).

[14] Interview with Major General James N. Mattis, in *Al-Anbar Awakening Vol. I: American Perspectives: U.S. Marines and Counterinsurgency in Iraq, 2004–2009*, ed. Timothy S. McWilliams and Kurtis P. Wheeler (Quantico, VA: Marine Corps University Press, 2009), 38.

[15] Ben Connable, *Embracing the Fog of War: Assessment and Metrics in Counterinsurgency* (Santa Monica, CA: RAND, 2012), xxi.

[16] Jason Campbell, Michael E. O'Hanlon, and Jacob Shapiro, "How to Measure the War," *Policy Review*, no. 157 (October/November 2009), 15–30.

[17] Eliot A. Cohen and John Gooch, *Military Misfortunes: The Anatomy of Failure in War* (New York: Free Press, 1996).

[18] Ibid., 222.

[19] Allan R. Millett, Williamson Murray, and Kenneth H. Watman, "The Effectiveness of Military Organizations," in *Military Effectiveness, The First World War, Vol. 1*, ed. Allan R. Millett and Williamson Murray (Boston: Allen and Unwin, 1988), 1–30.

[20] Allan R. Millett and Williamson Murray, "Lessons of War," *The National Interest*, Winter 1988/1989.

[21] Williamson Murray, *Military Adaptation: With Fear of Change* (New York: Cambridge University Press, 2012), 29–35. Murray notes that it is crucial to examine the problems associated with adaptation at the strategic level because that is where "statesmen and military leaders have found the greatest difficulties," and where the costs for adaptation often represent too high a price.

[22] Christopher J. Lamb et al., *Human Terrain Teams: An Organizational Innovation for Sociocultural Knowledge in Irregular Warfare* (Washington, DC: Institute for World Politics Press, 2013); and Christopher J. Lamb, Matthew Schmidt, and Berit G. Fitzsimmons,

MRAPs, Irregular Warfare and Pentagon Reform, INSS Strategic Perspectives 6 (Washington, DC: NDU Press, June 2009).

[23] See Theo Farrell, "Military Adaptation in War," in *Military Adaptation in the Afghanistan War*, ed. Theo Farrell, Frans Osinga, and James Russell (Stanford: Stanford University Press, 2013).

[24] Brooks, 34–42.

[25] On NSC evolutions, see David Rothkopf, *National Insecurity: American Leadership in an Age of Fear* (New York: PublicAffairs, 2014), 148–214. On proposals to adapt the NSC, see Jack A. LeCuyer, *A National Staff for the 21st Century* (Carlisle Barracks, PA: Strategic Studies Institute, December 2012).

[26] On coherence, see F.G. Hoffman, "Grand Strategy: Fundamental Considerations," *Orbis* 58, no. 4 (Fall 2014), 479–480.

[27] L. Elaine Halchin, *The Coalition Provisional Authority (CPA): Origin, Characteristics, and Institutional Authorities*, RL32370 (Washington, DC: Congressional Research Service, updated June 6, 2005).

[28] "President Names Envoy to Iraq: Remarks by the President in Photo Opportunity After Meeting with the Secretary of Defense," May 6, 2003, available at <http://georgewbush-whitehouse.archives.gov/news/releases/2003/05/20030506-3.html>.

[29] Nora Bensahel et al., *After Saddam: Prewar Planning and the Occupation of Iraq* (Santa Monica, CA: RAND, 2006), xvii–xviii.

[30] Thomas E. Ricks, *Fiasco: The American Military Adventure in Iraq* (New York: Penguin, 2006). Chapters 8 and 9 describe in detail the descent into violence.

[31] The Ottomans and the British both sought to rule Mesopotamia through Sunni Muslims.

[32] Ahmed S. Hashim, *The Sunni Insurgency in Iraq* (Washington, DC: Middle East Institute, August 15, 2003), available at <www.middleasti.org/scholars/editorial/sunni-insurgency.iraq>.

[33] John Abizaid specifically stated that the opposition was conducting a "classical guerrilla-type campaign against us. It's low-intensity conflict, in our doctrinal terms, but it's war, however you describe it." See Department of Defense News Briefing, July 16, 2003, available at <www.defense.gov/transcripts/transcript.aspx?transcriptid=2845>. See chapter one of this volume for a broader discussion of this issue.

[34] Christopher M. Schnaubelt, "After the Fight: Interagency Operations," *Parameters* (Winter 2005–2006), 48.

[35] Sandy Cochran and Kelly Howard, comps., "Multi-National Force–Iraq Chronology Reference," November 12, 2008, 17. Manuscript in possession of author. Hereafter, MNF-I Chronology.

[36] Ibid., 29.

[37] Ibid., 35.

[38] Bradford R. Higgins, "Joint Strategic Planning in Iraq: 'Optimism is not a Plan'—Needed Changes for a Long War," in *Towards a Comprehensive Approach: Integrating Civilian and Military Concepts of Strategy*, Forum Paper 15, ed. Christopher M. Schnaubelt (Rome: NATO Defense College, March 2011), 134.

[39] Ibid., 136. This was one of the results of the comprehensive review Zalmay Khalilzad ordered in July 2005.

[40] David Petraeus had previously commanded a division in the invasion of Iraq in 2003 and directed the rebuilding of Iraqi security forces as commander of Multi-National Security Transition Command–Iraq in 2004–2005.

[41] Conrad C. Crane, "Minting COIN: Principles and Imperatives for Combating Insurgency," *Air & Space Power Journal* (Winter 2007), 5.

[42] Secretary Donald Rumsfeld was still asking whether the United States was correct in calling Iraq an insurgency as late as June 13, 2006, when he sent a "snowflake" (or Secretary of Defense action note) to General George Casey, who replied on July 8, 2006, that "'insurgency' is very much a component of the struggle" in Iraq. For Rumsfeld's "snowflake," see MNF-I Chronology, 297; for Casey's reply, see MNF-I Chronology, 303. In 2006, General James L. Jones stated, "he believed that Rumsfeld so controlled everything, even at the earliest stages, that [the Joint Chiefs of Staff] were not generating independent military advice as they had a legal obligation to do." See Bob Woodward, *State of Denial* (New York: Simon & Schuster, 2006), 470.

[43] Gian P. Gentile, "Misreading the Surge Threatens U.S. Army's Conventional Capabilities," *World Politics Review*, March 4, 2008, available at <www.worldpoliticsreview.com/articles/1715/misreading-the-surge-threatens-u-s-armys-conventional-capabilities>.

[44] Crane, 19–23.

[45] Stephen D. Biddle, "Seeing Baghdad, Thinking Saigon," *Foreign Affairs*, March/April 2006, available at <www.foreignaffairs.com/articles/iraq/2006-03-01/seeing-baghdad-thinking-saigon>.

[46] *The National Security Strategy of the United States of America* (Washington, DC: The White House, March 16, 2006), 8.

[47] Peter D. Feaver states that the review effort that produced the *National Strategy for Victory in Iraq* was more of a tactical adjustment to an overall strategy that the Bush administration believed to be fundamentally sound rather than a thoroughgoing reformulation—Iraq Strategy 1.4 or 1.5, rather than 2.0. See Feaver, "Right to Be Right: Civil-Military Relations and the Iraq Surge Decision," *International Security* 35, no. 4 (Spring 2011), 100.

[48] Bob Woodward, *The War Within* (New York: Simon & Schuster, 2008), 4.

[49] Joseph A. Christoff, *Rebuilding Iraq: More Comprehensive National Strategy Needed to Help Achieve U.S. Goals*, GAO-06-788 (Washington, DC: Government Accountability

Office, July 2006), available at <www.gao.gov/new.items/d06788.pdf>.

[50] Stephen D. Biddle, interview by Frank G. Hoffman, January 23, 2015.

[51] Peter D. Feaver, interview by G. Alexander Crowther, November 18, 2008.

[52] Dwight D. Eisenhower realized soon after he took office that "time was critical, but did not see this as a reason for making a snap judgment. He wanted to make an informed decision, which he thought would be possible only if a proper methodology was used. He decided to conduct a systematic policy exercise that would review U.S. foreign policy objectives and recommend a course of action. The exercise came to be known as Project Solarium after the room in which Eisenhower made the decision to pursue it." See Tyler Nottberg, "Solarium for Today," The Eisenhower Institute, available at <www.eisenhower-institute.org/about/living_history/solarium_for_today.dot>.

[53] Fred Barnes, "How Bush Decided on the Surge," *The Weekly Standard*, February 4, 2008, available at <www.weeklystandard.com/Content/Public/Articles/000/000/014/658dwgrn.asp>.

[54] MNF-I Chronology, 264.

[55] Ibid., 266.

[56] Ibid., 275.

[57] Ibid., 279.

[58] Institute for the Study of War, "Operation Together Forward I," available at <www.understandingwar.org/operation/operation-together-forward-i>.

[59] MNF-I Chronology, 301.

[60] Ibid., 305.

[61] Ibid., 309.

[62] Edward Wong and Damien Cave, "Iraqi Death Toll Rose Above 3,400 in July," *New York Times*, August 15, 2006.

[63] "President Bush and Prime Minister Maliki of Iraq Participate in Press Availability," The White House, July 25, 2006, available at <http://georgewbush-whitehouse.archives.gov/news/releases/2006/07/20060725.html>.

[64] Ibid.

[65] MNF-I Chronology, 319.

[66] *Iraq Study Group Report* (Washington, DC: United States Institute of Peace, December 11, 2006), 15.

[67] Al Pessin, "U.S. Acknowledges Baghdad Security Plan in Trouble," *51VOA.com*, October 19, 2006; Institute for the Study of War, "Operation Together Forward II," available at <www.understandingwar.org/operation/operation-together-forward-ii>.

[68] Feaver, interview.

[69] Feaver, "Right to be Right," 102.

[70] Ibid.

[71] Barnes, "How Bush Decided."

[72] Peter Mansoor, *Surge: My Journey with General David Petraeus and the Remaking of the Iraq War* (New Haven: Yale University Press, 2010).

[73] Bing West, *The Strongest Tribe* (New York: Bantam, 2009), 202.

[74] "Text of U.S. Security Adviser's Iraq Memo," *New York Times*, November 29, 2006, available at <www.nytimes.com/2006/11/29/world/middleeast/29mtext.html?pagewanted=all&_r=0>.

[75] Feaver, "Right to Be Right," 104.

[76] Feaver, interview; Stephen J. Hadley, interview by Joseph J. Collins and Nicholas Rostow, October 7, 2014.

[77] "Rumsfeld's Memo of Options for Iraq War," *New York Times*, November 6, 2006.

[78] The Dayton process placed various Balkan actors on an airbase in Dayton, Ohio, where the United States and other outside players assisted the actors to achieve a compromise. This would require a neutral location where leaders from all sides could discuss the situation in isolation.

[79] "Press Conference by the President," The White House, November 8, 2006, available at <www.presidency.ucsb.edu/ws/index.php?pid=24269>.

[80] Feaver, interview.

[81] Peter Mansoor points out that this was the main security conclusion of the report.

[82] *Iraq Study Group Report.*

[83] Stephen Biddle et al., "Iraq: What Now? A Foreign Affairs Roundtable," *Foreign Affairs*, December 7, 2006, available at <http://adps.foreignaffairs.com/discussions/roundtables/iraq-what-now>.

[84] Ibid.

[85] Ibid.

[86] Ibid.

[87] Ibid.

[88] Peter Baker, "U.S. Not Winning War in Iraq, Bush Says for 1st Time," *Washington Post*, December 20, 2006.

[89] Barnes, "How Bush Decided."

[90] Jack Keane and Frederick W. Kagan, "The Right Type of 'Surge,'" *Washington Post*, December 27, 2006.

[91] "President's Address to the Nation," The White House, January 10, 2007, available at <http://georgewbush-whitehouse.archives.gov/news/releases/2007/01/20070110-7.html>.

[92] See Neil Smith and Sean MacFarland, "Anbar Awakens: The Tipping Point," *Military Review*, March–April 2008; John A. McCary, "The Anbar Awakening: An Alliance of Incentives," *Washington Quarterly* 32, no. 1 (January 2009); and Michael R. Gordon and Bernard Trainor, *The Endgame* (New York: Pantheon, 2012), chapter 14; Mansoor discusses the role of Petraeus and MNF-I in helping to spread the Awakening across large portions of Iraq.

[93] "Al-Sadr Declares Ceasefire in Iraq," *The Guardian* (London), August 29, 2006, available at <www.theguardian.com/world/2007/aug/29/iraq.usa>.

[94] Perhaps the best overall source for the Surge discussion is found in John R. Ballard, David W. Lamm, and John K. Wood, *From Kabul to Baghdad and Back: The U.S. at War in Afghanistan and Iraq* (Annapolis, MD: Naval Institute Press, 2012), 214–259.

[95] Seth G. Jones, "Afghanistan's Growing Security Challenge," in *State Building, Security, and Social Change in Afghanistan*, ed. Ruth Rennie (Washington, DC: The Asia Foundation, 2008); Seth G. Jones, "The Rise of Afghanistan's Insurgency: State Failure and Jihad," *International Security* 32, no. 4 (Spring 2008), 7–40; Antonio Giustozzi, *Koran, Kalashnikov and Laptop: The Neo-Taliban Insurgency in Afghanistan* (New York: Columbia University Press, 2008).

[96] Carlotta Gall, *The Wrong Enemy: America in Afghanistan, 2001–2014* (Boston: Houghton Mifflin Harcourt, 2014), 196.

[97] Ballard, Lamm, and Wood, 214–225; Ambassador Douglas Lute, interview by Richard D. Hooker, Jr., and Joseph J. Collins, March 11, 2015.

[98] Bob Woodward, *Obama's Wars* (New York: Simon & Schuster, 2010), 88–90; Peter Baker, "How Obama Came to Plan for 'Surge' in Afghanistan," *New York Times*, December 5, 2009.

[99] "White Paper of the Interagency Policy Group's Report on U.S. Policy Toward Afghanistan and Pakistan," Washington, DC, March 27, 2009, available at <www.whitehouse.gov/assets/documents/Afghanistan-Pakistan_White_Paper.pdf>.

[100] "Remarks by the President on a New Strategy for Afghanistan and Pakistan," The White House, March 27, 2009.

[101] Ibid., 1. See also Robert M. Gates, *Duty: Memoir of a Secretary at War* (New York: Knopf, 2014).

[102] Stephen D. Biddle, "Is it Worth it? The Difficult Case for War in Afghanistan," *The American Interest* 4, no. 6 (July/August 2009), 4–11.

[103] On Richard Holbrooke's role, see Vali Nasr, *The Dispensable Nation: American Foreign Policy in Retreat* (New York: Doubleday, 2013).

[104] Author discussion with Major General Gordon Davis, USA, November 25, 2014; Biddle, interview.

[105] Matthew C. Brand, *General McChrystal's Strategic Assessment: Evaluating the Operational Environment in Afghanistan in the Summer of 2009*, Research Paper 2011-1 (Maxwell Air Force Base, AL: Air University Press, July 2011).

[106] Biddle, interview.

[107] "COMISAF Initial Assessment," August 30, 2009, 1-1-1-3, available at <www.washingtonpost.com/wp-dyn/content/article/2009/09/21/AR2009092100110.html>.

[108] Stanley A. McChrystal, *My Share of the Task: A Memoir* (New York: Portfolio, 2013), 330.

[109] Woodward, *Obama's Wars*, 175–183; McChrystal, 316–338, on the review overall, and 333–334, on the leak; Bob Woodward, "McChrystal, More Forces or 'Mission Failure,'" *Washington Post*, September 21, 2009.

[110] McChrystal, 21.

[111] Woodward, "McChrystal," 1; Eric Schmitt and Thomas Shanker, "General Calls for More U.S. Troops to Avoid Afghan Failure," *New York Times*, September 21, 2009, A1.

[112] Karl W. Eikenberry and Stanley A. McChrystal, *U.S. Government Integrated Civilian-Military Campaign Plan for Support to Afghanistan*, August 9, 2009, available at <www.comw.org/qdr/fulltext/0908eikenberryandmcchrystal.pdf>.

[113] Scott Wilson and Ann Kornblut, "White House eyeing narrower war effort; Top officials challenge general's assessment," *Washington Post*, October 2, 2009; Rajiv Chandrasekaran, "Civilian, military officials at odds over resources needed for Afghan counterinsurgency," *Washington Post*, October 8, 2009, A1; Peter Baker and Eric Schmitt, "Several possible Afghan strategies, none a clear choice," *New York Times*, September 30, 2009, A14.

[114] Peter Baker, "Obama Meets Top Afghan Commander as He Mulls Change in War Strategy," *New York Times*, October 2, 2009, A1.

[115] McChrystal, 350.

[116] Peter Baker, Elizabeth Bumiller, and Thomas Shanker, "Obama Hears General's Troop Request for Afghanistan," *New York Times*, October 9, 2009, A10.

[117] Peter Baker, "Inside the Situation Room: How a War Plan Evolved," *New York Times*, December 6, 2009, A1; Anne Kornblut, Scott Wilson, and Karen DeYoung, "Obama Pressed for Faster Surge; Afghan Review a Marathon," *Washington Post*, December 6, 2009, A1.

[118] Woodward, *Obama's Wars*, 278. See also Leon Panetta with Jim Newton, *Worthy Fights: A Memoir of Leadership in War and Peace* (New York: Penguin, 2014).

[119] Carter Malkasian and J. Kael Weston, "War Downsized: How to Accomplish More with Less," *Foreign Affairs*, March/April 2012.

[120] M. Landler and J. Zeleny, "U.S. envoy's views reveal rifts on Afghan policy; Ex-general's opposition bolsters the case for those skeptical of troop buildup," *International Herald Tri-*

bune (London), November 14, 2009, 3; Eric Schmitt, "U.S. Envoy's Cables Show Worries on Afghan Plans," *New York Times*, January 25, 2010, A1.

[121] McChrystal, interview.

[122] Schmitt, "U.S. Envoy's Cables Show Worry."

[123] David Petraeus, interview by Joseph J. Collins and Nathan White, April 2, 2015; Stanley A. McChrystal, interview by Joseph J. Collins, Frank G. Hoffman, and Nathan White, March 27, 2015.

[124] Woodward, *Obama's Wars*, 225; Peter Baker, "How Obama Came to Plan for 'Surge' in Afghanistan," *New York Times*, December 5, 2009, A1.

[125] Kevin P. Marsh, "The Contemporary Presidency: The Administrator as Outsider: James Jones as National Security Advisor," *Presidential Studies Quarterly* 42, no. 4 (December 2012), 827–842. On the Secretary of Defense's concerns about an NSC process that takes an advocacy position, see Gates, 385. Michèle A. Flournoy, interview by Frank G. Hoffman and Joseph J. Collins, January 8, 2015.

[126] Peter Baker and Thomas Shanker, "A Pragmatist, Gates Reshapes Past Policies He Backed," *New York Times*, September 21, 2009, A1; M. Landler and Thomas Shanker, "Clinton and Gates Join Forces in Debate on Afghanistan Buildup," *New York Times*, October 13, 2009, A8. On the Secretary of State's views, see Hillary Clinton, *Hard Choices* (New York: Simon & Schuster, 2014), 129–149.

[127] Woodward, *Obama's Wars*, 235–237, 245, 272–273.

[128] John Burns, "McChrystal Rejects Scaling Down Afghan Military Aims," *New York Times*, October 2, 2009, A12; Woodward, *Obama's Wars*, 193–194.

[129] Elizabeth Bumiller and David Sanger, "3 Obama advisers favor more troops for Afghanistan," *New York Times*, November 11, 2009, A6; Art Spillius and B. Farmer, "Obama Wants Exit Strategy in New Plan; Decision on More Troops to Include Option for Leaving," *The Daily Telegraph* (London), November 13, 2009, A17.

[130] Panetta, *Worthy Fights*; Woodward, *Obama's Wars*, 158–159.

[131] Woodward, *Obama's Wars*, 172–174; Gates, 339, 350, 367.

[132] Anne S. Tyson and S. Wilson, "Gates Wants Leader's War Advice Kept Private; Admonition Follows Comments on War by U.S. Commander," *Washington Post*, October 6, 2009, A1.

[133] "An Interview with Admiral Michael G. Mullen, Chairman of the Joint Chiefs of Staff," *Joint Force Quarterly* 54 (3rd Quarter 2009). In this interview, the Chairman articulated a traditional perspective on civil military relations: "We execute policy. We do not make it or advocate for it. That said, I realize my role is advising policy as Chairman, but that advice is always private. And once the decision is made, we move out. That's what our military does, and we do it well. I would agree that we do need more of a focus on military ethics and civil-military relations in our schoolhouses."

[134] Thomas Shanker and Helene Cooper, "Obama meets Joint Chiefs to Review Afghanistan Strategy," *New York Times*, October 31, 2009, A7.

[135] Clinton, 148.

[136] Woodward, *Obama's Wars*, 338.

[137] Ibid., 271. Woodward suggests that Gates was the first to put a timeframe of 18–24 months for the U.S. commitment before withdrawals could begin. Lute, interview.

[138] Petraeus, interview; McChrystal, interview.

[139] Sheryl Gay Stolberg and Helene Cooper, "Obama Adds Troops, but Maps Exit Plan," *New York Times*, December 2, 2009, 1; Secretary Gates quoted in Huma Khan, "Gates Says Afghan Withdrawal Deadline May Be Delayed," ABC News, December 2, 2009.

[140] "Remarks by the President in Address to the Nation on the Way Forward in Afghanistan and Pakistan," U.S. Military Academy at West Point, December 1, 2009, available at <www.whitehouse.gov/the-press-office/remarks-president-address-nation-way-forward-afghanistan-and-pakistan>.

[141] Ibid.

[142] Ibid.

[143] Hillary Clinton and Leon Panetta, testimonies before the Senate Foreign Relations Committee, December 3, 2009, available at <www.foreign.senate.gov/hearings/afghanistan-assessing-the-road-ahead>.

[144] Admiral Mike Mullen and General David Petraeus, testimonies before the Senate Foreign Relations Committee, December 3, 2009, available at <www.foreign.senate.gov/hearings/afghanistan-assessing-the-road-ahead>.

[145] Karl Eikenberry, testimony before the Senate Foreign Relations Committee, December 3, 2009, available at <www.foreign.senate.gov/hearings/afghanistan-assessing-the-road-ahead>.

[146] Michael Hastings, "The Runaway General," *Rolling Stone*, June 22, 2010; Michael Shear, Ernesto Londono, and Debbi Wilgoren, "Obama Leaving Options Open on Firing McChrystal, Gibbs Says," *Washington Post*, June 22, 2010; McChrystal, 387–388.

[147] James P. Pfiffner, "Decision Making in the Obama White House," *Presidential Studies Quarterly* 41, no. 2 (June 2011), 244–262.

[148] Joel Achenbach, "In His Slow Decision-Making, Obama Goes with Head, Not Gut," *Washington Post*, November 25, 2009.

[149] Gates, 362; Woodward, *Obama's Wars*, 279.

[150] Feaver, "The Right to Be Right," 91.

[151] Meaning that, in the modern world, it is unlikely that either domestic audiences or the international community would tolerate the significant levels of violence that it would take to resolve political issues.

[152] There is a growing body of analysis that examines closely the "success" of the Surge. Some argue that it was an unalloyed success, some that it delivered diminished violence, and some that the Surge was a failure. There is also ongoing discussion that seeks to identify how Maliki failed. Some assert that he could not deliver a unified Iraq because of Sunni and Kurdish intransigence, some that he chose not to unify Iraq so that he could rule over a Shiite-dominated country, and others that he did succeed.

[153] Rich Lowry, "Bush's Vietnam Syndrome," *National Review*, December 27, 2006, available at <www.nationalreview.com/article/219591/bushs-vietnam-syndrome-rich-lowry>.

[154] Ron Suskind, *The Price of Loyalty* (New York: Simon & Schuster, 2004), 329.

[155] Feaver, "The Right to Be Right," 99n32, cites Heidi Urben, "'Decider' vs. 'Commander Guy': Presidential Power, Persuasion, and the Surge in Iraq," unpublished manuscript, May 12, 2008.

[156] His November 8, 2006, press conference indicated President Bush's feelings about a new approach and the need for new leadership. He also changed his level of direct interaction with Iraq. The MNF-I chronology shows that; between the mosque bombing of February 22 and the congressional elections, President Bush visited or had communications with General Casey 13 times. Between November 2006 and the change of command on February 10, 2007, he directly communicated with Casey 10 times, or over double the amount of direct interaction (once per 20 days before the elections, once per 9.5 days after).

[157] "The New Way Forward in Iraq," Fact Sheet, January 10, 2007, available at <http://georgewbush-whitehouse.archives.gov/news/releases/2007/01/20070110-3.html>.

[158] Daniel P. Bolger, *Why We Lost: A General's Inside Account of the Iraq and Afghanistan Wars* (New York: Houghton Mifflin Harcourt, 2014), 276.

[159] Mansoor, 2013.

[160] Rajiv Chandrasekran, "The Afghan Surge Is Over, So Did It Work?" *Foreign Policy*, October 2012.

[161] Joseph J. Collins, *Understanding War in Afghanistan* (Washington, DC: NDU Press, 2011), 72.

[162] The total costs of the campaign are well below Iraq's level, including 1,840 battle deaths, and over 20,037 wounded in action. See "Operation Enduring Freedom, U.S. Casualty Status: Fatalities as of October 24, 2014," available at <www.defense.gov/news/casualty.pdf>.

[163] For a map depicting casualty levels by province, see "Fatalities by Province," available at <http://icasualties.org/OEF/ByProvince.aspx>.

[164] Ibid.

[165] Afghan civilian totals are from the United Nations (UN) Office of the High Commissioner for Human Rights, *Afghanistan Mid-Year Report 2012: Protection of Civilians in Armed Conflict* (Kabul, Afghanistan: UN, July 2012), 1, available at <http://unama.unmissions.org/LinkClick.aspx?fileticket=-_vDVBQY1OA%3d&tabid=12254&language=en-US>.

[166] *Progress Toward Security and Stability in Afghanistan* (Washington DC: DOD, October 2014), A-3, available at <www.defense.gov/pubs/Oct2014_Report_Final.pdf>.

[167] On the character of the post-2009 fighting in Helmand Province, see Rajiv Chandrasekaran, *Little America: The War within the War for Afghanistan* (New York: Knopf, 2012); Jeffrey Dressler, *Counterinsurgency in Helmand* (Washington, DC: Institute for the Study of War, 2011); Bing West, *The Wrong War: Grit, Strategy, and the Way Out of Afghanistan* (New York: Random House, 2011).

[168] *Report on Progress Toward Security and Stability in Afghanistan and United States Plan for Sustaining the Afghanistan National Security Forces* (Washington, DC: DOD, April 2010), 11, available at <www.defense.gov/pubs/pdfs/Report Final SecDef 04 26 10.pdf>.

[169] Adapted from Ian S. Livingston and Michael E. O'Hanlon, *Afghanistan Index*, October 29, 2014, 8, figure 1.9, available at <www.brookings.edu/~/media/Programs/foreign-policy/afghanistan-index/index20141029.pdf?la=en>.

[170] Ronald E. Neumann, *The Other War: Winning and Losing in Afghanistan* (Washington, DC: Potomac Books, 2009).

[171] Collins, 70–71.

[172] "Fact Sheet: Bringing the U.S. War in Afghanistan to a Responsible End," The White House, May 27, 2014, available at <www.whitehouse.gov/the-press-office/2014/05/27/fact-sheet-bringing-us-war-afghanistan-responsible-end>.

[173] Jon Riley, "NATO Operations in Afghanistan 2008–2009: A Theatre-Level View," in *British Generals in Blair's Wars*, ed. Jonathan Bailey, Richard Iron and Hew Strachan (London: Ashgate, 2013), 246.

[174] *Progress Toward Security and Stability in Afghanistan Report* (Washington, DC: DOD, April 2014), 92, available at <www.defense.gov/pubs/April_1230_Report_Final.pdf>.

[175] Anand Gopal, *No Good Men Among the Living: America, the Taliban, and the War Through Afghan Eyes* (New York: Metropolitan, 2014), 273.

[176] Paul Shinkman, "Corruption Plagues Afghanistan Ahead of U.S. Withdrawal," *U.S. News and World Report*, December 27, 2013.

[177] Spencer Ackerman, "What Surge? Afghanistan's Most Violent Places Stay Bad, Despite Extra Troops," *Wired.com*, August 23, 2012, available at <www.wired.com/2012/08/afghanistan-violence-helmand>; Matt Waldman, "System Failure: The Underlying Causes of U.S. Policymaking Errors in Afghanistan," *International Affairs* 89, no. 4 (2013), 839.

[178] Stephen D. Biddle, "Afghanistan's Legacy: Emerging Lessons of an Ongoing War," *The Washington Quarterly* 37, no. 2 (Summer 2014), 73–86.

[179] Kevin P. Marsh, "A Tale of Two Surges: Conceptual Models of Foreign Policy and the Decisions to Adopt Troop Surges in the Iraq and Afghanistan Wars" (Ph.D. diss., Northern Illinois University, 2011).

[180] General George W. Casey Papers, Box #145, February 24, 2006, National Defense University Library Special Collections, Washington, DC.

[181] Higgins, 136.

[182] Casey Papers, Box #145, February 24, 2006.

[183] General Casey states that he was "informed about a review" on Iraq by General Peter Pace in October, "but, from my perspective, it did not begin in earnest until after Secretary Rumsfeld's resignation in early November." See George W. Casey, *Strategic Reflections* (Washington, DC: NDU Press, 2012), 135.

[184] At least 92 personal discussions, secure video teleconferences, and visits between February 2006 and February 2007.

[185] Feaver, interview.

[186] Hadley, interview.

[187] Hadley, interview; Petraeus, interview.

[188] Ibid.

[189] Ibid.

[190] Casey Papers, Box #145, June 14, 2006.

[191] Casey, *Strategic Reflections*, 37–38.

[192] "President Bush Nominates Dr. Robert M. Gates to be Secretary of Defense," The White House, November 8, 2006, available at <http://georgewbush-whitehouse.archives.gov/news/releases/2006/11/20061108-4.html>.

[193] Institute for the Study of War, *Timelines of the Surge in Iraq: December 2005–December 2008* (Washington, DC: Institute for the Study of War, n.d.), available at <www.understandingthesurge.org/wp-content/uploads/2009/10/Surge-timeline-1.pdf>.

[194] William Upshur, Jonathan Roginski, and David Kilcullen, "Recognizing Symptoms in Afghanistan: Lessons Learned and New Approaches to Operational Assessments," *PRISM* 3, no. 3 (June 2012), 89, available at <http://cco.dodlive.mil/files/2013/08/prism3-3.pdf>.

[195] Emily Mushen and Jonathan Schroden, *Are We Winning? A Brief History of Military Operations Assessment* (Alexandria, VA: Center for Naval Analyses, August 2014), ii.

[196] Stephen Downes-Martin, "Operations Assessment in Afghanistan is Broken," *Naval War College Review* 64, no. 4 (Autumn 2011). For further evaluation of conflict trends in Afghanistan, see Eric Gons et al., "Challenges of Measuring Progress in Afghanistan Using Violence Trends: The Effects of Aggregation, Military, Operations, Seasonality, Weather, and other Causal Factors," *Defense & Security Analysis* 28, no. 2 (June 2012).

[197] Lute, interview.

[198] Cited in Jonathan Schroden, "Operations Assessment at ISAF: Changing Paradigms," in *Innovation in Operations Assessment: Recent Developments in Measuring Results in Conflict*

Environments, ed. Andrew Williams et al. (The Hague, Netherlands: NATO Communications and Information Agency, n.d.); McChrystal, 2–20.

[199] We are indebted to Nathan White in the Center for Complex Operations at National Defense University for this insight.

[200] McChrystal; Panetta; and interviews with Flournoy, Lutes, Petraeus, and McChrystal.

[201] Frank Hoffman, "History and Future of Civil-Military Relations: Bridging the Gaps," in *The Past as Prologue: The Importance of History to the Military Profession*, ed. Williamson Murray and Richard Hart Sinnreich (New York: Cambridge University Press, 2006), 247–265.

[202] Rothkopf, 178–179.

[203] President Obama's strategic memorandum is provided as an annex in Woodward, *Obama's Wars*, 385–386.

[204] Ibid., 387. Emphasis added.

[205] Gates, *Duty*, 336.

[206] J. Alexander Thier, "The Making of a Constitution in Afghanistan," *New York Law School Law Review* 51, no. 7 (2007), 574–575.

[207] Christopher D. Kolenda, "Winning Afghanistan at the Community Level," *Joint Force Quarterly* 56 (1st Quarter 2010), 30–31. Kolenda was a key contributor to the McChrystal strategic assessment.

[208] To address the subnational governance issues identified during the strategy review process, the U.S. Government launched the District Development Program in 2010 and the Performance Based Governors Fund in 2011. Both depended on the cooperation of the Afghan Independent Directorate for Local Governance—part of the president's office—and faltered due to a lack of capacity and willingness at the national level to devolve resources and power to provincial and district governments. See Max Kelly, "Defeating Insurgency at the Grass Roots: Building Local Governance Capacity in Afghanistan" (unpublished paper, 2011); and Michael Shurkin, *Subnational Government in Afghanistan* (Santa Monica, CA: RAND, 2011).

[209] Upshur, Roginski, and Kilcullen; Downes-Martin.

[210] Ben Connable, "Learning from the Vietnam-era Strategic Assessment Failure," in *Innovation in Operations Assessment*, 16.

[211] Ibid.

[212] Casey, *Strategic Reflections*, 169–170.

[213] Ibid. Emphasis added.

[214] Paul David Miller, "Organizing the National Security Council: I Like Ike's," *Presidential Studies Quarterly* 43, no. 3 (September 2013), 592–606.

[215] Nathan White, "Challenges to Adaptation of U.S. Assessment Practices for Counter-insurgency in Afghanistan," International Studies Association conference paper, New Orleans, LA, March 2015.

[216] Petraeus, interview.

[217] James G. Stavridis, *The Accidental Admiral* (Annapolis, MD: Naval Institute Press, 2014), 64.

[218] Frank G. Hoffman, "Dereliction of Duty Redux? Post-Iraq American Civil-Military Relations," *Orbis* 52, no. 2 (Spring 2008), 217–235.

[219] Casey, *Strategic Reflections*, 165.

[220] Janine Davidson, "The Contemporary Presidency: Civil-Military Friction and Presidential Decision Making: Explaining the Broken Dialogue," *Presidential Studies Quarterly* 43, no. 1 (March 2013), 129–145.

[221] Linda Robinson et al., *Improving Strategic Competence, Lessons from 13 Years of War* (Santa Monica, CA: RAND, October 2014).

[222] General Martin E. Dempsey, interview by Richard D. Hooker, Jr., and Joseph J. Collins, January 7, 2015.

[223] Flournoy, interview.

[224] Colin S. Gray, *The Strategy Bridge: Theory for Practice* (New York: Oxford University Press, 2010).

[225] Dempsey, interview.

[226] Hadley, interview.

[227] Dempsey, interview; reinforced in both Flournoy and Lute, interviews.

[228] Dempsey, interview.

[229] "Admiral Mike Mullen's Speech on Military Strategy, Kansas State University, March 2010," Manhattan, KS, March 3, 2010, available at <www.cfr.org/defense-strategy/admiral-mullens-speech-military-strategy-kansas-state-university-march-2010/p21590>.

[230] Dempsey, interview.

[231] Dempsey, interview.

[232] Petraeus, interview; Dempsey, interview.

[233] Ali Khedery, "Why We Stuck With Maliki—and Lost Iraq," *Washington Post*, July 3, 2014.

[234] Emile Simpson, *War from the Ground Up: Twenty-First Century Combat as Politics* (New York: Oxford University Press, 2012).

[235] "Admiral Mike Mullen's Speech"; Thom Shanker, "Joint Chiefs Chairman Readjusts Principles on Use of Force," *New York Times*, March 3, 2010.

[236] Ibid.

[237] Ibid.

[238] Williamson Murray, *Military Adaptation in War, With Fear of Change* (New York: Cambridge University Press, 2011), 37.

[239] Feaver, "The Right to Be Right."

[240] Robinson et al.

[241] Richard Hart Sinnreich, "Victory by Trial and Error: Britain's Struggle Against Napoleon," in *Successful Strategies, Triumphing in War and Peace from Antiquity to the Present*, ed. Williamson Murray and Richard Hart Sinnreich (New York: Cambridge University Press, 2014), 446.

3

NATIONAL-LEVEL COORDINATION AND IMPLEMENTATION: HOW SYSTEM ATTRIBUTES TRUMPED LEADERSHIP

By Christopher J. Lamb with Megan Franco

Thidchapter explains and evaluates how well the national-level decisionmaking process guided the war efforts in Afghanistan and Iraq.
President George W. Bush explained operations in Afghanistan and
outlined the administration's response to the terror attacks of September 11,
2001, when he addressed a joint session of Congress on September 20.[1] The
President announced two great objectives: first, shutting down terrorist camps
that existed in more than a dozen countries, disrupting the terrorists' plans,
and bringing them to justice; and second, preventing terrorists and regimes
that seek weapons of mass destruction from threatening the United States and
the world. The President stated that to achieve these objectives, the United
States would have to wage a lengthy war "unlike any other we have ever seen."[2]
His strategy would use "every resource at our command—every means of diplomacy, every tool of intelligence, every instrument of law enforcement, every financial influence, and every necessary weapon of war—to the disruption
and to the defeat of the global terror network." This unprecedented effort to
integrate every tool available would entail a broad geographic scope in which
"every nation, in every region" would be forced to decide whether it supported
efforts to defeat "every terrorist group of global reach."

President Bush's speech was widely acclaimed, and over the next decade
and a half his intent has been achieved in some respects. The United States has
prevented another strategic attack by al Qaeda, greatly reduced the effectiveness of that terrorist organization, and orchestrated many lesser operational

successes. Even so, it became clear in the years following the President's speech that the United States could not wage the war he described or achieve the goals he set. Instead, as explained in previous chapters, the United States ended up with extended campaigns in Afghanistan and Iraq that squandered resources, diminished public support for the war, and arguably generated as many terrorists as they eliminated.[3] The United States has disengaged from its campaigns in Afghanistan and Iraq, but the threat of catastrophic terrorism identified by President Bush is still present.

In this chapter, we pose and answer fundamental questions. We ask how senior leaders identified the problem confronting the Nation and how they intended to solve it. We also address whether senior leader decisions constituted a strategy and whether they were able to coordinate and implement their decisions well. In the concluding section, we offer an overarching explanation for why it was not possible for the President to execute the war effort he originally described and why the U.S. performance in Afghanistan and Iraq has been so problematic.

Our decisionmaking analysis was senior leader–centric. Our primary sources were 23 senior leader descriptions of the decision process.[4] We concentrate on issues that senior decisionmakers deemed critical and their explanations for how they managed disagreements about how to proceed in the wars. We adopt a choice-based approach to analyze senior leader decisionmaking, consistent with their accounts that depict the decision process as a purposeful activity designed to solve problems.[5] Our approach has several important implications that, from the reviews we have received to date, are not obvious and need to be stated. Our purpose is not to criticize or defend specific decisions that senior leaders made. Instead, we examine whether these decisions met minimum requirements for good strategy, and if not, whether this shortcoming compromised the ability to achieve desired goals. We do not argue that a different understanding or approach would have been better. Instead, we consider whether leaders were able to execute their preferred approach as envisioned and adjust it in light of changing circumstances, and, if not, why not. Similarly, we do not speculate about senior leader motives or probe their psychological profiles. We take at face value their assertions that they wanted a strategy to defeat terrorism and acted with that intent.[6] Thus, we do not consider, as many have, whether the President or members of his

Cabinet were driven by a psychological need or other motives to address unfinished business with Saddam Hussein left over from the first Gulf War.[7] In sum, we examine factors that limited the ability of senior leaders to generate and implement coherent national strategy rather than argue in favor of alternative policies and strategies.

We concentrate on the first decade of war from 2001 through 2010 for several reasons. The most consequential decisions were made fairly early on. In addition, our primary sources deal mostly with decisions made during this period. More to the point, important decisions made later in the decade about how to wind down the wars in Afghanistan and Iraq are taken up in other chapters. Decisions to surge U.S. forces in Iraq and Afghanistan are taken up in the previous chapter, and decisions on how to transition the lead to host-nation forces are reviewed in a following chapter. We do not ignore decisions that led to successes. On the contrary, we make a point of noting successes in each decision area we investigate. However, in keeping with a lessons learned effort, we focus on explaining problems rather than successes.

Our findings are organized into four categories that are interrelated but examined sequentially: concepts, command, capabilities, and constraints. By *concepts*, we mean the national strategy and concepts of operation that explain what the United States hoped to achieve in Afghanistan and Iraq and how. *Command* denotes the collective attempts to orchestrate unified support for implementing senior leader strategy and plans. *Capabilities* are the tools (or "means") needed to execute strategy and plans. The final category—*constraints*—covers additional factors that senior leaders believe complicated the war effort. The constraints include strategy conundrums and other social and political factors that leaders believe limited the efficacy of the decisionmaking process and outcomes.

The analysis reveals some significant limitations in national decisionmaking that endured across the Bush and Barack Obama administrations. Two are especially important. Many senior leaders admit we have not agreed on the nature and scope of the terrorism threat or how to defeat it. They also are in near-complete agreement that the United States was not able to act with unified purpose and effort to achieve set objectives. We discuss the absence of unified effort primarily in the section on command, but we also demonstrate its impact in the section on capabilities. We also found a persistent inability to generate the full range of capabilities required for success, or in some cases, to do so in a timely fashion. Overall, we conclude that critical strategy handicaps, insufficient unity of effort, and, to a lesser extent, missing or late-to-need capabilities for irregular warfighting offer a compelling explanation for why the United States was not able to fully achieve its goals in Afghanistan and Iraq.

Concepts

Following 9/11, President Bush and his senior advisors were preoccupied with formulating a response to safeguard the Nation from more attacks. The desired output from senior leader decisionmaking was an effective national security strategy for protecting the country and defeating terrorism. Evaluating their decisionmaking therefore requires identifying criteria for what constitutes good strategy. We used the three basic elements of strategy that Richard Rumelt advocates: a penetrating diagnosis of the key problem to be solved, a corresponding guiding approach to solve the problem, and a set of coherent supporting actions for implementing the approach.[8] The analysis needs to identify the root cause of the problem that must be dealt with to obtain success. The preferred approach must overcome the problem based on an advantage or asymmetry and be discriminating enough to direct and constrain action. The supporting actions must be clear, prioritized, and feasible given scarce resources. Rumelt offers convincing explanations for how and why many leaders and organizations ignore or otherwise fail to meet these elementary requirements.

In evaluating the strategy decisions that guided the war on terror, we looked primarily at major decisions rather than official strategy documents. As some senior leaders have confessed, despite all the energy that goes into producing official strategy documents, they are generally ignored.[9] They are consensus products intended to serve bureaucratic and public policy purposes.[10] They tend to enumerate expansive and unrealistic strategic objectives.[11] Real strategy—to the extent it exists—resides in the minds of the key decisionmakers. As General George W. Casey, Jr., USA (Ret.), advises, "The decisionmaking process at the national level is idiosyncratic at best," and not as rigorous as the process military officers use. General Casey's experience with policy and strategy in Washington taught him "not to expect written direction from civilian leaders."[12] He referred to a few key policy documents but developed his initial campaign plan based upon verbal discussions with the President and

Secretary of Defense. Because real strategy is not codified, it sometimes can be difficult to identify. Fortunately, senior leaders have shared a great deal of their thinking on their strategy to combat terrorism.

Identifying the Root Problem

Senior decisionmakers viewed the U.S. interventions in Afghanistan and Iraq as extensions of the war on terror. Their assessment of the terror attacks on 9/11 resolved a longstanding dispute about terrorism. For decades, pundits argued over whether terrorists were capable of and inclined to launch mass-casualty attacks. Some analysts believed most terrorists would not do so because it would elicit a massive response and undermine political support for their cause, thus proving counterproductive. Terrorists groups that wanted mass casualty attacks were believed to be technically incapable of executing them. Others experts were more pessimistic. They thought the proliferation of knowledge in the information age was enabling "catastrophic terror" and observed that some groups with technical competence such as al Qaeda were advocating it.

The 9/11 attacks seemed to resolve this debate in favor of the pessimists. Senior leaders in the Bush administration settled on the urgent need to prevent another attack, particularly one involving the use of weapons of mass destruction. In President Bush's 2002 State of the Union address, he noted American forces in Afghanistan had found "detailed instructions for making chemical weapons, surveillance maps of American cities, and thorough descriptions of landmarks in America and throughout the world." These findings confirmed the war against terror would not end in Afghanistan and in fact was "only beginning." They also reinforced the President's conviction that we had to destroy terrorist organizations and prevent "terrorists and regimes who seek chemical, biological or nuclear weapons from threatening the United States and the world."[13]

These objectives served well as a summary agenda, but they did not pinpoint the nature and scope of the problem. Did the United States need to eliminate terrorism and its state sponsors everywhere, or just all terrorist groups? Only terrorist groups with the capability to use weapons of mass destruction, the intent to do so, or both? Or just the strain of Islamic extremist groups that had perpetrated the 9/11 attacks—or, more specifically, the organization that executed the attacks, namely, al Qaeda? The answers to these questions carried major implications for the type of effort the United States would have to mount and the resources required. Answers to these questions would determine whether an extended war in Afghanistan and intervention in Iraq were necessary, and whether state sponsors of terrorism such as Iran, or states such as North Korea with weapons of mass destruction that carried out terror attacks, had to be defeated or otherwise engaged. The more broadly the problem was defined, the greater the effort required to solve it.

In the short period between the 9/11 attacks and President Bush's speech to Congress on September 20,[14] the administration settled on an expansive and somewhat artful phrase to depict the scope of the security threat. President Bush declared, "Our enemy is a radical network of terrorists, and every government that supports them. Our war on terror begins with al Qaeda, but it does not end there. It will not end until every terrorist group of *global reach* has been found, stopped and defeated [emphasis added]." Conjoining terrorists and state sponsors broadened the scope of the war well past al Qaeda. Moreover, in this same speech, and often thereafter, the President cast the struggle in terms of freedom and tyranny, between those "who believe in progress and pluralism, tolerance and freedom" and those who do not. The President's definition of the problem and the enemies to overcome was broad but limited by two clarifications. The expression "axis of evil" defined the short list of noteworthy state sponsors of terrorism as Iran, Iraq, and North Korea.[15] The other limitation was the expression "global reach." This description indicated that only terrorist groups capable of attacking the United States had to be destroyed, rather than all terrorist groups, many of which had narrower agendas that did not directly threaten the Nation.

A key predicate of President Bush's approach was the belief that successful terrorist attacks with weapons of mass destruction would be calamitous. One senior administration official later explained that the President's strategy was broadly preventive and not narrowly punitive because senior leaders assumed they were at war with a global network, that the terrorists were bent on mass destruction rather than just political theater, and finally that sustaining a series of 9/11-type attacks "could change the nature of our country."[16] The dire consequences of such an attack required the United States to take the offensive, including preemptive military action and other extraordinary measures even if the probability of a successful mass casualty terrorist attack was low. This assumption was widely debated as "the one percent doctrine."

After taking office, the Obama administration made a point of narrowing the definition of the problem and thus the scope of the necessary response. President Obama identified the need "to disrupt, dismantle, and defeat al Qaeda in Pakistan and Afghanistan" and "prevent their return to either country in the future," thus limiting the war geographically and redefining the list of enemies the United States had to defeat. As Hillary Clinton puts it, "By refocusing so specifically on al Qaeda, as opposed to the Taliban insurgents . . . the President was linking the war back to its source: the 9/11 attacks."[17] In this regard, the scope of the war effort precipitated by the attacks on 9/11 was curtailed under the Obama administration.

It is not clear from strategy pronouncements or tactics employed, however, that President Obama envisions the *nature* of the threat differently. Some hoped the Obama administration would redefine the threat as a political problem whereby the enemy tried to get the United States to overreact in ways that alienated support from other nations and thus restricted U.S. freedom of maneuver and ability to marshal resources. The proper countervailing strategy would be to maintain widespread support and isolate the terrorists within the community of Islam (*umma*).[18] In this vein, some argued for abandoning controversial policies that alienated domestic and international opinion. Administration officials believe they put more emphasis on international cooperation and strategic communication,[19] but the major change in strategy did not materialize.[20] Perhaps the administration believed it had to first extricate the United States from large-scale operations in Iraq and then Afghanistan. If so, this has taken longer than anticipated and been set back by the rise of the Islamic State of Iraq and the Levant.

What is clear in retrospect is that lack of agreement on the nature and scope of the threat compromised strategy from the beginning. Members of the Bush administration, for instance, disagreed about the scope of the threat.[21] Some argued the threat was broad and transnational and required an equally broad response. Some others, who initially agreed with that view, came to believe the threat was so broadly defined that it undermined international cooperation. They consider the term "axis of evil" regrettable because it made negotiating with those powers difficult and/or expanded the scope of the war on terror beyond what could be sustained politically at home and abroad.[22] Others believe lack of clarity about the nature and scope of the catastrophic terrorist threat inclined leaders to focus on tactical operations but left the main threat unaddressed, if not stronger.[23] The contentious early debate over whether the United States needed to eliminate the regime in Iraq was a strong indication that the U.S. definition of the *strategic threat* was contentious at best.

Looking back, several senior leaders acknowledge the United States still has not identified its strategic problem well,[24] and in particular its religious origins. Some note the most threatening terror groups are found in deviant strains of Islam, while others depict the problem as "a clash within Islamic civilization between Sunni moderates and Sunni extremists."[25] Either way, the United States has not recognized the religious connection. Islamic allies object to the expression "Islamic terror" for the same reason Christians would object to the expression "Christian terror"; they consider it an oxymoron and a grossly counterproductive one that offends those whose support we seek and that could be misconstrued to extend legitimacy to terrorists. It also is common to acknowledge that non-Muslim voices are not credible in a debate over the meaning, direction, and permissible behaviors within Islam.

In any case, this tension between frank acknowledgment that terror has some popular appeal in Islamic communities and the political and strategic communication advantages of ignoring that connection continues to complicate U.S. strategy. General Martin Dempsey, who notes he has been accused of being both anti-Islamic and pro-Islamic, observes, "We as a Nation just haven't been able to have a conversation about . . . the threat of violent extremist organizations that also happen to be radical Islamic organizations."[26] Furthermore, he argues that until we understand the threat "in its totality" and find the right vocabulary to describe it, we cannot defeat the threat—at best, we can only contain it.[27]

Choosing an Approach to Victory

The second key element of any effective strategy is agreement on how to solve the root problem based on an advantage or asymmetry. When the root problem is poorly defined, the approach to solving it is equally problematic. This proved true for overall strategy in the war on terror, and by extension, for the

U.S. interventions in Afghanistan and Iraq. Senior leaders wanted to stop state support for terrorism and thought that deposing some regimes that supported terrorism would contribute to that objective. However, they disagreed on how important it was to ensure that good governance followed the deposed regimes. Was good governance in Afghanistan and Iraq an essential element of the war on terror, or a distraction that wasted resources? This question—never answered—reveals confusion about the nature and origins of the catastrophic terrorism threat and how it should be defeated.

The United States tried to create a comprehensive strategy for combatting terror that would address such questions but never succeeded. The official public strategy defined the problem too broadly with too many dimensions. It lumped the assassin of President William McKinley in with al Qaeda and cited underlying conditions of terror as diverse as "poverty, corruption, religious conflict and ethnic strife."[28] The National Counterterrorism Center tried to create a classified strategy, but failed.[29] Departments and agencies could not agree on a discriminating approach to defeating such a broad threat. Instead, they agreed to a long list of objectives that left them free to pursue their own priorities as they understood them. The failure to cohere around a common understanding of the terror problem and its solution complicated the interventions in Afghanistan and Iraq.

In Afghanistan, the strategy was never clear. The President and his advisors were cheered by news of terrorist leaders captured or killed,[30] but otherwise they had difficulty establishing objectives for the war effort. One early telltale sign of this confusion was the disagreement about whether to welcome or resist a rapid Northern Alliance seizure of Kabul. Some thought that if the Northern Alliance was too successful it would precipitate "intertribal fighting and score-settling" with the possibility that "chaos would reign."[31] Others were happy to see a quick collapse of the Taliban, which they thought would facilitate efforts to eliminate al Qaeda in Afghanistan. This difference of opinion revealed uncertainty about what we were trying to accomplish. A friendly, stable, effective Afghan government was preferable, but was it possible and essential for success in the war on terror? Without an answer to this question, it was difficult to answer a related question: how much priority should be given to eliminating the Taliban? Too much concern with the Taliban would take the focus off al Qaeda and might allow it to reemerge stronger elsewhere.[32] The opposite concern was that failure to destroy the Taliban would give al Qaeda an extended sanctuary and a new lease on life.[33] The debate boiled down to differences over the nature of the threat. Were the Taliban and al Qaeda allies of convenience, or cohorts in a global campaign that was threatening the United States? If they were allies of convenience, we could afford to bypass the Taliban and concentrate on al Qaeda; if the Taliban were an intrinsic part of the global terrorist network, they needed to be defeated.

During this initial period, senior military leaders understood their tactical objectives—attacking Taliban forces and capturing or killing terrorists—but they were uncertain about U.S. strategy for the war on terror.[34] Over time, the U.S. commitment to effective governance in Afghanistan increased, but not because strategy was clarified. Instead, it resulted from ad hoc decision-making in response to the reconstitution of the Taliban as an effective insurgent force. An ineffectual Afghan government left the Taliban and their terrorist allies free to operate, which was not deemed acceptable. Even though President Obama in his 2009 West Point speech narrowed the U.S. goal in Afghanistan to "disrupt, dismantle, and defeat al Qaeda," he specified three subordinate objectives that tied al Qaeda to the fortunes of the Taliban and Afghan government. He stated that we would deny al Qaeda a safe haven, reverse the Taliban's momentum and prevent the overthrow of the government, and strengthen Afghan capacity to take lead responsibility for the country's future. The three objectives were progressively less clear cut and more subject to debate as to whether they had been achieved. "Deny al Qaeda a safe haven" is easier to assess than the sufficiency of a "strengthened" Afghan government and its security forces. More to the point, even a strong case for good progress in all three objectives leaves open the question of whether the United States was committed to a friendly, stable, and effective Afghan government or instead wanted political latitude for an "expeditious exit."[35] As General Stanley A. McChrystal, USA (Ret.), notes, the United States never had a "clear strategic aim" in Afghanistan.[36] Instead, it backed into counterinsurgency to prevent tactical reversals to its counterterrorism agenda. It provided ever-increasing amounts of support to Kabul, but the purpose and importance of the extended Afghan campaign remained poorly understood, controversial, and not clearly connected to the broader U.S. counterterrorism strategy.

Lack of agreement on the nature and scope of the terror problem was even more deleterious in the case of Iraq. The limited commitment of U.S. leaders to a democratic government in Baghdad was telegraphed in the official list of U.S. goals, which stated the desired endstate was an Iraq that "encourages" the building of democratic institutions.[37] Over time, it became increasingly less clear whether the United States was intervening in Iraq to punish a state sponsor of terrorism, eliminate a potential source of weapons of mass destruction for terrorists, or promote democracy and stimulate cultural changes throughout the region to diminish the appeal of terrorism. The confusion led to divergent levels of commitment to postwar reconstruction and governance,[38] undermined public support, and confused military commanders in Iraq about what they were trying to accomplish. General Casey, the commander with the longest tenure, admits that he did not understand the strategic goals of the intervention.[39]

Initially the Department of Defense (DOD) put all of its energy into developing plans to defeat Saddam Hussein's military forces but resisted preparing for a long, large American occupation to ensure good governance. During informal conversations in the Pentagon, senior civilian leaders made it clear that DOD needed to withdraw forces from Iraq so it could be prepared for possible next moves in the war on terror.[40] This made sense given the broad scope of the war depicted by the President. However, Department of State leaders, as well as the special envoy for Iraq and some military leaders, were convinced that preventing chaos in Iraq was necessary and would require a substantial U.S. commitment.

These unreconciled differences led to bitter infighting between the two departments, especially about postwar planning.[41] The two departments also disagreed about using expatriate Iraqi leaders, disbanding (or not reconstituting[42]) the Iraqi army, and the extent of de-Ba'athification. Divergent views on the need for "nation-building" also fueled much of the controversy over appropriate operational concepts for the interventions in both Afghanistan and Iraq. That debate polarized around two questions: whether the United States should concentrate on counterterrorism or counterinsurgency—and if the latter, which approach?

Some argued counterterrorism—that is, killing and capturing terrorists and key supporters—was more important and practical than defeating insurgents. The United States developed a refined counterterrorist capability that has proved adept at identifying, targeting, and eliminating key terrorists.[43] The most controversial aspects of the counterterrorism operational concept are the means used to acquire intelligence and the procedures for deciding which individuals to kill. The great attraction of counterterrorism is that it directly engages the enemy, manifests unambiguous results, and is less expensive in lives and materiel than counterinsurgency.

No one objected to robust counterterrorism, although specific tactics and operations were contested. The debate was about whether killing and capturing individual terrorists were sufficient for solving the problem of catastrophic terrorism. The Bush administration believed the answer was no and wanted to force states to stop supporting terrorists. After the campaigns in Afghanistan and Iraq led to insurgency and civil war, and especially after the failure to find substantial weapons of mass destruction in Iraq, the Bush administration broadened the agenda by placing greater emphasis on promoting democracy. It was the first task identified in the 2006 National Strategy for Combating Terrorism.[44] The counterreaction from some in the Obama administration was to argue the United States should retreat from nation-building and concentrate on counterterrorism. Other Obama officials argued this made sense in Iraq, but that counterterrorism in Afghanistan was insufficient for reasons nicely summarized by former Secretary of State Hillary Clinton:

> *The problem with this argument was that if the Taliban continued to seize more of the country, it would be that much harder to conduct effective counterterrorism operations. We wouldn't have the same intelligence networks necessary to locate the terrorists or the bases from which to launch strikes inside or outside Afghanistan. Al Qaeda already had safe havens in Pakistan. If we abandoned large parts of Afghanistan to the Taliban, they would have safe havens there as well.*[45]

Some argued that ignoring the insurgency in Iraq would be a mistake for similar reasons. Chaos in Iraq would open the country as a staging base for future terrorist plots and destabilize the Middle East, leading to more conflict that terrorists could exploit.[46]

Those arguing that counterinsurgency was a necessary component of the war on terror debated the most effective operational concept. Historically there are two. One is to brutalize the population into abandoning support for insurgents and informing the government on their identity and whereabouts. If the population will not cooperate, it is isolated and punished. Economic warfare, concentration camps, massacres, and wholesale slaughter have all been used for this purpose. This approach is not politically sustainable in the United States today or in most other countries, so the second approach was adopted.

The U.S. counterinsurgency approach was to provide security for the population so they are free from fear of reprisals, construct an elaborate intelligence apparatus to reveal and penetrate the insurgent organization, use enough discriminate force to keep insurgents on the defensive without creating collateral damage that alienates the population, and make enough of an effort to counter popular grievances to reinforce the legitimacy of the host government and diminish the appeal of the insurgency. This approach requires multiple elements of power working in harmony, deep sociocultural knowledge of the target population, perseverance, and other subsidiary, situation-specific capabilities.

This type of counterinsurgency is much harder for an outside power such as the United States intervening in another country such as Afghanistan or Iraq. It is best to push the host-nation security forces to the front of the effort because they know the country, culture, language, and insurgents better than the United States ever could. The United States had to sell the second counterinsurgency agenda to the host nation and transfer capabilities to execute it, and do so well enough to generate enough progress to retain political support at home and abroad.

A "lite" version of counterinsurgency puts less emphasis on the need to protect and convince the population. Instead, the emphasis is on decapitating the leadership of the insurgency. The hope is that if the insurgent or terrorist organization is built around charismatic leaders, eliminating the leadership will lead to the collapse of the organization. Scholarship on this issue is inconclusive,[47] but this approach has not worked well in the ongoing war on terror. When U.S. special operations forces (SOF) became adept at exploiting all-source intelligence to target enemy leaders, some hoped that their proficiency would collapse enemy organizations. High-volume special operations did degrade the terrorist and insurgent organizations but never rendered them ineffective, as leaders in the SOF community came to understand.[48]

Rumelt argues that a strategic approach to solving a problem should be based on an advantage or asymmetry. In part, the debate over counterterrorism versus counterinsurgency addressed this issue. Those supporting counterterrorism believed it played to U.S. strengths, whereas counterinsurgency played into the hands of the enemy. The rebuttal was that the scope of the problem and the role played by state sponsors of terrorism left the United States with no choice but to fight insurgents who supported terrorists and would do so even more boldly if they controlled nation-states. The point to make here is that neither the Bush nor the Obama administration resolved the debate, and based their strategies on asymmetric U.S. advantages.

Supporting Actions to Implement the Chosen Approach
The third requirement for effective strategy is a set of prioritized actions that are clear and feasible given scarce resources. Many discrete actions taken by departments and agencies to advance the war effort were successful. The Central Intelligence Agency executed the front end of Operation *Enduring Freedom* well with SOF assistance. DOD managed the first phases of Operation *Iraqi Freedom* with historic success. The Department of Treasury, Federal Bureau of Investigation, and later the Department of Homeland Security embraced new missions and changed their organizational cultures to execute those missions. SOF and the Intelligence Community tracked down individual terrorist and insurgent leaders with increasing success. Other pockets of productivity included seizing terrorist financial assets and strong cooperative agreements with foreign governments.

As laudable as these high-performance supporting actions were, they did not add up to strategic success because they were not orchestrated, replicated, and reinforced in support of a good guiding strategy. Disagreement or confusion about the threat and how it is to be addressed generates corresponding disarray in the action agenda. Absent agreement on the root problem and approach to resolving it, decisionmaking proceeds ad hoc. This proved the case in both Afghanistan and Iraq. Subordinates could not act upon Presidential intent if the strategy for success was not clear. They had to wait to see what the President would decide next. If circumstances would not permit delay, they had to do what they thought best, which occasionally encouraged not only innovation but also inconsistency and friction.

For example, in the first National Security Council (NSC) meeting on operations in Afghanistan, policy positions were established on freeing women from oppression and on humanitarian assistance. Women's rights were necessary because "we felt an obligation to leave [the Afghans] better off" than before. President Bush also asked whether U.S. forces could drop food before bombs because he wanted to show the Afghan people that the U.S. intervention was different from the earlier one by the Soviet Union.[49] These policy preferences could have been part of a broader strategy to safeguard international political support for U.S. counterterrorism, or an element of counterinsurgency strategy designed to secure enough Afghan popular support to operate against terrorists in Afghanistan, or just personal preferences promoted by individual senior leaders. Absent a clear overarching strategy, subordinates could not make reasoned judgments about supporting actions and their relative priority.

Assumptions, Options, and Adjustments

The preceding argument is that the failure to identify the origins of the threat and related failure to clarify the importance of ensuring good governance after deposing regimes in Afghanistan and Iraq were key errors in strategy. Our findings challenge other explanations for poor performance in Afghanistan and Iraq, including the belief that senior leaders based their decisions on optimistic assumptions, made them without examining a sufficient range of options, or failed to adjust their decisions as circumstances changed. Planners extol the virtue of clarifying critical assumptions, analyzing alternative courses of action, formulating options in case assumptions prove wrong and in anticipation of subsequent developments (that is, answering the "what if" and "what next" questions),[50] and adjusting as the situation evolves. Military researchers in particular are quick to observe when these prerequisites for good decisionmaking are ignored or poorly conducted. Sometimes they are *too* quick, assuming rather than demonstrating senior leader assumptions.[51]

Assumptions, options, and adjustments are linked because assumptions can drive options that then become courses of action to be adjusted as circumstances unfold. Space limitations preclude in-depth examination of all the decisionmaking mistakes attributed to senior leaders in these areas, but we can assess some of the most prominent ones. One frequently cited example of a flawed assumption was the expectation that Iraqis were hungry for democracy, would greet American forces as liberators, and would remain calm and law abiding while their future was decided; that invading Iraq would be like liberating France in 1944.[52] General John Abizaid, USA (Ret.), refers to this expectation as a "heroic" assumption that compromised operations in Iraq.[53] This thesis is made credible by senior leaders who downplayed the costs and difficulties associated with occupying Iraq and emphasized they were unknowable.[54]

Where optimistic assessments were made, they appear to have been communication strategies designed to dampen opposition to the war. Senior leaders believed the ultimate costs of the war could not be predicted, and they wanted to downplay them in testimony to Congress and the public because they thought the war made strategic sense.[55] Worrying about the potential for civic unrest and general lawlessness is a routine concern of U.S. leaders planning foreign interventions, but American foreign interventions since World War II reveal how difficult it is to predict the level of popular resistance to U.S. forces.[56] Organized insurgencies in response to intervention would be worst-case scenarios at one end of the spectrum, whereas civil unrest and looting are commonplace. In the case of Iraq, senior leaders were well warned about and cognizant of the potential for lawlessness but not for organized insurgent resistance.

In any case, leaders were not guilty of rosy expectations of Iraqi gratitude and goodwill. They thought the majority Shiite population would welcome Saddam's ouster but the Sunnis much less so, and that in any case whatever welcome U.S. forces received would not last. Intelligence on Iraq predicted a "short honeymoon period" after deposing Saddam, and other national security organizations expected the same. Decisionmakers in Defense, State, and the White House worried about an extended American occupation precisely because they thought it would be costly and irritate the local population. This is why many senior leaders preferred a "light footprint" approach in both Afghanistan and Iraq.[57] As many commentators have noted, there were multiple planning efforts prior to the war by State, Defense, and other national security institutions that underscored how difficult the occupation might be.[58] These insights found a ready audience in the Bush administration, which came to office disdaining extended nation-building missions and warning that the U.S. military was "most certainly not designed to build a civilian society."[59]

Yet there were deep disagreements among senior leaders about how best and how fast to pass authority to the Iraqis while reducing U.S. presence. The DOD solution was a short transition period for military forces with a quick turnover of authority to Iraqi expatriates.[60] Secretary of Defense Donald Rumsfeld supported diverse efforts to anticipate nightmare scenarios that might derail the war effort, so he was not averse to considering ways plans could go awry.[61] He knew extended occupations could be costly, complicated, and counterproductive.[62] His way of avoiding the problem was to transfer it to the host nation to manage with assistance from other parties. He was well known for his bicycle analogy,[63] arguing that in teaching someone to ride a bicycle you have to take your hand off the bicycle seat. Secretary Rumsfeld argues the United States has a habit of trying to do too much for too long for other countries, exhausting itself and irritating and corrupting the host nation:

> *I understood that there were times when the United States would not be able to escape some national-building responsibilities, particularly in countries where we had been engaged militarily. It would take many years to rebuild societies shattered by war and tyranny. Though we would do what we could to assist, we ultimately couldn't do it for them. My view was that the Iraqis and Afghans would have to govern themselves in ways that worked for them. I believed that political institutions should grow naturally out of local soil; not every successful principle or mechanism from one country could be transplanted in another.[64]*

In other words, Rumsfeld thought those who believed the United States could export democracy and prosperity were the ones making rosy assumptions.[65] He favored an early handoff to the North Atlantic Treaty Organization (NATO) in Afghanistan, which he got.[66] In Iraq he wanted U.S. commanders "to accept as much risk getting out of Iraq as they had taken getting in." When commanders asked what that meant, they were told to "accelerate the withdrawal of forces."[67] Rumsfeld's staff warned him about postwar lawlessness,[68] but he believed it was best managed by parties other than the U.S. military, preferably other countries or international organizations recruited by the State Department, and eventually the Iraqis themselves.[69] In his memoirs, Rumsfeld argues that he wanted State to take more responsibility for the postwar effort (even though it was clear that the department could not effectively do so) and notes he had recommended for months that Ambassador L. Paul Bremer—the President's special envoy to Iraq—report to the President through State and not Defense.[70] He practiced what he preached, discouraging preparations for postwar lawlessness, a four-star headquarters to organize and oversee the occupation, and the flow of additional ground forces to theater once victory over the Iraqi military was assured.[71] In short, Rumsfeld was skeptical about the ability of the United States to engineer a stable and prosperous Iraq regardless of effort, and he wanted someone else in charge of that mission.

The Department of State, including Secretary Colin Powell and Ambassador Bremer, did not want an extended occupation of Iraq, either; in fact, Bremer notes it "was certain to be a short occupation."[72] However, these leaders believed that it would difficult to find others willing to take responsibility for the future of Iraq and that the United States would have to do so since it had engineered the war. After the acrimonious international debate over deposing Saddam, it was important to stop the hemorrhaging of political support for the war on terror, something a chaotic Iraq would accelerate and a stable Iraq would help reduce. Thus, State wanted the speed and scale of U.S. postwar activities commensurate with the U.S. interests at stake. It thought the quickest way out of Iraq was to make the maximum effort to stabilize it following the termination of large-scale fighting, which meant a large ground force for security, plenty of development assistance, and as much international support as could be mustered. Secretary Powell was well known for his approach to overseas interventions, which postulated that a large force and effort early on make them more manageable. He had no illusions about the possibility of postwar disorder; he warned the President on just this point. Secretary Powell and Ambassador Bremer repeatedly emphasized the importance of security and lamented not only the unwillingness of DOD to provide more troops but also State's inability to provide the number, quality, and duration of civil administrators needed to put Iraq back on its feet.[73]

In short, neither State nor DOD based their approaches to postwar Iraq on wishful thinking. On the contrary, they worried about how difficult an occupation could be. The fact that postwar governance and stability could be tough and costly informed White House thinking on the extent to which the United States should commit itself to a stable, prosperous, and democratic Iraq:

> *"So, if we get rid of Saddam, what is our obligation to* [the] *Iraqi people? Is it Saddamism without Saddam, or, putting it another way, a strong military leader within the existing system that simply agrees that he will not support terror, and will not develop* [weapons of mass destruction], *will not invade his neighbors, and will be not quite as brutal to his own people as Saddam was. Is that okay?" There was a conversation, and the President's view was we would get rid of Saddam Hussein for national security reasons, not because we were promoting democracy out of the barrel of a gun. We were going to have to remove him for hard national security reasons, but then what was our obligation to the Iraqi people? And the President said: "We stand for freedom and democracy. We ought to give the Iraqi people a chance, a chance with our help, to build a democratic system." And that's how the democracy piece got in, not that it had to be a Jeffersonian democracy, not that it had to be in our image, not that we wouldn't leave until the job is done, but we would give them a chance. And once we got into it, we realized that there had to be a democratic outcome because that was the only way you would keep the country together.*[74]

Thus, the President was committed to a good-faith but not an open-ended effort.[75] This limited commitment was understandable if good postwar governance was a desirable but not vital interest of the United States. The value of good postwar governance was then relative to its cost, which was unknowable in advance.[76]

Trying to assess the importance of a single planning assumption like how difficult postwar governance would be quickly leads to debate about other corollary assumptions. It soon becomes clear that senior leaders disagree about which assumptions were most important. While former Secretary of Defense Robert Gates and General Abizaid underscore the assumption of short, relatively easy occupations, former Deputy National Security Advisor Stephen J. Hadley and Ambassador Bremer underscore the importance of the assumption that Iraqi units would hold together well enough to help with postwar security.[77] Former Vice President Dick Cheney, Secretary Rumsfeld, and former Under Secretary of Defense for Policy Douglas J. Feith call attention to the assumption that U.S. forces would alienate local populations (something both the Bush and Obama administrations debated).[78] A RAND study notes that there were two key assumptions, one of which was that senior military commanders believed civilian authorities would be responsible for the postwar period.[79] Still others questioned the assumption that democracy could be imposed on foreign countries and cultures. Academics disagree on this issue but generally assert that "it depends" on the country in question and the level of commitment of the occupying power.[80]

The President's decision to give Iraqis a chance at democracy because it was the right thing to do but not a vital interest meant State and DOD could not ignore the postwar mission. However, it also left plenty of wiggle room for disagreements about how the mission should be conducted. The two departments obliged. They disagreed over the importance of ensuring good governance in Afghanistan and Iraq, over the appropriate level of U.S. commitment to this mission, over how it should be carried out, and over which department would do what to execute postwar tasks. These disagreements should not have been a surprise; they had been a longstanding bone of contention between the two departments. Consistent with previous experience,[81] President Bush did not resolve the differences.

The President gave the lead for postwar planning to DOD to preserve "unified effort." But he also promised Ambassador Bremer that he would have the authority and time he needed to stabilize Iraq (that is, take the Department of State approach). As the situation deteriorated, State was increasingly adamant about security and DOD was increasingly adamant about early departure for U.S. forces.[82] State increased its appeals for more troops, while Rumsfeld's generals told him irregular warfare was an intelligence-dependent mission and that more troops would be counterproductive. President Bush reiterated his promise to support more time and resources for Iraq when Bremer worried that DOD was setting him up to take responsibility for failure by pushing an accelerated schedule for turning over authority to the Iraqis.[83] The NSC staff refereed the debates between State and DOD, looking for ways to effect compromises. The views of the two departments were not reconciled and the success of the postwar mission was compromised—not because of optimistic assumptions about Iraqi sentiments but because differences between strong departments were not managed well, a topic we examine in great detail in the next section of the chapter.

Another common complaint is that senior leaders fail to consider a wide range of options. Academic research has long noted the deleterious tendency to lock in on one option rather than considering a wide range of possibilities before choosing a course of action.[84] In general, senior leaders were sensible to this danger.[85] General Dempsey notes that friction and disagreement among senior leaders are good because they ensure that a wide range of perspectives is considered, and this certainly seems to describe decisionmaking in both the Bush and Obama administrations. With a couple of exceptions, it is clear that both administrations went to great lengths to make sure a range of options was considered before making key decisions.

Criticism about a restricted range of options converges on two key decisions. First, it is often asserted the Bush administration erred in not considering options for managing security better in Iraq after the end of large-scale fighting with the Iraqi army. But as we have just argued, senior leaders did not ignore an obvious problem area; they were just unable to resolve differences over what to do about it.[86] The postwar lawlessness was widely anticipated even if the rapid rise of the Sunni insurgency was not, and the failure to prepare for postwar civil unrest helped kick-start the insurgency. In turn, the failure to prepare well for lawlessness was in part a result of the failure to reconcile the two alternative approaches to managing the problem preferred by the Department of State and the Department of Defense.

The second major complaint concerns bureaucracies deciding on a preferred course and then engineering White House approval without a fair hearing of alternatives. This occurred in both the Bush and Obama administrations and most notably when discussing whether to surge U.S. forces to quell the insurgencies. These decisions are covered at length in the previous chapter. However, to recapitulate, the charge is that "the military produced too few and too narrow of options."[87] When President Bush "raised the idea of more troops going to Iraq . . . all of the chiefs unloaded on him, not only questioning the value of additional forces but expressing concern about the impact on the military if asked to send thousands more troops."[88] Similarly, Pentagon war planners resisted President Obama's request for "every option and contingency" and instead, "like characters in the Goldilocks story," provided three options with the first and last grossly flawed so that only their preferred course of action—the middle one—made any sense at all.[89]

Interestingly, it can be argued that the Pentagon's premature closure on its preferred options for the Surge relates to key assumptions. A major assumption among uniformed and civilian defense leaders was that the mere presence of U.S. forces alienated the population. General Abizaid made this point,[90] and Secretary Rumsfeld agreed. He cites approvingly the analysis by Douglas Feith—that the broader impression of an overbearing U.S. presence was more to blame for unrest in Iraq than de-Ba'athification or the disbanding of the Iraqi army. Senior military leaders in Iraq—even those who took counterinsurgency seriously—also believed the U.S. presence was an irritant, which inclined them to focus on the goal of transferring capacity and responsibility for counterinsurgency to host-nation forces. If "our exit strategy ran through the Iraqi security forces," it was logical to argue, "we needed to double down on the Iraqis and not on our own forces."[91] Using American forces would signal to Iraqis that the United States would always underwrite their poor decisions.

Those supporting the Surge questioned the veracity of this assumption,[92] and when it was deemed a success in Iraq, defense leaders embraced the opposite assumption, arguing a larger U.S. presence could have a calming effect by demonstrating resolve (not unlike the original military argument for going in with a large force).[93] Uniformed leaders with this viewpoint were promoted, and new civilian leadership argued for a Surge in Afghanistan. Beyond the Pentagon, however, many new civilian leaders in the Obama administration thought the previous assumption about the irritating nature of a U.S. force presence was more realistic. They argued that "[m]ore troops and more fighting would alienate Afghan civilians and undermine any goodwill achieved by expanded economic development and improved governance."[94]

Some participants in the Surge decisions believe the White House misinterpreted the unanimity of opinion among defense leaders on the value of a Surge as a "'military bloc' determined to force the commander in chief's hand."[95] Some also argue there was a time lag that made the Pentagon resistance seem worse than it was to the White House.[96] There is room for debate on these issues. The notable point is that the simple act of internally coordinating a major department's position on a key issue for Presidential decision can be or appear to be an attempt to limit the President's options. The perception that the military bureaucracy was cooking options was a major point of friction between military and civilian authorities. However, it did not prevent the White House from hearing alternative views.[97] Therefore, in our view, the major problem in decisionmaking was not generating options and alternative views but the failure to reconcile those competing views productively. This was true for postwar planning, and it proves true for most other key decisions we review elsewhere in this chapter.

The last prerequisite for good decisionmaking we review—adjusting decisions in light of changing circumstances—seems to have been a much greater challenge. One reason for this is that it was difficult to come up with good indicators of success or failure. Before adjusting previous decisions, leaders had to agree on how things were changing and why. This was difficult. The same evidence—for example, levels of violence—could be used to support arguments that we were winning or losing. The positive assessment was that the opposition was making a pitched fight and would lose; the negative assessment was that the opposition was mobilized and growing and could fill its ranks no matter how many were killed. To make such complicated assessments of progress required an in-depth knowledge of Afghan and Iraqi politics and culture that the United States lacked (a point we return to later).[98]

Difficulties finding clear-cut metrics for progress notwithstanding, it does appear there were occasions when leaders resisted new evidence that challenged their existing convictions (cognitive dissonance). Secretary Rumsfeld, for example, was slow to recognize the emergence of an insurgency[99] in Iraq even though he later applauded General Abizaid for bringing the changed circumstances to his attention.[100] In addition, Hadley notes the White House was slow to reassess options when the Iraqi army melted away.[101] On the other hand, in response to changed circumstances, the White House was willing to pull in experts to learn about the demands of counterinsurgency. Commanders who applied time-tested counterinsurgency methods and enjoyed field success as a result might find themselves briefing the President, Vice President, Secretary of Defense, or other senior military and civilian leaders.[102]

Some leaders such as Vice President Cheney, Secretary Rumsfeld, and other defense leaders complain the NSC process made it difficult to adjust policies in light of new developments.[103] They argue National Security Advisor Condoleezza Rice imposed compromises that obscured a clear articulation of options on how to manage the war in Iraq. As we discuss, Dr. Rice denies this. It is interesting that in the Obama administration, Cabinet officials sometimes complained about the opposite tendency. Secretaries Clinton and Gates, for instance, suggest the Obama administration looked at options in Afghanistan "from every conceivable angle" and perhaps past the point of marginal additional benefit.[104]

We believe the record on senior leader adaptation to evolving circumstances is mixed. The innovative dimension of the Surge decisions is discussed in the previous chapter, and we review other notable successes and failures to innovate in the rest of this chapter. In summary, however, it seems clear that the willingness to consider alternative options and courses of action in response to evolving local conditions varied by leader, issue, and strength of the organizational culture resisting change.

In sum, there is room for improvement on adaptability, something General Dempsey and General McChrystal believe is quite important. They observe that in dynamic irregular warfare challenges, the key to success is not prognosticating well at the outset but adapting and innovating faster than the adversary.[105] The U.S. national security bureaucracy was not nimble in this respect. The lack of a clear strategy and bureaucratic conflict contributed to sluggish performance in Afghanistan and Iraq in several ways. For example, the lack of coherent strategy was a major factor undermining the U.S. ability to command and control the war effort for greatest effect. We examine this topic in the next section.

Command

Unified effort is important because working at cross-purposes is inefficient and often ineffective as well. The assumption that unified effort is useful reflects a decisionmaking bias in favor of coherence "based on the principles of rationality, causality, and intentionality."[106] This bias inclines "reformers" to "advocate more systematic attempts to define objectives, establish knowledge about the world, coordinate among different aspects of a decision, and exercise control in the name of some central vision."[107] The reformer perspective that favors unified effort is consistent with our assumption that senior leader decisionmaking was "choice based" and an instrumental activity designed to defeat terrorism. It also is consistent with the purpose of this current volume: identifying lessons from experience.

The conceptual failures reviewed in the previous section were a major impediment to unified effort, but not the only one. Other organizational limitations also diminished the ability of senior leaders to generate unified effort, which was a multidimensional challenge. International cooperation required diplomacy; partnership among the executive, judicial, and legislative branches required political action; collaboration between executive branch departments and agencies required Presidential intervention; coherent efforts within departments and agencies required good leadership from Cabinet officials; and so on. Here our focus is on unified effort within the executive branch, where there were successes and failures.

To be clear, we are not talking about disagreements per se, but rather the persistence of unresolved differences that lead to conflicting behaviors. Good decisionmaking requires a range of views, but once a decision has been made the entire organization needs to implement the decision with unified effort. Sometimes this happened.[108] However, senior leaders in both the Bush and Obama administrations often cite friction between national leaders and organizations as the Achilles' heel of the U.S. war effort. Few other topics generate so much piercing commentary from senior leaders as problems with the chain of command and interagency coordination, which we refer to as vertical and horizontal unity of effort issues.[109] Beginning with vertical unity of effort, we consider impediments to unified effort at three levels—decisionmaking at the national level (meaning between the White House staff and organizations constituting the National Security Council); within departments and agencies, particularly the Pentagon; and in the field (that is, Afghanistan and Iraq).

Vertical Unity of Effort

Vertical unity of effort refers to the lines of authority from the President down through the departments and agencies of the national security system. Our concern is with the way the President's guidance and instructions are communicated by senior leaders and implemented by subordinates in the executive branch. The necessity and challenge of delegating authority in the national security system have been well recognized for decades.[110] The President can involve himself in a miniscule portion of the decisions made throughout the national security system. Like all leaders commanding large organizations, he must issue broad guidance and count on subordinates to implement the guidance consistent with his intent and extant circumstances.

To make delegated authority work, there must be unity of command, which the U.S. military considers a principle of war. The Constitution provides for unity of command by making the President commander in chief of the Armed Forces and chief executive of the executive branch of government. Nevertheless, multiple forces limit the President's ability to generate unified effort. Problems arise when there is confusion about who is in charge of what; when the President's guidance is neglected or reinterpreted; and when the President is not able to review and issue clarifying instructions in a timely manner as circumstances evolve. These types of complications to vertical unity of effort were evident in the war on terror at multiple levels.

Confusion about who was in charge of various efforts arose early and continued throughout the war. President Bush was frustrated when he discovered DOD and the Central Intelligence Agency (CIA) each thought the other had the lead for operations in Afghanistan.[111] The mixup was due in part to the nature of the nontraditional threat, which required responses from multiple departments and agencies and raised doubts about which organization would lead the effort. President Bush and President Obama tried to eliminate such uncertainty by assigning "czars" in Washington or special envoys overseas to lead interagency missions. Some argue this practice led to bureaucratic conflict in Washington and confusion abroad about who spoke for the President.[112] In Afghanistan and Iraq, senior leader accounts suggest the performance of czars and special envoys was mixed and changed over time.[113] L. Paul Bremer was the most controversial such figure. Bremer's appointment did not simplify the President's job. Instead, it accentuated disagreements among State, Defense, and White House staffs about who was in the chain of command between the President and Bremer. The origins of Bremer's substantive policy preferences were disputable.[114] However, what seemed clear was that Bremer "was convinced that he worked for the President," even though his terms of reference stated he worked for the Secretary of Defense.[115] Senior DOD leaders insist the confusion about Bremer's reporting chain sidetracked the entire mission in Iraq.[116] President Obama's special envoy to Afghanistan and Pakistan caused similar consternation when, "reporting to [Secretary Clinton] but working closely with the White House," White House officials "saw his [Richard Holbrooke's] efforts to coordinate among various government agencies as encroaching on their turf."[117]

Senior officials also offer examples of Presidential guidance being ignored, exceeded, resisted, or misinterpreted to the detriment of coherence as it passed through the bureaucracy.[118] President Bush believed the Secretary of State "wasn't fully on board with [his] philosophy and policies,"[119] and the Vice President notes that on occasion both the Secretary of State and Secretary of Defense exceeded Presidential guidance.[120] George Tenet asserts the President's guidance on cutting funding to certain Iraqi exile groups was ignored.[121] Secretary Clinton argues that some of her initiatives were held up by White House officials who "wanted to be sure that State wasn't trying to usurp the White House's role as the primary coordinator of activity across the various agencies, especially when it came to communications." Clinton states these officials were out of step with the President, who had been asking for "this kind of plan for more than a year."[122] The President and White House officials in both the Bush and Obama administrations believed Pentagon leaders sometimes were not supportive of the President's agenda. Cheney points to "ongoing resistance inside the Pentagon and at [U.S.] Central Command to the surge strategy,"[123] and both secretaries of State and Defense acknowledge the Obama White House felt "boxed in" by Pentagon demands for more troops in Afghanistan.[124]

The trouble Presidents have ensuring unified effort down the chain of command is replicated at the level of Cabinet officials. Multiple sources, including the Chairman of the Joint Chiefs of Staff, indicate the commander of U.S. Central Command (USCENTCOM) would not take postwar planning seriously as directed by himself and the Secretary of Defense.[125] "Big organizations are just difficult to manage," states Secretary Rice in her memoirs. "As Secretary of Defense Bob Gates and I used to say to each other, only half-jokingly, 'You never know what your building is doing until it's too late.'"[126] Unified effort was also an issue among deployed military forces, which may surprise those who thought Goldwater-Nichols Department of Defense Reorganization Act of 1986 reforms solved "the age-old" military command problem "of too many high-ranking generals with a hand on the tiller."[127] Secretary Gates is forthright in acknowledging command relationships in Afghanistan were a "jerry-rigged arrangement [that] violated every principle of the unity of command." Some U.S. forces reported to the commander of the International Security Assistance Force in Kabul, others "to a separate U.S. three-star general, who in turn reported to the four-star commander of Central Command," and still others to the commander of U.S. Special Operations Command (USSOCOM).

The lack of joint command and control contributed to the inability of the Army and Air Force, and to some extent the Marine Corps, to adequately cooperate on the battlefield.[128] Overlapping and ad hoc command arrangements in Afghanistan also are a major reason SOF worked at cross-purposes with larger campaign objectives. Kill/capture operations took precedence over the indirect approach to counterinsurgency, even though there was broad agreement among the U.S. national security and USSOCOM leadership that the opposite was necessary.[129] In 2008, a 6-week interagency review found that in Kandahar Province alone there were 10 separate chains of command managing 10 separate warfighting efforts.

Similarly, before General McChrystal assumed command in Afghanistan in 2009, he reviewed an incident where Afghan civilians were inadvertently killed. He found:

> *There was an Afghan force that had a Marine Special Operations Command . . . element working with it, which didn't own the battlespace, but was out there doing its own thing. There was a Special Forces regional taskforce, which was also operating in the area, but was different from the battlespace owner. And then there were the forces that dropped the bomb which killed the civilians. He found that there were at least five players in the proximity of the incident, but nobody was in charge. The different entities didn't even have the requirement to keep each other informed of what they were doing.*[130]

This kind of disunity of command persisted until Secretary Gates ordered it rectified in the summer of 2010, nearly 9 years after the war started.[131] Gates considered getting "all American forces (including both special operations and the Marines) under the U.S. theater commander [and] at last establishing unity of command," an accomplishment akin to securing the Holy Grail.

Strong subordinate organizations resisted unified command, and their cultures also undermined unified effort in other ways. General Casey was concerned about the willingness of U.S. ground forces to embrace counterinsurgency principles. He thought Army and Marine Corps organizational cultures would "hamper our ability to accomplish the mission" because they were focused on the use of force. He knew he was "attempting to change deeply embedded Service culture and that [he] would have to change the mindset of the force," but "underestimated how long this would take."[132] Service cultures also complicated coordination of air-ground operations. General Richard Myers, USAF (Ret.), believes the lack of jointness in this area was a command failure that cost brave Americans their lives. He told General Tommy Franks, USA, then commander of USCENTCOM, that it was "absolutely unacceptable," and believes Franks took immediate action to fix the problem.[133]

As important as it is to pursue the senior leader's intent, subordinate units also need the latitude to achieve objectives consistent with extant circumstances. While many brigade commanders never comprehended or supported counterinsurgency doctrine, others improved on the preferred approach to counterinsurgency.[134] Then-Colonel Julian Alford, USMC, is a case in point. His unexpected success in pacifying al-Qaim near the Syrian border in 2005 drew the attention of General Casey, who visited Alford repeatedly and asked him to help educate other commanders on counterinsurgency methods.[135] Other notable Marine commanders emulated Alford with success, including Lieutenant Colonel William M. Jurney in Ramadi in 2006 and Lieutenant Colonel William Mullen III in Fallujah in 2007.[136] Similarly, a series of Army field commanders achieved unexpected counterinsurgency success by reaching out to local authorities and indigenous forces to partner on securing the local populations. Captain Jim Calvert in Qaim, Colonel Robert Brown in Mosul, Colonel H.R. McMaster in Tal Afar, and Colonel Sean MacFarland in Ramadi are all notable in this respect. In essence they were challenging policy and strategy established by superiors in their chain of command:

> Instead of communicating an intention to leave Iraq to Iraqis, Mac-Farland expressed commitment to their cause. He explained that if the Iraqis stood up for themselves, he and his forces would stay until they were "secure from al Qaeda and the Persians [Iranians]." He promised

to create a Sunni police militia that would become part of the Iraqi government but stay in Ramadi to protect their homes and families. To do so, MacFarland required "non-standard funding sources" available through interagency contacts. . . . In what MacFarland would later describe as "the game changer," Ramadi's police force increased from 150 to 4,000 in a matter of months. Consequently, intelligence and counterinsurgency capabilities improved and eventually responsibility for security operations began transitioning to the Iraqis.[137]

Simply put, MacFarland reversed existing policy, which was to tell the Iraqis, "You stand up, and we'll stand down."[138] Instead, he promised, "if you stand up, we'll stand by you." The other successful field commanders did the same.

The national security system's ability to learn and adapt to emerging conditions is reviewed in the previous chapter. Here we note there were some examples of learning in the field that should be encouraged. Field commanders were given the latitude to apply guidance as they thought local circumstances demanded, and some did so in innovative and successful ways. The Chairman's white paper on "mission command" philosophy, derived from warfighting experience over the past decade, explicitly argues the point that in complex and dynamic environments, subordinates should be encouraged to innovate more and given the latitude to do so.[139]

Innovation is risky when commander's intent is not well understood or commanders are not inclined to give subordinates much latitude. It could be misinterpreted as disloyalty to the chain of command and their preferred approaches. Concerning the decision to surge forces, General Casey concludes:

In retrospect, I believe that I should have directly offered the President a broader range of options for achieving our objectives in Iraq. I had discussed different options for improving the security situation with the Secretary of Defense and Chairman. . . . In the end, I only presented the President the course of action we selected—accelerated transition—and I believe that I should have offered him a wider range of options to meet his policy needs.[140]

General Casey knew that his DOD superiors and all the Service chiefs did not support the Surge and preferred greater efforts to hand off the security mission to Iraqi forces. Providing realistic alternatives to their preferred approach for the President's consideration would require ignoring his superiors' policy preferences and could have been interpreted as jumping the chain of command.

Alford, McMaster, MacFarland, and other successful field commanders faced the same dilemma working under Casey.[141] Yet they realized local Iraqi leaders could not afford to support American forces and the new government if the forces were trying to leave and the government looked like it would collapse. Success required convincing locals that the United States was "in it to win it," defined as not walking away until the government could manage its own security. Thus, these commanders had to turn the prevailing counterinsurgency approach on its head. As noted previously, instead of stating U.S. forces would stand down as the Iraqis took responsibility for security, they assured local Iraqis that if they stood up to defend themselves, U.S. forces would stand by them until the enemy was defeated. Some general officers such as General McChrystal also innovated well in trying circumstances.[142]

Innovation needs to be recognized, rewarded, and quickly replicated. In most cases the successes were recognized; they were so glaring they could hardly be ignored. Lessons from successful commanders also were shared both formally and informally (for example, Jurney learned directly from Alford, and MacFarland from McMaster). However, the record on rewarding and replicating these tactical successes was spotty. Some, but hardly all, successful field commanders were promoted by their parent organizations, and sometimes only begrudgingly.

The replication of these successful examples was even more limited. General Casey was right to be concerned about U.S. ground forces accepting counterinsurgency principles that ran against their organizational cultures. At best, the U.S. military adopted proven counterinsurgency techniques slowly and unevenly.[143] More importantly, however, tactical successes were not replicated because the methods they relied upon challenged prevailing policy and strategy. Tactical partnering with local forces could fuel sectarian sentiments and undermine formal Iraqi governmental structures that the United States was committed to supporting. It also often involved working with local leaders with checkered pasts or who were judged by U.S. leaders or intelligence to be marginal players, and it ran counter to the policy of transferring responsibility for security to Iraqi military forces as fast as possible, which was based on the assumption that the mere presence of U.S. forces was an irritant to be minimized as a matter of priority.[144] For all these reasons, the tactical successes of Marine and Army field commanders in late 2004 and 2005 failed to prompt a rapid reassessment of policy and strategy assumptions.

If mission command is going to take root and become a useful element of U.S. military culture, we need to consider the broader organizational implications of the concept. We need to better understand why some officers are inclined to innovate and learn from others; what it would take to make their examples more common if not the norm; and especially how to assess and replicate more rapidly successful innovation from the bottom up when it challenges existing senior leader assumptions.

It also needs to be acknowledged that innovation can backfire, especially where the commander's intent is not clear. Ambassador Bremer secured wide discretionary authority from the President without clear guidance on the purpose of occupying Iraq. His most controversial decisions—handling expatriate Iraqi leaders, disbanding (or not reconstituting) the Iraqi army, and de-Ba'athification—were so contentious because it was not clear whether they were consistent with Presidential intent.[145] Indeed, some argue Bremer was chosen because he was a take-charge kind of person who could operate without guidance: "In Bremer, the administration saw a hands-on and assertive administrator: a veritable proconsul who would grab hold of the turmoil that was Iraq and get the Bush administration's program there back on track."[146]

Some historical accounts lionize special envoys, "czars," and other national security officials for working around the limitations of the current system to generate good outcomes.[147] Recent studies of the national security system, however, warn that policy entrepreneurs constitute a "roll of the dice." They often have limited access to all available resources, rely upon questionable legal authorities, pursue policies based on faulty but unchallenged assumptions, and make poor use of subject matter experts and other institutional expertise.[148] Considered in the context of broader system attributes, turning over decisionmaking to an assertive, high-profile special envoy is more akin to mission roulette than mission command. Policy entrepreneurs such as Ambassador Bremer or Ambassador Richard Holbrooke are neither heroes nor villains. They are courageous, experienced leaders forced by circumstances and assignment to gamble the Nation's welfare and their reputations without a clear understanding of national objectives or much control over the combined forces the United States can bring to bear upon the problems they are assigned to resolve. When they succeed they are lionized; when they fail they are denigrated, and often their careers are destroyed.[149] Forced to work with uncertain authority, control, and situational awareness, the odds are not stacked in favor of their success.

More oversight to ensure accountability is the usual fix for subordinates generating poor outcomes, but in the current system, that tends to generate charges of micromanagement. Everyone is in favor of good oversight in principle, which requires leaders to take responsibility for what happens under their authority and fix problems rather than assign blame when things go awry. At the same time, everyone loathes micromanagers far removed from the problem who tell their subordinates not only what to do but also how to do it. In fact, it is more common for Washington insiders to rail about micromanagement than lack of oversight. For example, a group of senior leaders with much experience in both the Bush and Obama administrations has argued the United States has no hope of success in countering the Islamic State of Iraq and the Levant unless it overcomes the crippling problem of "tight Washington tactical control of decisions in the field of the sort so beloved by bureaucratic Washington departments and power centers."[150]

Getting the balance right between helpful oversight and unhelpful micromanagement is difficult in the current system for multiple reasons.[151] For one thing, a clear difference between the two is often discernable only in retrospect as the consequences of leader interventions (or lack thereof) emerge. The White House's orchestration of the Surge in Iraq and Secretary Gates's insistence on producing Mine-Resistant Ambush Protected (MRAP) vehicles are cases in point. Most people consider these interventions helpful oversight in retrospect because they appeared to work. On the other hand, most people now believe the CIA's Rendition, Detention, and Interrogation program did not receive sufficient oversight even though it was approved by the President, Vice President, National Security Advisor, and U.S. Attorney General, and reviewed by the chairmen and ranking Members of the Senate and House intelligence committees. Since no attack comparable to 9/11 has materialized, the unpopular program is now often described as ineffectual and unnecessary.

It may be difficult to distinguish between good oversight and micromanagement before outcomes are evident, but some general observations are possible. First, there is an interesting consistency in how senior leaders describe the difference between helpful oversight and unhelpful micromanagement; they appreciate the value of giving guidance more than receiving it. In times past, disarmament experts used to quip that a weapon is offensive or defensive depending upon which end of the barrel a person stands at. Similarly, we can jest that leader interventions are oversight or micromanagement, depending upon which end of the guidance pipeline a person stands at. This witticism has an empirical basis; senior leaders complain about guidance from superiors but see their own guidance to subordinates as helpful. They also demonstrate great sensitivity to higher authority requesting information from their subordinates but themselves seek unfiltered information from lower echelons of their organizations.

For example, Dr. Rice complained that Secretary Rumsfeld was hypersensitive when her staff went to sources in the field and the Pentagon for "routine" information, but she also threatened to resign when she thought DOD bypassed her to get Presidential approval on military commissions to try detainees.[152] Secretary Rumsfeld advocated delegated authority, but he also handpicked senior general officers for positions in the Pentagon, objected to the latitude Ambassador Bremer was given as the President's representative in Iraq, tried to bypass the Ambassador in Poland,[153] and subjected his own subordinates—including his Deputy Secretary of Defense—to such close scrutiny that they were afraid to speak up without his permission. "Fed up with the National Security Council staff's micromanagement," Secretary Gates cut off their contact with his forces in the field, but when he visited Afghanistan and Iraq, he liked to meet with unsupervised lower ranking officers to get ground truth.[154] Gates also was frustrated that President Obama would not accept the unanimous decision by his senior uniformed advisors on troop levels in Afghanistan, but at the same time was dismayed that the entire uniformed leadership of the Pentagon did not support his position on the urgent need to acquire better armored vehicles and other material.[155] Secretary Clinton's memoir suggests that she needed direct communication with the President to overcome White House staff interference with her plans, but she also fought to ensure Ambassador Christopher Hill's weekly message to the President went through her.[156] General Franks threatened to resign over unwarranted interference from the Secretary of Defense and bristled over critiques of his war plans by Service chiefs, but he had a reputation for insisting on being well informed on his subordinates' activities and demanding stringent compliance.[157]

Another insight is that the higher one goes in the national security system, the more pronounced the ostensible aversion to micromanagement, so much so that the sentiment constrains good oversight. There is common agreement that the White House (that is, NSC staff) should make policy but not get involved in the details of managing national security issues. In noting his job was to make sure plans were comprehensive and consistent with his strategic vision, but not to manage logistics or tactical decisions, President Bush stated he remembered how deleterious it was for President Lyndon Johnson to pick bombing targets in Vietnam.[158] Another historical example that White House officials cite as a caution against micromanagement is the Iran-Contra Affair. A Presidential Special Review Board headed by Senator John Tower investigated the incident during the Reagan administration and recommended several corrective measures, including an injunction against NSC staff implementing policy or conducting operations. In the same way that President Johnson's picking bombing targets is invoked as shorthand for civilian meddling in military matters,[159] Iran-Contra is routinely offered up as substantiated proof that the NSC staff should never delve into operational matters but instead leave those details to Cabinet officials.[160]

Experience in the war on terror suggests that we have "overlearned" the lessons of Iran-Contra, but senior leaders are slow to embrace this insight for fear of being labeled micromanagers. Condoleezza Rice and Stephen Hadley are cases in point. Dr. Rice explains in her memoir how Iran-Contra informed her views and those of her deputy, Hadley, who had served as counsel to the Tower Commission. Together they resolved to carry out the President's agenda through and not around Cabinet secretaries.[161] Thus, President Bush and his national security staff began their tenure determined to make policy but delegate well and let the system worry about implementation details. This same commitment to empowering subordinates also inclined President Bush to grant maximum flexibility to his man on the ground in Iraq, Ambassador Bremer.[162]

Yet when failure loomed, the President, Rice, and Hadley developed a keen appreciation for the value of detailed oversight even though it meant being accused of micromanagement. Rice saw the White House needed "better connectivity" with Bremer and his staff in Baghdad, and to get it she created the Iraq Stabilization Group headed by a "black belt in bureaucratic politics." This led to intense friction with the Secretary of Defense, the accusation that she was interfering in the chain of command, and also a short-lived reprimand from the President. President Bush objected to Dr. Rice summoning Ambassador Bremer to Washington to explain next steps in Iraq because he knew there would be fallout from bypassing Secretary Rumsfeld, who was sensitive to "what he thought to be White House interference in the chain of command." Rice told the President she could cancel Bremer's trip, but added, "Don't be surprised when the United States has a new plan for Iraq's political transition that you haven't seen." The President relented and asked when Bremer was coming.[163] Rice remained sensitive to the charge of micromanagement, however, admitting she was "far deeper into operational matters than [she thought] wise." Yet she ended up being glad she intervened.[164]

Similarly, Hadley remains convinced that the Tower Commission's injunction against NSC staff getting involved in operations remains "absolutely true." At the same time, he admits that the Iraq strategy could not succeed "if we gave it to the bureaucracy to be executed in the ordinary course [of business] because it would not get done in time." So he concludes, "the one thing we've learned since the Tower Commission report" is that "the NSC has the responsibility to ensure that policy decisions . . . are actually implemented and executed effectively." Hadley considers effective oversight of decision implementation (that is, operations) a "new frontier for the interagency process," and he experimented with alternative means of providing it. First he created an Afghan Operations Group—an interagency team with offices in the Department of State—and later he appointed a czar (Lieutenant General Douglas Lute, USA) with "a direct line to the President."[165] Insider accounts of decisionmaking indicate he later took a much more hands-on personal role in engineering the White House intervention that led to the Surge.[166]

There will always be an "eye of the beholder" dimension to distinguishing helpful oversight from unhelpful micromanagement. However, several insights may assist future leaders on this difficult topic. First, experienced leaders make a distinction between gathering information and intervening to direct subordinate behaviors. Since authority can be delegated, but not responsibility,[167] it is incumbent upon leaders to stay well informed about progress toward objectives, identifying anything or anybody that is impeding success. All leaders, from the President to the local commander and Ambassador in the field, must understand well whether the collective endeavor they supervise is succeeding or failing. In arguing the Secretary of Defense has to master details and understand issues, Secretary Gates distinguishes between "micro-knowledge" and micromanagement. A poorly informed Secretary of Defense is a "kept" man at the Pentagon, enjoying the trappings of power but "without the knowledge or influence to effectively lead."[168] In essence this was the same point Dr. Rice made to President Bush when he bristled at her bringing Ambassador Bremer to Washington; the White House had to know what Bremer was planning to do next. Getting such information from the bureaucracy can be difficult. Hadley notes that during the Obama administration, trying to get inside information from DOD on options for a Surge cost two senior leaders their careers.[169]

When leaders do move beyond information collection to intervene with amplifying guidance—especially over the objections of subordinates—they need to make sure they do so for the right reasons. They should override subordinate concerns when they are convinced their broader field of vision gives them insights that those further down the chain of command lack; that with their privileged perspective they can see that the larger enterprise is at risk if some particular actions are not taken. Micromanagement occurs when leaders tell a subordinate what to do based on personal past experience or some other prejudice rather than their broader field of vision. Good oversight is based on contextual insights from a higher level, whereas micromanagement second-guesses a subordinate without the detailed knowledge of immediate circumstances that are known to the subordinate. The assumption here is that requirements for success visible from the higher level drive and thus trump the importance of outcomes at a lower level. If this assumption does not hold, as is sometimes the case when tactical results enable strategic outcomes, leaders must be especially averse to overriding subordinates with better knowledge of local conditions.

Finally, many senior leaders believe a good decisionmaking process can make helpful oversight more common and hurtful micromanagement less likely. For example, a common prescription for good teamwork is to promote vibrant debate and information-sharing before the senior leader decision is made, and unified effort to achieve the leader's intent and objective after he or she makes the decision.[170] Since information can be used to further the interests of subordinates rather than leaders (often referred to as the principal-agent problem), mutual trust is essential to make this general approach work—a point emphasized in the Chairman's white paper on mission command.[171] This is true of operations in Afghanistan and Iraq. Delegated authority worked best where trust was most prominent (for example, within some Ambassador–joint force commander pairings, some interagency field teams hunting high-value targets, and within the U.S. military chain of command that allowed field commanders to apply general guidance in specific circumstances as they saw fit).

Trust relationships across organizational boundaries take time and often prove fragile if not reinforced through relationships, process, and common cultures. As SOF like to say, "You can't surge trust." Yet properly nurtured, what once was perceived as unhelpful micromanagement may eventually be seen as helpful collaboration. General Franks's opinion of Secretary Rumsfeld's supervision of his war plans evolved in this manner.[172] Trust relationships also can deteriorate. Trust levels between CIA Director George Tenet and the Bush White House fell so far that cooperation between the two was impossible, and President Obama's confidence in DOD and uniformed leadership also deteriorated over the course of his first administration. Similarly, some interagency task forces chasing high-value targets collapsed when trust relationships were broken.[173] Overall, mistrust was a significant problem at multiple levels of the national security system and especially during planning and execution of Iraq operations.[174]

As we have seen, vertical unity of effort was a problem even though the U.S. national security system benefits from legal structures that ensure unity of command and from common organizational norms—especially but not exclusively in DOD—that support unified command and effort. Generating horizontal unity of effort across diverse departments and agencies with divergent missions and cultures was even more difficult and more consequential as well.

Horizontal Unity of Effort

Stated broadly, *horizontal unity of effort* refers to the way discrete organizations cooperate for common purposes when they are not accountable to the same authority, or when they are too far removed from a common authority to receive effective oversight. More narrowly, horizontal unity of effort in national security discourse refers to how well departments and agencies in the executive branch collaborate to accomplish national objectives or, in common parlance, interagency cooperation. The legal structures, authority relationships, and organizational norms in the national security system are much better established for vertical than for horizontal unity of effort, so it is not surprising the latter was more problematic. Poor horizontal collaboration was a major performance impediment because so many of the subsidiary objectives and tasks in the war on terror—such as attacking terrorist leaders, countering their narrative and promoting ours (that is, strategic communications), and interrupting terrorist financing—depended upon interagency cooperation. Conversely, some of the greatest successes in the war on terror were the result of collaboration across departmental lines.

DOD-CIA cooperation is most often cited as an example of interagency success, both the operational collaboration at the beginning of operations in Afghanistan and then the later and more general fusion of all-source intelligence with special operations to hunt enemy leaders. Another important area marked by notable interagency cooperation was some of the Department of State and DOD partnerships forged between Ambassadors and theater commanders. Ambassador Zalmay Khalilzad and Lieutenant General David Barno, USA, in Afghanistan (2003) and Ambassador Ryan Crocker and General David Petraeus, USA, in Iraq (2007) made strenuous efforts to collaborate,[175] which contributed to their making progress against the insurgencies during their tenures.[176] There were other interagency successes in countering terrorist financing and securing international cooperation.[177]

Unfortunately, these types of success were as sporadic as they were critical. According to senior leader accounts—and many "lessons learned" efforts as well[178]—interagency conflicts handicapped U.S. national security performance. President Bush deplored interagency squabbling, argued it hurt his administration's credibility, and noted he was unable to end it.[179] His Cabinet-level officials also attributed poor outcomes to the lack of cooperation between departments and agencies. Conflict between DOD and State was particularly severe, but there was substantial friction between the National Security Advisor and Cabinet officials. In the Bush administration, Secretary Gates was able to work well with Dr. Rice,[180] and in the Obama administration, Gates worked well with Secretary Clinton. However, even when those relationships were relatively harmonious there was substantial conflict between other national security components, including enduring tension between the White House and Cabinet officials, between senior intelligence officials vying for control of intelligence assets, and between Ambassadors and military commanders in the field.

Successful interagency cooperation efforts took time to develop, had to be nurtured, and were fragile and prone to deterioration. DOD-CIA cooperation is a case in point. The idea to embed SOF with the Northern Alliance came from the CIA and worked well. However, as DOD flowed conventional military units to theater, the ad hoc cooperation between the CIA and SOF subsided, which contributed to command and control problems in Operation *Anaconda*.[181] Interagency cooperation in hunting important enemy leaders has been maintained with great effort, but it too is subject to interruption.[182] General McChrystal observes no interagency alliance was "as infuriating or as productive" as his relationship with the CIA, and that "more than once" he had to be stopped "in moments of utter frustration, from severing all ties" with the agency.[183] There is always a price to be paid for being slow to generate interagency cooperation when missions demand it, and sometimes the price is quite high. Many argue, for example, that the postwar administration of Iraq was fatally flawed by interagency strife.[184]

Postwar planning was led by DOD. Putting one department or agency in the lead is the typical U.S. Government means of managing interagency missions. Even if a good ad hoc working relationship has been forged on the fly, leaders prefer designating a "lead agency" as soon as possible. The President insisted on knowing whether DOD or the CIA had the lead for operations in Afghanistan. DOD acknowledged the CIA's initial lead but demanded that it transition to DOD as forces flowed to theater.[185] The lead agency approach can work when there is a consensus that one department or agency has the preponderance of expertise needed to manage a mission. For example, other departments recognized the Treasury Department as the right lead for the interagency effort to counter terrorism financing. However, the traditional lead agency approach does not work well for nontraditional missions such as counterterrorism and counterinsurgency, which by their very nature require intense ongoing interdepartmental cooperation and have no obvious organizational lead. In such circumstances, lead departments and agencies may restrict participation by others to minimize their ability to interfere, and those not in the lead may restrict their support to save resources or avoid responsibility for outcomes they cannot control. Thus, in the words of one seasoned NSC staff person, "lead agency" almost always devolves into "sole agency"[186] as centrifugal organizational forces—desire for autonomy, different mandates and cultures, personality conflicts—militate against interagency cooperation.

Both postwar planning and the reconstruction effort led by the State Department are good examples.[187] DOD excluded State subject matter experts from its postwar planning team fearing they would not support its "light footprint" approach that assumed a quick turnover to Iraqi authorities.[188] Most sources agree that State-DOD relations reached their nadir as a result. Ironically, State and Defense positions on the need for State Department expertise on postwar reconstruction reversed over time but the interagency friction remained. After State regained the lead for reconstruction in Iraq, Ambassador Hill concluded the large number of Foreign Service personnel assigned to the task was unnecessary and only done "because the military wanted it that way." DOD demanded that State "step up" and join the war effort by providing ever greater numbers of personnel even though, in the Ambassador's view, "finding meaningful work for them was a challenge." The Ambassador wanted to reduce U.S. presence and let the Iraqis work out their own future (the initial DOD position), but most of all to diminish the overbearing role of DOD and return the lead for bilateral relations to State.[189]

The importance and difficulty of generating interagency cooperation were well recognized by senior leaders. It is doubtful any topic generates a greater degree of senior leader consensus than the assertion that irregular warfare requires effective orchestration of all elements of power, unless it is the related observation that the United States failed to meet this requirement well. Senior leaders in both the Bush and Obama administrations recognized the importance of interagency cooperation and offer examples of how the war effort was compromised by inadequate unity of effort. Some commentators opine that interagency conflict is a significant problem only in Washington, where big egos and budgets are in play, or only in the field, where coordinated actions count. In reality it was a liability at all levels of the national security system and among numerous departments and agencies, although some relationships were more fraught with friction than others.

At the national level, conflict between the Department of State and DOD was most remarked upon. There is a long history of such tension. Secretary Gates noted that for most of his career, "the Secretaries of State and Defense weren't speaking to one another."[190] Dr. Rice, who served both as National Security Advisor and Secretary of State, considers infighting between the two departments almost endemic. In an extended discussion, Rice explains the quarreling as a result of the huge disparity in resources that requires State to rely on DOD assets and the tendency of Defense to meddle in foreign policy. Rice discounts cultural differences, but other observers believe they also play a role. She also notes that during the first Bush term, State-DOD tensions were exacerbated by personal distrust between Secretaries Rumsfeld and Powell.[191] During the Obama administration the relationship was less contentious, but tension between the White House and DOD was more so. In both administrations, there were interagency cooperation problems between other departments and agencies besides State and Defense.

Poor relations among the White House, DOD, and Intelligence Community (IC) are another longstanding problem area at the national level. Many observers note the tendency for the IC and DOD to disagree about intelligence priorities as well as the frequency of conflicts between the IC and White House. The White House is concerned that the IC is trying to influence policy with the way it shades its products or even playing politics with intelligence assessments to the disadvantage of the White House. The IC (mainly CIA) in turn worries that the White House wants to skew intelligence assessments to support policy or, if things go poorly, blame the IC for poor assessments that failed to predict critical factors. These types of allegations ignore the inherent difficulties involved in predicting the future and divining the intentions and capabilities that are the closely guarded secrets of other countries. When leaders bandied these accusations about, they destroyed relationships, diminished cooperation, and contributed to a poisoning of public discourse about U.S. strategic options and progress in the war.[192]

Interagency collaboration is a significant problem in Washington where the only person with the authority to resolve such disputes is the President. Hence, it is not surprising to find interagency coordination is more of a problem the further the participants are removed from direct Presidential supervision. At the regional level, the struggle between State and DOD again stands out.[193] Secretary Rice complains that regional combatant commanders "sometimes act quite independently, developing their own relationships with foreign leaders and bringing their influence to bear on issues that at best cross and at worst shatter the lines between diplomacy and security policy." The huge disparity in resources that combatant commanders can marshal compared to Ambassadors comes up in this context. Ambassador Hill recounts how a joint task force commander and his staff shook their heads in disbelief when he explained State would have a hard time coming up with $12 million for the police training program, and then went ahead and funded the effort themselves.[194]

The resource disparity between State and DOD may contribute to what many fear is the "militarization" of foreign policy, but differences in organizational cultures also play a role. Combatant commanders are mission-focused in a way that can incline them to run roughshod over what they consider minor problems. A passage from the deputy commander of USCENTCOM is instructive in this regard:

> *When it came to slow, bureaucratic foreign diplomacy we couldn't waste any time. We had immediate requests to make, and we couldn't afford to go through a million proper foreign channels and wait for a response. We were going to talk to who we wanted to, when we wanted to, and get answers immediately.* For most of our ambassadors overseas, this was a culture shock. *I would call and say we needed to talk to a certain foreign minister, president, emir, or appropriate head of state. I'd tell them to go directly to that president and tell him that in two hours he would be talking to Vice President Cheney or Secretary Powell, and to be prepared to discuss issues such as runways, overflight rights, access to ports and transportation systems, fuel at airports, security at airports and seaports, and help with air defense. We talked to who we needed to, got the answers we needed, and got the job done (emphasis added).*[195]

State acquiesced to this way of doing business in the aftermath of 9/11 when a consensus in favor of forceful action helped smooth over historic interdepartmental differences. State also agreed to a set of strategic communication themes for Operation *Enduring Freedom* even though they originated in DOD. However, after a few weeks, State had second thoughts about the themes and fought to revise them.[196] By the time the United States was preparing for Operation *Iraqi Freedom*, interagency differences of opinion on communication themes were so sharp that none could be agreed upon. The United States went to war with each department putting out its own storyline. Similarly, as time passed State insisted that bilateral discussions with foreign governments revert to well-established practices managed by State.

Interagency relationships in the field were also slow to develop, fragile, and subject to great variance. We noted that the chemistry between our teams of Ambassadors and joint force commanders was in some cases productively catalytic but more frequently corrosive and sometimes explosive.[197] The point to make here is that interagency success and failure were not just a function of personal relationships; even Ambassadors and joint force commanders intent on working well together found it a challenge because their departments assessed the situation differently and had different priorities and different cultures. General Casey underscores this point. He notes Presidential guidance emphasized that helping Iraq through the transition to democracy would take "the full commitment of all agencies," and that "in all activities, the Chief of Mission and Commander, USCENTCOM shall ensure the closest cooperation and mutual support."[198] Nevertheless, Casey asserts the guidance:

> *did not create the unity of command necessary for the effective integration of civil-military efforts in successful counterinsurgency operations. The Ambassador and I would have to create the unity of effort required for success. This would prove a constant struggle as the two supporting bureaucracies—State and Defense—often had differing views. Things would get more complex as we increasingly brought the new Iraqi government into the effort. The political and economic effects, so necessary to sustaining our military success, would be outside of my direct control.*[199]

The "often differing views" of State and Defense ensured the large array of small interagency groups assembled in Afghanistan and Iraq struggled to be productive. Interagency high-value target teams were hit and miss but improved over time. The same is true of Provincial Reconstruction Teams, although they never reached high levels of effectiveness. Ambassadors objected to State personnel reporting to military officers, but the teams were mostly staffed by DOD personnel in any case.

Ambassador Ronald Neumann, former U.S. Pacific Command Commander and Director of National Intelligence Admiral Dennis Blair, and former USSOCOM Commander Admiral Eric Olson agree with General Casey's contention that interagency unity of effort was a difficult proposition even when senior leaders wanted to get along:

> [We] *know personally most of those involved in leading the long wars in Iraq and Afghanistan. They are to a person—whether military officers or civilian officials—diligent and dedicated patriots. They have often worked across departmental lines to integrate security, governance and economic-assistance programs to achieve real successes. However, when officials and officers in the field did not get along, the deficiencies of the system allowed their disputes to bring in-country progress to a halt. What is needed is an overall system that will make cooperation and integration the norm, not the exception.*[200]

The Special Inspector General for Afghanistan Reconstruction agrees that the inability to forge unified effort in the field remains a critical shortcoming even after 15 years of war. He lamented the gap:

> *between high-level strategic documents and the various projects and programs being implemented. This lack of "implementation/operational planning"—making sure that U.S. activities in Afghanistan actually contribute to overall national goals there—threatens to cause agencies and projects to work at counter purposes, spend money on frivolous endeavors, or fail to coordinate efforts to maximize impact.*[201]

General McChrystal agrees, arguing that the United States cannot do something as difficult as Afghanistan "without one person in charge"—something "the U.S. still doesn't have right."[202] McChrystal's insistence that the problem demands a structural fix is noteworthy. He is lauded as an example of how good leadership alone can overcome interagency conflicts because of his virtuoso performance in forging informal unified effort in the hunt for senior terrorist and insurgent leaders. Yet one of his major strategic lessons from years of war is that we cannot have unified effort without formal unity of command. Neumann, Blair, and Olson concur, arguing this lesson has yet to be learned and applied:

> *Despite thirteen years of experience—and innumerable opportunities to learn lessons from both successes and mistakes—there have been few significant changes in our cumbersome, inefficient and ineffective approach to interagency operations in the field.* [Our] *current decision making framework is an ineffective, stove piped diplomatic, military and intelligence chain of command relying on complex Washington decision making procedures that operate by committee. It often produces confusion, mixed signals and slow reactions.*[203]

No remedial action has been taken to fix our deficiency in horizontal unity of effort because the consensus that it is a major problem has not been matched by agreement on what to do about it. The literature cites numerous factors as sources of interagency conflict, inter alia, policy differences,[204] personality clashes,[205] organizational turf battles,[206] resource disparities,[207] and differences in organizational mandates and cultures.[208] Many senior leaders believe enlightened leadership is sufficient to solve the problem. Senior leaders underscore the importance of personal relationships and, by extension, the importance of picking the right subordinates to lead important missions that require interagency collaboration (that is, people who respect one another and are inclined to work well together).[209] Senior leaders also often state their conviction that if they ensure good relations with a counterpart from another department or agency, the resultant cooperation will trickle down to their subordinates.

This was Secretary Gates's view, and it is a common one. Elaborating on his observation that Secretaries of State and DOD tend not to get along, Gates argues, "When it comes to government, whether it works or not often depends on personal relationships." He thought repairing interagency relationships would be easy in part because he had "a unique set of personal relationships stretching back decades." He also knew that if he got along with Secretary

Clinton, "it would radiate throughout our departments and the rest of the government."[210] Secretary Rumsfeld states similar things in explaining how early tensions were resolved over whether DOD or CIA would lead operations in Afghanistan:

> *There had always been deep-seated anxieties at the CIA about the much larger Defense Department. Though I know Tenet did not feel this way, some at the CIA did not want to be seen as subordinate to the Department of Defense. Tenet and I were conscious of the challenge that all presidents have in getting the various agencies of the government to work jointly. But we both felt that close, visible personal cooperation between the two of us at the top could ease them and encourage a joint approach for those down the chain of command.*[211]

Also discussing the DOD-CIA relationship, Lieutenant General Michael DeLong, USMC (Ret.), who served as General Franks's deputy until he retired in 2003, agrees with Secretary Rumsfeld on the importance of the senior leader relationships following 9/11. He asserts close personal relationships between USCENTCOM's uniformed leaders and the top civilians in the CIA and DOD ensured "the relationship between the CIA and the military was the best it had ever been."[212] Some strong personal relationships existed from the beginning, and others were built over time. Secretary Clinton relates how some key staff personalities supporting the President grew from a "team of rivals" into "an unrivaled team."[213] Either way, as Secretary Rice notes, "it helps enormously to have Cabinet secretaries who work well together."[214] Some senior leaders even assert "relationships matter most of all," and "if you can't develop a relationship of trust and credibility you won't be successful in making a contribution to national security."[215]

Good senior leader relations are desirable, and when they are problematic, interdepartmental cooperation can be abysmal. However, as General Casey argued, good relationships are far from a sufficient condition for interagency success. An obvious problem with asserting that interagency collaboration is only a function of good personal relationships is the way many strong personal relationships degenerated when relied upon for interagency collaboration. Many of the relationships touted in the preceding references deteriorated and became quite antagonistic. President Bush's national security team was considered a "dream team"[216] because they knew and respected each other. However, some relationships became problematic and others, such as Tenet's relationship with the White House staff, deteriorated beyond repair.[217] Similarly, many assumed that Ambassador Karl Eikenberry and General McChrystal would work well together since they shared a common military background, but they did not. In fact, the record suggests it is difficult to predict whether any given Ambassador–joint task force commander relationship will work.

Asserting that good interagency collaboration is a function of personal relationships levies a heavy—perhaps impossible—burden on leaders. It implies the converse is also true—that if there is poor interagency coordination, it must be a leadership problem. Dr. Rice makes just this point, stating, "the distrust between [Rumsfeld] and [Powell] . . . made the levels below the secretaries largely incapable of taking decisions." Senior leaders try to avoid ad hominem attacks,[218] but if they argue collaboration is just a function of relationships, the failure to collaborate must be explained by reference to leader relations. Someone must be responsible for the poor relationships that torpedo interagency cooperation, and the people writing their memoirs tend to believe they are not the source of the problem.

One way to sidestep the issue of personalizing interagency conflicts is to blame the "process" for creating friction. Indeed, a poorly run national security coordination process is the second most common explanation for poor interagency collaboration in senior leader accounts. Secretary Gates was advised by an experienced Pentagon leader that decisionmaking in the Pentagon "is like the old Roman arena—gladiators come before the emperor to battle and you decide who is the winner. Someone needs to make sure the process within the arena is fair, transparent, and objective," which many believe it was not.[219] If we add "and definitive," this assessment would summarize the complaints the Vice President, Secretary of Defense, and his subordinates had about the way the interagency decisionmaking process was run in the Bush administration.[220]

These leaders assert Dr. Rice made a point of seeking compromises instead of elevating unresolved differences of opinion to the President for resolution.[221] They believe the resultant compromises produced more than just ambiguity or confusion. If one department was allowed to win the argument over strategy and another the argument over tactics, the inevitable result was incoherence.

Under Secretary Douglas Feith, for example, laments the "interagency discord of the kind that confounded the President's Iraq policy from the outset of the Administration," and argues tension between State and DOD "became worse over time, in part because basic differences . . . were papered over again and again and never actually resolved."[222] These senior leaders also complain the Secretary of State facilitated the tension by not disagreeing in meetings but then making his case out of court with either the President or the press.[223]

The argument against consensus decisionmaking in interagency bodies has been made many times, as has the assertion that some departments do not "play fair" by trying to circumvent formal decisionmaking bodies.[224] In fact, Dr. Rice levies the same charge against DOD. She observes that Rumsfeld and Powell "did not confront each other face-to-face, let alone in front of the President." Instead, she states:

> *Don* [Rumsfeld] *would send memos (snowflakes, we called them) that implicitly—and sometimes explicitly—criticized what State or the NSC was doing. Often those memos reflected discussions that had already taken place, but they left the impression that it was Don imparting new wisdom or making an important recommendation. In meetings, he would ask Socratic questions rather than take a position. This led to tensions with and frustrations for Colin* [Powell].

In reality, it is common for Cabinet officials to press important issues for resolution by the President when they believe the President's inclinations favor their positions, and to delay or otherwise end-run the process when they fear a quick decision would go against them.

But as Dr. Rice insists, this tendency to accelerate, retard, or work around the formal decisionmaking process was not the real problem. There is a more fundamental "supply/demand" issue when it comes to Presidential adjudication. As Rice notes, the departments were generating more disputes than the President could hope to resolve:

> *The NSC should intervene when there is a policy disagreement among the departments or when they cannot coordinate among themselves. But the NSC cannot do so on every single issue every day, or the system*

would grind to a halt, wallowing in inefficiency. Most of the time the Department of Defense and the State Department need to find a way to work together—at all levels.[225]

Dr. Rice states that Defense officials did not appreciate this imbalance in demand for Presidential decisions and the supply of Presidential time available to adjudicate differences. According to Rice, DOD officials also did not appreciate the political downside of numerous Presidential interventions. Secretary Rumsfeld accused her of inserting herself in the chain of command, mistakenly "assum[ing] that I was substituting my own preferences for the views of the principals . . . that I kept seeking consensus when the President should have been given a decision memo—so that he could just decide." In reality, she explains, the President was informed on the debates and either asked her to "try one more time to find common ground," or "told me what he wanted to do." For political reasons, including the way a Presidential resolution of a fight between Cabinet officials would be portrayed in the press, it was often preferable to have the National Security Advisor deliver the decision rather than the President.

Although most of the discussion about horizontal unity of effort in Afghanistan and Iraq involves interagency coordination, there was a horizontal unity of effort issue within DOD involving war plans that features prominently in senior leader accounts. It was a horizontal rather than vertical unity of effort issue because the law assigns multiple senior leaders in DOD a role in war plans. General Franks emphasizes the fact that the chain of command for executing a plan runs from the President to the Secretary of Defense to the combatant commander. He recognized the law gives the Chairman responsibilities for reviewing combatant commander war plans and preparing joint logistic and mobility plans in support of them, but he resented commentary on his plan from the chiefs of staff of the military Services and Under Secretary of Defense for Policy.[226]

Yet both the law and practical politics give the chiefs and Under Secretary a role in war plans. By law the Under Secretary of Defense for Policy prepares written policy guidance for contingency plans and reviews them for consistency. Congress instituted this requirement after surveying much historical evidence supporting the contention that military plans and operations often are not in sync with larger national policy and strategy objectives. USCENTCOM's treatment of postwar planning justifies congressional concerns about the need for a tight linkage between national strategy and military plans. Franks's lack of interest in postwar planning was an irritant not only to the Chairman but also to the Under Secretary of Defense for Policy, who tasked his own staff with postwar planning and attempted to coordinate it with USCENTCOM. The command was not interested, and either Feith or his superiors (the Deputy Secretary of Defense or Secretary of Defense) chose not to press the issue with Franks. In retrospect, the Under Secretary acknowledged he should have contested the issue more forcefully.[227]

Similarly, the law mandates that the Chairman will present the views of the Service chiefs concurrently to the President, National Security Council, Homeland Security Council, or Secretary of Defense, as the case requires. The law also requires the Chairman to "communicate, as appropriate, the requirements of the combatant commands to other elements of the Department of Defense." For these and other reasons, including the political imperative for the President to check with all the chiefs before launching a war, General Myers argues:

> *The Joint Chiefs had to be fully informed on the CENTCOM plan. We all had a legal obligation to provide military advice to the President and National Security Council, and this advice had to be based in part on the details of the operational plan. No President or Secretary of Defense would approve a war plan without getting the Joint Chiefs' opinion.*[228]

As Vice President Cheney notes, reforms in the Goldwater-Nichols law ensure a clear division of labor between the military chiefs who prepare forces for the future and the combatant commanders who employ them in current operations.[229] Judicious tradeoffs in resource allocation must be made between prevailing in current fighting and preparing well for future operations. Thus, the Secretary of Defense and the President needed to hear both sets of opinions.

Franks and his deputy believed the chiefs were offering parochial rather than constructive criticism of his war plan for Iraq: "The Air Force representative insisted that the Air Force, not the Navy, should provide the main bombing support. The Navy insisted that more carriers were needed. The Army insisted we needed more ground troops."[230] Franks interpreted the comments from the chiefs as narrow, partisan efforts to push their Services to the front of the fight so they could "advance their share of the budget at the expense of the mission." He worried that complaints from the chiefs would slow his plan or force revisions that did not make sense from a joint perspective. He later told Secretary Rumsfeld, "No operation that is totally satisfying to any one service is truly a *joint* operation." He insisted the issue at stake was "unity of command."[231] It was his onerous job to make tradeoffs between the many functional capabilities that the Services offered and integrate them into a plan that would best accomplish the joint mission. Franks needed broader strategic perspective from the chiefs, not a reiteration of Service preferences.

These bitter differences about the development of the Afghan and Iraq war plans highlight a key problem for horizontal unity of effort. Well organized and led, cross-functional teams can be productive. Yet there is always the danger that those representing the different functional areas of expertise will give priority to protecting their parent organizations' equities rather than assisting in the process of making the necessary tradeoffs to produce an integrated and coherent approach to solving the problem. Attention to two prerequisites for success can help avoid this problem. First, it needs to be evident to all members that the team leader is focused on team rather than personal or parent organizational goals. Second, the functional representatives must transfer their loyalty from protecting their parent organizations' equities to successfully accomplishing the mission at hand. The two prerequisites are related. If it appears that a leader is acting in a self-serving manner, members are more apt to give priority to protecting their organizational equities, reasoning that doing so is in the larger interest.

In the case of General Franks and his three-star subordinate Service component commanders responsible for executing his plan, these prerequisites were met and the team worked well. The President asked each subordinate commander on the eve of the invasion of Iraq if he fully supported the joint plan, and each responded he did. General DeLong asserts that Franks succeeded because he made it clear he would not favor his own Service:

> *He was one of the most joint-oriented commanders I had ever met; he never once favored his Army background. . . . [W]e achieved another victory that few people realize, one that will have long-lasting repercussions on our military for time to come: true joint operations. . . . The*

Afghan and Iraq wars exhibited the best examples of joint operations I had ever seen. We broke the parochialism . . . due in large part to the mood that Franks set.[232]

However, the cross-functional group one level up from Franks that was responsible for reviewing USCENTCOM plans did not work so well. There was insufficient trust between team members and the Secretary of Defense. Franks and DeLong insist the Service chiefs were not offering "objective, balanced" feedback. The chiefs objected to the plan for Afghanistan and again to the plan for Iraq for the wrong reasons, according to USCENTCOM leaders. They were "there to look out for [their] own service—to raise money for supplies and weapons, and to recruit and train [their] forces."[233] Over time, the tension between Franks and the chiefs subsided as General Myers intervened to improve the relationships. Myers believed "one of [his] most important jobs would be to keep Tom Franks and the Joint Chiefs talking to each other and pulling together."[234] Although the process was tortuous and took time, he seems to have succeeded insofar as USCENTCOM received support it needed from the Services. Even USCENTCOM came to believe that a better plan emerged from all the give and take. According to DeLong:

This was a collaborative effort. As Franks said: "This was not a Tommy Franks plan. This was not a Don Rumsfeld plan. There was not friction between Franks and Rumsfeld on this plan. This was a national plan. It involved the service chiefs; it involved the service secretaries; it involved the president himself; it involved Don Rumsfeld; it involved me; it involved all of our staffs. I think we benefited from the fact that we had a long planning cycle, an opportunity to get ready.[235]

In the case of the tension between Franks and the Under Secretary for Policy Feith, it increased over time, as Secretary Rumsfeld failed to manage this critical relationship. General Franks was offended by the mere presence of the Under Secretary when he first briefed the Secretary of Defense on his concept for the USCENTCOM war plan. Franks states that he "generally ignored" Feith and that he was thankful that Rumsfeld "never allowed Feith to interfere in my business."[236] Thus, with the Secretary's acquiescence, USCENTCOM made a point of excluding key elements of Rumsfeld's staff from the planning process. One consequence is that the chances for reconciling differences over postwar planning were diminished.

Capabilities

The President's September 20, 2001, speech promising a "lengthy campaign unlike any other we have ever seen" implied that nontraditional capabilities would be required to defeat a nontraditional enemy. The President even cited examples. He mentioned law enforcement would need additional tools, and intelligence capabilities to expose enemy plans would have to be improved. Over the next decade, many new or augmented capabilities were used in Afghanistan, Iraq, and elsewhere with great success. Some capabilities were resident in the system but had to be pulled forward, proliferated, and employed better. This was the case with SOF, which senior leaders extol as making a critical contribution in the war on terror.[237] Other capability sets were altogether new. Some were or still are exceedingly controversial, such as enhanced interrogation techniques. Others, such as the armed drone program managed by DOD, were so successful that some decisionmakers wanted to alter strategy to take advantage of them.[238] And in some cases, such as Provincial Reconstruction Teams, performance problems were ameliorated but too slowly.

Although increasing capabilities or developing new ones took resources, in general this was not a major impediment. Congress generously made funds available. As one Senator complained to the Secretary of Defense in 2005 about the slow development of a key capability:

> *Over the last two years, Congress has provided more than $200 billion in supplemental appropriations for the wars in Iraq and Afghanistan . . . in addition to the more than $400 billion we spend each year on defense. . . . It is unbelievable, and quite frankly unacceptable, that American personnel face shortages of anything at this point.*[239]

The United States faced some technical challenges with new capabilities but in general these were not insurmountable obstacles either. The far more significant problem was that decisionmakers were unable to agree on the capabilities needed, or else the departments and agencies resisted providing them.

Departments and agencies often did not want to invest the time, effort, and resources necessary for new or enhanced counterterrorist and counterinsurgency capabilities.

For example, following the attacks on 9/11, the Department of the Treasury took its historical position of advising against attacking terrorist finances. Treasury worried that doing so would invite retaliation on U.S. financial institutions. The President overrode that concern and insisted that Treasury lead an effort to attack terrorist financing.[240] To its credit, Treasury soon mounted what is considered one of our most effective interagency counterterrorist efforts. In other cases, the results were insufficient or downright unsatisfactory.

Failing to produce capabilities required for success is a matter of grave importance. Senior leaders must ensure the means for executing their strategy are available and consistent with the ways they choose to defeat the enemy. It is not possible to catalogue and extract lessons from every capability that decisionmakers had to manage in the war on terror. Here we concern ourselves with capabilities that senior leaders stated were essential for success but were unable to generate due to limitations in decisionmaking processes. There are five such capability areas mentioned often by senior leaders as inadequate to need, all of which are controversial to some extent: special intelligence, sociocultural knowledge, strategic communications, specialized equipment, and civil-military administrative capacity.

Special Intelligence

Senior leaders described U.S. operations in the war on terror, Afghanistan, and Iraq as "intel-dependent" or "intel-centric." The urgent requirement for good intelligence was evident at several levels. First, superior, fine-grained, and timely intelligence—the kind that special operations require—was needed to target terrorists and insurgents. Second, the enemy's decisionmaking process had to be penetrated well enough to anticipate plans and programs and foil them, particularly given the enemy's intent to launch mass casualty attacks and use weapons of mass destruction. Finally, and at a deeper level, sophisticated cultural, social, and political intelligence was needed to inform U.S. leaders on what to target and when and how. The first-, second-, and third-order effects of removing any given person from the battlefield as opposed to monitoring his activities and plans had to be understood. Without this kind of intelligence, we would not be able to operate in a manner that would achieve success over the longer term by reducing the popular support that sustains the enemy's cause, organizations, and agendas.

Concerning the first level of intelligence required, the United States was able to produce a quantum leap forward in all-source intelligence integration with ongoing operations. A major effort was mounted to develop new types of intelligence and share more intelligence—that is, to move from the "need-to-know" principle to a "need-to-share" approach. Over time, the fusion of timely all-source intelligence and operations became a great success. When mistakes were made—and many were—it was generally due to poor command decisions about whether the available intelligence justified a decision to launch an operation or, in the midst of an operation, which targets to engage. Despite some notable and all-too-public failures during raids on enemy leadership cadres, the fusion of timely all-source intelligence and operations allowed U.S. forces to keep enemy organizations on the defensive and gave the United States tremendous leverage.

How well we penetrated enemy plans and programs is shrouded in secrecy for obvious reasons, but some general observations are possible. Best intelligence indicated that 9/11 was just the first of a series of attacks against the United States that al Qaeda wanted to execute. So in general, the dearth of successful follow-on strikes against the U.S. homeland suggests the United States did a good job of disrupting or anticipating enemy plans. The same can be said for the U.S. ability to overcome organized resistance in Afghanistan and Iraq. However, there are major exceptions. One was the failure to anticipate the switch to guerrilla tactics following the defeat of the adversary's organized military forces. CIA Director Tenet testified to Congress in March 2002 that we were entering a second, more difficult phase of operations in Afghanistan "with smaller units that intend to operate against [us] in a classic insurgency format."[241] However, DOD did not act upon this insight.

Similarly, DOD was slow to anticipate, prepare for, and respond to the rise of an insurgency in Iraq. Numerous experts warned of the potential for large-scale civil unrest following the occupation of Iraq, including Secretary Rumsfeld's own staff.[242] Secretary Rumsfeld argues DOD had to prepare for many possible calamities in Iraq, and that the first mention of possible "protracted guerrilla war" was an op-ed by someone "removed from the intelligence community."[243] CIA

Director Tenet argues the IC was prescient and predicted "Iraqi patience with an extended U.S. presence after an overwhelming victory would be short."[244] Yet the issue was not "how right" intelligence predictions of an uncertain future were, but whether intelligence foresaw the possibility of large-scale civil unrest and whether DOD prepared accordingly. If DOD had taken the postwar planning mission seriously along with the warnings of potential civil unrest, it would have been much better prepared to prevent or control the emergence of the insurgency. Among other things, it could have prevented the widespread looting and lawlessness that the CIA believed encouraged the insurgency[245] and done more to secure the weapons and arms depots abandoned by the defeated Iraqi army, which also contributed to the virulence of the insurgency.

The other major exceptions were the failure to uncover plans for the original attacks on 9/11 and then later, in 2003, to accurately surmise Iraq's weapons of mass destruction programs prior to invading the country. The common sense understanding is that the failure to anticipate a major attack on the United States, or to get the principal casus belli for war with Iraq wrong, is ipso facto a strategic intelligence failure. Such events are certain to generate conspiracy theories, second-guessing, and numerous retrospective technical insights on how the IC could have performed better.[246] It is also common to consider far less momentous intelligence issues in retrospect and declare the intelligence was either "right" or "wrong" rather than more or less likely at the time. For example, in recounting how U.S. planes missed an early attempt to eliminate Saddam Hussein with bombs, President Bush states the intelligence was wrong and "a harbinger of things to come."[247]

The natural penchant for evaluating intelligence after the fact as right or wrong is understandable. After the fact it is manifest that al Qaeda posed a threat to the homeland, that an insurgency arose, and that Saddam was not where we thought he might be at a particular point in time. Yet this natural tendency to grade intelligence "predictions" has unfortunate side effects. It can have a caustic effort on relations between senior intelligence officials and policymakers, encourage the blame game, and poison the decisionmaking environment. In the worst cases, both sides end up parsing the written documents and recounting what they said in meetings to justify their records. Logic is thrown out the window as senior leaders struggle to score debating points. Certainly this happened in the Bush administration.[248]

The third respect in which Afghanistan and Iraq were "intel-dependent" national security missions touches upon the first two. Locating terrorists and insurgents and penetrating the enemy's decisionmaking process require yet another capability area that bedevils the U.S. national security system: sociocultural knowledge. The United States lacked sufficient quantities of this kind of expertise not only in the IC, but elsewhere as well. Moreover, it was difficult to tap or generate sociocultural knowledge quickly, so throwing money at the problem was a poor remedy. Because this shortfall went well beyond requirements for good intelligence, we treat it as a separate capability shortfall in the next section.

Sociocultural Knowledge

Most senior leaders do not mention shortfalls in knowledge about the social and cultural dimensions of Afghanistan and Iraq in their memoirs. DOD is an exception. Both civilian and uniformed senior leaders came to regret how little we knew about Afghanistan and Iraq, their populations, and current conditions before invading those countries.[249] Secretary Gates offers a representative assessment:

> *Nearly always, we begin military engagements—wars—profoundly ignorant about our adversaries. . . . We did not grasp that after eight years of war with Iran, the Gulf War with us, and twelve years of harsh sanctions, the Iraqi economy, society, and infrastructure were shattered. The facade of Saddam's regime misled us with regard to what we were letting ourselves in for, just as his facade with respect to possessing weapons of mass destruction misled us. We had no idea of the complexity of Afghanistan—tribes, ethnic groups, power brokers, village and provincial rivalries. So our prospects in both countries were grimmer than perceived, and our initial objectives were unrealistic. And we didn't know that either. Our knowledge and our intelligence were woefully inadequate. We entered both countries oblivious to how little we knew.[250]*

Even after we had been in country for some time, we found it difficult to fathom the motives of host-nation officials or discern reliable indictors of popular behaviors.[251] As one flag officer notes, we can find where a person is but "not have a clue where that person derived his strong feelings against the United States from."[252] The sampling of influential scholarly literature we consulted also tends to stress lack of cross-cultural knowledge as a major shortcoming explaining poor results in Afghanistan and Iraq.[253]

What DOD leaders came to understand over time was that social, political, and cultural knowledge was just as important, if not more so, than information on military, economic, infrastructure, and institutional issues. Such country-specific expertise became a scarce commodity after Afghanistan and Iraq were invaded and occupied. What is often called "regional expertise" was suddenly needed in large quantities by the diplomatic, intelligence, and military communities. Unlike some colonial powers dealing with insurgencies in decades past, the United States did not have a ready-to-hand group of loyal administrators savvy in the ways of the foreign populations. In fact, the United States had few regional experts who could speak local languages and knew the current social and political scenes well.

The need for sociocultural knowledge is a staple in literature on irregular warfare, including counterterrorism. Assessing the 9/11 attacks, it was evident terrorists were able to exploit both the conveniences of modern infrastructure and their access to restricted social and political lines of communication that the United States could not tap or even monitor well. Terrorists used the *hawala* money transfer system and a global network of mosques to share resources and information. They also recruited from family, ethnic, and religious communities that were not easily penetrated by Western intelligence. Whereas U.S. leaders tend to think of strategic communication as a national-level enterprise, the terrorists promulgated their most effectual propaganda largely at the level of the individual *imam* or tribal elder where American credibility and influence are quite limited. Thus, in "security, recruiting, and communicating, traditional social networks provide our enemies with significant advantages."[254]

These same types of advantages were exploited by insurgents in Afghanistan and Iraq. As General Myers noted, it was "nearly impossible for a Westerner to penetrate the convoluted webs of tribal and clan loyalty that made up Iraqi society,"[255] and thus to know how best to influence key decisionmakers and local populations. Calls for sociocultural expertise grew more urgent as it became clear there would be no early exits from Afghanistan or Iraq.

Field commanders taking casualties from improvised explosive devices (IEDs) wanted to find the bombmakers and the bombs. Identifying the network of contacts that supported bombmaking and better understanding what inclined people to make or fail to report bombs required in-depth social, political, and cultural intelligence. Moreover, as new brigades rotated in and replaced those completing their tour of duty, they often had to reacquire sociocultural knowledge the hard way, amounting to 12 one-year campaigns rather than one 12-year campaign for U.S. forces.[256] Soon brigade commanders were requesting means to secure, retain, and transfer better sociocultural knowledge among units. As General Peter Chiarelli, USA (Ret.), would later note, "I asked my Brigade Commanders what was the number one thing they would like to have had more of, and they all said cultural knowledge."[257]

As field commanders such as General Chiarelli and General Petraeus were promoted and added their voices to the chorus of irregular warfare experts arguing for improved sociocultural knowledge, numerous programs were initiated to meet the demand, ranging from electronic devices that facilitated entry and storage of sociocultural knowledge to Human Terrain Teams, which were small groups of social scientists trained to deploy with brigades and advise commanders on behaviors that would help them isolate insurgents from popular support. These efforts were even better funded after the U.S. forces adopted population-centric counterinsurgency concepts that required them to understand popular sentiments well enough to interact with the indigenous people in ways that inclined the populace to support rather than resist U.S. objectives. However, as the report *A Decade of War* argues, our ability to operate in this domain was limited:

> *Because the traditional intelligence effort tended to focus on enemy groups and actions, it neglected "white" information about the population that was necessary for success in a population-centric campaign. Local commanders needed to know information about ethnic and tribal identities, religion, culture, politics, and economics. Intelligence products provided information about enemy actions but were insufficient for other information needed at the local level.[258]*

As an influential article further explains, in a counterinsurgency, small units must supply key intelligence to higher commands rather than the other way around. In large force-on-force conventional combat:

> *Satellites, spy planes, and more arcane assets controlled by people far from the battlefield inform ground units about the strength, location, and activity of the enemy before the ground unit even arrives. Information flows largely from the top down. In a counterinsurgency, the flow is (or should be) reversed. The soldier or development worker on the ground is usually the person best informed about the environment and the enemy.*[259]

Thus, all soldiers must collect intelligence for higher level analysts who create "comprehensive narratives" for each area that "describe changes in the economy, atmospherics, development, corruption, governance, and enemy activity" to inform higher levels in the chain of command.[260]

The critical importance of what came to be called "human terrain" or "the human domain" was evident not only at the small-unit level but also in the way U.S. leaders interacted with their host-nation counterparts. Prior to the war, U.S. officials debated and disagreed about which Iraqi expatriates to support, but in reality they were guessing about which ones might prove acceptable to the Iraqi people.[261] Once U.S. forces occupied Iraq, they had to appoint local officials without understanding the political consequences.[262] U.S. leaders were split over whether to select a governing group for Iraq by fiat, via regional caucuses, or through national elections. It was assumed that elected leaders would be more legitimate,[263] but elected leaders also might be more sectarian and desire a future for Iraq different from what the United States preferred. Indeed, the longer we stayed in Iraq, the more we realized our objectives were not identical with those of host-nation leaders. Having U.S. interests prevail to the extent possible meant we had to make our relationship with host-nation leaders "transactional and conditional,"[264] something that requires an adroit mix of leadership, unified effort among all U.S. elements of power, and sociocultural savvy.

Defeating the insurgents, partnering with host-nation officials, and winning popular support all were impossible tasks without a profound understanding of local social and political relationships at all levels. The need for cultural understanding has been cited as one of the "top 5" lessons learned from the wars in Afghanistan and Iraq,[265] a view echoed by many senior leaders.[266] During his confirmation hearing before taking command of U.S. and NATO forces in Afghanistan in June 2010, General Petraeus told Congress that the decisive terrain in counterinsurgency was "the human terrain."[267] General Raymond Odierno, Chief of Staff of the Army, stated the main lesson he learned in Iraq was that the best-equipped army in the world can still lose a war if it does not understand the people it is fighting.[268] General Robert Cone, Commander of the Army's Training and Doctrine Command, argues, "The human domain must be the centerpiece of our future efforts,"[269] and the Army has committed to making that so.[270] In May 2013, the Chief of Staff of the Army, the Commandant of the Marine Corps, and the USSOCOM commander signed a white paper that underscores the importance of "human domains" and the need for "better integrating human factors into the planning and execution of military operations."[271]

Despite all the high-level attention this capability area has received, there are two reasons to be concerned that U.S. forces will not have superior sociocultural knowledge available in the future. First, sociocultural knowledge cannot be surged. The language skills and knowledge of local social networks take time to develop. Some experts insist no worthwhile sociocultural knowledge can be generated quickly, while others believe there are different types and levels of sociocultural knowledge that take different amounts of time and effort to produce. Either way, no one recommends waiting until the conflict begins and then trying to produce such knowledge on the fly. Figuring out how to sustain and surge sociocultural knowledge at reasonable costs is a formidable organizational challenge in the best of circumstances.

Second, the U.S. military's traditional pattern of behavior on sociocultural knowledge is reasserting itself. The military often develops sociocultural expertise at great cost and too late to ensure success. Leaders then abandon the hard-won capability as part of postconflict budget reductions or out of deference to prevailing American strategic culture, which emphasizes readiness for major force-on-force conflicts. From American colonists to American revolutionaries to irregular operations during the Civil War to the Army's conflicts with Native Americans to American interventions in the Philippines and Central America to Cold War "brush-fire" conflicts to post–Cold War contingencies during the 1990s and our recent interventions in Afghanistan and Iraq, this has been the costly pattern the United States has followed. And it is now being repeated.

Much of the organizational architecture developed to provide sociocultural knowledge to U.S. forces is being dismantled. The Army's Irregular Warfare Center was closed in 2014, and the Human Terrain Team program is being phased out. Those officers participating in the Afghanistan-Pakistan Hands Program are not being promoted at rates comparable to the rest of the Army. The organizational and cultural reasons why DOD is turning its back on sociocultural knowledge are complex but can be explained by the institution's singular focus on conventional warfare. We return to this issue in discussing material shortfalls, but the summary explanation is that American strategic culture in general (to include Congress and public opinion) undervalues the importance of irregular warfare skills such as sociocultural knowledge in favor of concentrating on other factors such as technology, small-unit combat skills, and large-scale military maneuver training.[272] The unfortunate prognosis is that the United States will remain "deaf, dumb, and stupid" as it engages the world.[273]

Strategic Communications

Strategic communications is another capability area important for irregular warfare. The reason is simple: without some element of popular support, it is difficult for terrorists to survive and impossible for insurgents to do so. Hence, every effort must be made to convince the population that any support—even passive support—is not in its interests. While this line of reasoning seems straightforward and is supported by experts on irregular warfare, it was not a proposition embraced by senior leaders. Many acknowledge the disastrous implications of negative propaganda and perceptions—for example, often citing the consequences of Abu Ghraib or rhetorical missteps such as the expression "axis of evil"[274]—but only a handful give the importance of U.S. strategic communications serious attention in their writings: Secretaries Rice, Rumsfeld, and Clinton and Under Secretary Feith. There are several reasons for this.

Americans are prone to believe that actions speak louder than words and that success generates goodwill while failure does the opposite. Generals believe that defeating the enemy will encourage friends and that failure to do so emboldens enemies and inclines fence-sitters to lean toward the enemy. The diplomat's equivalent of this is to argue that policies generate support or resistance and no amount of packaging or "spin" will fool our foreign counterparts.[275] Beyond these generalizations, there are other objections to putting too much stock in managing communications. U.S. foreign policy elites tend to believe public opinion at best complicates a steady hand on the strategy tiller. In turn, the public distrusts any U.S. Government management of information for fear that it will be twisted and used in attempts to control the body politic. Overall U.S. culture is not comfortable with managed information at all, preferring a "free market place of ideas" without interference from governmental institutions.

Moreover, there is a wide consensus that strategic communications is not an American strength. Some question whether it is even possible to have a strategic communication strategy without a larger overarching strategy for the wars in Afghanistan and Iraq. Others believe we do not have the sociocultural knowledge needed to assess our target audiences and message effects and that we are too self-absorbed to focus on foreign audiences (suggesting, for example, that the White House tends to confuse strategic communications with the President's public affairs effort). Some also argue that American moralism and unilateralism incline us to discount the value of strategic communications. Americans tend to believe they and their government are different and better and that our motives are transparent and thus easily discerned from our actions. Furthermore, many believe foreign cultures embrace double standards that make it impossible for the United States to compete in strategic communications. Utter lack of restraint on the part of terrorists is seen as justifiable frustration or evidence of U.S. weakness, whereas a rare case of excess force on the part of American forces is seen as typical and evidence of massive arrogance and evil intent. In other words, some suggest foreign attitudes are so entrenched that attempts at persuasion are hopeless.

For all these reasons, we tend not to do strategic communications well—something more than 15 major reports are in unanimous agreement about. Virtually all those reports conclude the U.S. Government does not have a strategic communications strategy worthy of the name, lacks the expertise to execute a strategy, has no dedicated organization for doing so, and expends far too little resources to mount a serious strategic communications effort. Constant dollar spending on public diplomacy has declined since 1994 despite the bump in spending following 9/11. By 2007, the United States was spending about what France did on public diplomacy. DOD spent far more on television and newspapers for U.S. forces than it spent on military information support operations (formerly psychological operations). On top of all that, the three primary strategic communication disciplines in the U.S. Government—public affairs, public diplomacy, and military information support operations—feuded with one another to a dysfunctional extent. Senior public affairs leaders torpedoed the Office of Strategic Influence in the early days of the war on terror.[276] After that, most of the effort was contracted out and earned a reputation for spotty, if not deplorable, performance.

Even so, as victory proved elusive in Afghanistan and Iraq, DOD increasingly emphasized the importance of strategic communications. The 2006 Quadrennial Defense Review emphasized that "[v]ictory in the long war ultimately depends on strategic communication by the United States and its international partners." DOD, and according to some accounts the CIA as well,[277] spent years trying to encourage the Department of State to take the lead and mount a better strategic communications effort. By 2009, however, the lack of progress had disillusioned some DOD leaders. For example, the Chairman of the Joint Chiefs of Staff was fed up with the "cottage industry" that had grown up around the strategic communications mission. Admiral Mike Mullen published an article that argued the United States should just communicate its strategic intent through its actions and normal coordination processes. Mullen stated that if the United States made good policies and ensured its actions were consistent with those policies, it would not need a special effort to sell its image aboard. He cited the Great White Fleet's voyage around the world and the Marshall Plan as examples. Americans could simply show up and do the right thing because it is, "well, the right thing."[278] Admiral Mullen's approach was quite consistent with historic American norms and no doubt resonated with many Americans who believe actions speak louder than words and do not require a strategic communications bureaucracy for their interpretation.

Those who study irregular war and strategic communications argued the contrary case. As one response to the admiral's article noted, "However benign our behavior seems to us, it helps to explain it to others." The Great White

Fleet's mission was so open to misinterpretation that it created "a first-class war scare" in Japan and the United States that had to be defused by careful diplomacy. The Marshall Plan similarly was open to interpretation, with some arguing it constituted "a declaration of war by the United States for control of Europe."[279] Research indicating that many, if not most, Afghans do not know about the events of 9/11 or relate them to the presence of American forces in their country suggests that even in the information age, American interventions are still subject to gross misinterpretation.[280] Admiral Mullen's "frustration over poorly coordinated and poorly performing organizations currently trying to do strategic communications" was understandable. Yet many have argued that abandoning a strong and specialized strategic communications effort would be a mistake:

> *Because terrorists . . . can further their agenda in part by offering a hostile narrative about the United States, we need to emphasize strategic communications more rather than less. It is true that the American example is a great one and that the world is often indebted to the United States for its expenditures of blood and treasure. But it is also true that our actions and intentions, even when strategically and morally sound, will not always be easily recognized as such by foreign audiences, which is why the image of a great nation needs its custodians, and those custodians need a good organization to support them.*[281]

Secretary Gates and CIA Director Leon Panetta finally found a willing partner in Secretary Clinton, who made strategic communications an area of emphasis. She argued the ideological battle is slow and incremental but important. It drove her crazy, she stated, that "we were losing the communications battle to extremists living in caves." She had her staff develop a strategy and a new Center for Strategic Counterterrorism Communications. Despite some initial resistance from White House staff, President Obama was supportive, and Secretary Clinton got the center and her strategy off the ground.[282] While Clinton's initiatives represented progress, the body of expert opinion argues the United States still has a long way to go to improve performance in strategic communications. Many argue that the independent U.S. Information Agency that existed during the Cold War needs to be resurrected.[283]

Specialized Equipment

Other departments and agencies developed or purchased new equipment for operations in Afghanistan and Iraq, but equipment shortfalls were a larger concern for DOD and the hundreds of thousands of personnel it deployed in those contingencies. DOD has a "mission first" culture, and superb efforts were mounted to push new equipment forward to those fighting in Afghanistan and Iraq. Army and Marine ground forces at the small unit level received the kinds of equipment previously only available to SOF: body armor, latest generation night vision goggles, intra-squad communications gear, tactical satellite radios, tactical unmanned aerial vehicles, and so forth. For example, we went from having 8 unmanned aerial vehicles in Iraq in 2003 to 1,700 by 2008.[284] To get these kinds of capabilities to the troops quickly, the Pentagon created new organizations and streamlined procedures. Congress encouraged these efforts by making copious amounts of funding available.

Nevertheless, in the course of adjudicating requests from commanders in the field and figuring out the best way to respond, differences of opinion emerged on what kinds of additional capabilities made the most sense and how affordable they were. There were also complaints from Congress about the speed with which the Pentagon fielded equipment to the troops. The issue exploded like a flash bang grenade in the public consciousness when a young Soldier complained to Secretary Rumsfeld that vehicles did not have sufficient armor to deal with enemy ambushes. Rumsfeld was pilloried for his response that you "go to war with the Army you have." The comment was accurate but begged the question of whether U.S. forces should have been better prepared for irregular war, and worse, seemed to indicate nothing could be done to improve the situation, which infuriated Congress and the public.

As it turned out, the real issue was not going to war with the Army we had, but going to war with the bureaucracy we had. Both Secretary Rumsfeld and Secretary Gates had to overcome entrenched resistance inside the Pentagon to provide better armor for troops in the field.[285] Gates in particular ended up agreeing with General Franks's complaint that the Joint Chiefs of Staff were so focused on future requirements that it skewed their ability to offer good advice on fighting the war at hand. Given the law's clear division of labor between the military chiefs who prepare their Services for the future and the combatant commanders who employ them in current operations, it is not surprising that there is tension between the parties. The tension can be healthy if both sides have an adequate voice in resource allocation decisions and if the process enables Pentagon leaders to make judicious tradeoffs between the two sets of priorities. Favoring one or the other too much puts American security at risk, sooner or later. Secretary Gates argued that it was sooner. He waged a sustained and public battle against the tendency to favor investments in future military capabilities at the expense of doing what was necessary to win current wars, a malady he labeled "next-war-itis."[286]

Secretary Gates reached this conclusion after wrestling with the Pentagon bureaucracy over a number of equipment issues, but especially tactical intelligence, reconnaissance, and surveillance (ISR) assets and MRAP vehicles.[287] In the case of theater ISR, Gates contended with the Air Force. He created Task Force ODIN (Observe, Detect, Identify, and Neutralize) to press for more ISR delivered to theater with greater urgency. In the case of MRAPs, Gates confronted the Army and Marines, and also his own staff. Both equipment issues preoccupied him, but due to space limitations, we summarize only the MRAP saga.[288] These large, heavy vehicles were up to 10 times more expensive than adding armor to Humvees and up to 3 times more expensive than up-armored Humvees, but they were 400 percent more effective at preventing casualties if hit by an IED. Commanders in the field wanted them, but senior civilian and military leaders in the Pentagon did not. As one well-respected flag officer argued, "It is the wrong vehicle, too late, to fit a threat we were actually managing."[289]

In reality, U.S. casualties from IEDs increased substantially in absolute numbers from the time requests for MRAPs from commanders in the field arrived at the Pentagon in mid-2004 until Secretary Gates intervened in May 2007. Gates heard multiple arguments against MRAPs, the most "significant [being] that no one at a senior level wanted to spend the money to buy them." He overrode their objections and made MRAPs the Pentagon's number-one acquisition priority.[290] After that, the acquisition system was able to field large numbers of MRAPs within 18 months—an accomplishment often described as an industrial feat not seen since World War II. The costs were staggering—$25 billion for the Iraq deployments—but MRAPs quickly made an impact. When they began to flow to Iraq in November 2007, almost 60 percent of U.S. casualties were attributed to IEDs. Just a little over a year later with 10,000 MRAPs in country, only about 5 percent of casualties were attributable to IEDs, despite the fact that insurgents were making a point of targeting MRAPs with IEDs for symbolic reasons. Insurgents tried to defeat MRAPs by liberal use of their most advanced IEDs, the use of which jumped 40 percent between February and March 2008 as MRAPs entered Iraq in large numbers. Yet deaths from those advanced IEDs dropped 17 percent during the same period. In short, testimony by flag officers to Congress in March 2007 that MRAPs could cut casualties by perhaps as much as two-thirds was well founded.[291]

The decision to deploy MRAPs has been applauded as a case of stellar oversight and an example of egregious micromanagement. The Secretary and Congress sided with field commanders and irregular warfare experts inside the Pentagon who thought the vehicles were a bargain. Service chiefs and their subordinates responsible for assessing requirements and building future military capability thought MRAPs were a boondoggle. The case against MRAPs was that they met a transitory requirement. They were not needed given the plan to pull U.S. forces back and push Iraqis to the front of the fight. They were not an elegant solution to IEDs, which required stopping those making and emplacing the bombs. Besides, the enemy could just build bigger bombs, it was argued. The expensive MRAPs also would threaten the future of the joint light tactical vehicle, which was important for future forces.

The counterarguments were that MRAPs met the immediate need to reduce casualties. U.S. public support had plunged with rising casualties that seemed disproportionate to the progress and stakes in Iraq. The argument that the enemy would just build a bigger bomb makes no sense. By that logic, no military anywhere would ever use armor for anything. Armor has value not because it is invulnerable but because it makes the enemy's job harder and our job easier, which is what MRAPs did. Finally, replacing the crew of a Humvee cost two to three times more than buying an MRAP ($2.5–$3 million versus $1 million), so they were cost effective. Furthermore, Congress was eager to fund the MRAPs and it was not self-evident they would decrement other programs to do so.

It is impossible to definitely resolve the question of whether MRAPs were "worth it," but several conclusions do seem clear. MRAPs were never a silver bullet for defeating IEDs or the only element of force protection important in irregular warfare. Yet they were a valid requirement, saved lives, and made a difference even as insurgent violence was winding down. They would have made a bigger contribution if deployed earlier. Secretary Gates was right to cite the MRAP experience as prima facie evidence of the Pentagon's inability to balance conventional and irregular warfare capabilities, which he attributes to the inertia inherent in large hierarchical organizations that militates against adaptation. Like all large bureaucracies, military organizations:

> *force their members to apply numerous fixed techniques and procedures in the erroneous belief that this would enhance effectiveness. Yet it has just the opposite effect because the rank-and-file relies on a fixed routine instead of using judgment and experience. The mission of the institution is increasingly forgotten or ignored. The chiefs of various departments or sections create veritable fiefdoms of power and influence and try to devise ways to protect and expand their authority and power. They are also often resistant to any change because change is considered a threat rather than an opportunity.*[292]

In the case of MRAPs, the Pentagon's bureaucratic culture reinforced the tendency to channel decisionmaking into enclaves where special interests prevailed over broader strategic considerations. The only leaders in a position to override these Pentagon organizational proclivities and intervene with cross-cutting, integrative oversight over the diverse Pentagon functional areas were the Secretary and his Deputy and the Chairman and the Vice Chairman. Their divergent views on MRAPs were notable.

Secretary Gates (and the congressional armed services committees) could see the need for the MRAPs, but the Chairman and Vice Chairman could not. Most senior military officers writing about the war ignore the MRAP controversy,[293] yet it is a major feature in Secretary Gates's memoir. This difference between the top civilian and military leaders on MRAPs is best explained by the U.S. military's aversion to irregular warfare. Secretary Gates, confronted with this attitude, resolved to change it:

> *Beginning in the spring of 2007, I resolved to make senior civilian and military leaders in the Pentagon lower their eyes from future potential wars and turn aside from day-to-day politics and bureaucratic routine*

to focus on the wars right in front of them, in Iraq and Afghanistan.
Effectively waging war on our enemies on those battlefields would also
require successfully waging war on the Pentagon itself.[294]

Gates wanted the Pentagon to embrace preparedness for irregular warfare and
institutionalize niche capabilities for the same.[295] It has yet to do so, and in
that regard, the MRAP case is a "tell-tale" event. It sends a clear warning signal about the Pentagon's capacity for adaptation and fielding equipment in
response to nimble adversaries, particularly in nontraditional mission areas
such as irregular warfare.

Civil-Military Administrative Capacity

Another critical capability recognized as necessary for success in Afghanistan
and Iraq was the wide range of civil administrative skills necessary for improving governance.[296] These skill sets ranged from overseeing development
projects to training police forces to advising local politicians on how to run
fair elections. As Stephen Hadley notes, in the decades following Vietnam, the
United States reformed its military forces until they were the best in the world,
but it "did not make a similar effort to develop the capabilities we need to do
post-conflict operations." The military's small civil affairs force is mostly in the
Reserves, and it is insufficient to need. So these "largely civilian capabilities"
must be tapped elsewhere in the U.S. Government and private sector. However, "we have not developed a systematic way to identify, train, exercise, deploy,
do lessons learned, and improve" these capabilities. "We just haven't done it.
And so every time we have one of these, whether it's Bosnia, Afghanistan, Iraq,
or the 2011 Arab Awakening," we start from scratch.[297]

DOD, operating with a downsized and professionalized post-Vietnam
military, does not want to take on these responsibilities. At the same time,
it recognizes the importance, so it wants others to do them. When it became
clear that other countries, international organizations, and nongovernmental
organizations were unwilling or incapable of providing the requisite capabilities for civil-military administration, a huge effort was mounted to have the
Department of State provide them. When it became clear State could not do
so, or at least not quickly and in sufficient quantity and quality, DOD argued
it should assume responsibility for some mission-critical civil-military duties.

Police training is one such example. Disputes over who should control the police training effort generated much friction between DOD and State. Development projects were another area of contention, with differences of opinion on whether projects should serve short-term military or political objectives or longer term development goals. New organizations such as the interagency Provincial Reconstruction Teams did not work well; there was squabbling over which department should lead the teams and difficulty manning them. Often the teams were de facto DOD constructs because only it had the manpower to populate them.

In the past, such requirements led to the creation of new organizations and mandates, but in the Afghanistan and Iraq wars, we tried to meet the need by obtaining more flexible authorities for DOD and State. These authorities helped but did not solve the problem. The misadventures of the Coalition Provisional Authority in Iraq and other ad hoc civilian assistance efforts have been laid bare in inspector general reports that are hair-raising for the amount of waste they document, but more so for the consequences of the mismanagement.[298] Over time, greater civilian capacity was generated and coordination problems were ameliorated, but we never were able to produce sufficient quantity or quality of personnel to meet the need.[299]

The failure to tackle this capacity shortfall is hard to explain. Senior leaders characterized the issue as critical—indeed, a national imperative. Much was written about it, but little was done. Pondering this inertia, Secretary Gates and others made reference to Ambassador Robert Komer's insights in his classic study on Vietnam. Against great bureaucratic opposition, Komer built and led a unique, large, hybrid civil-military administrative structure in Vietnam (that is, Civil Operations and Revolutionary Development Support, or CORDS) and used it to great effect, albeit too late to make a decisive difference in the war. Komer is not cited as a model for emulation so much as for his explanation as to why too little was done too late to make a difference. Like Gates, he blamed the failure on "institutional inertia," but also cited a "shocking lack of institutional memory" and the "notable dearth of systematic analysis of performance."[300]

Views differ on how best to overcome institutional inertia in this area. Some leaders advocate an effective civilian reserve force that can be called up in times of need.[301] Others have argued we need standing capacity to launch the effort and build upon, and that we had an appropriate start in the Department of State but not sufficient funding. For example, James Stephenson, a senior U.S. Agency for International Development official in Iraq, argued:

> We still need to create the standing capacity to aid failing and failed states, even those at war. . . . The State Department Coordinator for Reconstruction and Stabilization (S/CRS) is supposed to lead this effort, but Congress has repeatedly refused to provide adequate funding for S/CRS to perform its mission. . . . Establishing such an organization is not difficult; it requires only national will and funding from Congress. An available field force of experienced, committed civilian practitioners is already contemplated and within reach. S/CRS has planned for civilian advance teams that would deploy both with the military and in circumstances where there is no military presence, but it has no funding to adequately implement the concept. Without a standing capacity, our civilian response will continue to be ad hoc and, too often, inadequate.[302]

Stephenson criticized Congress for not providing funding, but others question whether State was ever committed to the mission.[303] The lack of congressional action could reflect the fragile political support for the wars, skepticism about the value of building new bureaucracy to deal with hopefully transitory problems, the view that over time Provincial Reconstruction Teams would prove capable of doing the job,[304] or resistance from existing departments and agencies that wanted the mission. What is certain is that when it comes to providing civil-military administrative capacity for irregular warfare, we have retrogressed from the time Komer ran CORDS in Vietnam and seem incapable of correcting the problem.

Constraints

National security decisionmaking often requires balancing one objective against others. Senior leader accounts underscore the extent to which efforts to achieve one goal were constrained by efforts to achieve another. Managing such strategic tensions was a major challenge. For example, several senior leaders note the difficulty of convincing people in Iraq that this time the United States was serious about removing Saddam by force if necessary when the

Nation also was compelled to pursue the normal diplomatic posturing that suggested a lack of resoluteness.[305] Similarly, Vice President Cheney argues that waffling about U.S. commitment to prevail in Iraq shored up domestic political support in some places, but it also made the job of our military leaders in the field more difficult.[306] Secretary Gates observes that in order to support General Petraeus on the Surge of military forces in Iraq, he had to suggest ending it in Washington so it would not look like an open-ended commitment to increased force levels.[307] George Tenet notes the tradeoff between a postwar Iraq leadership that had legitimacy and leaders we thought we could control.[308] Under Secretary Feith relates concerns that advance work on postwar planning for Iraq might have undermined the public perception that we were giving the United Nations and diplomacy a real chance to succeed.[309]

General Myers also notes the way strategic objectives militate against one another, generating paradoxes that "require artful execution of strategy." He believes it is impossible to eliminate such tensions but feels they can be "balanced and mitigated in the policymaking process,"[310] assuming a superior decisionmaking process is in place. Unfortunately, as General Myers notes, several other constraints complicated the decisionmaking process in Afghanistan and Iraq. Poor civil-military relations are a case in point. Several senior military leaders note the uncanny ability of military and civilian leaders to talk past one another, with the military demanding clear objectives and civilian leaders wanting a range of options and associated costs before deciding what could and should be accomplished.[311] Misunderstandings fueled by these political and cultural differences undermine trust, teamwork, and thus decisionmaking.[312]

Another such factor raised by senior leaders is the broader political environment prevailing in Washington.[313] In ways not true following Pearl Harbor or other national catastrophes, the public discourse over the war on terror was damaged and has not recovered despite multiple national investigations designed to clear the air with copious fact-finding.[314] General Myers argues the quality of the national strategy debate has been degraded:

> *Unfortunately, in my view, as a nation we haven't been able to engage in this public discourse since the summer before the 2004 national elections when the efforts in Iraq and Afghanistan became much more polit-*

icized, much more partisan. The strident and often vitriolic language on both sides of the debate made such discourse difficult, if not impossible. The media were just an amplifier for this partisan discourse. . . . Our national security debate has to be elevated.[315]

Perhaps worse than the partisan politics is the tendency of senior leaders to position themselves to be able to blame others for poor outcomes. The early fault-finding over intelligence warnings of 9/11 was eclipsed by an even more fractious debate over intelligence used to justify the invasion of Iraq. Taken as a whole, finger-pointing is corrosive. Instead of a serious public debate about national security issues of great consequence, there is a lot of posturing to advance or undermine reputations that trivializes the issues at stake. Feith argues the country was unable to have the strategy debate it needed following 9/11, but even worse, the decision process was so flawed that it was impossible to have a good strategy debate even within the administration.[316] Hadley, Myers, and others believe this remains the case: "We have not really had a no-kidding, depoliticized conversation about what it takes to keep this country safe, consistent with our laws and consistent with who we are as the American people."[317]

If social mores have changed to allow unabashed criticism of colleagues in memoirs, so too has the willingness to leak information—classified or not—to the press, a trend that some note is an international habit as well.[318] Leaders who lament leaks often try to counteract their effect by leaking countervailing information themselves. Some journalists and academics justify leaks as a contribution to transparency, but this argument is suspect. The accuracy of the leaked information has to be questioned, but it also is clear that leaks can drive senior leaders into smaller decisionmaking groups with no note-takers or notes taken, thus diminishing longer term historical transparency.[319] In any case, it is hard to find a single senior leader account that does not lament leaks for the damage they do to the decisionmaking process. Leaks embittered senior leaders toward one another, hurt careers, endangered operations and operators, encouraged some senior officials to resign, undermined the U.S. reputation overseas, and hurt national security.[320] Tenet calls leaks the "IEDs of inside the Beltway warfare."[321] Leaks help fuel the supercharged, ad hominem political environment that trivializes matters of supreme importance. That,

239

combined with the press penchant for racing to expose malfeasance before all the facts are in, contributes to the tendency to regard any unfortunate event as prima facie evidence of incompetence.

For example, Secretary Clinton notes the December 30, 2009, suicide bombing that killed seven CIA officers produced quick criticism of "poor tradecraft," forcing a quick defense of the agency by its director. General Franks makes a similar point about intense criticism of Operation *Anaconda*, which gave rise to complaints about "breakdowns and blunders" that cost lives. To put the eight troops who lost their lives during the combat operation in perspective, he notes the hundreds of Americans killed in egregious World War II accidents and asks, given the high stakes and the reality that war with a determined enemy is unpredictable, whether we need a better sense of perspective about the costs of war.[322] We must sympathize with senior leaders in this regard. While it is important to confront calamities with transparency and openness to assess how they can be prevented in the future, the immediate cries of ineptitude can encourage the opposite: a rush to justify and move past the episode. General Franks made a point of noting no matter how much he disagreed with other leaders on occasion, he never doubted their "loyalty or motivations." That is probably a good starting point for analysis of any unfortunate turn of events in the national security realm.

Conclusions

The analysis in this chapter challenges some popular explanations for what went wrong in Afghanistan and Iraq. Some argue victory was impossible because host-nation officials we partnered with were flawed. However, the senior leaders we consulted do not believe this was a critical factor. As General Petraeus notes, "You go to war with the Host Nation you have, not just the one you'd like."[323] We also argue that flawed intelligence about the Iraqi weapons of mass destruction, the dilapidated state of Iraqi public services, and other intelligence shortcomings were not the main reason the United States found it difficult to achieve its objectives. We certainly needed better and different kinds of intelligence, but no one faulty intelligence prediction explains poor performance in Afghanistan and Iraq. Perhaps the most common explanations for failure that we challenge relate to individual decisionmakers and their decisions.

When things go wrong it is natural to blame leaders, reasoning that things would have gone better if they had made better decisions. This is especially true when senior leader decisions are controversial, as was the case with Iraq. As commentators often note, Iraq was a war of choice that should not have been initiated without being prepared for all likely developments, especially postwar lawlessness. It also is understandable that poor outcomes are often linked to common decisionmaking errors such as erroneous assumptions, improper analogies, tunnel vision, and cognitive dissonance. Almost by definition when things go badly, these types of limitations are in play to some extent.

For example, at some level, it is true that senior leaders did not anticipate how hard it would be to achieve what they set out to do. Shocked by 9/11, they settled on the reasonable conclusion that in the information age it was increasingly likely that terrorists operating with the avowed intention of attacking the United States with weapons of mass destruction could do so. They wanted to reduce that threat with an international campaign against terror that included attacking not only the terrorists but also states inclined to support them, and Iraq was a better target in that regard than Iran or North Korea. Full of conviction in the aftermath of 9/11,[324] the widespread attitude was "as much as it takes for as long as it takes."[325] What earnest, dedicated senior leaders discovered was that much more than firm convictions and overwhelming resources was required to pursue this agenda successfully.

It is clear from assessing and comparing diverse senior leader accounts that U.S. leadership was not able to formulate a real strategy for victory, implement it with unified effort, or provide the capabilities necessary. It is stunning to realize that after 15 years of war, senior leaders note that we still do not have a strategy for defeating the enemy and in fact do not agree on who or what the enemy is; that within weeks of 9/11, the President knew the U.S. response would require an unprecedented integration of all elements of national power, which he was unable to provide; that after immense amounts of spending, the United States still could not field the capabilities experts argue are required for success in irregular war; and worse, that so much magnificent effort and so many resources were wasted for these reasons.

These limitations provide a better explanation for poor performance in Afghanistan and Iraq than the assertion that any one decision, no matter how important, was flawed due to unrealistic assumptions, tunnel vision, or cognitive dissonance. The collective explanatory weight of the three limitations we identify is commensurate with the magnitude of the performance puzzle posed by the history of the wars. The United States expended prodigious amounts of blood and treasure, swept enemy forces from the field, and targeted terrorists and insurgent leaders on an industrial scale, but exercised little influence over outcomes. This reality is comprehensible when one realizes we had no guiding strategy, worked at cross-purposes, and did not furnish the capabilities necessary for irregular warfare. Many leaders were frustrated by such impediments and, on occasion, they were able to mitigate or temporarily overcome them. But in the main, these problems persisted through 15 years of war.

The first handicap—lack of an adequate strategy—may elicit yawns. The cognoscenti often decry the lack of strategy but are ignored by senior leaders who promulgate lists of goals and work toward them purposefully, believing that should suffice. Yet as we have shown—and as a significant number of senior leaders now relate in their memoirs—the United States needs a strategy, beginning with a precise definition of the problem posed by 9/11. Preventing terrorists from obtaining and using weapons of mass destruction is a workable ersatz definition, but it has lost support over time and never was sufficient for guiding operations in Afghanistan and Iraq.[326] The United States backed into counterinsurgency to prevent tactical reversals to its counterterrorism agenda. Senior leaders never agreed on whether or why stabilizing those countries was a vital interest. The failure to identify the problem we were trying to solve condemned the United States to incremental decisions and half-hearted commitment, and retarded unified effort and fielding capabilities needed to win the wars.

Sociopolitical constraints help explain the absence of strategy. Senior leaders do not put real strategy in official strategy documents because doing so alienates important constituencies and opens them to criticism that they have misdiagnosed the problem or chosen too narrow a means for solving it. The political risks of real strategy are so onerous that it is now common to confuse strategy with goal-setting and "assume strategy is a big-picture overall direction divorced from any specific action."[327] Leaking information about senior leader deliberations, civil-military tensions, and poisonous partisan politics all reinforce this trend, driving clear thinking further underground. Leaders want deep discussions on problems and solutions, but promulgating discriminating choices increases their political vulnerability.[328]

Another reason strategy is difficult to generate is that Presidents are successful politicians but not necessarily good strategists, and they are more attuned to the need to preserve political support than the importance of strategy. This last point is critical because the U.S. national security system is President-centric. The President is the chief executive and commander in chief, and only he can resolve contentious strategy issues among Cabinet officials. But, as discussed earlier in this chapter, the President is also a "commander in brief" who has limited time to devote to managing even the most important security issues. Those close to President Bush note his effectiveness increased during his second term as he devoted more time to managing Iraq,[329] and that effective war management fell off when a new President first underestimated the importance of his personal involvement.[330]

The second handicap—insufficient unified command and effort—is also a shopworn shibboleth, but again, one with profound consequences. Our greatest, most persistent, most deleterious implementation problem was our inability to integrate the vast capabilities resident in the national system for best effect. Indeed, we were not even able to achieve unified command of all *military* forces in Afghanistan until 10 years of war had passed. This resultant disunity of effort was a persistent source of trouble and wasted effort. From the National Security Council to Ambassadors and field commanders in Afghanistan and Iraq, we failed to productively resolve competing perspectives, priorities, and practices. Thus, we often achieved less than possible or even worked at cross-purposes, as was true in the case of postwar planning for Iraq. In the past, we have sometimes overcome the costs of doing business this way and managed to "win ugly" by attacking problems with astounding amounts of resources. In Afghanistan and Iraq, this inefficient approach was unsustainable, particularly because no one was sure how important success in those endeavors was or how to measure it.[331]

The third handicap—failure to provide the capabilities demanded by irregular warfare—is more controversial but no less consequential. Special intelligence, sociocultural knowledge, strategic communications, specialized equipment, and civil-military administrative capacity were essential but not sufficient for success. Given the absence of a strategy and unified effort, a better effort to provide these capabilities would not have pacified Afghanistan or Iraq. Even so, fielding these capabilities would have contributed to progress and reduced the costs borne by those fighting the wars. Some senior leaders mounted herculean efforts to squeeze better capabilities out of a reluctant bureaucracy. We tried to highlight where they succeeded, but clearly the United States still has shortcomings in these areas that will handicap any future irregular warfare operations it undertakes.

Senior leaders ultimately are responsible for these limitations, but it is also important to acknowledge that leaders are not in complete control of outcomes and that they are constrained to make their decisions within an organizational and political system with behaviors they do not fully control. For these reasons, good outcomes are not always the result of great decisionmaking, and bad outcomes are not always the result of flawed decisionmaking. It also is important to note that the criteria and standards for judging senior leader decisionmaking are biased toward high-profile failure and tend to shift depending on whether commentators are looking forward or backward.[332] In retrospect, when it is clear actual developments were not well prepared for and handled, critics often reverse-engineer senior leader decisions and conclude they must have relied on biased assumptions and wishful thinking, and overlooked obvious problems for which they should have better prepared. However, when advising on future courses of action, pundits are more likely to sympathize with the difficulty of predicting developments and assert that leaders have to adjust quickly because some assumptions always prove wrong and unexpected developments always arise.

Recognizing these biases, we examined the decisionmaking process as senior leaders experienced and described it, and we assessed their national-level decisionmaking with more enduring criteria. We asked whether they had a strategy, implemented it with unified effort, and provided the means for its execution. We believe it would have been much easier for the United States to make the right decisions or recover from poor ones if these criteria were met. From the decisionmakers' own accounts, we know that these criteria were not met and that performance in Afghanistan and Iraq suffered as a result.

These national-level coordination and implementation handicaps are so serious that many senior leaders conclude the U.S. national security system needs major reform.[333] Fixing unified command problems is a case in point.

Many leaders have called for reforms to correct the absence of any "effective, consistent mechanism that brings a whole interagency team to focus on a particular foreign policy issue."[334] General Myers states the case clearly:

> *The issue to date, and certainly through my tenure in the Joint Chiefs of Staff, is that below the President there is no one person, head of a department, or head of an agency who has been tasked with or is responsible for the strategic direction and integration of all elements of national power, so the United States can properly execute a strategy for Iraq, Afghanistan, or a global counterinsurgency. And while there are people who are tasked to do parts of this job, nobody brings it all together. In particular, nobody has the authority and influence needed across the whole U.S. government to be responsible, and held accountable, for strategic planning and execution. We need some new constructs and some new matrixed organizations.[335]*

General McChrystal makes the same point. For complex problems such as Afghanistan and Iraq, he warns, "If you don't get a unity of command, you are going to fail." He considers the confused military commands in Afghanistan "lunacy" but notes they were fixed after 10 years of war, something that cannot be said for confused interagency command, which persists to this day. Secretary Rumsfeld, Secretary Gates, Ambassador Neumann, Admiral Blair, Admiral Olson, and others agree and propose reforms to fix the problem.[336]

However, the national security system may not be reformed any time soon. Thus, as many argue, it is imperative for rising senior leaders to understand the system we have, work within its limits, and attempt to mitigate its shortcomings.[337] On this score, a word of warning against complacency or despair is in order. Complacency is the greater temptation. Many seem to believe the United States is too large or powerful to fail, or hope the kinds of problems identified here could be corrected with a simple change of leadership. It also seems true that many practitioners have become inured to the system's shortcomings and are not aware of their impact. As one expert notes, we have a pronouncement-practice gap; we promulgate strategy documents that postulate unified effort as an essential precondition for success, even though "as a government we have proven incapable of 'whole of government operations.'"[338]

General Casey experienced this firsthand. He received Presidential guidance emphasizing the need for "the closest cooperation and mutual support"[339] among departments and agencies working in the field, but he was not given the means to generate it. Similarly, we intone the virtues of jointness but do not require it in the planning and execution of military operations.

Pessimism about these performance limitations is not helpful, either. We have to hope they can be managed better if they are well understood by a new generation of national security leaders. In this vein, it is worthwhile enumerating some key insights from the analysis in this chapter that can assist future leaders in managing complex national security problems.

- General Casey correctly notes national-level decisionmaking was not as rigorous as the process military officers used, but that does not mean it is incomprehensible. Senior leaders need to study the national security system, its processes, and its strengths and weaknesses so they can better participate in the process.[340]

- The U.S. national security system has many strengths. Over the past 15 years of war, U.S. successes were usually a function of departments and agencies conducting their core missions well, or leaders finding ways to generate new levels of interdepartmental cooperation on nontraditional missions. This suggests that departments have deep capacities to execute their core missions, but that we must recognize when a mission demands interagency collaboration and make special provisions for it.

- Real strategy is hard. We pay so much lip service to strategy, and so readily embrace public policy documents as a substitute for strategy, that many senior leaders do not recognize its absence. Real strategy is not the result of compromise, even though its execution can involve compromise. Real strategy requires exacting depictions of the essential problem and a clear choice among competing solutions to guide means developed and employed.

- The first step in real strategy is distilling the problem to its essential elements, which is hard for both substantive and political reasons. Not agreeing on the nature of the terrorist threat we are trying to defeat cripples our performance. The U.S. shortfall in sociocultural knowledge exacerbates this strategy limitation but is not the sole reason for it. Instead, political and organizational proclivities make this a common strategy failing.

■ America's well-diagnosed penchant for incrementalism and "gut" calls is not a substitute for strategy. Real strategy in the current system must emerge from the minds of senior leaders who agree on its essential elements. The President and his national security staff have no greater responsibility than ensuring this happens, but busy and inexperienced Presidents and National Security Advisors overwhelmed with managing day-to-day activities often fail to perform this task.

■ Trust is a prerequisite for good national security and military strategy because it is a critical prerequisite for good teams. Trust must be cultivated among senior leaders because the decision-making environment in Washington and organizational cultures throughout the national security system militate against it. Trust takes time to build and is fragile. Providing a real range of viable options to senior leaders increases trust; leaking information destroys trust.

■ "No strategy for dealing with current or emerging threats, however good, is likely to be fully successful" without the ability to generate better unified effort.[341] Yet senior leaders should not expect the formal national security staff process to resolve all important interagency differences. Presidents do not have the time to referee all such disputes and are disinclined to accept the political baggage that goes along with doing so. Working around the system to engineer a direct relationship with the President can produce a backlash from bypassed parties that leads to mission failure. The key is to identify the most critical issues and ensure they are resolved, and then be prepared to forge a new unified effort in response to changed circumstances.

■ Insufficient unity of effort is not just a "civilian" or interagency problem. It also is a challenge for the Pentagon and military operations. DOD was not able to generate enough of a team effort across its various fiefdoms for war planning, postwar planning, war resourcing, or command and control of military forces in the field. These limitations compromised the effectiveness of U.S. military operations and wasted resources. In this respect, the Pentagon has a "strategy formulation and execution problem" of its own that requires attention.

■ Managing interagency operations well is a critical senior leader skill. Complex security problems are now more common, and complex problems are interdisciplinary and thus interagency problems. Some of the greatest successes in the war were the result of collaboration across departmental lines. Interagency collaboration did not occur when leaders followed the traditional lead agency approach or selected ostensibly compatible personalities. Managing across organizational boundaries is a complex skill that requires, among other things, working hard to build relationships with counterparts, comprehending the decisionmaking styles of superiors, and developing trust within top leadership circles.[342] It also behooves senior leaders to study those cases where predecessors have forged a high degree of interagency cooperation.

■ As we try to demonstrate by referring to a variety of successes and failures, including interagency high-value target teams, postwar planning, and the MRAP experience, leaders who want to manage complex, cross-functional (to include interagency) problems well must curb organizational tendencies to maximize autonomy. They must be prepared to take initiative and innovate, not only within their functional areas of specialization but also across Service and departmental boundaries.

■ As we discussed when contrasting good oversight with poor micromanagement, too many leaders advocate empowering subordinates while restricting information flow and retaining approval authority for problem-solving. To forge vertical unity of effort and execute an effective mission command approach, leaders must distinguish oversight from micromanagement:

- Good oversight requires leaders to stay well informed about progress and identify any critical impediments. Leaders need to worry less about controlling information flow and more about identifying impediments to progress that jeopardize their mission. When they move to eliminate obstacles, leaders need to make sure they override subordinate concerns only when their broader perspective gives them insights their subordinates lack.

- Deleterious micromanagement occurs when leaders overrule a subordinate based on personal past experience or some other prejudice rather than their broader field of vision. In such cases the leader fails to exploit his broader contextual understanding and also squanders the subordinate's greater knowledge of immediate tasks and circumstances.

- Senior leaders need to better appreciate the limits of the current system's ability to understand foreign social and political structures—and the fact that this kind of knowledge cannot be generated quickly or organized well on the fly. Leaders must act in advance to institutionalize an effective and expandable sociocultural knowledge base. New organizations to provide sociocultural knowledge seem expensive until the alternative is considered, something the past 15 years of war should have made painfully clear.

- More generally, senior leaders charged with managing irregular war must be prepared to fight for capabilities they will need to be successful. The U.S. national security system is not well organized to conduct extended irregular warfare missions. The departments and agencies dislike irregular warfare and resist creating organizations and programs to provide capabilities tailored to its demands.

Some people hope we will just avoid irregular foes or complex contingencies such as Afghanistan and Iraq because the system is not optimized for performance in those circumstances. However, the senior leaders we consulted agree that the need to manage such problems cannot be ruled out and may well be unavoidable. Others hope the system will be reformed to allow leaders to employ its vast capabilities with greater success against such problems, but emerging leaders most likely will go to war again with the system we have rather than one we might prefer. Still others are counting on new leaders to make the system work better, but that may depend on how well we educate our rising leaders on the peculiar strengths and weaknesses of our national security system.

Greater emphasis on senior leader education is justified given the nature of the serious system handicaps identified in this chapter. The need for real strategy, unified implementation of the same, and the ability to provide the means required by one's strategy are so much a matter of common sense that they may strike the reader as superficial bromides. It all seems so obvious. Yet grasping and acting upon the obvious have exceeded our reach. Ambassador Komer made this point about insights he offered on our performance in Vietnam: "If these rather generalized lessons seem like restating the obvious, one need only recall how little we actually practiced them."[343] Indeed. That is the thing about learning; it cannot be said to have taken root until it is applied. Unless we act upon these often-repeated insights, we will endure and endure again these same performance liabilities to the detriment of those we send into harm's way. If we fail to act upon these well-documented insights about our performance, we are inviting, if not condemning, future leaders to relive and relearn what so many brave men and women sacrificed to illuminate.

Notes

[1] George W. Bush, "Address to a Joint Session of Congress and the American People," Washington, DC, September 20, 2001.

[2] Ibid.

[3] As noted in chapter six of the current volume, between 2004 and 2014, Islamic terrorist groups increased from 21 in 18 countries to 41 in 24 countries. In retrospect, General David Petraeus observes that a top lesson from the experience in the war is that one must "ask if what you are doing will take more bad guys off the street than it creates." David Petraeus, interview by Joseph J. Collins and Nathan White, March 27, 2015.

[4] The memoirs and interviews from senior leaders include George W. Bush, *Decision*

Points (New York: Crown Publishers, 2010); Dick Cheney with Liz Cheney, *In My Time: A Personal and Political Memoir* (New York: Threshold Editions, 2011); Condoleezza Rice, *No Higher Honor: A Memoir of My Years in Washington* (New York: Crown Publishers, 2011); Thomas J. Ridge and Larry Bloom, *The Test of Our Times: America Under Siege and How We Can Be Safe Again* (New York: Thomas Dunne Books, 2009); Hillary R. Clinton, *Hard Choices* (New York: Simon & Schuster, 2014); Robert M. Gates, *Duty: Memoirs of a Secretary at War* (New York: Knopf, 2014); Donald Rumsfeld, *Known and Unknown: A Memoir* (New York: Sentinel, 2011); George C. Tenet with Bill Harlow, *At the Center of the Storm: My Years at the CIA* (New York: HarperCollins, 2007); Leon E. Panetta with Jim Newton, *Worthy Fights: A Memoir of Leadership in War and Peace* (New York: Penguin, 2014); Henry H. Shelton with Ronald Levinson and Malcolm McConnell, *Without Hesitation: The Odyssey of an American Warrior* (New York: St. Martin's Press, 2010); Richard B. Myers with Malcolm McConnell, *Eyes on the Horizon: Serving on the Front Lines of National Security* (New York: Threshold, 2009); Tommy Franks, *American Soldier* (New York: Regan Books, 2004); Michael DeLong with Noah Lukeman, *A General Speaks Out: The Truth about the Wars in Afghanistan and Iraq* (St. Paul, MN: Zenith Press, 2007); George W. Casey, *Strategic Reflections: Operation* Iraqi Freedom*, July 2004–February 2007* (Washington, DC: NDU Press, 2012); Stanley A. McChrystal, *My Share of the Task: A Memoir* (New York: Portfolio/Penguin, 2013); Douglas J. Feith, *War and Decision: Inside the Pentagon at the Dawn of the War on Terrorism* (New York: Harper, 2008); L. Paul Bremer with Malcolm McConnell, *My Year in Iraq: The Struggle to Build a Future of Hope* (New York: Simon & Schuster, 2006); and Christopher R. Hill, *Outpost: Life on the Frontlines of American Diplomacy* (New York: Simon & Schuster, 2014). We also benefited from the project's personal interviews: Stephen J. Hadley, interview by Joseph J. Collins and Nicholas Rostow, October 7, 2014; Martin E. Dempsey, interview by Richard D. Hooker, Jr., and Joseph J. Collins, January 21, 2014; John Abizaid, interview by Joel Rayburn, September 19, 2014; Stanley A. McChrystal, interview by Joseph J. Collins and Frank G. Hoffman, April 2, 2015; and Douglas Lute, interview by Richard D. Hooker, Jr., and Joseph J. Collins, March 10, 2015.

[5] A statement of method and a list of sources are available upon request. In short, we relied on James G. March's observation that most decisionmaking theory typically assumes decisions are either "choice-based or rule-based." We adopted a choice-based decisionmaking that pursues a "logic of consequences" whereby leaders attempt to select courses of action that will improve their circumstances based on expected results. We thought this was appropriate given that the 9/11 terror attacks were unprecedented in kind and effect, and that neither President George W. Bush nor President Barack Obama was an experienced foreign policy practitioner, factors that we presume made basic decisions about the war on terror less subject to rule- and identity-based decisionmaking. See James G. March and Chip Heath, *A Primer on Decisionmaking: How Decisions Happen* (New York: Free Press, 1994), viii–vix.

[6] This does not mean we accepted all senior leader assertions at face value. They use "communication strategies" on occasion and make weak arguments on others. For example, while in office Under Secretary of Defense for Policy Douglas Feith told James Fallows

that media reports of interagency friction among senior leaders was exaggerated: "In our interview Douglas Feith played this down—maintaining that press reports had exaggerated the degree of quarreling and division inside the Administration." But in his memoir, Feith acknowledges the opposite. See James Fallows, "Blind into Baghdad," *The Atlantic*, January 1, 2004; and Feith, 53ff.

[7]   We acknowledge the abundant evidence that some senior leaders immediately focused on Iraq after 9/11, but accept their explanations for why they did so. General Myers, General Franks, and General DeLong do the same and also say they agree that Iraq was an appropriate target given the U.S. strategy in the war on terror.

[8]   Richard P. Rumelt, *Good Strategy, Bad Strategy: The Difference and Why It Matters* (New York: Crown Business, 2011).

[9]   Gates, 14, 446; Rice, 152–153.

[10]   Christopher J. Lamb, "Pentagon Strategies," in *Challenges in U.S. National Security Policy: A Festschrift Volume Honoring Edward L. (Ted) Warner*, ed. David Ochmanek and Michael Sulmeyer (Arlington, VA: RAND, 2014).

[11]   Lute, interview.

[12]   Casey, 165, 169–170.

[13]   See Feith, 51; and Rice, 150, where she notes, "In October 2001 we'd seen credible reporting that terrorists would again attack the United States, perhaps with a radiological or nuclear weapon. The President sought in the 2002 State of the Union to place all of this into context and to make clear that the United States could defend itself only by taking on the proliferation challenge."

[14]   Bush, "Address."

[15]   Four months later a senior administration official gave a speech that could be interpreted as expanding the list to include Cuba, Libya, and Syria. Then–Undersecretary of State John R. Bolton asserted there were "three other state sponsors of terrorism that are pursuing or that have the potential to pursue weapons of mass destruction or have the capability to do so in violation of their treaty obligations." See John R. Bolton, "Beyond the Axis of Evil: Additional Threats from Weapons of Mass Destruction," May 6, 2002, available at <www.heritage.org/research/lecture/beyond-the-axis-of-evil>.

[16]   Feith, 507.

[17]   Clinton, 132–133.

[18]   Myers's strategic arguments could be interpreted in this manner. Myers, 292–298.

[19]   Clinton, 189, 199–200.

[20]   Jack L. Goldsmith, *Power and Constraint: The Accountable Presidency after 9/11* (New York: Norton, 2012).

[21]   For example, see Shelton, 437ff, 441–442, 444–445.

[22] Rice, 151.

[23] Myers, 212–214, 291, 298.

[24] Rumsfeld, 723; Myers, 291. Myers sees the terrorist threat as the equivalent of a global insurgency.

[25] Abizaid, interview.

[26] Dempsey, interview.

[27] Ibid.

[28] *National Strategy for Combating Terrorism* (Washington, DC: The White House, February 2003), 5–6.

[29] Christopher Lamb and Erin Staine-Pyne, *9/11, Counterterrorism, and the Senior Interagency Strategy Team: Interagency Small Group Performance in Strategy Formulation and Implementation*, IAS-003 (Washington, DC: The Simons Center for Interagency Cooperation, April 2014).

[30] Bush, *Decision Points*, 365; Rumsfeld, 528, 631; Cheney, 435–436.

[31] Tenet, 217–218; also Cheney, 340–341.

[32] Myers, 212, 214.

[33] Rumsfeld notes that General David Barno and Ambassador Zalmay Khalilzad made this case when recommending the shift from counterterrorism to counterinsurgency operations. See Rumsfeld, 686. See also Hy S. Rothstein, *Afghanistan and the Troubled Future of Unconventional Warfare* (Annapolis, MD: Naval Institute Press, 2006).

[34] Myers, 213.

[35] See Joseph J. Collins, "After the Afghan Surge: Rapid Exit or Better Peace?" *Small Wars Journal*, July 15, 2014.

[36] McChrystal, interview. The deleterious impact of the absence of a clear strategic aim is his number one strategic lesson from 15 years of war.

[37] See the discussion in chapter one and below where we note, "the President committed the United States to make a good-faith but not open-ended effort" in Iraq.

[38] The confusion about commitment led to some artful wordsmithing, with some emphasizing "that we will be here as long as it takes to do the job, and not a day longer," and others emphasizing, "At the same time, we should make sure we don't leave a day earlier." See Bob Woodward, *State of Denial* (New York: Simon & Schuster, 2006), 209.

[39] Casey, 154.

[40] Conversations between the author and senior leaders in the Pentagon where he served as Deputy Assistant Secretary of Defense for Resources and Plans during the first George W. Bush administration.

[41] Nora Bensahel, "Mission Not Accomplished: What Went Wrong with Iraqi Reconstruc-

tion?" *The Journal of Strategic Studies* 29, no. 3 (June 2006), 453–473.

[42] Bremer thought reconstituting "Saddam's army would have set off a civil war." Bremer, 224.

[43] Christopher J. Lamb and Evan Munsing, *Secret Weapon: High-value Target Teams as an Organizational Innovation*, INSS Strategic Perspectives 4 (Washington, DC: NDU Press, March 2011).

[44] *National Strategy for Combating Terrorism* (Washington, DC: The White House, September 2006).

[45] Clinton, 138.

[46] For example, see *National Security Strategy of the United States of America* (Washington, DC: The White House, March 2006), 12.

[47] A noteworthy skeptic is Jenna Jordan, "When Heads Roll: Assessing the Effectiveness of Leadership Decapitation," *Security Studies* 18, no. 4 (2009), 719–755; and "Attacking the Leader, Missing the Mark: Why Terrorist Groups Survive Decapitation Strikes," *International Security* 38, no. 4 (Spring 2014), 7–38.

[48] McChrystal, *My Share of the Task*, 161–162.

[49] Rice, 91.

[50] Planning for such possibilities is called "branches and sequels" in military planning parlance. See *Military Decision Making Process–Multinational Planning Handbook*, Version 2.4–Handbook, Supports MNF SOP Version 2.4 (Honolulu, HI: Multinational Planning Augmentation Team Secretariat/U.S. Pacific Command, January 2009); see also Field Manual 101-5, *Staff Organization and Operations* (Washington, DC: Headquarters Department of the Army, May 1997). Assumptions for campaign planning "should be reasonable" but are "assumed to be true in the absence of proof." Arguably, planning assumptions, which are often derived from strategic assumptions, are less speculative (for example, whether an ally will allow U.S. forces to operate from its territory). Joint Publication 5-0, *Joint Operation Planning* (Washington, DC: The Joint Staff, August 11, 2011), IV-7.

[51] For example, otherwise excellent studies by the Center for Strategic and International Studies (CSIS) and RAND overemphasize flawed assumptions in the authors' view. See Anthony H. Cordesman, *American Strategic, Tactical, and Other Mistakes in Iraq: A Litany of Errors* (Washington, DC: CSIS, April 19, 2006), available at <http://csis.org/files/media/csis/pubs/060419_iraqlitany.pdf>; and Nora Bensahel et al., *After Saddam: Prewar Planning and the Occupation of Iraq* (Santa Monica, CA: RAND, 2008). See discussion in previous notes.

[52] Abizaid, interview. President Bush in his memoir notes the difficult but positive histories of postwar Germany, Japan, and South Korea. He explains that he understood Iraq was different, but states, "With time and steadfast American support, I had confidence that democracy in Iraq would succeed." Bush, *Decision Points*, 357.

[53] Gates, 115; Abizaid, interview.

[54] Vice President Cheney and Deputy Secretary of Defense Paul Wolfowitz are most frequently cited in this respect, but some sources (for example, Fallows) refer vaguely to "OSD officials," presumably meaning Feith or his special plans office. General Abizaid, for example, specifically mentions Feith's optimism that Iraqis would welcome U.S. forces. See Abizaid, interview. Yet RAND asserts that "senior policymakers throughout the government held to a set of fairly optimistic assumptions about the conditions that would emerge after major combat and what would be required thereafter." RAND only cites Cheney and Wolfowitz, however, and somewhat incongruously elsewhere underscores all the pessimistic studies conducted by diverse elements of the bureaucracy. Bensahel et al., *After Saddam.*

[55] The author's office produced a short analytic piece for Wolfowitz prior to the war that reviewed past predictions of casualties and war costs prior to U.S. interventions. The memorandum demonstrated there was significant variance between predictions and actual costs, and it received a compliment from the Deputy Secretary.

[56] RAND, for example, somewhat inexplicably asserts senior leaders held rosy assumptions about how easy the postwar security challenges would be and yet notes, "it should be clear from U.S. interventions not just in Iraq, but in Afghanistan, Kosovo, and Bosnia, that wars do not end when major conflict ends." Indeed, which is why it is suspect to assume seasoned leaders were unaware of it. Similarly, it notes that wrong assumptions were "not unreasonable" but "were never seriously challenged . . . despite a predilection for questioning virtually all operational military assumptions from several directions, and despite the existence of alternative analyses within the government." Ultimately, RAND concludes, "The problem, therefore, was not that the U.S. government failed to plan for the postwar period. Instead, it was the failure to effectively coordinate and integrate these various planning efforts." Bensahel et al., *After Saddam,* 236–237, 243.

[57] Hadley, interview.

[58] See Fallows.

[59] Condoleezza Rice, "Campaign 2000: Promoting the National Interest," *Foreign Affairs,* January/February 2000. See also Feith, *War and Decision,* 101.

[60] Rumsfeld, 482–483; Franks, 393. Feith reviews the expatriate issue at length. He argues:

It is remarkable that key U.S. officials believed that the Iraqi externals were the chief danger the United States had to guard against in post-Saddam Iraq. Yet the main idea behind the transitional civil authority was precisely to guard against the externals dominating the post-Saddam political scene in Iraq. Why should that have been a goal of U.S. policy at all? When challenged on this point, top [Department of] State and CIA [Central Intelligence Agency] officials responded that the leaders of the external groups were not skilled enough and, moreover, lacked legitimacy. Rumsfeld, Wolfowitz and I considered State's view presumptuous and dangerous. We did not see what right or interest the United States had in serving as Iraq's occupier for an extended period just because some U.S. officials labeled the external leaders illegitimate.

He also argues that the Department of Defense (DOD) was proved right insomuch as five key expatriate Iraqis were later appointed and elected in Iraq and proved influential. See Feith, 279, 281.

[61] General Abizaid notes, as do many others, that Rumsfeld held meetings where everyone was asked to identify their top 10 concerns about how the war effort might go awry. Abizaid, interview.

[62] Rumsfeld notes a sophisticated argument from his staff on this point and an early warning that the Department of State disagreed with it. Rumsfeld, 484. At the time, there was discussion in Pentagon hallways that Rumsfeld also wanted U.S. forces out of Iraq quickly so they could reconstitute and be prepared for whatever next steps in the war on terror the President might direct.

[63] Rumsfeld's staff frequently heard him use this analogy, and Hadley states he heard it at least 10 times until "finally on the 11th time the President said: 'Yeah, Don, but we cannot afford to have the bicycle fall over.'" Still, Hadley notes the President understood Rumsfeld's point, stating, "Casey and Rumsfeld are right. Ultimately, the Iraqis have to win this and take over, but we can't get from here to there, given where we are; we need a bridge to get the violence down and to allow people then to start the political process again." Hadley goes on to note that that was "what the Surge in Iraq was; it was a bridge." Hadley, interview.

[64] Rumsfeld notes he learned this lesson from the failed intervention in Lebanon in the early 1980s. Rumsfeld, 483.

[65] Feith also argues State was guilty of unrealistic assumptions for believing the United States could run Iraq for years until a "credible" Iraqi leadership emerged. Feith, 277, 370, 468. Some retired generals also have argued the United States should have deposed Saddam and then just left irrespective of conditions. General Dempsey disagrees. Like President Bush, he argues such a course of action would not be consistent with "who we are as a nation." "Out of a sense of both obligation, responsibility to protect although that is not really doctrine, but also compassion—we will assist those who have been defeated to reestablish themselves in a more moderate and inclusive, responsible way." Dempsey, interview.

[66] Rumsfeld pleads guilty to not having "a plan for full-fledged nation building" and insists that such a plan and effort would have been "unwise, well beyond our capability, and unworthy of our troops' sacrifice." Rumsfeld, 683.

[67] Dempsey, interview; Abizaid, interview.

[68] Rumsfeld believed in the value of second-guessing assumptions. Rumsfeld, 665ff; Feith, 48.

[69] Feith notes DOD argued early on for international forces in both Afghanistan (97, 101) and Iraq, where as early as February 2003, DOD was arguing that "the sooner we get international police in Iraq the better." But Feith concludes, "U.S. diplomacy on Iraq lacked

consistency, conviction, energy, or creativity" (249, 365).

[70] Rumsfeld, 526ff. Rumsfeld states it is a canard that he cut State out of postwar planning and explains that he wanted State more involved in the execution of the occupation. He does not acknowledge that planning and execution are two different activities.

[71] Rumsfeld's staff even refused initially to accept the designation of U.S. forces as occupiers—which conferred legal authorities as well as obligations—and instead insisted U.S. forces were liberators, not because they made optimistic assumptions but because they did not want U.S. forces obligated to the postwar security and development missions. General Franks agreed with Rumsfeld on these points. Dempsey, interview; Abizaid, interview. Rumsfeld's preferences were rigorously consistent in this regard, as every source we consulted emphasizes. Hadley, interview; Dempsey, interview; Abizaid, interview; Lute, interview; Fallows.

[72] Bremer, 125; see also 117.

[73] Ibid., 125, 226.

[74] Hadley, interview. Hadley goes on to note that as the United States got deeper into Iraq its motives moved from altruism to opportunity. The idea that Iraq could become a model for the Middle East began to take hold: "because in the Middle East it was either Sunnis oppress Shia, or Shia oppress Sunnis, and both of them beat up the Kurds. We wanted to show that Sunni, Shia, and Kurds could work together in a democratic [framework], develop a common future, where the majority ruled but the minority participated and had protections."

[75] This led to qualified statements of support for postwar governance. For example, Feith, in his testimony to Congress, outlined five specific objectives for the postwar period, two of which were war on terror objectives (eliminating weapons of mass destruction and terrorists' infrastructure), another two which were to reassure Iraqis we would neither partition their country nor "occupy or control them or their economic resources," and the last which was to "*begin* the process of economic and political reconstruction, *working to put Iraq on a path* to become a prosperous and free country" (author's emphasis). Having made it clear that the commitment to postwar governance was limited, Feith stated that the United States would need a "commitment to stay as long as required to achieve the objectives," but also "a commitment to leave as soon as possible, for Iraq belongs to the Iraqi people." See Bensahel et al., *After Saddam*, 43.

[76] This is why General Dempsey notes senior military leaders must accept that in protracted campaigns assumptions and objectives will change and they have to "adapt the campaign accordingly." "Sometimes changing objectives is portrayed as mission failure, when in fact in a protracted campaign the likelihood of renegotiating objectives is 100 percent." Dempsey, interview.

[77] Hadley, interview; Bremer, 27. Secretary Gates agrees, stating that the "fundamental erroneous assumption was that both wars would be short."

[78] In the Bush administration, a major conceptual roadblock for the Surge was the

widespread perception that the mere presence of U.S. forces alienated the population. This thinking prevailed among senior civilian leaders in DOD. Secretary Rumsfeld, for example, cites approvingly the analysis by Feith that concludes it was not de-Ba'athification or the disbanding of the Iraqi army that gave rise to an insurgency but rather the broader impression of an overbearing U.S. presence. Senior military leaders in Iraq—even those who were taking counterinsurgency seriously—also believed the U.S. presence was an irritant, which inclined them to focus on the goal of transferring capacity and responsibility for counterinsurgency to host nation forces. Some leaders in the Obama administration believed the same way about a Surge of forces in Afghanistan, believing "more troops and more fighting would alienate Afghan civilians and undermine any goodwill achieved by expanded economic development and improved governance." Rumsfeld, 514; Clinton, 140.

[79] Bensahel et al., *After Saddam*, xviii.

[80] Both Andrew J. Enterline and Alexander B. Downes note a range of opinions on the topic. Enterline's analysis concludes, "The survival of imposed democracy is by no means assured. Instead, the survival of democracy is strongly conditioned by the process by which the regime is imposed and the social and economic conditions present in the state hosting the imposed polity." Downes's more recent research published in 2013 is more pessimistic, arguing that "interveners will meet with little success unless conditions in the target state—in the form of high levels of economic development and societal homogeneity, and previous experience with representative governance—are favorable to democracy." See Andrew J. Enterline and J. Michael Greig, "The History of Imposed Democracy and the Future of Iraq and Afghanistan," *Foreign Policy Analysis* 4, no. 4 (October 2008), 321–347; and Alexander B. Downes and Jonathan Monten, "Forced to Be Free? Why Foreign-Imposed Regime Change Rarely Leads to Democratization," *International Security* 37, no. 4 (Spring 2013), 90–131.

[81] DOD routinely argues that it will take care of organized resistance and that the State Department ought to provide for civil order after major operations are completed. The typical pattern is that the issue is not resolved prior to the intervention, and when civil unrest recorded by media embarrasses the White House, the President orders DOD to step in and provide security. Often during the interregnum much damage is done to host-nation infrastructure and U.S. reputation. This problem was recognized after the fact in Panama, Somalia, Haiti, Bosnia, and many other U.S. military interventions.

[82] See Bremer, 106, 157, 188, 205–209.

[83] Ibid., 209.

[84] Irving Janis and Alexander George have conducted classic scholarship in this area.

[85] Virtually all senior leaders in memoirs emphasize their appreciation for and insistence on a wide range of options being considered before making key decisions. See, for example, Gates, 222; Casey, 22, 29, 143; DeLong, 22 (where he notes that the United States even sought advice from the Russians about Afghanistan); Franks, 373, 389, 394.

[86] As Fallows argues, the problems that arose in Iraq "were precisely the ones its own expert agencies warned against," so "the Administration will be condemned for what it did with what was known" and not for what it failed to anticipate.

[87] Lute, interview.

[88] Gates, 39.

[89] Clinton, 133.

[90] Abizaid, interview.

[91] Dempsey, interview.

[92] For example, Cheney, 439.

[93] General McChrystal makes this point in his interview, arguing the Surges should never have been necessary. The Iraq Surge sent an important signal of resolve that was backed up by the senior leaders; Afghanistan was much more problematic in that respect. Although McChrystal thought it was essential to avoid losing Afghanistan, he believed that it was not backed up by the same type of resolve, and people could feel it: "Afghans could feel it, the Taliban could feel it, and the allies could feel it." McChrystal, interview.

[94] Clinton, 140.

[95] Gates, 365.

[96] Petraeus notes that senior military leaders were acting on and publicly supporting previous Presidential decisions unaware that the President was actually reconsidering his options, which made it seem as if they were making their case publicly so as to limit the President's options, which was not the case. Petraeus, interview.

[97] Bush demanded new options as the situation continued to deteriorate (or fail to improve, according to some). As Hadley and Lute argue, if the Pentagon does not give real options to the President, he will get them elsewhere. Bush, *Decision Points*, 364; Hadley, interview; Lute, interview.

[98] Joel Rayburn, *Iraq after America: Strongmen, Sectarians, Resistance* (Stanford: Hoover Institution Press, 2014).

[99] Fallows recounts Rumsfeld's answer on April 11, 2003, when asked why U.S. soldiers were not stopping the looting: "Freedom's untidy, and free people are free to make mistakes and commit crimes and do bad things. They're also free to live their lives and do wonderful things, and that's what's going to happen here." Fallows believes the Secretary's embrace of uncertainty became a "reckless evasion of responsibility. He had only disdain for 'predictions,' yes, and no one could have forecast every circumstance of postwar Baghdad. But virtually everyone who had thought about the issue had warned about the risk of looting. U.S. soldiers could have prevented it—and would have, if so instructed."

[100] Abizaid notes he reported on the insurgency and need to get control and maintain presence to the point where "I thought I was going to get fired early." He also observes that the Army, as well as Secretary Rumsfeld, wanted the war to be over. Abizaid, interview.

[101] Hadley, interview. Others also note the poor communications between the Pentagon and the field at this juncture.

[102] Bush, *Decision Points*, 365; Cheney, 430; Rumsfeld, 364.

[103] Cheney, 440–441, 449; see also discussion and notes below.

[104] Gates observes that the decisionmaking process can be too stark and uncompromising, and that some consensus is necessary. Gates, 384–385; Clinton, 130, 133.

[105] Dempsey, interview; McChrystal, interview. General McChrystal stated that "strategically, his thinking evolved away from the direct use of military power to a focus on what was in people's minds. The winner, he thought, would be the person who understood the problem the quickest and adapted to it—those who learned fastest."

[106] The quotations and discussion in this paragraph draw upon March and Heath, 205–206, where they discuss the "Garbage Can Model" of decisionmaking. This model is more valuable for its descriptive than its explanatory power, in the opinion of the author.

[107] There are different approaches to decisionmaking that do not value unified effort so much. Some practitioners (or "pragmatists") argue leaders could and should exploit impediments to unified effort to further their agendas. Still others believe advantages can be found in the "flexible implementation, uncoordinated actions, and cognitive confusion" that characterize lack of unified effort.

[108] For example, there were noteworthy pockets of interagency success. The Institute for National Strategic Studies at the National Defense University has published a set of such studies, arguing they point the way forward for better interagency collaboration.

[109] For example, see Bush, *Decision Points*, 88, where the President relates his frustration with interagency "squabbling" and how despite his efforts to eliminate it, "nothing worked"; Rice, 16, 22, where she tied interagency friction to poor relations between Powell and Rumsfeld and their mutual "distrust," which led to dysfunction and nearly brought things "to the breaking point"; Clinton, 24, where she notes, "the traditional infighting between State and Defense . . . in many previous administrations had come to resemble the Sharks and the Jets from *West Side Story*"; Rumsfeld, 525, 527–528, where he blames failures in Iraq on Rice's inability to manage the interagency process correctly, explains his repeated recommendations "that they institute chances to improve the President's most important national security body" but states that "there [was] little or no improvement" and that the dysfunction continued to "undermine our nation's policies"; Gates, 92, 341, where he acknowledges "lack of institutional cohesion at the top of the government" and relates that upon arriving he and his staff found "interagency planning, coordination and resourcing are, by far, the weakest link" for U.S. operations in Afghanistan; Myers, 301–305, where he asserts that the United States cannot deal effectively with 21st-century threats, that good integration in operations is the exception and not the rule, and that no strategy is "likely to be fully successful" without better interagency coordination; Franks, 375–376, where he notes, "insufficient trust between the departments" of State and Defense, "deep and inflexible commitment to their own ideas [that] was disruptive and

divisive," and a Washington bureaucracy that "fought like cats in a sack"; and McChrystal, 116, 118, where he admits that "Early on, counterproductive infighting among the CIA, State Department, Department of Defense, and others back in Washington" threatened the Afghan campaign, and that "more than once, my most trusted subordinates had to stop me, in moments of utter frustration, from severing all ties with our 'Agency Brothers.'"

[110] Henry M. Jackson, *The Secretary of State and the Ambassador: Jackson Subcommittee Papers on the Conduct of American Foreign Policy* (New York: Praeger, 1964), 7–8.

[111] Rice, 92.

[112] Gates, 295.

[113] For example, Gates supported the idea of a war czar initially. Later, he concluded the person selected for the role was a disappointment. He believed the czar began second-guessing commanders in the field, contributing to Presidential mistrust of the uniformed military leadership, and leaking to the press (67, 338, 364, 430, 482, 500). However, he did not like special envoys (295), while Secretary Clinton did (29). Hadley believed the war czar worked well and only declined in effectiveness under the Obama administration because the czar's access to the President was curtailed. Hadley, interview.

[114] For example, Abizaid believes Bremer thought the Iraqi army was anti-democratic and that he had a decided preference for smaller Iraqi forces and in particular weak or no Sunni forces. Thus, he clashed with General Petraeus when Petraeus was trying to build up such forces in Mosul. He speculates that Bremer believed a continuance of organized military power loyal to Sunni leaders would doom representative government in Iraq. Abizaid, interview.

[115] Ibid.

[116] Rumsfeld, 510, 522–523, 527, 532; Feith, 496ff.

[117] Clinton, 29, 140–141.

[118] The ability of the President to get his policies implemented by the bureaucracy has been identified as a key issue for many decades. See Jackson, 3–36. In the case of Iraq and Afghanistan, both President Bush and President Obama believed the Pentagon resisted their desire for alternative options for troop increases. Also, many senior Bush administration leaders argue that Bremer exceeded the authority granted him by the President. See, for example, Rice, 242; and Feith, 496–497. Cheney (380–381) asserts that Secretary Powell exceeded the President's guidance on the Israeli-Palestinian peace process and that (478–479) Secretary Gates did the same, "speaking for himself and not reflecting U.S. policy," when he "informed the king [of Saudi Arabia] that the president would be impeached if he took military action against Iran." Cheney notes the President had not yet decided about next steps on Iran, and Gates in effect was curtailing the President's options by suggesting to a key ally that military operations were impossible. According to General Myers (225), General Franks ignored guidance to prepare postwar planning. Finally, according to Cheney (454), General Casey would not support the President's Surge.

[119] Bush, *Decision Points*, 90.

[120] Cheney, 380, 478.

[121] Tenet, 446.

[122] Clinton, 190.

[123] Cheney, 457.

[124] Gates, 364–365, 367; Clinton, 133.

[125] Myers, 425.

[126] Rice, 20.

[127] Unless otherwise noted, citations in this paragraph are from Gates, 206, 478. For discussion of the consequences of disunity of effort flowing from confused command arrangements, see Christopher J. Lamb and Martin Cinnamond, *Unity of Effort: Key to Success in Afghanistan*, Strategic Forum No. 248 (Washington, DC: NDU Press, October 2009).

[128] Abizaid, interview. Petraeus agrees the lines of authority were confused in Afghanistan. Petraeus, interview.

[129] McChrystal, interview. McChrystal observed that special mission units sometimes "would go in and hit a target, maybe there would be a firefight, but the impact on stability of that area might be negative." For some data on this, see Lamb and Cinnamond, 7.

[130] McChrystal, interview.

[131] Lute, interview.

[132] Casey, 62. Casey at least recognized the issue. Others, such as Gates, were altogether surprised that the U.S. Army had forgotten after Vietnam how to do counterinsurgency. Gates, 28.

[133] Myers, 212.

[134] Thomas E. Ricks, *Fiasco: The American Military Adventure in Iraq* (New York: Penguin, 2006), 420–424; Peter Baker, *Days of Fire: Bush and Cheney in the White House* (New York: Anchor, 2013), 489–490; Bob Woodward, *The War Within: A Secret White House History 2006–2008* (New York: Simon & Schuster, 2008), 36–38; Michael R. Gordon and Bernard E. Trainor, *The Endgame: The Inside Story of the Struggle for Iraq, from George W. Bush to Barack Obama* (New York: Pantheon Books, 2012), 240–246.

[135] Gordon and Trainor, 172–173.

[136] Frank G. Hoffman, "Learning While Under Fire: Military Change in Wartime" (Ph.D. diss., King's College London, 2015).

[137] Lamb and Munsing, 31.

[138] This policy was recognized and articulated by the President. Bush, *Decision Points*, 356.

[139] Martin E. Dempsey, "Mission Command," April 3, 2012.

[140] Casey, 144.

[141] Lieutenant Colonel William F. McCollough, USMC, is an example from Afghanistan of a field commander who proved able to innovate and excel at counterinsurgency. See Michael T. Flynn, Matt Pottinger, and Paul Batchelor, *Fixing Intel: A Blueprint for Making Intelligence Relevant in Afghanistan* (Washington, DC: Center for a New American Security, 2010), 13ff.

[142] McChrystal, *My Share of the Task*; and other citations.

[143] See Scott R. Mitchell's revealing article, "Observations of a Strategic Corporal," *Military Review*, July/August 2012. The issue of whether commanders embraced counterinsurgency doctrine is reviewed at greater length in Christopher J. Lamb, James Douglas Orton, Michael Davies, and Ted Pikulsky, *Human Terrain Teams: An Organizational Innovation for Sociocultural Knowledge in Irregular Warfare* (Washington, DC: Institute for World Politics Press, July 2013).

[144] Gordon and Trainor, 172–173. This is how Gordon and Trainor explain Casey's failure to support Colonel Blake Crowe, who wanted to replicate Alford's success. Other histories, however, dispute the extent to which the chain of command supported, ignored, or resisted the successful field commanders. For example, Ricks agrees with Gordon and Trainor, but Major General John R. Allen, USMC, asserts the Marine Expeditionary Force supported Colonel MacFarland's efforts. See Timothy S. McWilliams and Kurtis P. Wheeler, eds., *Al-Anbar Awakening, Volume I, American Perspectives: U.S. Marines and Counterinsurgency in Iraq, 2004–2009* (Quantico, VA: Marine Corps University Press, 2009), 229; and Thomas E. Ricks, *The Gamble: General David Petraeus and the American Military Adventure in Iraq, 2006–2008* (New York: Penguin Press, 2009), 60–63.

[145] After the fact, in his memoir, President Bush notes he was not comfortable with the option of quickly turning over political control to Iraqi expatriates rather than holding elections, but he seems ambivalent about the other two decisions. Bush, *Decision Points*, 249, 259.

[146] Also, "Rumsfeld had sought to block some of Jay Garner's picks because they were State Department Arabists who might be less than ardent supporters of Bush's bold plan to remake Iraq. With Bremer, he would not have that problem." Michael R. Gordon and Bernard E. Trainor, *Cobra II: The Inside Story of the Invasion and Occupation of Iraq* (New York: Pantheon, 2006), 546.

[147] See an account of Anthony Lake as a heroic policy entrepreneur in Ivo H. Daalder, *Getting to Dayton: The Making of America's Bosnia Policy* (Washington, DC: Brookings Institution Press, 2000), 167ff. Daalder cites John Kingdon on policy entrepreneurs who seize windows of opportunity. See John W. Kingdon, *Agendas, Alternatives, and Public Policies* (Boston: Little, Brown, 1984).

[148] *Forging a New Shield* (Arlington, VA: Project on National Security Reform, 2008), 126, 146.

[149] Hadley notes that he asked quite a few people to take the war czar job, and they all turned it down understanding the risks involved: "Douglas Lute was willing to do it. He is a hero in my view." Hadley, interview.

[150] Ronald E. Neumann, Dennis Blair, and Eric Olson, "A New Plan: Make U.S. Foreign Policy Swifter, Stronger and More Agile," *Defense One,* September 20, 2014; and Dennis Blair, Ronald E. Neumann, and Eric Olson, "Fixing Fragile States," *National Interest,* August 27, 2014.

[151] Feith notes, "No mathematical formula can tell the Secretary of Defense and the President precisely where strategic supervision ends and improper micromanagement of military operations begins." Rumsfeld seems to agree, arguing it is a process and that the National Security Advisor must "oversee the implementation of the president's decisions, ensuring that they are carried out effectively," which "requires careful balance to avoid the extremes of disengagement and micromanagement." Feith, 109; Rumsfeld, 324, 720.

[152] Rice, 18. Feith claims Franklin Miller of Rice's staff "often reached directly into civilian and military offices at the Pentagon rather than going through channels—asking questions, and giving what some took to be orders, in a way that flouted the chain of command and therefore irritated Rumsfeld." Feith, 276. Stephenson agrees: "Frank Miller continued to hammer away at me. Bill Taylor helped us in every way he could, but I was under a lot of pressure. We received a call from Sarah Lenti, an aide to National Security Advisor Condoleezza Rice. Ms. Lenti wanted a status report every other day on each of the [U.S. Agency for International Development] electricity generation projects including daily movements (or not) of the V94. She also wanted a weekly telephone call. We were told that Dr. Rice required briefings every other day. I thought it overkill, but we did it. It was just one more example of what we referred to as the 'eight-thousand-mile screwdriver.'" Stephenson, 116–117.

[153] Hill, 198.

[154] Gates, 482.

[155] Gates also resented the National Security Advisor giving the President advice on matters of mutual interest to the CIA and Defense without informing him. Gates, 352.

[156] Clinton, 190; Hill, 357.

[157] Rice, 18, 106, 245; Rumsfeld, 299–300, 512, 523; Rice, 20, 242–243; Delong, 20, 45; Franks, 300, 545; Gates, 120, 122, 133, 361–362, 364–367, 578, 585–586; Franks, 262, 300–301, 440ff, 461–462. See also Ricks, 33, where one disgruntled staff officer describes U.S. Central Command as "two thousand indentured servants whose life is consumed by the whims of Tommy Franks"; and Myers, 220, where he states that after one session with the Secretary, "Franks stormed into my office and threw his cap across the room. . . . He said, 'Chairman, if these sessions continue like this, I'll quit. I don't need the hassle.'" For issues involving Secretary Clinton and reporting from the field to the National Security Council staff, see Gates, 482; and Hill, 357. For yet another example of this phenomenon, see Steve Coll's assertion that Admiral William J. Fallon was "uneasy" about video meetings between President Bush and General Petraeus because "the Admiral was Petraeus's superior, and the videoconferences did not conform to a normal chain of command." Coll, "The General's Dilemma: David Petraeus, the Pressures of Politics, and the Road out of Iraq," *The New Yorker,* September 8, 2008. There are exceptions to the penchant to

safeguard information from subordinates. General Casey actually wanted his subordinates to have direct contact with the National Security Advisor when she visited. Casey, 137.

[158] Bush, *Decision Points*, 194–195.

[159] This sensitive issue—criteria for picking targets—came up in a discussion between Secretary Rumsfeld and General Franks, and inclined Franks and his deputy to consider Rumsfeld a micromanager. DeLong, 20.

[160] There are many references to Iran-Contra in senior leader accounts from the past decade. For several, see Rice, 14; Bremer, 245; and Gates, 352, where he asserts, "no one in the White House had any business going to the president with such a recommendation without going through the established interagency process. This was part and parcel of an increasingly operational National Security Staff in the White House and micromanagement of military matters—a combination that had proven disastrous in the past."

[161] Rice, 14–15.

[162] Ibid., 211–212.

[163] Ibid., 245; Rumsfeld, 242–243.

[164] Rice, 243–245; Rumsfeld, 526; Feith, 470.

[165] Hadley also asked the CIA to prepare an integrated plan for how all elements of U.S. power could be harnessed to arrest the decline of Iraq. Hadley, interview; Tenet, 435.

[166] See the previous chapter's description of decisionmaking on the Surge.

[167] Edgar F. Puryear, *American Generalship: Character Is Everything: The Art of Command* (Novato, CA: Presidio, 2000), 280–281.

[168] Gates, 578. Others have made this distinction as well. See Gail Harris and Pam McLaughlin, *A Woman's War: The Professional and Personal Journey of the Navy's First African American Female Intelligence Officer* (Lanham, MD: Scarecrow Press, 2010), 126.

[169] He was referring to General Lute and Gen. James E. Cartwright, USMC. Hadley, interview. Lute notes that the position he was in made it impossible to stay on the right side of the Chairman. Lute, interview.

[170] Feith makes this point, for example. Feith, 272.

[171] The Chairman's white paper notes that delegated authority within broad commander's intent works best within teams that share a high degree of trust. Dempsey, "Mission Command."

[172] Franks, 309, 341, 362, 384, 546; DeLong, 88.

[173] Lamb and Munsing, 45.

[174] Rice makes the point emphatically that the Secretary of State and Secretary of Defense did not trust one another (16), but the same was true of Pentagon leaders and Bremer, and Bremer and many of his subordinates in the Coalition Provisional Authority (see, for example, Stephenson, 34–36).

[175] General Casey also emphasized that he viewed his relationship with Ambassador John Negroponte "as my most important relationship, and we spent quite a bit of time together." Casey, 10–11, 67.

[176] Bush, for example, attributes the success of the surge to superb coordination between our civilian and military efforts. Bush, *Decision Points*, 393.

[177] Myers, 270.

[178] For example, see Christopher S. Chivvis et al., *Initial Thoughts on the Impact of the Iraq War on U.S. National Security Structures* (Santa Monica, CA: RAND, 2014); Elizabeth Young, "Decade of War: Enduring Lessons from a Decade of Operations," *PRISM* 4, no. 2 (March 2013); Matthew R. Hover, "The Occupation of Iraq: A Military Perspective on Lessons Learned," *International Review of the Red Cross* 94, no. 885 (Spring 2012), 339–346; Todd Greentree, "Bureaucracy Does Its Thing: U.S. Performance and the Institutional Dimension of Strategy in Afghanistan," *Journal of Strategic Studies* 36, no. 3 (March 2013), 325–356; David Mitchell and Tansa George Massoud, "Anatomy of Failure: Bush's Decisionmaking Process and the Iraq War," *Foreign Policy Analysis* 5, no. 3 (July 2009), 265–286.

[179] Bush, *Decision Points*, 88.

[180] Hadley, interview.

[181] Rothstein, 176ff. Sean Naylor's account of the operation records the breakdown in interagency information-sharing, but other accounts attribute problems to lack of jointness (or vertical unity of effort). See Sean Naylor, *Not a Good Day to Die: The Untold Story of Operation Anaconda* (New York: Berkley Books, 2005); and Mark G. Davis, "Operation Anaconda: Command and Confusion in Joint Warfare" (Master's thesis, School of Advanced Air and Space Studies, 2004).

[182] See Lamb and Munsing.

[183] McChrystal, *My Share of the Task*, 118.

[184] This is the thesis of Stephenson in *Losing the Golden Hour*.

[185] Myers, 170–171; Franks, 280; Rumsfeld, 375–376.

[186] *Forging a New Shield*, 160; cited in Fletcher Schoen and Christopher J. Lamb, *Deception, Disinformation, and Strategic Communications: How One Interagency Group Made a Major Difference*, INSS Strategic Perspectives 11 (Washington, DC: NDU Press, 2012), 114.

[187] Special Inspector General for Iraq Reconstruction (SIGIR), comp., *Hard Lessons: The Iraq Reconstruction Experience* (Washington, DC: U.S. Independent Agencies and Commissions, 2009); SIGIR, *Learning from Iraq* (Washington, DC: U.S. Government Printing Office, 2013).

[188] There is general agreement that the nadir of Defense-State relations occurred when the Secretary of Defense rejected State experts willing to serve on its postwar planning team. Rice, 210; Feith, 386–389.

[189] Hill, 295–296, 334–336, 348.

[190] Cited in Clinton, 24.

[191] Rice, 15–22.

[192] Tenet, 358, 364–367; Rice, 198; Cheney, 367–368, 404–405.

[193] Differences between the Departments of State and Defense at the regional level have been the subject of some notable books by journalists who believe the tensions between the departments and their disparities in resources have led to an increasingly militarized American foreign policy. See Dana Priest, *The Mission: Waging War and Keeping Peace with America's Military* (New York: Norton, 2003); and Stephen Glain, *State vs. Defense: The Battle to Define America's Empire* (New York: Crown Publishers, 2011).

[194] Hill, 354.

[195] DeLong, 28.

[196] The author was assigned the lead within DOD for coordinating information operations until the Under Secretary of Defense for Policy could find someone to do the job full-time and stand up what came to be called the Office of Strategic Influence.

[197] Rumsfeld states that Bremer and LTG Ricardo Sanchez, USA, were barely on speaking terms and that LTG Karl Eikenberry, USA, "moved his military headquarters out of the U.S. embassy in Kabul [during Ambassador Neumann's tenure], reversing the close civil-military linkage that Barno and Khalilzad had forged" (510, 689). Bremer also notes that he and General Sanchez were not in sync. It should be noted that Ambassador Neumann indicates he worked well with Eikenberry. Bremer, 186; Ronald E. Neumann, *The Other War: Winning and Losing in Afghanistan* (Washington, DC: Potomac Books, 2009).

[198] National Security Presidential Directive (NSPD), "United States Government Operations in Iraq," May 11, 2004, available at <www.fas.org/irp/offdocs/nspd/nspd051104.pdf>.

[199] Casey, 7–8.

[200] Blair, Neumann, and Olson.

[201] Special Inspector General for Afghanistan Reconstruction, "High-Risk List," December 2014, available at <www.sigar.mil/pdf/spotlight/High-Risk_List.pdf>.

[202] McChrystal, interview.

[203] Blair, Neumann, and Olson concentrate on failures in Afghanistan and Iraq, but they make the point that operations elsewhere were suffering from the same disunity of effort. For example, concerning Yemen, Congressman Ted Deutch (D–FL) noted, "U.S. assistance to Yemen totaled $256 million for Fiscal Year 2013, but these funds come from 17 different accounts, all with very different objectives." He asked a fundamental question that went unanswered: "What exactly is our long-term strategy for Yemen?" (12–13).

[204] General Abizaid, for example, notes the tendency of the press to put undue emphasis on personality clashes between himself and Bremer or between Bremer and General Sanchez when in reality the conflicts were about policy issues. Abizaid, interview.

[205] See Rice's discussion of the personal differences between Rumsfeld and Powell (5–22).

[206] For example, Franks argues tension between State and Defense arose from overlapping missions (375), and Rice makes the same point (15–16). For another example, Rumsfeld argues State would not relinquish the police training mission to DOD even though it did not have the "attention, resources, and focus" to do the mission successfully. In contrast, Secretary Clinton quotes Secretary Gates as explaining their good relationship as the result of his "being willing to acknowledge that the Secretary of State is the principal spokesperson for United States foreign policy" (25).

[207] This is a common thesis from Department of State leaders; see Rice and Hill.

[208] Rice states endemic conflict between secretaries of State and Defense is "not, as some might think, because State is from Venus and Defense from Mars," referring to a popular article that explained the organizational cultural differences between those two departments. Her evidence for the assertion was that often the "secretary of state is more willing to use force than the Pentagon." However, most observers do not consider willingness to use military force a good indicator of cultural differences between State and Defense (15).

[209] For example, Secretary Gates believes the wrong choice for Deputy Secretary of State complicated unity of effort in the Obama administration (289). Many other senior leader accounts similarly underscore the importance of choosing the right people to generated unified effort (for example, Bush, *Decision Points*, 89–90; Rice, 15; Rumsfeld, 299–300, 687; McChrystal, *My Share of the Task*, 168).

[210] Gates, 92.

[211] Rumsfeld, 375–376.

[212] DeLong, 74.

[213] Clinton, 28.

[214] Rice, 15.

[215] Dempsey, interview. General Dempsey also notes that developing trust requires understanding a superior's or colleague's leadership and decisionmaking style. He notes the three Secretaries of Defense he has worked with are significantly different in this regard. Hadley makes a similar observation, noting the difference between Rumsfeld and Gates, both of whom were strong secretaries but with different styles. Gates was willing to be more of a team player, "and there was a level of trust between Gates, Condi and me." Hadley, interview.

[216] "The Bush All-Stars," *New York Times*, January 22, 2001. The *Times* noted that from the Republican viewpoint, "President George W. Bush has assembled a national security dream team, featuring Dick Cheney as vice president, Colin Powell as secretary of state, Donald Rumsfeld as secretary of defense and Condoleezza Rice as national security adviser."

[217] Tenet, 358, 364–365. See also Cheney, 404–405, 416.

[218] Even General Franks, known for being straightforward, made a point of saying he "never doubted the loyalty or the motivation" of other leaders and that he did not want to apportion blame for any perceived misdeeds (544–545).

[219] Gates, 21. See also Tenet, 447. Tenet asserts, "We did not have . . . an integrated and open process in Washington. . . . Quite simply, the NSC [National Security Council] did not do its job."

[220] Cheney, 449, 462–463; Rumsfeld, 325–329; Feith, 245, 250, 283, 385, 527. Rumsfeld depicts several specific process limitations that he believed undermined unity of effort, including an NSC penchant for "avoiding detailed records" to assuming agreement if no objections to an NSC summary of conclusions were made explicit.

[221] Bremer also noted Rice sought compromise over the two options for transfer of political authority to Iraqis (205–207).

[222] Feith, 385.

[223] Rumsfeld, 324; Feith, 62.

[224] A classic argument to this effect is offered by Senator Henry Jackson: *Organizing for National Security: Inquiry of the Subcommittee on National Policy Machinery, Senator Henry M. Jackson, Chairman, for the Committee on Government Operations, United States Senate*, 3 vols. (Washington: U.S. Government Printing Office, 1961); and Henry M. Jackson, ed., *The National Security Council: Jackson Subcommittee Papers on Policy Making at the Presidential Level* (New York: Praeger, 1965).

[225] Rice, 15.

[226] Franks, 274–277, 330.

[227] The author raised the need to prepare for postwar disorder in a staff meeting with Under Secretary Feith because of lessons learned in a study on Operation *Just Cause* conducted by Fletcher School Professor Richard H. Shultz, Jr., for his office years earlier. The study was later published as *In the Aftermath of War: U.S. Support for Reconstruction and Nation-Building in Panama Following* Just Cause (Montgomery, AL: Air University Press, 1993). Feith mentions the resulting postwar planning effort in his memoir (362–366).

[228] Myers, 175.

[229] Cheney, 452.

[230] DeLong, 26.

[231] Franks, 277–278.

[232] DeLong, 27, 135–136.

[233] Ibid., 26, 89.

[234] Myers, 175.

[235] DeLong, 88. See also Myers, 220.

[236] Franks, 330. Feith notes that U.S. Central Command had advisors from State and CIA but none from his office in the Pentagon, which he believes is one reason the schism opened between USCENTCOM and Policy (371).

[237] From the President down, many senior leaders single out special operations forces for praise and recognize their special importance in irregular war. Some also acknowledge their overwhelmingly disproportionate casualty rates. Gates, for example, notes some special mission unit casualty rates reached 50 percent. See Bush, *Decision Points*, 92; Cheney, 334; Shelton, 441; Gates, 267; Feith, 96, 112.

[238] Secretary Clinton did not take this position, but see her discussion of drones (183–184).

[239] Senator John Kerry, cited in Christopher J. Lamb, Matthew J. Schmidt, and Berit G. Fitzsimmons, *MRAPs, Irregular Warfare, and Pentagon Reform*, Occasional Paper 6 (Washington, DC: NDU Press, June 2009), 6.

[240] Shelton, 440–441.

[241] Rothstein, 97.

[242] See discussion on postwar planning for large-scale civil unrest in Iraq in previous notes.

[243] Rumsfeld, 521. Feith also asserts a major intelligence failure in not predicting the insurgency, and enumerates a list of CIA intelligence failures in Iraq (276, 517).

[244] Tenet, 425.

[245] Ibid., 433.

[246] For example, the Commission on the Intelligence Capabilities of the United States Regarding Weapons of Mass Destruction made 74 recommendations on how to improve intelligence, 69 of which were accepted and acted upon by the Bush administration.

[247] Bush, *Decision Points*, 254.

[248] See Tenet's discussion of his debate with policy officials over whether Iraq and al Qaeda had an operational relationship (350–364, 371–372, 480).

[249] For example, Myers, 253; Franks, 354.

[250] Gates, 589.

[251] General Abizaid notes, for example, that we were slow to realize Iraqi leaders were undermining our efforts to build a truly national army, observing that they wanted sectarian forces "and we weren't smart enough to see it." It also has been observed that well after the fact we realized school attendance was a good indicator of local violence. Locals kept children home from school when they expected trouble.

[252] McChrystal, interview.

[253] For example, William Rosenau, "Counterinsurgency: Lessons from Iraq and Afghanistan," *Harvard International Review* 31, no. 1 (Spring 2009); Young; John A. Nagl, *Knife Fights: A Memoir of Modern War in Theory and Practice* (New York: Penguin Press, 2014); and Greentree.

[254] David Tucker makes this case well, as have many others. See David Tucker and Christopher J. Lamb, *Restructuring Special Operations Forces for Emerging Threats*, Strategic Forum No. 219 (Washington, DC: NDU Press, January 2006).

[255] Myers, 253.

[256] Dempsey, interview.

[257] General Lieutenant General Peter Chiarelli, Commanding General, Multi-National Corps–Iraq, *Mapping the Human Terrain (MAP-HT)* J/ACTD, FY 07 J/ACTD Candidate, PowerPoint, undated.

[258] *Decade of War, Volume I: Enduring Lessons from the Past Decade of Operations* (Suffolk, VA: Joint and Coalition Operational Analysis, June 15, 2012).

[259] Flynn, Pottinger, and Batchelor.

[260] Ibid.

[261] Feith argues this was a principal source of interagency discord (389–401).

[262] See DeLong's discussion of the Chalabi controversy (90) and Bremer on appointment of local Iraqi officials (27).

[263] Bremer describes this debate (224–226).

[264] Dempsey, interview.

[265] Colonel Robert Forrester, deputy director of the Center for Army Lessons Learned, cited in Drew Brooks, "Lessons Learned in Iraq War Will Apply in Future Conflicts," *The Fayetteville Observer* (North Carolina), January 1, 2012.

[266] General Petraeus, for example, still lists understanding local culture, leadership, social issues, politics, and human terrain as a primary requirement for future success in military operations. In fact, he insists that it is necessary "to really understand the country that you are going to invade in a very granular and nuanced way." Lute makes the same point. Petraeus, interview; Lute, interview.

[267] Leo Shane III and Kevin Baron, "Petraeus Confirmation Hearing, Live," *Stars and Stripes*, June 29, 2010.

[268] Doyle McManus, "McManus: A smaller, smarter military: The best-equipped army in the world can still lose a war if it doesn't understand the people it's fighting," *Los Angeles Times*, April 22, 2012.

[269] David Vergun, "Leaders Look at Army of 2020 and Beyond," Army News Service, September 14, 2002.

[270] See also Dan Cox, "An Enhanced Plan for Regionally Aligning Brigades Using Human Terrain Systems," *Small Wars Journal*, June 14, 2012; and Sydney J. Freedberg, Jr., "Army Makes Case for Funding Culture Skills beyond Coin," *AOL Defense*, July 2, 2012.

[271] Raymond T. Odierno, James F. Amos, and William H. McRaven, *Strategic Landpower: Winning the Clash of Wills* (Washington, DC: DOD, 2013).

[272] Colin S. Gray, *Irregular Enemies and the Essence of Strategy: Can the American Way of War Adapt?* (Carlisle Barracks, PA: Strategic Studies Institute, March 1, 2006), 34.

[273] McChrystal, interview.

274 Bush, *Decision Points*, 89; Rice, 196–197.

275 Ambassador Christopher Hill demonstrates the classic Foreign Service Officer attitude while acknowledging the need to do better: "greater public diplomacy became the cure for why the popularity of the United States had fallen so precipitously during the time after the Iraq invasion. Even though it was the policy that needed improvement, there was no question that our diplomats needed to do a better job of explaining and reaching out to nontraditional audiences" (189–190).

276 Feith, 171ff.

277 Clinton, 188–189.

278 Mike Mullen, "Strategic Communication: Getting Back to Basics," *Joint Force Quarterly* 55 (4th Quarter 2009).

279 Daniel Yergin, *Shattered Peace: The Origins of the Cold War and the National Security State* (Boston: Houghton Mifflin, 1977), 324.

280 The author is indebted to Norine McDonald for this observation. See Yaroslav Trofimov, "Many Afghans Shrug at 'This Event Foreigners Call 9/11,'" *Wall Street Journal*, September 8, 2011.

281 Schoen and Lamb, 118–120.

282 Clinton, 190, 200–201.

283 Feith makes this recommendation (511ff).

284 Gates, 266. Elsewhere in this volume we note General Dempsey's assertion that an Army captain had more access to national intelligence in 2008 than he did as a division commander in 2003.

285 Rumsfeld considered the armored vehicle issue an acquisition problem (645, 648), but Gates understood the problem was much larger and involved Pentagon decisionmaking more generally. For a review of both see Lamb, Schmidt, and Fitzsimmons.

286 Thomas P. Barnett, "Pentagon Malady: 'Next-War-Itis,'" *Time*, March 6, 2013.

287 The data in the following discussion come from Lamb, Schmidt, and Fitzsimmons.

288 On MRAPs, see especially Gates, 119–126; for intelligence, surveillance, and reconnaissance, see Gates, 126–135.

289 Lamb, Schmidt, and Fitzsimmons.

290 Gates, 118–119.

291 Lamb, Schmidt, and Fitzsimmons.

292 Milan Vego, "On Military Creativity," *Joint Force Quarterly* 70 (3rd Quarter 2013), 84.

293 Petraeus might be considered an exception of sorts since he went on record supporting field commander requests for MRAPs. Kris Osborn, "Petraeus Praises MRAPs," *Defense News*, April 14, 2008, 4.

[294] Gates, end of chapter 3.

[295] Ibid., 448.

[296] Bush, *Decision Points*, 381; Clinton, 149; Myers, 253, Bremer, 114, 125.

[297] Hadley, interview.

[298] SIGIR, *Hard Lessons*.

[299] On quality, see Stephenson, 16.

[300] Robert W. Komer, *Bureaucracy Does Its Thing: Institutional Constraints on U.S.-GVN Performance in Vietnam* (Santa Monica, CA: RAND, 1972).

[301] Feith, 519.

[302] Stephenson, 150–151.

[303] Hill's memoir provides insights about the way career personnel in the State Department think of this mission area. He resented the persistent calls for a civilian surge, believing Iraq should be left to the Iraqis to run. He thought it was hard to find meaningful work for all the civilian staff shoved into Iraq (335–337).

[304] Senior leaders argue the Provincial Reconstruction Teams eventually got the job done (for example, Rumsfeld, 687), and they did improve and made a contribution. However, close examinations of their performance identify numerous problems and unsatisfactory performance. One of the better such studies is a 2008 House Armed Service Committee effort: U.S. House of Representatives, the House Armed Services Committee, Subcommittee on Oversight and Investigations, *Agency Stovepipes vs. Strategic Agility: Lessons We Need to Learn from Provincial Reconstruction Teams in Iraq and Afghanistan*, April 2008.

[305] Hadley, Bremer, and Feith, with Feith noting the concern originated with President Bush. Hadley, interview; Bremer, 26; Feith, 317. This concern is overemphasized by these leaders. General Franks told the President that regional leaders understood the United States was conducting contingency planning but that the President had not yet made a decision on whether to go to war (388). Similarly, even outside observers note other countries knew the United States was planning military operations. Rather than detracting from diplomatic efforts, this type of planning made U.S. threats credible and gave added incentives for diplomats to reach agreements. There is no reason that would not hold every bit as true for postwar planning as for the large-scale invasion and war planning. See Fallows.

[306] Cheney, 371, 457–458, 460.

[307] Gates, 50.

[308] Tenet, 419.

[309] Feith, 317; Hadley, interview.

[310] Myers, 297.

[311] Dempsey, interview; Petraeus, interview.

[312] McChrystal underscored the lack of team trust among senior leader echelons in particular. McChrystal, interview.

[313] See Bremer, 209, 235–236; Feith, 273, 514; Tenet, 364–365, 443; Clinton, 188.

[314] Laurence H. Silberman makes the argument, for example: "The Dangerous Lie That 'Bush Lied,'" *Wall Street Journal*, February 8, 2015, A13.

[315] Myers, 297–298.

[316] Feith, 527.

[317] Hadley, interview.

[318] Clinton notes foreign leaks undermined diplomacy (165); Myers notes the same (182).

[319] Hadley states that once or twice a week he would invite the Vice President, Secretary of State, Secretary of Defense, Chairman, CIA Director, and Director of National Intelligence to his office for candid discussions of tough issues with "no note-takers" and "no leaks." Other senior leaders also comment on the value of such small, restricted groups. Cheney, for example, cites Hadley's small group meetings and observes the best decisionmaking was done with no aides present to minimize the chance of leaks. Hadley, interview; Cheney, 468.

[320] For example, Cheney argues a State leak caused major problems (407) and that leaks hurt careers (409); Bremer and the President note leaks are a persistent problem (Bremer, 227); Tenet's resignation was fueled in part by what he believed were White House leaks (481); Hadley argues leaks expose operational details that incur risks to the operations and those executing them (Hadley, interview); Franks notes Rumsfeld insisted on working in small groups because of leakers (344) and that leaks about Iraq war planning were incredibly injurious (385) and complicated his relationship with senior civilians (441); DeLong states leaks about Yemen hurt us (74); Gates notes leaks were a big problem, particularly in the Obama administration (152, 370), which infuriated the President (298, 328), and that in advance of the Osama bin Laden raid, everyone was terrified there would be a leak that would spoil the operation (542).

[321] Tenet, 434.

[322] Franks, 382–383.

[323] David Petraeus, interview by Frank G. Hoffman, December 31, 2014.

[324] Hadley mentioned the determination among national leaders immediately following 9/11 to defend the country, stating they were "strong willed" about it and, in retrospect, "should have listened a lot more carefully to our regional friends and allies seeking the counsel of other countries." Hadley, interview.

[325] Lute, interview; Franks, commenting on President Bush and Secretary Rumsfeld (374).

[326] Preventing terrorists from acquiring weapons of mass destruction is still a critical objective but one that has lost its place of central importance. In discussing the future

security environment and risks, the Chairman has noted that the consequences of a terrorist attack "are relatively insignificant in terms of national survival." Martin E. Dempsey, "Risky Business," *Joint Force Quarterly* 69 (2nd Quarter 2013), 3.

327 Rumelt, 6.

328 This issue was briefly discussed in the opening of the chapter.

329 Hadley, interview.

330 Lute, interview; Petraeus, interview.

331 Rayburn.

332 Another indication that the impact of critical assumptions is often exaggerated is the tendency to focus on just those ostensibly responsible for untoward developments. For example, much greater attention has been paid to the assertion that naïve optimism explains the invasion of Iraq than to the assumption that a successful terrorist attack against the United States with weapons of mass destruction would change the American way of life. Yet the latter is a far more consequential assumption for the Bush administration's entire approach to the war on terror, a critical difference between the Bush and Obama administrations, and a more foundational issue for future counterterror strategy.

333 The author concurs, but notes the methodology used in this chapter is biased toward reform. The decisionmaking methodology we used was "choice-based" and assumes decisionmaking is an instrumental activity. The corollary assumption is that unified effort is useful, which reflects a bias in favor of coherence and in turn inclines us to sympathize with "reformers" who "advocate more systematic attempts to define objectives, establish knowledge about the world, coordinate among different aspects of a decision, and exercise control in the name of some central vision." This bias is probably appropriate for a "lessons learned" effort but needs to be acknowledged. For a discussion of the bias, see March and Heath, 205–206.

334 Cited in Lamb and Munsing, 7.

335 Myers, 302.

336 McChrystal, interview. For Rumsfeld, see National Commission on Terrorist Attacks Upon the United States, *The 9/11 Commission Report: Final Report of the National Commission on Terrorist Attacks Upon the United States Including the Executive Summary* (New York: Norton, 2004); Neumann, Blair, and Olson; Secretary Gates noted in 2007 "that if we are to meet the myriad challenges around the world in the coming decades, this country must strengthen other important elements of national power both institutionally and financially, and create the capability to integrate and apply all of the elements of national power to problems and challenges abroad" (emphasis added). Robert Gates, "Remarks as Delivered by Secretary of Defense Robert M. Gates," Manhattan, KS, November 26, 2007.

337 Dempsey notes one such insight is that most changes are effected through budget adjustments and thus in conjunction with budget cycles rather than events in the field. Dempsey, interview.

[338] Kori Schake, "QDR 2010: What Exactly Was the Point?" in *Economics and Security: Resourcing National Priorities*, ed. Richmond M. Lloyd (Newport, RI: Naval War College, 2010); and Kori Schake, "Security and Solvency," *Orbis* 58, no. 3 (Spring 2014), 310–325.

[339] NSPD.

[340] There are several good sources on national security system behaviors. See *Forging a New Shield*.

[341] Myers, 305.

[342] Dempsey, interview.

[343] Komer's modern-day counterpart, Todd Greentree, makes the same point: "There is nothing revolutionary in the practical fixes suggested below. Most of the lessons were learned in Vietnam and are being relearned today." See Greentree.

4

Raising and Mentoring Security Forces in Afghanistan and Iraq

By T.X. Hammes

Security force assistance played a leading role in both Afghanistan and Iraq, where local security forces were often spoken of as "our ticket home" or "our exit strategy." The effort to raise, train, equip, field, and advise army and police forces eventually became the center of gravity in both theaters. Yet for some years, the effort was ad hoc, under-resourced, and complicated by internal bureaucratic struggles in Washington and by corrosive corruption and mismanagement within host-nation governments. If the United States were to undertake similar efforts in the future, the quality and effectiveness of its security force assistance programs will again play a decisive role in achieving successful outcomes.

While there are many similarities, there are also significant differences between the efforts in Afghanistan and Iraq as well as between the army and police in each country. This chapter deals in turn with Afghan National Security Forces (ANSF)—the army, national police, and village police program—and then the Iraqi army and national police. It includes some discussion of the efforts to establish effective ministries of defense and interior in both countries.

Each section tracks the effort chronologically, which most effectively highlights some of the key issues the training teams struggled to overcome. As with all lessons-learned efforts, this one focuses on the problems encountered in the examined period. However, one remarkable success cannot be denied: Starting from scratch in functionally destroyed nations, the coalitions, led by the United States, raised, trained, and equipped an Afghan security force of over 350,000 personnel and an Iraqi force of over 625,000. These are truly remarkable accomplishments and speak highly of the dedication and talent of the military and civilian personnel who made this happen. It is even more remarkable given the enormous obstacles they had to overcome—from the absence of institutions in both countries to the complex nature of U.S. bureaucratic processes. Subsequent events in both countries indicate that host-nation politics will remain the dominant factor in the effectiveness of future advisory efforts.

Afghan National Security Forces

The difficulties in raising these forces started at the beginning of U.S. involvement in Afghanistan. The rapid U.S. response to the 9/11 attacks meant the planners focused on defeating the Taliban and al Qaeda and understandably had little time to consider postconflict governance. This oversight was exacerbated by the fact that senior leaders in the Department of Defense (DOD) did not give much thought to who would govern Afghanistan and how after the Taliban were removed.

Not until mid-October 2001 was Richard Haass, then with the Department of State Policy Planning Staff, named the U.S. Government's coordinator for the future of Afghanistan. He notes that there was a "clear reluctance" to think about providing security or extending the reach of the central government, which may have been based on the George W. Bush administration's skepticism about nation-building.[1] In fact, well before the initial campaign had concluded, Secretary of Defense Donald Rumsfeld had shifted the DOD focus. On November 27, Rumsfeld called General Tommy Franks, USA, U.S. Central Command (USCENTCOM) commander, to discuss the status of military planning—for Iraq.[2] The shift of resources further degraded planning for the governance of Afghanistan.

Rather than attempt to govern as an occupying power, the United States turned to the United Nations (UN). Under UN auspices, the International Conference on Afghanistan (the Bonn Conference) was convened in December 2001. It established an Afghan Interim Authority, and on December 20, 2001, the UN adopted Security Council Resolution 1368, which established the International Security Assistance Force (ISAF).[3] The original ISAF mandate was to provide security for Kabul and train Afghan security forces. No provision was made for an ISAF security presence outside of Kabul. For their part, U.S. forces remaining in country were focused on the counterterrorism mission of killing or capturing surviving members of al Qaeda and the Taliban. In short, no one was responsible for the security of the Afghan people except the Afghan Interim Authority, which had no national security forces and had to contend with the numerous armed militias present in Afghanistan. While the Bonn Agreement established a goal of a 50,000-person Afghan National Army (ANA) and a 62,000-person Afghan National Police (ANP),[4] it provided no resources to meet those goals.

The next month, January 2002, at the Tokyo Donor's Conference, the mission to develop Afghan security forces and disarm the militias was established on a lead nation basis. Italy was responsible for establishing the legal system— drafting the laws and establishing the courts. Germany was responsible for the police. The United Kingdom led the anti-narcotics efforts. Japan assumed the mission of disarmament, demobilization, and reintegration (DDR) of the militias. The United States took on the job of raising the army.[5]

Afghan Army

Under the ISAF mandate to raise security forces, the United Kingdom (as the first nation commanding) and then Turkey (as the second nation) did not wait for the United States to start training Afghans. During each nation's turn as ISAF commander, it trained a single battalion (*kandak*). The U.S. effort started in February 2002, when a team led by Major General Charles Campbell, USA, USCENTCOM Chief of Staff, did an initial evaluation of Afghan plans for the army. U.S. Special Forces, however, did not arrive to fulfill the U.S. mission as lead nation for training the Afghan army until May 2002. Special Forces detachments began to work with small units in various parts of the country. The program was not centrally directed, nor did it attempt to build the national institutions necessary to develop an effective army. It was not until October 2002 that Major General Karl Eikenberry, USA, arrived as Chief of the Office of Military Cooperation–Afghanistan (OMC-A) with the mission of building the Afghan army. He realized the mission would require more resources than Special Forces could provide; they had done well in forming platoons, companies, and battalions, but the Afghan army needed to progress beyond battalions to brigade-, corps-, and national-level functions. Eikenberry noted that the Afghan army lacked a recruiting force, trainers, living facilities, equipment, and any form of logistics or personnel support, all of which are fundamental to forming an army. OMC-A was literally building the Afghan army's supporting base even as it was training and deploying the combat units of the army.

Eikenberry established Task Force (TF) Phoenix, which would use a U.S. Army infantry brigade to train the Afghan army.[6] Indicative of the expedient nature of the effort, OMC-A received the 2nd Brigade of the 10th Mountain Division to execute its mission. The brigade consisted of the brigade headquarters, one infantry battalion, and a logistics battalion. Upon arrival in country, it was augmented by individuals and training teams from the Marine Corps, National Guard, and nine different countries to form TF Phoenix. An essentially ad hoc organization executing a mission it had not trained for, 2nd Brigade also had a change of command only 2 weeks before it deployed in May 2003.

The brigade took over directly from the Special Forces units. It started by establishing a centralized training location in Kabul. Up to this point, Special Forces Soldiers had been training small units of Afghans in the field. TF Phoenix focused on training at the company and battalion levels while starting to build brigade and corps staffs. However, an infantry brigade is not manned with personnel appropriate to establish national-level institutions, so that mission was contracted out to Military Professional Resources, Incorporated (MPRI). By the time the brigade left in December 2003, it was sending platoons, companies, and *kandaks* out to conduct operations with the 1st Brigade of the 10th Mountain Division. Working with MPRI, it was also forming the brigade and corps staffs.

During this 6-month period, the task force also handed the 4-week basic training course over to the Afghans, supported by American advisors. During the same period, the French ran the officers' course, and the British ran the noncommissioned officer (NCO) course, each of which ran separately. When NCO and basic training courses graduated, the NCOs joined the troops and formed companies. They worked together on small-unit tactics until the longer officers' course graduated, at which point the officers and the U.S.-embedded training teams joined the companies. Three companies formed a kandak, which began a unit-training program to prepare for combat. Given the significant differences between the military cultures of Britain, France, and the United States, there were inevitable issues when the officers, NCOs, and troops began to work together. This problem was further exacerbated by the significant number of officers who had been trained by the Soviets. Once certified, the unit was paired with a U.S. battalion and deployed to the field. Some units were also assigned to Kabul and thus did joint patrolling with ISAF.

A critical challenge for OMC-A was the integration of former mujahideen fighters and commanders into the national army. Naturally, militia commanders and the political leaders they supported were reluctant to relinquish control to the national army. For the United States and donor nations, there was serious concern about moving potential war criminals into the new Afghan army. For the Afghans, the concern was the ethnic balance of the force and the potential for its dominance by a single group. Thus, Eikenberry and his Afghan counterpart had to carefully screen applicants prior to assigning them to key billets. They then spent 3 weeks briefing every political leader in Kabul, from the president and four vice presidents to cabinet members to faction leaders.[7] Those who were not integrated were "theoretically" processed by the DDR program run by the Japanese.

The ongoing war and resultant lack of overall security, however, ensured the Afghan DDR was not fully effective. Lorenzo Striuli and Fernando Termentini succinctly highlighted the requirements for a successful DDR program. They noted:

- fighting in the theater of interest must be completely or at least nearly ended, and a significant peacekeeping force must be deployed to ensure no renewal of conflict
- all former fighting factions must be included in the process because, without disarming all combatants, the potential for conflict renewal remains high
- sufficient resources must be assured for the duration of the process because an incomplete reintegration of former belligerents leaves a dangerous situation in postconflict societies.[8]

None of these requirements was achieved by 2002 in Afghanistan or even by the end of 2014. As a result, despite a series of well-funded programs, ISAF, the UN Development Programme, and the Afghan government have failed to disarm the numerous militias that have plagued Afghanistan. The DDR effort succeeded in quarantining warlord tanks and artillery. However, it was functionally impossible to collect all the small arms, to include machine guns, mortars, and rocket-propelled grenades. Thus, militia activities were curtailed, but the militias could not be eliminated. In fact, some were incorporated into the ANSF, and their loyalties remain split between the national government and their militia leaders.

Despite the continued presence of the militias, TF Phoenix was tasked with raising the Afghan army. As the task force expanded to meet the train, equip, and advise mission, Brigadier General F. Joseph Prasek, USA, assumed command. Even as TF Phoenix worked to field the new Afghan army, insurgents began their first attacks against the coalition and new Afghan government in April 2002.

At the Bonn II Conference in December 2002, the Afghan government and donor nations agreed the army would expand to include "(1) 43,000 ground combat troops based in Kabul and four other cities, (2) 21,000 support staff organized in four sustaining commands . . . (3) Ministry of Defense [MOD] and general staff personnel, and (4) 3,000 air staff to provide security transportation for the President of Afghanistan."[9] In contrast to the small army envisioned by the Bonn II Conference, Afghan defense minister Marshal Fahim called for a force of 200,000 to 250,000 troops to provide security for the entire nation.[10] Donor nations refused to consider this much higher number. Ironically, by 2011, ISAF was building the ANSF to a total of over 350,000 personnel.

Upon 2nd Brigade's departure in December 2002, the expanded mission was passed to a National Guard brigade. Throughout this period, MPRI conducted the training for corps headquarters and the MOD.[11] During the same timeframe, the Taliban as well as local guerrilla groups continued a low-level insurgency from bases inside Pakistan. By fall 2003, the U.S. strategy was clearly failing. Taliban elements were moving freely through most of the south and east, unchallenged by any Afghan government presence. Security had deteriorated to the point that the United Nations and aid organizations were pulling their people out of the south and southeast.[12] The Taliban had recovered from its initial setbacks and was taking the offensive. As 2004 started, the situation in Afghanistan was deteriorating as insurgent attacks increased steadily.

In response, from late 2003 to 2005 OMC-A focused on building the Afghan National Army. Basic training was formalized and established at 8 weeks with training base throughput capacity increasing steadily. Efforts continued to build effective headquarters above brigade level—that is, corps headquarters and national institutions. By July 2005, however, the ANA had reached a strength of only 24,300 trained and equipped, with 6,000 more in training—less than half the force authorized in the December 2002 Bonn Conference. Over this period, training for the newly raised infantry battalions was standardized at 14 weeks (6 weeks individual training, 6 weeks advanced training, and 2 weeks of collective training). Despite being undermanned and lacking resources, OMC-A planned to complete training the then-authorized 46,000 soldiers by the fall of 2007.

In its June 2005 report on Afghan security, the Government Accountability Office (GAO) noted that U.S. funding for the ANA started at only $179.2 million in 2002 but rapidly increased to over $2 billion by 2005. Despite the major increase in funding, the GAO stated, "efforts to establish sustaining institutions, such as a logistics command, needed to support these troops have not kept pace. Plans for completing these institutions are not clear." It went on to note the estimated total bill for police and army to be $7.2 billion, with $600 million needed annually for sustainment.[13] The GAO report also noted that OMC-A struggled with the numerous changes in the plan for the ANA as well as consistent shortages of training personnel. OMC-A had never been staffed at more than 71 percent of its approved personnel level.[14]

One of the key challenges was the steadily increasing level of violence in Afghanistan. As attacks on Afghan and coalition forces increased, leaders made the logical choice to increase the size of the Afghan army and police. With each increase, more trainers were needed, but before each new requirement was filled, the increased threat led to plans for further increasing ANSF strength.

On July 12, 2005, OMC-A was renamed the Office of Security Cooperation–Afghanistan (OSC-A). Despite the identified problems with manning and planning, its responsibility was expanded to include the entire Afghan security sector. In addition to training the ANA, OSC-A would assume responsibility for reforming the Afghan National Police.[15] Inevitably, the expanded mission required more resources. GAO noted that OSC-A requested $7.6 billion for 2007, more than the estimated total bill in June 2005.[16] This amount was to cover the cost of 70,000 ANA soldiers and 82,000 police, as well as the expansion and professionalization of the MOD and sustaining institutions. Even as OSC-A raced to build the ANA, the Taliban were increasing their attacks, requiring OSC-A to upgrade the equipment it was providing to ANSF.

In April 2006, OSC-A was redesignated as Combined Security Transition Command–Afghanistan (CSTC-A). It retained responsibility for training the army and police as well as mentoring the ministries of defense and interior. Unfortunately, the security situation continued to deteriorate, particularly in relation to attacks focused on ANSF and coalition forces. Improvised explosive device incidents increased from 844 in 2005 to 2,215 by 2007.[17]

While North Atlantic Treaty Organization (NATO) reports indicated major progress in training the Afghan army during 2007–2008, GAO was much less optimistic. In its June 2008 report, it noted:

The United States has provided over $10 billion to develop the ANA since 2002; however, less than 2 percent (2 of 105 units) of ANA units are assessed as fully capable of conducting their primary mission. Thirty-six percent (38 of 105) are assessed as capable of conducting their mission, but require routine international assistance, while the remaining ANA units (65 of 105 units) are either planned, in basic training, or assessed as partially able or unable to conduct their primary mission. Building an Afghan army that can lead security operations requires manning, training, and equipping of personnel; however, U.S. efforts to build the ANA have faced challenges in all of these areas. First, while the ANA has grown to approximately 58,000 of an authorized force structure of 80,000—nearly three times the 19,600 Defense reported in 2005—the ANA has experienced difficulties finding qualified candidates for leadership positions and retaining its personnel. Second, while trainers or mentors are present in every ANA combat unit, less than half the required number are deployed in the field. Defense officials cited an insufficient number of U.S. trainers and coalition mentors in the field as the major impediment to providing the ANA with the training to establish capabilities, such as advanced combat skills and logistics, necessary to sustain the ANA force in the long term. Finally, ANA combat units report significant shortages in approximately 40 percent of critical equipment items, including vehicles, weapons, and radios. Some of these *challenges, such as shortages of U.S. trainers and equipment, are due in part to competing global priorities, according to senior Defense officials. Without resolving these challenges, the ability of the ANA to reach full capability may be delayed.*[18]

In its 2008 report to Congress, CSTC-A stated it was working closely with the Afghan government on three lines of operation to develop the ANSF: "(1) build and develop ministerial institutional capability; (2) generate the fielded forces [*sic*]; and (3) develop the fielded forces."[19] CSTC-A noted the target end-strength for the ANA had been increased to 80,000 and the ANP to 82,000.[20] This was yet another in a continuing series of rapid increases in target end-strength for the ANA. It would also require fielding different kinds of units: "13 light brigades, a mechanized brigade, a commando brigade, a headquarters and support brigade, enabling units and the initial operation of an air corps."[21]

To assist in filling the shortage of trainers, the North Atlantic Council announced the formation of NATO Training Mission–Afghanistan (NTM-A) as an integral part of ISAF on June 12, 2009. NTM-A stood up formally on November 21 of that year. The command was a NATO organization that included personnel from 37 nations and was led by a U.S. lieutenant general who was dual-hatted as the commander of CSTC-A, which remained a U.S. command and was the administrative conduit for U.S. funds.[22] While providing a significant reinforcement in personnel, NTM-A also had an expanded mission to:

provide higher-level training for the ANA, including defence colleges and academies, and [...] be responsible for doctrine development, as well as training and mentoring for the ANP. This will reflect the Afghan Government's policing priorities and will complement existing training and capacity development programmes, including the European Union Police Mission and the work of the International Police Coordination Board.[23]

However, NTM-A would not provide advice or training for the Afghan ministries. That mission remained the responsibility of CSTC-A. Keeping track of the collective NATO and individual national caveats concerning training and funding added to the complexity of the mission.

In August 2009, General Stanley A. McChrystal, USA, the new ISAF commander, concluded his own initial commander's assessment. In particular, the pessimistic report noted the failure to focus on the population, which General McChrystal believed to be the center of gravity for the conflict:

> [The Afghan government] *and ISAF have both failed to focus on this objective. The weakness of state institutions, malign actions of power-brokers, widespread corruption and abuse of power by various officials, and ISAF's own errors, have given Afghans little reason to support their government. These problems have alienated large segments of the Afghan population. They do not trust the* [Afghan government] *to provide their essential needs, such as security, justice, and basic services.*[24]

In short, the NATO/ISAF effort in Afghanistan had lost ground since 2003. McChrystal stated that the size of the army needed to be 240,000, triple the size noted in the 2008 CSTC-A report to Congress. In addition, the ANP strength needed to almost double to 160,000.[25] However, by 2010, the international community and the Afghan government had agreed to strengths of only 171,600 for the ANA and 134,000 for the ANP. Furthermore, NTM-A was manned at only 52 percent of its authorized strength.[26]

Even as the international community refused to expand the army to the level McChrystal requested, the International Crisis Group's analysis of the progress of the training program to date indicated continuing major problems:

> *Despite billions of dollars of international investment, army combat readiness has been undermined by weak recruitment and retention policies, inadequate logistics, insufficient training and equipment and inconsistent leadership. International support for the ANA must therefore be targeted not just toward increasing the quantity of troops but enhancing the quality of the fighting force. Given the slow pace of economic development and the likelihood of an eventual drawdown of Western resources, any assessment of the future shape of the army must also make fiscal as well as political sense. Although recent efforts to consolidate the training command structure under the NATO Training Mission-Afghanistan (NTM-A) are encouraging, the U.S. emphasis*

on rapid expansion of the army, in response to the growing insurgent threat, could strain NTM-A resources and outpace the capacity of Afghan leaders to manage an inherently unwieldy system.[27]

In its 2009 report to Congress, GAO noted significant progress for the ANA in that 18 of its 72 units were now rated fully capable and 26 were capable with support. (It did not say why the total number of units had decreased from the 105 reported the previous year.) It noted that DOD identified the primary limitation on progress as the shortage of training personnel. It had only half of the 2,225 personnel needed to train the ANA at the approved level of 79,000 soldiers. This shortage was likely to get more severe with the newly approved strength increase for the ANA.[28]

In 2010, the International Crisis Group noted that from 2008 to 2010, the target date for 134,000 trained troops had been brought forward at least twice, first from 2013 to 2011, and then to October 2010. While recruiting had kept pace, shortfalls in NCOs and officers with specialized skills in medicine, transportation, and logistics were hindering growth.[29]

Lieutenant General William Caldwell, USA, who commanded NTM-A/CSTC-A from November 2009 to November 2011, noted that the following elements complicated NTM-A efforts to raise and train the ANA:

- eighty-six percent illiteracy rate: required teaching recruits and officer basic reading skills
- eighteen years of conflict: led to hoarding and survival mentality
- focus on quantity over quality in recruiting and training: resulted in need for retraining
- ANA negative growth: resulted in creating a recruiting command
- leadership shortfalls and challenges: led to creation of multiple schools and courses (officer/NCO schools)
- minimal oversight and accountability: required top-to-bottom review of inventory processes and the inculcation of an ethos of stewardship

- struggling sustainment: required creation of a logistics system from the national level to the local unit-level distribution
- high attrition: required extensive improvements to all soldier support systems, including the recruiting system
- lack of a manufacturing base: required creation and development of local suppliers; creation of the Afghan First program to build indigenous manufacturing for ANSF uniforms, boots, and other military materiel
- substandard pay: required constant dialogue with Afghan leadership to increase pay in all ranks to a living wage to reduce opportunities for corrupt behavior
- endemic corruption: mandated leadership changes, review of ethical standards
- tribal tensions: presented unique assignment challenges
- substandard equipment: required immediate procurement, acquisition, and maintenance efforts, including a mindset change from replacement to repair
- inadequate standards to evaluate training and operations (35 percent weapons qualification rate): required creation and enforcement of standards
- numerous language barriers among themselves and NATO: complicated training.[30]

Despite these challenges, Dr. Jack Kem, Deputy to the Commander of NTM-A, reported that by August, the ANA had reached the October 2010 goal of 134,000 and the ANP was at 115,000, exceeding the goal of 109,000. NTM-A had either corrected or managed the long list of problems while dramatically increasing the strength and competence of the ANA. New goals had been established for October 2011 of an ANA of 171,600 and ANP of 134,000.[31] A key part of the effort was a literacy program designed to bring 50 percent of the ANSF to third-grade reading and comprehension levels. One reason for the emphasis on literacy was the ANA and ANP needed to be able to read and write to operate in the way they were being trained. This emphasis on literacy training continued through 2010. GAO noted that ANA "staff members' low literacy levels hinder their ability to use computers, effectively manage staff functions, and exercise command and control. Partnering is essential to provide necessary supervision and oversight of planning for supplies (i.e., fuel and ammunition)."[32]

ISAF still reported significant progress in establishing an accountability system for vehicles and equipment. One major issue remained the ethnic balance of the forces. In a nation that is roughly 40 percent Pashtun,[33] NTM-A had only succeeded in raising the number of southern Pashtuns to 4 percent of the force.[34] Given the historic animosity between the southern Pashtun and the Northern Alliance (Uzbek, Tajik, Hazara, and so forth), this was not a surprising result. Most southern Pashtun perceived the ANA as an occupying force and thus were resistant to joining. Insufficient numbers of southern Pashtuns has remained a problem for ANA to this day.

Even as NTM-A met recruiting and training goals for 2011 early, the security situation continued to deteriorate in some parts of the country. With the withdrawal of ISAF looming and operational demands for troops in the field increasing, the target strengths for both ANA and ANP were increased:

In August 2011, a larger target size of 352,000 (195,000 ANA and 157,000 ANP) was set, to be reached by November 2012. The gross size of the force reached approximately that level by the end of September 2012, and remains at levels just below those targets. That figure does not include the approximately 30,000 local security forces.[35]

Furthermore, there was some increase in reported capabilities with 7 percent of the units reported as "independent with advisors," as were 9 percent of the ANP units. Also, the number of units had increased dramatically—to 219 ANA and 435 ANP units.[36] But the change of metric from "fully capable" in 2008 reports to "independent with advisors" in 2012 makes it difficult to compare the actual capabilities of the forces at the two different times. Also during 2012, the Army and Marine Corps began deploying Security Force Assistance Advisory Teams to facilitate the transition of all operations to Afghan forces. The relative priority the Services placed on transition teams versus U.S. operational units remained an issue. As was the pattern throughout our time in Afghanistan, advisory teams were formed late—sometimes actually in-country—and often without the appropriate mix of rank and skills.[37]

GAO went on to state that there was little or no progress in developing the critical ministries of Defense and Interior:

We have previously reported that limited capacity in the Afghan Ministries of Defense (MOD) and Interior (MOI)—which oversee the ANA and ANP, respectively—present challenges to the development and sustainment of capable ANSF. For instance, MOI faced challenges, such as a lack of consolidated personnel databases and formal training in properly executing budget and salary functions. In April 2012, DOD reported that the MOD was assessed as requiring some coalition assistance to accomplish its mission, an assessment unchanged since October 2010, while the MOI was assessed as needing significant coalition assistance— an assessment unchanged since 2009. Additionally, DOD reported that the ministries face a variety of challenges, including, among others, MOD's lack of human capital in areas requiring technical expertise and MOI's continuing problems with corruption.[38]

By early 2013, GAO was reporting shortfalls in promised funding for future Afghan security forces and inadequate staffing by the Services of the Security Force Assistance and Advisory Teams.[39] Each of these failings had been identified for years, but NATO had been unable to address them. At the end of 2014, NTM-A completed its mission and was replaced by a NATO-led mission titled Resolute Support:

This mission will not involve combat. Its support will be directed primarily to Afghan ministries and institutions, as well as the higher command level of the Afghan security forces. . . . Approximately 12,000 personnel from both NATO and partner nations will be deployed in support of the mission. The mission is planned to operate with one central hub (in Kabul/Bagram) and four spokes in Mazar-e Sharif, Herat, Kandahar and Jalalabad.

Key functions will include:

- *Supporting planning, programming and budgeting;*
- *Assuring transparency, accountability and oversight;*

- *Supporting the adherence to the principles of rule of law and good governance.*[40]

Although NTM-A has become Resolute Support, the United States has maintained CSTC-A. However, its focus is on advising and assisting Afghans at the ministerial level. CSTC-A no longer has a direct role in the training, equipping, or employing ANSF.

A lively debate continues as to whether the ANSF can hold its own against a resurgent Taliban. Few question the ability of the ANA to fight. In fact, the fighting spirit and capabilities of the ANA have been demonstrated over the last two fighting seasons. Despite increased attacks and high casualties, ANA remains an aggressive, effective fighting force. This represents one of the most positive aspects of the current situation. Unfortunately, many observers question the ability of its institutions to sustain the combat forces. Thus, both the U.S. and NATO missions will focus on assisting the ministries with these critical sustaining functions. While Afghan forces have clearly continued to fight hard (as indicated by their casualties), the military outcome remains in question. As NATO forces have withdrawn from the country, the security situation has worsened. On July 9, 2014, for instance, the United Nations announced that Afghan civilian casualties in the first half of 2014 surged to the highest level since 2009.[41] By the end of November 2014, the *Washington Post* reported there were more attacks in Kabul during 2014 than in any year since the U.S.-backed Northern Alliance seized the capital city in 2001.[42] But the rate of attacks fell off sharply in January and February of 2015. A key indicator will be the results of the 2015 fighting season.

Afghan Police

Afghanistan has never had a strong or effective civilian police force. Whatever progress was made in developing a civilian police force during the 1970s was lost during the more than two decades of conflict that followed. Following the defeat of the Taliban in the fall of 2001, anti-Taliban Northern Alliance commanders were quick to exploit the power vacuum and filled many of the district and provincial police forces with private militias that had little or no police training or experience. The daunting challenge confronting police reformers in the spring of 2002 was to create an effective civilian police force from an untrained entity manned primarily by factional commanders and their militias who had little or no equipment or infrastructure, who were unpaid or underpaid, and who operated within the corrupt and factionalized institutional structure of the Ministry of Interior (MOI).[43]

With this as a background, representatives of the Afghan people and donor nations signed the Bonn Agreement on December 5, 2001. Annex I included authority to raise a police force that all agreed should be "a multiethnic, sustainable, and countrywide 62,000-member professional police service."[44] As noted earlier, Germany assumed the lead nation role for forming the Afghan police at the January 2002 conference in Tokyo. It acted quickly by organizing a donor nations' conference in Berlin by February. Germany's plan focused on training senior police officers in a 3-year course and police NCOs in a 1-year course at the Kabul Police Academy. It did not plan to provide any training or mentoring for the vast majority of police officers who were ordinary patrolmen.

U.S. leaders believed that police would be critical to maintaining order in Afghanistan and that the German program was moving too slowly. So, despite Germany's role as lead nation, the United States established a police training program. For bureaucratic and legal reasons, the Department of State's Bureau of International Narcotics and Law Enforcement was designated as the program manager for the Afghan police. Since the bureau lacked the personnel to actually conduct the training, it contracted with DynCorp Aerospace Technology to train and equip the police, advise the MOI, and provide infrastructure assistance to include constructing several police training centers.[45] DynCorp had won previous contracts to train police forces in Bosnia and Haiti. The initial U.S. program was a "train the trainers" program. Experienced Afghan police officers completed a 3-week instructor development course taught by DynCorp advisors. They then conducted the 8-week basic training course for new police officers as well as the 2-week refresher program for veteran officers. For comparison, in 2008, police in Bosnia-Herzegovina, a much more literate and less violent society than 2002 Afghanistan, received 25 weeks of initial training.[46] Highway and border police each received an additional 2 weeks of training. While this provided some basic skills training, the contract did not provide for the essential post-training mentoring that had been critical in other programs. For comparison, both the New York and Los Angeles police departments require a 6-month basic training course and a significant period of on-the-job, one-on-one mentoring before an officer is considered ready for duty. Brazil reformed its police training in 2007 to require 380 to 500 hours while Ukraine requires 6 months.[47] Further exacerbating the problem in Afghanistan, the requirement for interpreters cut the actual instruction time by at least half, leading to an inevitable decrease in quality.

Even more damaging to the effort was the fact that U.S. trainers could not vet the men who were assigned as police officers. Most were not trained police but attained the jobs either because they were "police" after the collapse of the Mohammad Najibullah government or because specific powerbrokers in Afghanistan insisted they get the job. Many were illiterate and had never been in a classroom.

By January 2005, Germany and the United States had trained more than 35,000 national, highway, and border police using the dual programs. They expected to meet the goal of training 62,000 by December 2005.[48] Despite the optimistic projections, by July 2005 senior leaders believed the police training was not progressing well. As part of the reorganization of the U.S. effort in Afghanistan, responsibility for police training was transferred from the Department of State to DOD so that OSC-A became responsible for training all Afghan National Security Forces. At the time of the turnover, the ANP were organized in multiple branches. The largest, the Afghan Uniformed Police, were responsible for day-to-day law enforcement countrywide and scheduled to increase from 31,000 to 45,000 personnel. The Afghan Border Police, with 18,000 personnel, were tasked with manning 13 border posts and patrolling the border. Theoretically, the Afghan National Civil Order Police (ANCOP) were to be responsible for maintaining civil order in Afghan's largest cities and acting as a reserve for crisis. In fact, because its officers received more training, better equipment, and better vetting than other police agencies, ANCOP were often used as an auxiliary to the Afghan military in combat operations. The last two branches were the Afghanistan Highway Police and Counter Narcotics Police of Afghanistan.[49] Due to exceptional corruption, the Afghan Highway Police were subsequently dis-established.

In a further reorganization of the advisory effort, Germany's role of training and advising senior police officers was assumed by the European Union Police Mission (EUPOL) Afghanistan in the summer of 2007.[50] The EUPOL mission is to "contribute to the establishment of a sustainable and effective civilian police, which works together with the Afghan justice system to improve the local population's safety. The mission monitors, mentors, advises and trains at the level of senior management of the Afghan MOI, Afghan Ministry of Justice, Afghan Attorney General's Office, in Kabul and in several regions."[51] Recently, the European Union decided to extend EUPOL Afghanistan to the end of 2016.

EUPOL Afghanistan focused on training senior officials of the MOI and senior police officers with an emphasis on coordination and cooperation among various elements of the Afghan judicial system. Unfortunately, it was unable to fill about half of the allotted training slots and actually assigned many of their personnel to Provincial Reconstruction Teams rather than the ANP training program.

The fact that CSTC-A also provided training and mentoring for senior police officials created both coordination and execution problems since it and EUPOL Afghanistan had fundamentally different understandings of the role of police in counterinsurgency. Because it provided the bulk of both financial and personnel resources for the ANP, CSTC-A was the primary driver of the police training program. In late 2007, it initiated the Focused District Development (FDD) plan. Under this plan, all police officers were withdrawn from a district, replaced with Afghan National Civil Order Police, and then put through a 2-month training program before returning to their districts.[52] CSTC-A was enthusiastic about the progress of those police units that had participated in the program. A news release stated, "Initial reviews suggest that FDD is working, albeit slowly. Districts that have completed FDD have experienced a 60 percent decrease in civilian casualties."[53] This optimism may have been premature. The January 2008 Afghanistan Study Group Report, led by General James L. Jones, USMC (Ret.), and Ambassador Thomas R. Pickering, noted:

The ANP are severely underfunded, poorly trained, and poorly equipped. Many months go without pay because of corruption and problems with the payroll system. In parts of the country the police are seen as a greater cause of insecurity than the Taliban. . . . U.S. assistance needs to go beyond equipping and training, and be directed towards embedding foreign police officers into Afghan units.[54]

In June 2008, a DOD assessment showed that not one Afghan police unit out of 433 was fully capable of performing its mission; over three-fourths of them were assessed at the lowest capability rating.[55] In 2010, the Special Inspector General for Afghanistan Reconstruction (SIGAR) called into question the validity of the mission-capable rating system in its entirety. It noted that the Baghlan-e Jadid police district had been rated capable of independent operations (CM1 in the rating system) upon completion of the FDD plan in June 2009. However, when the SIGAR team asked to visit the district, still rated CM1, in March 2010, they were told it was "not secure" and "overrun with insurgents" to the point the Baghlan-e Jadid police force "had withered away."[56]

The problems were not limited to the police. It is a well-established fact that police reform must be accompanied by reform across the judicial system. Unfortunately, it is also clearly more difficult to educate the large numbers of judges, lawyers, clerks, and prison officials than it is to raise basic police forces. This was further exacerbated by the fact that the U.S. Government provided massive resources to the police in comparison to the relatively limited resources dedicated to supporting the other elements of the justice system. Without effective court and prison systems, even competent police operations have little or no impact on security. In its mostly pessimistic 2008 report, the Afghan Study Group noted important advances in the Afghan justice system: "The heads of the major justice sector institutions—the Supreme Court, the Ministry of Finance, and the Office of the Attorney General—have all been replaced with competent, moderate reformers."[57] At the time, Transparency International's Corruption Perception Index rated Afghanistan 172 out of 179 countries. Despite intensive efforts, the reformers had limited success. By 2013, Afghanistan was tied with Somalia and North Korea for last place.[58]

In his initial commander's assessment of August 2009, General McChrystal noted that 8 years into the conflict, "the ANP suffers from a lack of training, leaders, resources, equipment, and mentoring. Effective policing is inhibited by the absence of a working system of justice or dispute resolution; poor pay has also encouraged corruption."[59] He pushed for the police training contract to be moved from State to DOD to improve the quality of the training. This decision meant DynCorp, which had been selected by State and had held the contract for the previous 7 years, would not be eligible to bid on retaining it. In response, DynCorp sued in Federal court. Despite numerous audits over the years that indicated major problems with DynCorp trainers and the obvious lack of progress on the part of the ANP, DynCorp won the suit and then won the subsequent rebid of the contract.[60] In effect, a Federal court overturned the decision of the ISAF commander in Afghanistan and forced him to continue using a contractor that had consistently failed to execute its mission.

McChrystal was not the only senior official who felt the ANP was not progressing. In March 2009, Special Envoy Richard Holbrooke "characterized the ANP as 'inadequate,' 'riddled with corruption,' and the 'weak link in the security chain.'"[61] In a joint report, the Royal United Services Institute and Foreign Policy Research Institute noted that "even by the Afghan government's own admission, problems remain. Institutional and individual competence to tackle crime remains low, while corruption, police criminality and abuses of power are pervasive. Failing to provide sufficient civil security, the police are unable to fulfil their potential role as a key appendage to the reconstruction effort."[62]

The formal establishment of NATO Training Mission–Afghanistan in November 2009 was an effort to correct some of these problems through better coordination of ANSF training. Although NTM-A stood up and was tasked with police and military training for Afghan forces, CSTC-A remained a separate command because NTM-A could not provide trainers for the ministries nor could it administer the U.S. funds provided for the Afghan security forces. Thus, NATO caveats and U.S. laws required the continued existence of CSTC-A. However, to ensure the two commands worked well together, a single officer was dual-hatted to command both organizations.

While improving the coordination of the various training elements, the shift of police training responsibility to NTM-A highlighted an ongoing dispute concerning the proper role of the ANP. Critics of ISAF's use of the police believed the ANP were being misused as "little soldiers" and improperly assigned "to isolated posts without backup" and, as a result, "suffered three times the casualties of the ANA."[63] They focused on the need for a police force capable of enforcing the rule of law in postconflict Afghanistan rather than as a counterinsurgency force. In contrast, proponents of assigning the police nationwide as a paramilitary security force understood the need for professional police but believed that until the security situation improved significantly, the ANP had to focus on the counterinsurgency security mission. In fact, in those areas that were relatively secure, to include most Afghan cities, there was a critical need for an effective police force focused on the rule of law. At the same time, the higher literacy requirements inherent in community policing mean the training pipeline must be longer to allow for significant literacy education of even patrol officers. However, such a force simply could not survive in heavily contested districts. Many Afghan political and police leaders saw the police in a different light. To them, the police had to focus on protecting the regime and government personnel—not the population. This tension has never been formally resolved.

Unification of the command enhanced the coalition strengths that assisted the police training program—such as the Italian Carabinieri trainers who, unlike the British or Americans, were part of a professional national police force. While former U.S. and British police officers brought experience to the mission of training local law enforcement, they lacked the knowledge of operating in a national police force that maintains paramilitary capabilities.

Unfortunately, there were also numerous challenges. Despite the assignment of CSTC-A/NTM-A as the de facto lead for police training, "smaller bilateral missions and the European Police Mission (EUPOL) [continued] pursuing its own mandate."[64] This divergence of national mandates for police training reflected only one small aspect of the coordination issues involved in conducting a counterinsurgency campaign with over 40 nations participating.

In addition to the problems created by dysfunction within the coalition effort to support the police, the SIGAR noted that as late as January 2015, the MOI was unable to track the number of personnel it employs or whether they are getting paid. The U.S. response has been to once again attempt to "implement a fully functional electronic accounting and personnel tracking system."[65]

This action, over 10 years into the effort to build an effective police department, highlights one of the problems the United States faces when training a foreign force. U.S. planners continually try to install relatively sophisticated computerized systems to track personnel, pay, and equipment. The transparency provided by such systems is seen by U.S. personnel both as a management tool and an anticorruption tool. For instance, an effective system will show how many personnel are actually in a unit—and thus eliminate payment to "ghost" soldiers. It will also allow for more effective accountability of equipment and consumables such as fuel. This reduces the losses to black market activities. Unfortunately, many Afghans, to include senior officers, do not want this level of transparency. They require the funds acquired through fraud to function in their organizations—and in too many cases, simply to enrich themselves. Furthermore, the shortage of literate, numerate, and computer-savvy personnel in the ANSF is simply insufficient to operate and maintain these systems.

Local Police Initiatives

While not technically an element of the Afghan National Security Forces, any discussion of Afghan security must include the various local police initiatives that have been made across the country. The collapse of the Taliban government left local policing in the hands of various warlords and militias. The men who filled these jobs were not trained policemen. The United Nations' initial plan called for a national police force to be trained, equipped, and deployed under lead nation supervision. Unfortunately, this project was started from a low baseline and would inevitably take a great deal of time. With a deteriorating security situation and insufficient ANA/ANP forces to protect the rural population, ISAF commanders from the local to the national level turned to militia/local men to provide security. Over the last decade, the United States and ISAF have made several attempts to form local militia units similar to the "Sons of Iraq" concept that was successful in that country. These local militias were referred to as police but, if trained at all, were trained as paramilitary units by soldiers, not policemen.

A series of programs was tried: Afghan National Auxiliary Police (2005), Afghan Public Protection Program (2007), Community Defense Forces (2009), Community Defense Initiative/Local Defense Initiative (2009), Interim Security for Critical Infrastructure (2010), Village Stability Operations (2010), and finally, consolidation under the Afghan Local Police (ALP) Program (2010).[66] Some reports from the field extolled the virtues of locally recruited police/militias.[67] Other reports have consistently detailed abuses, such as corruption, assault, rape, and murder, by local police/militias.[68] This is inevitable in a nation as diverse as Afghanistan where the coalition support to local programs varies widely. In addition, in those areas with mixed populations with longstanding animosities, the police/militias are seen as another source of power in local conflicts. Even Special Forces teams living with the locals are hard-pressed to understand the local politics well enough to ensure a neutral security force. Despite these challenges, the policy of having Special Forces teams live with ALP units resulted in major improvements in their performance and professionalism. The teams dedicated a great deal of effort to vetting the individual militia members through local community leaders. This effort, plus their continued mentoring and presence, ensured that the ALP provided better security than the numerous previous programs.

However, significant problems remained, in particular the difficulty of assuring the loyalty of ALP units to the government or their adherence to their function as neutral enforcers of the law rather than as partisan militia in local disputes. As a result, the U.S. Embassy in Kabul forbade U.S. diplomats from meeting with tribal leaders to discuss tribal "pacts," ruling out on-the-ground contact with local defense groups concerning counterinsurgency and counterterrorism chiefly out of concern that local defense groups might spur intertribal conflict and eventually oppose the national government.[69]

Each of the problems with the ALP has been magnified by the withdrawal of the Special Forces advisors. In some areas, Special Forces were replaced by Afghan special forces teams, which simply lack the resources available to their U.S. counterparts. Because the ALP lacks supporting institutions to provide pay, equipment, fuel, spare parts, and ammunition, some have been forced to turn to extortion to survive.[70]

Continuing Problems

From the beginning, the police training program has suffered from a number of significant problems. Insufficient manning, disagreement over the police mission, corruption, and the weakness of the justice system have degraded the program since its inception. The GAO's Afghanistan Security Report of March 2009 noted CSTC-A was short over 1,500 police trainers.[71] Three years later, a subsequent GAO report noted ANP instructor manning levels still reflected a 46.5 percent shortage.[72] Despite the increased focus on ANSF development by successive ISAF commanders—General McChrystal, General David Petraeus, USA, General John Allen, USMC, and General Joseph Dunford, USMC—

manning levels for police trainers never approached even the modest levels requested by NTM-A. In his 2011 study, William Rosenau reported:

> *the capabilities, performance, and leadership of the Afghan National Police (ANP)—like other Afghan institutions—differed from district to district, province to province, and region to region. In the view of a British police advisor in Lashkar Gah, the ANP showed signs of a growing commitment to serving and protecting the public. Specialized police units such as the Afghan National Civil Order Police (recruited on a national basis and provided with intensive and sustained advice, training, and support) displayed considerable professionalism and prowess. In many districts, however, the local police remained hobbled by drug addiction, endemic corruption, and poor leadership.*[73]

A different and equally significant disagreement has existed over whether the police should be centrally controlled from the MOI in Kabul or should be controlled locally in the form of local police. In some areas, district and provincial police chiefs have become a power unto themselves. Lieutenant General Abdul Raziq, the current chief of police for Kandahar Province, has succeeded in reducing Taliban attacks in the province by two-thirds. However, questions about Raziq's human rights record as well as the source of his newfound wealth have followed him since he appointed himself as chief of police of Spin Boldak.[74]

As early as 2006, when the United States began to advocate increasing ANP strength from 62,000 to 82,000, some partner nations expressed:

> *concern that the focus of reform efforts is shifting away from establishing a civilian police force to a paramilitary or counter-insurgency force. . . . The most fundamental issue that must be resolved for police reform efforts to succeed in Afghanistan is the need for a shared vision of the role of the ANP, and a shared strategy on how to achieve that vision. In particular, there is a need to reconcile the "German vision" of the police as a civilian law and order force, and the "U.S. vision" of the police as a security force with a major counter-insurgency role.*[75]

Perhaps the greatest challenge in working with the MOI and the ANP has been corruption. Despite focused efforts by donor nations and the ISAF command element, corruption has remained a major issue for Afghanistan as a whole and the police in particular. Organizations as disparate as Transparency International, the World Bank, and the Asia Foundation have consistently reported *increasing* levels of corruption in Afghanistan from 2005 to the present.[76] The continuing and deleterious nature of corruption in the ANP has been the subject of dozens of government, academic, and think-tank reports. A recent Google search of the specific phrase "Afghan police corruption" brought 226,000 hits. If one takes the quotes off, it brings over 1 million hits. Nor are there indications the Afghans have a plan for dealing with this problem. In December 2013, Thomas Ruttig of Afghan Analysts Network noted, "The Ministry of Interior—known for its systematic sale of positions—has, according to the oversight body SIGAR, completely stopped its anti-corruption reforms."[77]

Despite the prevailing corruption, Michelle Hughes, a former DOD official who has field experience in 12 countries, reports there are reasons for both optimism and pessimism concerning the future of the ANP. On the positive side:

- The international community's heavy investment in police education, training, mentoring, and equipping has led to a large, increasingly effective police force.
- Public trust and confidence in the ANP are the highest they have been in 7 years.
- The Afghan Minster of Interior has developed his own 10-year vision to make the police an essential public service.
- Afghan officials are becoming the greatest proponents for the professionalization of the police as a law enforcement service.

However:

- There has been little progress toward action to take the ANP to the next level of professionalism. The effort continues to be ad hoc, disaggregated, and poorly defined.

- The MOI lacked an effective personnel management system. Not surprisingly, the heavily automated one established by the co-alition was less than successful. As a result, in late December 2014, Resolute Support and the Afghan government unveiled the new Afghanistan Human Resources Information Management System.[78]
- The MOI lacks the capability for planning, programming, and budget execution.[79]

There are other developments that do not bode well for the police. Despite repeated reports from U.S. Government agencies noting major deficiencies and fraud in previous DynCorp contracts,[80] the company was awarded new contracts in 2015 to "provide advisory, training and mentoring services to the Afghan Ministry of Interior (MoI/Afghanistan National Police) and the Afghanistan Ministry of Defense (MoD/National Army)."[81]

Key Issues for the Future of ANSF

In April 2014, DOD expressed optimism concerning the ability of the Afghan security forces to deal with the Taliban. Unfortunately, the optimism had to be tempered with significant caveats:

ANSF capability is no longer the biggest uncertainty facing Afghanistan. Since taking the lead for security operations nationwide in June 2013, the ANSF demonstrated an ability to overmatch the Taliban consistent-ly, with limited ISAF support. The sustainability of gains to date will be dependent on a number of factors, to include: Afghan ownership of the security and economic problems facing their country to date; the out-come of the presidential elections and Afghanistan's ability to reach in-ternal political equilibrium, international financial support after 2014; the ability of the new Afghan government to put in place the legal struc-tures needed to attract investment and promote growth; and the size and structure of the post-2014 U.S. and NATO presence.[82]

Later in the report, DOD noted that "the logistics and facilities depart-ments for the MOD and MOI still require coalition assistance and are expect-ed to continue to require support in the near future."[83]

For its part, the Congressional Research Service (CRS) noted that funding will remain a major challenge for the ANSF. The CRS noted the discrepancy between currently pledged funds and those funds actually needed to maintain the ANSF at the 352,000 men deemed necessary for security:

On the assumption that the post-2014 ANSF force would shrink to 228,000, it was determined that sustaining a force that size would cost $4.1 billion annually. The United States pledged $2.3 billion yearly; the Afghan government pledged $500 million yearly; and allied contributions constituted the remaining $1.3 billion. The Afghan contribution is to rise steadily until 2024, at which time Afghanistan is expected to fund its own security needs. However, the apparent U.S. and NATO decision to keep the ANSF force at 352,000 produced revised funding requirement levels of about $6 billion per year.

With respect to the funding requirements for a 352,000 person force, the Administration has requested $4.1 billion for the ANSF for FY [fiscal year] 2015. At the NATO summit, partner countries reaffirmed pledges of about $1.25 billion annually for the ANSF during 2015–2017. The $500 million Afghan contribution would apparently be required to reach the $6 billion requirement for 2015, although Afghan government revenues have fallen due to the election dispute, and it is not clear that Afghanistan has the funds to honor its financial pledge for the ANSF.[84]

Perhaps an even greater challenge will be maintaining ANSF professionalism and end-strength. As of late 2013, 31.4 percent of the Afghan National Security Forces do not reenlist each year.[85] With an end-strength goal of 352,000, ANSF will have to recruit, train, and equip 110,528 new personnel every year—more than the 2013 recruiting goal for the U.S. Army and Marine Corps combined.[86]

In late 2014, SIGAR released a list of seven high-risk programs that are particularly vulnerable to fraud, waste, and, abuse. Number one on the list was corruption and rule of law. Number three on the list was the Afghan National Security Forces.[87] All of this comes at a time of increasing disillusionment among NATO and other ISAF members. In December 2014, the Alliance was "struggling to find 4,000 non-American troops for the coming year. It is 1,200 short. . . . It would be a band-aid, however. There is no military solution to the insurgency, as NATO's failure to defeat the Taliban shows."[88]

On January 1, 2015, ISAF completed its mission and the NATO-led mission named Resolute Support was launched to provide training, advice, and assistance for the Afghan security forces and institutions.[89]

Iraqi Army

Prior to the invasion, Pentagon planners made a key assumption about the Iraqi army. They believed that upon conclusion of hostilities, it would come back on duty and thus provide for the security of Iraq. Ambassador L. Paul Bremer's decision to disband the army invalidated this assumption. The debate about the decision to disband the army has been fully explored in numerous sources. Its importance for this discussion is the fact that the planners had no branch plan if this key assumption proved false.

With no viable security forces, the violence in Iraq steadily increased. Almost immediately upon disbanding the army, the Coalition Provisional Authority (CPA), as the governing authority of Iraq, decided it had to build a new one. However, it lacked the expertise to do so and thus had to turn to the Pentagon to request personnel. The inevitable result was an ad hoc organization. Furthermore, the disbandment of the army combined with the de-Ba'athification decision created enormous difficulties for those tasked with raising the new Iraqi army.

It was not until late May 2003 that Major General Paul Eaton, USA, was tasked with creating that army. He would not execute the mission as part of the U.S. Army but as a member of the CPA. He was briefed on his mission in May and arrived in Baghdad on June 13. At that point, he had a staff of five and minimal guidance. Nor was there any plan to provide additional resources.[90]

Upon arrival, Eaton was told the CPA had already determined that the Iraqi army would be oriented toward foreign threats to its own borders.[91] To reassure its neighbors, its logistics support would all be provided by civilian contractors whose contracts prohibited delivery of any support more than 80 miles from the home station of the Iraqi unit.[92] In short, the new Iraqi army would not have sufficient logistics support to be a threat to any of its neighbors. However, it was unclear how civilian logistics firms would deliver supplies to battalions and companies in combat.

The initial CPA plan was to create three motorized Iraqi divisions. At the time, the CPA was envisioning a 3-year period before allowing control of Iraq to revert to Iraqis. Thus, it allowed a year for fielding the first 12,000-man division. Then it would dedicate the second year to the establishment of two more Iraqi divisions.[93] Eaton developed the Coalition Military Assistance Transition Team (CMATT) joint manning document based on these planning factors. The CPA also placed some distinct restrictions on Eaton's efforts to raise a new Iraqi army. No brigadier or higher from the old army could return since they were also Ba'athists. (Keep in mind the Iraqi army had almost 10,000 brigadiers. By law, the U.S. Army can have no more than 231 total general officers from brigadier general to full general.) The army should also match the ethnic/religious makeup of Iraq—60 percent Shia, 20 percent Kurd, and 20 percent Sunni. (While Kurds are both Sunni and Shia, their primary identity is Kurdish, and therefore the CPA sought ethnic/religious balance based on the 60/20/20 formula.) Recruiting for the army specifically stated that it would fight external enemies only and would not be involved in any actions against the Iraqi people. While this made sense in reducing the Iraqis' fear of a new army, it created significant problems in early 2004 when the Second Battalion was ordered to Fallujah to support coalition forces in their fight against Iraqis. Finally, there was no punishment for desertion. At any point, a soldier could simply decide he no longer wanted to be part of the army and leave without fear of disciplinary action.

While the CPA struggled to reestablish the Iraqi army, the increasing violence drove coalition military commanders to take the initiative and begin raising, training, and equipping Iraqi units for local security. Coalition ground commanders needed Iraqis to augment their security efforts and did not feel they could wait for the first Iraqi army units to be fielded. In the fall of 2003, the CPA supported these decisions and allowed the establishment of Iraqi Civil Defense Corps units. The training of these units, soon re-designated the Iraqi National Guard, was determined by individual U.S. divisional commanders. Initially, training periods varied from 3 days to several weeks. Employment was also up to the individual commander. Some paired Iraqi National Guard units with their own forces. Others left the units to operate on their own.

Eaton and his small team had to start from scratch: develop all Iraqi army facilities, to include finding their own offices, phones, and computers; establish recruiting offices; find trainers; procure every item of equipment for the new soldiers and their bases; and have 1,000 men in training by August. While building the Iraqi army, the team also had to build its own organization—the CMATT. Eaton requested and was promised military trainers, but only four actually reported—two Britons and two Australians. Since Combined Joint Task Force 7 (CJTF 7), the military command in Iraq, did not work for the CPA, it could not be tasked to train Iraqi security forces (ISF) nor even required to provide augmentees to CMATT. This highlighted one of the major problems CMATT faced. Nearly everything it needed had to come through military channels, but it lacked influence in the Pentagon. CMATT worked for the CPA under Ambassador Bremer, who did not have a good relationship with Lieutenant General Ricardo Sanchez, USA, the CJTF 7 commander. Eaton believes a key issue in the slow start to training the Iraqi army was the fact that CMATT was essentially an orphan in the military system. It lacked a four-star sponsor who could force the Pentagon to take action in support of the training effort.[94]

Partially due to personnel shortages, primary training responsibility was outsourced to Vinnell Corporation. This was both a blessing and a curse. Vinnell had a good record working with Arabic-speaking soldiers and had provided training for the Saudi Arabian National Guard for 25 years:

> [Vinnell's] *force-generation methods included the training of Iraqi officers in Jordan at a non-commissioned officers' academy and a "recruit training" academy in Kirkush, Iraq. Trained and equipped Iraqi forces would then be used to train additional forces. The contractors would deliver "trained units" and "trained leaders" to larger Iraqi army formations. Because of the Geneva Convention, as well as legal and regulatory concerns, the contractors would not become embedded advisors once the initial training was complete and Iraqi units moved on to combat operations.*[95]

Besides fielding and training the Iraqi units, Vinnell moved quickly to provide essential services to the new Iraqi army—recruiting, mess, laundry, maintenance, refurbishing base buildings, and so forth. Unfortunately, by December 2003, it was obvious that an army trained by contractors alone was not meeting the requirement. Training attrition in the First Battalion was nearly 50 percent. The April 2004 breakdown of the Iraqi Second Battalion when it was ordered to Fallujah to assist U.S. forces confirmed the shortfalls in training, equipment, and leadership.[96] What the Vinnell trainers could not do was instill the soldier's ethos in the Iraqi recruits. In response, CMATT developed a plan to use coalition noncommissioned officers to provide the "soldier" aspect of training. However, even when the joint manning document was produced, CMATT was manned at less than 50 percent strength. Furthermore, many personnel were assigned for 3- to 6-month tours, which were too brief for the personnel to truly understand the situation and have an impact. Again, without a four-star sponsor to push the Pentagon, CMATT could not overcome its low manning priority in the joint personnel system.

Compounding the training and personnel shortages, the slow release of funding for facilities and equipment by the Pentagon continually disrupted the plan. The slow construction of barracks meant that billeting space became the pacing item for producing Iraqi army units. Since all military bases had been thoroughly looted when the Iraqi army was dissolved, barracks rooms, offices, mess halls, armories, ranges, medical facilities, motor pools, and other facilities had to be built or refurbished so that Iraqi army units had somewhere to move after basic training.[97] Even when funding was released, the shortage of contracting officers led to both delays and quality control problems on the construction and logistical support contracts. The shortage of qualified translators contributed to further delays since, for good reason, the legally binding contract was in Arabic but had to be translated to English for processing in the CPA system. Inevitably, translation errors led to misunderstandings and disputes—from minor disputes over mess hall menus to major disputes over the condition and date of turnover of major Iraqi bases from the contractor to the Iraqi army.

Despite CMATT's severe shortage of personnel, the CPA decided that the training for the Iraqi police was progressing so badly that it transferred responsibility for the program to CMATT in March 2004. Just prior to that, the CPA changed the tasking to CMATT from raising one division in 3 years to raising three divisions in 1 year. The sudden requirement for the understrength CMATT staff to both triple the production of army units and revise and implement a nationwide program to raise, train, and equip police obviously had a negative impact on the entire training program for Iraqi security forces. Beset with many problems at the outset, CMATT under Major General Eaton was nevertheless able to establish a foundation for much of the rapid expansion of the ISF that Multi-National Security Transition Command–Iraq (MNSTC-I) would lead over the next few years.

With the dissolution of the CPA and transfer of authority to the Iraqis imminent, National Security Presidential Directive 36, dated May 11, 2004, detailed the new command arrangements in Iraq. With respect to support to the ISF, it stated, "The Secretary of State shall be responsible for the continuous supervision and general direction of all assistance for Iraq. Commander, US-CENTCOM, with the policy guidance of the Chief of Mission, shall direct all United States Government efforts and coordinate international efforts in support of organizing, equipping, and training all Iraqi Security Forces."[98] In June 2004, CMATT was redesignated as MNSTC-I. Commanded by Lieutenant General David Petraeus, it remained responsible for developing the MOD, MOI, and ISF—military and police.

With only 45 days to prepare, General George W. Casey, Jr., USA, took command of Multi-National Force–Iraq on July 1, 2004. Indicative of the turbulence he faced, he noted that in his 32 months in command, he served with three Iraqi governments, two Secretaries of Defense, two Chairmen of the Joint Chiefs of Staff (CJCS), two Ambassadors, four Multi-National Corps–Iraq (MNC-I) commanders, and two MNSTC-I commanders.[99] Continuity clearly was not a characteristic of the multinational effort in Iraq from June 2004 to February 2007. As he took over, Casey found there were only about 30,000 trained police on duty, only 3,600 of 18,000 border guards had weapons, and only 2 infantry battalions had reached an initial operating capability. His new plan called for 135,000 trained police, 32,000 border guards, and 65 infantry battalions.[100]

Believing he had eliminated the insurgent sanctuaries in Baghdad and Fallujah in 2004, Casey concluded that the now 80 Iraqi infantry and special operations force battalions, with embedded U.S. advisors, could begin to assume the security mission. He was concerned that keeping U.S. forces in the lead would hamper the willingness and ability of the Iraqis to take over. Thus, he focused MNC-I on partnering with and mentoring the Iraqis. As part of the process of forcing the Iraqis to lead, two U.S. brigades were withdrawn from Iraq without replacement. Unfortunately, security continued to deteriorate, particularly after the al-Askari mosque bombing in February 2006. Casey stopped the withdrawal of U.S. forces and focused on securing Baghdad. The conflict was shifting from an insurgency against the government to a sectarian civil war between Sunni and Shia.

On the positive side, the previous years of effort by MNSTC-I were beginning to pay off in the rapidly expanding numbers of Iraqi security forces. By January 2006, in its report to Congress, DOD stated 98 Iraqi and special operations forces (SOF) battalions were conducting counterinsurgency operations across Iraq. Almost 107,000 Iraqi soldiers, sailors, and airmen had been trained, and 82,000 police were in the field. This expansion followed a reduction in the number of U.S. Army combat brigades in early 2006 from 17 to 15.[101] The report went on to cite numerous statistics to show the progress being made in the political, economic, and security spheres in Iraq. But it could not finesse the fact that the weekly total number of attacks had almost tripled in the last 2 years.[102]

By late 2006, the Iraqi army had grown to about 138,000, an end-strength increase of almost 30 percent in less than a year.[103] Unfortunately, the early decision to focus on building a light infantry force to face external enemies meant the Iraqi army displayed serious weaknesses. It consisted almost entirely of light infantry battalions supported by motor-transportation regiments. It included only one mechanized brigade, part of which was equipped with tanks and infantry fighting vehicles donated by Eastern European countries. As a result, there was a wide disparity between the lightly equipped Iraqi army forces and the more heavily equipped U.S. forces trying to accomplish similar missions. In addition, the Iraqi army mirrored the sectarian and ethnic divisions that plague the country. Kurds, Sunni Arabs, and Shiite Arabs usually served in battalions that consisted largely or exclusively of their own groups. Furthermore, there was "no judicial system within the Iraqi Army to assure discipline, and soldiers can refuse orders with impunity."[104]

The police forces grew even more rapidly, reaching a total strength of 188,200 by November—a remarkable 129 percent growth.[105] As could be expected with such rapid growth, both MOD and MOI forces were "hampered by immature logistics and maintenance support systems, sectarian and militia influence, and the complex security environment."[106]

DOD noted that 2007 witnessed the continued rapid growth of Iraqi security forces, with the army reaching 194,233 trained personnel and the police reaching 241,960, with plans to expand to over 270,000 in the military and over 307,000 in the MOI:

> *The Coalition's four main areas of emphasis in developing the MoD and MoI and their forces remain . . . (1) developing ministerial capacity; (2) improve the proficiency of the Iraqi forces; (3) build specific logistics, sustainment and training capacities; and (4) support the expansion of the MoD and MoI forces. Special problems within these areas include corruption and lack of professionalism, sectarian bias, leader shortfalls, logistics deficiencies, and dependence on Coalition forces for many combat support functions.*[107]

The history of the U.S. Surge in Iraq has been covered extensively elsewhere and will not be covered in detail here. Yet it is important to note that in addition to rapidly expanding the ISF prior to and during the surge period, MNSTC-I, during the tenure of Lieutenant General Martin Dempsey, USA, from September 2005 to June 2007, also drove quality improvements that enabled Iraqi forces to play a key role in surge operations and hold their own against anti-coalition forces. A strong focus on force generation paid major dividends in this timeframe. MNSTC-I's extensive use of the foreign military sales program also accelerated the flow of modern military equipment to the ISF, transforming army and police units in about 2 years from a force mounted principally in civilian pickup trucks to one equipped with 3,200 up-armored Humvees by the end of 2008. Entire divisions, such as the 11th and 14th, were assembled and employed in action in as little as 12 months.[108] While many of the problems cited above were not fully solved, ISF units nonetheless far outnumbered U.S. and coalition troops, particularly in the crucial Baghdad operations, and on the whole performed successfully. They deserve a fair portion of credit for the eventual success of the Baghdad security plan and the major reductions in violence that followed across Iraq.

The rapid expansion of the ISF does not tell the full story. A major success story of the Surge was the formation of the Sons of Iraq. By late 2007, 91,000 volunteers had signed up. By mid-2008, the *Washington Post* reported that violence had decreased from 1,400 incidents per day to only 200.[109] With violence decreasing to early-2005 levels, the concern among Sunnis turned to integrating the Sons of Iraq into the official security forces of Iraq. The Shia-dominated government was not eager to incorporate so many men who were recently their enemies.[110] Less violence and an army and police force of over 530,000 meant the Shia also perceived much less need for the Sons of Iraq as separate forces. They did not want them integrated into the Iraqi army.[111]

Over the next year, violence continued to decrease even as U.S. forces started to draw down. By early 2009, the steadily increasing application of resources to raising and training the Iraqi army resulted in an army of almost 200,000, augmented by police forces of over 380,000. Operational units were improving but still required coalition support for intelligence, communications, engineering, and close air support. There also remained serious concerns about the ability of the MOD and MOI to execute the full range of their duties. While retention and recruiting looked good for meeting future goals, the ministries' development was slow and uneven.[112]

By June 2010, Iraqi forces had grown to 625,000, and DOD believed they were on track to achieve minimum essential capability in all areas except logistics and sustainment, with continued problems in planning, budgeting, and procurement. Furthermore, while the ISF would not be ready to fight an external enemy by the December 2011 deadline for the withdrawal of all U.S. forces, they were sufficiently prepared for internal security.[113] U.S. forces withdrew on time, and the U.S. Government's interest in Iraq declined precipitously until the sudden and rapid collapse of the two Iraqi army divisions responsible for the defense of Mosul in June 2014.

This collapse illustrated the difficulty of overcoming cultural and political realities when building another nation's army. With the departure of American advisors, "the army became [former prime minister Nouri al-] Maliki's private militia,"[114] according to Major General Eaton. As such, it discriminated against non-Shia, often functioning as an enforcement arm of Shiite political parties. The political reality for the Sunni in particular meant that the Islamic State in Iraq and the Levant (ISIL) might in fact be the lesser of two evils. The U.S. advisory effort was unable to change the culture of the Iraqi army. David Zucchina of the *Los Angeles Times* reported, "Officers in one of many units that collapsed in Mosul, the 2d Battalion of Iraq's 3d Federal Police Division, said their U.S.

training was useful. But as soon as their American advisors left, they said, soldiers and police went back to their ways. 'Our commanders told us to ignore what the Americans taught us,' Shehab said. 'They said, "We'll do it our way."'"[115]

Recent actions by the U.S., allied, and Iraqi governments have started the rebuilding process for the Iraqi army. As both an indicator of the significant challenges and a sign of sincere reform, Prime Minister Haider al-Abadi stated that a preliminary investigation has revealed 50,000 "ghost" soldiers on MOD rolls. He expects the continuing investigation to find more such soldiers.[116]

Iraqi Police

Reconstituting the Iraqi police as a force that served and protected the Iraqi people was always going to be a major challenge. Under Saddam, "The [Iraqi police] had been the bottom of Saddam's bureaucratic hierarchy of security agencies and suffered from years of mismanagement, deprivation of resources, and lack of professional standards. . . . Iraqis saw the [police] as part of a cruel and repressive regime and described its officers as brutal, corrupt, and untrustworthy."[117]

The complete lack of a U.S. plan for rebuilding the police greatly magnified the already daunting challenge. With disorder rising in Iraq, the Departments of Justice and State hastily initiated the process in May 2003 by dispatching a six-member team of police executives to assess the needs of the Iraqi police. That team recommended 6,000 international civilian police trainers and advisors be recruited and deployed to Iraq immediately. On June 2, 2003, Ambassador Bremer approved the plan but lacked the funds to implement it.[118] This was the first indicator the United States would consistently under-resource police training in Iraq. Recognizing the importance of an effective police force to the future of Iraq and seeing little progress to that point, USCENTCOM Commander General John Abizaid, USA, recommended to Bremer that the U.S. military assume responsibility for police training in September 2003. Despite his inability to resource the training through CPA, Bremer opposed the transfer of responsibility, and thus training remained the responsibility of the CPA for the time being.

Nonetheless, in October, CJTF 7 Commander Lieutenant General Sanchez told a senatorial delegation that 54,000 police were on duty. When Bremer inquired about the police training, he was told, "The Army is sweeping up half-educated men off the streets, running them through a 3-week train-ing course, arming them, and then calling them 'police.'"[119] Bremer directed Sanchez to stop training police. However, the CPA still could not provide a viable alternative training program. It took until December 2003 for the first 24 police trainers to arrive. Not until March 2004 did the United States de-cide to provide 500 police trainers through a DynCorp contract with the State Department. In the same month, the Civilian Police Advisory Training Team (CPATT) was established and subordinated to CMATT. Thus, the badly un-derstaffed CMATT was given responsibility for both the army and the police. While CMATT remained under the authority of the CPA and not the military, the transfer of authority for the police highlighted a fundamental disagree-ment between the military and the Departments of State and Justice police trainers, who felt strongly that the training should focus on developing a com-munity policing service dedicated to enforcing law and order:

> *The problem was that the U.S. military and State/DOJ* [Department of Justice] *civilian police advisors had markedly different goals for the Iraqi police. This divergence of views meant that there was no common understanding among U.S. agencies about the mission of the Iraqi po-lice. It also meant a divergence between the training provided to mem-bers of the Iraqi Police Service and their utilization in the field.*
>
> *State policymakers and DOJ police trainers were intent on creating an efficient, lightly armed, civilian Iraqi Police Service (IPS) that utilized community-policing techniques and operated in conformity with West-ern, democratic standards for professional law enforcement.*
>
> *Beyond utilizing the IPS in a counter-insurgency role, the U.S. military was determined to create an internal Iraqi security force that could pro-tect itself and deal with the insurgency and hostile militias, ultimately permitting a U.S. withdrawal.*[120]

The initial CPA training program had in fact focused on community po-licing. To reinforce this point, they renamed the Iraqi National Police the Iraqi Police Service. However, with the rising violence, the military commanders responsible for security in Iraq believed the Iraqi police needed to be a militarized counterinsurgency force able to support coalition forces in the field. This was the primary driver behind CJTF 7's efforts to raise 54,000 local police. After the insurgency was put down, the force could be reoriented to a community policing force. This disagreement was not resolved with the transfer of police training to CMATT. Nor did the reorganization provide any immediate increase in resources for the police. By June 2004, as the CPA prepared to turn governance over to the Iraqis, there were still fewer than 100 civilian police trainers in Iraq.[121] Upon the departure of the CPA, authority over the police reverted to the Ministry of the Interior. However, MNSTC-I remained the primary force behind recruiting, training, equipping, and fielding the police.

With the rising violence dramatically illustrated by the coordinated Sunni attacks on coalition forces in Fallujah, Baghdad, Ramadi, Samarra, and Tikrit, as well as the Mahdi army offensive in Najaf and Sadr City, the under-trained, under-equipped Iraqi police collapsed in many areas. To fill the gap, MN-STC-I Commander Lieutenant General Petraeus authorized 750-man police battalions composed mostly of Sunnis who were former Iraqi special forces soldiers. Once raised and equipped, they were immediately dispatched to fight alongside coalition units. At the same time but without coordinating with the United States, Minister of Interior Falah Hassan al-Naqib started recruiting police commando units from the same source and using them in independent operations. The appearance of Naqib's forces on the battlefield surprised the coalition, but they proved effective.[122]

On May 3, 2005, there was another transfer of power as the Iraqi transitional government replaced the Iraqi interim government. Bayan Jabr Solagh (also known as Baqir Jabr al-Zubeidi), a senior official of the Shiite Supreme Council of the Islamic Revolution of Iraq (SCIRI), was appointed Minister of Interior. He consolidated the numerous ad hoc police battalions/commando units into the Emergency Response Unit (a special weapons and techniques battalion), 8th Police Mechanized Brigade (3 motorized battalions), Public Order Division (4 brigades/12 battalions), and Special Police Commando Division (4 brigades/12 battalions).[123] At the same time, Jabr appointed leaders of the Badr Brigade, SCIRI's armed wing, to the ministry and key police commands. He recruited thousands of Shia to replace Sunnis and effectively turned the Iraqi police into a Shiite militia that was free to kidnap, torture, and murder Sunnis.[124]

In response, MNSTC-I declared 2006 to be "the Year of the Police" and started a major effort to reorganize training and discipline in the force. It convinced the MOI to combine the U.S.-created public order battalions with the Iraqi-created commando units in a single national police force that would be named the Iraqi National Police. It would have more training and equipment and serve as a backup to the Iraqi Police Service, the lightly armed street police created by the State/Justice training team:

> *With this reorganization, the Ministry of Interior forces consisted of the Iraqi Police Service, the National Police, the Department of Border Enforcement, the Center for Dignitary Protection, and the MOI's portion of the Facilities Protection Service. (The MOI is planning for the eventual incorporation of an estimated 150,000 members of the Facilities Protection Service who currently reside in other ministries.)*[125]

However, the deep civilian distrust of the new Iraqi National Police meant this effort failed to curb the violence against Sunnis—and the response of their militias against Shias. The next major coalition effort to reform the police followed the next transition of power between Iraqi governments in response to the December 15, 2005, national elections. It took almost 6 months for the political parties to agree to the appointment of Nouri al-Maliki as prime minister in May 2006. Due to political infighting, he was unable to name a new Minister of Interior until June 2006. In an effort to reform the police, Jabr was replaced as MOI by Jawad al-Bulani, who was given deputies from the Dawa, Badr, and Kurdish parties. In effect, this was an effort to establish a set of checks and balances within the MOI. Conspicuously absent was a Sunni deputy. Further reinforcing Sunni concerns about the police, Jabr did not leave government but merely moved laterally to the Ministry of Finance, where he controlled the police funding and actual payment of police salaries.[126]

In October 2006, with clear evidence the Iraqi National Police were participating in torture and murder, the United States took action. U.S. forces removed the entire 8th Brigade of the 2nd National Police Division from duty and arrested its officers. In 2007, all 9 Iraqi national police brigade commanders and 18 of 27 battalion commanders were replaced for sectarian behavior, and all national police units were retrained by Italian Carabinieri.[127] For some policemen, it was the first training they had ever received. While this represented a major effort to provide supervision and training to convert the Iraqi National Police from an armed wing of the Shiite political parties to a genuine national police force, there were still insufficient trainers to align with most Iraqi police. The violence against the Sunni population continued.

At the same time that MNSTC-I, through CPATT, was working to improve the quality of the Iraqi National Police, the long-term efforts to provide training and mentoring to other police elements began to bear fruit. By November 2006, 117 training teams had been assigned to the Iraqi Police Service, which consisted of patrol, traffic, station, and highway police who handled law enforcement in the 18 provinces. As local police, the Iraqi Police Service ethnic and religious makeup was generally representative of their communities.[128] MNSTC-I also had Police Transition Teams (PTTs), National Police Transition Teams, Border Transition Teams, and Customs and Border Support Teams mentoring the various police agencies across the country. These police transition teams were generally composed of 11 to 15 members. Three to four of the members were contractor police trainers hired by the U.S. State Department, while the rest consisted of military personnel. These teams conducted joint PTT/Iraqi Police Service patrols in order to improve the performance of the Iraqi Police Service.[129]

In conjunction with the efforts to mentor Iraqi police in the field, MNSTC-I worked to develop the institutional skills necessary for the MOI to successfully run the police forces. During 2006 and 2007, the ministry gradually assumed responsibility for personnel, logistics, finances, and internal affairs. Corruption and sectarianism created severe problems. By July 2007:

> *Iraq's MOI had become a "federation of oligarchs" with various floors of the building controlled by hostile militia groups. According to the report, police officials moved between floors protected by heavily armed bodyguards and internal power struggles were settled by assassination in the parking lot. . . . the congressionally mandated "Independent Commission on the Security Forces of Iraq" stated that Iraq's MOI was crippled*

by corruption and sectarianism, and posed the main obstacle to developing an effective police force in Iraq.[130]

The effort to build the MOI had suffered from the same tension as all advisory efforts in Iraq. Some advisors focused on getting it done for them. Others focused on helping them do it themselves. None had been able to address the underlying political infighting among the Iraqis.

Yet by December 2007, the Surge meant that DOD could report reduced levels of violence in most parts of Iraq. It could also report progress in police force generation, police operational success, and reform efforts. The MOI continued to take on more responsibility for planning, budgeting, personnel, and logistics. CPATT now fielded 247 PTTs but was still 17 percent short of requirements. CPATT focused on Baghdad, placing a PTT in every station, but in other parts of the country the ratio was as low as one PTT for seven police stations. The MOI consisted of over 370,000 personnel in the ministry, Iraqi Police Service, Iraqi National Police, and other elements. But in its quarterly report to Congress, DOD had to admit that "the Ministry remains hampered by corruption, sectarianism and logistics deficiencies."[131] While police forces continued to grow quickly, there was little political will to reform.

Progress continued in most areas over the next year. The December 2008 DOD report to Congress noted that the MOI had demonstrated improved performance in all ministerial functions—particularly planning, budgeting, and execution of the budget. It noted that despite poor performance in Basra during March and April 2008, the Iraqi Police Service improved with each subsequent operation. In addition, 18 of the 33 Iraqi National Police battalions were capable of operating with only limited coalition support. Only one battalion was rated at the lowest level. Another 13 battalions were being formed with a stated goal of one Iraqi National Police brigade per province. On the negative side, the MOI failed to coordinate its operations well with MOD.[132]

By far the most important area of improvement was in depoliticizing the MOI. In June 2006, Prime Minister Maliki replaced the highly sectarian Jabr with Jawad al-Bulani, a technocrat who worked hard for 3 years to reduce the political and actual fighting within the ministry. In 2009, the U.S. Institute of Peace (USIP) reported that he had dramatically reduced the divisiveness within the ministry while also improving its effectiveness. The key question was whether the reforms could be made permanent in order to withstand further changes in leadership or government.[133]

Even as USIP was finalizing its report, Maliki was in the process of quietly removing inspectors general in numerous Iraqi ministries. The *New York Times* reported:

> *Whatever the precise tally, the events have begun provoking accusations that Mr. Maliki, who has never been an advocate of having his government's inner workings scrutinized, might leave the posts vacant or stack them with supporters of his party, Dawa. The secrecy surrounding the moves has magnified suspicions that the government aims to cripple the oversight mechanisms put in place after the invasion.*[134]

The MOI continued to increase in strength. By October 2011, the Special Inspector General for Iraq Reconstruction reported that the Iraq police had 325,000 personnel; Facilities Protection Service, 95,000; Training and Support, 89,900; Department of Border Enforcement, 60,000; Iraq Federal Police, 45,000; the Oil Police, 31,000; and the counterterrorism force, 4,200, for a total of 650,000 police.[135]

After his 2010 reelection, Prime Minister Maliki did not reappoint Bulani but instead personally assumed the roles of Minister of Interior, Minister of Defense, and Minister of National Security. Throughout his 7-year tenure, Maliki has implemented a divide-and-conquer strategy that has neutered any credible Sunni Arab leadership. Under intensifying pressure from government forces and with dwindling faith in a political solution, many Sunni Arabs have concluded their only realistic option is a violent conflict increasingly framed in confessional terms.[136]

This partially explains the rapid advance of ISIL into the Sunni-dominated areas of western Iraq. The Iraqi military and police forces had been so thoroughly pillaged by their own corrupt leadership that they all but collapsed in spring 2015 in the face of the advancing ISIL militants, despite roughly $25 billion worth of American training and equipment over the past 10 years and far more from the Iraqi treasury. Now the pattern of corruption and patronage in the Iraqi government forces threatens to undermine a new American-led effort to drive out the extremists, even as President Barack Obama is doubling to 3,000 the number of American troops in Iraq.[137]

Training Teams

In Afghanistan, the initial advisory effort consisted of the Central Intelligence Agency and SOF teams inserted to support the Northern Alliance militias in the campaign to drive the Taliban out of Afghanistan. At this point, the advisory effort was the main effort for U.S. forces in Operation *Enduring Freedom*. Once the initial campaign was over, the emphasis shifted to operations conducted by U.S. forces. As noted earlier, initial efforts to raise Afghan forces were improvised. TF Phoenix took over training the Afghan army and was followed by OMC-A. The commanders understood the need for advisors and formed Embedded Training Teams (ETTs) to work with each kandak. The teams were initially assigned to a kandak after it completed its training cycle, but in March 2005, ETTs began to be assigned to kandaks on the first day of training.[138] When NATO became more involved in training Afghan forces, they formed NATO Operational Mentor and Liaison Teams. In time, 27 nations provided trainers to these 13- to 30-person teams, which were assigned to kandaks as well as brigade and corps headquarters.[139] Despite the international effort, the ANA never received sufficient numbers of advisors. By 2008, the GAO reported that:

> *While trainers or mentors are present in every ANA combat unit, less than half the required number are deployed in the field. Defense officials cited an insufficient number of U.S. trainers and coalition mentors in the field as the major impediment to providing the ANA with the training to establish capabilities, such as advanced combat skills and logistics, necessary to sustain the ANA force in the long term. Finally, ANA combat units report significant shortages in approximately 40 percent of critical equipment items, including vehicles, weapons, and radios. Some of these challenges, such as shortages of U.S. trainers and equipment, are due in part to competing global priorities, according to senior Defense officials. Without resolving these challenges, the ability of the ANA to reach full capability may be delayed.[140]*

In 2010, drawing on the experiences of Iraq and Afghanistan, the Secretary of Defense directed the services to develop the Afghanistan-Pakistan (AFPAK) Hands Program to improve the knowledge and continuity of the advisors who were to be assigned to Afghanistan and Pakistan. On September 3, the Chairman of the Joint Chiefs of Staff published CJCS Instruction 1630.01, directing the establishment of the program:

> *Afghanistan/Pakistan Hands: A cadre of military and civilian personnel who receive regional language, culture, and counterinsurgency (COIN) training for deployment to key billets in Afghanistan or Pakistan. APH personnel are placed in key positions where they will engage directly with Afghan and Pakistani officials and the population. Upon completion of their in-theater deployment, APH will be assigned to a key out-of-theater billet where their in-country experience will be applied to work Afghanistan or Pakistan regional issues.*[141]

AFPAK Hands proved a success. As the commanders came to understand the program, they began to request these personnel because the language, cultural, and historical training they received made them more effective advisors.[142] The program could not provide sufficient numbers of advisors for the large and rapidly growing Afghan National Security Forces, so the Services continued to improve their own programs. In 2013, as U.S. forces shifted to the advisory effort, GAO summarized how the United States had provided advisors for ANSF:

> *In addition to conducting security operations, ISAF forces have long been training and advising the ANSF both in training centers and at unit locations after they have been formed and fielded. For the U.S. contribution, DOD has used a variety of approaches to provide U.S. forces to carry out the advise and assist mission. For example, prior to 2010, the advising mission in Afghanistan was primarily conducted with transition teams. These teams did not exist as units in any of the services' force structures and were instead comprised of company and field grade officers and senior non-commissioned officers who were centrally identified and individually selected based on rank and specialty.*

As previously reported, the demand for these leaders created challenges for the services because, among other things, the leaders were generally pulled from other units or commands, which then were left to perform their missions while understaffed. In part as a means of alleviating these challenges, the Army developed the concept of augmenting brigade combat teams with specialized personnel to execute the advising mission, and began deploying these augmented brigades in 2010. In early 2012, based on requests from ISAF as part of its shift to a security force assistance mission, the U.S. Army and Marine Corps began to deploy small teams of advisors with specialized capabilities, referred to as SFA [security force assistance] advisor teams, which are located throughout Afghanistan, to work with Afghan army and police units from the headquarters to the battalion level, and advise them in areas such as command and control, intelligence, and logistics. U.S. advisor teams are under the command and control of U.S. commanders within ISAF's regional commands.[143]

In Iraq, commanders at levels from battalion to division quickly grasped the requirement to provide advisors and support to the units operating in their areas until the Iraqi ministries could mature to the point they could do the job. They did so on their own initiative starting with the Iraqi Civil Defense Corps (later redesignated as the Iraqi National Guard). For its part, the Coalition Provisional Authority integrated Iraqis into the CPA structure for running the country. Upon the CPA's departure, the coalition continued to provide civilian and military advisors at senior levels. It also attempted to provide advisory teams down to the battalion level for Iraqi forces. Since this was a wartime requirement with no corresponding peacetime force structure except for SOF, the advisors were often drawn from the units in combat. Initially drawn from the U.S. and willing coalition units in country, the advisors provided both expertise to the host-nation forces and insights to U.S. commanders on what those forces and ministries were doing. Obviously, drawing officers from U.S. units in combat was not an optimal solution. In response, the Pentagon directed the Services to build Military Training Teams to embed in Iraqi units.

Both the Army and Marine Corps had difficulty finding enough advisors to fill the team billets. While the Services occasionally carefully picked advisors (including a few screened for command positions), the mission generally fell to Reserve units. Initially, the advisors were organized into 39 10-man Advisor Support Teams that were assigned to each of the newly raised Iraqi army divisions.[144] Over time, team sizes were increased, with the Marine Corps assigning up to 40 members per team.[145] Unfortunately, these teams continued to be formed for the most part by assembling individual augmentees, who identified major problems with the program: they did not receive adequate preparation before deployment; they lacked guidance and authority; and the chain of command was rarely clear.[146]

As the Iraqi army improved, the training team focus changed from basic skills to training the Iraqis to operate independently of coalition support. As lower level units improved, the advisory focus shifted to higher level commands and critical support functions until the time of the final withdrawal of all U.S. advisory teams.

In both countries, similar efforts were made to provide advisors to the police forces. However, as noted earlier, police advisory efforts were seriously complicated by the divergence of views between military and civilian personnel concerning the proper training, equipping, and employment of police. An even greater problem was the dispersion inherent in police operations. Unlike military forces that generally functioned out of battalion or larger bases, many police were assigned to small stations spread over the entire country. While it was feasible to provide advisors to headquarters, provincial, district, and large city police stations as well as special units like the ANCOP, it was simply impossible to provide advisors to most police stations to allow close advising and joint patrolling. In response, some individual coalition combat units teamed up with local police in both theaters. Furthermore, entire deployed military police units were often tasked specifically to support the host-nation police. In short, efforts were made to provide advisors whenever possible, but police advising, by its very nature, is a much more challenging proposition than advising military forces. Police advisory efforts were therefore less effective than armed forces advisory efforts.

In both Iraq and Afghanistan, the complete destruction of the security forces institutions and infrastructure made it obvious that the newly formed security forces would need U.S. advisors and trainers. Since there was no plan to provide them for either country, initial efforts were ad hoc and took many forms. As each theater matured, the process for assigning, training, equipping, and deploying trainers became more formal. As requirements were clarified, the Services attempted to move from individual assignment/deployment to deployment as teams. Despite the clear importance of advisors to the effective functioning of host-nation forces, advisory duty was not seen as career enhancing as service with a U.S. unit. This made finding personnel for the teams even more challenging. Moreover, the presence of numerous coalition partner nations in each theater drove a requirement for significant numbers of officers and NCOs to be assigned as liaison teams between U.S. units and the coalition units operating in proximity. The liaison effort also suffered from "ad hoc–racy."

Despite major efforts by the Services and deployed units, the advisory effort never reached the required levels of personnel, often failed to match needed skills to the assigned billets, and usually failed to provide effective team training and uniform equipping prior to deployment.[147] Yet advisors had a major positive impact—and the AFPAK Hands revealed the much greater impact that could have been achieved by dedicating more resources and affording advisory efforts a higher priority.

Insights
Iraq and Afghanistan are fundamentally different societies and presented very different challenges to those trying to raise, train, and equip their security forces. However, the most important insights that can be drawn from these campaigns are the same.

Insight 1: Have a Plan
This painfully obvious lesson should not have to be stated. Yet in both campaigns, efforts to establish security forces were ad hoc. While it may have been excusable for initial plans to be based on hasty estimates and poor understandings of the societies involved as well as the threats, the fact is that in both countries, it took years before realistic plans were developed to provide appropriately sized forces.

For different reasons, in Afghanistan and Iraq there was no plan to establish host-nation security forces. When the requirement became obvious, initial plans were not well grounded in reality, resulting in a severe underestimation of the number of host-nation security forces required and an initial failure to provide sufficient personnel and resources to train even those inadequate forces. It took 18 months to get 2nd Brigade, 10th Mountain Division, to Afghanistan to start a serious training program for the army. Police training and organization have remained serious problems up to the present. In Iraq, it took months even to establish the CMATT, which was never properly manned or funded but was nonetheless suddenly assigned responsibility for police training almost a year after the invasion. In both Iraq and Afghanistan, the State Department decided to hire DynCorp to handle police training rather than requesting assistance from the U.S. Department of Justice's International Criminal Investigative Training Assistance Program, which was used to train police in Bosnia and Kosovo.

In each case, successive plans increased the number of security forces to be recruited, trained, and equipped, but resourcing never caught up with the plan. Also in each case, command and control arrangements changed frequently with the eventual assignment of all security force training to the military command.

The lack of a plan meant that the key decision—whether to keep the existing security forces and build on them or start from scratch—was not taken until after Phase III operations. In both countries, the security forces were built from the ground up—and in Iraq, this reversed a major planning assumption. At the same time, in both nations many militias remained active and outside the command of the government. The planning process must decide which elements of any existing security forces to retain and what role militias and private military companies will play. While ideally neither entity will exist, in reality the very instability that leads to outside intervention means the government has proved incapable of providing security. Inevitably, subnational communities will turn to militias to defend themselves. Many businesses and other nongovernmental organizations, both domestic and international, will have no choice but to turn to private military contractors for security. In fact, when militias were ordered disbanded, some simply reappeared as private security companies. They could not all be banned because the government simply could not provide security.

A key element of any plan must be the advise-and-assist effort. These programs require large numbers of senior officers and NCOs and thus place a disproportionate strain on the personnel resources of the services and civil organizations that provide advisors. The plan must account for providing sufficient numbers with appropriate skills and provide time to train them *before* deployment.

A final caution is that either building or improving another nation's security forces will take longer than planned.

Insight 2: Understand the Problem to Be Solved

A frequent error seen in dealing with interactively complex problems is a failure to clearly understand the real problem that has to be solved. In Iraq, initial efforts were focused on creating an army to defend the country from external enemies. This approach continued long after the insurgency was a clear and rapidly growing threat. In Afghanistan, the effort to create a centralized army and police force increased tensions between ethnic and tribal groups and the central government. In both cases, attempts to solve the wrong problem exacerbated the underlying real problem of insurgency.

The initial misunderstanding of the problem was compounded by the often repeated idea that host-nation security forces were our "ticket out." This was based on the incorrect assumption that if the United States could simply form effective security forces, it would have accomplished the mission—a fundamental misunderstanding of the political, social, and economic conditions in both countries. The key insight is that security forces are essential but insufficient.

In both theaters, a serious effort to understand the problem was long delayed. In Iraq, it was not until Petraeus took over, and in Afghanistan not until the 2008 Bush administration review, that the U.S. Government made a serious effort to understand each conflict and devise an appropriate solution. The Obama administration conducted its own review in 2009 in its attempt to understand the problem. This highlights the fact that despite major efforts to understand a complex problem, planners may still define it incorrectly. The U.S. efforts to transfer the population-centric approach used in Iraq to Afghanistan did not result in the dramatic improvements in security seen in Iraq. Bluntly stated, a flawed understanding of the political and social dynamics in Afghanistan led us to the approach of "population-centric counterinsurgency." The Afghanistan Surge did not significantly reduce the levels of violence there.[148] In both nations, failure to understand the conflict cost lives and years of effort.

Magnifying the difficulty of developing security forces is the fact that political, economic, and social conditions define what is possible in each case. The mission of the security forces can be clearly defined only after the problem is understood. The lack of clarity was most noticeable in the different approaches to police training taken by the State and Justice departments' training teams as opposed to those taken by the DOD team. But even within DOD, there was strong disagreement about the mission and hence the force structure of both the Afghan and the Iraqi armed forces. Similarly, due to a poor understanding of the actual problems in Iraq, the initial plan for the army was to build an army to fight a nonexistent external threat. Unfortunately, that army was not sufficiently organized, trained, or equipped to deal with the actual internal threat.

Insight 3: Understand that the Situation Will Change and Develop Branches and Sequels Concurrently with the Primary Plan

All insurgencies are wicked problems, the very nature of which means the problems will change as various players interact with each other. These changes often invalidate initial assumptions. Thus, a critical element of planning must be developing branches and sequels to compensate for invalid assumptions.

In each theater, the deteriorating security situation led to rapidly changing estimates of the situation and subsequent changes in planning. Each change included an increase in the proposed size and composition of the host-nation security forces. However, there is little indication that branch plans were developed to cover the eventuality that the situation would continue to worsen and larger host-nation forces would be needed. Thus, each increase had to be planned and executed from scratch.

The frequent changes led to reorganizations of the U.S. and coalition command arrangements. The confusion inherent in the constantly changing arrangements was exacerbated by the short tours of most trainers. It was difficult for the host-nation personnel to establish relationships with their coalition counterparts. Furthermore, the mix of government and contract training personnel contributed to fragmentation of coalition efforts. Finally, the training and mentoring establishments never received the number of personnel required by their tables of organization. Another complication was that personnel without the required knowledge or skill were often assigned in an effort to fill those billets.

While these problems could not have been overcome by effective branch and sequel planning, the impact could have been lessened by reducing the time needed to respond to each change.

Insight 4: Understand the Culture That Drives the Societies in Conflict

Coalition efforts in both nations seemed to be based on the idea of a two-sided conflict—the government versus the insurgents. The reality in both cases was much more complex. Ethnic, political, religious, institutional, and cultural differences drove much of both conflicts. Coalition failure to understand these underlying factors dramatically reduced the effectiveness of counterinsurgency efforts because the coalition failed to establish political structures appropriate for the individual nations.

In fact, the historical record of outsiders overcoming deep ethnic, religious, and cultural schisms within any society is poor. This is not a new factor, nor should it have been a surprise. In both nations, the United States attempted to build ethnically balanced national security forces. In both nations, there was great resistance to this idea. In Afghanistan, we still have not succeeded in enlisting sufficient southern and eastern Pashtun to balance the force ethnically. While the April 2014 DOD *Report on Progress Toward Security and Stability in Afghanistan* shows the ANA has succeeded in recruiting Pashtuns in proportion to the population,[149] other sources note that most of the Pashtuns have been recruited from the north and that the southern and eastern Pashtun remain severely under-represented[150] and even viewed as outsiders because they cannot speak the local version of Pashtu.[151] This is a particular problem since most of the security incidents occur in the south and east.

In Iraq, shortly after our departure, Maliki began transforming the army and national police into Shiite-dominated forces that answered to him. Again, neither development should be surprising. In the past, decades of outside rule have been required to create the national institutions that can manage sectarian and ethnic tensions (think India). Understanding the impact of these issues requires a major effort during the initial phase of understanding the problem. Failure to do so will often result in outsiders taking actions that magnify rather than reduce those problems.

Any proposed solution must be functional within the cultural context in which it must operate. In both nations, the United States selected courses of action that were not appropriate to those cultures. A Joint and Coalition Operation Analysis report noted that the planned endstates were based largely on U.S. expectations instead of those consistent with the host nation and mission. For example, the planned endstate for Afghanistan was envisioned as a strong central government, despite only one instance of such a government in Afghan history—the extremely repressive rule of Amir Abdul Rahman Khan from 1880 to 1901—and a lack of broad popular support for that system of governance.[152] Despite this history, the Afghans at the Bonn Conference chose to adopt the 1964 Afghan constitution. Subsequent actions indicate the Hamid Karzai government assumed that Afghanistan could best be ruled by a central government with the power to reach into every district in the nation. This assumption, questionable at best, drove the structure, training, and organization of the MOD, MOI, and the security forces themselves. In a highly decentralized, multiethnic, multicultural, multi-religious society, security forces of the central government, especially those from a different group, are often distrusted and actively resisted.

At the Loya Jirga, Karzai sought a government based on the Afghan constitution of 1964. The Loya Jirga supported him. The constitution envisioned an Afghanistan with a Western-style justice system and planned to develop the police accordingly. Unfortunately, in 2002 Afghanistan lacked almost all elements of a Western justice system—and thus the initial concept for policing was severely flawed. Without effective courts and prisons to include sufficient numbers of trained judges, lawyers, clerks, corrections officers, and other personnel, police can function only as a poorly trained and equipped paramilitary security force.

In Iraq, the United States failed to understand the depth of the hostility between the Shiite and Sunni communities. In creating a highly centralized security force, it created a force that Maliki could control and use to suppress Sunni political participation in the government of Iraq.

Perhaps the single most challenging cultural problem in both nations was corruption—as the West understands it. Almost every after action report noted corruption as siphoning off a major portion of resources as well as placing unqualified personnel in key billets from district to national levels. The problem, of course, is figuring out what is considered corruption in the specific culture and what is considered greasing the wheels or a moral obligation to take care of family. In both countries, the reality remains that without the exchange of funds or favors, projects do not get completed. Clearly, we will have to deal with corruption in future efforts. However, we must understand what represents wasteful corruption and what represents necessary transactions or even moral obligations for that society. We should remember that while we may abhor contractors offering money to government officials to procure contracts, an outsider might think the U.S. lobbying system looks remarkably similar. Money is paid to a lobbyist or directly to an election campaign, and certain laws or programs are approved.

One of the cultures we must take into account is our own. For instance, DOD planning culture is based around accomplishing a mission. It assumes that there is a solution for the problem and that the solution can be expressed as an essentially linear plan. Unfortunately, both Iraq and Afghanistan are distinctly nonlinear, interactively complex problems. Thus, the first and most difficult step should have been to define the problem we were trying to solve and then develop an agreed-upon solution. Instead, U.S. decisionmakers made flawed assumptions about both countries and leapt immediately into military planning. Not surprisingly, in both countries the U.S. understanding of the situation was slow to develop and then changed frequently. It was not until 2007 that the Office of the Secretary of Defense even openly stated that Iraq was an insurgency/civil war. From this understanding, it devised the Surge that led to a dramatic decrease in violence. While some may question the Surge's long-term impact, there is no question it provided the Iraqis with breathing space to reach a political solution. The fact that they fell back to sectarian violence several years after the departure of U.S. forces does not alter this observation.

Another U.S. cultural requirement is a senior sponsor for host-nation security forces. Ensuring sufficient resourcing from the Pentagon requires the personal attention of a four-star officer. Throughout both wars, training security forces was not a mission the U.S. Armed Forces were organized, trained, or equipped well to execute. They were even less prepared to establish the necessary civilian defense institutions to manage and supervise those forces. Thus, the U.S. defense bureaucracy had to be forced to do something alien. Any attempt to force a bureaucracy to execute a function outside its design requires senior leaders with the ability to force not only their organization but also others to respond quickly to rapidly changing events. (Recall the lack of progress in fielding Mine-Resistant Ambush Protected vehicles until very senior DOD officials took personal interest.) It was not until the security forces programs in both nations got this level of attention that resource shortages were alleviated. Unfortunately, particularly for police programs, personnel shortages were never really solved.

The U.S. Government has a tendency to default to police as the "frontline" in any counterinsurgency operation. This tendency was heavily reinforced in the 2006 edition of Field Manual 3-24, *Counterinsurgency*. Unfortunately, doctrinal attitudes about the police role in counterinsurgency are based heavily on British experiences. In the primary cases—Malaya and Northern Ireland—Britain was the governing power and had spent centuries establishing the British system of policing and justice. Thus, police were culturally less threatening than army personnel to the native populations. However, in many parts of the world, the police are the most oppressive and corrupt element of the host-nation government.

As noted earlier, the Iraqi police were the bottom of the barrel of Saddam's security forces. Corrupt, hated, and trained only to enforce fear of the government, these were the people to which the United States first gave weapons and put back on the street with authority to use deadly force in its name. In Afghanistan, various militia commanders simply declared their own people to be the police force. A fundamental lesson is that the police are not the default security force in a counterinsurgency. The United States should field and support police forces only in those areas where they are culturally appropriate. They may not be appropriate nationwide. While police may be seen as legitimate in better developed urban areas, they may be seen as a force of government oppression in rural areas.

Insight 5: Structure Ministries and Forces Appropriate to the Problem and the Societies in Conflict

In both countries, the United States developed ministries and forces modeled on U.S. institutions. The political, economic, and social (cultural) conditions of these countries made U.S. approaches problematic and unsustainable without a significant U.S. presence. Compounding the problem was a failure to understand that the actual organization and functioning of the ministries of defense and interior are inevitably tied to the political and social structures of the host nations. This was particularly damaging since ministerial development is both more critical and much more difficult than fielding forces. In both countries, the coalition attempted to establish apolitical, merit-based technocratic ministries. The domestic political situations and vicious conflicts within the governments meant this was an unattainable goal. The rapid takeover of the Iraqi ministries by Shiite militants illustrates the fact that structures designed and imposed by outsiders are unlikely to sustain themselves in this type of political climate.

This fact dramatically complicates any advisory effort. U.S. advisors can only train what they know, so advisors must be educated in different ways to organize ministries and forces before they deploy. If U.S. advisors are to assist existing ministries and forces, it is also essential they understand those organizations and their cultures prior to deploying. Planners should assume developing and executing such a program—to include basic language training—will take at least a year. If advisory tours remain 1 year in length, this will effectively double the personnel requirement for advisory efforts.

From the outset, any program to raise, train, and equip a host-nation security force must be focused on how it must function after the departure of the United States. Unfortunately, in both countries, the United States attempted to build a national security enterprise modeled on its own. This was particularly visible in how we organized and trained the armed forces. Like all militaries, the U.S. Armed Forces are the product of unique historical and cultural conditions. The success of U.S. forces is heavily attributed to both technology and NCO leadership. Naturally, we sought to inculcate both those values into the Iraqi and Afghan forces. Yet in both cultures, the concept of someone who is socially and militarily inferior to another providing instruction, correction, and honest advice to his social or military superior is an alien concept. While a professional NCO corps has been essential to the success of the U.S. military, it has been neither necessary nor desired in other successful militaries. In the same vein, U.S. forces seek a technological edge—even at the expense of much greater training and maintenance requirements. A typical example was the selection of the G222 transport aircraft for the Afghan air force. While this aircraft met a definite Afghan need for in-theater airlift, its complexity was simply more than the Afghans could manage. As a result, despite a purchase price of $486 million for 20 aircraft, all eventually were sold for scrap for $32,000 total.[153]

An integral and perhaps the most important part of any plan to build another nation's security forces are command relationships. In both theaters, responsibility and command relationships for the vital mission of host-nation security forces started as ad hoc arrangements. In both theaters, the early frequent changes in host-nation civilian governments inevitably led to changes in the host-nation personnel responsible for security. In Afghanistan, constantly changing relationships between the national commanders and ambassadors for coalition members, NATO command, and U.S. command caused confusion and delays.

In both Iraq and Afghanistan, coalition trainers showed remarkable creativity and tenacity in trying to build armed forces in the image of the United States. However, trying to impose a merit-based, technologically savvy, equipment-intensive approach onto societies where relationships and social standing have a heavy bearing on organizational behavior proved a bridge too far.

One of the biggest shortcomings of the MOI and police training programs was the imbalance of resources between police and other elements necessary for a legal system. Police are only one piece of the rule of law. Without effective courts, court administrators, and prison systems, police operations have little effect. In both nations, U.S., coalition, and host-nation security personnel frequently expressed frustration over the fact that those they arrested were often released in a matter of hours. While these releases were at times legitimate, they were often tied to corruption or incompetence in the rest of the legal system. If there is not an effective method for trying and imprisoning violators, then the Western concept of policing simply will not work.

Both police training programs were further hampered by the confusing U.S. legal authorities concerning training police overseas. In an effort to prevent perceived abuses such as torture and extrajudicial executions by U.S.-trained police in the 1950s through the 1970s, Congress passed laws restricting how U.S. support could be provided to overseas police. Given the continuing need for police training globally, Congress included a long list of exceptions to permit subsequent police training to be funded. In the intervening decades, executive branch officials have had to be creative to work around those restrictions in Somalia, Iraq, and Afghanistan. Yet no matter how creative the work-around, the result was less than ideal. These restrictive laws still exist and will be the starting point for any future police training program. To date, they have prevented the United States from developing a coherent international police assistance program and instead force ad hoc programs to be developed each time the need arises.

In both Iraq and Afghanistan, we found ourselves fighting a well-equipped, aggressive insurgency. Yet we initially built police forces appropriate for community policing in an essentially pacified area. In both nations, there were locations where such police were appropriate, but for the most part we failed to match police training, equipment, and structure to the tactical situation they faced. In fact, we consistently sent police to stations in contested or insurgent-controlled areas that infantry forces could not hold. The inevitable result was that police suffered much higher casualty rates than either indigenous or foreign military forces. It is essential that appropriate security conditions are established *before* assigning community police. If the situation is too dangerous for police to operate effectively, security must be provided by military or at least paramilitary police units until security conditions improve.

Insight 6: Develop Effective, Accurate, and Appropriate Metrics to Inform Senior Decisionmakers

U.S. military culture combines two factors that reinforce each other and negatively affect metrics programs. First, the Services enforce short tours. Almost all after action reports from Vietnam highlighted the short tour as a major deficiency. Many noted that "the U.S. didn't have 10 years of experience in Vietnam. It has one year's experience ten times." In Iraq and Afghanistan, 1 year was considered a long tour, with many units spending only 6 months in country and individual staff offices on tours as short as 3 months. Thus, planners should assume the Services will not impose long tours in future conflicts.

Short tours reinforce the second issue, which is optimistic reporting. British ambassador Sherard Cowper-Coles noted, "the military system of six-month combat tours seemed intentionally designed to compel officials to produce overly positive assessments. The pattern was always the same. At the beginning of each tour, the newly arrived commander would declare the situation grave. He would then implement a new short-term plan, which he would declare a success."[154]

To be fair, the short tours prevented a commander from gaining a deep understanding of his area of operations. Thus, it was natural that he would be uncertain at the beginning of a tour but gain confidence as his relatively superficial understanding of the situation increased. And of course, the vast majority of successful military commanders are optimists by nature. Yet another element of military culture reinforced the normal optimism of a successful officer: the fitness report as commander in combat would be one of the most important of an officer's career and would be influenced heavily by his own reporting of success or failure in his area. Thus, institutional approaches drove commanders to overly optimistic reporting.

Despite these contradictions, metrics were considered central to the U.S. command's understanding of the fight in both theaters. The United States dedicated a great deal of effort to developing an effective set of metrics to allow commanders to understand the situation on the ground and track changes. Yet as Lieutenant General Daniel Bolger, USA (Ret.), notes, "The problem with numbers in Afghanistan related to the overall difficulty of combat reporting. All the computers and spreadsheets on earth couldn't change that basic old rule: garbage in, garbage out."[155]

The lack of language skills, short tours, enforced optimism, and sheer complexity of the political, social, and economic environment made accurate measurement nearly impossible. Bolger's observation is strongly supported by Ben Connable's deeply researched *Embracing the Fog of War: Assessment and Metrics in Counterinsurgency*, which revealed the fatal flaws in the system ISAF used to track progress in the campaign and the ANSF.[156] This problem is not new. Similar reports concerning the Hamlet Evaluation System in Vietnam questioned the reliability of the data collected there. The optimistic reporting was partially responsible for General William Westmoreland's 1967 declaration that there was "light at the end of the tunnel," just before the Tet Offensive exploded across Vietnam.[157]

The durability of this problem is reflected by the wide discrepancy between the generally optimistic reports from the Pentagon and the often pessimistic reports from GAO, CRS, and other independent organizations. Yet the fact remains that metrics have been a major factor in political and military decisions in wars such as these. It is critical that an effective method for determining, reporting, and interpreting metrics be developed. As always, the most difficult metrics will be those involving intangibles such as quality of the force. In both theaters, the number of trained and fielded forces was closely monitored. In both, the commanders struggled with evaluating the quality of the forces and the quality of the interior and defense ministries.

Conclusion

No serious plans for indigenous forces had been prepared for either Afghanistan or Iraq. The mission to create those forces was assigned to ad hoc organizations that, despite herculean efforts, were constantly behind the power curve. For the first few years, each plan was overcome by events before it was even approved and resourced. Even when the emphasis shifted to indigenous forces, the training commands and Embedded Training Teams remained well understrength. Furthermore, the personnel system never really adjusted to either place people with the right backgrounds into the commands or to provide time to assemble, properly train, and then deploy the Embedded Training Teams as units.

The primary highlight of the entire training effort was the ingenuity, adaptability, courage, and persistence of the personnel assigned. Working against incredible handicaps, not the least of which was trying to create forces that mirror-imaged those of the West, they succeeded in raising, training, equipping, and deploying major security forces. The relative success or failure of those forces rests with the political leadership of the host nations and the continued provision of resources for those forces to operate according to the organization and training they received.

Notes

[1] Richard N. Haass, *War of Necessity, War of Choice: A Memoir of Two Iraq Wars* (New York: Simon & Schuster, 2009), 198.

[2] Bob Woodward, *Bush at War* (London: Pocket Books, 2004), 300.

[3] United Nations Security Council Resolution 1368 (September 12, 2001), available at <www.refworld.org/cgi-in/texis/vtx/rwmain?docid=3c4e94557>.

[4] Combined Security Transition Command–Afghanistan (CSTC-A), "United States Plan

for Sustaining the Afghanistan National Security Forces, June 2008," 5, available at <www.defense.gov/pubs/united_states_plan_for_sustaining_the_afghanistan_national_security_forces_1231.pdf>.

[5] Tim Bird and Alex Marshall, *Afghanistan: How the West Lost Its Way* (New Haven: Yale University Press, 2011), 119.

[6] "Interview with Lieutenant General Karl Eikenberry," in *Eyewitness to War Volume III: U.S. Army Advisors in Afghanistan*, ed. Michael G. Brooks (Fort Leavenworth, KS: Combat Studies Institute Press, 2009).

[7] Ibid., 40.

[8] Lorenzo Striuli and Fernando Termentini, "Afghanistan: Disarmament, Demobilization and Reintegration," Rome, Analisi e Ricerche Geopoliticiche sull'Oriente, Osservatoria sull'Asia minor, central e meridionale, September 2008, available at <www.argoriente.it>.

[9] Government Accountability Office (GAO), *Afghanistan Security: Efforts to Establish Army and Police Have Made Progress, but Future Plans Need to Be Better Defined* (Washington, DC: GAO, June 2005), 6.

[10] Bird and Marshall, 114.

[11] Interview with Mike Milley, in *Eyewitness to War Volume III*, 95–111.

[12] Robert B. Oakley and T.X. Hammes, *Securing Afghanistan: Entering a Make-or-Break Phase?* INSS Strategic Forum 205 (Washington, DC: NDU Press, March 2004), 4.

[13] GAO, *Afghanistan Security: Efforts*, 3.

[14] Ibid., 15.

[15] Frederick Rice, "Afghanistan Unit Takes on New Mission, Name," American Forces Press Service, July 13, 2005, available at <www.defense.gov/news/newsarticle.aspx?id=16650>.

[16] GAO, *Securing, Stabilizing, and Reconstructing Afghanistan: Key Issues for Congressional Oversight* (Washington, DC: GAO, May 2007), 13.

[17] North Atlantic Treaty Organization (NATO), *Progress in Afghanistan: Bucharest Summit 2–4 April 2008* (Brussels: NATO Public Diplomacy Division, 2008), 4, available at <www.isaf.nato.int/pdf/progress_afghanistan_2008.pdf>.

[18] GAO, *Afghanistan Security: Further Congressional Action May Be Needed to Ensure Completion of a Detailed Plan to Develop and Sustain Capable Afghan National Security Forces* (Washington, DC: GAO, June 2008, 3).

[19] CSTC-A, 6.

[20] Ibid., 4.

[21] NATO, *Progress in Afghanistan*, 8.

[22] National Defence and the Canadian Armed Forces, "NATO Training Mission-Afghanistan," available at <www.forces.gc.ca/en/operations-supporting-docs/ntm-a.page>.

[23] NATO, "NATO Training Mission–Afghanistan," April 4, 2009, available at <www.nato.int/cps/en/natolive/news_52802.htm>.

[24] Stanley A. McChrystal, "COMISAF's Initial Assessment," August 30, 2009, 2–4, available at <www2.gwu.edu/~nsarchiv/NSAEBB/NSAEBB292/Assessment_Redacted_092109.pdf>.

[25] Ibid., 2–15.

[26] Office of the Special Inspector General for Afghanistan Reconstruction (SIGAR), *Actions Needed to Improve the Reliability of Afghan Security Force Assessments* (Arlington, VA: SIGAR, June 29, 2010), 2, available at <www.sigar.mil/pdf/audits/2010-06-29audit-10-11.pdf>.

[27] International Crisis Group (ICG), "A Force in Fragments: Reconstituting the Afghan National Army," Asia Report 190, May 12, 2010, ii.

[28] GAO, *Afghanistan: Key Issues for Congressional Oversight* (Washington, DC: GAO, April 2009), 20, available at <www.gao.gov/new.items/d09473sp.pdf>.

[29] ICG, "A Force in Fragments," 17.

[30] Statement of Lieutenant General William B. Caldwell IV, USA, to the Committee on Oversight and Government Reform Subcommittee on National Security, Homeland Defense, and Foreign Operations, September 12, 2012, 2–3, available at <http://oversight.house.gov/wp-content/uploads/2012/09/Caldwell-Testimony.pdf>.

[31] Jack Kem (Deputy to the Commander, NATO Training Mission–Afghanistan), interview by Greg Bruno, "Long Road Ahead for Afghan Security Forces," *CFR.org*, August 17, 2010, available at <www.cfr.org/afghanistan/long-road-ahead-afghan-security-forces/p22805>.

[32] Department of Defense (DOD), *Report on Progress Toward Security and Stability in Afghanistan* (Washington, DC: DOD, November 2010), 31, available at <www.defense.gov/pubs/november_1230_report_Final.pdf>.

[33] Thomas Barfield, *Afghanistan: A Cultural and Political History* (Princeton: Princeton University Press, 2010), 24.

[34] Cheryl Pellerin, "Afghan Security Forces Grow in Numbers, Quality," American Forces Press Service, May 23, 2011, available at <www.defense.gov//news/newsarticle.aspx?id=64044>.

[35] Kenneth Katzman, *Afghanistan: Post-Taliban Governance, Security, and U.S. Policy*, RL30588 (Washington, DC: Congressional Research Service, October 9, 2014), 27–28, available at <http://fas.org/sgp/crs/row/RL30588.pdf>.

[36] GAO, *Afghanistan Security: Long-standing Challenges May Affect Progress and Sustainment of Afghan National Security Forces* (Washington, DC: GAO, July 24, 2012), 2.

[37] Ibid., 8–9.

[38] Ibid., 6.

[39] GAO, *Afghanistan: Key Oversight Issues* (Washington, DC: GAO, February 2013), 20.

[40] "NATO-led Resolute Support Mission in Afghanistan," *Security-Risks.com*, November 29, 2014, available at <www.security-risks.com/security-trends-south-asia/afghanistan/nato-led-resolute-support-mission-in-afghanistan-3920.html>.

[41] UN Assistance Mission in Afghanistan (UNAMA), *Afghanistan: Midyear Report 2014: Protection of Civilians in Armed Conflict* (Kabul: UNAMA, July 2014), available at <http://unama.unmissions.org/LinkClick.aspx?fileticket=m_XyrUQD-KZg%3d&tabid=12254&mid=15756&language=en-US>.

[42] Sudarsan Raghaven, "Taliban Brings War to Afghan Capital, Threatening Stability and Endangering Foreigners," *Washington Post*, November 30, 2014, available at <www.washingtonpost.com/world/asia_pacific/in-afghanistan-taliban-fighters-attack-foreign-compound-in-capital/2014/11/29/f0aef902-77d4-11e4-a755-e32227229e7b_story.html>.

[43] Andrew Wilder, *Cops or Robbers? The Struggle to Reform the Afghan National Police*, Issue Paper Series (Kabul: Afghanistan Research and Evaluation Unit, July 2007), vi, available at <www.areu.org.af/Uploads/EditionPdfs/717E-Cops%20or%20Robbers-IP-print.pdf>.

[44] "Summary of the Afghan National Police," Program for Culture and Conflict Studies, Naval Postgraduate School, available at <www.nps.edu/programs/ccs/National/ANP.html>.

[45] GAO, *Afghanistan Security: Efforts*, 8.

[46] David H. Bayley and Robert M. Perito, *The Police in War: Fighting Insurgency, Terrorism, and Violent Crime* (Boulder, CO: Lynne Rienner, 2010), 112.

[47] Peter C. Kratcoski and Dilip K. Das, eds., *Police Education and Training in a Global Society* (Plymouth, UK: Lexington, 2007), 10, 192.

[48] GAO, *Afghanistan Security: Efforts*, 19.

[49] Wilder, 11–13.

[50] "Summary of the Afghan National Police."

[51] European Union External Action, "What is EUPOL Afghanistan?" available at <www.eupol-afg.eu>.

[52] CSTC-A, 4.

[53] "Afghan National Police," Institute for the Study of War, available at <www.understandingwar.org/afghan-national-police-anp >.

[54] James L. Jones and Thomas R. Pickering, co-chairs, *Revitalizing our Efforts, Rethinking our Strategies*, Afghan Study Group Report, 2nd ed. (Washington, DC: Center for the Study of the Presidency, January 30, 2008), 34. Emphasis in original.

[55] GAO, *Afghanistan Security: U.S. Efforts to Develop Capable Afghan Police Forces Face Challenges and Need a Coordinated, Detailed Plan to Help Ensure Accountability* (Washington, DC: GAO, June 18, 2008).

[56] Brummet, 13.

[57] Jones and Pickering.

[58] Transparency International, Corruption Perceptions Index 2013, available at <www.transparency.org/cpi2013/results>.

[59] McChrystal, 2–15.

[60] Spencer Ackerman, "Mercs Win Billion Dollar Afghan Cop Deal. Again." *Wired.com*, December 21, 2010, available at <www.wired.com/2010/12/controversial-firm-snags-another-billion-dollar-afghan-police-deal/>.

[61] Robert M. Perito, "Afghanistan's Police: The Weak Link in Security Sector Reform," U.S. Institute of Peace Special Report, Washington, DC, August 2009, 2, available at <www.usip.org/sites/default/files/afghanistan_police.pdf>.

[62] Royal United Services Institute and Foreign Policy Research Institute (FPRI), *Reforming the Afghan National Police* (Philadelphia: FPRI, n.d.), i, available at <www.fpri.org/docs/ReformingAfghanNationalPolice.pdf>.

[63] Perito, "Afghanistan's Police," 1.

[64] Michelle Hughes, "The Afghan National Police in 2015 and Beyond," U.S. Institute of Peace, Washington, DC, May 2014, 2, available at <www.usip.org/sites/default/files/SR346_The_Afghan_National_Police_in_2015_and_Beyond.pdf>.

[65] Missy Ryan, "Afghan Police Problems Cited," *Washington Post*, January 12, 2015, A14.

[66] Human Rights Watch, *Afghanistan: "Just Don't Call It a Militia"—Impunity, Militias, and the "Afghan Local Police"* (New York: Human Rights Watch, September 2011), 15, available at <www.hrw.org/sites/default/files/reports/afghanistan0911webwcover_0.pdf>.

[67] David Axe, "NATO Cancel Afghan Cop Program," *Wired.com*, April 10, 2008, <www.wired.com/2008/04/nato-cancels-af>.

[68] Human Rights Watch.

[69] Daniel Glickstein and Michael Spangler, "Reforming the Afghan Security Forces," *Parameters* 44, no. 3 (Autumn 2014), 101.

[70] Margherita Stancati, "Left Unmoored, Afghan Local Police Pose New Risk," *Wall Street Journal*, March 24, 2014, available at <http://online.wsj.com/articles/SB10001424052702304679404579459270523670760>.

[71] GAO, *U.S. Programs to Further Reform the Ministry of Interior and National Police Challenged by Lack of Military Personnel and Afghan Cooperation* (Washington, DC: GAO, March 2009), 11.

[72] DOD, *Report on Progress Toward Security and Stability in Afghanistan* (Washington, DC: DOD, December 2012), 53, available at <www.defense.gov/news/1230_Report_final.pdf>.

[73] William Rosenau, *Acknowledging Limits: Police Advisors and Counterinsurgency in Afghanistan* (Alexandria, VA: Center for Naval Analyses; Quantico, VA: Marine Corps Uni-

versity Press, 2011), 95, available at <www.cna.org/sites/default/files/research/Police%20 Mentor_Layout%204.pdf>.

[74] Declan Walsh, "Powerful Afghan Police Chief Puts Fear in Taliban and Their Enemies," *New York Times*, November 1, 2014.

[75] Wilder, x.

[76] Civil Military Fusion Center, "Corruption and Anti-Corruption Issues in Afghanistan," February 2012, 6; Transparency International.

[77] Thomas Ruttig, "Some Things Got Better—How Much Got Good?" Afghanistan Analysts Network, December 30, 2013, available at <www.afghanistan-analysts.org/some-things-got-better-how-much-got-good-a-short-review-of-12-years-of-international-intervention-in-afghanistan>.

[78] Terri Barriere, "New automated personnel management system unveiled," NATO Afghanistan–Resolute Support, RS News, available at <www.rs.nato.int/article/news/new-automated-personnel-management-system-unveiled.html>.

[79] Hughes.

[80] Bryan Rahija, "Woes Continue for Afghan National Police Training Program," The Project on Government Oversight, August 18, 2011, available at <http://pogoblog.typepad.com/pogo/2011/08/woes-continue-for-afghan-national-police-training-program.html>.

[81] DynCorp, "DynCorp International Awarded Afghan Training and Mentoring Contracts," January 8, 2015, available at <www.dyn-intl.com/news-events/press-release/dyncorp-international-awarded-afghan-training-and-mentoring-contracts/>.

[82] DOD, *Report on Progress Toward Security and Stability in Afghanistan* (Washington, DC: DOD, April 2014), 5, available at <www.defense.gov/pubs/April_1230_Report_Final.pdf>.

[83] Ibid., 27.

[84] Katzman, 27–28.

[85] Ibid., 27.

[86] DOD, *Report on Progress Toward Security and Stability in Afghanistan* (Washington, DC: DOD, October 2013), 48.

[87] SIGAR, *High Risk List* (Arlington, VA: SIGAR, December 2014), 1, available at <www.sigar.mil/pdf/spotlight/High-Risk_List.pdf>.

[88] "Afghanistan: So long, good luck," *The Economist*, November 29, 2014, 36.

[89] North Atlantic Treaty Organization, "Resolute Support Mission in Afghanistan," February 27, 2015, available at <www.nato.int/cps/en/natohq/topics_113694.htm>.

[90] Paul Eaton, interview by T.X. Hammes, October 14, 2014.

[91] Author's personal experience when serving with the Coalition Military Assistance Transition Team in 2004.

[92] Ibid.

[93] Frederick Kienle, "Creating an Iraqi Army from Scratch: Lessons for the Future," American Enterprise Institute, May 25, 2007, 2, available at <www.aei.org/publication/creating-an-iraqi-army-from-scratch/>.

[94] Eaton, interview.

[95] Kienle, 2.

[96] Ibid.

[97] Eaton, interview.

[98] National Security Policy Directive 36, "United States Government Operations in Iraq," May 11, 2004, 2, available at <http://fas.org/irp/offdocs/nspd/nspd051104.pdf>.

[99] George W. Casey, Jr., *Strategic Reflections: Operation* Iraqi Freedom *July 2004–February 2007* (Washington, DC: NDU Press, 2012), 1–3.

[100] Ibid., 39.

[101] DOD, *Measuring Stability and Security in Iraq* (Washington, DC: DOD, February 2006), 3–4, available at <www.defense.gov/home/features/Iraq_Reports/docs/2006-02-Report.pdf>.

[102] Ibid., 27.

[103] DOD, *Measuring Stability and Security in Iraq* (Washington, DC: DOD, November 2006), 31, available at <www.defense.gov/pubs/pdfs/9010Quarterly-Report-20061216.pdf>.

[104] Ibid., 58.

[105] Ibid., 31.

[106] Ibid., 32.

[107] Ibid., 30–31.

[108] Andrea R. So, "A Multi-National Security Transition Command-Iraq Status Report," Institute for the Study of War, Georgetown University, June 20, 2008, 2.

[109] "Timeline: The Iraq Surge, Before and After," *The Washington Post,* available at <www.washingtonpost.com/wp-srv/nation/thegamble/timeline>.

[110] DOD, *Measuring Stability and Security in Iraq* (Washington, DC: DOD, December 2008), iv.

[111] Ibid., 31.

[112] Ibid., 31–32.

[113] Ibid., viii–ix.

[114] David Zucchina, "Iraq Troops Doubt Own Army Despite U.S. Training, Aid," *Los Angeles Times*, November 3, 2014, A1.

[115] Ibid.

[116] Loveday Morris, "50,000 'ghost soldiers' found in Iraq's army," *Washington Post*, December 1, 2004, A14.

[117] Robert M. Perito, "The Iraqi Federal Police: U.S. Police Building under Fire," U.S. Institute of Peace, October 2011, 2, available at <www.usip.org/sites/default/files/SR291_The_Iraq_Federal_Police.pdf>.

[118] Bruce R. Pirnie and Edward O'Connell, *Counterinsurgency in Iraq, 2003–2006* (Santa Monica, CA: RAND, 2008), 49.

[119] Ibid., 49–50.

[120] Robert Perito, "Policing Iraq: Protecting Iraqis from Criminal Violence," U.S. Institute of Peace, June 2006, 2, available at <www.usip.org/publications/policing-iraq-protecting-iraqis-criminal-violence>.

[121] William H. McMichael, "Retired Civilian Police Officer Praises Troops, Slams U.S. Government Planning," *Army Times*, May 7, 2007.

[122] Perito, "The Iraqi Federal Police," 4–5.

[123] D. J. Elliott, "Training the Iraqi National Police," *The Long War Journal,* July 3, 2007, available at <www.longwarjournal.org/archieves/2007/07/iraqi_national_police.php>.

[124] Perito, "The Iraqi Federal Police," 5–6.

[125] DOD, *Measuring Stability and Security in Iraq*, November 2006, 33.

[126] Perito, "The Iraqi Federal Police," 7.

[127] John J. Kruzel, "Reform, Training Initiatives Improve Iraq's National Police," American Forces Press Service, October 31, 2007.

[128] DOD, *Measuring Stability and Security in Iraq* (Washington, DC: DOD, March 2007), 32, available at <www.defense.gov/pubs/pdfs/9010_March_2007_Final_Signed.pdf>.

[129] DOD, *Measuring Stability and Security in Iraq,* November 2006, 32–33.

[130] Robert Perito and Madeline Kristoff, "Iraq's Interior Ministry: The Key to Police Reform," U.S. Institute of Peace, July 2009, 1.

[131] DOD, *Measuring Stability and Security in Iraq* (Washington, DC: DOD, March 2007), 34, available at <www.defense.gov/pubs/pdfs/9010_March_2007_Final_Signed.pdf>.

[132] DOD, *Measuring Stability and Security in Iraq*, December 2008, 32–42.

[133] Perito and Kristoff, 3.

[134] James Glanz and Riyahd Mohammed, "Premier Is Quietly Firing Fraud Monitors," *New York Times,* November 17, 2008, available at <www.nytimes.com/2008/11/18/world/middleeast/18maliki.html?=&_r=1&>.

[135] Special Inspector General for Iraq Reconstruction (SIGIR), *Quarterly Report to the United States Congress* (Arlington, VA: SIGIR, October 30, 2011), 54, available at <http://

cybercemetery.unt.edu/archive/sigir/20131001093855/http://www.sigir.mil/files/quarter-lyreports/October2011/Report_-_October_2011.pdf>.

[136] ICG, "Make or Break: Iraq's Sunnis and the State," Middle East Report No. 144, August 14, 2013, i–ii, available at <www.crisisgroup.org/~/media/files/middle%20east%20 north%20africa/iraq%20syria%20lebanon/iraq/144-make-or-break-iraq-s-sunnis-and-the-state.pdf>.

[137] David D. Kirkpatrick, "Graft Hobbles Iraq's Military in Fighting ISIS," *New York Times*, November 23, 2014, available at <www.nytimes.com/2014/11/24/world/middleeast/graft-hobbles-iraqs-military-in-fighting-isis.html?ref=world&_r=1>.

[138] Mirtha Villarreal, "Embedded Training Teams Making History in Afghanistan," DOD News, March 21, 2005, available at <www.defense.gov/News/NewsArticle.aspx-?ID=31140>.

[139] NATO Headquarters Brussels, "Fact Sheet: NATO's Operational Mentor and Liaison Teams (OMLTs) October 2009," available at <www.nato.int/isaf/topics/factsheets/om-lt-factsheet.pdf>.

[140] GAO, *Afghanistan Security: Further Congressional Action May Be Needed*, 3.

[141] Chairman of the Joint Chiefs of Staff Instruction 1630.01, "Afghanistan/Pakistan Hands (APH) Program," September 3, 2010, 2, available at <http://citeseerx.ist.psu.edu/viewdoc/download;jsessionid=955C05A775806BB20F6B6906A1698E1B?-doi=10.1.1.366.4268&rep=rep1&type=pdf>.

[142] Steven Heffington, "AFPAK to APAC Hands: Lessons Learned," *War on the Rocks*, January 7, 2014, available at <http://warontherocks.com/2014/01/afpak-to-apac-hands-lessons-learned/?singlepage=1>.

[143] GAO, *Security Force Assistance: More Detailed Planning and Improved Access to Information Needed to Guide Efforts of Advisor Teams in Afghanistan* (Washington, DC: GAO, April 2013), 3–4, available at <www.gao.gov/assets/660/654289.pdf>.

[144] William Rosenau et al., *United States Marine Corps Advisors: Past, Present, and Future* (Alexandria, VA: Center for Naval Analyses, August 2013), 37, available at <www.hqmc.marines.mil/Portals/138/Hip%20Pocket%20Briefs/CNA,%20USMC%20Advisors%20 Aug2013.pdf>.

[145] Ibid., 40.

[146] Ibid., 46–49.

[147] GAO, *Iraq and Afghanistan: Actions Needed to Enhance the Ability of Army Brigades to Support the Advisory Mission* (Washington, DC: GAO, August 2011), 2, available at <www.gao.gov/new.items/d11760.pdf>.

[148] Tyler Jost, *Defend, Defect or Desert? The Future of the Afghan Security Forces*, Policy Brief (Washington, DC: Center for a New American Security, January 2015), 4, available at <www.cnas.org/sites/default/files/publications-pdf/CNAS_Afghan_ANF_policybrief_Jost. pdf>.

[149] DOD, *Report on Progress Toward Security and Stability in Afghanistan*, April 2014, 38.

[150] Vanda Felbab-Brown, "Afghan National Security Forces: Afghan Corruption and the Development of an Effective Fighting Force," testimony before the House Armed Services Committee's Subcommittee on Oversight and Investigations, August 2, 2012, available at <www.brookings.edu/research/testimony/2012/08/02-afghanistan-security-felbab-brown#>.

[151] Donald J. Planty and Robert M. Perito, "Police in Transition in Afghanistan," U.S. Institute of Peace, February 2013, 5, available at <www.usip.org/sites/default/files/SR322.pdf>.

[152] Joint and Coalition Operational Analysis (JCOA), *Decade of War, Volume I: Enduring Lessons from the Past Decade of Operations* (Suffolk, VA: JCOA, June 15, 2012), 16.

[153] Josh Hicks, "A $486 million fleet, now $32,000 in scrap," *Washington Post*, October 13, 2014, A15.

[154] Jack Fairweather, *The Good War: The Battle for Afghanistan 2006–14* (London: Jonathan Cape Ltd, 2014), 248.

[155] Daniel Bolger, *Why We Lost: A General's Inside Account of the Iraq and Afghanistan Wars* (New York: Houghton Mifflin Harcourt, 2014), 391.

[156] Ben Connable, *Embracing the Fog of War: Assessment and Metrics in Counterinsurgency* (Santa Monica, CA: RAND, 2012).

[157] Terry H. Anderson, "The Light at the End of the Tunnel: The United States and the Socialist Republic of Vietnam," *Diplomatic History* 12, no. 4 (1988), 443–462, available at <http://dh.oxfordjournals.org/content/12/4/443.extract>.

5

9/11 AND AFTER: LEGAL ISSUES, LESSONS, AND IRREGULAR CONFLICT

By Nicholas Rostow and Harvey Rishikof

What I fear is not the enemy's strategy, but our own mistakes.

—Pericles[1]

Great cases, like hard cases, make bad law. For great cases are called great not by reason of their real importance in shaping the law of the future, but because of some accident of immediate overwhelming interest which appeals to the feelings and distorts the judgment.[2]

—Northern Securities Co. v. United States, 1904

Rather than examining all legal issues and controversies since 2001 that have generated lessons,[3] this chapter focuses on three in particular. The first part of the chapter focuses on the use of force because it helped frame the period that began on September 11, 2001. The next part concerns detention policies because they have been a locus of controversy almost from the moment of the first arrest or capture. Some commentators now contend that the subsequent wish to avoid controversy associated with detention appears to have led the United States more often than not to kill rather than capture. The second part then examines interrogation policy and techniques before moving on to the third part, which considers the legal impact of unmanned aerial vehicles as an example of the effect of advanced technology on law. The use of these vehicles has touched a nerve because of the novelty of the platform. The chapter concludes by summarizing the lessons identified and makes recommendations for future handling of legal issues.

The Relevancy of Law and Lessons to Be Learned

Law permeates American strategy and tactics by defining the permissible space in which the United States may act and prescribing how it should act. The law, therefore, was relevant to the decision to engage in a "war" against terror after September 11, 2001, and to all operations, including detention, flowing from that decision.

The fact that law is important to Americans dates to the earliest English settlements in the 17th century. Nearly two centuries later, in 1803, the Supreme Court reminded its audience in *Marbury v. Madison* that "The government of the United States has been emphatically termed a government of laws, and not of men."[4] In implementation of this idea, the Constitution and laws apportion authority within the government to make decisions for the United States. They also define—sometimes broadly, sometimes in infinite detail—the boundaries limiting the reach of such decisions, identify permissible instrumentalities available to decisionmakers, and clarify ways to use such instruments. In addition, as part of "the supreme Law of the Land,"[5] treaty obligations—some of which like the 1949 Geneva Conventions and the United Nations (UN) Charter have been incorporated into U.S. law by statute[6]—recognize that the United States is part of a larger community.[7] We recall these essential features of U.S. Government and society because they imbue American strategy and tactics. Senior political and military leaders are part of this system of values and need to bear this fact in mind. The law grants substantive authority to act. It creates process, which is essential to decisionmaking, good or bad. It embodies and proclaims the values of a society—that is, "the pattern of behavior deemed right."[8]

Looking back over the past decade and a half and taking full advantage of hindsight, we can begin to see what the U.S. Government did well, could have done better, and should not have done at all. A starting point is the fact that the 9/11 attacks seemed to come out of nowhere, leaving government officials scrambling to prevent what they were certain would be additional attacks and simultaneously trying to discover what had hit their country. Adding to the pressure-cooker atmosphere, the anthrax attacks of September

17–18, October 2, and October 9, 2001, and the crash of American Airlines Flight 587 in Queens, New York, on November 12, 2001 (which turned out to be a nonterrorist event), followed 9/11 in short order. In addition, daily reports of numerous potential attacks against the United States at home and abroad came to certain White House and other officials. The reports reflected real-time information originating inside and outside the Nation. They included little or no analysis in part because it was not clear that such analysis would have predicted the September 11 attacks, and nobody wanted again to take the risk of relying on such analysis. It was a time of extraordinary anxiety, and the heightened focus on preventing future attacks, which has lessened over time, still remains.[9] Although the Federal Bureau of Investigation (FBI) closed its inquiry into the anthrax attacks in 2010,[10] some commentators dispute the 2006 conclusion that one man, who committed suicide, was responsible for the anthrax crimes.[11]

To say that after 9/11 government officials went to bed every night terrified of a repetition of an attack when they awoke is a cliché. It also is an understatement. This observation is not to excuse but to help explain. After all, government officials during the Cold War probably feared they would wake up to nuclear war.[12] That said, we appreciate that an atmosphere of fear and the reality of the increased stress it brings are obstacles to sound government decisionmaking. Government officials report that the mood was to take any steps deemed necessary to prevent additional attacks. Process and law appeared in the circumstances almost as if they were expensive luxuries.[13]

Every aspect of the U.S. response to the 9/11 attacks raised significant legal issues. First, it was necessary to secure American public officials and government buildings, clearly an executive branch responsibility under the Constitution. Second, the government employed all available resources to hunt for the perpetrators of the attacks. In the first days after September 11, this effort took a variety of forms, including what appeared to be indiscriminate arrest and detention of suspects, which raised issues of probable cause.[14]

Third, once the government pinpointed the source of the attacks, an international use of force became a likely option. Legal issues permeate all uses of military force. Domestic and international authorities and rules, including the international law governing the use of force (*jus ad bellum*) and the laws of war (also known as Law of Armed Conflict or international humanitarian law) (*jus in bello*) govern. They frame the context in which policy, political, and moral responsibilities are discharged in connection with an international use of force.[15]

Fourth, intelligence collection and analysis, at home and abroad, was and is essential in responding to terrorist attacks. How intelligence is collected and against whom or what involves legal issues of the first importance. Since 2001, we have seen that how those legal issues are addressed affects the government's credibility, the ability to prosecute, and relations with most important allies and friends. When an administration ignores or misinterprets the law, it causes costly and unwanted distraction with long-lived effects. Leaks of real secrets—how the U.S. Government conducts intelligence collection and operations—have further undermined the legitimate effort to shore up security against future terrorist attacks. As intelligence operations against terrorists foreseeably may involve detention and interrogation, intelligence planning needs to include detention and interrogation protocols just as military planning should.

Fifth, the last 14 years have been rife with detention issues. How should one characterize as a legal matter those who are detained? How were they arrested or captured? How long are they to be detained in a conflict with no foreseeable termination? What are appropriate means for holding terror suspects pending prosecution or interrogation for intelligence purposes? What if the urgent need for intelligence causes the adoption of interrogation methods that make prosecution impossible or even violate domestic and international law? The question of what to do with suspected perpetrators when captured in the course of military or foreign intelligence operations should be examined early in the operational planning process. After capture is not the optimal moment to analyze policy options.

The U.S. Government disposes of an array of instruments with which to combat terrorists. Not all are, or need to be, military or intelligence-related. The Federal, state, and local response to terrorist attacks such as those carried out in Oklahoma City in 1995 involved a variety of intelligence responses in order, among other things, to determine whether the attack was international or domestic, part of a program of attack or an isolated incident, and the action of a large or small band. In the Oklahoma City bombing, law enforcement methods brought the perpetrators to justice in the U.S. criminal law system, which concluded with incarceration and execution. Had the perpetrators been operating from a foreign country with the assistance of that country or from a part of a country outside governmental control, it might have been necessary for the U.S. Government to consider a military response.

The Use of Force

Uses of military force involve domestic and international law. The Constitution is the principal source of authority for the President and Congress to determine to use force internationally. As a matter of law, the United States is committed by domestic and international law to respect the international regime for the lawful use of armed force.

Afghanistan and Al Qaeda

U.S. domestic law governs how the United States takes decisions with respect to the international use of force. Under the Constitution, executive power is vested in the President, who also is commander in chief of the Armed Forces.[16] Since the days of George Washington, scholars and practitioners, including judges, have acknowledged that the President has the authority and responsibility under Article II of the Constitution to direct the Armed Forces to defend the country.[17] The President may or may not seek congressional support depending on the politics and situation of the moment.[18] Attempts to legislate an outcome of this political process in advance, as with the 1973 War Powers Resolution, have failed.[19] Politicians have not allowed the nominal law to constrain their constitutional, political options for addressing a crisis. The fate of President Barack Obama's proposed resolution authorizing the use of force against the Islamic State of Iraq and the Levant (ISIL) illuminates this point about the Constitution in action:[20] it appears that the proposal is not moving forward in Congress and that both the President and Congress agree that the President has sufficient existing authority, including the 2001 Authorization for Use of Military Force, to direct military operations against ISIL and other groups in the Middle East that the President determines threaten the United States.[21]

The domestic authority to use force against the government of Afghanistan, al Qaeda, and others involved in some way with the 9/11 attacks came both from the President's constitutional responsibilities under Article II and from a congressional resolution authorizing the use of the "Armed Forces against those responsible for the recent attacks against the United States and its citizens."[22] The United States treated the events as armed attacks, giving rise to the right to use force in self-defense against the perpetrators and the government of the territory from which they came—Afghanistan.[23]

Having determined that al Qaeda, with the assistance or acquiescence of Afghanistan, conducted the attacks, the President, independently of Congress, could direct the Armed Forces into action against the known and suspected perpetrators as a reasonable action given the absence of alternatives designed to prevent a repetition and to bring the situation creating the right of self-defense to an end.[24] The attacks so shocked the government and the country that it was clear that Congress would stand with the President and would want to be seen as doing so. The 2001 Authorization for Use of Military Force constituted both a statement of solidarity and authorization. As Justice Robert H. Jackson wrote in his concurring opinion in the Steel Seizure Case of 1952, the President operates at the zenith of his powers when explicitly supported by Congress.[25] *Explicit* does not mean by appropriations but by joint resolution.[26] The 2001 authorization put President George W. Bush in the strongest possible legal (and political) position to confront the attackers.

The resolution authorized the President "to use all necessary and appropriate force against those nations, organizations, or persons he determines planned, authorized, committed, or aided the terrorist attacks that occurred on September 11, 2001, or harbored such organizations or persons, in order to prevent any future acts of international terrorism against the United States by such nations, organizations or persons." By its terms, this resolution fulfilled the requirements of the 1973 War Powers Resolution.[27] Not only did the 2001 authorization cement the domestic authorization for U.S. military operations in Afghanistan in 2001, it also was broad enough to allow military operations against those who carried out or supported the September 11 attacks, including "nations, organizations, or persons he determines . . . *aided* the terrorist attacks" *in order to prevent a repetition*.[28] Both the Bush and Obama administrations have argued that this resolution authorizes military operations, even more than 14 years after September 11, against entities the President concludes may have had a role in the 2001 attacks and to prevent a repetition of them. The resolution's language, they argued, also encompassed capture and interrogation, which are foreseeable consequences of a use of force. The breadth of the resolution's language was consistent with past open-ended congressional resolutions authorizing the use of force.

The day after the attacks, the UN Security Council adopted a resolution affirming the inherent right of self-defense at the same time it unequivocally condemned the terrorism of the day.[29] In response to the attacks, for the first time in its history, the North Atlantic Treaty Organization (NATO) invoked Article 5 to render assistance to one of its members suffering armed attack.[30]

Iraq

In October 2002, Congress adopted a joint resolution authorizing the use of force against Iraq.[31] Its preamble harked back to Iraq's invasion of Kuwait in 1990. The 2002 resolution also made the following points in arguing the legal case for the use of force: Iraq had not complied with UN Security Council resolutions and continued to support terrorist organizations and attack U.S. and other air forces implementing the resolutions; Iraq, having used weapons of mass destruction before[32] and having harbored and supported terrorists, constituted a threat to the national security of the United States; Iraq had tried to kill former President George H.W. Bush; and prior resolutions expressed the sense of Congress supporting U.S. military enforcement of UN Security Council resolutions adopted after the 1991 Gulf War.

The 2002 resolution authorized the President "to use the Armed Forces of the United States as he determines to be necessary and appropriate in order to (1) defend the national security of the United States against the continuing threat posed by Iraq; and (2) enforce all relevant United Nations Security Council resolutions regarding Iraq."[33] The resolution, like the 2001 Authorization for Use of Military Force, specifically fulfilled War Powers Resolution requirements.[34] This resolution, therefore, provided congressional approval of the 2003 campaign against Iraq and satisfied all domestic law requirements for those military operations. Whether the President had authority to act without such congressional authorization remains a hypothetical question and need not concern us.

President Bush apparently thought the military buildup that turned out to be preparation for the 2003 invasion would strengthen the hand of diplomats.[35] In 1991, the UN Security Council adopted Resolution 687 that set forth the conditions Iraq had to meet in order to bring an end to the council's authorization to use force to enforce the resolutions responding to Iraq's invasion and purported annexation of Kuwait. The wording of the congressional resolution aligned with this approach.[36]

Ultimately, the issue for the administration in 2003 was whether to invade Iraq despite substantial international criticism and whether to take the criticism and advice seriously. The United States proceeded to act—after all, it alone had suffered attack on September 11—against Iraq because the President and Congress saw the world through the prism of the attacks. Every risk was magnified. The two political branches of the U.S. Government seemed unwilling to seriously consider the advice of longstanding allies with different perspectives on Iraq and the risks and consequences of an invasion.

International Law Governing the Use of Force in Afghanistan and Iraq

Regarding the U.S. use of force in Afghanistan, the authorities are clear or as reasonably clear as they ever are. Iraq was different. While the President's domestic authority to order the invasion of Iraq in 2003 was clear and uncontroversial as a result of the congressional resolution of 2002, the international legal authority was the subject of controversy, not least because of the advocacy of "preemptive" self-defense in the 2002 National Security Strategy.[37]

As an independent state in the international system, the United States enjoys all the legal rights other states do. The UN Charter sets forth fundamental norms for international relations, binding on all states. They are part of U.S. statutory law.[38] The UN Charter provides that states may use force *only* in exercise of "the inherent right of individual or collective self-defence if an armed attack occurs" or pursuant to UN Security Council authorization.[39] The use of the word *inherent* means that the Charter brought forward to the UN era the customary law requirement that any use of force in self-defense fulfill the principles of necessity and proportionality. Once a decision is made to use force, military operations must conform to the laws of war.

A rule of reason operates with respect to the law governing the decision to use force and conduct military operations. With respect to the principle of necessity, force may be used in self-defense "if an armed attack occurs" when, taking into account the totality of the circumstances, it is unreasonable to suppose a nonforcible response will achieve the lawful goal of self-defense—the end to the situation giving rise to the right to use of force defensively. What is proportional force also must conform to a rule of reason: that minimum *degree* of force reasonably calculated to achieve the lawful *goal* of force. As an operational matter, the tactical use of force should distinguish between combatant and noncombatant targets. Civilians may not be targeted.[40]

Under the laws of war, prisoners must be treated with humanity, no matter whether they lawfully enjoy combatant status or not.[41] Lawful combatants, for example, are entitled to treatment as prisoners of war (POWs). Unlawful combatants and others must be treated humanely but may be subject to prosecution for doing what would be lawful under the laws of war if done by lawful combatants—for example, killing. They do not enjoy "combatant immunity."[42]

As we have seen, the United States, with the implicit endorsement of the UN Security Council and the explicit concurrence of its NATO Allies, treated 9/11 as armed attacks to which it could respond with proportional uses of force. This judgment should have provided the basis for categorization and treatment of detainees from the outset, just as it did with respect to who or what could be the target of military operations. Together with the congressional resolution authorizing the use of force against the perpetrators, these actions signaled international agreement with the U.S. President's decision to give Afghanistan an ultimatum to deliver Osama bin Laden and other al Qaeda leaders to the United States for trial or "share in their fate."[43]

International legal authorities for the U.S.-led invasion of Iraq in 2003 were more open to debate than U.S. domestic law authorities. Unlike in 1990–1991, the UN Security Council did not provide explicit authorization to use force against Iraq in 2001–2003. The Security Council resolution on Iraq prior to the invasion in March 2003, Resolution 1441 (2002), adopted on November 8, 2002,[44] found Iraq to be in "material breach" of its obligations under prior binding UN Security Council resolutions. Resolution 1441 was the ninth such Security Council finding since 1991.

Whether it could or should be read as an authorization is a matter on which experts have disagreed.[45] "Material breach," according to the Vienna Convention on the Law of Treaties, which the United States always has regarded as an accurate statement of the customary international law of treaties and thus binding on the United States, vitiates the multilateral agreement and, if all the parties agree, entitles one party to treat it as suspended or terminated.[46] Resolution 1441 provided that unanimous agreement. On the other hand, some have argued that the Security Council should have made that judgment, not individual states acting on the basis of the view that the 1991 authorization has continued in force because the Security Council had never rescinded it.[47]

A principal U.S. legal theory made much of this UN Security Council finding of material breach. In 1990, the Council had authorized the use of force against Iraq to uphold and implement its resolutions responding to Iraq's August 1, 1990, invasion of Kuwait.[48] After the 1991 Gulf War, Resolution 687 set conditions that Iraq had to meet for the authorization to use force no longer to be in effect.[49] Those conditions not having been met, the United States and the United Kingdom (and the Legal Counsel to the United Nations in the 1990s) understood the 1990 authorization to remain in effect in 2002.

Detention

U.S. detention policy and practice after the attacks of September 11, 2001, have involved two unrelated but important elements. The first concerns domestic detention. The second involved detention of those captured in or near theaters of military operations against al Qaeda and its supporters and those suspected of terrorist connections or activities and residing or transiting foreign countries. Though the two kinds of detention raise different legal issues, U.S. conduct in each of these areas suggests several lessons to be learned.

Domestic Detention

In the immediate aftermath of the September 11 attacks, the United States relied on broad interpretations of statutes in order to detain aliens and U.S. citizens. These statutes were written in a different era and context. As then–Assistant Attorney General Michael Chertoff stated in 2001:

> *In past terrorist investigations, you usually had a defined event and you're investigating it after the fact. That's not what we had here. . . . From the start, there was every reason to believe that there is more to come. . . . So we thought that we were getting information to prevent more attacks, which was even more important than trying any case that came out of the attacks.*[50]

He also noted, "We're clearly not standing on ceremony, and if there is a basis to hold them we're going to hold them."[51] Attorney General John Ashcroft was more explicit still: "We have waged a deliberate campaign of arrest and detention to remove suspected terrorists who violate the law from our streets."[52] One assumes that he meant that persons who were suspected of terrorism were arrested for nonterrorism offenses, not on the basis of suspicion only.

Under the Immigration and Nationality Act of 1952, as amended, aliens found either inadmissible or removable for terrorist activity are subject to mandatory detention until deportation.[53] According to a 2002 FBI affidavit concerning the investigation into 9/11:

> *the FBI identified individuals whose activities warranted further inquiry. When such individuals were identified as aliens who were believed to have violated their immigration status, the FBI notified the Immigration and Naturalization Service (INS). The INS detained such aliens under the authority of the Immigration and Nationality Act. At this point, the FBI must consider the possibility that these aliens are somehow linked to, or may possess knowledge useful to the investigation of, the terrorist attacks on the World Trade Center and the Pentagon.*[54]

Fourteen years after September 11, the logic of the affidavit—the assumption that aliens who had violated their immigration status were or might be connected to terrorist threats—is clear. In 2001, everyone wanted to know what the FBI knew. Few questions were asked about the Bureau's factual basis for arrests or how it obtained information. That is a lesson in itself. Government reticence about answering legitimate questions, just like government intimidation of people to make them afraid to ask questions, puts the people's freedom and real security at risk.[55]

The government also invoked the Material Witness Statute as authority to detain.[56] In relevant part, the statute provides:

> *If it appears from an affidavit filed by a party that the testimony of a person is material in a criminal proceeding, and if it is shown that it may become impracticable to secure the presence of the person by sub-*

poena, a judicial officer may order the arrest of the person and treat the person in accordance with the provisions of section 3142 of this title. . . . Release of a material witness may be delayed for a reasonable period of time until the deposition of the witness can be taken.[57]

In 2011, the Supreme Court held that motive is irrelevant in determining whether a particular use of the statute was constitutional.[58]

The use of the Immigration and Nationality Act and Material Witness Statute after 9/11 resulted in more than 1,000 arrests, ending in prosecutions chiefly for document or immigration fraud. Some 400 persons were charged; 39 were convicted of terrorism-related offenses.[59] While the constitutional norm for arrest is "probable cause" leading to a judicial warrant, there are exceptions where "reasonable suspicion" exists.[60] The Supreme Court has alluded to the possibility of a broader exception when terrorism is suspected.[61] Attorney General Ashcroft defended the policy and practice by quoting Attorney General Robert F. Kennedy's willingness to arrest organized crime figures for "spitting on the sidewalk if it would help in the battle against organized crime."[62]

In September 2001, the U.S. Government believed that if it did not act quickly, another attack would follow. On the other hand, terrorist attacks or other such shocks require professionalism and vigilance from everyone to minimize unintended consequences, including and perhaps especially with respect to the rule of law. The imperative of such vigilance in the context and wake of chaos is another important lesson to be learned.

Detention as a Result of Armed Conflict

Detention is a foreseeable feature of military operations and counterterrorism operations generally. It requires answers to three questions, preferably before the operations take place: What are the circumstances of the detention, and, if they involve an armed conflict, what kind of armed conflict is involved? What are the rights and protections of the detainees? What is the appropriate governmental department that should be responsible for the detention process?

In all cases, the state is responsible. It has to decide how to discharge that responsibility. The Third Geneva Convention Relative to Prisoners of War sets forth requirements that the responsible body must follow.[63] In military operations, armed forces take and hold prisoners until the state decides otherwise. The armed forces are not the only governmental body that may do so; the state may designate other organizations as responsible or create an organization for the purpose of exercising responsibility with respect to detainees.

The following sections provide possible answers to these questions within the framework of what is commonly referred to as the "war on terror" and define the detention options available to the United States under the laws of war following the September 11 attacks. Those options include detaining the alleged attackers and their co-conspirators as prisoners of war as a matter of U.S. policy; detaining the alleged terrorist actors as unlawful combatants engaged in combat or combat-related activities, therefore subject to prosecution; and detaining civilians to remove them from the battlefield for their own protection. Regardless, treatment of detainees in the first two cases would be governed by Common Article 3 of the four 1949 Geneva Conventions, which means, at a minimum, humane treatment.[64] Prosecution, whether in military or civilian courts, would depend on admissible evidence.

The United States is a party to the most important treaties governing the conduct of military operations, including the four Geneva Conventions of 1949, which are at the core of the laws of war. Article VI, Clause 2, of the Constitution makes treaties part of "the supreme law of the land."[65] This clause requires the United States to follow a treaty even if its language indicates that it is not self-executing, meaning that it cannot be enforced in U.S. courts without implementing legislation.[66] Parts of the Geneva Conventions have been adopted as U.S. statutes in the Uniform Code of Military Justice.[67]

The 1949 Geneva Conventions are second only to the UN Charter in terms of numbers of states-parties. Authoritative decisionmakers therefore regard elements of the conventions as having become part of customary international law, binding on all states and participants in the international system whether they have become parties to the conventions.[68] In 1977, an international conference concluded two Protocols Additional to the 1949 Geneva Conventions, Protocol I dealing with international armed conflict and Protocol II dealing with noninternational armed conflict. The United States is not a party to protocols I and II but regards elements as accurately codifying customary international law. The protocols as a whole do not represent customary international law.[69]

One must evaluate the detentions during the Afghan and Iraq conflicts through the lens of the laws of war. For much of the period 2001 to 2005, the administration went to great lengths to avoid doing so.[70] It further appears that experts in the laws of war and the law governing interrogation were excluded from the decisionmaking process.[71] This result-oriented process led to erroneous decisions that have damaged the reputation of the United States and compromised the international and multilateral effort to combat terrorism.

International Armed Conflict. The Geneva Conventions and Additional Protocols of 1977 envision two types of armed conflict: an international armed conflict and a noninternational armed conflict. An international armed conflict involves at least two states in armed conflict with each other.[72] Additional Protocol I will apply to the extent a state party to the conflict has ratified it or regards specific provisions to be accurate restatements of customary international law. The United States has not ratified Additional Protocol I in part because it confuses the distinction between military and civilian targets and humane treatment of prisoners. The protocol would extend lawful combatant status, as a matter of law, to those whom the United States and others regard as terrorists or other unlawful combatants not entitled to POW status upon capture. A "farmer by day, fighter by night"[73] does not constitute a lawful combatant in the American view; rather, such a person is an unlawful combatant directly participating in hostilities.[74]

The Third Geneva Convention sets forth in detail criteria for lawful combatant status. They include the following:

> *Prisoners of war, in the sense of the present Convention, are persons belonging to one of the following categories, who have fallen into the power of the enemy:*
>
> *(1) Members of the armed forces of a Party to the conflict as well as members of militias or volunteer corps forming part of such armed forces. (2) Members of other militias and members of other volunteer corps, including those of organized resistance movements, belonging to a Party to the conflict and operating in or outside their own territory, even if this territory is occupied, provided such militias or volunteer corps, including such organized resistance movements, fulfil the following conditions:*

(a) that of being commanded by a person responsible for his subordinates;
(b) that of having a fixed distinctive sign recognizable at a distance;
(c) that of carrying arms openly;
(d) that of conducting their operations in accordance with the laws and customs of war.[75]

If one is captured when fighting but does not meet these and similar criteria set forth in Article 4 of the Third Geneva Convention, one is not a lawful combatant and thus subject to prosecution for murder and/or accessory to murder. Although such a person does not enjoy POW status, as a matter of law, he must be treated humanely. A prisoner of war or someone held pursuant to Common Article 3 is entitled to not only humane but also respectful treatment.[76] Detention of a POW lasts "until the cessation of active hostilities,"[77] but POWs undergoing judicial punishment may be repatriated before the end of the sentence.[78]

If one is not a lawful combatant, one is a mere fighter or "unprivileged belligerent" or unlawful combatant, not entitled to POW status upon capture. A member of the armed forces in conflict with an unlawful combatant may target the unlawful combatant in battlefield or other circumstances permitting the use of lethal force. In addition, on capture, an unlawful combatant is subject to prosecution for engaging in criminal acts that would be lawful for a lawful combatant to undertake (for example, killing). Lawful combatant status alone gives an individual the right to engage in hostilities without committing murder or being an accessory to murder.[79] The violent acts of an unlawful combatant usually constitute criminal acts.[80]

The legal options considered above do not exhaust detention options or issues. In Iraq, for example, the United States found itself detaining Iraqis and others and having to categorize them by group affiliation and determine which law(s) to apply. Providing adequate facilities for the number of persons detained, maintaining security inside the facility as well as security from external attack, and conducting status review consume resources and carry high strategic risk. If detention operations appear to be a failure and conducted contrary to law and morality, as was the case at Abu Ghraib in 2003–2004, public support for the military campaign as a whole may erode and do so quickly. As a matter of policy, the United States could treat all detainees captured in connection with the wars in Afghanistan and Iraq and global counterterrorism operations as POWs.[81] The detaining state could determine whether a conflict is international or noninternational, what mix of international and domestic law to apply, and whether treatment is humane under the Geneva Conventions.[82] In addition, it might decide to use tribunals to try alleged violators of the laws of war.

Guantanamo Bay. One of the most important lessons to identify and learn concerns the use of Guantanamo Bay Naval Base as a detention facility for persons captured in the war on terror. The decision to hold detainees there seems to have been made to minimize the U.S. constitutional rights of detainees and to maximize the government's freedom with respect to the treatment and interrogation of such detainees. Despite the voluminous memoir literature covering the period, we know little about how the decision was made and why.[83] Douglas Feith's memoir mentions the reason for establishing a facility at Guantanamo Bay was to avoid detainee petitions for writs of habeas corpus. The goal was to extract intelligence about future terrorist operations from those held there without benefit of legal counsel or other due process. This plan failed because it was predicated on a legal belief based in immigration law that a facility not on U.S.-owned territory was outside the Constitution,[84] which the Supreme Court held to be incorrect.[85] According to Feith and Donald Rumsfeld, Rumsfeld predicted that detention would become a serious political and legal issue and for that reason did not want the Department of Defense to be responsible.[86]

The use of Guantanamo Bay as a prison for detainees has been severely criticized since 2001.[87] It was not necessary to house detainees there. One could just as easily have held them in theater or given responsibility for detention to our Afghan or Iraqi allies.[88] Alternatively, one could have put detainees in a facility in the territorial United States, as was the practice with respect to POWs during World War II. The latter option would have had foreseeable consequences. The government could have prepared for issues in advance and, therefore, reduced their impact on policy and politics.

As the Supreme Court decided in 2004,[89] detainees do have the right to petition for a writ of habeas corpus. That decision has imposed resource costs on the United States, but they apparently have not been high. Few detainees have obtained their freedom using this avenue, although detainees have been released pursuant to diplomatic agreement with other countries.[90] The use of ordinary district courts to try terrorist cases has proved feasible and successful, but moving the detainees to the districts for trial has proved politically impossible.[91]

The military commissions thus far have proved cumbersome and subject to innumerable legal objections and practical difficulties. The United States brought the first detainee to Guantanamo Bay in January 2002 and the last in March 2008. The United States has held approximately 780 detainees there since 2002. As of April 2015, 122 remained. Fifty-six are approved for release. Military commissions have convicted eight (six by plea agreement). An additional 29 are designated for trial, and 34 are being held indefinitely. The annual cost of the facility per detainee is approximately $3 million.[92]

Procedural and due process issues have hindered the prosecution at Guantanamo. In 2012, the District of Columbia Circuit Court reversed the conviction of Salim Hamdan on the grounds that the crime of material support did not exist as a war crime under international law at the time of the conduct.[93] Such issues were not anticipated but should have been because the commissions had to be created from scratch, including creating workable and fair rules of procedure.[94] In response to critics, Congress in 2009 amended the original 2006 Military Commissions Act. Critics continue to argue that the government should try detainees in ordinary Federal courts and that the failure to do so is a sign that the cases are not strong. Defenders of commissions point to security threats, the risk of disclosing classified information, and the fairness of the amended procedures since 2009. Still an open legal question is the "extent to which constitutional guarantees apply to aliens detained at Guantanamo."[95] Pursuant to the Supreme Court holding in *Hamdan v. Rumsfeld*,[96] Common Article 3 of the Geneva Conventions applies. Thus, detainees are entitled to a hearing and trial before a duly constituted court vested with procedural and judicial guarantees. Comparison between the procedural safeguards of the two courts yields few material differences. Differences that exist include such subjects as search and seizure, a difference that reflects the character of armed conflict. In the end, the Supreme Court will determine whether, as a matter of U.S. law, military commissions provide adequate due process. If the court holds that they do, such a result still may not have an impact on international opinion, which seems to have calcified in opposition.[97]

For all the failings and headaches associated with the detentions, there have been practical benefits to the detention experience. The United States has learned how to build and maintain a first-class detention facility, suited to a detention population unique to the American prison system. While the detention facilities at Guantanamo Bay do not run on ordinary corrections principles, this fact does not seem to put them at a higher risk of prison upheaval than other prisons. Visiting congressional delegations, the media, and the International Committee of the Red Cross provide continual observation of the treatment of detainees. Over time, the United States has learned how to operate such a facility and obtain information from detainees about plans for prison disruption. Detainees no longer have information relevant to current terrorist operations.

Detention at Guantanamo has raised the question of duration. A "war against terror" could last an extremely long time. Under the Third Geneva Convention, prisoners of war may be held until "the cessation of active hostilities."[98] Does the detaining power alone have the right to decide when release will not result in a return to a battlefield? This question has yet to be answered, even as the United States attempts to close the Guantanamo facility by sending detainees elsewhere, knowing that some released detainees have resumed fighting the United States and its partners.[99]

One of the most controversial U.S. practices at the facility is the implementation of a "no-suicide" policy. To prevent suicide, facility personnel must conduct 24-hour surveillance of the detainees and force-feed them when they go on hunger strikes.[100] In addition, as a Federal district judge noted on November 7, 2014, common sense and decency have not always prevailed in the treatment of detainees, even those in a physically debilitated condition as a result of hunger striking.[101] Critics of the facility and practices there have threatened to complain to doctors' licensing boards alleging violations of professional ethics. As a result, doctors have had to preserve anonymity.[102]

The Guantanamo Bay detention facilities remain unique among both U.S. prisons and detention facilities for those captured in the course of hostilities. They are expensive, due to the fact that over 2,000 personnel are caring for fewer than 125 detainees.[103] The facility now raises the question: what is the U.S. standard for defining the meaning of "treated humanely" in Common Article 3 of the four Geneva Conventions of 1949? Is it the treatment those detainees receive today in Guantanamo?[104]

Noninternational Armed Conflict. A noninternational armed conflict is what the language suggests: confined within the borders of a country. The categorization depends on geography because the laws of war have not applied in civil wars historically unless one side decides to abide by them, as in the case of the American Civil War.[105] Captives in civil wars in the past tended to receive harsh treatment. Common Article 3, affording all persons captured in a noninternational armed conflict humane treatment, did not formally become the standard until 1949. Even under the 1949 Geneva Conventions, the detaining authority determines whether treatment is humane, although it may be subjected to criticism if its treatment is not obviously humane. The United States has been criticized more for housing detainees in Guantanamo Bay than because of routine treatment methods. In 2002, the Bush administration announced that it would treat detained Taliban and al Qaeda fighters in a manner "consistent with the Geneva Conventions."[106] According to Douglas Feith, this position reflected his views and those of the Chairman of the Joint Chiefs of Staff, General Richard B. Myers, not the Department of Justice, General Counsel of the Department of Defense, Counsel to the President, or Counsel to the Vice President.[107] The latter were reluctant to adopt a position that might confer legitimacy on al Qaeda and Taliban activities and constrain the range of interrogation options available.[108] The position Feith and Myers successfully opposed may have reflected a misunderstanding of the requirements of the Geneva Conventions with respect to interrogation. In 2001–2002, the administration's process for preparing a position on law of war issues circumscribed discussion, excluding those lawyers—the Judge Advocates General in particular—who are most expert in the area. In this regard, an analogy might be a discussion of anti-trust law without the benefit of anti-trust lawyers. Feith, who had studied the Geneva Conventions and the 1977 protocols in the 1980s, was sufficiently expert to carry the day. Feith argued that the Geneva Conventions specified how to treat those who were captured and whether they were entitled to POW treatment. In any case, all were entitled to humane treatment.[109]

In 2006, well after the initial reaction to the 9/11 attacks and the overthrow of the Taliban and Saddam Hussein, the Supreme Court clarified the U.S. position with respect to the legal character of the conflict with al Qaeda and the treatment of its members or affiliates. The Supreme Court held that, as a matter of U.S. law, the United States is engaged in a global, noninternational conflict with al Qaeda.[110] As such, detainees are not entitled to POW status as a matter of law but must be humanely treated consistent with Common Article 3 of the 1949 Geneva Conventions. Of course, the fact that the United States may deny alleged al Qaeda conspirators POW status operates as a floor rather than a ceiling on its legally permissible treatment options. For policy reasons rather than legal obligation, the United States could have chosen to afford al Qaeda detainees POW status and the accompanying protections under international and domestic constitutional law. In addition, the United States could arrest and prosecute detainees under domestic criminal law. Assembling a prosecutable case is sometimes difficult if interrogators and jailers have mistreated the defendant. Evidence of criminality may be hard to find by examining terrain and plumbing the memories of troops. Nonetheless, Federal court trials of terrorists have succeeded.[111] The court thus vindicated Myers and Feith. A lesson to draw from this episode is that the government avoided error because of the coincidence of Feith's expertise. A more inclusive legal process would have made luck unnecessary.

Interrogation: Hard Cases Make Bad Law

After September 11, the U.S. Government's most important goal was to prevent a repetition of the attacks. Therefore, as soon as arrests or captures were made, the government sought information from detainees regarding future plans. Leaders of the plot to commit the attacks of 9/11 and other al Qaeda members were most likely to possess this information; hence, the label "high-value detainees" applied.[112] The detention of such persons and the pressing need for information seemed to justify "enhanced interrogation techniques."[113] The President himself chose the methods from a list.[114] His conclusion, based on advice, was that waterboarding would be an acceptable exception to all the norms and laws regarding interrogation. In prior conflicts dating even to the Spanish-American War, the United States deemed such practices torture.[115] These actions were to be carefully monitored and "were only applied to a handful of the worst terrorists on the planet, including people who planned the 9/11 terrorist attacks and who, among other things, were responsible for journalist Daniel Pearl's death."[116] To date, only Central Intelligence Agency (CIA) interrogators have waterboarded detainees.[117] The Agency instituted health protocols to ensure that no permanent harm was done.[118]

The CIA and executive branch proclaimed the value of these interrogations after the interrogation of Khalid Sheikh Mohammed—an alleged mastermind of the 9/11 attacks. The Bush administration announced that high-value detainees could provide information that would save thousands of innocent lives and "more than twenty plots [that] had been put in motion by al-Qa'ida against U.S. infrastructure targets" had been uncovered through these interrogations.[119] CIA Director George Tenet pointed to the capture and interrogation of Khalid Sheikh Mohammed as one of the greatest CIA successes and wrote that "none of these successes would have happened if we had to treat KSM [Khalid Sheikh Mohammed] like a white-collar criminal—read him his Miranda rights and get him a lawyer who surely would have insisted that his client simply shut up."[120] Other administration officials followed the same general line of explanation without disclosing the details of what the interrogation disclosed.[121]

The interrogation program provoked outrage.[122] Defenders point to extreme circumstances as justification—for example, the placement of a nuclear weapon in a city.[123] Defenders of "enhanced interrogation techniques" (later deemed to be torture by President Obama[124]) need to make the case that alternatives would not have worked. Professional interrogators assert that all one needs is time to obtain reliable information from most prisoners.[125] The Bush administration believed that time was what it lacked. According to Tenet, the CIA obtained Justice Department approval for the interrogation techniques it used and briefed the chairs and ranking Members of the congressional intelligence committees.[126]

In 2014, the then-Democratic majority of the Senate Select Committee on Intelligence issued a report on the interrogations and CIA conduct. The report disputed the Agency claim that only three detainees were subject to waterboarding.[127] The report also disputed that interrogation techniques had proved an effective means of acquiring intelligence or gaining the cooperation of detainees. In response to this conclusion of the committee majority, CIA Director John Brennan stated, "the cause and effect relationship between the use of EITs [enhanced interrogation techniques] and useful information subsequently provided by the detainee is, in my view, unknowable."[128] The committee majority report also accused the CIA of systematic misrepresentations about the program. Brennan denied this allegation.[129]

Prohibition on Torture

Domestic and international law have relevancy to interrogation of those seized in connection with international military and other operations. With regard to those detained as a result of counterterrorism operations, including military operations, since September 11 discussion has focused on the Convention against Torture and Other Cruel, Inhuman or Degrading Treatment or Punishment and implementing legislation in the United States.

The United Nations Convention against Torture defines *torture* as:

> *any act by which severe pain or suffering, whether physical or mental, is intentionally inflicted on a person for such purposes as obtaining from him or a third person information or a confession, punishing him for an act he or a third person has committed or is suspected of having committed, or intimidating or coercing him or a third person, or for any reason based on discrimination of any kind, when such pain or suffering is inflicted by or at the instigation of or with the consent or acquiescence of a public official or other person acting in an official capacity. It does not include pain or suffering arising only from, inherent in or incidental to lawful sanctions.*[130]

The United States ratified the convention with a Senate-approved understanding that torture meant an act "specifically intended to inflict severe physical or mental suffering" resulting from the intentional infliction or threat of infliction, or infliction or threat of infliction on a third person, of severe physical or mental pain or suffering.[131] The Federal Torture Act implementing this convention was adopted in 1994 and incorporated the understanding as statutory language.[132] The Torture Statute imposed criminal penalties on actions against "one who specifically intends to inflict severe physical pain or mental pain or suffering."[133] Since 1992, the United States also has been a party to the International Covenant on Civil and Political Rights, which prohibits "torture or . . . cruel, inhuman or degrading treatment or punishment."[134] The question became: What is torture?

The Memoranda on Torture

For a number of years prior to the September 11 attacks, the CIA had sought legal opinions as protection when undertaking missions that likely would be particularly dangerous or politically controversial, or both. The claim of acting in accordance with legal advice is a defense in the event of criminal investigations of CIA activities.[135] The Justice Department Office of Legal Counsel is the executive branch authority on the meaning of U.S. law. Executive departments and agencies therefore seek its legal opinion. In summer of 2002 and again in May 2005, the CIA requested an Office of Legal Counsel opinion to safeguard against potential criminal and civil penalties against individuals involved in interrogating high-value detainees. The Office of Legal Counsel provided the requested opinions in several controversial legal memoranda.[136]

These memoranda reviewed U.S. anti-torture statutes and proposed interrogation techniques. First, they concluded that the Fifth and Eighth Amendments of the Constitution do not extend to alien combatants when held outside the United States.[137] Second, they asserted that certain Federal criminal statutes do not apply to properly authorized interrogations of enemy combatants.[138] Third, the memoranda interpreted 18 U.S.C. § 2340—the statute making it a criminal offense for any person outside the United States to commit or attempt to commit torture—not to apply to interrogations conducted within the United States or permanent military bases such as Guantanamo Bay.[139] Furthermore, the memoranda interpreted § 2340 to define torture narrowly, requiring intentional acts resulting in "death, organ failure, or serious impairment of bodily functions."[140] Fourth, al Qaeda and associated forces "are not entitled to the protections that the Third Geneva Convention provides to prisoners of war."[141] By redefining the legal standard for torture to equate with acts resulting in death or organ failure and ignoring the validity of the Geneva Conventions, the memoranda seemingly put aside existing law on torture. After arguing against what appeared to be settled law, the memoranda did not include an assessment of likely public, including international, reactions.

Reactions to the Memoranda

Strong criticism greeted the June 2004 public release of the Office of Legal Counsel memoranda on torture.[142] Top administration officials immediately began to distance themselves from it. Congress and the administration acted to strengthen the existing prohibitions on torture by U.S. officials. The memoranda were withdrawn, reaffirmed in 2005, and withdrawn again. Nonetheless, in 2005, the Attorney General reaffirmed the lawfulness of the use of harsh interrogation techniques. Ultimately, the Supreme Court reached conclusions contradicting those in the memoranda. The memoranda nevertheless have continued to be part of the debate about the legality of torture.[143]

Congress. During his nomination hearing for U.S. Attorney General, Michael Mukasey commented on the memoranda, stating that "worse than a sin, it was a mistake."[144] Subsequent administration actions reflect such an opinion of the memoranda. Much of the current legal framework for interrogating terrorist detainees was established as a reaction to the memoranda. In 2005, Congress passed the Detainee Treatment Act, commonly referred to as the McCain Amendment,[145] which sought to enforce U.S. international obligations by explicitly prohibiting all executive departments and agencies from subjecting detainees under U.S. Government control to "cruel, inhuman, or degrading" treatment, consistent with international law.[146] Additionally, the law limited interrogation techniques only to those listed in the U.S. Army Field Manual.[147] At the same time, Senator John McCain (R-AZ) publicly announced that the bill did not rule out harsh treatment in case of an emergency such as imminent attack or even when faced with a hostage rescue scenario.[148]

Hamdan. In June 2006, the Supreme Court held that the United States is obligated to adhere to the prohibition on torture in Common Article 3 of the 1949 Geneva Conventions.[149] In *Hamdan v. Rumsfeld*,[150] the Supreme Court held that Article 3 applied to the conflict with al Qaeda and prohibited subjecting detainees to violence, outrages upon personal dignity, torture, and cruel or degrading punishment. Thus, *Hamdan* gave notice that the Office of Legal Counsel's memoranda were incorrect.

A year later, President Bush issued Executive Order 13340, reinforcing existing legal prohibitions on torture.[151] However, another controversial Office of Legal Counsel opinion overshadowed this order. The opinion concluded that six "enhanced interrogation techniques," when used with specified conditions and safeguards, could be employed by the CIA against high-value detainees belonging to al Qaeda without violating either the McCain Amendment or Article 3 of the Geneva Convention.[152]

The Obama Administration. On January 22, 2009, on his second full day in office, President Obama issued his own executive order concerning detainee interrogation, rescinding Bush's order and closing many avenues for interrogation left open by the Bush administration. The order banned enhanced interrogation and instructed all U.S. agencies that the only authorized interrogation techniques were those listed in the Army Field Manual. Much like the Bush administration's executive orders and memoranda on torture, President Obama's stance also has met with criticism and provoked debate. Some argue that his position on interrogation has gone too far, overly constraining American efforts to obtain valuable information from terrorist suspects. Such criticisms focus in particular on the President's rejection of enhanced interrogation techniques. The arguments claim that since all interrogation methods used now must conform to the standards of the Army Field Manual, America's enemies can prepare themselves to resist these methods, thereby rendering interrogations less effective sources of valuable intelligence. Furthermore, many argue that, in the case of an emergency when time is of the essence, it may be necessary to use harsh interrogation techniques to obtain necessary intelligence.[153]

Lessons from Interrogation Policy

The magnitude of the September 11 attacks was unprecedented, as were the shock and fear it generated. In this time of emergency, when suspects refused to talk, it was to some extent inevitable that the Bush administration would use extreme measures to obtain any information that could protect American lives, including extrajudicial means such as enhanced interrogation techniques and torture. That such interrogation techniques will be used regardless of the law (or their historical record of effectiveness) does not render them legal. The U.S. interrogation policy brings us back to an important lesson from the first decades of the 21st century: the need for a disciplined and inclusive interagency process as a check on action that in retrospect seems impulsive rather than carefully considered.[154]

First, some commentators believe it should be permissible to engage in torture/enhanced interrogation techniques. Advocates of this position argue that such techniques should be used only if circumstances require them and if rigorous procedures, including congressional oversight, exist. In such a case, the government would be arguing that it was permitted by a legal doctrine of necessity. Such procedural steps are necessary so as to publicly emphasize compliance with domestic and international law. The U.S. Government should seek to establish domestic rather than international procedures and processes to follow before engaging in enhanced interrogations.[155] This process should include review by independent legal specialists, particularly given the complex questions of international humanitarian law that interrogation inevitably raises. Transparency also must be provided such that the other branches of government are capable of providing meaningful oversight of the interrogations.

Second, some argue that if the President is going to act extrajudicially, a limited duration must be established under which the employment of extraordinary measures such as enhanced interrogation may reasonably be used.[156] The President cannot have an unlimited timeframe during which he legally may act out of necessity as commander in chief; the ticking bomb actually must tick. When the emergency passes and no threat to U.S. citizens seems imminent, military and civilian personnel must be prohibited from engaging in harsh techniques.

Third, military and nonmilitary personnel must be trained to conduct interrogations in a manner that is consistent with domestic and international law.[157] They must be aware of the potential consequences of interrogation. Such training is especially important given that U.S. law provides legal protections against criminal and civil actions only when U.S. agents "did not know that the [interrogation] practices were unlawful and a person of ordinary sense and understanding would not know the practices were unlawful."[158] A good faith reliance on advice of counsel is an important factor in considering the reasonableness of such actions[159] but is not a substitute for adequate training.

Fourth, the executive branch itself needs greater internal oversight so that it is aware of the actions taken by the military or the Intelligence Community. It took the senior levels of the Bush administration nearly 4 months to learn of the "shocking and clearly illegal" events in the military detention facility at Abu Ghraib.

Influencing the debate are the following questions and how they are answered: Do the interrogation techniques—torture—work? Such techniques have been used since time immemorial, which suggests the perpetrators believe some useful information always will be obtained. Are such techniques of interrogation politically defensible in a democracy, particularly the United States? The Golden Rule is the norm but is not followed by many enemies of the United States. Should the United States, as a matter of policy, follow that rule whether enemies do so? Finally, what role should morality play? Is torture consistent with what Americans think they are or what they think their government should do?

The exchanges among the majority and minority of the Senate Select Committee on Intelligence and the CIA have neither answered all the questions nor put to rest the controversy about the use of enhanced interrogation techniques and the effectiveness of such techniques. We conclude that the United States should respect the normative regime against torture set forth in the convention and implementing statute, and that if a President deems it necessary to authorize conduct that varies from that normative regime, he or she should be prepared to defend the action by making a necessity defense. If the President is not prepared to take that step, that fact would suggest that deviating from the norm is not necessary or otherwise justified.[160]

High-Tech Sniping: The Targeted Killing Controversy

In the wake of the 9/11 attacks, first the Bush administration and then the Obama administration have insisted, without much controversy or opposition, that the United States is engaged in an armed conflict with al Qaeda, its associates, and any state that supported it. This characterization of the conflict does not mean law enforcement methods would never be used, especially as the perpetrators had engaged in prosecutable crimes. Rather, it acknowledges the need for a spectrum of methods to defend the country and prevent a repetition of the attacks. As a result, from the outset, the conflict engaged the President's constitutional authorities and responsibilities as commander in chief and the use of U.S. armed force against al Qaeda. Determining lawful targets for the armed forces takes place in this context.[161]

The 2001 Authorization for Use of Military Force explicitly gives the President power to target individuals determined to bear responsibility for the attacks. The laws of war permit the targeted killing of lawful targets (indeed, the laws of war prefer targeted killings because they demonstrably respect or attempt to respect distinctions between combatants and noncombatants and military and civilian targets), and the history of warfare is in large part the history of soldiers trying to kill identifiable soldiers on the opposing side. At the same time, applying the standard involves more than just applying a yardstick. For example, a difficult issue of appraisal involves determination of who or what might be considered to be directly participating in hostilities.[162]

The 9/11 attacks highlighted the danger posed by terrorist safe havens in remote parts of the world. Unmanned aerial vehicles (UAVs), because of their technological qualities, have come to be a weapon of choice in targeting commanders and leaders of al Qaeda and other terrorist groups at war with the United States. They can loiter over a target for long periods, permitting the acquisition of precise targeting data. They fire precision weapons, thus permitting substantial limitation of collateral damage. They do not put friendly pilots or soldiers at risk because they are unmanned. They can attack persons hiding in areas difficult to reach by soldiers. For these reasons, President Bush, and, more frequently, President Obama have used UAVs in fighting terrorists. Then–CIA Director Leon Panetta called armed UAVs "the only game in town in terms of confronting or trying to disrupt the Al Qaeda leadership."[163]

Despite the advantages provided by UAVs and their demonstrated effectiveness, their use has engendered much debate.[164] So long as the targeted killing is carried out consistently with the legal principles from the laws of war set forth in this chapter, we see no more difficulty with the practice than with the sort of sniping that killed Admiral Nelson at the Battle of Trafalgar.

The Lawful Target

The 2001 Authorization for Use of Military Force gave the President appropriate guidance as well as discretion. Its grant of authority "to use all necessary and appropriate force"[165] limited the President's authority to use the military instrument to those situations where police action, by the United States or the state in which the terrorist is found, is impossible. It was neither necessary nor appropriate to use the Armed Forces to track down and arrest Timothy McVeigh for the 1995 Oklahoma City bombing. Attacks by UAVs in London or Paris or Moscow would be inappropriate as well as unnecessary. A use of force against Osama bin Laden was "necessary and appropriate" given the lawfulness of the target under the laws of war and the circumstances of his location, including the lack of cooperation by the host government or inability of the host government to discharge its international legal responsibilities with respect to the use of force from its territory.

Military operations conducted by the United States must conform to U.S. legal obligations. The Uniform Code of Military Justice incorporates that law in so far as it is set forth in treaties to which the United States is a party, such as the four 1949 Geneva Conventions, or in customary international law.[166] U.S. military operations are conducted with the benefit of legal advice offered by Judge Advocates General assigned to commands in the field, the headquarters of combatant commanders, and Washington, DC.

The principal sources of law in this area are the 1949 Geneva Conventions and those sections of Additional Protocol I of 1977 that the United States regards as an accurate codification of customary international law. At the core of this body of law are the principles of necessity, proportionality, distinction, and humanity.

Necessity. The military necessity requirement "arises predominantly from customary international law."[167] Military objectives are defined in Article 52 of Additional Protocol I as "those objects which by their nature, location, purpose or use make an effective contribution to military action and whose total or partial destruction, capture or neutralization, in the circumstances ruling at the time, offers a definite military advantage."[168] This principle recognizes the legitimate interest in ending hostilities through victory.[169] At the same time, since the first effort to codify a nation's view of the laws of war during the American Civil War, states have recognized that "[m]ilitary necessity does not admit of cruelty—that is, the infliction of suffering for the sake of suffering."[170]

Proportionality. The principle of proportionality "requires that damage to civilian objects . . . not be excessive in relation to the concrete and direct military advantage anticipated."[171] Thus, belligerents are required to weigh the military objective potentially achieved against the loss of civilian life and damage to civilian property. When determining whether a belligerent met this standard, one employs a "reasonable commander" standard—that is, "one must look at the situation as the commander saw it in light of all known circumstances."[172]

Distinction. The principle of distinction is central to the modern laws of war. It obligates military commanders to distinguish between military and civilian objectives.[173] This principle requires combatants to discriminate between military and civilian targets, direct their attacks at other combatants and military targets, and protect civilians and civilian property to the extent reasonable.[174] Attacks that are not directed at military objects or that employ a method or means of combat that cannot be directed—so-called indiscriminate attacks—are forbidden.[175] Belligerents must be distinguishable from civilians and "refrain from placing military personnel or materiel in or near civilian objects or locations."[176]

While Protocol I directs belligerents to meet a "feasibility" standard in regard to operations—for example, "those who plan or decide upon an attack" must do "everything feasible" to ensure they are not attacking civilians, civilian objects, or items or individuals who enjoy special protection; to "take all feasible precautions" when choosing weapons and tactics to minimize incidental injury and collateral damage; and to select that military objective from among those yielding a "similar military advantage" that "may be expected to cause the least danger to civilian lives and to civilian objects"[177]—the United States certainly does not recognize this requirement as part of customary international law however much it tries to adhere to it in operations and uses a quantum of force that seems reasonable under the circumstances.[178]

Humanity. The principle of humanity or avoidance of "unnecessary suffering" limits the ability of combatants to adopt certain "means of injuring the enemy."[179] Consistent with the principle of necessity, inflicting "suffering, injury, or destruction not actually necessary for the accomplishment of legitimate military purposes" is prohibited.[180] The humanity principle is comprised of three parts: it prohibits use of "arms that are per se calculated to cause unnecessary suffering"; it prohibits use of "otherwise lawful arms in a manner that causes unnecessary suffering"; and those prohibitions apply only when the unlawful effect is specifically intended.[181]

The State Department Legal Advisor, Harold Koh, explained the Obama administration's position with respect to adherence to these principles in military operations in 2010. He stated that the United States applied "law of war principles," including:

> *First, the principle of distinction, which requires that attacks be limited to military objectives and that civilians or civilian objects shall not be the subject of the attack; and*

Second, the principle of proportionality, which prohibits attacks that may be expected to cause incidental loss of civilian life, injury to civilians, damage to civilian objects, or a combination thereof, that would be excessive in relation to the concrete and direct military advantage anticipated.[182]

If a target is lawful under the laws of war, a state may use weapons, including weapons delivered by UAVs against such targets. In this context, targeted killing is no more than high-tech sniping. As a matter of international law, when Afghanistan was unwilling or unable to take action against the perpetrators of the 9/11 attacks and similarly unwilling or unable to prevent future attacks, the United States not only had a right to use force in self-defense against those perpetrators, but also in fact had no choice if it were to defend itself against further attacks.

Critics have attacked the targeted killing program on the basis of its compliance with the law of war principles of distinction, proportionality, and necessity. Yet UAVs are currently among the most precise weapons to hit remote targets. Despite the sophistication of their technology, unmanned platforms do not and cannot replace people in the evaluation process by which a lawful target is identified, potential for civilian casualties is weighed, and after-action results are considered. Unmanned platforms nonetheless make distinguishing between military and nonmilitary targets and keeping collateral damage to a minimum easier than historically has been possible. UAVs offer other specific advantages that would seemingly make them preferable. They allow operators to make target-engaging decisions absent fear of death or the "fog of war." They also allow for process in a way that other weapons systems do not. For example, because a pilot is not in danger, the command center has additional time to debate a strike and weigh the prudence of striking a particular target.

Achieving effective distinction between military and civilian targets is a goal of contemporary laws of war. That UAVs provide an advantage to the side possessing them seems undeniable. But inequality in means of warfare is not disqualifying or illegal. Military commanders hope that the battle is unfair to their advantage. Regardless of whether jihadists are considered lawful combatants or unlawful noncombatant fighters, terrorists who actively take part in hostilities against the United States by plotting attacks are targetable.[183]

Further addressing these principles, the White House's May 23, 2013, fact sheet, "U.S. Policy Standards and Procedures for the Use of Force in Counterterrorism Operations Outside the United States and Areas of Active Hostilities," states that compliance with these four principles is integral to the overall standard that the United States uses in deciding whether to undertake a targeting operation against a particular terrorist target. That sheet asserts specifically:

> [L]*ethal force will be used outside areas of active hostilities only when the following preconditions are met: First, there must be a legal basis for using lethal force. . . . Second, the United States will use lethal force only against a target that poses a continuing, imminent threat to U.S. persons. . . . Third, the following criteria must be met before lethal action may be taken:*
>
> *1. Near certainty that the terrorist target is present;*
> *2. Near certainty that non-combatants will not be injured or killed;*
> *3. An assessment that capture is not feasible at the time of the operation;*
> *4. An assessment that the relevant governmental authorities in the country where action is contemplated cannot or will not effectively address the threat to U.S. persons;*
> *5. An assessment that no other reasonable alternatives exist to effectively address the threat to U.S. persons.*
>
> *Finally, whenever the United States uses force in foreign territories, international legal principles, including respect for sovereignty and the law of armed conflict, impose important constraints on the ability of the United States to act unilaterally—and on the way in which the United States can use force.*[184]

As currently conducted, unmanned attacks fall into two procedural categories. The Obama administration has tried to apply lessons it took from the Bush administration experience. It has been transparent, or at least reasonably transparent, with respect to determining who is targeted. After the targeted killing of American Anwar al-Awlaki in 2011, the administration released legal memoranda and a fact sheet providing parameters of its targeted killing procedure. Paired with subsequent news reports, a rough sketch has emerged of an intensive interagency process in which names are nominated and then debated. Lawyers are present to help decide whether to engage the targets.

Al-Awlaki's U.S. citizenship caused debate over whether targeted killing was subject to constitutional due process protections. Some[185] argue that individual targets require "notice" before they are attacked.[186] Others, like Samuel Adelsberg,[187] argue a neutral decisionmaker and additional inter-branch deliberation are required. Still others insist judicial review of targeting decisions is required. A last group, to which the authors of this chapter belong, do not consider such killings to involve judicial process at all. Being lawful targets as a matter of the laws of war, combatants can be killed in military operations.

A leaked Department of Justice white paper argues that a lethal operation against a U.S. citizen who is a senior operational leader of al Qaeda or an associated force, in a foreign country, outside the area of active hostilities, does not violate due process.[188] Use of force in such circumstances is justified as an act of national self-defense.[189] Additionally, an al Qaeda leader is a member of the cohort against whom Congress has authorized the use of necessary and appropriate force.[190] The fact that such a person also might be a U.S. citizen does not alter this conclusion.[191]

This analysis is consistent with Supreme Court cases holding that the military constitutionally may use force against a U.S. person who is part of enemy forces.[192] Applying the Supreme Court's balancing approach in *Mathews v. Eldridge*, the white paper concluded that lethal operations are permissible (that is, the government's interest would outweigh the private interest of the targeted citizen at issue), at least where an informed, high-level official of the U.S. Government has determined that the targeted individual poses an imminent threat of violent attack against the United States; where a capture operation would be infeasible (and where those conducting the operation continue to monitor whether capture becomes feasible); and where such an operation would be conducted consistent with applicable law of war principles. Similar determinations were expressed by Eric Holder[193] and President Obama.[194] Not so for Harold Koh, however, who in 2010 stated the targets were not entitled to due process.[195]

Conclusions

It is impossible now to say when the era that began on September 11, 2001, will end. Involved in continuous military and counterterrorism operations and subject to repeated terrorist attacks, the United States, its friends, and allies face a difficult future full of hard choices. How they should make those choices is set forth in their respective constitutions and the laws adopted pursuant to them. The body of relevant law includes international law. Our conclusions embody lessons identified and to be learned from the first 14 years of the period, which perhaps should be considered now as a condition of international life rather than a long war.

First, of course, the United States and others should prepare themselves for attack.[196] Such preparation means practice, as if one were doing fire drills at school, and development of plans for certain foreseeable situations involving substantial numbers of casualties or shocking events, such as the January 2015 murder of the *Charlie Hebdo* staff in Paris, that do not involve large numbers of people but strike at the heart of free expression.

Second, a regular and vigorous interagency decisionmaking process is essential. When an event occurs, whether terrorist, military, or natural, the pressure for speed will be enormous. That pressure squeezes out thinking and common sense. The latter are essential to successful response.

Third, legal planning must be included as part of operational planning. Thus, lawyers should be regarded as essential participants in the planning process, preparing their clients for legal issues along the way and advising them on how to address the issues as they come up. Such subjects as targeting, arrest, and detention inevitably will be part of any military and counterterrorist operations.

It is to be hoped that, as Philip Bobbitt has stated, "We have entered a period in which strategy and law are coming together."[197] In any event, it is desirable that we do so because the law expresses what society deems permissible strategy and tactics. The fusion of law and policy is at the core of political legitimacy and of the chief lessons we identify as important to learn in contemplation of future conflict.

Lessons to be learned by the United States from the response to the 9/11 attacks are easier to identify than to learn and implement; the lessons cross disciplines. They are not exclusively legal or military or tactical or strategic.

But because the law involves a process of authoritative decision, it is inextricable from what often is considered an exclusively "policy" process.

Embrace a Disciplined, Inclusive, Interagency Decisionmaking Process

Such process contributes to good government in ordinary times.[198] In a crisis, when one may be tempted to treat them as time-consuming luxuries, it is even more important. First impressions of reality usually are incomplete or wrong.[199] Particularly when, as in the case of the September 11 attacks, there is fear that they constitute the first of a series of surprise attacks, the impulse inevitably will be to seek shortcuts and demand instant results. A disciplined and inclusive interagency decisionmaking process should fit the circumstances and not be sidelined. The process should not seek consensus for its own sake, nor should it cut out those whose views are in a minority. It should ensure that issues presented to the President for decision reflect serious options, different points of view, and appropriate analysis, including the foreseeable consequences, costs, and benefits. And the options should be presented in a timely fashion. Numerous examples exist where such an approach was lacking in the period 2001–2014.[200] The dearth of process in the early days of the Bush administration was striking in the area of legal advice to the President. Counterterrorism, moreover, is a concept and subject that attracts exploitation and expansion to achieve unrelated objectives because of the difficulty in government of resisting any idea labeled "counterterrorism." A vigorous interagency process can keep unrelated subjects off the agenda and focus the issues to be addressed and choices to be made.

Embrace the Constitution and Fundamental International Norms

The Constitution has served the American people well for 228 years. For over a century, the United States has made support for the international rule of law a fundamental part of its foreign policy and a definition of its national interests. In the immediate aftermath of the 9/11 attacks and the commencement of military operations in Afghanistan in October 2001, the administration tried to work around the Constitution in the way it held and treated detainees. It arrested large numbers of people using statutory authorities never contemplated to be relevant to counterterrorism operations. Probably driven by fear of additional attacks and a belief that detainees had information about such attacks that had to be extracted at all costs, the administration refused humane treatment for all detainees despite the requirement of the 1949 Geneva Conventions.[201]

Administrations invariably find themselves enmeshed in unnecessary controversy when they do not adhere to the Constitution and respect legal standards. Decisions should not be made to avoid what, in the circumstances, may appear to be constitutional inconveniences such as due process.[202] One hears in defense of the conduct in the immediate aftermath of the September 11 attacks that the country was not attacked again, even though some things were done that courts subsequently held to be unlawful or an abridgement of constitutional due process. When government officials seek to evade the Constitution or fundamental international norms such as those governing the use of force or the treatment of prisoners, the result, more often than not, is poor decisionmaking and worse results. Another consequence is distortion of the public debate. In such circumstances, the focus tends to be on legal requirements and procedures, not the substance of the policy.[203]

Prepare and Plan for Detention Operations and Foreseeable Legal Issues in Advance

This third lesson has a number of parts. It concerns the need to include detention planning during the development of a military campaign plan[204] and to assign the best people to detention operations. As the Abu Ghraib abuses showed, failed detention policies can have strategic consequences.[205] In the course of developing a plan for the detention, interrogation, and treatment of detainees, the United States also must sort out, to the extent it can in advance, the complex legal environment it almost certainly will confront during military operations abroad. What kind of conflict is involved as a matter of law? How should one categorize the enemy for purposes of the Geneva Conventions and other relevant and applicable bodies of law? In the event of occupation of even a part of a country, one foreseeably may become involved in detention operations not related to the battlefield. Afghanistan involved issues of Afghan, U.S., and International Security Assistance Force jurisdiction and applicable international law. Iraq brought home the complexity of meeting the requirements of the Third (prisoners of war) and Fourth (civilians) Geneva Conventions in an environment of ongoing violence, political upheaval, and difficult logistics. The fact that the United States and its military partners are party to different treaties containing rules for armed conflict, including detention and treatment of detainees, alone creates significant operational issues. It is essential that, to the extent foreseeable and possible, commanders and their operations not be trapped in likely legal thickets. Legal planning, therefore, should be an integral part of military planning.

The authors would like to express their gratitude to Jesse Lemon, Brittany Albaugh, Christopher Carlson, and Tara J. Pistorese for excellent research assistance in connection with all phases of the development of this chapter. They also would like to express their gratitude to Judge James E. Baker for reading an early draft and providing most helpful suggestions. Of course, he bears no responsibility for this chapter.

Notes

[1] Thucydides, *The Peloponnesian War*, trans. Rex Warner (Baltimore: Penguin Books, 1972), 122.

[2] *Northern Securities Co. v. United States*, 193 U.S. 197, 401 (1904) (Holmes, J., dissenting).

[3] See, for example, Benjamin Wittes, *Law and the Long War: The Future of Justice in an Age of Terror* (New York: Penguin, 2008).

[4] *Marbury v. Madison*, 5 U.S. (1 Cranch) 137, 163 (1803).

[5] U.S. Const. art. VI.

[6] The War Crimes Act of 1986 in part codified Common Article III of the Geneva Conventions. 18 U.S.C.A. § 2441. The United Nations Participation Act of 1945 (UNPA) authorizes U.S. participation in the United Nations, including to fulfill UN Charter obligations specifically under Art. 41. 22 U.S.C.A. § 287.

[7] Some important attributes—sovereignty, for example—of every country, including the United States, result from the workings of the international system and international law. See Morton A. Kaplan and Nicholas deBelleville Katzenbach, *The Political Foundations of International Law* (New York: Wiley, 1961).

[8] Eugene V. Rostow, *The Ideal in Law* (Chicago: University of Chicago Press, 1978), 1. Also, "Roman jurists thought law could not be defined at all—that it pervaded society

too deeply, and in so many ways, that the idea of law could never be captured in a single perspective." Ibid.

9   Conversation with C. Dean McGrath, Jr., Deputy Chief of Staff, Office of the Vice President, 2001–2005.

10   Department of Justice, *Amerithrax Investigative Summary: Released Pursuant to the Freedom of Information Act* (Washington, DC: Department of Justice, 2010), available at <www.justice.gov/archive/amerithrax/docs/amx-investigative-summary.pdf>.

11   Jeanne Guillemin, *American Anthrax: Fear, Crime, and the Investigation of the Nation's Deadliest Bioterror Attack* (New York: Times Books, 2011), 245–249.

12   On his last day in office, Secretary of State Dean Rusk remarked to his colleague Eugene Rostow, the Under Secretary of State for Political Affairs, that there had been no nuclear wars on his watch, thus revealing the importance of that concern during his 8 years in office.

13   See, generally, Gabriella Blum and Philip B. Heymann, *Laws, Outlaws, and Terrorists: Lessons from the War on Terrorism* (Cambridge: MIT Press, 2010).

14   See the Constitution Project, *Report on Post-9/11 Detentions* (Washington, DC: Liberty and Security Initiative of the Constitution Project, June 2, 2004), available at <http://constitutionproject.org/pdf/report_on_post_9_11_detentions2.pdf>.

15   See, for example, Yoram Dinstein, *The Conduct of Hostilities under the Law of International Armed Conflict*, 2nd ed. (Cambridge: Cambridge University Press, 2010). "Laws of war" or "law of armed conflict" are more precise terms than "international humanitarian law" and therefore preferred.

16   U.S. Const. art. II, §§ 1–2.

17   See, for example, Harold Hongju Koh, *The National Security Constitution: Sharing Power after the Iran-Contra Affair* (New Haven: Yale University Press, 1990); Eugene V. Rostow, *President, Prime Minister, or Constitutional Monarch?* McNair Paper No. 3 (Washington, DC: NDU Press, 1989); Henry Bartholomew Cox, *War, Foreign Affairs, and Constitutional Power, 1829–1901* (Cambridge: Ballinger, 1984); Abraham D. Sofaer, *War, Foreign Affairs, and Constitutional Power: The Origins* (Cambridge: Ballinger, 1976); Louis Henkin, *Foreign Affairs and the Constitution* (Mineola, NY: Foundation Press, 1972); Edward S. Corwin, *The President: Office and Powers, 1787–1957* (New York: New York University Press, 1957); Robert F. Turner, "The Constitutional Framework for the Division of National Security Powers among Congress, the President, and the Courts," in *National Security Law*, ed. John Norton Moore and Robert F. Turner (Durham, NC: Carolina Academic Press, 2005), 779–841.

18   Robert F. Turner, "The Authority of Congress and the President to Use the Armed Forces," in *National Security Law*, 843–884; *Marbury*, 137; *Youngstown Sheet & Tube Co. v. Sawyer*, 343 U.S. 578 (1952); Robert F. Turner, "Truman, Korea, and the Constitution: Debunking the 'Imperial President' Myth," *Harvard Journal of Law and Public Policy* 19, no. 2 (Winter 1996), 533; Louis Fisher, "The Korean War: On What Legal Basis Did Truman Act?" *American Journal of International Law* 89, no. 1 (1995), 21.

[19] Turner, "The Constitutional Framework;" Turner, "The Authority of Congress."

[20] Letter from the President to Congress, February 11, 2015, enclosing a draft joint resolution authorizing for 3 years the use of force, not including "enduring offensive ground combat operations."

[21] Stephen W. Preston, "The Legal Framework for the United States' Use of Military Force Since 9/11," remarks at the annual meeting of the American Society of International Law, April 10, 2015, available at <www.defense.gov/Speeches/Speech.aspx?SpeechID=1931>.

[22] S.J. Res. 23, September 18, 2001. Pub.L. 107-40, 115 Stat. 224 (2001) (hereafter Authorization for Use of Military Force Against Terrorists or, AUMF).

[23] Letter from John D. Negroponte, U.S. Permanent Representative to the United Nations, to the President, UN Security Council, October 7, 2001, available at <http://avalon.law.yale.edu/sept11/un_006.asp>. Letter fulfilled obligation under Article 51 of the UN Charter to report defensive uses of force to the Security Council.

[24] James E. Baker, *In the Common Defense: National Security Law for Perilous Times* (Cambridge: Cambridge University Press, 2007).

[25] *Youngstown Sheet & Tube Co.*, 635–636 (1952) (Jackson, J., concurring). See also Baker, 40–44.

[26] War Powers Resolution, 50 U.S.C. § 1547 (a) (1) (1973).

[27] AUMF § 2 (b) (1). On the constitutionality of at least parts of the War Powers Resolution, see *Immigration and Naturalization Service v. Chadha*, 462 U.S. 919 (1983).

[28] Emphasis added.

[29] UN Doc. S/RES/1368 (September 12, 2001). The International Court of Justice (ICJ) Advisory Opinion on the Israeli wall or security fence took a different view and denied that the attacks that caused Israel to build the wall gave rise to an international law right of self-defense. See Legal Consequences of the Construction of a Wall in the Occupied Palestinian Territory, Advisory Opinion, 2004 I.C.J. 136 (July 9), available at <www.icj-cij.org/docket/files/131/1671.pdf>. On the limited import of an ICJ Advisory Opinion, see Legality of the Threat or Use of Nuclear Weapons, Advisory Opinion, 1996 I.C.J. 226, 237, para. 17 (July 8), available at <www.icj-cij.org/docket/files/95/7495.pdf>.

[30] On September 12, 2001, the North Atlantic Treaty Organization (NATO) invoked Article 5 (April 4, 1949), available at <www.nato.int/cps/en/natolive/official_texts_17120.htm>. Article 5 provides:

The Parties agree that an armed attack against one or more of them in Europe or North America shall be considered an attack against them all and consequently they agree that, if such an armed attack occurs, each of them, in exercise of the right of individual or collective self-defence recognised by Article 51 of the Charter of the United Nations, will assist the Party or Parties so attacked by taking forthwith, individually and in concert with the other Parties, such action as it deems necessary, including the use of armed force, to restore and maintain the security of the North Atlantic area.

*Any such armed attack and all measures taken as a result thereof shall immediately be re-
ported to the Security Council. Such measures shall be terminated when the Security Council
has taken the measures necessary to restore and maintain international peace and security.*

[31] H.J. Res. 114, Oct. 16, 2002. Pub. L. 107-243, 116 Stat. 1498 (2002) (hereafter Iraq
AUMF).

[32] Iraq repeatedly deployed chemical weapons during its 8-year war with Iran. The first
documented case was the November 1980 chemical bombing of the city of Susangerd. By
February 16, 1984, Iraq had used chemical weapons against Iran at least 49 times, killing
at least 109 and injuring hundreds of others. In 1991, the Central Intelligence Agency
(CIA) estimated that Iran had suffered thousands of deaths from Iraq's use of chemical
weapons. On March 16, 1988, the Iraqi regime used chemical weapons against its own
Kurdish population in the city of Halabja. The attack killed between 3,200 and 5,000 people and injured 7,000 to 10,000 more. Margret A. Sewell, "Freedom from Fear: Prosecut-
ing the Iraqi Regime for the Use of Chemical Weapons," *St. Thomas Law Review* 16 (2004),
365–393.

[33] Iraq AUMF.

[34] Ibid.

(c) WAR POWERS RESOLUTION REQUIREMENTS—

*(1) SPECIFIC STATUTORY AUTHORIZATION—Consistent with section 8(a)(1) of
the War Powers Resolution, the Congress declares that this section is intended to constitute
specific statutory authorization within the meaning of section 5(b) of the War Powers Resolution.*

*(2) APPLICABILITY OF OTHER REQUIREMENTS—Nothing in this joint resolution
supersedes any requirement of the War Powers Resolution.*

[35] Stephen J. Hadley, interview by Joseph J. Collins and Nicholas Rostow, October 7, 2014.

[36] The authoritative U.S. view was set forth by State Department Legal Adviser William H.
Taft IV and his colleague, Todd F. Buchwald, in "Preemption, Iraq, and International Law,"
American Journal of International Law 97, no. 3 (July 2003), 557–563. Articles by John
Yoo, Richard N. Gardner, Richard A. Falk, Miriam Sapiro, Thomas M. Franck, Tom J. Far-
er, and Jane E. Stromseth appeared in the same issue of the journal, discussing the same
subject from different points of view and therefore illuminating the scope of the dialogue
about legality. The U.S. Naval War College *International Law Studies*, 80 (2006), edited
by Richard B. Jacques, provides the same insights through articles by Ruth Wedgwood,
Thomas M. Franck, Nicholas Rostow, Yoram Dinstein, Marco Sassoli, W. Hays Parks, Jeffrey K. Walker, Adam Roberts, Michael N. Schmitt, M.H. MacDougall, Wolff Heintschel
von Heinegg, Hyun-soo Kim, D.L. Grimond and G.W. Riggs, Alan Baker, Jean-Philippe
Lavoyer, John F. Murphy, Jan Hladik, David E. Graham, and Charles H.B. Garraway on
issues in international law and military operations arising from the Iraq campaign and
war on terror.

[37] *The National Security Strategy of the United States of America* (Washington, DC: The

White House, September 2002), 9, available at <www.state.gov/documents/organiza-tion/63562.pdf>. The use of the term *preemptive* was unfortunate and seemed to mark a break with the historical U.S. position that the international law of self-defense included a right of anticipatory self-defense, as had been established by Daniel Webster in 1841 and adhered to by every administration since then. The documents establishing this interpretation of international law are in the *Caroline* file, available at <http://avalon.law.yale.edu/19th_century/br-1842d.asp>. As Professor Yoram Dinstein, formerly twice the Stockton Professor of International Law at the Naval War College, frequently argues, if the 2002 National Security Strategy had used the word *interceptive*, it would have *preempted* problems. The National Security Strategy is a political, not a legal, document.

[38] UNPA.

[39] UN Charter Article 51, which reads:

Nothing in the present Charter shall impair the inherent right of individual or collective self-defence if an armed attack occurs against a Member of the United Nations, until the Security Council has taken measures necessary to maintain international peace and security. Measures taken by Members in exercise of this right of self-defence shall be immediately reported to the Security Council and shall not in any way affect the authority and responsi-bility of the Security Council under the present Charter to take at any time such action as it deems necessary to maintain or restore international peace and security.

On the controversies over the meaning of "armed attack," see Yoram Dinstein, *War, Aggression, and Self-Defence,* 5th ed. (Cambridge: Cambridge University Press, 2011), 196–277; Nicholas Rostow, "International Law and the Use of Force: A Plea for Realism," *Yale Journal of International Law* 34, no. 2 (Summer 2009), 549.

[40] See Dinstein, *Conduct,* throughout; Myres S. McDougal and Florentino P. Feliciano, *Law and Minimum World Public Order: The Legal Regulation of International Coercion* (New Haven: Yale University Press, 1961).

[41] U.S. courts, administrations, and the Department of Defense use the term *unlawful combatant.* As a matter of law, there is no such person. One either is a combatant or a noncombatant. If one is a combatant, one may, as a matter of law, engage in activities that otherwise would constitute murder. If one is a noncombatant, one may not engage in such conduct without incurring risk of prosecution. *Fighter* would be a more neutral term than unlawful combatant and would make the distinction clear. The Obama administration uses the term *unprivileged belligerent,* which approximates the same idea. See *Ex Parte Quirin,* 317 U.S. 1 (1942); Dinstein, *Conduct,* 33. Rather than insist on usage that readers may find unfamiliar, we adopt the common parlance of *lawful* and *unlawful* combatants to distinguish between combatants, who enjoy the privilege of killing as a matter of interna-tional and domestic law, and noncombatants, who do not enjoy such privilege and are not entitled, as a matter of law, to prisoner of war status on capture.

[42] The Third Geneva Convention in effect contains a roadmap for treating detainees.

[43] George W. Bush, "Address to a Joint Session of Congress and the American People,"

Washington, DC, September 20, 2001.

44 UN doc. S/Res/1441 (2002), November 8, 2002.

45 Jane Stromseth, "Law and Force After Iraq: A Transitional Moment," *American Journal of International Law* 97, no. 3 (July 2003), 628.

46 Vienna Convention. The Constitution defines *treaty* more narrowly than international law. Therefore, the United States is not a party to the Convention. Vienna Convention on the Law of Treaties, 1155 U.N.T.S. 331, 8 I.L.M. 679, *entered into force* January 27, 1980, available at <http://www1.umn.edu/humanrts/instree/viennaconvention.html>; Robert Dalton, "Treaties and Other International Agreements," in *National Security Law*. With respect to material breach, Article 60 of the Vienna Convention provides that:

A material breach of a bilateral treaty by one of the parties entitles the other to invoke the breach as a ground for terminating the treaty or suspending its operation in whole or in part. 2. A material breach of a multilateral treaty by one of the parties entitles:

a. The other parties by unanimous agreement to suspend the operation of the treaty in whole or in part or to terminate it either: i. In the relations between themselves and the defaulting State, or ii. As between all the parties; b. A party specially affected by the breach to invoke it as a ground for suspending the operation of the treaty in whole or in part in the relations between itself and the defaulting State; c. Any party other than the defaulting State to invoke the breach as a ground for suspending the operation of the treaty in whole or in part with respect to itself if the treaty is of such a character that a material breach of its provisions by one party radically changes the position of every party with respect to the further performance of its obligations under the treaty. 3. A material breach of a treaty, for the purposes of this article, consists in: a. A repudiation of the treaty not sanctioned by the present Convention; or b. The violation of a provision essential to the accomplishment of the object or purpose of the treaty. 4. The foregoing paragraphs are without prejudice to any provision in the treaty applicable in the event of a breach. 5. Paragraphs 1 to 3 do not apply to provisions relating to the protection of the human person contained in treaties of a humanitarian character, in particular to provisions prohibiting any form of reprisals against persons protected by such treaties.

Thus, Iraq's action, in the U.S. and United Kingdom (UK) view, meant that the 1990 UN Security Council authorization to use force remained in force, allowing "Member States co-operating with the Government of Kuwait . . . to use all necessary means to uphold resolution 660 (1990) and all subsequent relevant resolutions and to restore international peace and security in the area." UN doc. S/Res. 678 (1990), November 29, 1990. On the UK view, see "The Written Answer of the Attorney General, Lord Goldsmith, to a Parliamentary Question on the legal basis for the use of force in Iraq," March 17, 2003, UK Foreign and Commonwealth Office.

47 Thomas N. Franck, "What Happens Now? The United Nations after Iraq," *American Journal of International Law* 97, no. 3 (2003), 613; Patrick McLain, "Settling the Score with Saddam: Resolution 1441 and Parallel Justifications for the Use of Force Against Iraq," *Duke Journal of International Law* 13, no. 1 (2003), 233, 249. Paragraph 34 of UN Security

Council Resolution 687 (1991) ("Decides to remain seized of the matter and to take such further steps as may be required for implementation of the present resolution and to secure peace and security in the region") meant the Security Council alone could decide when the authorization in Resolution 678 (1990) could be invoked; for a different interpretation of the Security Council Iraq resolutions, see Nicholas Rostow, "Determining the Lawfulness of the 2003 Campaign Against Iraq," *Israel Yearbook on Human Rights* 34 (2004), 15–34; Sean D. Murphy, "Assessing the Legality of Invading Iraq," *Georgetown Law Journal* 92, no. 4 (2004), 173–272; Jules Lobel and Michael Ratner, "Bypassing the Security Council: Ambiguous Authorizations to Use Force, Cease-fires and the Iraqi Inspection Regime," *American Journal of International Law* 93, no. 1 (1999), 124 (absence of, or ambiguity in connection with, question of Security Council authority).

[48] UN doc. S/Res. 678 (1990) (November 29, 1990); Taft and Buchwald, "Preemption." See also Rostow, "International Law."

[49] UN doc. S/Res. 687 (1991) (April 3, 1991).

[50] Quoted in Stephen Dycus et al., *National Security Law*, 5th ed. (New York: Wolters Kluwer, 2011), 733.

[51] Ibid., 734.

[52] Ibid.

[53] 8 U.S.C. §§1182(a)(3)(B), 1227(a)(4)(B), as amended (2001).

[54] Affidavit of Michael E. Rolince, U.S. Department of Justice, Executive Office for Immigration Review, Immigration Court, quoted in Dycus et al., 739–740.

[55] On June 17, 2015, the Second Circuit Court of Appeals held that "The Constitution defines the limits of the Defendants' [former prison wardens Dennis Hasty, Michael Zenk, and James Sherman, former Attorney General John Ashcroft, former Federal Bureau of Investigations Director Robert Mueller, and former Immigration and Naturalization Service Commissioner James W. Ziglar] authority; detaining individuals as if they were terrorists, in the most restrictive conditions of confinement available, simply because these individuals were, or appeared to be, Arab or Muslim, exceeds those limits. . . . Holding individuals in solitary confinement twenty-three hours a day with regular strip searches because their perceived faith or race placed them in group targeted for recruitment by al Qaeda violated the detainees' constitutional rights." See Turkmen, et al. v. Hasty, et al., Nos. 13-981, 13-999, 13-1002, 13-1003, 13-1662 at *106-07 (2nd Cir. June 17, 2015), available at <www.ca2.uscourts.gov/decisions/isysquery/16c71149-0fdd-4844-b140-d197f4bd3118/9/doc/13-981_complete_opn.pdf#xml=http://www.ca2.uscourts.gov/decisions/isysquery/16c71149-0fdd-4844-b140-d197f4bd3118/9/hilite/>.

[56] 18 U.S.C. §3144, as amended (1986).

[57] Ibid.

[58] *Ashcroft v. Al-Kidd*, 563 U.S. __ (2011), 131 S. Ct. 2074 (2011) ("Efficient and even-handed application of the law demands that we look to whether the arrest is objectively

justified, rather than to the motive of the arresting officer."), quoted in Dycus et al., 757.

[59] Dycus et al., 738.

[60] The police may arrest based on "articulable suspicion that the person has been, is, or is about to be engaged in criminal activity." *United States v. Place*, 462 U.S. 696, 702 (1983). "'[R]easonable suspicion of criminal activity,' short of probable cause, only 'warrants a temporary seizure for the purpose of questioning limited to the purpose of the stop.'" *Florida v. Royer*, 460 U.S. 491, 498 (1983). Quoted in Dycus et al., 735. In 2006, Congress amended the Immigration and Nationality Act to permit arrest and detention of aliens on suspicion of illegal status.

[61] *Zadvydas v. Davis*, 533 U.S. 678 (2001).

[62] Quoted in Dycus et al., 738. British local authorities are said to use cameras installed as part of the effort to fight terrorism to enforce recycling laws.

[63] Geneva Convention Relative to the Treatment of Prisoners of War, August 2, 1949, reprinted in Adam Roberts and Richard Guelff, eds., *Documents on the Laws of War*, 3rd ed. (Oxford: Oxford University Press, 2000), 244ff.

[64] Geneva Convention for the Amelioration of the Condition of the Wounded and Sick in Armed Forces in the Field, August 12, 1949, Art. 3, reprinted in Roberts and Guelff, 198–199:

In the case of armed conflict not of an international character occurring in the territory of one of the High Contracting Parties, each Party to the conflict shall be bound to apply, as a minimum, the following provisions:

(1) Persons taking no active part in the hostilities, including members of armed forces who have laid down their arms and those placed hors de combat by sickness, wounds, detention, or any other cause, shall in all circumstances be treated humanely, without any adverse distinction founded on race, colour, religion or faith, sex, birth or wealth, or any other similar criteria.

To this end, the following acts are and shall remain prohibited at any time and in any place whatsoever with respect to the above-mentioned persons:

(a) violence to life and person, in particular murder of all kinds, mutilation, cruel treatment and torture;

(b) taking of hostages;

(c) outrages upon personal dignity, in particular humiliating and degrading treatment;

(d) the passing of sentences and the carrying out of executions without previous judgment pronounced by a regularly constituted court affording all the judicial guarantees which are recognized as indispensable by civilized peoples.

(2) The wounded and sick shall be collected and cared for.

An impartial humanitarian body, such as the International Committee of the Red Cross, may offer its services to the Parties to the conflict.

The Parties to the conflict should further endeavor to bring into force, by means of special agreements, all or part of the other provisions of the present Convention.

The application of the preceding provisions shall not affect the legal status of the Parties to the conflict.

This Common Article appears in the three other 1949 Geneva Conventions dealing with Wounded, Sick, and Shipwrecked Members of Armed Forces at Sea, Prisoners of War, and Civilians in Time of Armed Conflict. Ibid., 223–224, 245, 302.

[65] U.S. Const. art. VI.

[66] *Medellin v. Texas*, 128 U.S. 1346 (2008).

[67] Article 134 of the Uniform Code of Military Justice, the "general article," allows the military to import noncapital Federal criminal statutes and charge them in a military court-martial. 10 U.S.C. §934. Art. 134 (1956). Thus, Article 134 incorporates the War Crimes Act of 1996.

[68] See, for example, Roberts and Guelff, 196. *See also* Dinstein, *Conduct*, chapter one; W. Michael Reisman and Chris T. Antoniou, *The Laws of War* (New York: Vintage, 1994), xix–xxi; Theodor Meron, "The Geneva Conventions as Customary Law," *American Journal of International Law* 81, no. 2 (April 1987), 348–370.

[69] On the U.S. position with respect to parts of Protocols I and II, see Michael J. Matheson, then Deputy Legal Adviser, U.S. Department of State, "The United States Position on the Relation of Customary International Law to the 1977 Protocols Additional to the 1949 Geneva Conventions," *American University Journal of International Law and Policy*, vol. 2 (1987), 415, 419. See also Kenneth Anderson, "Wall Street Journal Mistaken About the Obama Administration and Protocol I?" *TheVolokhConspiracy.com*, available at <http://volokh.com/2011/03/08/wall-street-journal-mistaken-about-the-obama-administration-and-protocol-i/> (comments by John Bellinger III, formerly Legal Adviser to the National Security Council, 2001–2005, and Legal Adviser to the Department of State, 2005–2009, on the Obama administration decision to be guided by Article 75 of Protocol I, pertaining to humane treatment of detainees, even though the United States is not a party to Protocol I, and Article 75 does not codify customary international law). See also Nicholas Rostow, "The World Health Organization, the International Court of Justice, and Nuclear Weapons," *Yale Journal of International Law* 20, no. 1 (1995), 151, esp. 163–173, and citations therein.

[70] Adam R. Pearlman, "Meaningful Review and Process Due: How Guantanamo Detention is Changing the Battlefield," *Harvard National Security Law Journal* 6, no. 1 (2015), 255; but see Donald Rumsfeld, *Known and Unknown: A Memoir* (New York: Sentinel, 2011), 563–569, for a different view of the decisionmaking process.

[71] Jack Goldsmith, *The Terror Presidency: Law and Judgment inside the Bush Administration* (New York: Norton, 2007), 22.

[72] Dinstein, *War*, 5–8.

73 Special Rapporteur on Extrajudicial, Summary or Arbitrary Executions, Study on Targeted Killings, Addendum, UN doc. A/HRC/14/24/Add.6 (May 28, 2010) (by Philip Alston). See also Nicholas Rostow, "The Laws of War and the Killing of Suspected Terrorists: False Starts, Rabbit Holes, and Dead Ends," *Rutgers Law Review* 63, no. 4 (2011), 1215, 1225.

74 Dinstein, *Conduct*, 146–155.

75 1949 Geneva Convention III Art. 4.

76 1949 Geneva Convention III specifies in detail how prisoners of war (POWs) are to be treated, cared for, and protected. Article 75 of Additional Protocol I of 1977 sets forth minimum "Fundamental guarantees" with respect to treatment. The Obama administration has decided to follow this Article out of a sense that it is right. John Bellinger, "Obama's Announcements on International Law," *Lawfareblog.com*, March 8, 2011, available at <www.lawfareblog.com/2011/03/obamas-announcements-on-international-law>. Common Article 3's requirements are set forth in note 66.

77 1949 Geneva Convention III Art. 118.

78 Ibid., Art. 115.

79 Jens David Ohlin, "When Does the Combatant's Privilege Apply?" *OpinioJuris.org*, August 1, 2014, available at <http://opiniojuris.org/2014/08/01/combatants-privilege-apply/>. See also Dinstein, *Conduct*, 33–61.

80 Ibid.

81 Defense Department usage is *enemy prisoners of war* because it uses POW to mean, among other things, a "privately owned weapon."

82 In the U.S. case, the conditions of detainees in Guantanamo Bay are much improved compared to when the facility consisted of essentially a fenced-in tennis court.

83 An exception is Douglas J. Feith, but he does not spend much time on the decision. See note 108 below. See also Pearlman, "Meaningful Review."

84 Douglas J. Feith, *War and Decision: Inside the Pentagon at the Dawn of the War on Terrorism* (New York: HarperCollins, 2008), 159.

85 *Boumediene v. Bush*, 553 U.S. 723(2008).

86 Feith, 160; Rumsfeld, 561–573.

87 Louis Begley compared it to Devil's Island, the notorious French prison in Guiana where Dreyfus was held. *Why the Dreyfus Affair Matters* (New Haven: Yale University Press, 2009), 31ff ("the United States' own Devil's Island in Guantanamo").

88 Rumsfeld, 561–573.

89 *Hamdi v. Rumsfeld*, 542 U.S. 507 (2004).

90 Seven Uighurs contested a Combat Status Review Tribunal determination that they were "enemy combatants." The District of Columbia Circuit Court of Appeals held that there was insufficient evidence to hold them. The government therefore had to release

them, transfer them, or conduct a new hearing. Four eventually went to Bermuda. *Huzaifa Parhat v. Gates*, 532 F.3d 836 (D.C. Cir. 2008).

[91] *National Defense Authorization Act for Fiscal Year 2013*, 10 U.S.C. § 801 note (2012); *National Defense Authorization Act for Fiscal Year 2014*, 10 U.S.C. § 801 note (2013).

[92] There were 242 detainees in Guantanamo Bay at the beginning of the Obama Presidency. Department of Defense Office of Military Commissions, Human Rights Fact Sheet, March 2015, available at <www.mc.Mil/home>.

[93] *Hamdan v. United States*, 696 F.3d 1238 (D.C. Cir. 2012).

[94] President Bush established the first post–September 11, 2001, military commissions and accompanying guidelines. Military Order, November 13, 2001, "Detention, Treatment, and Trial of Certain Non-Citizens in the War Against Terrorism," *Federal Register* 66 (November 16, 2001), 57833, available at <https://federalregister.gov/a/01-28904>.

[95] Jennifer K. Elsea, *Comparison of Rights in Military Commission Trials and Trials in Federal Court* (Washington, DC: Congressional Research Service, March 21, 2014).

[96] *Hamdan v. Rumsfeld*, 548 U.S. 557 (2006).

[97] Ibid. A substantial number of lawyers and millions of dollars have been devoted to making the commission a legitimate forum for prosecution.

[98] Geneva Convention III, Art. 118; Roberts and Guelff, 289.

[99] Carol Rosenberg, "Why Obama Can't Close Guantanamo," *Foreign Affairs*, December 14, 2009, available at <www.foreignaffairs.com/articles/136781/carol-rosenberg/why-obama-cant-close-guantanamo>.

[100] Senator Diane Feinstein, among others, has criticized this practice. See Andy Worthington, "Sen. Dianne Feinstein Urges Pentagon to End 'Unnecessary' Force-Feeding at Guantánamo," *EurasiaReview.com*, April 14, 2015, available at <www.eurasiareview.com/14042015-sen-dianne-feinstein-urges-pentagon-to-end-unnecessary-force-feeding-at-guantanamo-oped>. It is not evident that facility personnel have an alternative if the detainees are not to be permitted to kill themselves.

[101] *Dhiab v. Obama*, No. CV05-1457(GK), 2014 WL 5795483 (D.D.C. November 7, 2014).

[102] In 2010, Nicholas Rostow was told this information officially during a trip to Guantanamo Bay as part of review, on behalf of the President and Secretary of Defense, of the treatment of detainees.

[103] James Risen and Matt Apuzzo, "C.I.A. on Path to Torture, Chose Haste over Analysis," *New York Times*, December 15, 2014, A1.

[104] International Committee of the Red Cross, "Treaties and State Parties to Such Treaties," available at <www.icrc.org/applic/ihl/ihl.nsf/INTRO/475?OpenDocument>. Article 75 of 1977 Protocol I Additional to the Geneva Conventions of 12 August 1949 Relating to the Protection of Victims of International Armed Conflicts, June 8, 1977, Art. 75, contains a lengthy elaboration on Common Art. 3 of the 1949 Geneva Conventions. Roberts and

Guelff, 463–466.

[105] Dycus et al., 235. See the Lieber Code, Instructions for the Government of Armies of the United States in the Field (1863), originally published as General Orders No. 100, War Department, Adjutant General's Office, on April 24, 1863, reprinted in Dietrich Schindler, *The Laws of Armed Conflicts: A Collection of Conventions, Resolutions, and Other Documents*, 4th rev. ed. (Leiden: Martinus Nijhoff Publishers, 2004).

[106] Statement of the White House Press Secretary, February 7, 2002.

[107] Feith, 161–165; Lisa L. Turner, "The Detainee Interrogation Debate and the Legal-Policy Process," *Joint Force Quarterly* 54 (3rd Quarter 2009), 42–46.

[108] Feith, 162.

[109] Ibid., 161–163.

[110] *Hamdan v. Rumsfeld*, 548 U.S. 557, 630 (2006).

[111] For example, *United States v. Yunis*, 924 F. 2d 1086, 1089 (D.C. Cir. 1991).

[112] See Memorandum from Steven G. Bradbury, Principal Deputy Assistant Attorney General, Office of Legal Counsel, U.S. Department of Justice, to John Rizzo, Senior Deputy General Counsel, CIA 14 (May 10, 2005) available at <www.fas.org/irp/agency/doj/olc/techniques.pdf>.

[113] John A. Rizzo, *Company Man: Thirty Years of Controversy and Crisis in the CIA* (New York: Scribner, 2014).

[114] Hadley, interview.

[115] Paul Kramer, "The Water Cure," *The New Yorker*, February 24, 2008, available at <www.newyorker.com/magazine/2008/02/25/the-water-cure>.

[116] This insurance against harming the victim of waterboarding raises the question: did the detainee know, and if so, did it affect the result of the interrogation? The silence on the results of the waterboarding, except in most general terms, is deafening. See George Tenet with Bill Harlow, *At the Center of the Storm* (New York: HarperCollins 2007), 242.

[117] CIA interrogators presumably were acting under a covert action finding. In addition, they were acting pursuant to a legal opinion by the Office of Legal Counsel at the Justice Department.

[118] U.S. Congress, Senate, Senate Select Intelligence Committee, Committee Study of the Central Intelligence Agency's Interrogation Program, 113th Cong., 2nd sess., 2014, available at <www.washingtonpost.com/wp-srv/special/national/cia-interrogation-report/document/>.

[119] Tenet, 250.

[120] Ibid., 255.

[121] Richard Cheney, interview by Timothy Russert, *Meet the Press*, September 16, 2001, available at <www.whitehouse.gov/vicepresident/news-speeches/speeches/vp20010916.

html>. Cheney stated, "we have to work through sort of the dark side." Testimony of Cofer Black to Joint House and Senate Select Intelligence Committee, September 26, 2002, available at <www.fas.org/irp/congress/2002_hr/092602black.html>. Black stated, "All I want to say is that there was 'before' 9/11 and 'after' 9/11. After 9/11 the gloves come off." Also see James P. Terry, *The War on Terror: The Legal Dimension* (Lanham, MD: Rowman and Littlefield, 2013), 73–77, who weighs the claims for the results of enhanced interrogation against results. Terry, who served as Legal Counsel to the Chairman of the Joint Chiefs of Staff under Colin Powell pointed out that some advocates of the treatment of Khalid Sheikh Mohammed believe that he provided valuable information that saved lives but undermine their case because the plots he claimed to have helped foil were disrupted before he was captured.

[122] Stephen Grey, *Ghost Plane: The True Story of the CIA Torture Program* (New York: St. Martin's Griffin, 2006), 242–243; Henry Shue, "Torture," in *Torture: A Collection*, ed. Sanford Levinson, rev. ed. (Oxford: Oxford University Press, 2004), 55 (moral absolutism recognized by the European Court of Human Rights); Jeannine Bell, "'Behind This Mortal Bone': The (In)effectiveness of Torture," *Indiana Law Journal* 83, no. 1 (2008), 339 (arguing torture is neither effective nor in a nation's best interest); David Luban, "Liberalisms, Torture, and the Ticking Bomb," *Virginia Law Review* 91, no. 6 (2005), 142 (stating ticking bomb scenarios are a device to rationalize and institutionalize torture); Jane Mayer, *The Dark Side* (New York: Doubleday 2008), 213.

[123] Fritz Allhof, "Torture Warrants, Self-Defense, and Necessity," *Public Affairs Quarterly* 25, no. 3 (July 2011); Alan M. Dershowitz, *Why Terrorism Works: Understanding the Threat, Responding to the Challenge* (New Haven: Yale University Press, 2002); John T. Parry, "Torture Warrants and the Rule of Law," *Albany Law Review* 71, no. 3 (2009), 885–906.

[124] Zeke Miller, "Obama: 'We Tortured Some Folks,'" *Time*, August 1, 2014.

[125] Steven M. Klienman, "The Promise of Interrogation v. the Problem of Torture," *Valparaiso University Law Review* 43, no. 4 (2009), 1577–1587.

[126] Tenet, 242.

[127] One member of the minority voted with the majority. Majority Report, 31 n. 145 reports that an overseas detention facility had equipment for conducting waterboarding. The committee found no evidence that someone had been waterboarded at the site, but committee suspicions were aroused by finding evidence of paraphernalia. The committee majority did not believe what CIA said on the subject. See note 121, at 6.

[128] CIA, "Remarks as Prepared for Delivery by CIA Director John O. Brennan in response to the Senate Select Committee on Intelligence Study on the Former Detention and Interrogation Program," December 11, 2014, available at <www.cia.gov/news-information/speeches-testimony/2014-speeches-testimony/remarks-as-prepared-for-delivery-cia-director-john-o-brennan-response-to-ssci-study-on-the-former-detention-and-interrogation-program.html>.

[129] Ibid.

[130] United Nations Convention against Torture and Other Cruel, Inhuman or Degrading Treatment or Punishment, ¶ 1, G.A. Res. 39/46, U.N. GAOR, 39th Sess., Supp. No. 51, at 197, U.N. Doc. A/39/51 (1984). The UN Convention against Torture requires all signatories to make torture a crime.

[131] Dycus et al., 914.

[132] 18 U.S.C. §§ 2340–2340A (2000).

[133] Ibid.

[134] International Covenant on Civil and Political Rights, Art. 7 (1966) (the United States became a party in 1992), 999 U.N.T.S. 171.

[135] Daniel L. Pines, "Are Even Torturers Immune from Suit? How Attorney General Opinions Shield Government Employees from Civil Litigation and Criminal Prosecution," *Wake Forest Law Review* 43, no. 1 (2008), 93–160; A. John Radsan, "Sed Quis Custodiet Ipsos Custodes: The CIA's Office of General Counsel?" *Journal of National Security Law & Policy* 2, no. 2 (2008), 201–252.

[136] Memorandum for John Rizzo, Acting General Counsel of the Central Intelligence Agency, August 1, 2002, from Jay S. Bybee, Assistant Attorney General, Office of Legal Counsel, Department of Justice (withdrawn December 30, 2004, by Acting Assistant Attorney General Daniel Levin); Memorandum for Alberto R. Gonzales, Counsel to the President, from Jay Bybee, August 1, 2002 (withdrawn by Levin memorandum); Memorandum from John C. Yoo, Deputy Assistant Attorney General, Office of Legal Counsel, to William J. Haynes II, General Counsel of the Department of Defense, "Military Interrogation of Alien Unlawful Combatants Held Outside the United States," March 14, 2003, available at <www.aclu.org/files/pdfs/safefree/yoo_army_torture_memo.pdf>. This memo was produced by John Yoo and signed by Jay Bybee (withdrawn by Levin memorandum).

[137] Haynes memorandum, 6–10.

[138] Ibid., 11–47.

[139] Ibid., 1–2, 32–47.

[140] Ibid., 39, 1, 36–47.

[141] Executive Order 13440, "Interpretation of the Geneva Conventions Common Article 3 as Applied to a Program of Detention and Interrogation Operated by the Central Intelligence Agency," July 20, 2007, available at <http://fas.org/irp/offdocs/eo/eo-13440.htm>.

[142] Julie Angell, "Ethics, Torture, and Marginal Memoranda at the DOJ Office of Legal Counsel," *Georgetown Journal of Legal Ethics* 18, no. 3 (2005), 557–568; George Harris, "The Rule of Law and the War on Terror: The Professional Responsibility of Executive Branch Lawyers in the Wake of 9/11," *Journal of National Security Law & Policy* 1, no. 2 (2005), 409–452; Luban, 1425–1453; "The Bush Administration and the Torture Memo: What on Earth Were They Thinking?" *Economist*, June 17, 2004.

[143] Reaction to Yoo's memorandum by fellow Republicans within the Office of Legal Counsel (OLC) is illuminating. Jack Goldsmith, who headed the OLC from 2003 to 2004, stated

that Yoo's memo was "riddled with error" and a "one-sided effort to eliminate any hurdles posed by the torture law." Daniel Levin, who headed the OLC after Goldsmith, described his initial reaction to Yoo's memo as "this is insane, who wrote this?" See David D. Cole, "The Sacrificial Yoo: Accounting for Torture in the OPR Report," *Journal of National Security Law & Policy* 4, no. 2 (2010), 455.

[144] "Nomination of Michael Mukasey to Be the Attorney General of the United States: Hearing of the Senate Committee on the Judiciary," Federal News Service, October 17, 2007.

[145] Department of Defense Emergency Supplemental Appropriations to Address Hurricanes in the Gulf of Mexico, and Pandemic Influenza Act, 2006 (P.L. 109-148); the National Defense Authorization Act for FY 2006 (P.L. 109-163).

[146] See generally 13 No. 2 Human Rights Brief 39-40 (2006).

[147] See P.L. 109-148, Title X, Sec. 1002 (2005); P.L. 109-163, Title XIV, Sec. 1402 (2006).

[148] S. Amend. 1556 to S. 1042, 109th Cong. (2005), reprinted in 151 Congressional Record S8889 (July 25, 2005).

[149] Geneva Convention Relative to the Treatment of Prisoners of War Art. 3, August 12, 1949, 6 U.S.T. 3116, 75 U.N.T.S. 135.

[150] 548 U.S. 557 (2006).

[151] Executive Order 13340.

[152] Department of Justice, Office of Legal Counsel, "Memorandum Regarding Application of the War Crimes Act, the Detainee Treatment Act, and Common Article 3 of the Geneva Conventions to Certain Techniques That May Be Used by the CIA in the Interrogation of High-level Al Qaeda Detainees," July 20, 2007.

[153] Luban, 1425 (ticking bomb scenarios rationalize and institutionalize torture); Kate Kovarovic, "Our 'Jack Bauer' Culture: Eliminating the Ticking Time Bomb Exception to Torture," *Florida Journal of International Law* 22, no. 2 (2010), 251.

[154] See Goldsmith, 166–168 (impact of fear).

[155] See Alan M. Dershowitz, "Is There a Torturous Road to Justice?" *Los Angeles Times*, November 8, 2001, B19 (judges should be allowed to issue "torture warrants," thus permitting the use of torture within our legal system rather than "outside of the law"); but see Oren Gross, "Are Torture Warrants Warranted? Pragmatic Absolutism and Official Disobedience," *University of Minnesota Law Review* 88, no. 4 (2004), 1481, 1487 ("preventive interrogational torture is far too complex to be addressed by definitional juggling").

[156] Philip B. Heymann and Juliette N. Kayyem, *Long-Term Legal Strategy Project for Preserving Security and Democratic Freedoms in the War on Terrorism* (Cambridge: MIT Press, 2004) (determining an emergency exception based upon President showing "an urgent and extraordinary need").

[157] See Charles Krauthammer, "The Truth About Torture," *Weekly Standard*, December 5, 2005, available at <www.weeklystandard.com/content/public/articles/000/000/006/400rh-qav.asp>.

[158] P.L. 109-148, Title X, Sec. 1004; P.L. 109-163, Title XIV, Sec 1404.

[159] Ibid.

[160] As long ago as *Marbury v. Madison*, the Supreme Court opined that not only was the government of the United States a government of laws, but that "It will certainly cease to deserve this high appellation, if the laws furnish no remedy for the violation of a vested legal right" 5 U.S. (1 Cranch) 137, 163. At the same time, the court observed, "by the constitution of the United States, the President is invested with certain important political powers, in the exercise of which he is to use his own discretion, and is accountable only to his country in his political character, and to his own conscience" 5 U.S. at 165–166. In the context of a Presidential decision to torture a detainee, these statements beg the question: is such a decision a political act in which case the President is accountable politically, or is it a violation of a legal right not to be tortured, in which case the President would be accountable in a court? In our judgment, however one answers, the President is accountable for his or her acts. Under the Constitution, there exists no unaccountable power. See also Blum and Heymann, 130.

[161] In law enforcement operations, the standards for the use of lethal force are entirely different. Blum and Heymann, esp. chapter 4.

[162] Dinstein, *Conduct*, 146–152.

[163] Pam Benson, "U.S. Airstrikes Called 'Very Effective,'" *CNN.com*, May 18, 2009, available at <www.cnn.com/2009/POLITICS/05/18/cia.pakistan.airstrikes>.

[164] Blum and Heymann, chapter 4.

[165] Joint Resolution, "Authorization for Use of Military Force," September 18, 2001, Pub. L. 107-40 (S.J. Res. 23).

[166] See, for example, Field Manual 27-10, *The Law of Land Warfare* (Washington, DC: Headquarters Department of the Army, 1956); Army Regulation 190-8, "Enemy Prisoners of War, Retained Personnel, Civilian Internees and Other Detainees," October 1, 1997, § 1.1(b)(4) (stating that, should conflicts arise, the Geneva Conventions take precedence over the regulation).

[167] Ibid.

[168] Protocol I, Art. 48; Roberts and Guelff, 447.

[169] Ibid.

[170] U.S. War Department, General Orders No. 100, the Lieber Code of 1863, Art. 16 (1863). For example, the 1907 Hague Convention (IV) respecting the Laws and Customs of War on Land, Annex, Art. 23, prohibits treacherous killing or wounding or using weapons causing unnecessary suffering. Roberts and Guelff, 77. The 1907 Hague Conventions are part of customary international law. Dinstein, *Conduct*, 15.

[171] Protocol I, Art. 51 (5)(b); Roberts and Guelff, 449.

[172] Jeff A. Bovarnick et al., *Law of War Deskbook* (Charlottesville, VA: International and Operational Law Department, U.S. Army Judge Advocate's Legal Center and School, 2011), 156.

[173] See generally Dinstein, *Conduct*, 8.

[174] Bovarnick, 154.

[175] Protocol I, art. 51(4); Roberts and Guelff, 448–449.

[176] Bovarnick, 155.

[177] Ibid.

[178] Ibid., 155–156.

[179] Ibid., 157.

[180] Ibid.

[181] Ibid.

[182] Harold Hongju Koh, address to the Annual Meeting of the American Society of International Law, March 25, 2010, available at <www.state.gov/s/l/releases/remarks/139119.htm>.

[183] Ibid.

[184] The White House, "Fact Sheet: U.S. Policy Standards and Procedures for the Use of Force in Counterterrorism Operations Outside the United States and Areas of Active Hostilities," May 23, 2013, available at <www.whitehouse.gov/the-press-office/2013/05/23/fact-sheet-us-policy-standards-and-procedures-use-force-counterterrorism>.

[185] See Mike Dreyfuss, "My Fellow Americans, We are Going to Kill You: The Legality of Targeting and Killing U.S. Citizens Abroad," *Vanderbilt Law Review* 65, no. 1 (2012), 249.

[186] Cf. *Hamdi v. Rumsfeld*, 542 U.S. 507, 597 (2004) (Thomas, J., dissenting).

[187] Samuel S. Adelsberg, "Bouncing the Executive's Blank Check: Judicial Review and the Targeting of Citizens," *Harvard Law & Policy Review* 6, no. 2 (2012), 437–459.

[188] Department of Justice, "Lawfulness of Lethal Operation Directed against a U.S. Citizen who is a Senior Operational Leader of Al-Qa'id or an Associated Force," published by NBC News on February 4, 2013.

[189] Ibid.

[190] Ibid.

[191] Ibid.

[192] Ex parte Quirin, 317 U.S. 1 (1942).

[193] Robert Chesney, "Text of the Attorney General's National Security Speech," March 5, 2012, *Lawfareblog.com*, available at <www.lawfareblog.com/2012/03/text-of-the-attorney-generals-national-security-speech/>.

[194] "Remarks by the President at the National Defense University," Washington, DC, May 23, 2013, available at <www.whitehouse.gov/the-press-office/2013/05/23/remarks-president-national-defense-university>.

[195] *Al Aulaqi v. Obama* (D.D.C. 2010) seems to indicate that judicial inquiry into such process is a nonjudiciable political question. In *Al Aulaqi*, Judge Bates held that Anwar Al-Aulaqi's lawsuit seeking to enjoin the U.S. Government from targeting his son was nonjusticiable under the political question doctrine because "[j]udicial resolution of the 'particular questions' posed" would require [it] to decide complex issues such as "whether . . . Anwar Al-Aulaqi's alleged terrorist activity render[ed] him a concrete, specific, and imminent threat to life or physical safety" and "whether there are means short of lethal force that the United States could reasonably employ to address any threat that Anwar Al-Aulaqi poses to U.S. national security interests." These questions, Judge Bates stated, would require the court take into account military, strategic, and diplomatic considerations—for example, to "assess the merits of the President's (alleged) decision to launch an attack on a foreign target"—that it was simply not competent to handle. Thus, the extent to which due process conflicts with U.S. Government's targeted killing program may remain in the realm of academics but not courts. *Al-Aulaqi v. Panetta*, No. 12-1192 (D.D.C. July 18, 2012).

[196] Blum and Heymann, 189–193.

[197] Philip Bobbitt, "Playing by the Rules," *The Guardian*, November 15, 2003.

[198] Baker; Tower Commission, *Report of the President's Special Review Board* (New York: Bantam Books, February 27, 1987), parts I and II.

[199] This insight goes as far back at least as Thucydides, *The Peloponnesian War*, bk. I, ch. I, 24.

[200] For example, Hadley, interview.

[201] Each of the four Geneva Conventions of 1949 contains a common Article 3 requirement of humane treatment of persons detained who are not entitled to the protections afforded prisoners of war, that is, combatants as defined in the Third Geneva Convention. The conventions are reprinted in Roberts and Guelff. During the early part of 2002, there was significant debate as to whether to consider treating captured Taliban or al Qaeda personnel as prisoners of war under the Third Geneva Convention of 1949. The initial decision to declare all captured enemy soldiers to be "unlawful combatants"—not entitled as a matter of law to be treated as prisoners of war—appears to have been the result, at least in part, of a mistaken reading of the Geneva Conventions. A memorandum went to President Bush with a significant error. The memorandum stated that, under the Geneva Conventions, an interrogator could ask only a prisoner's name, rank, and serial number, when in fact the convention provides that a prisoner of war is only required to provide that information. The interrogator may ask whatever question he or she wishes. The President naturally felt such constraints would have been untenable under the circumstances created by the September 11 attacks. But the Geneva Conventions would not have imposed those constraints in the first place. Author conversation with William Lietzau, former Deputy Assistant Secretary of Defense for Rule of Law and Detainee Policy.

[202] Feith, 159, "And government lawyers argued that a facility on non-U.S.-owned territory would likely not be subject to habeas corpus petitions by detainees."

[203] For example, the American debate about the 2011 Libya campaign for the most part concerned the applicability of the War Powers Resolution, not the wisdom of the effort to oust Muammar Qadhafi.

[204] Martin E. Dempsey, interview by Richard D. Hooker, Jr., and Joseph J. Collins, January 15, 2015.

[205] When the Abu Ghraib story broke in the press, a 19-year-old Marine watching television reports stated, "Some assholes have just lost the war for us." Thomas E. Ricks, *Fiasco: The American Military Adventure in Iraq* (New York: Penguin Press, 2006), 290.

6

Reflections on Lessons Encountered

Richard D. Hooker, Jr., and Joseph J. Collins

This volume is an effort to capture, at the strategic level, useful lessons from America's long and painful experiences in Iraq and Afghanistan. Earlier chapters explore in detail a range of the important strategic dimensions and dynamics of these campaigns. In this chapter, we render an early accounting of the costs and gains, followed by more general observations that may inform the soldier/statesman and strategist when facing similar complex challenges. In particular, we focus on three major strategic events: the decisions to invade Iraq in 2003, to surge in Iraq in 2006, and to surge in Afghanistan in 2009. Our audience is that cohort of present and future senior military leaders, as well as those advising them, who operate at the apex of civil-military relations, the politico-military interface where all key strategic decisions are made. The task has been daunting, not least because we find ourselves far enough removed from events to lend a measure of clarity, but not so far as to permit true objectivity. This is not history, at least not yet, nor is it revealed truth. But it is, we hope, something of a beginning on a journey of discovery.

Two Campaigns: A Complex Balance Sheet

Iraq and Afghanistan loom large in the popular consciousness as the long, grinding conflicts that, along with the economic collapse of 2008, dominated American political life in the years following 9/11. Both were separate and distinct cases, yet each was inextricably involved with the other, usually as a competitor for resources. Both began as more or less conventional state-on-state military interventions but evolved quickly into full-blown counterinsurgencies. Both involved large coalitions, massive security assistance programs, and bitterly divided ethno-sectarian groups, challenging attempts to employ a "comprehensive approach" that could unite civil and military action across the effort. Both featured weak, corrupt host-nation governments.

Yet there were also important differences. Iraq featured greater wealth, a more advanced infrastructure, less daunting logistical challenges, different tribal and ethno-sectarian dynamics, and more human capital. Afghanistan, lacking oil and other natural resources, was desperately poor and vulnerable to outside intervention, while its harsh climate and topography made military operations difficult. As in Vietnam, the U.S. military was forced to adapt its doctrine, training, and equipment in nonstandard ways, while the civilian component strained to build host-nation capacity.

With this as context, we state unequivocally that the wars in Afghanistan and Iraq carried high costs in blood and treasure. More than 10,000 American Servicemembers, government civilians, and contractor personnel have been killed, and well over 80,000 have been wounded or injured, many seriously. Veterans and Servicemembers suffering from post-traumatic stress disorder or traumatic brain injury add hundreds of thousands more to the casualty count. Our allies and partners, not including host nations, count over 1,400 dead. In Iraq alone, at least 135,000 civilians were killed, mostly by terrorists and insurgents.[1] In Afghanistan, from 2009 to 2014, nearly 18,000 civilians were killed, over 70 percent at the hands of the enemy.[2] The effects of these wars, at home and abroad, will be felt for many years to come.

The direct costs of these campaigns are $1.6 trillion, which in the main were covered not by revenues but by deficit spending. More complex, long-term estimates exceed $4 trillion.[3] The U.S. Armed Forces—especially its ground forces—experienced extraordinary stress and have yet to recover. That process has suffered from the simultaneous challenges of sequestration, downsizing, and the requirements of new and pressing conflicts.

Fourteen years after 9/11, any attempt to accurately gauge political losses and gains from the wars in Iraq and Afghanistan is problematic. The costs appear high and the benefits slight, though long-term outcomes remain uncertain. Iraq, thought to have been stabilized in 2011 when U.S. and coalition troops withdrew, now faces partition and a strong pull into an Iranian orbit. Though al Qaeda in Iraq was defeated, the Islamic State in Iraq and the Levant (ISIL) has emerged as an even stronger threat, further destabilizing Iraq, Syria, and the region as a whole. Afghanistan under the new Ashraf Ghani administration remains a work in progress, its future after the withdrawal of the International Security Assistance Force (ISAF) in question.

Looking back at this remove, the costs seem clear, painful, and excessive, while the benefits are unclear or still beyond the horizon. Throughout, the Armed Forces performed with courage and competence, retaining the trust and confidence of the American people. Yet success in both campaigns is elusive. Progress in Afghanistan and Iraq, in the words of General David Petraeus, USA (Ret.), still appears fragile and reversible.

There have been solid gains. Saddam Hussein's tyranny, aggression, and lust for weapons of mass destruction (WMD) are history. Al Qaeda in Afghanistan and Pakistan has been all but destroyed. The Taliban have been checked, although their various branches remain a potent force in both Afghanistan and Pakistan. Because of the dedicated work of our Intelligence Community, Armed Forces, Department of Homeland Security, and national law enforcement establishment, al Qaeda has been unable to repeat the catastrophic attacks of September 2001. This is a crowning achievement of the Long War, and one that should not be discounted.

Both Afghanistan and Iraq have been liberated from highly oppressive regimes. They have also been introduced to democracy. More immediately, both nations have received generous help in reconstruction. Afghanistan, for example, had been at war for nearly 24 years before the United States and its partners helped to oust the backward and highly authoritarian Taliban regime. The devastation of the country in 2002 stands in great contrast to the effects of U.S. and allied reconstruction efforts, which have significantly improved the quality of life for Afghan citizens.[4]

Al Qaeda terrorism, however, has morphed from a single hierarchical organization to a set of interlocking networks. There are now al Qaeda rivals, such as ISIL, that have significant capabilities, and there are other violent extremist organizations, especially in North Africa and the Horn of Africa, that have declared themselves to be members or affiliates of al Qaeda. Lieutenant General Michael Flynn, USA (Ret.), former head of the Defense Intelligence Agency, noted, "In 2004, there were 21 total Islamic terrorist groups spread out in 18 countries. Today, there are 41 Islamic terrorist groups spread out in 24 countries."[5] While we may have prevented major terrorist attacks against the homeland since 9/11, we have no reason to be complacent.

In geostrategic terms, our intervention in Iraq has accelerated the Sunni-Shia conflict that now rends the Middle East. Saddam was an odious tyrant, but his Iraq represented a powerful counterweight to Iranian hegemonic aspirations. Iran has been the winner, as a weakened and fractured Iraq, dominated by Shia political forces, is now heavily influenced by Tehran. The intense sectarianism that followed the U.S. departure from Iraq enabled the rise of ISIL in the years that followed, with grave consequences for the region and the world.

It is important to note that neither Iraq nor Afghanistan was originally a counterinsurgency (COIN) campaign. Both interventions unseated existing governments, to be replaced by new leaders, nascent governance structures, and a bewildering array of international aid organizations that flooded these countries with money and advisors. A practical working democracy, competent ministries, and the rule of law did not materialize quickly, frustrating the desire to hand over governance and security responsibilities and withdraw. In both cases, the opposition was defeated but not destroyed. Over time, strong insurgent forces were reconstituted to contest host-nation governance and coalition security forces. U.S. leaders were slow to acknowledge the nature and character of these conflicts as they evolved into true insurgencies, though subsequent adaptations were rapid and effective, especially at the tactical and operational levels.

In Afghanistan, a sober assessment shows that while the Afghan people are clearly better off than they were under the Taliban, and while Afghanistan is no longer a safe haven for al Qaeda, the Taliban were not eliminated. In the Hindu Kush, the new Ghani regime, backed by an army that has succeeded at great costs in three fighting seasons, has reduced friction in the coalition and is fighting hard to improve governance and reduce corruption. Nevertheless, the future stability and prosperity of Afghanistan remain in some doubt. In Iraq, in the 3½ years subsequent to the U.S. withdrawal, the Nouri al-Maliki government adopted intensely sectarian practices, weakened its army, and opened the door for ISIL. In both Iraq and Afghanistan, our military efforts were able to set conditions and create space for a resolution of the political issues that had impelled both insurgencies in the first place. This must be seen as a major accomplishment. Unfortunately, both the Iraqi and Afghan political establishments lacked the will and capacity to fully exploit these gains. Internal corruption and inadequate democratic structures, grafted onto traditionally authoritarian and tribal cultures, prevented stable power-sharing solutions in Iraq and inhibited them in Afghanistan. Thus, the military gains achieved were not enough to enable political solutions, despite the commitment of huge sums and the sustained efforts over many years of coalition diplomats and development experts. Herein lies a powerful lesson: by itself, the military instrument cannot solve inherently political questions, absent the total defeat of an adversary and its reconstruction from the ground up. This is unlikely in all but the most extreme cases.

There is, however, a larger context. The ideological and sociological seeds of Islamist terrorism and insurgency are found in the larger war between fundamentalist and more moderate camps and a struggle for political modernization in a greater Middle East much in need of reform.[6] This suggests that the conflict in which we have been engaged for the past 14 years will continue, albeit in new forms.

The Long War has become a longer war; as Clausewitz noted, the results of war are never final.[7] Those who crave a final accounting of the wars in Iraq and Afghanistan will have to wait decades to get it. It is, however, possible to offer judgments and observations that may be helpful to the rising generation of senior military leadership. Both civilian and military leaders are required to cooperate to make effective strategy, yet their cultures vary widely. As noted elsewhere, the dialogue is an unequal one, with the power of decision residing exclusively with the President and the civilian leadership. Nevertheless, the role of senior military leaders is critical. If military professionalism means anything at all, those leaders possess expert knowledge not available anywhere else. By law and precedent, they have a right to be heard. Navigating this terrain represents the art of generalship at its most challenging. Success derives from intellectual preparation, decades of experiential learning and high success in leading complex military organizations, a decided character that is sturdy and self-confident while also open to new ideas, an advanced grasp of higher strategy, and a strong moral-ethical compass. Not all who rise to the top of the military hierarchy are so equipped.

Case Analysis

While a comprehensive discussion of findings and observations is found in earlier chapters and in a separate annex, Operations *Iraqi Freedom* and *Enduring*

Freedom represent distinct case studies in how policy and strategy are made, each a rich vein to be mined. Immediately following the 9/11 attacks, an urgent consensus formed demanding a military response. In the case of Afghanistan, time was short, and only limited interagency discussion took place before military forces were in motion. In a sense, our approach to the campaign was always, in Helmuth von Moltke's felicitous phrase, a "system of expedients" as the interagency community adapted and evolved to changing conditions and to the reality that for many years, Afghanistan was a secondary priority to Iraq. Only in 2010 did Afghanistan become the primary theater of war.

The opportunity for planning and preparation was far greater in the case of Iraq. Here the case for war was less clear, the higher prioritization less convincing, the military less enthusiastic. Perhaps the most basic of strategic questions—what is the problem to be solved?—became a football to be kicked around for the next several years, with the answer ranging from destruction of WMD to preventing a nexus of terror to establishing democracy in the heart of the Arab world. Many key assumptions—that Saddam's WMD program presented a clear and present danger, that Iraqi reconstruction would pay for itself, that the majority Shiite population would welcome coalition forces as liberators, that working through Iraqi tribal structures could be safely ignored, that a small footprint could be successful, that large-scale de-Ba'athification was needful and practical, that a rapid transfer to Iraqi control was possible—proved unfounded, dislocating our strategy and the campaign. The failure to plan adequately and comprehensively for the postconflict period ushered in a new, dangerous, and intractable phase that saw a rapid descent first into insurgency and then into intense sectarian violence.[8] National decisions linking strategic success to corrupt and incapable host-nation governments—the primary drivers of the insurgencies in the first place—proved a major brake.

What was the appropriate role for senior military figures in this regard? The answer lies partly in the degree to which military leaders at the politico-military interface are expected to limit their advice to purely military matters—to delivering "best military advice" only, leaving aside political, economic, legal, and other dimensions for others to weigh. This is a recurring theme in civil-military relations, dating to the 1950s if not earlier, that has not yet been fully resolved. Political leaders may believe, and some clearly do, that military officers are ill-equipped to operate in this environment:[9]

[M]ilitary officers are ill-prepared to contribute to high policy. Normal career patterns do not look towards such a role. . . . half-hearted attempts at irregular intervals in an officer's career to introduce him to questions of international politics produce only superficiality and presumption and an altogether deficient sense of the real complexity of the problems facing the nation.[10]

An alternate perspective, voiced by President John F. Kennedy but with roots in Clausewitz, holds that military officers engaged at the highest levels have not only a right but also a duty to take into consideration the context of critical national security issues, including their political, diplomatic, and economic dimensions, lest their military advice be rendered useless or impractical. President Kennedy specifically urged—even ordered—the military, from the Joint Chiefs right down to academy cadets, to eschew "narrow" definitions of military competence and responsibilities, take political considerations into account in their military recommendations, and prepare themselves to take active roles in the policymaking process.[11]

We take the latter view. For the Chairman of the Joint Chiefs and combatant commanders, there is no "purely military" question, no neat distinction between different dimensions of strategy and policy. They are conjoined. In this regard, we do not find in the record convincing evidence of vigorous debate or respectful dissent from senior military leaders on the key questions raised above, though admittedly all rise above the purely military. Nor do we see them as apparent only in hindsight. The military operations leading to the overthrow of Saddam were outstandingly successful, a tribute to superb military leadership and to the Armed Forces as a whole. Nevertheless, the basic assumptions upon which our national and campaign strategies for Iraq were based were flawed, with doleful consequences.[12] The primary responsibility must lie with the political leaders who made them. But senior military leaders also have a voice and real influence as expert practitioners in their fields. In the case of the decision to invade Iraq, this influence was not used in full.

This dynamic speaks fundamentally to how we make strategy in America and how our civil-military relations are ordered. Despite criticism of the military as "praetorian" or "out of control,"[13] deference to civilian control is real, especially when dealing with strong civilian personalities. The example of

407

early success in Afghanistan with limited forces empowered proponents of a similar approach for Iraq, as did the heavy support by the administration for "transformational" thinking about armed conflict. In terms of organizational culture, and our experience in Vietnam notwithstanding, the Armed Forces were more predisposed to sharp, decisive, conventional operations than protracted irregular ones. These factors help explain, in part, the approaches taken by senior military leaders in the run-up to Iraq.

A separate but related case is President George W. Bush's decision to surge in Iraq in 2006, made against the recommendations of the military chain of command. The ultimate success of the Surge remains open to debate. Some argue that the Surge precipitated a major reduction in violence, creating conditions for a political settlement that ultimately failed when U.S. forces withdrew in 2011. Others see the crisis in Iraq today as evidence that the Surge along with the Anbar Awakening were only tactical successes with temporarily positive effects that were undone later by the political failures of the Maliki administration. While these differing perspectives will not be resolved, the role played by senior military leaders at this time illuminates both the strengths and weaknesses of America's unique approach to making strategy.

The year 2006 was difficult for the United States and the coalition in Iraq. The February 22 bombing of the al-Askari mosque led to an extraordinary spike in violence. By most accounts Iraq began to degenerate into open civil war, a conflict that the new Maliki government was unwilling or unable to control. Several attempts to stabilize Baghdad failed. That summer, officials with the National Security Council staff began to push for a "policy review." In November, the administration was dealt a strong rebuff in the midterm elections, leading to the resignation of Secretary Donald Rumsfeld. In early December, the bipartisan Iraq Study Group released its report, stating that "the situation in Iraq is grave and deteriorating."[14]

Aware that the success of the campaign was in doubt, President Bush reached out to a number of advisors, both in and outside the formal military and political chains. He was provided essentially with three options: to accelerate the withdrawal of American troops and the handover to Iraqi security forces, to pull back from the capital and allow the factions to fight it out, or to surge forces dramatically to regain the initiative and reestablish security.[15] With some variations, most senior military officials favored the first option.[16] In the case of the Joint Chiefs of Staff, their views were undoubtedly colored by their Title 10 responsibilities to preserve a force weakened by years at war as well as concerns about readiness to meet other contingencies should they erupt. Other senior commanders genuinely believed that more U.S. troops would only inflame local opposition from both sides. In the end, the President elected to surge five Army brigades to the capital and 4,000 Marines to Anbar Province in western Iraq, with a mandate to focus strongly on securing the population.

In so doing, President Bush chose not to adopt the military advice provided by the formal chain of command, opting instead for the Surge option recommended by outside advisors. Moving swiftly, he replaced Secretary Rumsfeld with Robert Gates, installed General Petraeus as his new field commander, announced an increase in the size of the Army and Marine Corps, directed an associated "civilian surge," and expedited the deployment of the fresh troops. To their credit, senior military leaders supported the President's decision and its implementation, helping to enable a 95 percent reduction in violence and setting conditions for an eventual transition to Iraqi control. This achievement staved off defeat and a precipitous withdrawal, perhaps the best outcome available under the prevailing circumstances.

Any scholar assessing this period must confront the fact that in this case, the President, as commander in chief, disregarded the best military advice proffered by the Joint Chiefs, combatant commander, and theater commander. (To be fair, President Bush encountered opposition from the State Department, Congress, and his own party as well.) Plumbing the depths of this paradox requires more space than we have here, but a true understanding has many dimensions. Many of the three- and four-star generals engaged in Iraq in 2006 spent most of their careers focused on conventional warfighting and not on counterinsurgency; indeed, the debate on the efficacy and applicability of COIN doctrine continues to this day. Most of them had specific responsibilities and frames of reference that did not encompass the President's wide field of view. It is also worth noting that by late 2006, the President had been engaged and focused on Iraq for at least 4 years and was by then experienced, highly knowledgeable, and possessed of his own firm views.[17] The recommendations of senior military leaders can be seen as grounded in their particular backgrounds, sets of experiences, and personal perspectives, none of which mirrored the President's.

A fair rendering of this episode might conclude that at bottom, the system worked as it should. For his part, President Bush was careful to solicit the views and inputs of his most senior military and civilian advisors and weighed them carefully. This give-and-take was clearly helpful to all concerned. Yet he also went outside the circle of formal advisors to ensure that all points of view were brought forward. His ultimate decision was clear and unambiguous, and he generously supported the requests of his military commanders. Against strong opposition in Congress and much criticism in the media, he displayed a persistence and determination that proved most helpful to the theater commander and chief of mission charged with implementing his strategy. In his time in office, much went wrong in Iraq, and observers have found much to criticize. By any standard, and the ultimate outcome in Iraq notwithstanding, this decision and its implementation must stand as a high point in President Bush's administration and a successful example of civil-military interaction.

Three years later, President Barack Obama found himself in a similar quandary in Afghanistan. For several years, a resurgent Taliban had pressed U.S. and North Atlantic Treaty Organization (NATO) forces. This prompted an increase in troop strength in 2008, bringing the full contingent of coalition forces to 68,000. As U.S. troop numbers in Iraq came down and as the security situation in Afghanistan worsened, the new administration authorized another 21,000 U.S. troops in February 2009 and in June replaced General David McKiernan with General Stanley A. McChrystal, who was thought to be a commander with greater skills in counterterrorism and counterinsurgency.[18] After conducting his own strategic review, McChrystal requested a further 40,000 troops, warning that "failure to provide adequate resources risks . . . mission failure."[19]

This episode provoked serious debate and discussion in the interagency community and has been widely covered in the memoirs of senior officials. At issue was the split between White House officials who opposed a large increase and military officials who supported it. (Secretary Gates found himself somewhat in the middle, straddling the divide and attempting to manage an increasingly fractious process.)

A deeper question was the approach adopted by senior military officials during policy deliberations. At the time and later, the President, his senior staff, and other civilian officials expressed dismay at apparent attempts to influence the military's preferred course of action, partly by making the case outside normal policy channels and partly by a failure to provide a range of feasible options.[20] Several events fueled this perception. A September 4, 2009, *Washington Post* article quoted General Petraeus as stating that success in Afghanistan was unlikely without many more troops. In a presentation given in London on October 1 to the International Institute for Strategic Studies, General McChrystal affirmed his recommended COIN strategy and his request for troops, publicly airing his preferred course of action and refuting others in advance of any Presidential decision. More damaging, however, was the leak of McChrystal's strategic assessment to the media, which essentially predicted the war would be lost if ISAF was not heavily reinforced.[21] In his memoir, Secretary Gates described the President as "infuriated."[22] Though neither saw any calculated plan, both Gates and the Chairman of the Joint Chiefs of Staff, Admiral Mike Mullen, expressed frustration at these media missteps.

Understanding this period requires a grasp of a number of dynamic interactions. The Obama administration was new, with its national security team still shaking itself out. The President, Vice President, Chief of Staff, and Secretary of State had just come from Congress, where aggressive questioning in committee was the norm, a sharp contrast to the previous 8 years. As most new administrations are, the Obama team was keen to assert civilian control. In contrast, the Secretary of Defense, Chairman, and U.S. Central Command commander had extensive experience, their views shaped by years of involvement in the Long War and particularly by the perceived success of the surge in Iraq. Though a new four-star, General McChrystal had served extensively in both Iraq and Afghanistan and probably believed he had been given a mandate to move in a new direction as McKiernan's replacement. These and other factors contributed to quite different frames of reference and at times a clash of perspectives that proved difficult for all concerned.[23]

The final decision, to add an additional 30,000 troops to ISAF to resource a population-centric COIN strategy, was announced by the President at West Point on December 1. With NATO force additions, the total surged coalition force was 140,000 personnel. This gave General McChrystal much of what he had asked for, albeit with a limited timeline; the Surge troops would redeploy in only 18 months. However, the bruising contest had lingering effects. When a *Rolling Stone* article quoting McChrystal aides as critical and even contemptuous of White House officials was published 6 months later, McChrystal was relieved and retired, as McKiernan had been, barely a year into his tour. At least in part, the President's decision had its roots in the civil-military conflict of the previous fall.[24]

As with the invasion of Iraq in 2003 and the Iraq Surge in 2006, these events represent policy- and strategy-making and civil-military relations at their most complex and challenging. We ascribe no unworthy motives to any of the key players. What seems clear, however, is that a perception formed in the minds of senior White House staff that the military had failed to bring forward realistic and feasible options, limiting serious consideration to only one, and that it had attempted to influence the outcome by trying the case in the media, circumventing the normal policy process.[25] These unfortunate developments affected both policy and strategy and fed lingering resentments that would prove deleterious in the months and years to come.

Findings and Observations

In considering from a strategic perspective the key lessons from the Long War, the scholar is almost compelled to say something about America's long history with counterinsurgency. Its roots in the American experience are deep. Where successful, as in the settling of the American West and in the Philippines, the methods used were often brutal and indiscriminate. More recently, in Vietnam, Iraq, and Afghanistan, our experiences have on the whole been difficult, costly, and indecisive. The ability of the enemy to fight from sanctuary, his unwillingness to present himself for destruction by our superior technology, the incapacity of host governments, and the loss of public support occasioned by protracted and indecisive combat all militated against clear-cut success. The historical record of large-scale, foreign expeditionary forces in counterinsurgencies is a poor one. While small-scale advise-and-assist missions have often been successful, large-scale expeditionary force COIN efforts do not play to American strengths and, if experience is any guide, are not likely to lead to success in securing U.S. strategic objectives.

More broadly, the normal military preference for overmatching force in armed conflict is often right, even as it commonly invokes opposition from civilian decisionmakers. Strong forces can smother friction, provide options, and avoid long, protracted conflicts that in the end may be far more expensive and casualty producing.[26] Yet making this case persuasively may be difficult when political leaders wish to portray lower costs, smaller footprints, more "transformational" approaches, or more moderate courses of action that provoke less violent criticism from either side of the political spectrum.[27] Each case is specific, but the lessons of history should not be easily discarded. Clear objectives accompanied by ample resources intelligently applied, with strong congressional and public support, typically evoke success.

The authors in this volume have attempted an assessment of strategic decisionmaking in Iraq and Afghanistan, but it will be years before a full accounting is possible. Many key issues, such as the gradual evolution of command and control structures, use of Provincial Reconstruction Teams, challenge of coalition partner caveats, and many others, deserve a fuller and more comprehensive assessment. The foregoing discussion, supported by interviews with a number of prominent civilian leaders and four-star officers, nevertheless sheds light on U.S. successes and failures and suggests the following as concluding thoughts for consideration.

Military involvement in national security decisionmaking at the best of times carries an element of tension inherent in civil-military relations. At times during the Long War, this tension was compounded unnecessarily. Civilian decisionmakers can benefit from a better understanding of the complexity of military strategy and the military's need for clear planning guidance. For example, strategy often founders on poorly defined or overly broad objectives that are not closely tied to available means, and here military leaders could and should play a key role.

Senior military officers for their part require a deep understanding of the policy/interagency process, an appreciation for the perspectives of civilian counterparts, and a willingness to embrace, and not resist, the complexities and challenges inherent in our system of civilian control. Vigorous debate and a clear presentation of military perspectives are essential for informed and successful strategy. Best military advice should be provided, nested within a larger appreciation of the strategic context and its political, economic, diplomatic, and informational dimensions. This conversation must be carried on in confidence, respecting the prerogatives of civilian leaders with whom the ultimate decision rests.

In most cases, civilian leaders look for a range of feasible options from the military, framed by clear cost and risk estimates, each of which could achieve the policy objective. In cases where the objective is unclear or unachievable, military leaders should press for clarity or state clearly that available resources could not support a successful outcome. Pressing for a commitment to success, defined as achieving sustainable political outcomes worthy of the sacrifices made, does not abrogate the civil-military compact. Rather, it reflects the gravity of any decision for war and the need for a determined commitment to prevail.[28] In so doing, it is helpful to consider that, in general, civilian policymakers do not come from a military planning background and that formulating specific goals and objectives is often an iterative process based on discussion and consensus.[29] In this regard, domestic political considerations often intrude and should be expected by military leaders.

In crafting policy and strategy, well-considered ideas matter and could often carry the day. Though time is scarce and resources precious, prior preparation and rehearsal are always good investments. Informed and articulate advocacy has a quality all its own, and skilled communicators with a convincing message are more likely to win acceptance. Department and agency cultures and interests are real, and they matter. But their positions could change through discussion and persuasion.

Policy and strategy take place in an operating universe that is highly sensitive to budget, election, and news cycles. They set the rhythm, the cadence, and the pace of political life. Career military officers are not always attuned to these realities, whereas civilian policymakers are. Awareness and flexibility with respect to this reality improve the quality and utility of military advice.

The art of generalship at the highest levels must also encompass an ability to understand and adapt to different Presidential and secretarial leadership styles and modes. Within a general interagency framework, each constructs decision settings composed of personalities and processes they find most helpful and congenial. These may, and often will, vary significantly from one administration to the next. At the four-star level, the ability to adapt to different civilian leadership styles is critical and may spell the difference between success and failure.

Four-star generals and admirals are practically by definition masters of Service and joint warfighting, but at the most senior levels, other attributes are necessary. These include interagency acumen, media savvy, a detailed understanding of congressional relations, a strong grasp of the defense planning, programming, and budgeting system, and skill in multinational environments. Normal career development patterns do not always provide opportunities to build these competencies. Sustained tenure in high-level command positions may also be a significant consideration.[30] In a number of the examples discussed in this volume, gaps in these skill sets contributed to poor outcomes that might have been prevented either by having different professional development and military and civilian education opportunities or by applying more refined selection criteria for specific, very high-level positions.[31]

At its core, strategy is all about making hard decisions, potentially raising issues of great moral or ethical significance. While the ultimate power of decision rests firmly in civilian hands, senior military officials have a duty to support effective and successful policy and strategy and to offer their best military advice and, if necessary, respectful dissent to help preclude strategic failure. As one senior four-star officer put it when interviewed for this study, "We have a sacred responsibility to provide best military advice. If we fail we concede that right."[32] Admirals and generals do not, of course, set aside personal and professional core values when they reach the pinnacle of responsibility. A strong moral compass is imperative when considering questions of war and peace.

National security decisionmaking is a highly personal endeavor relying heavily on trust relationships. These may take years to build but can be lost overnight. In this regard, General Colin Powell's admonition is useful: "Never let your ego get so close to your position that when your position goes, your ego goes with it." The interagency community at its apex is no place for hot tempers or the easily annoyed. A calm and steady temperament can be a real advantage. Today's policy adversary may be tomorrow's policy ally. As much as possible, senior leaders will find it advantageous to maintain good working relationships with civilian partners, even—or perhaps especially—when they find themselves on opposite sides of the issue.

If Afghanistan and Iraq are any guide, future wars will present national security decisionmakers with problems that will challenge their minds and souls. A lesson here for future senior officers is that there is no substitute for lifelong learning. The study of history, a broad grasp of all the instruments of national power with their strengths and weaknesses, confidence and a decisive character, and a fair portion of prudence and humility are all helpful when dealing with future commitments and challenges. There are no easy days and few simple problems for four-stars. Ultimately, they must deal with life-and-death decisions on a big stage. And while history does not repeat itself, there are age-old patterns that senior officers and politicians will always face. Sir Winston Churchill, writing in the years between the world wars, leaves us with this cautionary reminder:

> *Let us learn our lessons. Never, never, never believe any war will be smooth and easy, or that anyone who embarks on the strange voyage can measure the tides and hurricanes he will encounter. The Statesman who yields to war fever must realize that once the signal is given, he is no longer the master of policy but the slave of unforeseeable and uncontrollable events. Antiquated War Offices, weak, incompetent or arrogant Commanders, untrustworthy allies, hostile neutrals, malignant Fortune, ugly surprises, awful miscalculations—all take their seats at the Council Board on the morrow of a declaration of war. Always remember, however sure you are that you can easily win, that there would not be a war if the other man did not think that he also had a chance.*[33]

Notes

[1] Estimates of civilian dead in Iraq vary widely, with the low end at approximately 133,000. See "Costs of War," The Watson Institute for International Studies, Brown University, May 2014.

[2] United Nations Assistance Mission in Afghanistan (UNAMA), *Afghanistan: Annual Report 2014–Protection of Civilians in Armed Conflict* (Kabul: UNAMA, February 2015), 1–2, available at <http://unama.unmissions.org/Portals/UNAMA/human%20 rights/2015/2014-Annual-Report-on-Protection-of-Civilians-Final.pdf>.

[3] Costing Iraq and Afghanistan is imprecise because methodology can vary widely. For example, future interest payments and veterans' care in the out years are counted in some estimates and not in others. A detailed accounting of the costs related to the campaigns in Iraq and Afghanistan is found in annex A of this book.

[4] Highlights include an increase in adult life expectancy from 42 to 64 years, a decrease in maternal mortality from 1,600 to 327 per 100,000, a more than 10-fold increase in school attendance (including a 36 percent increase for girls), an increase in 1-hour access to health care from 9 percent to 60 percent, an increase in reliable access to electricity of 12 percent, and a growth in mobile phone subscribers from zero to 19 million. Statistics provided from various sources including Central Intelligence Agency, *The World Factbook*, available at <www.cia.gov/library/publications/the-world-factbook/index.html>; U.S. Agency for International Development, "Afghanistan Country Profile"; Ian S. Livingston and Michael O'Hanlon, *Afghanistan Index* (Washington, DC: The Brookings Institution, February 10, 2015), 20–23; "Afghanistan," *InternetWorldStats.com*, available at <www.internetworldstats.com/asia/af.htm>; and Jonathan Foreman, "Good News from Afghanistan," *Commentary*, July 1, 2014.

[5] James Kitfield, "Flynn's Last Interview: Iconoclast Departs DIA with a Warning," *Breaking Defense*, August 7, 2014, available at <http://breakingdefense.com/2014/08/flynns-last-interview-intel-iconoclast-departs-dia-with-a-warning/>.

[6] "In the next century few things will matter more than the battle for the soul of Islam; should fundamentalist brands triumph and become mainstreamed, the destabilizing effects throughout the Islamic world and the community of nations itself will be almost incalculable." R.D. Hooker, Jr., "Beyond *Vom Kriege*: The Character and Conduct of Modern War," *Parameters* 35, no. 2 (Summer 2005), 11.

[7] Carl von Clausewitz, *On War*, ed. and trans. Michael Howard and Peter Paret (Princeton: Princeton University Press, 1976 and 1984), book one, chapter one, 80.

[8] David Petraeus, interview by Joseph J. Collins and Nathan White, March 27, 2015.

[9] "[O]n politico-military issues . . . military officers may have little background and no strong views of their own." Douglas J. Feith, *War and Decision: Inside the Pentagon at the Dawn of the War on Terrorism* (New York: Harper, 2008), 371.

[10] John F. Reichart and Steven R. Sturm, ed., *American Defense Policy* (Baltimore: The Johns Hopkins University Press, 1987), 724.

[11] Jerome Slater, "Military Officers and Politics I," in Reichart and Sturm, 750.

[12] General John Abizaid, former commander of U.S. Central Command, refers to the "Heroic Assumption"—the expectation that the liberation of Iraq would resemble the liberation of France in 1944. Chief of Staff of the Army Operation *Iraqi Freedom* (OIF) Study Group, interview of Abizaid (unpublished), September 19, 2014.

[13] Historian Richard H. Kohn is a primary exponent of this view. See Richard H. Kohn, "Out of Control: The Crisis in Civil Military Relations," *The National Interest*, no. 35 (Spring 1994); *The Forgotten Fundamentals of Civilian Control of the Military in Democratic Government*, Project on U.S. Post–Cold War Civil-Military Relations, Working Paper No. 11 (Cambridge: John M. Olin Institute for Strategic Studies, June 1997); and "The Erosion of Civilian Control of the Military in the United States Today," *Naval War College Review* 55 (Summer 2002).

[14] James A. Baker III and Lee H. Hamilton, *The Iraq Study Group Report* (New York: Random House, 2006), xiii.

[15] George W. Bush, *Decision Points* (New York: Crown, 2010), 372.

[16] "In retrospect, I believe that I should have directly offered the President a broader range of options for achieving our objectives in Iraq. I had discussed different options for improving the security situation with the Secretary of Defense and Chairman. . . . In the end, I only presented the President the course of action we selected—accelerated transition—and I believe that I should have offered him a wider range of options to meet his policy needs." George W. Casey, Jr., *Strategic Reflections* (Washington, DC: NDU Press, 2012), 144.

[17] In addition to weekly meetings of the National Security Council on Iraq, President George W. Bush also received, and read, daily updates produced by the NSC Office for Iraq and Afghanistan.

[18] Robert M. Gates, *Duty: Memoirs of a Secretary of War* (New York: Knopf, 2014), 346.

[19] The President eventually ordered a troop surge of 30,000 as recommended by Secretary Gates, announcing his decision at West Point on December 1, 2009. See Bob Woodward, "McChrystal: 'More Forces or Mission Failure,'" *Washington Post*, September 21, 2009.

[20] "During September several events fractured what little trust remained between the senior military and the president and his staff." Gates, 367.

[21] See Woodward, "McChrystal."

[22] Gates, 368. The chapter dealing with these events is titled "Afghanistan: A House Divided."

[23] Douglas E. Lute, interview by Richard D. Hooker, Jr., and Joseph J. Collins, March 10, 2015. General Petraeus also described in some detail the chain of events that led to these misunderstandings. Petraeus, interview.

[24] Bob Woodward, *Obama's Wars* (New York: Simon & Schuster, 2010), 372–373.

[25] Lute, interview.

[26] Ibid. "For the United States, fighting a sustained conflict for less than vital national interests is a waning proposition."

[27] The authors are indebted to Professor Richard Betts for these insights.

[28] "Without strategy, there is no rationale for how force will achieve purposes worth the price in blood and treasure." Richard Betts, cited in H.R. McMaster, "The Uncertainties of Strategy," *Survival* (February–March 2015), 201.

[29] Martin E. Dempsey, interview by Richard D. Hooker, Jr., and Joseph J. Collins, January 7, 2015.

[30] Four-star theater commanders in Afghanistan averaged 12.8 months in command, compared to 17.2 months in Iraq and 30.8 months in Vietnam.

[31] A remarkable number of senior officers who played key roles in the Long War were selected for advanced civil schooling at top graduate schools early in their careers. This opportunity yielded rich dividends in their strategic development. They include Admiral James G. Stavridis, USN (Ret.); General Petraeus; General Peter W. Chiarelli, USA (Ret.); General Raymond T. Odierno, USA; General Dempsey; General Abizaid; and General John R. Allen, USMC (Ret.). Former Secretary of State and Chairman of the Joint Chiefs of Staff General Colin Powell might also be included. Other officers, most notably General James N. Mattis, USMC (Ret.), enjoy reputations as lifelong learners and self-taught strategists of the first rank.

[32] Lloyd J. Austin III, interview by Richard D. Hooker, Jr., April 7, 2015.

[33] Winston Churchill, *My Early Life: A Roving Commission* (New York: Scribner's, 1930, rpt. 1958), 232.

Annex A

The Human and Financial Costs of Operations in Afghanistan and Iraq

Sara Thannhauser and Christoff Luehrs

This annex provides both an assessment of the human and financial costs of the wars in Afghanistan and Iraq and a baseline for assessing broader strategic gains and losses from a decade-plus of war. It reviews official U.S. Government data and private studies that attempt to capture the direct costs of U.S. operations in Afghanistan and Iraq, as well as some of the related and projected costs associated with the operations such as healthcare and disability costs for veterans and interest on the debt. While the annex focuses specifically on U.S. costs, it also briefly reviews costs incurred by our allies, host-nation security forces, and local populations.

Many organizations, both public and private, have developed cost assessments for the wars. Some document the expense solely in terms of casualties and funds, while others attempt to include indirect costs such as environmental impact and macroeconomic costs. Individual governmental agencies (Department of Defense [DOD], Department of Labor, and Department of Veterans Affairs) have at various times issued numbers on the human and financial costs of the wars, but there has been no official publically available systematic report on war costs by these agencies. The Congressional Research Service (CRS), Congressional Budget Office (CBO), and Government Accountability Office (GAO) have published over 50 reports detailing the human and financial tolls. CRS has been relying on nonpublic DOD reports of war costs issued to the four congressional defense committees, as well as CRS, CBO, and GAO. In addition, Congress created the Office of the Special Inspector General for

Iraq Reconstruction (SIGIR) and Special Inspector General for Afghanistan Reconstruction (SIGAR) to document fraud, waste, and abuse.[1]

Academics and think tanks have also put forth considerable effort to document and assess the cost of both wars. The Center for Strategic and International Studies and Center for Strategic and Budgetary Assessments have produced several studies that document the costs of the wars.[2] The Watson Institute of International Affairs at Brown University hosts the Cost of War Project, which consists of more than 30 economists, anthropologists, lawyers, humanitarian personnel, and political scientists working to compile and conduct the first comprehensive analysis of these wars in terms of human casualties and economic costs.[3] Researchers in the John F. Kennedy School of Government at Harvard University have published extensively on the financial legacy of Iraq and Afghanistan, specifically highlighting how wartime spending decisions will impact future national security budgets.[4] Other organizations, such as the Iraq Body Count, look specifically at the civilians harmed or displaced by violence and how the wars have spilled into neighboring states.[5]

Given the number of estimates that exist, and the fact that each organization reaches its conclusions operating under varied assumptions and using different projection calculations, it is challenging to come up with a single definitive figure for the costs of the two wars. For the most part this annex relies on numbers provided from official government sources. However, where gaps exist in official data, this annex relies on figures and conclusions reached by some of the academic studies listed herein. Finally, in reality, determining an accurate ultimate cost sheet for the wars is an impossible endeavor at this point as the war in Afghanistan is ongoing, while U.S. efforts in Iraq against the Islamic State of Iraq and the Levant (Operation *Inherent Resolve*) were funded at $5 billion in the December 2014 Consolidated and Further Continuing Appropriation Act, 2015, with a further $8.8 billion requested for fiscal year (FY) 2016.[6]

Cost in Human Life

The number of U.S. Servicemember casualties of the campaigns in Iraq and Afghanistan pales in comparison to other wars such as World War I and World War II, nor does the toll from these campaigns come close to the cost in lives associated with the wars in Vietnam and Korea. Undoubtedly, the reduction in casualty numbers and high survival rates for seriously wounded troops can be attributed to the incredible advancements in the field of medicine, armored vehicles, body armor, and the asymmetric nature of the conflicts. However, it does not lessen the burden for those who lost loved ones or those whose lives are altered due to limb amputations, traumatic brain injuries (TBI), chronic severe depression, and/or post-traumatic stress disorder (PTSD). Moreover, American soldiers were not alone in making the ultimate sacrifice; U.S. civilian government personnel also gave their lives.[7]

Also shouldering the burden with U.S. soldiers and government employees were U.S. citizens, third-country nationals, and local nationals who served as contractors to U.S. Government agencies.[8] Finally, the cost of war must also take into account the number of lives that were lost on September 11, 2001. After all, it was the events of that day and the subsequent loss of 2,977 lives in New York City, Washington, DC, and Shanksville, Pennsylvania, that triggered the ensuing decade of war and its aftermath.

DOD Personnel

According to its own casualty report, DOD deaths (both military and civilian) reported for Operation *Enduring Freedom* (OEF), Operation *Iraqi Freedom* (OIF), and their follow-on operations total 6,855 lives (see table 1 for a historical comparison).[9] In August 2014, the United States lost its highest-ranking Soldier with the death of Major General Harold J. Greene, USA. He was the first American general killed in a combat zone since Vietnam.

Beyond the dead, 52,340 Servicemembers have been physically wounded in the wars. According to the Veterans Health Administration, 1,158,359 veterans of Afghanistan and Iraq have been treated for a wide range of medical issues, the vast majority of them as outpatients.[10] That number is likely to grow while operations in both theaters continue. The most frequent diagnoses of veterans have been musculoskeletal ailments, mental disorders, and "Symptoms, Signs and Ill-defined Conditions."[11] The three enduring and most debilitating ailments associated with these operations are traumatic brain injuries, major limb amputations, and PTSD. In terms of TBI, figure 1 documents the increase over the past decade of war. According to the Defense and Veterans Brain Injury Center, in 2000 there were a reported 10,958 cases of TBI. Between 2005 and 2012 (the peak of the war efforts in Iraq and Afghanistan),

Table 1. Overall Department of Defense Casualties (as of June 4, 2015)

Conflict	Servicemember Deaths	DOD Civilian Deaths	Servicemember Wounded in Action
World War I[a]	116,516		204,002
World War II	405,399		670,846
Korean War	36,574		103,284
Vietnam	58,220		303,644
Operation *Iraqi Freedom*[b, c]	4,411	13	31,951
Operation *New Dawn*[d]	66	0	295
Operation *Inherent Resolve*[e]	6	0	1
Operation *Enduring Freedom*[f]	2,351	4	20,069
Operation *Freedom's Sentinel*[g]	2	1	24
Total, 2001–2014	6,836	18	52,340

a. Defense Casualty Analysis System, "Principal Wars in Which the United States Participated—U.S. Military Personnel Serving and Casualties (1775–1991)," available at <www.dmdc.osd.mil/dcas/pages/report_principal_wars. xhtml>.

b. Department of Defense, Casualty Status, Fatalities as of June 15, 2015, 10 a.m. EDT, available at <www.defense. gov/news/casualty.pdf>.

c. Operation *Iraqi Freedom* includes casualties that occurred between March 19, 2003, and August 31, 2010, in the Arabian Sea, Bahrain, Gulf of Aden, Gulf of Oman, Iraq, Kuwait, Oman, Persian Gulf, Qatar, Red Sea, Saudi Arabia, and the United Arab Emirates. Prior to March 19, 2003, casualties in these countries were considered under Operation *Enduring Freedom*. Personnel injured in *Iraqi Freedom* who die after September 1, 2010, will be included in statistics from that operation.

d. Operation *New Dawn* includes casualties that occurred between September 1, 2010, and December 31, 2011, in the Arabian Sea, Bahrain, Gulf of Aden, Gulf of Oman, Iraq, Kuwait, Oman, Persian Gulf, Qatar, Red Sea, Saudi Arabia, and the United Arab Emirates. Personnel injured in *New Dawn* who die after December 31, 2011, will be included in statistics from that operation.

e. Operation *Inherent Resolve* includes casualties that occurred in Bahrain, Cyprus, Egypt, Iraq, Israel, Jordan, Kuwait, Lebanon, Qatar, Saudi Arabia, Syria, Turkey, the United Arab Emirates, the Mediterranean Sea east of 25° longitude, the Persian Gulf, and the Red Sea.

f. Operation *Enduring Freedom* includes casualties that occurred between October 7, 2001, and December 31, 2014, in Afghanistan, Guantanamo Bay (Cuba), Djibouti, Eritrea, Ethiopia, Jordan, Kenya, Kyrgyzstan, Pakistan, the Philippines, Seychelles, Sudan, Tajikistan, Turkey, Uzbekistan, and Yemen.

g. Operation *Freedom's Sentinel* includes casualties that occurred in Afghanistan after January 1, 2015.

Figure 1. Traumatic Brain Injury Over Time, 2000–2014 (as of August 19, 2014)

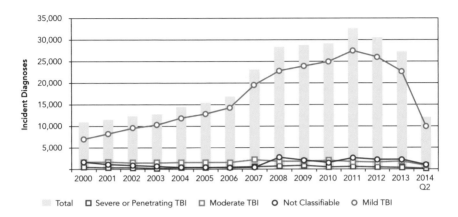

Source: Hannah Fischer, *A Guide to U.S. Military Casualty Statistics: Operation Inherent Resolve, Operation New Dawn, Operation Iraqi Freedom, and Operation Enduring Freedom*, RS22452 (Washington, DC: Congressional Research Service, November 20, 2014).

the average number of cases reported per year was 25,668.[12] The vast majority of TBI cases (85.8 percent) between 2000 and 2014 have been classified as "mild," with 8.6 percent classified as "moderate," and 2.6 percent as "severe or penetrating."[13]

Figure 2 documents major limb amputations due to battle injuries in OEF and OIF between 2001 and September 2014. From 2003 until the first quarter of 2009, the majority of the major limb amputations due to battle injuries occurred in OIF. In the second quarter of 2009, the trend changed and since that time the majority of the major limb amputations due to battle injuries have occurred in OEF. As of September 2014, 1,573 soldiers have lost a limb due to the wars in Afghanistan and Iraq.[14] By comparison, in Vietnam, 5,283 soldiers lost a limb.[15]

Both figures 1 and 2 illustrate a dramatic increase in these injuries at the height of the wars. Figure 3 documents the reported cases of PTSD among Servicemembers who deployed to Iraq and Afghanistan and those who did not. Between 2000 and 2014, there were a reported 36,321 cases of PTSD among Servicemembers who did not deploy. During that same time period, among soldiers who deployed to Afghanistan and/or Iraq, 128,496 cases of PTSD were reported.[16]

Figure 2. Major Limb Amputations Due to Battle Injuries in Operation *Iraqi Freedom*, Operation *New Dawn*, and Operation *Enduring Freedom*, 2001–2014 (as of September 1, 2014)

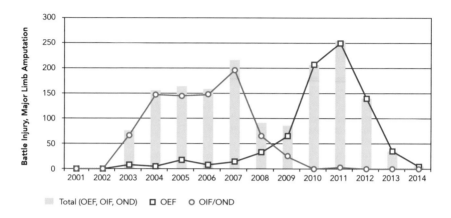

Source: Hannah Fischer, *A Guide to U.S. Military Casualty Statistics: Operation Inherent Resolve, Operation New Dawn, Operation Iraqi Freedom, and Operation Enduring Freedom*, RS22452 (Washington, DC: Congressional Research Service, November 20, 2014).

Figure 3. Annual Post-Traumatic Stress Disorder Diagnoses in All Services, 2000–2014 (as of September 5, 2014)

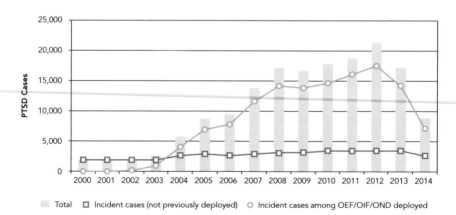

Source: Hannah Fischer, *A Guide to U.S. Military Casualty Statistics: Operation Inherent Resolve, Operation New Dawn, Operation Iraqi Freedom, and Operation Enduring Freedom*, RS22452 (Washington, DC: Congressional Research Service, November 20, 2014).

426

Many observers have voiced concerns that repeated deployments and shorter "dwell" times at home may have increased the mental health toll on Servicemembers, even as ongoing studies grapple with the exact nature of the causal link between the two.[17] According to a CRS report, between 2001 and 2011, the rate of mental health diagnoses among Active-duty Servicemembers increased approximately 65 percent.[18] Between 2000 and 2011, diagnoses of adjustment disorders, depression, and anxiety disorders (excluding PTSD) made up 26 percent, 17 percent, and 10 percent, respectively, of all diagnoses. Alcohol abuse and dependence disorders and substance abuse and dependence disorders made up 13 percent and 4 percent, respectively. PTSD represented approximately 6 percent of mental disorder diagnoses over this time period.[19] According to a 2012 Medical Surveillance Monthly Report, beginning in 2010, suicide has become the second leading cause of death for Active-duty Servicemembers, behind only war injuries.[20] Taken together, it is clear that in addition to loss of life there is a significant psychological cost of these wars affecting Servicemembers, veterans, and their families, and it will continue to have an impact for years to come.

U.S. Contractors

Unique to modern U.S. wars are the tremendous contributions of contractors working alongside U.S. military and government personnel. More so than any other wars in U.S. history, civilians worked together with military counterparts in Afghanistan and Iraq, providing a range of services including transportation, construction, base support, intelligence analysis, and private security. According to CRS, over the last decade in Iraq and Afghanistan contractors accounted for 50 percent or more of the total military force.[21] When accounting for the contractors hired by other government agencies such as the Department of State and U.S. Agency for International Development (USAID), it is fair to say that there have been more contractors on the ground in these countries than U.S. troops—even at the peak of these operations. And in such service, many civilian contactors were killed or injured. According to a report in the *New York Times*, the contractor with the highest war zone deaths is the defense giant L-3 Communications: "If L-3 were a country, it would have the third highest loss of life in Afghanistan as well as in Iraq; only the United States and Britain would exceed it in fatalities."[22]

Unlike the easily accessible and reliable figures documenting the loss in life of American Servicemembers, there is not an equally accurate account of contractor casualties. Under the Federal Defense Base Act, American defense contractors are obligated to report the war zone deaths and injuries of their employees—including subcontractors and foreign workers—to the Department of Labor and to carry insurance that provides employees with medical care and compensation. According to one expert, however, since many contractors do not comply with even the current reporting requirements, the true number of private contractor deaths may be far higher.[23] Moreover, while contractors have been killed in large numbers, a full and accurate accounting has not yet been conducted by DOD, Department of State, and USAID (although Congress instructed those agencies to do so).[24] Consequently, the numbers in table 2 are at best a sound, conservative estimate based on the Defense Base Act case summary reports through March 2015.

The U.S. Department of Labor's Office of Workers' Compensation Programs' Defense Base Act case summaries indicate that 1,592 contractors lost their lives in Afghanistan, and 1,620 in Iraq (see table 2). In terms of contractors injured in action, which the Department of Labor categorizes as "lost time 4 days or more," 13,813 were injured in Afghanistan and 18,309 in Iraq.[25] Other initiatives to collect data on contractor casualties find that these numbers are conservative. Efforts to better capture contractor casualties are ongoing. At the high end of the spectrum, the Cost of War Project estimates that 3,401 contractors died in Afghanistan and 3,481 in Iraq.[26] More in line with the Department of Labor numbers, an online blog called the *Defense Base Act Compensation Blog* cites 3,187 contractor deaths in Iraq and Afghanistan.[27] However, the blog cites a much higher injured figure of 86,375.

Only a small proportion of contractors working on U.S. Government contracts are U.S. citizens. In FY 2010, 24 percent of all contractors in Afghanistan and Iraq (including those working for DOD, State, and USAID) were U.S. nationals, 44 percent were local Iraqis or Afghans, and 32 percent were from third countries.[28] A 2013 CRS report found that roughly 30 percent of DOD contractors in theater were U.S. citizens in Iraq (early 2012) and Afghanistan (early 2013), respectively.[29] As a result, the bulk of contractor casualties are non-Americans. The majority have been Afghan and Iraqi nationals working under U.S. Government contracts.[30] Nationals from Fiji, Turkey, Nepal, and the Philippines have also died while serving as contractors for the U.S. Government.

While there are numerous studies on the mental impacts of Afghanistan and Iraq on Servicemembers, there is no parallel effort to capture the psychological toll on contractors. According to one report, injured contractors who are U.S. citizens have had a more difficult time getting care than returning Servicemembers. Contractors also lack the support network available to returning troops through Tricare or the Department of Veterans Affairs. Their care depends on getting workers' compensation payments, and they have often had to struggle with insurance companies to get quality care or even to get medical bills paid.[31]

Coalition Partners, Host-Nation Civilians, Nongovernmental Workers, and Journalists

In addition to American Servicemember fatalities, international coalition partners recorded 1,449 dead in Afghanistan and Iraq (the largest group was 632 British soldiers killed).[32] The groups that shouldered the greatest burden in these wars, however, were the local populations and security forces of Afghanistan and Iraq. As shown in table 2, it is difficult to provide exact numbers for these groups. Because different sources use different time periods and methodologies to arrive at their numbers, the estimates provided here should, to quote a CRS report on the subject, "be viewed as guideposts rather than statements of fact."[33] The ranges provided for local populations and security forces are based on (table 2, notes d, f) and represent conservative estimates from 25,729 to 35,470 security forces and 158,415 to 191,000 civilians killed. Beyond host-nation civilians, casualties were also recorded for nongovernmental (NGO) workers and journalists. According to the Cost of War Project, 393 NGO employees lost their lives in Afghanistan and Iraq, and 246 journalists were killed in both conflicts (table 2, note g).

It is far too early to assess the indirect impact of a decade-plus of war on host-nation civilians. Like soldiers, many suffer the same physical and psychological wounds from limb amputations to severe depression and PTSD. However, they often lack the medical support services to treat and mitigate the debilitating and devastating effects of these enduring injuries and ailments. Moreover, the culture of violence and sectarianism remains ever present and

Table 2. Overall Casualties, 2001–2015

Conflict	Operation *Iraqi Freedom*	Operation *Enduring Freedom*	Totals 2001–2015
Servicemembers[a]	4,483	2,353	6,837
DOD Civilians[a]	13	5	18
U.S. Government Civilians (non-DOD)[b]	6–12	10–15	16–27
Allied Troops[c]	319	1,130	1,449
Local Security Forces[d]	12,000	13,729–23,470	25,729–35,470
U.S. Contractors[e]	1,620	1,592	3,212
Host-Nation Civilians[f]	137,000–165,000	21,415–26,000	158,415–191,000
Journalists[g]	221	25	246
NGO Workers[g]	62	331	393

a. Figures as of June 15, 2015, 10 a.m. EDT. See Department of Defense, Casualty Status, available at <www.defense.gov/news/casualty.pdf>. Operation *Iraqi Freedom* includes casualties that occurred between March 19, 2003, and August 31, 2010, in the Arabian Sea, Bahrain, Gulf of Aden, Gulf of Oman, Iraq, Kuwait, Oman, Persian Gulf, Qatar, Red Sea, Saudi Arabia, and the United Arab Emirates. Prior to March 19, 2003, casualties in these countries were considered under Operation *Enduring Freedom*. Personnel injured in *Iraqi Freedom* who die after September 1, 2010, will be included in statistics from that operation. Also included for Iraq are Operation *New Dawn* (casualties that occurred between September 1, 2010, and December 31, 2011, in the Arabian Sea, Bahrain, Gulf of Aden, Gulf of Oman, Iraq, Kuwait, Oman, Persian Gulf, Qatar, Red Sea, Saudi Arabia, and United Arab Emirates) and Operation *Inherent Resolve* (casualties that occurred in Bahrain, Cyprus, Egypt, Iraq, Israel, Jordan, Kuwait, Lebanon, Qatar, Saudi Arabia, Syria, Turkey, the United Arab Emirates, the Mediterranean Sea east of 25° longitude, the Persian Gulf, and the Red Sea). *Enduring Freedom* includes casualties that occurred between October 7, 2001, and December 31, 2014, in Afghanistan, Guantanamo Bay (Cuba), Djibouti, Eritrea, Ethiopia, Jordan, Kenya, Kyrgyzstan, Pakistan, the Philippines, Seychelles, Sudan, Tajikistan, Turkey, Uzbekistan, and Yemen. Also included for Afghanistan is Operation *Freedom's Sentinel* (includes casualties that occurred in Afghanistan after January 1, 2015).

b. No central data point for U.S. Government (USG) civilian fatalities was identified. Numbers are derived from Department of State, Bureau of Diplomatic Security, *Significant Attacks Against U.S. Diplomatic Facilities and Personnel: 1998–2013* (Washington, DC: Department of State, May 2014), available at <www.state.gov/documents/organization/225846.pdf>. Ranges reflect ambiguities in reporting "U.S. citizen" versus "USG employee" deaths.

c. Figures as of June 11, 2015, available at <www.icasualties.org>.

d. There are multiple sources with considerable variation in data due to uncertain reporting. See "Afghanistan Index," The Brookings Institution, Washington, DC, available at <www.brookings.edu/about/programs/foreign-policy/afghanistan-index>; "Human Costs of War: Direct War Death in Afghanistan, Iraq, and Pakistan, October 2001–April 2015," *Costs of War*, available at <www.costsofwar.org/sites/default/files/%28Home%20page%20fig-

(Table 2 continued)

ures%29%20SUMMARY%20-%20Direct%20War%20Death%20Toll.pdf>; "Iraq Index," The Brookings Institution, Washington, DC, available at <www.brookings.edu/about/centers/middle-east-policy/iraq-index>.

e. Department of Labor, "Defense Base Act Case Summary by Nation," accessed March 31, 2015, available at <www.dol.gov/owcp/dlhwc/dbaallnation.htm>.

f. Iraq Body Count (IBC) records violent civilian deaths that have resulted from the 2003 military intervention in Iraq. Its public database includes deaths caused by U.S.-led coalition forces and paramilitary or criminal attacks by others. IBC is available at <www.iraqbodycount.org/about/>; "Human Costs of War"; United Nations Assistance Mission in Afghanistan, Reports on the Protection of Civilians, available at <http://unama.unmissions.org/Default.aspx?tabid=13941&language=en-US>.

g. Figures from "Human Costs of War: Direct War Death in Afghanistan, Iraq, and Pakistan, October 2001–April 2015."

the risk of new conflict is real as the recent advances of ISIL in Iraq have made all too obvious. In fact, the Iraq Body Count notes that 2014 has been the third deadliest year after 2006 and 2007 for Iraqi civilians.[34] In Afghanistan, the United Nations Assistance Mission in Afghanistan reported that 2014 saw the highest number of civilian deaths and injuries recorded in a single year since 2009.[35]

Cost in Dollars

How much does war cost? Experts have been devising elaborate methods to account for not only the direct obligations of war, but also projected costs from the interest on large promissory notes to the expanded long-term medical and healthcare costs required to support veterans. Two of the most prominent scholars in this area are Nobel Laureate economist Joseph Stiglitz and Linda Bilmes.[36] Stiglitz and Bilmes examined both the operational direct costs and future costs. They also delved into what they call the macroeconomic costs, such as the impact of higher oil prices on weakening aggregate demand and the link between oil prices and decisions of the Federal Reserve to loosen monetary and regulatory policy prior to the financial crisis.[37] Projections that include these macroeconomic considerations into their accounting of financial costs reach total cost estimates of up to $4.4 trillion dollars.[38] While these costs are real, they are often not trackable and require numerous assumptions for future projections.[39] For the purpose of this project, this section of the annex focuses on the direct obligations made to pay for the wars in Afghanistan and Iraq and provides examples for estimates of related costs for reference. This section does not delve into the costs incurred by coalition partners.

Figure 4. Estimated War Funding by Operation Fiscal Year 2001–2015 Request (in USD billions of Budget Authority)

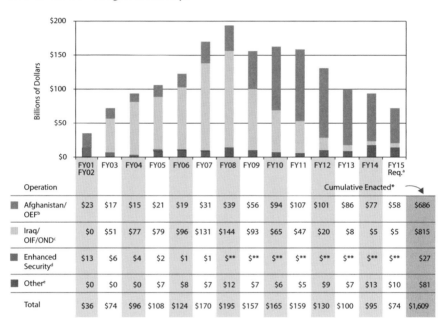

Operation	FY01 FY02	FY03	FY04	FY05	FY06	FY07	FY08	FY09	FY10	FY11	FY12	FY13	FY14	Cumulative Enacted* FY15 Req.ª
Afghanistan/ OEFᵇ	$23	$17	$15	$21	$19	$31	$39	$56	$94	$107	$101	$86	$77	$58 $686
Iraq/ OIF/ONDᶜ	$0	$51	$77	$79	$96	$131	$144	$93	$65	$47	$20	$8	$5	$5 $815
Enhanced Securityᵈ	$13	$6	$4	$2	$1	$1	$**	$**	$**	$**	$**	$**	$**	$** $27
Otherᵉ	$0	$0	$0	$7	$8	$7	$12	$7	$6	$5	$9	$7	$13	$10 $81
Total	$36	$74	$96	$108	$124	$170	$195	$157	$165	$159	$130	$100	$95	$74 $1,609

*Cumulative enacted (FY01–FY14). **Amounts to less than $200 million.

Source: Amy Belasco, *The Cost of Iraq, Afghanistan, and Other Global War on Terror Operations Since 9/11*, RL33110 (Washington, DC: Congressional Research Service, December 8, 2014).

a. Fiscal year (FY) 2015 reflects June 2014 request (amended) rather than initial placeholder request of $79.4 billion for Department of Defense (DOD); reflects resources not scoring level. Excludes $5.5 billion requested for Operation *Iraqi Freedom* in FY2015.
b. DOD refers to the Afghan War as Operation *Enduring Freedom*, primarily military and other operations in Afghanistan as well as in-theater support in neighboring countries and other counterterror operations (for example, the Philippines and Djibouti).
c. DOD referred to the Iraq War as Operation *Iraqi Freedom* until September 1, 2010, when U.S. forces transitioned from combat operations to advising, assisting, and training Iraqi forces. The mission was renamed Operation *New Dawn*, which ended December 31, 2011. On that date, all U.S. forces left Iraq; military personnel continuing to provide in-theater support were assigned to Operationf *Enduring Freedom*. Excludes new Operation *Inherent Resolve* request.
d. "Enhanced Security" covers cost of 9/11 attacks to DOD and New York City; referred to as Operation *Noble Eagle* by DOD.
e. "Other" includes DOD funding designated for a war emergency or Overseas Contingency Operation that is not tracked as a war cost, such as congressional additions for childcare centers, barracks improvements, additional C-130 and C-17 aircraft not requested, as well as unanticipated increases in basic housing allowances, fuel costs, modularity, or restructuring of Army brigades. In recent years, "Other" includes transfers by Congress from base budget operation and maintenance expenses to Title IX war funding.

Table 3. Costs of Major U.S. Wars (in 2011 USD billions)

World War I	$334
World War II	$4,104
Korea	$341
Vietnam	$738
Persian Gulf War	$102
Iraq, Afghanistan, war on terror	$1,529

Source: Stephen Dagget, *Costs of Major U.S. Wars*, RS22926 (Washington, DC: Congressional Research Service, June 29, 2010), 2.

Notes: Figures for World War I through Persian Gulf War in fiscal year (FY) 2011 USD. Figures for Iraq, Afghanistan, and war on terror from figure 4 converted to FY2011 USD.

Direct Overseas Contingency Operations Budget

In budget terms, the U.S. Government now describes the wars as Overseas Contingency Operations (OCO). According to the latest comprehensive CRS report on the costs of Iraq, Afghanistan, and other Long War operations since 9/11, the United States has obligated $1.6 trillion in OCO funds, most directed at DOD and Department of State.[40] Figure 4 provides an overview of estimated war funding by operation to date. Notably, operations in Iraq account for the lion's share of war costs, despite the fact that these figures do not yet include appropriations for Operation *Inherent Resolve*. Taken together, these costs make the campaigns since 9/11 the second most expensive war in U.S. history, as shown in table 3. Counting only direct OCO appropriations, America's longest war has already cost twice as much as its second longest engagement, Vietnam. Remarkably, a cost estimate for Vietnam that does account for additional costs (increased troop levels, debt-servicing, veterans' compensation, and pensions) through the year 2000 arrives at a total of $1.2 trillion.[41] This suggests that, even when comparing long-term and related costs for Vietnam only to the direct OCO appropriations since 2001, post-9/11 operations have already cost more and are likely to far outstrip the largest Cold War–era campaign.

Ongoing Commitments and Future Costs

With over 52,000 U.S. Servicemembers wounded, many of them require extensive medical care, which becomes the responsibility of the Department of Veterans Affairs (VA). According to a recent CRS estimate, the United States has spent $22.8 billion between 2001 and 2015 providing medical care to veterans of the Afghanistan and Iraq wars.[42] Beyond medical issues, some Servicemembers were injured so severely that they require disability benefits. The VA reported that over 700,000 Iraq and Afghanistan veterans received disability compensation through September 2013 and that the average annualized cost per patient rose from $8,100 to $12,900 between 2000 and 2013.[43] According to one estimate, the United States has spent $35 billion in disability payments to Iraq and Afghanistan veterans through the VA between 2001 and 2013.[44] The CBO puts the figure at $34 billion for 2001–2015.[45] While difficult to predict with a high degree of confidence, past experience suggests that these costs will continue for some time, decades after the wars themselves have ended. According to Linda Bilmes's estimate, the VA is projected to spend another $836.1 billion in medical care and disability benefits through 2053.[46] Others have criticized the underlying methodology for vastly exaggerating potential costs.[47]

A more conservative projection was offered by the Congressional Budget Office, which released a report that projects the costs of veterans care from 2011 through 2020.[48] The report cites two scenarios that operate under slightly different assumptions. In the first scenario, CBO assumes a smaller force deployed after 2013, which according to its estimate will result in $40 billion in projected expenditures. In the second scenario, CBO assumes a larger force presence post-2013, which drives its estimate up to $55 billion. Since the publication of this report, the United States has planned to leave 9,800 troops in Afghanistan through 2015, with smaller troop levels planned for 2016 and 2017. Given those numbers, it is more accurate to cite CBO scenario two figures as it accounts for a significant presence past 2013.

The $1.6 trillion cited in figure 4 represents OCO appropriations made from 2001 through fiscal year 2015. During the writing of this annex, $5 billion in OCO funds had been enacted for FY 2015 to fund Operation *Inherent Resolve* in Iraq, with an additional $8.8 billion requested for FY2016.[49]

Total Costs

The direct cost, measured by budget authority, of $1.6 trillion is a baseline figure when it comes to calculating the total costs of America's post-9/11 campaigns. The Cost of War Project puts the total economic cost at $4.4 trillion through FY 2014.[50] Bilmes projects a total cost of $4 to $6 trillion stating that this would make Afghanistan and Iraq "the most expensive wars in U.S. history."[51] Yet many methodological issues remain, particularly in the absence of official statistics to serve as a basis for projections. Moreover, the above quoted $4.1 trillion for World War II represent direct appropriations only. A more comprehensive approach along the lines of Bilmes and Stiglitz or the Cost of War Project would increase that figure dramatically. The fact remains that this has been the second most expensive war in the Nation's history by the most conservative estimates.

Other Costs and Constraints on the Future

There are many other costs associated with the wars. For example, a number of researchers are looking at environmental costs. At this point, research into these costs is preliminary at best, but there are some organizations that are starting to document environmental impacts of the war on water and soil pollution, toxic dust, greenhouse gas and air pollution from military vehicles, and war-related destruction of forests and wetlands.[52]

Perhaps the most difficult cost to assess is the constraints placed on future national security policymakers. The financial deficits incurred from the wars, combined with a slow economic recovery, could give policymakers pause before electing to engage in similar operations in the future. The Barack Obama administration has exercised great caution in applying military force (especially in terms of limiting American troop presence) in Libya, Mali, Syria, and Iraq. In 2012, the Obama administration announced that it would rebalance its national security priorities toward Asia, signifying a shift away from the war efforts in the Middle East and Southeast Asia. Yet as of 2015, the United States is still engaged in Afghanistan (Operation *Freedom's Sentinel*) and reengaged in Iraq (Operation *Inherent Resolve*) for which a combined $96 billion in OCO funds have been requested for FY 2016 at the time of writing.[53] The human toll and financial legacy of the wars in Afghanistan and Iraq will continue to shape how U.S. policymakers respond to future crises, and how the United States will reshape its military force.

Conclusion

Though the question that this annex attempts to answer appears basic in nature, the reality is that it is a problematic endeavor to capture all the direct, related, and projected costs associated with the wars in Afghanistan and Iraq. As such this annex only offers a point of departure based on a conservative review of official data and private studies. Two macro trends are obvious from the historical tables. One the one hand, the survival rates of U.S. Servicemembers in military operations have improved dramatically. On the other hand, those operations have become increasingly expensive. These fundamental realities will impact on future strategies as leaders decide if, when, and how to use military force.

In summation, the United States lost 6,837 Servicemembers, 34 to 45 government civilian employees, and 3,212 contractors in Afghanistan and Iraq. Over 52,000 soldiers and around 30,000 contractors were wounded or injured. Conservative estimates of the death toll among host-nation civilians and security forces range from 180,000 to almost 230,000. In terms of financial costs, the United States has spent at least $1.6 trillion dollars on the wars with estimates on the high end reaching almost three times that number. Operations are ongoing and a more accurate reckoning will have to wait until they are concluded. Nevertheless, these numbers do provide a baseline for assessing broader strategic gains and losses from the wars in Afghanistan and Iraq.

Notes

[1] See, for example, Special Inspector General for Iraq Reconstruction (SIGIR), comp., *Hard Lessons: The Iraq Reconstruction Experience* (Washington, DC: U.S. Independent Agencies and Commissions, 2009); SIGIR, *Learning from Iraq* (Washington, DC: U.S. Government Printing Office, 2013).

[2] Anthony H. Cordesman, *The U.S. Costs of the Afghan War: FY2002–FY2013* (Washington, DC: Center for Strategic and International Studies, 2012); Anthony H. Cordesman, *The Cost of the Iraq War: CRS, GAO, CBO, and DoD Estimates* (Washington, DC: Center for Strategic and International Studies, 2008); Steven M. Kosiak, *Cost of the Wars in Iraq and Afghanistan, and Other Military Operations Through 2008 and Beyond* (Washington, DC: Center for Strategic and Budgetary Assessments, 2008); Todd Harrison, *Impact of the Wars in Iraq and Afghanistan on the US Military's Plans, Programs and Budgets* (Washington, DC: Center for Strategic and Budgetary Assessments, 2009).

[3] See Watson Institute for International and Pubic Affairs at Brown University, available at <http://costsofwar.org/>.

[4] Linda J. Bilmes, *The Financial Legacy of Iraq and Afghanistan: How Wartime Spending Decisions Will Constrain Future National Security Budgets*, Faculty Research Working

Paper Series 13-006 (Cambridge, MA: Harvard Kennedy School, March 2013), available at <https://research.hks.harvard.edu/publications/workingpapers/citation.aspx?PubId=8956>.

5   Iraq Body Count (IBC) records violent civilian deaths that have resulted from the 2003 military intervention in Iraq. Its public database includes deaths caused by U.S.-led coalition forces and paramilitary or criminal attacks by others. IBC is available at <www.iraqbodycount.org/about/>.

6   Lead Inspector General for Overseas Contingency Operations, *Operation Inherent Resolve: Quarterly Report and Biannual Report to the United States Congress* (Washington, DC: U.S. Government Printing Office, December 17, 2014–March 31, 2015), 16–17, available at <https://oig.state.gov/system/files/oir_042915.pdf>.

7   No central data point for U.S. Government civilians killed was identified. Numbers here are derived from news reports and verified using the Department of State Diplomatic Security's "Significant Attacks Against U.S. Diplomatic Facilities and Personnel: 1998–2013," available at <www.state.gov/documents/organization/225846.pdf>.

8   For a breakdown of contractors by origin, see Moshe Schwartz and Jennifer Church, *Department of Defense Use of Contractors to Support Military Operations: Background, Analysis, and Issues for Congress*, R43074 (Washington, DC: Congressional Research Service [CRS], May 17, 2013), 23–24.

9   Department of Defense Casualty Analysis System, "Fatalities as of June 15, 2015, 10 a.m. EST," accessed at <www.defense.gov/news/casualty.pdf>.

10   Department of Veterans Affairs (VA), *Analysis of VA Health Care Utilization among Operation Enduring Freedom (OEF), Operation Iraqi Freedom (OIF), and Operation New Dawn (OND) Veterans* (Washington, DC: VA, June 2015), 5, available at <www.publichealth.va.gov/docs/epidemiology/healthcare-utilization-report-fy2015-qtr1.pdf>.

11   Ibid., 8. The phrase describes a catch-all category commonly used to diagnose outpatient populations.

12   Defense and Veterans Brain Injury Center, "DoD Worldwide Numbers for TBI [Traumatic Brain Injury]," available at <www.dvbic.org/dod-worldwide-numbers-tbi>.

13   See Hannah Fischer, *A Guide to U.S. Military Casualty Statistics: Operation Inherent Resolve, Operation New Dawn, Operation Iraqi Freedom, and Operation Enduring Freedom*, RS22452 (Washington, DC: CRS, November 20, 2014).

14   Ibid.

15   Ann Leland and Mari-Jana "M-J" Oboroceanu, *American War and Military Operations Casualties: Lists and Statistics*, RL32492 (Washington, DC: CRS, February 26, 2010), 9.

16   Fischer.

17   Katherine Blakeley and Don J. Jansen, *Post-Traumatic Stress Disorder and Other Mental Health Problems in the Military: Oversight Issues for Congress*, R43175 (Washington, DC: CRS, August 8, 2013), 53–57.

[18] Ibid.

[19] "Mental Disorders and Mental Health Problems, Active Component, U.S. Armed Forces, 2000–2011," *Medical Surveillance Monthly Report* 19, no. 6 (June 2012), 11–17.

[20] "Deaths by Suicide While on Active Duty, Active and Reserve Components, U.S. Armed Forces, 1998–2011," *Medical Surveillance Monthly Report* 19, no. 6 (June 2012), 7–10.

[21] Schwartz and Church.

[22] Rod Norland, "Risks of Afghan War Shift from Soldiers to Contractors," *New York Times*, February 11, 2012.

[23] Steven L. Schooner and Collin D. Swan, "Dead Contractors: The Un-Examined Effect of Surrogates on the Public's Casualty Sensitivity," *Journal of National Security Law & Policy* (April 16, 2012).

[24] Government Accountability Office (GAO), *Iraq and Afghanistan: DOD, State, and USAID Face Continued Challenges in Tracking Contracts, Assistance Instruments, and Associated Personnel*, GAO-11-1 (Washington, DC: GAO, October 2010), 41; see also Steven L. Schooner, "Why Contractor Fatalities Matter," *Parameters* 38 (2008), 78.

[25] Department of Labor, "Defense Base Act Case Summary by Nation," accessed March 31, 2015, available at <www.dol.gov/owcp/dlhwc/dbaallnation.htm>.

[26] "Human Costs of War: Direct War Death in Afghanistan, Iraq, and Pakistan, October 2001–April 2015," *Costs of War*, n.d., available at <www.costsofwar.org/sites/default/files/(Home%20page%20figures)%20SUMMARY%20-%20Direct%20War%20Death%20Toll.pdf>.

[27] "Civilian Contractor Casualty Count," *Defense Base Act Compensation Blog*, accessed August 18, 2014, available at <https://defensebaseactcomp.wordpress.com/civilian-contractor-casualty-count/>.

[28] Schooner and Swan.

[29] Schwartz and Church, 24–25.

[30] T. Christian Miller, "Foreign Workers for the U.S. Are Casualties Twice Over," *ProPublica.org*, June 19, 2009.

[31] T. Christian Miller, "Contractors in Iraq are Hidden Casualties of War," *Los Angeles Times*, October 6, 2009.

[32] See "Iraq Coalition Military Fatalities by Year" and "Afghanistan Coalition Military Fatalities by Year," accessed at <http://icasualties.org/>.

[33] Hannah Fischer, *Iraq Casualties: U.S. Military Forces and Iraqi Civilians, Police, and Security Forces*, R40824 (Washington, DC: CRS, December 6, 2011), summary.

[34] "Iraq 2014: Civilian Deaths Almost Doubling Year on Year," available at <https://www.iraqbodycount.org/analysis/numbers/2014/>.

[35] United Nations Assistance Mission in Afghanistan, "Civilian Casualties in Afghanistan

Rise by 22 Percent in 2014," February 18, 2015, available at <www.unama.unmissions.org/Portals/UNAMA/human%20rights/2015/18_Feb_2015-Press%20Release_2014_PoC-annual_report-Final-Eng.pdf>.

[36] On calculating the costs of war, see Joseph Stiglitz and Linda J. Bilmes, "Estimating the Costs of War: Methodological Issues, with Applications to Iraq and Afghanistan," in *Oxford Handbook of the Economics of Peace and Conflict*, ed. Michelle Garfinkel and Stergis Skaperdas (Oxford: Oxford University Press, 2012). On the long-term costs, see Joseph Stiglitz and Linda J. Bilmes, *The Three Trillion Dollar War: The True Cost of the Iraq Conflict* (New York: Norton, 2008); Linda J. Bilmes and Joseph Stiglitz, "The Long-Term Costs of Conflict: The Case of the Iraq War," in *The Handbook on the Economics of Conflict*, ed. Derek L. Braddon and Keith Hartley (Northampton, MA: Edward Elgar Publishing, 2011).

[37] Neta C. Crawford, "U.S. Costs of Wars Through 2014: $4.4 Trillion and Counting," *Costs of War*, June 25, 2014, available at <http://costsofwar.org/sites/default/files/articles/20/attachments/Costs%20of%20War%20Summary%20Crawford%20June%202014.pdf>.

[38] Ibid.

[39] For a discussion of differences in methodologies, see Amy Belasco, *The Cost of Iraq, Afghanistan, and Other Global War on Terror Operations Since 9/11*, RL33110 (Washington, DC: CRS, December 8, 2014), 3, including footnotes.

[40] Ibid., summary. The Congressional Budget Office (CBO) estimates a slightly higher total of $1.649 trillion in *The Budget and Economic Outlook: 2015 to 2025* (Washington, DC: CBO, January 26, 2015), 81.

[41] Richard M. Miller, Jr., *Funding Extended Conflicts: Korea, Vietnam, and the War on Terror* (Santa Monica, CA: Praeger Security International, 2007), 42–67.

[42] Ibid., 19.

[43] CBO, *Veterans' Disability Compensation: Trends and Policy Options* (Washington, DC: CBO, August 2014), 11–12.

[44] Bilmes, 6–7.

[45] CBO, *The Budget and Economic Outlook: 2015 to 2025* (Washington, DC: CBO, January 2015), 81.

[46] Bilmes, 6–7.

[47] CBO, "The Cost of War: A Comment on Stiglitz-Bilmes," April 8, 2008, available at <https://www.cbo.gov/publication/24762>.

[48] Heidi L.W. Golding, *Potential Costs of Health Care for Veterans of Recent and Ongoing U.S. Military Operations* (Washington, DC: CBO, June 27, 2011).

[49] Lead Inspector General for Overseas Contingency Operations.

[50] See "Economic Costs," *Costs of War*, April 2015, available at <http://costsofwar.org/article/economic-cost-summary>.

[51] Bilmes, 1.

[52] See "Environmental Costs," *Costs of War*, April 2015, available at <http://watson.brown.edu/costsofwar/costs/social/environment>.

[53] Amy Belasco, *Defense Spending and the Budget Control Act Limits*, R44039 (Washington, DC: CRS, May 19, 2015), 11.

Afghanistan Timeline

Pre-Soviet Intervention (1838–1978)

1838–1842	British forces invade and install Shah Shuja Durrani on the throne. He is assassinated in 1842. A major part of the British occupation forces are later destroyed near Gandamak during retreat toward Jalalabad. British triumph in subsequent fighting, but it is a pyrrhic victory. They leave altogether in the fall of 1842, allowing the deposed Dost Mohammed Barakzai to retake throne.
1878–1881	Second Anglo-Afghan War. As a result of this war, treaty is signed that grants Great Britain control of Afghan foreign affairs.
1919	Emir Amanullah Khan declares independence from London. Third Anglo-Afghan War begins.
1926–1929	Amanullah attempts to modernize Afghanistan, introducing several social reforms. Effort backfires and results in civil unrest. Amanullah flees.
1933	Mohammed Zahir Shah made king and Afghan monarchy holds for next four decades.
1953	General Mohammad Daud Khan named prime minister. His administration is remembered for his dependence on Soviet economic and military assistance and for Helmand Valley project, which greatly improved quality of life in southwestern Afghanistan.

1963	Mohammed Daud resigns as prime minister after border dispute with Pakistan.
1964	Constitutional monarchy is introduced and ratified by Zahir Shah in October, sparking political polarization and power struggles.
1973	Mohammed Daud returns to become president after seizing power in bloodless coup from his cousin, Zahir Shah. President Daud later distances himself from Soviet Union and seeks closer ties with West, as well as Saudi Arabia, Iran, and Egypt.
1978	Daud is deposed. He and his family are killed in a pro-Soviet coup. The People's Democratic Party comes to power, but is stymied by internal disputes and revolt by mujahideen groups.

Soviet Intervention (1979–1988)

1979 December	Soviet army launches invasion to bolster communist Afghan government.
1980	Babrak Karmal named ruler, supported by Soviet troops. Various mujahideen groups increase opposition to Soviet forces and fighting intensifies. The United States, Pakistan, China, Iran, and Saudi Arabia provide economic and military aid to mujahideen.
1985	Mujahideen groups form alliance against Soviet forces. Experts estimate that half of Afghanistan's population is now displaced by war, with many seeking refuge in Iran or Pakistan.
1986	The United States provides mujahideen with Stinger missiles, allowing them to shoot down Soviet aircraft. Mohammad Najibullah named as new head of Soviet-backed regime, replacing Babrak Karmal.

1988	Afghanistan, Soviet Union, the United States, and Pakistan sign peace accords, and Soviets initiate troop withdrawal.

Red Army Retreats (1989–2001)

1989	Last Soviet troops leave Afghanistan. Civil war continues as mujahideen work to overthrow Najibullah and the pro-Soviet regime.
1992	Najibullah's government falls, and destructive civil war follows.
1996	Taliban fighters take Kabul and institute a brutal rule, barring women from work outside the home and implementing Islamic punishments that include public stoning, amputation, and execution.
1997	Pakistan and Saudi Arabia recognize the Taliban regime as legitimate. Taliban fighters now control approximately two-thirds of country.
1998	U.S. launches missile strikes against suspected training bases of militant Osama bin Laden, the suspected leader of al Qaeda. Bin Laden is thought to have planned and financed the bombing of U.S. Embassies in Africa.
1999	United Nations (UN) Security Council adopts Resolution 1267, implementing financial sanctions against the Taliban. The group's funding, travel, and arms shipments are restricted in an effort to get the country to hand over bin Laden for trial.
2000 October 12	USS *Cole* is attacked by suicide bombers while anchored near port of Aden in Yemen. The attack is later attributed to bin Laden.
2001 September 9	Ahmad Shah Masood, leader of the main opposition to the Taliban—the Northern Alliance—is killed in

suicide attack by two al Qaeda operatives posing as news reporters.

U.S.-Led Invasion (2001–2003)

2001 September 11   Al Qaeda operatives hijack four commercial airliners, crashing two into the World Trade Center and one into the Pentagon. A fourth plane crashes in a field in Shanksville, Pennsylvania. Close to 3,000 people die in the attacks.

2001 September 17   Pakistani government officials in Kandahar request the surrender of bin Laden. Mullah Omar, the leader of the Taliban, refuses.

2001 September 18   Congress passes a joint resolution authorizing use of force against those responsible for attacking the United States on 9/11.

2001 October 7   The United States and Great Britain begin bombing al Qaeda and Taliban targets in Afghanistan. Training bases in Kabul, Kandahar, Kunduz, Farah, Mazar-e-Sharif, and Jalalabad are first to be targeted.

2001 November   Taliban regime is rapidly defeated after its loss at Mazar-e-Sharif to forces loyal to ethnic Uzbek leader Abdul Rashid Dostum. Over the next week, Taliban strongholds are overtaken after coalition and Northern Alliance offensives on Taloqan (11 November), Bamiyan (11 November), Herat (12 November), Kabul (13 November), and Jalalabad (14 November).

2001 November 14   UN Security Council passes Resolution 1378, which calls for a "central role" for the UN in establishing an interim government.

2001 December 5   Afghan factions agree to a deal in Bonn, Germany, for interim government.

2001 December 9	Taliban abandons Kandahar, which is generally seen as the end of the Taliban regime.
2001 December 3–17	Bin Laden is tracked to Tora Bora cave complex southeast of Kabul. Afghan militias engage in a fierce 2-week battle with militants. Bin Laden is thought to have left for Pakistan on 16 December.
2001 December 20	UN Security Council establishes the North Atlantic Treaty Organization (NATO)-led International Security Assistance Force (ISAF) with Resolution 1386.
2001 December 22	The Afghan Interim Authority—composed of 30 members and headed by a chairman—is inaugurated with a 6-month mandate followed by a 2-year Transitional Authority, after which elections are held. Hamid Karzai is sworn in as head of the interim government.
2002 January	First deployment of ISAF in the Kabul region.
2002 January 11	First group of al Qaeda and Taliban prisoners are sent to Guantanamo Bay, Cuba.
2002 March	Operation *Anaconda* begins as troops move into the Shah-i-Kot Valley in Paktia Province.
2002 April 17	President George W. Bush calls for the reconstruction of Afghanistan. Congress appropriates over $38 billion in humanitarian and reconstruction assistance to Afghanistan from 2001 to 2009.
2002 April	Former King Zahir Shah returns, but makes no claim to the throne. He dies in 2007.
2002 June 19	The Loya Jirga, or grand council, elects Karzai as head of interim government. Karzai appoints members of his administration, which is given a mandate to serve until 2004.
2002 November	The United States creates a civil affairs framework to coordinate reconstruction with UN and nongovernmental organizations with hopes of expanding the authority

of the Kabul government. Provincial Reconstruction Teams (PRTs) are stood up first in Gardez and followed by teams in Bamiyan, Kunduz, Mazar-e-Sharif, Kandahar, and Herat.

2003 March 20   The United States invades Iraq. This signals a pivot in American foreign policy away from Afghanistan toward the war in Iraq.

Elections and Return to Violence (2004–2008)

2004 January 4   Afghanistan's Loya Jirga approves a new constitution that creates a strong presidential system intended to unite the country's various ethnic groups.

2004 October 9   Presidential elections are held, and Karzai is declared winner after getting 55 percent of the vote. His closest rival, former education minister Younis Qanooni, receives only 16 percent.

2004 December 7   Karzai is officially sworn in as president of Afghanistan and begins a 5-year term in power.

2005 May 23   President Bush and Karzai announce the signing of a military agreement to give American forces full use of Afghan military facilities to prosecute the war against Taliban and al Qaeda fighters. The agreement also solidifies the strategic partnership between the United States and Afghanistan.

2005 September 18   More than 6 million Afghans vote in first parliamentary elections in more than 30 years. Nearly half of all Afghans casting ballots are women, and 68 out of 249 seats are set aside for female members of Afghanistan's lower house of parliament. In the upper house, 23 out of 102 seats are reserved for women, establishing this election as the most democratic in the history of Afghanistan.

2005 December	Newly elected Parliament opens.
2006 July	Intense fighting erupts in southern Afghanistan during summer months. Number of suicide attacks quintuples and remotely detonated bombings more than double.
2006 October	After expansions in September 2005 and July 2006, NATO takes command in the east from a U.S.-led co-alition force, and assumes complete responsibility for security across the whole of Afghanistan.
2006 November	At a summit in Riga, friction emerges between NATO member states over troop commitments to Afghanistan. Eventually, leaders agree to remove some national re-strictions on when, where, and how Alliance troops may be used.
2007 May	Mullah Dadullah, an important Taliban military com-mander, is killed during a joint operation by Afghan, U.S., and NATO troops in southern Afghanistan.
2007 August	UN reports that opium production is at a record high.
2008 June	Karzai warns that Afghanistan will deploy troops into Pakistan to combat Taliban militants if Islamabad fails to take action against them.
2008 July 7	Taliban launch a devastating suicide bomb attack against the Indian embassy in Kabul, killing more than 50.
2008 September	President Bush deploys an additional 4,500 U.S. troops to Afghanistan, in a move he calls a "quiet Surge."
2009 January	In testimony to Congress, U.S. Defense Secretary Robert Gates describes Afghanistan as the Obama administra-tion's "greatest test."
2009 February	NATO countries pledge increased military commit-ments in Afghanistan.

Annex B

New American Strategy (2009–2012)

2009 March 27	President Barack Obama announces an updated strategy for Afghanistan and Pakistan. An additional 21,000 U.S. Government personnel will train and assist Afghan security forces, and there will be increased support for civilian development.
2009 April	Responding to calls from U.S. military officials, NATO members agree to send an additional 5,000 troops to train troops and police.
2009 May 11	General Stanley A. McChrystal, USA, is named new U.S. and ISAF commander after the exit of General David McKiernan.
2009 July	Marines launch major offensive in southern Afghanistan involving 4,000 troops in Helmand Province.
2009 July 2	McChrystal issues a revised tactical directive that provides guidance and intent for employment of force, including tighter controls over U.S. airstrikes.
2009 August 10	McChrystal and Ambassador Karl W. Eikenberry release an Integrated Civilian-Military Campaign Plan for Support to Afghanistan, charting out the strategy to promote a more capable Afghan government and security force.
2009 August 20	Presidential and provincial elections are tainted by widespread Taliban attacks, spotty turnout, and claims of fraud.
2009 October 20	Karzai declared winner of August presidential election, after second-placed opponent Abdullah Abdullah pulls out before the runoff takes place.
2009 December 1	President Obama announces a decision to surge 30,000 additional U.S. troops to Afghanistan. He also states that the United States will begin withdrawing its forces by

	July 2011. NATO forces, around the same time, surge to 40,000.
2009 December	An al Qaeda double agent kills seven Central Intelligence Agency officials in suicide attack on a U.S. base in Khost.
2010 February	NATO-led forces launch Operation *Moshtarak* in an effort to establish government control of southern Helmand Province.
2010 June 23	McChrystal is replaced by General David Patraeus, USA, who officially takes command of U.S. and ISAF forces in July 2010.
2010 July	Whistleblowing Web site *WikiLeaks* releases thousands of stolen classified U.S. military documents covering military operations in Afghanistan and Iraq.
2010 August	Karzai accuses private security firms of operating with impunity and orders that they cease all operations. He later relaxes the decree.
2010 September 18	Parliamentary elections are tainted by Taliban violence and accusations of fraud, which delay the final results until 31 October.
2010 November	At a summit in Lisbon, NATO leaders agree to transfer security responsibility to Afghan forces by the end of 2014.
2011 January	Karzai completes the first official state visit to Russia by an Afghan leader since 1989.
2011 February	Afghanistan Rights Monitor reports that number of civilians killed since the 2001 invasion hit unprecedented levels. In 2010, at least 2,421 civilian Afghans were killed and over 3,270 were injured in conflict-related security incidents across Afghanistan.

2011 April	U.S.-based pastor burns a copy of the Koran and prompts nationwide protests in Afghanistan. UN workers and several Afghans are killed.
2011 April	Approximately 500 prisoners, including many former Taliban fighters, break out of prison in Kandahar.
2011 May 1	Bin Laden killed by U.S. forces in Pakistan.
2011 June 22	President Obama orders troop reductions of 33,000 by summer 2012, including 10,000 by the end of 2011.
2011 July	Karzai's half-brother and Kandahar governor Ahmed Wali Karzai is killed by an associate.
2011 September	Ex-President Burhanuddin Rabbani—a key negotiator in talks with the Taliban—is assassinated.
2011 October	As relations with Pakistan deteriorate after a number of attacks, Afghanistan and India complete a strategic agreement to increase security and development cooperation.
2011 November	Karzai secures the permission of tribal elders to negotiate a 10-year military agreement with the United States. The proposed deal permits U.S. troops to stay in the country beyond 2014.
2011 December	At least 58 people are killed in attacks at a Shiite religious site in Kabul and Shiite mosque in Mazar-e-Sharif.
2011 December 5	Pakistan and the Taliban refuse to attend the scheduled Bonn Conference on Afghanistan. Pakistan boycotts the event in response to a NATO airstrike that killed Pakistani soldiers on the Afghan border.
2012 January	Taliban agrees to open an office in Dubai in preparation for peace talks with the U.S. and Afghan governments.
2012 February	At least 30 people killed in protests about alleged destruction of copies of the Koran at the U.S. airbase in Bagram. Two soldiers are also killed in retaliatory attacks.

2012 March	Taliban suspend talks and accuse Washington of not fulfilling promises to take steps toward a prisoner swap. Sergeant Robert Bales, USA, murders 16 Afghan civilians during an unprovoked shooting spree in the Panjwai district of Kandahar.
2012 April	Taliban initiate their "spring offensive" with a bold attack on diplomatic quarter of Kabul. The government attributes attacks to the Haqqani Network. Afghan and NATO security forces kill 38 militants.

NATO Withdrawal Plan (2012–2014)

2012 May	NATO summit outlines plan to withdraw foreign combat troops by end of 2014. France decides to withdraw its combat mission by the end of 2012, a year earlier than scheduled.
2012 July	Donor countries pledge $16 billion in civilian aid to Afghanistan through 2016. The United States, Japan, Germany, and United Kingdom supply bulk of funds. Afghanistan acquiesces to new measures aimed at countering government corruption.
2012 August	U.S. military disciplines six Soldiers for destroying copies of the Koran and other religious texts in Afghanistan. They do not face criminal prosecution. Three Marines are also disciplined for a video in which the bodies of dead Taliban fighters were desecrated.
2012 September	The United States hands over Bagram high-security detention facility to the Afghan government, but retains custody over some foreign prisoners until March 2013.
2012 September	The United States temporarily halts training new police recruits to conduct background checks for possible ties to the Taliban following a series of "insider" attacks on foreign troops.

2013 February	Karzai and Pakistan's Asif Ali Zardari reach an agreement to work toward an Afghan peace deal within 6 months. They support the opening of an Afghan office for negotiation in Doha and urge the Taliban to do the same.
2013 March	Two former Kabul Bank officials, Sherkhan Farnood and Khalilullah Ferozi, are arrested for multimillion dollar fraud that nearly caused the collapse of the entire Afghan banking system in 2010.
2013 June	Afghan security forces assume responsibility for all military and security operations from NATO forces on the same day officials announce that the Taliban and the United States will resume negotiations.
2013 June	Karzai halts security talks with the United States because of the announcement of possible peace talks with the Taliban. Afghanistan vows to conduct independent talks with the Taliban in Qatar.
2014 January	Taliban suicide attack strikes a restaurant in Kabul's diplomatic quarter, constituting the worst attack on foreign civilians since 2001. Among the 13 victims is the country director for the International Monetary Fund.
2014 February	Start of presidential election campaign, marked by a rise in attacks by the Taliban.
2014 April	Presidential election results are inconclusive, and the election goes to a second round between Abdullah Abdullah and Ashraf Ghani, both candidates in the 2009 presidential elections.
2014 June	Second round of voting in the presidential election begins. More than 50 Afghans are reported killed throughout the country in various incidents during voting.

2014 July	Election officials initiate a recount of all votes cast in June's presidential runoff, following U.S.-mediated deal to end the political impasse between candidates.
2014 August	Despite U.S. mediation efforts by Secretary of State John Kerry, Ghani and Abdullah continue to dispute election results.
2014 September	Ghani and Abdullah sign a power-sharing agreement, ending 2-month audit of disputed election results. Ghani is declared president.
2014 October	The United States and United Kingdom formally end combat operations in Helmand Province. Opium poppy cultivation reaches record levels, according to U.S. experts.
2014 December	NATO concludes its 13-year combat mission in Afghanistan. Despite the official end to ISAF's combat role, violence continues across much of the country.
2015 January	NATO-led follow-on mission Resolute Support begins. Approximately 12,000 personnel provide training and support to Afghan security forces.
2015 March	President Obama delays American troop withdrawal from Afghanistan, following an appeal from President Ghani.
2015 May	Taliban representatives and Afghan officials meet in Qatar for informal peace talks. Both sides agree to continue the process at a later date, though the Taliban refuse to halt fighting until all foreign troops leave the country.

Sources: "Afghanistan Profile—Timeline," BBC News, May 7, 2015, available at <www.bbc.com/news/world-south-asia-12024253>; "Timeline: Major Events in the Afghanistan War," *New York Times*, June 22, 2011, available at <www.nytimes.com/interactive/2011/06/22/world/asia/afghanistan-war-timeline.html?_r=0>; "U.S. War in Afghanistan: 1999–Present," Council on Foreign Relations, n.d., available at <www.cfr.org/afghanistan/us-war-afghanistan/p20018>; "The War in Afghanistan: A Timeline," CBS News, available at <www.cbsnews.com/news/the-war-in-afghanistan-a-timeline/>; Ludwig W. Adamec, *Historical Dictionary of Afghanistan* (Lanham, MD: Scarecrow Press, 2012).

Annex C

Iraq Timeline

Significant Events Pre–Gulf War

1534–1918	Iraq territory is part of Ottoman Empire.
1917	Great Britain captures Baghdad from Ottoman Empire during its Mesopotamian Campaign in World War I.
1920	Great Britain, with support of the League of Nations, establishes modern state of Iraq.
1932	Iraq becomes fully autonomous state and admitted into League of Nations.
1939–1945	Great Britain's military forces reoccupy Iraq during World War II.
1958 July 14	Brigadier General Abd al-Karim Qasim topples monarchy in military coup, establishing the Republic of Iraq.
1963 February 9	Former Colonel Abd al-Salam Muhammad Arif becomes new head of government after former Prime Minister Abd al-Karim Qasim is overthrown and executed.
1964 July	Iraqi government nationalizes many key industries and businesses.
1966 April	President Abd al-Salam Muhammad Arif is killed in helicopter crash; his brother, Abdul-Rahman Arif, replaces him.
1968 July 17	Ba'athists topple Abdul-Rahman Arif's government; Ahmed Hassan al-Bakr assumes presidency.

1970s	Saddam Hussein begins to gain power and influence within the Ba'ath Party and government.
1970 March	Saddam completes an agreement with Kurdish leader, Mulla Mustafa al-Barzani, which effectively recognizes Kurdish identity and guarantees Kurdish independence within next 4 years.
1972 April	Saddam secures Iraq-Soviet Friendship treaty in Moscow.
1972 June	Iraq's government nationalizes oil fields of Iraq Petroleum Company.
1974	Iraq's government grants limited autonomy to Iraq's Kurdish region.
1979	Saddam forces President Ahmed Hassan al-Bakr to resign.
1980–1988	Iran-Iraq War spans 8 years. Iraq claims victory, but there is no clear winner.
1988 March	Iraq's military attacks Kurdish town of Halabjah with poison gas, killing thousands of civilians.
1990 August 2	Iraq invades Kuwait, prompting United Nations (UN) to impose economic sanctions in response to act of aggression.

Operation *Desert Storm*, 1990–1991

1990 August 6	UN Security Council passes Resolution 661 that places economic sanctions on Iraq. Resolution 665, passed soon after, authorizes embargo to enforce sanctions.
1990 November	UN Security Council passes Resolution 678 that demands Iraq withdraw from Kuwait by January 15, 1991. It empowers states to use military force to oust Iraq from Kuwait after deadline.

1991 January 12	U.S. Congress authorizes use of military force in conflict.
1991 January 16–17	Allied air campaign of Operation *Desert Storm* begins. Military operations to engage Iraqi forces in Kuwait involve coalition of 30 countries.
1991 February 23	Ground phase of Operation *Desert Storm* begins.
1991 February 28	Iraqi forces withdraw from Kuwait and Iraqi government accepts all UN resolutions passed resulting from invasion of Kuwait.
1991 March/April	Kurdish rebels in north and Shiite tribes in south rebel against central Iraqi government. Saddam's forces stifle rebellion with force.
1991 April 3	UN Resolution 687 passes, which set framework for ceasefire and created UN Compensation Fund.
1991 April 6	Ceasefire terms are agreed upon between Iraq and allied forces.
1991 April 7	Operation *Provide Comfort* begins to protect and assist Kurds in northern Iraq.
1991 June 9	First chemical weapons inspection in Iraq conducted by UN Special Commission on Iraq.
1992 August	A no-fly zone banning flights from Iraqi planes is implemented in southern Iraq.
1993 April	Saddam's agents fail in attempt to assassinate former President George H.W. Bush in Kuwait.
1993 June	U.S. Government conducts military strike on Iraqi Intelligence Service's headquarters in response to assassination attempt on President Bush.
1995 April	Iraq's oil exports moderately resume in "oil-for-food program" under UN Security Council Resolution 986.
1995 October	Saddam succeeds in winning referendum, which grants him power to remain president.

1996	The United States expands southern no-fly zone, just south of Baghdad.
1997 January 1	Operation *Northern Watch* implemented.
1998 October	Iraq refuses to further cooperate with UN Special Commission to Oversee the Destruction of Iraq's Weapons of Mass Destruction (WMD).
1998 December	U.S. and British military planes launch bombing campaign, Operation *Desert Fox*, intended to destroy and dismantle Iraq's WMD programs.
1999 February	A senior Shiite spiritual leader, Grand Ayatollah Sayyid Muhammad Sadiq al-Sadr, killed in Najaf.
1999 December	UN Security Council Resolution 1284 orders establishment of UN Monitoring, Verification, and Inspection Commission, which replaces UN Special Commission. Iraq does not accept resolution.
2001 February	U.S. and British warplanes conduct bombing campaigns in attempt to immobilize Iraq's air defense.
2001 September 11	Al Qaeda terrorists attack World Trade Center in New York and Pentagon with passenger airplanes, killing approximately 3,000 people. Another hijacked plane, intended to strike the White House, is brought down in rural Pennsylvania after brave actions by passengers.

2002–2003

2002 September 12	At UN General Assembly meeting, President George W. Bush asks world leaders to confront the "grave and gathering danger" of Iraq. British Prime Minister Tony Blair also releases report on Iraq's military capability.
2002 October	Congress, by wide majority, authorizes use of military force in Iraq.

2002 November 8	UN Security Council unanimously passes Resolution 1441. Iraq later agrees to weapons inspections, and UN weapons inspectors return.
2003 February 5	Secretary of State Colin Powell delivers presentation before UN Security Council, arguing that Iraq has WMD and advanced weapons programs.
2003 March 18	Diplomatic process ends and arms inspectors leave Iraq. President Bush gives Saddam and his sons 48 hours to leave.
2003 March 19	Allied forces bomb military targets and attempt to kill Saddam.
2003 March 20	U.S.-led invasion of Iraq begins. Effort is named Operation *Iraqi Freedom*.
2003 April 9	Saddam's rule is toppled and Baghdad comes under direct U.S. control.
2003 May 1	President Bush declares end of combat phase in Iraq on aircraft carrier USS *Abraham Lincoln*, under banner that reads "Mission Accomplished."
2003 May 23	Coalition Provisional Authority (CPA) announces that all public-sector employees affiliated with Ba'ath Party are to be removed from their positions.
2003 July 22	Saddam's sons, Uday and Qusay, are killed in Mosul in gun battle with Soldiers from 101st Airborne Division.
2003 August	Prominent Shiite leader Ayatollah Mohammed Baqr al-Hakim is killed by car bomb in Najaf. One hundred twenty-four people also killed.
2003 August 7	Car bomb at Jordanian embassy kills 18 people.
2003 August 19	Suicide bomber targets UN headquarters in Baghdad, killing 22 people and wounding at least 100. The UN Special Representative in Iraq, Sergio Vieira de Mello, is killed.

2003 December 14	Saddam, on the run for nearly 9 months, is captured by U.S. troops.

Insurgency

2004 January	Central Intelligence Agency former chief weapons inspector David Kay testifies at public congressional hearings that U.S. intelligence agencies failed to detect disarray and decline of Iraqi WMD program.
2004 March	During Shiite religious festival, suicide bombers kill 140 people in Baghdad and Karbala.
2004 March 31	Four private security contractors killed in Fallujah.
2004 April 28	Photos emerge that show American Soldiers forcing Iraqi prisoners into abusive and sexually humiliating positions at Abu Ghraib prison.
2004 April–May	Mahdi army and other Shiite militias loyal to cleric Muqtada al-Sadr engage coalition forces.
2004 June 28	CPA hands over its ruling power to interim government headed by Prime Minister Ayad Allawi.
2004 August	U.S. forces and insurgents loyal to Shiite cleric Moqtada al-Sadr fight in Najaf.
2004 November	U.S. forces lead offensive against pro-Saddam insurgents in Fallujah. A previous offensive in April 2004 was stopped for political reasons.
2005 January 30	Approximately 8 million Iraqis vote in elections for Iraq's newly formed National Assembly.
2005 April	Iraqi parliament selects Kurdish leader Jalal Talabani as president. A Shiite, Ibrahim Jaafari, is selected as prime minister.
2005 May	Civilian deaths from bombings and shooting related incidents rise to 672, up from 364 in April.

2005 June	Massoud Barzani is selected as the president of the Kurdistan Regional Government (KRG).
2005 August	The draft version of the new constitution is accepted by Shiite and Kurdish negotiators. Sunni representatives refuse.
2005 October 15	Iraqi citizens vote for new constitution that will create Islamic federal democracy. The new constitution is approved.
2005 December	First government and parliamentary elections take place since allied invasion.

Civil Unrest

2006 January–December	UN estimates that more than 34,000 civilians killed in violence in 2006, more than three times official Iraqi death toll estimates.
2006 February 22	Al-Askari Mosque in Samarra, one of the most important Shiite mosques in the world, is bombed. That event unleashes a wave of civil unrest and violence throughout the country.
2006 April 22	President Talabani forms new government with Shiite compromise candidate Nouri al-Maliki to end political stalemate. Maliki becomes prime minister.
2006 May and June	UN reports that more than 100 civilians are killed each day.
2006 June 7	U.S. airstrike kills al Qaeda's leader in Iraq, Abu Musab al-Zarqawi.
2006 November	Iraq and Syria reestablish full diplomatic relations. Car bombings in the Shiite neighborhood of Sadr City in Baghdad result in one of the deadliest attacks in Baghdad since 2003.
2006 November 5	Saddam is sentenced to death by hanging.

2006 December 30   Saddam is executed.

2007–2008

2007 January 10   President Bush announces the Surge strategy in Iraq. He orders over 20,000 Army and Marine forces to Baghdad, its suburbs, and Anbar Province. Iraqi forces and U.S. Government civilians also surge. Together with the Sunni Awakening, the Surge markedly reduces insurgent and sectarian violence in Iraq.

2007 February   Over 100 people killed in bombing attack in Baghdad's Sadriya Market.

2007 August   Political alliance formed supporting Prime Minister Maliki's government between Kurdish and Shiite parties. Sunni parties refuse to join.

2007 September   Security contractors with Blackwater kill 17 civilians in Baghdad.

2007 December 16   Great Britain transfers responsibility for Basra Province to Iraqi forces.

2008 January 13   Iraq's parliament passes legislation permitting some former Ba'ath party officials to work in public sector.

2008 March 2   President Mahmoud Ahmadinejad becomes first Iranian president to visit Iraq since Iraq-Iran War.

2008 March 24   Prime Minister Maliki orders Iraqi forces to disarm al-Sadr's Mahdi army in Basra, resulting in several hundred causalities.

2008 September 1   U.S. military forces transfer responsibility of Anbar Province to Iraqi forces. This is the first Sunni province returned to central government.

2008 November   Iraq's parliament approves security agreement with the United States, which states all U.S. troops are scheduled to leave Iraq by end of 2011.

2009–2011

2009 January	Iraq's security forces assume responsibility for security in Baghdad's Green Zone.
2009 February 27	President Barack Obama starts gradual withdrawal of U.S. forces. Approximately 50,000 troops to remain in Iraq until 2011.
2009 June 30	U.S. forces withdraw from Iraqi towns and cities and transfer security duties to Iraqi troops.
2009 July	Massoud Barzani is reelected president.
2009 December	Islamic State of Iraq claims responsibility for suicide bombings in Baghdad and attacks in August and October that kill nearly 400 people.
2010 January	A former senior official in the Saddam government, "Chemical" Ali Hassan al-Majid, is executed.
2010 March 7	Parliamentary elections take place.
2010 August 31	Last U.S. combat brigade leaves Iraq.
2010 September	A year after relations soured between Syria and Iraq, the countries restore full diplomatic relations.
2010 November–December	Talabani is reappointed president and Prime Minister Maliki retains his position.
2011 January	Al-Sadr returns to Iraq.
2011 February	Kurdistan's oil exports recommence after disagreement between KRG and central government over contracts with foreign firms and allocation of oil revenues.
2011 December 18	U.S. military forces complete withdrawal.

Post-U.S. Withdrawal

2012 March	Arab League holds first major summit in Iraq since fall of Saddam's government.
2012 April	KRG oil exports stop due to continued disagreement with central government oil contracts.
2012 September	Former Iraqi Vice President Tariq al-Hashemi is sentenced to death. He pursued safe haven in Turkey.
2012 November	Iraq's arms deal with Russia is canceled after allegations of corruption within Iraqi government.
2012 December	President Talabani suffers stroke and is treated in Germany. Sunnis take part in mass demonstrations throughout Iraq, protesting central government's marginalization of the Sunni minority.
2013 April	Iraqi troops attack a Sunni antigovernment protest camp in Hawija, resulting in over 50 casualties and sparking riots in surrounding areas.
2013 July	Hundreds of al Qaeda members, including senior leaders, escape from jails in Taiji and Abu Ghraib.
2013 September	KRG parliamentary elections take place. Kurdistan Democratic Party wins the elections. Islamic State of Iraq and Syria (ISIS) claims responsibility for series of bombings that hit Erbil, the capital of Kurdistan.
2014 January	Pro–al Qaeda fighters take control of Fallujah and Ramadi after months of fighting in Anbar Province. Iraqi forces are able to retake Ramadi.
2014 April	The Islamic Dawa Party, led by Prime Minister Maliki, wins a plurality at parliamentary election, but is unable to win a majority.
2014 June	ISIS seizes Mosul and other key towns in a lightening offensive. Thousands of civilians flee. The United States

and Iran both offer assistance to Iraqi government. ISIS renames itself the Islamic State and declares an Islamic caliphate covering territories in Syria and Iraq.

2014 September   Haider al-Abadi forms more diverse government, including Sunni Arabs and Kurds. Kurdish leadership tables its independence referendum. The United States announces and implements new strategy against Islamic State. U.S. Armed Forces launch airstrikes in support of Iraqi forces near Baghdad.

2014 December   Iraqi government and Kurdish leaders sign agreement on sharing Iraq's oil revenue and military assets.

2015 January   U.S.-led coalition completes over 900 airstrikes against Islamic State.

2015 March   Islamic State fighters lay waste to Assyrian archaeological sites in Nimrud and Hatra.

2015 April   Iraqi security forces regain control of Tikrit from Islamic State.

2015 May   Islamic State seizes Ramadi.

Sources: "Iraq Profile—Timeline," BBC News, available at <www.bbc.com/news/world-middle-east-14546763>; "Timeline of Key Events in Iraq and Afghanistan," Institute for the Study of War, July 16, 2010, available at <www.understandingwar.org/reference/timeline-key-events-iraq-and-afghanistan>; "Timeline of Major Events in the Iraq War," *New York Times*, October 21, 2011; "Phases of Conflict: Chronicling the Iraq War," *Washington Post*, 2005; "The Iraq War: 2003–2011," Council on Foreign Relations, 2014, available at <www.cfr.org/iraq/timeline-iraq-war/p18876>; Hala Fattah, *A Brief History of Iraq* (New York: Facts on File, 2009); Ronald J. Brown, *Humanitarian Operations in Northern Iraq, 1991 with Marines in Operation Provide Comfort* (Washington, DC: Government Printing Office, 1995); Michael A. Schiesl, *The Objectives of United States Military Intervention in Northern Iraq Between Operation Desert Storm and Operation Iraqi Freedom* (Fort Leavenworth, KS: Army Command and General Staff College, 2003); John A. Warden III, *The Air Campaign: Planning for Combat* (Washington, DC: NDU Press, 1998); John Yoo, "International Law and the War in Iraq," *American Journal of International Law* 97 (2003), 563–576; Adam Clymer, "Congress Acts to Authorize War in Gulf; Margins Are 5 Votes in Senate, 67 in House," *New York Times*, January 13, 1991; "The Operation Desert Shield/Desert Storm Timeline," Department of Defense News, August 8, 2000, available at <www.defense.gov/news/newsarticle.aspx?id=45404>; "Remarks of President Barack Obama—As Prepared for Delivery: Responsibly Ending the War in Iraq," Camp LeJeune, NC, February 27, 2009, available at <www.whitehouse.gov/the_press_office/Remarks-of-President-Barack-Obama-Responsibly-Ending-the-War-in-Iraq/>.

Contributors

Dr. Richard D. Hooker, Jr., is the Director for Research and Strategic Support and Director of the Institute for National Strategic Studies (INSS) at the National Defense University (NDU) in Washington, DC. As a member of the Senior Executive Service, Dr. Hooker served as Deputy Commandant and Dean of the North Atlantic Treaty Organization (NATO) Defense College in Rome from September 2010–August 2013. He is a member of the Council on Foreign Relations, International Institute of Strategic Studies, and Foreign Policy Research Institute, and is a Fellow of the Inter-University Seminar on Armed Forces and Society. Dr. Hooker taught at the United States Military Academy at West Point and held the Chief of Staff of the Army Chair at the National War College. He served with the Office of National Service at the White House under President George H.W. Bush, with the Arms Control and Defense Directorate at the National Security Council (NSC) during the administration of William J. Clinton, and with the NSC Office for Iraq and Afghanistan during the administration of George W. Bush. While at the NSC he was a contributing author to *The National Security Strategy of the United States.* His areas of expertise include Defense Policy and Strategy, the Middle East, NATO/Europe, and Civil-Military Relations. Dr. Hooker graduated with a BS from the United States Military Academy in 1981 and holds an MA and Ph.D. in International Relations from the University of Virginia. He is a Distinguished Graduate of the National War College, where he earned a Master of Science in National Security Studies and also served as a Post-Doctoral Research Fellow. His publications have been used widely in staff and defense college curricula in the United States, United Kingdom, Canada, and Australia, and include more than 50 articles and 3 books on security and defense-related topics. Dr. Hooker has lectured extensively at leading academic and military institutions in the United States and abroad. Prior to his retirement from Active duty, Dr.

Hooker served for 30 years in the U.S. Army as a parachute infantry officer in the United States and Europe. While on Active duty he participated in military operations in Grenada, Somalia, Rwanda, the Sinai, Bosnia, Kosovo, Iraq, and Afghanistan, including command of a parachute brigade in Baghdad from January 2005 to January 2006. His military service also included tours in the offices of the Chairman of the Joint Chiefs, Secretary of the Army, and Chief of Staff of the Army.

Dr. Joseph J. Collins is the Director of the Center for Complex Operations in INSS. He joined the National War College faculty in 2004 as Professor of National Security Strategy, where he taught military strategy, U.S. domestic context, and irregular warfare. He also directed the college's writing program. Prior to his decade at the National War College, Dr. Collins served for 3 years as the Deputy Assistant Secretary of Defense for Stability Operations, the Pentagon's senior civilian official for peacekeeping, humanitarian assistance, and stabilization and reconstruction operations. His team led the stability operations effort in Afghanistan. From 1998–2001, he was a Senior Fellow in the Center for Strategic and International Studies, where he did research on economic sanctions, military culture, and national security policy. In 1998, Dr. Collins retired from the U.S. Army as a colonel after nearly 28 years of military service. His Army years were equally divided between infantry and armor assignments in the United States, South Korea, and Germany; teaching at West Point in the Department of Social Sciences; and a series of assignments in the Pentagon, including Army Staff Officer for NATO and Warsaw Pact strategic issues, Special Assistant to the Chief of Staff of the Army, Military Assistant to the Under Secretary of Defense for Policy during Operation *Desert Storm*, and Special Assistant and Chief Speechwriter to the Chairman of the Joint Chiefs of Staff. Dr. Collins has also taught as adjunct faculty in the graduate divisions of Columbia University and Georgetown University. He is a life member of the Council on Foreign Relations. Dr. Collins holds a Ph.D. in Political Science from Columbia University and a BA from Fordham University. He is also an honor graduate of the Army's Command and General Staff College and holds a diploma from the National War College. Dr. Collins's many publications include books and articles on the Soviet war in Afghanistan, Operation *Desert Storm*, contemporary U.S. military culture, defense transformation, and homeland defense. His most recent publications include *Choosing War: The Decision to Invade Iraq and Its Aftermath* (NDU Press, 2008) and *Understanding War in Afghanistan* (NDU Press, 2011).

Dr. G. Alexander Crowther is the Deputy Director of and Cyber Policy Specialist in the Center for Technology and National Security Policy in INSS. He has extensive government service, including a decade each in the Cold War, post–Cold War, and post-9/11 eras. He has worked as a Western Hemisphere specialist, strategist, and political advisor. He served overseas eight times: three times in Latin America, twice in Korea, twice in Iraq, and once in Belgium. He has a variety of awards from the Department of Defense and Department of State as well as the Canadian government. His work at the strategic level includes tours at the Army Staff, Joint Staff J5 (Strategic Plans and Policies), and as a Research Professor at the Strategic Studies Institute at the U.S. Army War College. He was personally selected to be a Counterterrorism Advisor for the U.S. Ambassador to Iraq, Political Advisor for the Multi-National Corps–Iraq Commander, and Special Assistant for the Supreme Allied Commander, Europe. He was an International Security Studies Fellow at the Fletcher School of Law and Diplomacy. He is also an Adjunct Senior Political Scientist at the RAND Corporation and an Adjunct Research Professor of National Security Studies at the Strategic Studies Institute. Dr. Crowther has a BA in International Relations from Tufts University, an MS in International Relations from Troy University, and a Ph.D. in International Development from Tulane University.

Dr. Thomas X. Hammes is a Senior Research Fellow with the Center for Strategic Research in INSS. He is also an Adjunct Professor at Georgetown University. His areas of expertise include military strategy, future conflict, and insurgency. Dr. Hammes graduated with a BS from the U.S. Naval Academy in 1975 and holds an MA in Historical Research and a Ph.D. in Modern History from Oxford University. He is a Distinguished Graduate of the Canadian National Defence College. His publications include *The Sling and the Stone: On War in the 21st Century* (Zenith, 2006) and *Forgotten Warriors: The 1st Provisional Marine Brigade, the Corps Ethos, and the Korean War* (Modern War Studies, 2010). He has also published 14 book chapters and over 120 articles. His publications have been used widely in staff and defense college curricula in the

United States, United Kingdom, Canada, and Australia. Dr. Hammes has lectured at leading academic and military institutions in the United States and abroad. Prior to his retirement from Active duty, he served for 30 years in the U.S. Marine Corps to include command of an intelligence battalion, infantry battalion, and Chemical Biological Incident Response Force. He participated in military operations in Somalia and Iraq and trained insurgents in various locations.

Dr. Frank G. Hoffman is a Senior Research Fellow with the Center for Strategic Research in INSS. Prior, he was Deputy Director of the Office of Program Appraisal in the Department of the Navy from August 2009 to June 2011. Dr. Hoffman was commissioned as a second lieutenant in the U.S. Marine Corps in 1978. From 1978–1983, after graduating from both The Basic School and Infantry Officer Course, he served in a variety of line and staff positions in the 2nd and 3rd Marine divisions. He was a company commander and Head Tactics Instructor at the School of Infantry at Camp Lejeune from 1980–1982. From 1983–1986, he was assigned to Headquarters Marine Corps (HQMC) and served as a resource analyst. He transferred to civilian service, continuing at HQMC until 1991 as a defense analyst. From 1991–1998, he served at the Marine Corps Combat Development Command at Quantico, Virginia, as a national security analyst. He represented the Marine Corps on the Defense Science Board and Commission on Roles and Missions in 1995. Dr. Hoffman was then the Special Assistant to the Commanding General for national security affairs and the Director of the Marine Strategic Studies Group for 2 years. In 1999, the Secretary of Defense appointed Dr. Hoffman to the staff of the U.S. National Security Commission for the 21st Century, where he developed the commission's recommendations for the Department of Homeland Security. He served as a research fellow from 2001 to 2008 in the Center for Emerging Threats and Opportunities at the Marine Warfighting Laboratory where he was responsible for conducting assessments on future threats. He worked with U.S. Joint Forces Command, Allied Command Transformation, and British, Australian, and Israeli partners on alternative futures and wargames and experimentation activities. While at Quantico, Dr. Hoffman conducted studies on future threats, developed Service and joint concepts, and was a member of Strategic Vision Group, which wrote the Marine Corps' Vision and Strategy

2025. He was also a chapter author for Field Manual 3-24, *Counterinsurgency*. He served on the 2004 Defense Science Board for postconflict stability operations and lectured extensively at professional military education institutions in Japan, Taiwan, Austria, Denmark, Israel, and the United Kingdom. His publications include *Decisive Force: The New American Way of War* (Praeger, 1996), 10 book chapters, and 100 essays and articles in foreign policy and academic journals. Dr. Hoffman graduated with a BS in economics from the Wharton School at the University of Pennsylvania, an MEd from George Mason University, an MA in security studies from the Naval War College; and an M.Phil. and Ph.D. from King's College London.

Dr. Christopher J. Lamb is the Director of the Center for Strategic Research in INSS. He conducts research on national security strategy, policy and organizational reform, defense strategy, requirements, plans and programs, and special operations forces. Prior to joining INSS, Dr. Lamb served as the Deputy Assistant Secretary of Defense for Resources and Plans. He was responsible for strategic planning guidance, transformation planning guidance, contingency planning guidance, the Information Operations Roadmap, and oversight of combatant commander contingency planning. Dr. Lamb also has served as Director of Policy Planning in the Office of the Assistant Secretary of Defense for Special Operations and Low-Intensity Conflict, Deputy Director for Military Development on the Department of State's Interagency Task Force for Military Stabilization in the Balkans, and Director for Requirements and Plans in the Office of the Secretary of Defense. He led the Project for National Security Reform study of the national security system from 2007–2008, which produced the landmark report *Forging a New Shield*. Prior to joining the Department of Defense, Dr. Lamb was a Foreign Service Officer with tours in Haiti, the Ivory Coast, and the Pentagon. Dr. Lamb received his doctorate in International Relations from Georgetown University in 1986. From 1993 through 1998 he was an Adjunct Professor in the National Security Studies program at Georgetown University. Dr. Lamb is the author of numerous articles and books, many of which are used in joint professional military education courses. His recent research includes collaborative studies on national security and defense reform, interagency teams, military requirements and transformation, and special operations forces.

Contributors

Mr. Christoff Luehrs is a Research Analyst with the Center for Complex Operations in INSS. His work focuses on lessons learned from interagency operations in Afghanistan and Iraq. He is currently a Ph.D. candidate in the School of International Service at American University. Mr. Luehrs previously worked for the Center for Technology and National Security Policy in INSS on its Stability Operations Seminar series. Originally from Germany, Mr. Luehrs served in the German army, including a tour with NATO's Stabilization Force in Bosnia-Herzegovina. He holds a BA in War Studies and History and an MA in International Relations from King's College London.

Mr. Harvey Rishikof is Senior Counsel at Crowell & Moring, LLP, and the Co-Chair of the American Bar Association (ABA) National Task Force on Cybersecurity and the Law. Most recently he was Dean of Faculty at the National War College and held a joint appointment at the Drexel University Thomas R. Kline School of Law and College of Computing & Informatics. His last governmental position was Senior Policy Advisor to the Director of National Counterintelligence in the Office of the Director of National Intelligence. He specializes in national security law, civil and military courts, terrorism, international law, civil liberties, civilian/military relations, governmental process, and the U.S. Constitution. Mr. Rishikof's career includes experience in the private and public sectors and academia. He is a lifetime member of the Council on Foreign Relations and the American Law Institute. Mr. Rishikof is the Chair of the Advisory Committee for the ABA Standing Committee on Law and National Security. As Dean of the Roger Williams University School of Law (1999–2001), he introduced courses in national security law and the Constitution in cooperation with the Naval War College. Mr. Rishikof was Legal Counsel to the Deputy Director of the Federal Bureau of Investigation. As Administrative Assistant to the Chief Justice of the Supreme Court (1994–1996), Mr. Rishikof, a former Federal Court of Appeals Law Clerk in the Third Circuit for the Honorable Leonard I. Garth, served as Chief of Staff for the Chief Justice and was involved in general policy issues concerning the Federal court system. Mr. Rishikof has authored many articles, including "Morality, Ethics, and Law in the War on Terrorism (The Long War)" in *Countering Terrorism and Insurgency in the 21ˢᵗ Century: International Perspectives* (Praeger Security International, 2007). He also co-edited

The National Security Enterprise: Navigating the Labyrinth (Georgetown University Press, 2009) and *Patriots Debate* (ABA, 2012).

Dr. Nicholas Rostow is a University Professor at NDU and a Distinguished Research Professor with the Center for Strategic Research in INSS. He specializes in international and national security law and affairs and U.S. Government and international decisionmaking in foreign and national security policy. He is also a Senior Research Scholar at the Yale Law School. Prior to joining NDU in September 2010, Dr. Rostow served for more than 4 years as University Counsel and Vice Chancellor for Legal Affairs and tenured full professor at the State University of New York. His public service positions include General Counsel and Senior Policy Adviser to the U.S. Permanent Representative to the United Nations from 2001–2005; Charles H. Stockton Chair in International Law at the U.S. Naval War College in 2001; Staff Director of the Senate Select Committee on Intelligence from 1999–2000; Counsel and Deputy Staff Director to the House Select Committee on Military/Commercial Concerns with the People's Republic of China from 1998–1999 (the Cox Committee investigation of high technology transfers to China); Special Assistant for National Security Affairs to Presidents Ronald Reagan and George H.W. Bush, and Legal Adviser to the National Security Council under Colin Powell and Brent Scowcroft from 1987–1993; and Special Assistant to the Legal Adviser in the Department of State from 1985–1987. In this latter capacity, he served as Counsel to the President's Special Review Board (Tower Board), investigating the role of the National Security Council staff in the Iran-Contra Affair, and wrote a substantial portion of the Tower Board report (appendix D). Dr. Rostow has taught in the College of Law at the University of Tulsa, Fletcher School of Law and Diplomacy at Tufts University, and the Naval War College. He graduated from Yale with a BA *summa cum laude*, a Ph.D. in history, and a JD. His publications are in the fields of diplomatic history, international law, and issues of U.S. national security and foreign policy.

Ms. Sara Thannhauser is a Counterterrorism Specialist at the Department of the Treasury. From 2009 to 2014, she was a Research Fellow with the Center for Complex Operations in INSS, where she worked on national security issues involving irregular conflict, interagency affairs, and lessons learned from modern conflicts. Her duties included field research in Iraq and Afghanistan with both diplomats and military personnel. She assisted the Joint Staff and Office of the Secretary of Defense for Policy on counterinsurgency doctrine and policy in North Africa. Ms. Thannhauser also served as staff editor for the journal *PRISM.* She holds an MA in International Affairs from American University and a BA *summa cum laude* from Saint Bonaventure's University.